PUBLICATIONS
OF THE
ARMY RECORDS SOCIETY
VOL. 13

JOHN PEEBLES' AMERICAN WAR
1776–1782

The Army Records Society was founded in 1984 in order to publish original records describing the development, organisation, administration and activities of the British Army from early times.

Any person wishing to become a Member of the Society is requested to apply to the Hon. Secretary, c/o the National Army Museum, Royal Hospital Road, London, SW3 4HT. The annual subscription entitles the member to receive a copy of each volume issued by the Society in that year, and to purchase back volumes at reduced prices. Current subscription details, whether for individuals living within the British Isles, for individuals living overseas, or for institutions, will be furnished on request.

The Council of the Army Records Society wish it to be clearly understood that they are not answerable for opinions or observations that may appear in the Society's publications. For these the responsibility rests entirely with the Editors of the several works.

Captain John Peebles in 1778, aged 39, from the miniature in the Scottish United Services Museum. (Courtesy of the Trustees, National Museums of Scotland)

JOHN PEEBLES' AMERICAN WAR

The Diary of a Scottish Grenadier, 1776–1782

Edited by
IRA D. GRUBER

Published by
SUTTON PUBLISHING LIMITED
for the
ARMY RECORDS SOCIETY
1997

First published in the United Kingdom in 1998
Sutton Publishing Limited · Phoenix Mill · Far Thrupp · Stroud ·
Gloucestershire

British Library Cataloguing in Publication Data

A catalogue record for this book is available from the British Library

ISBN 0 7509 1791 1

Typeset in Ehrhardt
Typesetting and origination by
Sutton Publishing Limited.
Printed in Great Britain
at Bookcraft, Midsomer Norton, Somerset.

Contents

Maps

Preface

I first met John Peebles more than twenty-five years ago; that is, I first saw his diary of the War for American Independence among the Cunninghame of Thorntoun Papers in the Scottish Record Office. Like many other scholars who have come to appreciate Peebles as an intelligent, literate, and meticulous observer of the American War, I was soon relying on him to help me understand the British side of that war. Over the years, I returned repeatedly to his diary, becoming each time the more impressed with it and the more persuaded that it should be published. So it was that when I met Professor Ian Beckett at Princeton in the spring of 1993 and we talked of my editing a volume on the American War for the Army Records Society, I had only Peebles' diary to suggest. I was, and am, persuaded that it is among the best of all British diaries for the American War and that it is clearly the best of those that have not been published.

What made Peebles' diary so valuable was his long and persistent recording of events, great and small – not just the principal battles and campaigns but especially the details of British army life, the social and military rituals as well as the personal interactions that bound officers and men together through an increasingly discouraging war. He spent most of the American War with a battalion of British grenadiers in the middle colonies. He took part in and described General William Howe's West Chester campaign of 1776 (including the battles of White Plains and Fort Washington), the occupation of Rhode Island that December, the struggle for eastern New Jersey during the winter and spring of 1777, and the invasion of Pennsylvania (including the Battle of Brandywine and the opening of the Delaware River). He was subsequently with the army under Sir Henry Clinton as it withdrew from Philadelphia through New Jersey and fought at Monmouth in June 1778, relieved Rhode Island later that summer, campaigned along the Hudson River in 1779, and captured Charleston, South Carolina, in the winter and spring of 1780. He returned with Clinton to New York in June 1780 and remained there until October 1781 when he embarked with the fleet that tried unsuccessfully to relieve Lord Cornwallis at Yorktown, Virginia. This extensive service gave Peebles an unusual opportunity to assess the progress of the rebellion and British efforts to end it; even more important, it gave him ample time to record the mundane and repetitive transactions that shaped the British army in the American War and made it formidable even in a losing cause.

In this edition I have tried to present Peebles' diary just as he wrote it. The spelling, capitalization, and punctuation are his. The few additions to the text – an occasional mark of punctuation or an expansion of an obscure abbreviation – are within square brackets; and any deletions are described in footnotes or Appendix C. Nothing that was woven into the diary itself has been left out. But I have not included the many supplementary documents, lists, and accounts that Peebles included in his notebooks with his diary: the nautical logs, general and battalion orders, lists of promotions, rosters, duty assignments, and accounts of expenditures as well as extracts from books of history, literature, and poetry. I have chosen to exclude these supplementary documents because they more often encumber than illuminate Peebles' account. I have, in short, tried to present his diary – his view of the American War – as completely and reliably as I could.

In preparing this edition I have had the help of a number of institutions and individuals. The Army Records Society, particularly its secretary Professor Ian Beckett, first encouraged me to edit Peebles' diary and subsequently agreed to support its publication. Rice University, which has always sustained my scholarship quite generously, provided funds in this instance to assist in creating, verifying, and editing a typescript of the diary. The Scottish Record Office not only gave me permission to publish the diary but also found a quiet place where my wife and I could read the diary aloud, could check the whole of the typescript against Peebles' manuscript notebooks. And the William L. Clements Library of the University of Michigan allowed me to use its resources – its wonderful collections for the American War and its extraordinarily knowledgeable staff – in beginning to understand what Peebles wrote. John Dann, Arlene Shy, and John Shy each took a special interest in John Peebles and suggested ways of deciphering and presenting his text.

A number of other friends and scholars helped along the way. Paula Platt and Miguel Ramos created the initial typescript (from a microfilm copy); Michael Maas and Harvey Yunis provided translations of passages in Latin; Daniel Sherman did the same for those in French; Mary Winkler, Michael Winkler, Albert Van Helden, and Worth Estes collaborated in decrypting prescriptions and various medical and pharmaceutical terms; and William Bowman Piper identified many of the plays, poems, and novels that appear in Peebles' diary. My wife helped me in checking and correcting the typescript and in reading the typescript to find place names to be included in the maps as well as words and phrases to be clarified in the footnotes; David and Peggy Dillard proofread the corrected typescript; Linda Crist and Ian Beckett offered solutions to editorial problems and Elizabeth Lowry-Corry copyedited the typescript for the Army Records Society with unusual care and insight. I am grateful to all who helped but to none more than my wife, Pat, who has endured more than her share of scholarly campaigns.

Introduction

British army officers of the eighteenth century frequently had small leather-bound notebooks in their baggage, notebooks in which they recorded debts or other business transactions, made notes on their reading, kept company or battalion rosters, described tactical evolutions, and, sometimes, maintained a diary. Many of these notebooks, kept during the War for American Independence, have survived into the late twentieth century; and a remarkable number of them contain diary entries as well as other records of army officers' lives. Indeed, at least twenty such diaries for the American War have already been published.[1]

Although they were written by officers of nearly every rank and military speciality – by men of dissimilar tastes and talents and under a variety of circumstances – these diaries were remarkably alike. Most, to judge by what has survived, dealt with relatively short periods and with military operations at the beginning of the war. Only five of the twenty published diaries cover more than two years, and none of the others, more than eighteen months. Most diarists, apparently inspired by the novelty and high drama of the opening campaigns, concentrated on the war in New England and the middle colonies before 1779 – on battles, raids, and foraging expeditions as well as the movements of opposing forces. They often included impressions of the country and its people and estimates of the strength of the rebellion, but these impressions were clearly tangential. From generals like Sir Henry Clinton (commander-in-chief in North America 1778–82) and James Pattison (commandant of British artillery) to field grade officers like John Montresor (the chief engineer) and Major Frederick Mackenzie (of the 23rd Regiment) to company level officers like Captain John Barker (10th Regiment) and Captain William Bamford (40th Regiment), British officer diarists of the American War were preoccupied with military operations and with the earlier stages of the war.[2]

Captain John Peebles was interested in far more. For nearly six years he kept a diary that provided an unusually detailed and regular account of engagements from Fort Washington to Brandywine and Monmouth and from Verplanks Point to Charleston and Yorktown – an account that was the more valuable because it recorded his gradually changing impressions of the rebellion and of British efforts to end it. But what distinguished his diary from all others was his patient and persistent recording of ordinary events in his life and in the lives of other British soldiers. Better than any other observer of the American War, he provided an interior history of the British army in that war. Through his mundane reporting he made clear the importance that British officers attached to ritual and routine, to their duty as soldiers, to relations with each other, and to ties between officers and men – to the habits and skills and attachments that made the army effective through a long and discouraging war. Finally, he, better than others, showed that the army was not entirely alienated from the American people, that some British soldiers formed binding friendships with patriots and Loyalists alike.

* * *

When Peebles entered the War for American Independence in the spring of 1776, he was a thirty-six-year-old lieutenant in the 42nd or Royal Highland Regiment of the British army, the Black Watch. A Scot, in a quintessentially Scottish regiment, he was older and had served longer than most lieutenants of infantry regiments.[3] He had been born in Irvine, Ayrshire, on 11 September 1739. After receiving a sound, general education and, perhaps, some rudimentary training in pharmacy and in the treatment of the sick and wounded, he had served as surgeon's mate in North America for more than five years before being appointed an ensign in the Black Watch in the summer of 1763.[4] Because he was late beginning commissioned service in the line and because promotion was relatively slow in his regiment, he did not become a lieutenant until 1770 when he was thirty-one; and he would not be promoted again until 1777.[5] In short, when he sailed for North American in the spring of

1776, he was eight or nine years older and had served about three years longer than the average British lieutenant of infantry.[6]

John Peebles was also more broadly educated than most of his rank. He was certainly not the only officer with strong and diverse interests, but his were unusual. Apart from his experience as a surgeon's mate – and a residual curiosity about illness and medication – he had been a quartermaster in the 42nd and had developed a considerable range of intellectual interests and some literary skill. He read Montesquieu and a variety of political histories, made notes on the works of David Hume and Edward Gibbon, was filled with admiration for David Rittenhouse and his orrery, welcomed Adam Ferguson's visit to the Black Watch, and copied contemporary poetry into his journal.[7] No wonder that he would be chosen adjutant to his battalion of grenadiers or that he would become a clear, expressive diarist.

Just as Peebles was older and more broadly educated than most of his fellow officers so too was he better acquainted than most with Britain's American colonies. In more than nine years of service in North America, he had travelled widely, made friends with a number of colonists, and invested in American land. As a surgeon's mate in the Second Virginia Regiment (1758–9) and in the 77th or First Highland Regiment (1759–63) and then as an ensign in the 42nd (1763–7, after which he and the regiment went to Ireland), Peebles had travelled from Philadelphia and New York to Halifax, Louisbourg, and St. Johns.[8] He had come to know such prominent colonists as Nathaniel Gist of Virginia, John Allen of Pennsylvania, and John Foxcroft and Robert Magaw of New York. (Gist and Magaw became colonels in the Continental army; Foxcroft, who shared with Benjamin Franklin the postmaster generalship of North America from 1761, and Allen, son of Chief Justice William Allen of Pennsylvania, became Loyalists.)[9] Peebles even bought a 500 acre lot in the Cumberland Basin of Nova Scotia. And these were more than fleeting connections. On returning to America during the Revolution, Peebles regularly sought out and dined with 'old acquaintances,' inquired after others, and kept up with his lands in the Cumberland Basin.[10]

John Peebles was, then, by education and experience well

equipped to become a diarist of the War for American Independence. But he had other personal qualities and talents that emerge through his writing and that made him an especially effective observer of the American War. He was a healthy, responsible, and engaging man who, in addition to being able to make and keep friends, could gain entrance into a variety of societies. He took a compassionate interest in men and women of every station – in his fellow officers and their wives, in the rank and file of his regiment, and in the ordinary colonists, patriots and Loyalists alike, that he came to know. He sometimes allowed himself a caustic judgment; usually he was generous and sympathetic. Above all, he had the clarity of mind and ready store of words to record economically – even wryly – much of what he saw: off Long Island in the summer of 1776, a fine breeze brought three large ships 'bowling down' upon his slow moving convoy; at Philadelphia the following winter, he called on two married women and 'got a great dish of chat'; and in August 1780, after his men had camped in a widow's orchard, he observed that she would not 'make much Cyder this year.'[11]

What, then, does John Peebles tell us about the War for American Independence? Like all other British officer diarists, he describes in detail important battles that he took part in. Because there are many accounts of each of these battles, and because Peebles saw each from a relatively limited perspective, his version usually refines rather than adds substantially to our understanding. Thus he described the Battle of Brandywine in September 1777 as the 2nd Battalion of British Grenadiers saw it while driving the right wing of the rebel army from a succession of hills. At Monmouth in June 1778 he was with the 42nd (and the 3rd Brigade) which entered the battle late and tired and which fought inconclusively with rebel forces that were, by then, strongly posted.[12]

But on two occasions he was able to provide a more comprehensive – and more valuable – view of an engagement. During the attack on Fort Washington in November 1776, he was with the 3rd Battalion of British Grenadiers which was held in reserve on the east bank of the Harlem River and in a position to get a comprehensive view of the action. And at Charleston in April and May 1780, he took part in nearly every phase of the siege, recording in rich detail the

4

construction of the saps, parallels, and batteries and marking the progress of the British army as it dug its way toward the town and eventually forced the rebels to surrender.[13]

Similarly, with only two or three exceptions, John Peebles' accounts of minor engagements add little to what we know of those events in particular or of the 'petit guerre' in general. He took part in or saw dozens of skirmishes in New Jersey during the winter and spring of 1777, in Pennsylvania during the following year, and in Massachusetts and New Jersey in the late summer and autumn of 1778. These actions, initiated by foraging, raiding, and scouting parties, were sometimes large and costly, involving several thousand men and producing hundreds of casualties. Yet Peebles was usually satisfied with a brief summary of what happened.[14]

On two or three occasions he was moved to create remarkably detailed and coherent descriptions of events that must have been all too familiar and discouraging to the British and that were almost never fully described by their diarists. On 23 February, 1777, he led the advanced guard of a foraging party that marched from Amboy well beyond Woodbridge, New Jersey. Twice he and his men became separated from the main party of foragers, and each time they came under heavy attack. By the end of a long day of marching and fighting, he was the only one of twenty in the advanced guard who had not been killed or wounded. Feeling strongly that he had not been properly supported and that his men had been sacrificed to little purpose, he recorded the day's events with a thoroughness that is truly exceptional among British accounts of skirmishing in the American War.[15]

John Peebles' diary also adds to but does not transform our knowledge of British tactics and training in the American War. He recorded an occasional order requiring the infantry to form a two-rank line and to rely on their bayonets when attacking rebels in woods or lightly fortified positions. He summarized the results of inquiries into British defeats (usually ascribed to failures in communications rather than any fundamental flaw in tactics).[16] And he reported spending many days each winter and spring preparing for combat – marching, manoeuvering, and firing as companies and as battalions.[17] But only once in six years did he describe what manoeuvres the battalion performed (on another occasion he included a copy of his colonel's 'Rules for manoeuvering'); and his descriptions of engagements with the rebels convey little sense of what tactics or manoeuvres were being employed.[18]

Nor does Peebles' diary tell us much that we have not known of discipline in the British army during the American War. He complained throughout the war of plundering and desertion. Plundering seemed particularly serious when the army was on the march in Pennsylvania and South Carolina; and, he thought, the Hessians were more often guilty than the British.[19] But his own grenadiers continued to plunder while in winter quarters, stealing even from Loyalists who lived within British lines. Desertion also seemed to be worse when the army was campaigning in Pennsylvania, New Jersey, and New York or when troops feared that they were to be withdrawn from the colonies and redeployed to another theater of the war.[20] But no punishment or threat of punishment – no summary executions by the side of the road or lashes administered in front of the battalion – stopped either plundering or desertion for long.[21] Perhaps a part of the problem was that officers like Peebles, being sympathetic with their men, treated indiscipline with some tolerance or, at least, resignation. He clearly distinguished between picking ripe fruit and stealing a pig or cow and between being captured while drunk and going over to the enemy while sober.[22] In short, what Peebles has to say about discipline in the American War serves mainly to corroborate and refine what other British soldiers have said.

Peebles' diary refines what others have said about battles, tactics, and discipline; and in a few instances – the siege of Charleston, skirmishing in New Jersey – it does considerably more. But the principal value of his diary is not in his accounts of battles or his discussions of tactics and discipline. Rather it is in his persistent and detailed recording of his life and of the collective lives of his company and battalion through nearly the whole of the American War. Longer and more patiently than any other British officer, he kept track of his own changing attitudes toward the rebellion and the war as well as his interactions with other officers, common soldiers, loyal Americans, and close friends. This patient recording of events – day after day, year after year – reveals better than any other account of the war the importance of shared values, rituals, routines, and even diversions in shaping and sustaining an army through a discouraging war.

Consider first Peebles' own changing views of the rebellion. Although predisposed to dislike rebels, he gradually came to respect them and their determined resistance to the British army. From the beginning of his service in the American War, he was sympathetic with those colonists – especially Loyalists and Quakers – whose lives had been disrupted by the rebellion; and he remained friendly with 'old acquaintances' who had gone into rebellion.[23] Yet he repeatedly described rebels, or Yankees as he sometimes referred to them, as 'greedy & cunning' and 'insolent.'[24] He refused to believe that the cheering crowds that welcomed the British to Philadelphia were genuinely glad to see them; he considered members of Congress 'audacious wicked Rascals' and their public pronouncements, 'shrewd and Haughty'; and he described captured American soldiers as 'shabby looking fellows.' As late as 1780 he said the rebels defending Charleston had 'more impudence than any other people on earth.'[25] By then, however, he was beginning to show grudging respect to rebels. Those captured in Charleston were a 'ragged dirty looking set of People as usual, but more appearance of discipline than what we have seen formerly & some of their officers decent looking men.' Later that summer, he conceded that since France had entered the war, the rebellion had gained strength and British victory was by no means sure.[26]

As Peebles' respect for the rebels increased, his support for and confidence in what the British were doing declined. Until the Americans captured a British army at Saratoga and France recognized the new United States, John Peebles had been reasonably optimistic; he had few criticisms of British war aims or strategies. But when the British tried to make peace with the colonists by offering sweeping concessions and when they withdrew from Philadelphia and prepared to reduce their forces in North America, Peebles became critical of their new plans. Their overtures to Congress were, he thought, 'very humbling to Great Britain'; and their preparations for carrying on the war showed 'disorder, confusion, and undetermined councils.'[27] He was temporarily encouraged by British victories in South Carolina in 1780 – by the capture of Charleston in May and the destruction of an American army at Camden in August. Thereafter defeats and costly victories sapped his confidence. He increasingly called British actions 'stupid' or 'blameable'; he lamented the 'throwing away mens lives to very little purpose'; and in early October 1781 he received reports that Lord Cornwallis was secure at Yorktown with a skeptical 'hum.'[28]

Peebles probably would have been even more critical of the conduct of the war had he not been familiar with many senior officers. It is difficult to know how often company grade officers received invitations to dine informally with colonels and generals. It seems likely that John Peebles was favored more often than most lieutenants or captains – perhaps because he was older, better educated, and more experienced than most, perhaps because he was an agreeable person and had introductions from his former commanding officer and Ayrshire neighbor, Lieutenant-General Archibald Montgomerie, Earl of Eglintoun.[29] Whatever the source of his favor, Peebles did dine frequently and informally with generals: at least six times with the commander-in-chief, Sir Henry Clinton, four times with Charles Earl Cornwallis, and once or more with six other generals.[30] Such familiarity did not bring Peebles rapid promotion or keep him from expressing frustration with his hosts. But he clearly judged his acquaintances more generously than he did the British government, senior naval officers, and renegades like Benedict Arnold.

In describing the informal dinners that helped bind officers together during the American War, Peebles also provided rare glimpses of senior officers at ease. These are, for the most part, tantalizingly brief sketches of powerful men but the kind of sketches that help establish the tastes, habits, and character of men who are known primarily through their writings, actions, and formal portraits. Lord Cornwallis, a most aggressive and effective commander who was to have the misfortune of being trapped at Yorktown in 1781, appeared to John Peebles consistently polite, temperate, and relaxed while presiding over small and elegant dinners.[31] Baron Riedesel, who had commanded the foreign contingent in the British army that surrendered at Saratoga in 1777, was 'a genteel polite man & esteem'd a good officer & Speaks English tollerably well.'[32] Sir Henry Clinton, commander-in-chief 1778–82, was far more relaxed as a host than as a commanding general. On one occasion he was late for dinner because he was 'playing ball'; on others he was 'complaisant & in good humor' or even 'very facetious.' But John Peebles saw a much more anxious Clinton who was obsessed with his reputation – a Clinton too busy to come down to dinner yet able to take an hour and a half explaining to Peebles that he was not responsible for Cornwallis' surrender at Yorktown or his own failures to take Charleston in 1776 or Rhode Island in 1780.[33]

Informal dinners were only one of many social events that sustained the British army in America. The army also observed a number of anniversaries – royal, national, ecclesiastical, and military – that reminded officers and men of their obligations to king and country and their special ties to one another. And no one has provided a more sustained or full account of these observances than John Peebles. His patience in noticing year after year that the army was celebrating the Queen's birthday or St Andrew's Day or the Battle of Brandywine – his care in describing what might have seemed to others commonplace events – has created a unique testament to the value the British placed on ritualistic observances, to their conviction that a regular reaffirmation of common obligations and purposes was essential to keeping an army together and making it a sound fighting force.

The most formal of the army's celebrations were those associated with the monarchy and the royal family. The king, King George III, was the head of the army: he signed the most important documents and regulations, chose the men who commanded his forces, and approved appointments and promotions.[34] Officers, in turn, swore to obey the king and his regulations; and they renewed their obligations symbolically by celebrating the queen's and king's official birthdays (18 January and 4 June), the coronation and accession of George III (22 September and 25 October), and the Restoration of the monarchy (29 May).[35] They marked these anniversaries with parades, twenty-one gun salutes, formal dinners, and – for the queen's birthday – balls. And when one of the king's younger sons, Prince William, came to America as a midshipman in 1781, they received him with a royal salute and a parade.[36]

Less formal but no less important to the army were celebrations of the patron saints of England, Ireland, Scotland, and Wales. The British government carefully recorded the nationality of the officers and men in each of its regiments, presumably to ensure or, at least, to anticipate the loyalty of each regiment. Although well over half of the common soldiers in the army at the beginning of the American War were English (60 per cent to 24 per cent Scottish and 16 per cent Irish), the officers were more evenly drawn from the three nations (42 per cent English to 27 per cent Scottish and 31 per cent Irish).[37] Thus the British were careful to celebrate the patron saint's day of each of their constituent nations, including Wales, whose officers and men were not distinguished in the official returns from the English but who were identified with the 23rd Regiment or Royal Welsh Fusiliers. These celebrations took slightly different forms. St Patrick's Day (17 March) and St George's Day (23 April) began with processions, led by someone impersonating the saint, and ended with drinking and dining. St David's Day (1 March) was remembered with a 'copious libation,' and St Andrew's Day (30 November) with formal dinners for the officers and hard drinking bouts for the rank and file.[38] In 1781 when Sir Henry Clinton hosted a St Andrew's Day dinner at headquarters, some forty-five senior officers gathered for special Scottish dishes, music by a band and a piper, and toasts to the 'Brother Saints' and to King George III: 'May our Royal Master be serv'd as well as he is lov'd. by all the Sons of those Saints we have given . . . .'[39]

In addition to its celebration of royal and national anniversaries, the British army affirmed its common purposes on a number of other occasions – a few religious and secular, most, military. Although John Peebles and his comrades rarely went to church together except for funerals, they observed Christmas and New Year's Day with a suspension of routine duties and special dinners.[40] They were much more likely to celebrate military than religious or secular events. They received news of British victories with feu de joie; they remembered important, earlier victories with commemorative dinners; they nourished the traditions of their battalions and regiments with other ceremonial meals and much 'noisy mirth'; and they marked the arrival of senior officers and changes in command with salutes and elaborate, even extravagant, entertainments. When Sir William Howe resigned his command in the spring of 1778, the army and navy staged a mischianza or medley of festivities to say farewell: a procession on the Delaware, a tournament in which knights contested for the honor of maids in Turkish gowns, a grand march through triumphal arches, a dance sustained by the music of a hundred instruments, a fireworks display, and a supper in a hall built for the occasion. Such events, expensive and foolish as they might have seemed, did remind officers that they had a separate, special calling.[41]

John Peebles has provided, then, a wonderfully complete record of those ceremonial occasions when British officers affirmed their loyalty to king and country and their special obligations as commissioned officers. But he was interested in and described far more than celebrations of royal anniversaries, patron saints' days, British victories, and changes in command. He carefully recorded the ordinary social events that not only provided pleasure and recreation for officers whenever the army came to rest but also gave officers opportunities to know one another better and to develop friendships that would sustain them through the strains of subsequent campaigns. He, better than any other British observer of the American War, has described how officers drew together in pursuit of pleasure: in dining and drinking, enjoying casual entertainments, putting on balls and plays, and finding diversion outdoors.

No pleasure was more important to British officers of all ranks than communal dining and drinking. Although they were not required to dine together – a few chose to live with their wives or mistresses – most officers chose to mess with friends or with their regiment or battalion; and some joined clubs that provided for more elaborate meals once or twice a week.[42] Officers who did not join a mess found it expensive and difficult to repay social obligations, especially to afford the quantity and quality of wines that were expected by guests. Indeed, dinners, which began at three in the afternoon and which might include delicacies like oysters or turtles, frequently led to evenings of hard drinking.[43] John Peebles repeatedly complained of officers drinking too much, of their being 'fou' (drunk) or foolish. On one particularly raucous occasion some thirty-one officers drank seventy-two bottles of claret, eighteen of Maderia, and twelve of port – together with some porter and punch. No wonder Peebles reported 'much noise & little fun, staid till 10 & left them dancing in the dirt . . . .' But he valued communal dining and drinking and was miserable when not a part of a mess.[44]

Frequently after dinner, Peebles and his fellow officers enjoyed casual entertainments – music, dancing, or games that could be undertaken without extensive preparations or equipment. Flutes or fiddles were enough for an informal concert or a dance, particularly in the countryside or on board a ship.[45] And the games that officers played were quite simple. A deck of cards could sustain four people through an evening of whist; three dice were enough for two playing at passdice; and a grin or grimace alone would do for a grinning match.[46] Even outdoor games like cat (played with two sticks) and sackracing required nothing that could not be easily found or fashioned around an army. Although Peebles refused to play for high stakes, he regularly joined other officers in an informal dance or game: 'the fiddle struck up & we all fell a dancing . . . we staid late'; 'play'd dollar whist . . . & won 8'; 'had a great match at Cat for a dinner they beat us £4 . . . .'[47]

These informal diversions were the most usual but by no means the only entertainment for British officers in the American War. Officers who spent their winters in cities like Philadelphia or New York cooperated to support a variety of elaborate entertainments. They rented and decorated rooms where they could assemble to talk, drink and gamble in the evenings and where they could hold an occasional concert or ball. They paid for public rooms by seasonal subscriptions and concerts and balls by subscriptions or tickets. They allowed the Hessians to run a gambling table, to make a substantial profit while providing, John Peebles thought, very expensive entertainment.[48] And, each winter, officers of the army and navy together with their wives and mistresses put on plays for the benefit of the widows and orphans of common soldiers. (Their taste and, perhaps, talents ran toward farces with no more than an occasional Shakespearean tragedy or an eighteenth century comedy of manners.)[49] Although Peebles might grumble about the cost of a subscription, the age and appearance of women attending a ball, or the quality of acting in a particular play, he and many other officers continued to support these entertainments throughout the war.[50]

So too did they continue to find diversion together outdoors. These were relatively young and vigorous men, accustomed to taking large amounts of exercise; and when not on the march with the army, they pursued outdoor diversions in every season. They walked together prodigious distances – as much as sixteen or eighteen miles a day – to see the countryside, find fresh food, take a meal at a tavern, 'work off the fumes' of a night of hard drinking, recover from a voyage or improve 'the digestive powers.'[51] They went hunting for quail, ducks, meadowlarks, robins, woodcocks, plover, and squirrels; and they rode after foxes or the scent of foxes.[52] In summer those camped by the ocean went bathing; in winter those in the middle colonies went sleighing; and throughout the year those who could buy and keep a horse went riding.[53] They organized competitions – some relatively simple like an hour or two of putting the stone or playing golf, others more complicated like a week of horse racing on Long Island for substantial prizes.[54] These varied and pleasant diversions kept Peebles and other officers together when they were not campaigning, nurturing their friendships and feelings of camaraderie.

And friendship clearly seems to have prevailed among the officers that Peebles knew best; at least in nearly six years of service in North America, the officers of the 42nd and British Grenadiers were far more often cooperative than contentious. They did have an occasional petty disagreement over the value of a commission or the choice of quarters, and there were at least two among them who could be difficult: Lieutenant James Cramond, who 'had a pride a Vanity & a temper that prevented his being liked in the Regt. or esteem'd in the army . . . ,' and Brigadier-General Thomas Stirling, who sometimes wielded authority selfishly or vengefully.[55] There were also a number of circumstances that could be frustrating for any British officer: not just the unexpected strength of the rebellion, the length of the war, and the emerging weaknesses in British policy but also the persistent difficulty of controlling soldiers in a revolutionary war. Yet, to judge by Peebles' diary, disagreements and expressions of frustration were exceptional; the officers he knew best kept up their spirits and settled their differences amicably through nearly six years of the American War.

So too did they work effectively with their subordinates. Although officers held themselves apart, socially, from the rank and file in the eighteenth-century British army, they did feel bound to the common soldiers of their companies and regiments; and they and their men developed in time a valuable camaraderie. At least, John Peebles' diary conveys a greater sense of mutual dependence between officers and men than might seem likely in so hierarchical an organization as the British army of the American War. It was not just that he and his men shared the dangers and drudgery of war – the long marches, sudden skirmishes, large and exhausting battles, prolonged sieges, and periods of frustrating inactivity – or that they celebrated the same royal, national, and military anniversaries. It was also that over time he and they developed attachments to one another – genuine concern and sympathy for each other – that sustained them through the most difficult circumstances, that kept them together even when overrun in combat. Peebles cared for his own wounded and saw that deserving men were declared invalids; he rebuked himself for becoming so angry that he struck a soldier and repeatedly criticized other officers for wasting lives through their own incompetence or ambition; he intervened to shield a noncommissioned officer from unjust punishment; and he developed a close working relationship with Sergeant and Mrs Donald McCraw who looked after his cooking, washing, and household accounts. No wonder that when he addressed his company for the last time, both he and they were deeply moved.[56]

Officers and men were also bound together by disease, and Peebles more consistently than any British officer diarist of the American War has charted the collective health of the army. He and his company were exceptionally healthy. Only two or three times during nearly six years of service did he complain of even a trivial illness (pimples or a headache), and only once were very many in his company too sick to do their duty – in the late summer and autumn of 1779 when more than fifty of the eighty men in the 42nd Grenadiers company were ill.[57] The rest of the army was not quite so fortunate. In the spring of 1777 it was afflicted with a very contagious dysentery ('flux') and fever that persisted for more than three months; in the fall of 1779, with headaches, pains, and intermittent fever ('ague') that rendered whole units unfit for service and lasted for another three months; and in September 1780 with a brief and less pervasive recurrence of the aches and fevers of the previous year that on this occasion struck the civilian population particularly hard.[58] Yet by comparison with some eighteenth-century armies and with contemporary civilian populations, the British army in the War for American Independence seems to have enjoyed relatively good health.[59]

Although Peebles took a keen interest in the health and welfare of his men – although he and they became firmly attached to each other during the American War – his closest friends were his fellow officers and their families. He and John Rutherfurd had liked one another since they first met in 1763. During the American War, they were in different companies of the Black Watch and saw little service together. But they were able to meet frequently during winters in Philadelphia and New York. Peebles dined regularly with Rutherfurd and his wife, accompanied them to concerts, and sometimes stayed overnight with them.[60] He also relied on Rutherfurd's advice in seeking promotion and his help in protecting and transferring funds. When the Rutherfurds went home in December 1781, Peebles sorely missed 'the happy little couple.'[61] But he did not lose touch with them. Thirty years later he was still corresponding with Rutherfurd, sharing news of old friends from the 42nd, of their growing families, and of the changing circumstances of their lives.[62]

However much John Peebles saw of his fellow officers, he did not depend on them exclusively for companionship during the American War. He had many friends among the colonists. Some were 'old acquaintances' – people he had met during his prior service in America – others were relatively new friends.[63] With most, with nearly a dozen Loyalist families, he established ties that would last throughout the war.[64] Peebles may have had more American friends than most British officers; he may have been less pretentious and more genuinely concerned with the colonists than many of his colleagues. He certainly had the breadth of interests and engaging manners that made him a welcome guest. But his success in making and keeping friends among the colonists was not unique and suggests that British officers did not uniformly turn friends, or potential friends, into enemies.

John Peebles knew best the Ludlows of Queens County, Long Island. He began visiting George Duncan Ludlow and his brothers during the summer of 1778. Ludlow had been a judge of the New York Supreme Court before the war and he was to become superintendent of the Court of Police on Long Island in 1780, perhaps the most powerful civil office on Long Island under British military government and one that brought both enemies and large profits.[65] Peebles regularly dined with the judge; slept at his house; enjoyed his entertaining and instructive conversation; borrowed his books; danced and went riding with his wife; and – on leaving America in 1782 – agreed to correspond with him. Judge Ludlow may have valued the protection that John Peebles and his grenadiers could offer, and Peebles may have enjoyed being included in the Judge's grand entertainments; but the two clearly liked one another and had enough common interests to sustain a friendship beyond Peebles' service in America.[66] Peebles also liked and admired Judge Ludlow's brothers – Lieutentant-Colonel Gabriel Ludlow, an agreeable companion who commanded the 'best looking' battalion of Loyalists that Peebles had seen, and Daniel Ludlow, 'a sharp keen hand' and a fine host.[67]

John Peebles did not see any other American family quite so often as he did the Ludlows, yet he came to feel close to at least another three. He considered Dr Ogden of Jamaica, Long Island, an 'old acquaintance' when in November 1778 he was assigned temporarily to live in his house. The Ogdens may well have thought Peebles a suitable match for their daughter Polly; at least he and Polly were soon dancing and talking nonsense, she was sending him a present, and Mrs Ogden was insisting he stay overnight. Then, Dr. Ogden died and the flirtation ended. Peebles continued to visit and assist the family until he went home in 1782.[68] Peebles had known the Ogdens' neighbors, Major and Mrs Cortland, since January 1779, perhaps longer. He particularly liked 'that happy family,' visited them when they were ill, dined with them 'en famille', and gradually became quite close to them. When he told Mrs Cortland that he was resigning his commission and going home, 'she burst out a crying.'[69] Although Peebles had known John Foxcroft earlier, perhaps in the 1760's, he did not renew that friendship until the summer of 1781 when the grenadiers were camped near Foxcroft's house on Wallabout Bay. Thereafter, the friendship flourished; and during his last months in America, Peebles saw more of the Foxcrofts than any other American family. Foxcroft, who had once shared the postmaster-generalship of British North America with Benjamin Franklin, regularly invited Peebles to dinners and parties that included some of the most prominent Loyalists in the colonies.[70]

It is clear that close ties with other British officers and American Loyalists were important to John Peebles – that they sustained him throughout his service in the American War. But so too did ties with his Scottish family and friends. His few surviving letters and his diary show that he corresponded regularly with at least half a dozen people in Ayrshire and that he was ever glad to see and to help friends from home who were with British forces in the colonies.[71] He rarely let a packet or a friend depart without writing to his fiancée, Anna Hamilton, his father, John Peebles, or one of his Irvine friends. He told them about the war, inquired about friends and relations, and shared his hopes for the future. Occasionally, he sent more than a letter: money for his father, a portrait of himself for Anna, or apples and seedlings for his friends Dick Marshall, Tom Arthur, and the Earl of Eglintoun.[72] And he treasured their replies: 'din'd with my little friends, a party there, they wish'd me to stay the Eveng, but I came home to Camp to read my letters over again.' Through six years of immersion in the British army and the American War, he never lost touch with Aryshire or forgot his obligations there.[73]

Indeed, by the winter of 1781 John Peebles had begun to value his Scottish connections above those to the British army. By then

17

he had acknowledged that the war was not going well – that the rebellion was gaining strength and British efforts to suppress it were becoming increasingly ineffectual. He was also sure by then that he wanted to marry Anna Hamilton. With the war dragging on inconclusively and with his career in the army faring no better, he decided to sell his commission, quit the army, and make a new life for himself and Anna in Scotland. He was then forty-one and she forty; if they were to have a prospect of having children, he could wait no longer. But when he tried to sell his commission, he found his colonel, Brigadier-General Stirling, not just unwilling to give his consent but positively hostile to all Peebles' proposals.[74] It was with increasing frustration, even desperation, that Peebles had to wait another year – until Stirling left the 42nd Regiment – to sell out, leave the army, and go home to Scotland.[75]

Once home, John Peebles lost no time in marrying Anna Hamilton and in building a most satisfying life with her. Anna's father, who was collector of the customs at Irvine, provided them with a dowry of £1,000 and a house. He may also have helped John secure an appointment in the customs service as surveyor for the port of Irvine, a post he was to hold for decades.[76] John, in turn, was to take a leading role in the Hamilton family once Anna's father and brother were dead (as executor to her brother's estate for many years after 1798) and in the Ayrshire militia during the wars of the French Revolution and Napoleon (as major and later captain of the Irvine Volunteers).[77] By 1804 he and Anna were able to arrange for their only child, Sarah, to marry a prominent local landowner, Lieutenant-Colonel John Cuningham of Caddel and Thorntoun House, and to begin to know talented grandchildren.[78] Although Peebles never became collector of the customs at Irvine as he had hoped, he continued to earn a comfortable living as surveyor and to enjoy good health well into his seventies (friends admired his excellent memory of events in the American War and his physical vigour, his ability to walk five or six miles at a stretch).[79] Anna died in 1812, at the age of seventy-one, and John in 1823, at eighty-four. He left his daughter and son-in-law an estate of nearly £5,000 and a remarkable diary of his service in the American War.[80]

Abbreviations

John Peebles used many abbreviations in his diary, and he took little trouble in standardizing them. (Grenadiers, for example, appears as Grs., Grrs., Grenrs. and Grenadrs.) Even so, it is relatively easy to understand most of his abbreviations, and in those cases where it is not, brief explanations are included in footnotes. A key to the initials he used to identify regular correspondents (TA, Fr, AH) and officers within his regiment is included at the beginning of Appendix A (Biographical Notes); and the meaning of initials used to indicate the direction of the wind, course being steered, or sails being carried may be checked in Appendix B (see compass card and sail plan for a square rigger). Abbreviations employed in the footnotes for modern scholarly sources (names of manuscript collections, titles of books and articles) are defined in the first reference to each source.

THE BRITISH ISLE

0   20   40   60   80
MILES

S C O T L A N D

Hebrides or Western Isles

Edinburgh

Glasgow
Greenock
Kilmarnock
Saltcoats
Ailsa
A Y R
Frith of Clyde

Craighlaw
Whithorn
Copeland Id
Whitehaven

ISLE of MAN

Dublin   Drouth
Liverpool

I R E L A N D

CO.
WEXFORD
CO.
CORK

E N G L A N D

W A L E S

Tuskar
Rock

ST GEORGES CHANNEL

London
Cosham

C. Clear

Portsmouth

Plymouth   Tor Bay

Falmouth

E N G L I S H   C H A N N E L

Chapter I

'again surpriz'd to find the fleet & army gone'

Greenock to New York
12 April to 5 August 1776

On April 12, 1776, Lieutenant John Peebles marched with his regiment, the 42nd or Royal Highland Regiment of the British army, from Glasgow to Greenock, Scotland. The next day he and his regiment, known informally as the Black Watch, embarked on transports in the River Clyde to begin a voyage to North America. They were on their way to join other forces in putting down a rebellion that had broken out in thirteen of Great Britain's American colonies. By then, the conflict between mother country and colonies – the War for American Independence as it would eventually be known – was entering a new and more destructive phase. The British had precipitated fighting in the spring of 1775 after years of quarrelling over taxes, individual liberties, and the imperial constitution. To sustain their authority with a minimal show of force, they had sent a small detachment of troops to confiscate military stores at Concord, Massachusetts. The ensuing battles of Lexington and Concord and Bunker Hill, nominal and costly British victories, did far more to rouse than to intimidate the colonists. Representatives of the thirteen colonies met in Philadelphia to define their grievances and to organize an army, a Continental army under the command of George Washington, to oppose the British at Boston. The British responded by declaring the colonies in rebellion, imposing a blockade on their ports, and assembling an army of some 35,000 regular soldiers to isolate and crush resistance in New England. John Peebles and the 42nd Regiment were, then, one small part of the unprecedented reinforcements flowing west across the Atlantic in the spring of 1776 – one small part of the army that the British were assembling in North America.

Although Peebles began a diary on the day that he marched to Green-ock, he did not record his feelings as he prepared to leave for America. Had he done so he might well have expressed some mixture of appre-hension, frustration, and even optimism. Apart from the hazards of an extended voyage in a crowded sailing ship, of life within an army that had only a primitive understanding of illness and epidemics, and of combat that sometimes claimed up to two-fifths of those engaged, Peebles could anticipate a separation of many months from family and friends. Notwithstanding earlier service in North America and Ireland, he remained close to his father, his sister and her growing family, and a number of old friends in his native town of Irvine and other nearby communities of Ayrshire, Scotland. He may have felt particular frustra-tion at the prospect of prolonged separation from Anna Hamilton, the daughter of the collector of customs at Irvine and his 'dear little friend.'[1] He and Anna (the A.H. of his diary) may not have been formally engaged to marry when he sailed for America in April 1776, but they already cared deeply for one another, and if they hoped to marry and have children, they would have to do so before too long. She was then thirty-six and he, thirty-seven.

Even so, Peebles may have had a sense of optimism when he sailed, a sense that the war would soon be over and that, while it lasted, it would provide unusual opportunities for promotion. He had few illusions about the colonists' loyalty to the crown, yet like many of his fellow officers he was confident that the British army could promptly defeat any rebel forces and end dreams of American independence.[2] He may also have hoped that the war would advance his career. Because he had served as a surgeon's mate for nearly six years before being commissioned an ensign in the line and because promotion was unusually slow in his regiment, Peebles was older and had served longer than most other lieu-tenants in the British army. It is possible that his advancement had been further slowed by his lack of money and social standing. But he had been able to pay for his lieutenancy in 1770; he had support from one of the leading men of Ayrshire, Lieutenant-General Archibald Montgo-merie, Earl of Eglintoun; and he went to America ambitious for promo-tion – for an opportunity to purchase a captaincy in his regiment. Although he never seems to have sought promotion outside his regi-ment, he could expect that casualties throughout the army and the cre-ation of new regiments would draw officers away from, and create vacancies within, his own regiment. He could also hope that he would have opportunities to distinguish himself in combat, gaining thereby the notice and favor of his superiors and their support when vacancies did occur. In short, the prospect of serving in an American war brought Peebles opportunities as well as anxieties and frustrations.

What he could not have foreseen when he embarked at Greenock was where or when he might enter the war. The British government and its commander-in-chief in North America, General William Howe, had agreed that the army would remain at Boston until reinforced and would then proceed to New York to open the campaign of 1776 against New England.[3] Thus Peebles and his regiment sailed for Boston in late April. No one in Britain yet knew that Howe had been driven from Boston in March or that he had sailed to Halifax, Nova Scotia, to await supplies before going on to New York.[4] So it was that Peebles and his regiment – indeed the whole of what was called the Highland reinforcement – embarked on a far longer voyage than they or anyone expected, a voyage that was prolonged by poor communications, unfavorable winds and currents, and ordinary delays that afflicted ships under convoy. Although Peebles and his regiment would reach Boston in just over six weeks (a remarkably short passage), they would be another ten weeks on board their transports before joining Howe at New York in early August. Their passage made clear many of the difficulties that the British faced in attempting to put down a rebellion 3,000 miles from home.[5]

Greenock to New York
12 April to 5 August 1776

On Friday the 12th April 1776 the Regt. march'd from Glasgow to Greenock to Embark, but the Wind blowing too high it was put off for that day. Saturday morning being more moderate we Embark'd early and were all safe on board by 10 o'Clock; The Baggage arrived the same day in Gabbards [that is, in lighters] from Glasgow and was put on board the respective ships.

Sunday 14th the Flora Frigate arrived in the Evening for a Convoy for the Transports, Capt. Brisbane Commander.

Monday we heard that we were to wait for Frasers Regt. who were now assembled at Glasgow, and having much to do in forming the Companies & modelling the two Battalions would not be ready to march for eight or ten days.[6]

Tuesday the Masters of Transport were each furnish'd with a Printed paper of signals from Capt. Brisbane by which Boston was appointed a Rendevous in case of separation. The Ocean an arm'd Transport on which the Agent Lt. Henry was on board appointed to sail in the Center, & the Venus, another arm'd Transport in the Rear both for Frasers Regt. Our transports were The Brilliant Colo: Sterling, The Thomas, Major Murray, The Thames Major Grant with the Grenadrs., The Houston Capt. McKenzie Light Infantry, The Peggy Capt. Grahams, The Bowman Capt. Erskins The Oxford Capt. Smiths, The Minerva Major McPhersons The Glasgow Capt. C Grants The Neptune the Genls. & the Joseph & Henry with some odd men the Qr.Mr. & Adjutant – Eleven ships for our Regt. & double that number for Frasers two battalions, and one The Globe for an Hospital Ship for both Regts.[7]

Wednesday the 17th. and for a week after the Wind not fair, could not have saild if ready, employed in finishing the cloathing making cartridges & completing our Sea Stores –

Thursday the 25th. Frasers Regt. arrived from Glasgow and

24

Embark'd that afternoon, pretty late before they got all on board, Stout, raw, & irregular. Friday & Saturday employed in taking the Remains of our Baggage on board having some appointments just arrived from London.

Sunday the 28th. The Blue Squadron that is the 42d weighed anchor and turn'd down to Gourock Road, from the tail of the Bank.

Monday 29th. The White Squadron (Frasers) with the Flora weighed & came down to us on which we all got under Sail & turn'd the Clough about 2 P.M. a fine fleet in all 35 sail, a steddy breeze N.N.W. at 10 abreast with Elsa, made the Copland light.[8]

Tuesday 30th. fine weather saw the Isle of Man, the Whole fleet in sight steering SSW.

Wednesday May 1st. fine weather whole fleet in sight, the wind NW off Dublin Bay.

Thursday May 2d 1776 This last 24 hours fine weather all sail sett saw Howth bearing about WNW. the whole Fleet in sight Standing off & on & tacking by signals from the Man of War, the wind coming round to SW & hazy

Friday May 3d. moderate weather all sail sett the whole Fleet in sight turning out of the Channel, at 2 P.M. saw the highlands of Wexford bearing W.N.W. – in the evening lost sight of land reckon ourselves without Tuscar, weather thick spoke with a sloop bound for Rotterdam

Saturday May 4th the weather hazy and a heavy sea from the Wward. Carrying Double Reeff'd Topsails. at six handed top-sails blowing a smart gale, the Fleet in sight some far ahead – at 8 The Flora handed topsails & sett Mizon, then blowing very hard & a high cross sea.[9] did not forget Saturday night a Strong gale under low sail at noon Cape Clear N Dist: 8 or 10 leagues from which we take our departure

Sunday May 5th. a smart Gale double reefd The sea runing high & ship'd a good deal of water the whole fleet in sight

Handed TS blowing very hard & a very high sea   The Troops much incommoded with the water below when the hatches shut hot & stinking,   all sick most ship'd a great deal of water – a pig wash'd overboard, a goat (poor Betsy) drown an 14 fowls, the Thames a watery B _ the Flora out of sight & great part of the Fleet

Monday May 6th   Carrying Courses the Sea running very high & cross   12 [p.m.] sett closs reef'd main TS 4 [a.m.] sett closs reef'd fore & mizzon Topsails & jibb   8 [a.m.] six sail in sight   12 [a.m.] Let a reef out of the TS & set the main top most stay sail

Tuesday May 7th. Carrying double reef'd TS   jib & main T stay sail   2 [p.m.] let the double reef out of the topsails,   15 sail of the fleet in sight

Wednesday May 8th. Fair weather carrying whole TS & stay sails   16 Sail of the fleet in sight. a birth day. 10 [p.m.] single reef'd the TS & stowed the Midde Stay S & Miz: topmost stay S   8 [a.m.] let the reef out of the TS & set the Mid. stay S & Miz: topmost stay S

Thursday May 9th   Carrying whole TS jib & staysails   18 Sail of the fleet in sight   spoke to some of them

Friday May 10th   fair Wr. & light winds,   all sail sett   smooth water   16 sail of fleet in sight   4 [a.m.] got up the maintop Gal-antyard

Saturday 11th May   Clear Wr. & light winds   Carrying all Sail, that part of the fleet we saw yesterday are ahead except the Glasgow whom we spoke – all well
   at Noon had an Observation Latt. 44.57

Sunday 12th May   Clear Wr. & light winds   carrying Studden sails   the Glasgow in Company & 5 or 6 sail to windward   10 [a.m.] down steering sails, 8 sail in sight from the masthd. had an observation Latt 44.45.

Monday 13th. May   a fine light breeze   the Glasgow in Com-

pany & 3 sail to windward not far off – Steering Sails Sett   6
[a.m.] one sail to leeward & two a great way ahead having run
ahead of the Glasgow & the 3 to windward   resolved to stand up
and join
   an Observation Latt 43.54

Tuesday May 14th. Shorten'd Sail for the ships a stern – spoke
the Glasgow & Minerva[;] the Peggie & Bristol in Company,
agreed to steer West till we come to Latt [Long?] 40. – 6 [a.m.]
The above 4 ships still in Company   att Noon Cloudie no Observation

Wednesday 15t. May   fair weather and a fine breeze   carrying
whole topsails & some Staysails, – the above 4 sail in Company
at 4 P.M. spoke the Glasgow & Peggie, all well, the Peggie saw a
Brig which they supposed to be a Yanky   2 [a.m.] sett two fore
Steering sails   6 [a.m.] the above 4 sail in Company the Peggie
astern   at noon had an Observation Latt 42.14

Thursday 16th May   a fine steddy breeze & smooth water, the
above 4 Ships in Compy in the Eveng saw a hawk flying about
the ships, it Perched at last on our Mizzen top, & was catch'd by
one of the sailors   suppose from the Western Islands[10]   2 [a.m.]
Carrying Steering Sails   6 [a.m.] the little fleet of 5 sail keeps
together at noon had an Observation Lat.41.38

Friday 17th May   fine weather & light winds all sail sett, the
same ships in Company. – our hawk made its escape & flew to
another ship – as pleasant sailing as if we were in the trade
winds & every thing else very agreeable   at 10 P.M. had a Review
of the Mens arms and appointed them to their alarm stations,
about 80 on deck. Lt. P. Qr. Deck[,] Lt. Gr: foreCastle[,] Lt. Gil:
main D[eck],   the beds up to try how they wd. cover the men in
case of actions – at Noon had an Observation Latt: 41.43

Saturday 18th May. fair Wr. light breeze & smooth water   the
little fleet together – Saw a Sail to S. wd. bearing down upon us,
the ship ordered to be clear'd & man'd,   12 rounds given to the
men. she prov'd to be a large Man of war white pennant, but she

did not come near enough to know of what nation, Steering to the N.E. N.B. our Men were orderd to load & cock the two guns[11] – in the Eveng the hawk returned & was caught. – The men order'd to draw their charge & clean their firelocks, the shot taken out of the 2 Guns & the Powder fired off at Noon had an observation Latt 41.20

Sunday May 19th. the forepart of this 24 hours fair weather all sail sett the 4 ships still in Comy at 10 P.M. haul'd down steering sails – a jovial Saturday night – at 2 of the morng handed topsails At Noon had an observation courses & winds as per Log – Latt.41.24 –

Monday 20th May this last 24 hours the fore & middle part fair weather, for the most carrying single reef'd TS & Gib & stay sails handed – the four sail still in company, mostly dull sailors – at 8 A.M. saw a large ship standing to eastward small rain & looks thick, at Noon the wind check'd about to N.W. wore ship – no observation

Tuesday 21st. May fair weather forepart Carryg Double reef'd TS – a head Sea, the little fleet of 4 sail still in Company, but obliged to wait for them now & then by turns – The latter part all sail sett. – Spoke 3 of our fleet. the Peggie caught some Bonita, we saw no fish but a few Rudderfish & 1 Shark At Noon had an observation Lat.40.48

Wednesday 22d May fair weather all sail sett the 4 Ships still in Company, spoke with them all in the course of the day – all well Handed middle stay & mizen TS 2 [a.m.] hand Gib & topmost stay sail, a small breeze 4 [a.m.] Double Reef'd Topsails, fresh gale 6 [a.m.] showers & foggy 8 [a.m.] handed Miz: TS at Noon had an observation close reef'd TS hald up Miz: &c to wait for the fleet Lat. 41.11

Thursday 23d May in the fore part of this 24 Hours thick foggy Wr. & blowing pretty hard Carrying fore sail main sail & M. topsail waiting for the Sternmost Ships the Peggy & Minerva – At 6 P.M. handed main topsail at 7 Wore ship the

wind checking about to N.W. with a shower at 8 clear sett Topsails – the 4 Ships in view the Bristol to windw'd & astern the
Glasgow, astern, the Peggy close by, the Minerva to Leew'd, At
Noon had an observation, almost calm & a tumbling sea Latt.
40.59.

Friday 24th May But little wind the forepart of this last 24
hours Carrying single reef'd main TS & double reef'd fore, a
very cross tumbling sea the 4 ships still in sight – The Wind
freshens & came on a smart breeze at 7 A.M. see a Brig steering
to the N.E.d she came down among us but did not speak, put out
a St. Georges jack, at 10 handed topsails a very cross sea & thick
weather, towards noon more moderate sett topsails closs reef'd –
had no observation

Saturday 25th. May The afternoon mostly thick & rainy
weather & blowing a smart breeze carrying the 3 close reef'd
topsails, a high cross sea – one of our little fleet missing suppos'd
to be the Peggy Eason – at 6 P.M. wore ship to Sod. at 8 handed
Miz:topsail blowing a Smart Gale – N:B: had an excellent seapye
[that is, sea-pie] for dinner Three Ships in sight one of them far
astern see fowls every day they call them sheer water's saw a
Swallow yesterday at Noon had observation Lat. 41.00

Sunday 26th. May fair weather & a fresh breeze from the
Northwestw'd. going under easy sail waiting for the other ships
3 off the weather Qr. & one far astern which prov'd to be the
Peggy she came up with us at night about 10, we then made
more sail & got ahead again – at 8 A.M. saw a ship right ahead &
standing to the Nd. of Ed. she came down pretty near us & put
up french colours but did not come near enough to speak her –
The Glasgow a great way astern all this morng At Noon had an
observation Lat.40.00 the breeze takes off

Monday 27th May This last 24 hours the fore part fair
weather & little or no wind some time calm, the Courses hauled
up – the little fleet of 4 sail in sight – at 8 P.M. wore ship & sett
the courses, came on rain, – at 10 handed TS blowing a smart
Breeze & very dirty had no observation –

Tuesday 28th. May first part little Wind, much rain, & high sea, Carrying Courses waiting for the ships astern at 6 P.M. Sett TS double reef'd a rainy dirty night – in the morning clear'd up & turned out a fine day – The 4 ships in sight the Glasgow a great way astern, waited under easy sail for her coming up a fine light breeze at Noon had an observation Lat. 41.27 –

Wednesday 29th May the fore part of this 24 hours fair Weather & light Winds spoke the Glasgow just as we were going to dinner – all well see a good many porposes, & two or three kinds of birds, Sheer waters, boatswains, and Pitterals – the fleet all up out reef's & sett steering sails at 12 Rain hauled down steering-sails, hard rain & a smart breeze towards morng. The little fleet scatter'd again, the Minerva & Bristol off the weather bow, one far to leeward & 1 off the W[eathe]r.Q[uarte]r. a good way astern at Noon had an observation Lat. 41.45

Thursday 30th May first part thick weather & a smart breeze carrying single reef'd TS & The Minerva & Bris[tol] off the Wr. Qr. The Peggy astern the Glasgow off the lee beam a good way off – at 4 very foggy the ships all out of sight at 6 clear, all in view after 8 thick fog wore ship at 2 got a head of the fleet, stowed jib & stay sail in the morng the Peggy and Brist not far astern, the other two a good way off. little wind – at 8 AM see a strange sail fr: Masth. to So:wd. at 12 the sail a head seen from Deck at Noon had an observation Lat. 41.33 –

Friday 31st May fore part Calm. at 6 a little breeze from the No.Wd at 8 rainy continued almost all night, the breeze pretty smart, single reef'd Topsails, at 12 handed Miz: topsail & at 4 AM set him again at 8 AM little wind the bristol & Peg a little ahead spoke the latter near Noon all well they say Long. 53 the Glasgow far astern at noon had an observation Lat. 41.20

Saturday June 1st 1776 fair weather and light breezes ahead of the little fleet with single reef'd topsails in the night still moderate Topsails sett – the latter part of this 24 hours almost calm, the 5 ships close together, see two strange sail to the Northeastward, standing to the westwd. a good distance off – The ship springled with vinegar being the third time this voyage – at Noon had an observation   Lat. 41.18

Sunday June 2d. the fore part Calm & fair Wr. about 4 see a sail to Westwd bearing down upon us, the Minerva & us lay to for her, about 6 she fell in with the fleet & appears to be the Neptune she spoke the Minerva (being to windward) & hauled up to the wind; the 2 sail to leeward seen from the deck appear to be Brigs & probably of our fleet as they are standing as we do – in the eveng spoke the Bristol   she sprang her for TS yard, & had another rig'd out,   we then sternmost – in the morng ahead & to windward of the whole the Peggy sails well today – the 2 sail to leeward almost out of sight from the mast head – at Noon had an observation   Lat. 41.46

Monday 3d. June   fine weather & a pretty good breeze   the little fleet close together, towards Evening the breeze freshen'd, double reef'd our Topsails & haul'd down staysails, the sea pretty rough during the night
   The Neptune a great way to leeward the rest pretty well together, reefs out. spoke the Minerva near 12 all well, saw a no. of fowl & a penguin   At Noon had an observation   Lat. 42.17

Tuesday 4th. June   moderate weather with flying fogs, some-times carryg all sail, & sometimes the courses haul'd up – The Little fleet all in sight   driving & rolling about in a Calm – at 8 a breeze sprung up, spoke the Glasgow, all well;   let them all go ahead except the Bristol whom we spoke likewise & in the morng spared her a piece of wood for a spritsail yard – The Wr. cool foggy & showery – saw a Swallow – At Noon had an observation Lat. 42.29

Wednesday 5th. June   a fine breeze which increas'd towards eveng & blew smartly; between 3 & 4 split our fore Topsail & bent another – the little fleet in Company – saw two Cutties – the fore part of this 24 hours being the Anniversary of the King's birthday was celebrated with joy & festivity,[12] but it blowing pretty hard & a rough sea,   there was much tumbling

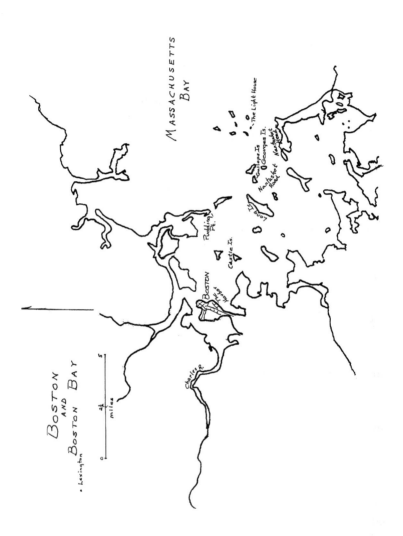

about in the cabin to the great damage of table chairs and glasses, & some broken ribs & other bruizes – see a good deal of sea-weed – remarkably cold   at Noon had an observation Lat. 42.11

Thursday 6th June   the weather clear fair & cold spoke the Neptune at 4 P.M. all well they saw only one of the fleet (a Brig of Frazers) since they parted the first storm – the rest of our little fleet astern – whole topsails & staysails smooth water   between 6 & 7 about ship & stood to the northward   the Minerva far to leeward – see a Gull   at Noon spoke the Peggy, all well except the damage of the King's birthday – had an obsern   Lat. 41.17.

Friday 7th. June   fore part fair weather & light winds,   all sail sett, the little fleet in Company, – at 8 spoke the Minerva, all well, Discovered Capt. Dunlop, – some cabbin sufferings on the Kings birthday – he calls himself in Longi:63. & odd & Lat 41.10 at Noon – Topgallant sail, & some stasails taken in to wait for the rest of the ships – the morning thick & rainy, 3 ships astern & 2 off the Wr. beam – about 10 see a Gannet   rainy   at Noon thick weather no observation

Saturday 8th. June   moderate weather & flying fogg; all sail sett the other ships sometimes out of sight tho' not far off – at 7 P.M. sounded & found bottom on 40 fathom, sand & small stones supposed to be St. Georges Bank – Spoke the Peggie,   she sounded on 32 fathom – at 11 wore ship – at 3 AM sounded again & had 20 fm. small sand – The latter part a smart breeze, single reefed TS   the rest of the fleet in sight & to leeward   at Noon had an observation   Lat. 42.11.

Sunday 9th. June   this last 24 hours fair Weather & cold, fore part a smart breeze   carrying single reef'd topsails – in the eveng spoke the Peggie & agreed to ware at 8 & stand off, which we all did,   at 2 AM. wore ship to westard – The little fleet all in sight in the morning but much scatter'd, the Minerva Glasgow & Neptune a great way to Leeward – The Weather clear and very cold for the season   see a good many Gannits – at Noon had an observation   Lat. 41.52

Monday 10th. June fair weather & light winds Carrying all sail, the little fleet in sight, 3 far to leeward – at 4 P.M. See the Land from Masthead, in two hours quite plain, which we take [to] be Cape Codd, see two strange sail, the ships to leeward hauls up, – stood on under easy sail all night our little fleet got close together, at 4 AM was close in with the Cape got out anchor & Bent Cables & stood up the Bay, 4 of the other ships ahead the Peggy to leeward – at 10 AM. made the Light House & saw two sail standing out, which proved to [be] the Milford frigate 28 Guns & the Arm'd Brig Hope coming out to meet us the Brig boarded some of the headmost ships & gave them pilots, the frigate did not speak any of us – Informed that the fleet & army left Boston about the 17th. March & went to Halifax –

Tuesday 11th June fair weather little or no Wind the little fleet ahead, a one PM. caught 3 Haddocks, at 3 pass'd the Light House, at 4 came to an Anchor in Nantasket Road where we found the Renown 50 Guns, & 2 transports of the 71st. the Mayflower & Peggy, they took the little schooner thing coming in that morning – the Commanding offrs. of ships went on board, the comr. (Capt. Banks), & heard the News of Boston being aband. likewise in the harbour a small Brig (the Yanky Hero) taken by the Milford a few days ago after a smart engagement. a great many Yanky boats looking at us within shot at 9 AM. went on board the Renown with Majr. Grant to breakfast with Comr. got all the news, he expects to be attacked soon with row Gallys & fire rafts went ashore with the Com on an Island, engaged to dine with him

Wednesday 12th June fair wr. & warm lying at anchor, the armd Brig at the Light house, the frigate out, hear'd firing – see the Provincials at Work on Pudding Point & Castle Island – at 2 PM. a flag of Truce from Boston went on board the Renown without being stopp'd in her way, their ostensible reason, to enquire after the state of their prisoners taken in the Hero, but more probably to view our situation & numbers, din'd on board Capt Banks Major Gr Major Mc. & the two flag of truce Gentln. who were reserv'd & cunning as the Yankies generally are, they had no Authority to treat of a Cartel and went off after drinking a few Glasses of wine – today hoisted out our long boat to water & sent the women ashore to wash, on the Island opposite Nantasket village St Georges island one house on it made an hospital of, the Comr has Cows & sheep and a little Garden there   Major & Mrs. Gr dind on board the Commodore, on this day wednesday which should be thursday By the sea journal[13]

Thursday 13th. June a good many men ashore from each ship except ours, awkward squads to exercise, on Gallops Island   the Weather hot   Visited several of the ships and went on shore,   the Yankies looking at us from every hill near us – the long boat ashore watering & with the women washing on Georges Island – some people seen buzy at work on Long Island in the Eveng. – several visits from the other ships   all well, except a few men – The Arm'd Brig the Hope out yesterday in pursuit of the Yanky Privateers,   chased one in to Marblehead, but she came out soon after attended with 3 or 4 more & a number of boats & pursued the Brig in their turn   the Brig made a Signal for assistance but the Como. said he had none to send, she returned to Nantasket Road in the Eveng.   having taken a small schooner with Oysters – the Brig commanded by Lieut Dawson who seems to be active in anoying the Enemy who we hear have offer'd a Reward of £5000 for his head,   he brought in 3 gentlen., who deserted from Boston – about 12 o'clock the Commodore came on board of us on a visit to the Commdg Officer & his Lady, – acquainted us that some of the 71st. Transports was taken, by the Provinicals & the Troops march'd to Boston; suppos'd to be the Venus,   the intelligence came by 3 people who deserted from Boston yesterday to the Arm'd brig,   they say the Provincials have thrown off all dependence on G Britain & abuse the king –

On Friday morning the 14th. June being ready at 5 to go ashore to Gallops Island wt. the long boat full of men,   we recd a Message from the Com: not to send any men ashore the Provincials being seen in numbers on the next Island at work,   went immediately and delev this order to the other ships, & to desire the inmost ships to move out, in about an hour after the Enemy began to fire from a Battery on Long Island, on which the Transports were ordered to get under way & stand down to the light house, they continued firing on us with 3 Guns & one Mortor while in their reach, the Renown return'd a few shot & slip'd anchor, we fir'd six or eight shot (6 Prs.) at Nantasket Village & the people on the heights, & Renown fir'd there likewise on her way but without effect also – we were not long come to at the light house when the Enemy fired upon the fleet from the opposite shore, we all got under way again, almost calm, & the Com: made a signal for Masters (which was not taken notice of having receiv'd no orders) he sent for the Comd Officer, went on board with him where we receiv'd orders to go to sea immediately & observe the same signals we had from the Flora, Halifax the Rendevouz – the shot flying about – the Yankies exulting on the Hills – four sail in sight in the Bay – the Light house deserted & set on fire which soon after blew up with a great explosion about noon – the 4 sail proves to be the Milford & 3 of our fleet, the Henry & Joseph & 2 of Frazers, they fell in about one, & stood on with the rest of the fleet they had seen Privateers

Saturday 15th June (by sea accot.) The Fleet standing out of the Bay consisting of 17 sail viz 2 men of war 2 arm'd Brigs 11 transports & 2 Schooners, – at 6 PM. took our departure from Light House island, bearing from us NWBN 1/2W distance 4 leagues, the Como: made a signal for all ships to come under his stern in the Eveng, which being comply'd with stood on under easy sail, Renown ahead. the Milford in the Rear – the Morng thick fog a Gun every hour from the Com: answd with Musquets & drums, accordg to instructions, the Renown close by & several of the fleet seen now & then when fog clears a little –

N:B: the Yanky Privateers followed us out of the Bay, looking on at a distance; a good deal of firing of Cannon ashore –

Sunday 16th. June foggy Wr. little or no wind, going to & fro thro' the fleet watching the Como. motions who made several private signals, – the Hope bore down to him, & the frigate sent her boat aboard, & soon after stood away to the So-wd. & W-wd. – Between 5 & 6 the Bristol and Renown ran foul of each other the former lost her Bowsprit & driver bomb [boom] & tore her main topsail &ca the Renown sent her boat aboard & they began to rig out again, – a dirty wet night, – driving up among the fleet, got abreast of the Com; he fir'd a Gun at us at 4 AM. the fleet all in sight & pretty compact, the frigate we suppose return'd to Boston Bay – going under double reef'd topsails only, and jogging on after the Como an officers watch on deck at night. Lt. P. at Noon had a Glance of the Sun by which Lat. 43.40

Monday 17th. June the fleet of 16 sail all in sight following the Como. at an awfull distance, turning thick & foggy he began to fire fog Guns at 5 P.M. & continued till one in the morning, when it cleared up a little so as could see the Light & some of the fleet –
One of the little Schooners amissing, and the Bristol a good way astern, the fleet gathering up about the commo. & lying to for those astern – flying fog every now & then quite thick – no observation – an officer's watch on deck at night Lt. Gr.

Tuesday 18th. June thick foggy weather, the fleet in Company but 'hid now & then with fogs Commo: firing hourly Guns – all sail sett but little wind, tryed to fish but no bottom with 80 fathom line
an officers watch on deck Lt. Gil: The fog clear'd away this morning and had a fine sun for observation at Noon, but were too late abegining The Peggy observed in 42.55 the Glasgow in 43.00 –

Wednesday 19th. June fair weather & a fine light breeze the fleet of 15 sail in Company; in the Eveng. the Neptune being to windwd made the Signal for seeing a strange sail, which the Com. repeated & hove to, the fleet ran up pretty close to him & threw topsails to the Mast, as the sail approach'd she made like a man of war, & fir'd two Guns, see another sail along with her, we lay to for about an hour, then the Com: bore away & stood his Course, the strange sail fir'd an other Gun after 10 P.M. – a good deal of lightning in the night, an officers watch Ens. [Charles] Nor[man]. 49[th.], the strange sails seen in the morng but the before noon out of sight, the whole of the last 24 hours a tumbling sea from westwd. at noon had an observation Lat. 43.27 –

Thursday 20th. June fair weather & light winds steering sails out fore & aft. the whole of our fleet in sight, – at 7 see the land bearing N. to NE. – The Como: ahead alter'd his course at 8, after heaving to a little for the sternmost ships to come up. a fine night no officers watch on deck – in the morning 4 sail of the fleet far astern & to leewd. viz the Bristol, Glasgow, & little schooner, the hope Brig wt them at Noon had an observation Lat. 44.09 –

Friday 21st. June clear fine weather little wind see the land off the lee bow, at 8 PM see the land in islands, stood off the Wr. being thick foggy, at 4 AM. 6 guns to ly to on the starboard tack, little or no wind & very foggy catch'd a great number fish cod & Hallybutt in the fore noon see the land very plain close by not above a league off, and saw 2 sail in shore and to eastward, one of them very large. NB what with tacking lying to and hawling to & from the shore calms & fog we seem to be lost in our reckoning at noon had an observation Lat. 44.46

Weather mostly thick & foggy clearing up a little now & then Saturday 22d. June clear'd up a little see most of the fleet, the land in sight near us little wind & foggy a large sail standing out towards us – about 3 PM. the Com. saluted him with 13 Guns which was return'd by the other with 11 – a double Decker – our Com: hawled down his broad Pendant & hoisted a long one, at 6 PM. spoke the Henry and Joseph all well – plenty of fish, they inform'd us the ship saluted was the Eagle[,] Lord Howe from England, having been told so by another of the transports – at 8 PM tack'd to westwd.[14] a thick foggy night, an officers watch on deck – Lt. P. – in the morng caught fish plenty, see 10 or 12 sail the 2 men of war ahead, very little wind, see the land all along the starboard side as we ly to w:wd. – at Noon too foggy to get an observation

Sunday 23d. June clear'd up a good deal, see the land very plain & close by, but nobody knows it. little wind most of the fleet in sight – about 2 PM a signal to tack, stood off – about 3 a Signal to come in under the Como. stern: tack'd after 6 got a peep of the land, tack'd & stood off, at 9 P.M. the Com: haild us, told us not to come so near ask'd if we had seen the admiral, that it was Ld. Howe in the Eagle ask'd for Major & Mrs. Gr[ant]: at 10, tack'd again the night foggy an offrs. watch on deck Lt. Gr: – see the land all the morng stood off & on turning to windwd. the fleet pretty close together the Admiral to windwd standing to the Land, a little before Noon made the Harbours mouth & soon after see the Town, the Admiral lying to at Noon had an observation off Halifax Lat 44.39. –

Monday 24th. June the weather clear & a fine breeze standing in for the Harbour, the Renown went up to the Eagle who was lying to, & then stood off. The Transports entered the harbour about 3 PM. & stood up leaving the men of war in the offing; about 4 came to an anchor opposite the Town; the Commg. offr. went ashore to report, but the Govr. (Capt. Arbuthnot of the Navy) was gone on board the Admiral & the Genl. (Massey) out walking – orders. neither offr. nor soldier to go ashore – an offrs. watch on Deck Lt. Gil: – a fine Morng & warm – leave to go ashore except an offr. pr. ship went ashore in the forenoon, met some old acquaintances, Alister List Mr. A. &ca. deliver'd letters to Mr. Douglas & Mr. Brymer, view'd the Town & Citadel hill not much alteration on the former & a small 8 gun battery on the latter – about 800 Marines, 2 Compys of 14th & 2 of R. H. Emigrts & a Subs. Detachmt of Artillery dined with Alister List
    again surpriz'd to find the fleet & army gone from Halifax & no body here knows where the Admiral gone to sea again

Tuesday 25th. June the weather warm, the long Boat out a

watering at the Dockyard, went ashore & dined with Mr. A: every thin[g] very dear in this place Mutton Lamb or Veal 1/ the lb. & other things in propor: Rum cheap, wine reasonable – call'd at Mrs. Mos. but did not see Miss – but saw my little favr Jeany A: now Mrs. Cochran, pretty but Yankyfied – NB. the People in this Province not much better affected to Governmt than the others, but kept under – an order for the Awkward men & some more to go ashore to Exercise – ships of war in Harbour – the Niger Capt. Arbuthnot Lt. Govr. the Renown Capt. Banks, the Mercury Capt. Montague a Sloop & 2 arm'd Brigs, the Hope & Hero

Wednesday 26th June   very warm, wrote to Dick Marshall & A.H. to go by a ship bound for London[15] – went ashore and din'd wt. Capt. McKay 65th. a genteel Mess – Signal from the Niger frigate (the Comodore here) for Masters of Transports – orders to deliver up their empty Water Casks, & make ready to sail at shortest notice – a Detachmt from each ship ashore at Exercise – sent Sergt. Black to the Hospital on Georges island, poor man ill of a Consumption – the 65t. Regt. drafted   the officers going home next week – arms ashore reparring by the ordinance

Thursday 27th. June   warm & pleasant wr.   a good many men ashore at exercise, under the charge of an officer from each ship – went ashore & din'd wt. Mr. Brymer a Navy com. Agent Secry – the Milford arriv'd wt. a small prize – the Boston Station quite unguarded now, she saw nothing of either of the fleets except the Venus whom she sent to New York – wrote Tom Ar[thur]. & sent the letters on board the ship for London – Willie D[unlop]: came aboard in the Eveng. took a fillup – a rumour of some of the 71st being taken – Gave the Men some money to accot. a dollar to those clear of debt, & half to the others   Bot a small sheep for the Mess 40/[16]

Friday 28th. June   agreeably warm,   ashore early in morng with the men at Exercise, walk'd to the head of N.W. arm &ca. embark'd about noon, bot a Cask of Rum from Mr. Brymer 38 gals. at a dollar, good Rum but thick   my turn to stay aboard, the

Majr. & Sp: dines at the Govrs. the rest on board the Renown –
told by the Govr. we sail tomorrow

A transport of Hessians arrived, & brought in a prize with her,
a sloop   they parted with the fleet 27 May – Got some more
water on board, – orders for Every Body to be on board tonight
in case of sailing tomorrow

Saturday 29th. June   a very hot day, none of the troops
went ashore today to Exercise   I went ashore to get somethings
for the Mess, & dined with Capt. Ramsay 14th. Reg.
exchanged some guineas for Dollars – in the afternoon a black
cloud with thunder & lightning, & then a heavy shower which
cool'd the air – no signal made for sailing today   the Men of
war does not seem to be [in] a hurry – all hands on board,
some rain in the night

Sunday 30t. June   heazy weather & a light breeze at NE, a
Signal in the morning for preparing to sail,   The Milford
weighed & went down near the Mouth of the Harbour & came to
an anchor – about 9 A:M: a Signal for Weighing when the whole
of our fleet weighed & got under sail, the wind at E: veering
round to S.E.   a fine breeze for turning out   Several of the
Transports got below Georges island, but the Como: could not
make it out, so hove out a signal about one for the whole to come
to an anchor on whh those that were down turn'd back & came
to above Georges island, a smart breeze at S.S.E.

Monday 1st. July   The Weather being thick & the wind not
fair made no attempt to get out, the Milford still at anchor down
below – In the afternoon arrived the Brune frigate from Portsmouth in 8 weeks, & 2 transports of Hessians   they left the rest
of their fleet off the Coast, and are expected in tomorrow or next
day,   some say their destination was for Rhode island, but on
intelligence at sea bore away for Halifax – The Hessians seem to
be good looking men, but mostly Recruits I am told & many of
them excellent marksmen

Tuesday 2d. July   thick weather   the wind still about S. &

41

S.S.E. no hopes of getting out – last night a Schooner arrived from Quebec with letters to Genl. Massey acquainting him that Genl. Carleton on the arrival of the Troops from England had proceeded up the River & dispossess'd the Rebels of their Posts at St. Peters lake, & the mouth of the River Sorrel & taken about 200 Prisoners, with their Genls. Thomson & Arnold, with little or no loss on our side, that the Rebels had Pillaged & abandoned Montreal which was taken possession of by Genl. Carleton, – that a Comy. of the 8th. Regt. Capt. Forster & some Indians had come down from Oswegatchie & taken a Post at the Cedars and 500 Prisoners whom they dismissed[17] – this day arrived a large ship with part of the 2d. Regt. of Guards on board

Wednesday 3d. July   a Wet & foggy morning   so thick we could not see the Town, sent our long boat for water got one load by noon & sent her off again – the wind coming about the west-ward & clearing up the Como: made a signal for sailing about 3 P.M.   the fleet got all under way immediately & stood out to sea about 22 or 23 sail, (the Renown & an arm'd schooner) 12 of Highlander. 4 of Guards & Hessians the rest private mercht. men following the army with stores, &ca.   at the mouth of the Harbour a signal from the Renown for all ships to come under his stern we were all pretty close up before dark – at 8 P.M. Cape Sambrough Light House bore S.W. distance one league from which we take our departure   the mouth of the Harbour NNW   Lat. left 44.40   Longi. 63.30

N:B: wrote a memorial to the Lt. Govr. about my land at Cumberland which I intended to deliver tomorrow but on the signal being made for sailing sent it enclosed to Genl. Massey with a card from Major Grant begging the favr. of him to give it in & back it. & acquaint us of its fate – No rendezvous given out, the Masters of Transports furnish'd with sealed orders which they are not to open but in case of separation –

Thursday 4th. July   sea reckoning,[18] left Halifax Harbour as mention'd above, later our Departure at 8 P.M. Cape Sambrough S.W. dist. 1 league, Halifax NNW the Como: ahead, a light in his poop, the fleet pretty close up, the night clear, little wind,   at

4 A.M. clear, about 16 sail of strange ships seen to Eastwd supposed to be part of the Hessian fleet. Our Como: took no notice of them, our fleet in sight except the Milford, who we suppose is gone off to her station in Boston Bay – see a sail standing to the Northwd a topsail schooner the Como: does not mind her – he fired a shot at the Mermaid for shooting ahead – the strange fleet out of sight – at noon had an observation Lat. 44.14.

Friday 5th. July clear weather & light winds the whole fleet in sight but pretty much scattered. the Como: made the Signal for coming under his stern twice but the ships to leeward could not get up & he wd. not bear down to them, in the Eveng a signal for making sail not properly minded, – at 4 AM clear the fleet in sight but far asunder, at 8 foggy, which continued till near noon when it cleared; note Wm. McIntosh's child died this morng. Had a Review of Arms & Ammunition &ca. all in good firing order except 1 or 2, each man has 18 rounds – at noon the fleet tack'd by signal, still scatter'd – Had no observation being buzy with ye Review of Arms &c

Saturday 6th. July clear weather & a light breeze the fleet 24 sail all in sight most of them pretty close up. the Glasgow a good way to leeward, spoke the Peggy & Minerva in Eveng all well, close up with the Como: whole Topsails – a fine clear night, little wind & smooth water, – But about 3 A.M. came on a heavy squall at S.S.W. with lightning & rain, all sails down and clew'd up snug except the wing of the foresail; it lasted half an hour, – at 8 & 9 foggy but clear'd up by 10, saw all the fleet, some ahead of the Como: all carrying double Reef'd Topsails since the squall. – at noon had an observation Lat. 43.14. –

Sunday 7th. July fair weather & light winds the whole fleet in sight & pretty compact, several of them ahead of the Como:. in the Eveng a signal to let us know he would carry lights before 9 P.M. it turn'd thick and we had fog guns as usual till it clear'd up about The Morning clear weather & cool, little wind, the whole fleet in sight, some to leeward about 10 the Como: sett his top gallantsails, & we did so too, at 11 spoke the Peggie all

43

well going to breakfast – spoke the Bristol at Noon had an observation Lat: 42.12. then tacked

Monday 8th. July fair & clear little or no wind all sail sett, at 6 & 8 P.M. lying to under the Comos. stern as p signal he hail'd some of the ships next him to enquire what they were. the fleet all in sight. – the night clear & starry Betwixt 4 & 8 AM. hard rain – at 8 tack'd little wind, most of the fleet ahead of the Como: the forenoon almost calm – at noon cloudie could not see the sun the air warm & sultry –

Tuesday 9th. July calm & sultry, the fleet all in sight lying every way, between 1 & 2 P.M. a Boat from the Peggy to go & see a man very ill, found him in a very uncommon state almost speechless & insensible V:S: [Venesection] & Epispast[ic] [that is, bleeding and blistering] – at 6 P.M. a signal for all masters to go on Board the Como: they got another Paper of sealed orders not to be open'd but in case of separation. the Como. lying to, the fleet crowding up to him, about 7 came on a thick fog – at 8 a signal to make sail after lying by 8 guns & a fog gun every hour till midnight when it cleared up the morng clear & little wind all the fleet in sight & ahead, the Como: close by. at noon had an observation Lat. 41.45

Wednesday 10th. July Clear weather, smooth water & light winds, the fleet all in sight, mostly ahead of the Commodore, all sail sett. – at 8 P.M. tacked and stood to the westward, the wind light & veering – the Night clear & starry with a fine view of the Milky way – in the morning a gentle breeze sprung up from the So-ward, the Wr. clear and the fleet in sight as the day advanced, it come on cloudy, & about 10 AM. began to rain a little & distant thunder – about 11 the Peggy fired 3 Platoons which we suppose is burrying the man yt. was ill – at Noon heavy rain had no observation

Thursday 11th. July forepart heavy rain, but not much wind. the fleet all in sight, but a good deal scattered, in the Eveng. it clear'd up and came on a fine night starry & clear, double Reef'd topsails. sometimes the Courses haul'd up during the heavy showers – a tumbling sea in the night a fine breeze, the Como: off the Weather bow – in the morng 1 of the Grrs. fell down in the fore hold, & hurt himself a good deal – the fleet greatly scatter'd today only 20 sail in sight at noon had an observation Lat. 40.33

Friday 12th. July fore part clear & warm weather little wind & smooth waters. the fleet all in sight carrying topgallant sails. the fore part of the night a good deal of lightening & some clouds. the Como: close by, down top gallantsails & reeff topsails. a light in his poop as usual – between 2 & 3 came on a heavy squall of wind & rain all sails clew'd up, but it did not last long, at 4 wore ship a Gale came on from the Westwd. veering to Nowd. & continued to blow very smart all the morning with a high sea, the fleet much scattered about 15 sail in view the Como: not to be seen – at noon had an observation Lat. 40.10. –

Saturday 13th. July the Gale continues about 4 P.M. the gale takes off & the sea falls, out some reeffs – 20 sail in sight but no word of the Como: most of the fleet to windwd. of us some bearing down, 4 or 5 ships with yr. Colors out as if for a strange sail, but we see none – tack'd & stood in amongst the fleet, then put about again. – clear weather & light wind carrying whole topsails &ca – no appearance of the Como: yet who seems to have lost his fleet, we having 20 sail in Company – between 7 & 8 descried the Como: from the Masthead bearg. NE from us, 2 sail with him we bore away down to him and about noon came under his stern as per signal He asked why didn't you tack t'other night when I made ye. signal buz – at noon had an observation Lat. 39.26

Sunday 14th. July warm weather & a breeze from the Westwd. 23 sail in sight, the arm'd schooner missing. the signal still out for coming under his stern, & 3 times repeated with Guns, but not properly minded by many of the Transports who ly to far to windard of him: a fine Eveng all sail sett. towards night tried to tack on order to get nearer to the Como: but the ship wd not stay – the Como & most of the fleet astern & to windward – about

1 AM. a hard squall of wind & rain but did not last long. foress & topsails, and Reeff'd – about 8 AM. another hard Squall of wind & Rain which lasted about 1/4 of an hour, bore away & clew'd up, the Como: has an Ens. at Mizzon topmast head, vide signals   at Noon had an observation. Lat. 40.4

Monday 15th. July first part clear, towards Eveng. cloudy with Lightening & very warm,   the fleet in sight,   at 4 a signal to tack, put about & stood to the South Eastwd.   a signal to come under his stern, which was in part obeyed, but some far to leeward,   at 8 P.M. came on a heavy squall of Wind & Rain which continued in a hard Gale, clearing up at short intervals   at 9 bore away, the main sheet gave way, & clew line block   the sail a good deal torn, & wt difficulty handed, laid the ship to under a foresail, the foresheet gave way likewise, bent a new one   it continued to blow hard the whole night increased every now & then with a squall, & heavy rain, in the morng only 4 or 5 ships to be seen, & the Gale not abated, with almost constant hard rain, & a tumbling sea; lost our only sheep overboard which was become very tame & a great pet, nor does the Gale yet take off   at noon when it Rains & blows

Tuesday 16th. July the first part blowy, the latter end of the Gale, which abates in the afternoon, & towards night quite moderate, made sail with a gentle breeze from NW. see the Como: & 8 or 9 Sail, some to windwd & some to leewd,   bore away for the Como: about a league off. note in the afternoon got down the old mainsail & bent a new one – the night clear & moderate, the sea fallen & but little wind, the morning fair & warm   see the Como about the same distance as he was last night   8 or 9 Sail in view – see a great number of Dolphin & some Shark's, tried to catch 'em but have not yet succeeded – drying beds & cloaths & setting up the Rigging   at noon had an observation Lat. 39.29 –

Wednesday 17th. July serene & moderately warm little or no wind, 9 Sail in sight including the Como: & ourselves – a number of Dolphin all about ye ship   got a slight harpoon made with which I struck a large Dolphin had hauled him halfway up the side, but the prong of the geeg straitned & let him fall – see the ship with the Guards has suffered something in the Gale about her main topmast or top Gallant mast – spoke the Henry & Joseph all well – Note. our milk goat died suddenly today, supposed from a blow – the night clear with a fine breeze as per Log, which dyed away about 8 AM. – the 9 sail still in sight. the Como: close by. the Wear. warm and little or no wind, see a good many flying fish but no dolphin today yet – at Noon had a late observation Lat. 39.43

Thursday 18th. July fair weather & warm, the little fleet of 9 Sail in sight some a good way to Leeward, the Como: going under easy sail waiting for them – about 8 P.M. he wore ship & stood to the Northward for about an hour, the better to pick up the leewd ships at 9 put about again & stood to the southward per signal the Night Clowdy & some appearance of squalls, but pass'd over lightly – the morng warm & sultry, & little wind, see sixteen sail to windwd bearing down to us with a frigate, about 8 AM. they fell in with us & proove to be those of our fleet we lost Sunday night the frigate we don't yet know. she sent her boat on board the Como. they lay to together awhile then made sail, the frigate astern at noon had an observation. Lat. 38.53

Friday 19th. July fair weather & warm, after dinner spoke the York McVea[19] who told us the frigate that join'd was the Flora who fell in with part of our fleet on tuesday, when she had only the Glencairn & Porter Snow with her, & had separated from the Ocean Houston & 5 or 6 more a few days ago in a fog, the Flora with them had been in Boston Bay 4 or 5 days, but finding it evacuated took down the light the Yankie's had put up, and came away witht being molested. they were 16 days from thence when they fell in with our ships & scarce of water the Transports spared her some – McVea told us something about some of our transports being taken, but Foster of the Peggie who was likewise on board the Flora said he heard nothing of it – at 8 P.M. wear'd & stood to the So:wd. all night & E.wd. at 6 about again, about 7 came on a pretty smart breeze which increased to close reef'd TS the fleet of 24 sail in sight & pretty well up we miss the Jos: & Henry & some others; most of the fleet close reef'd,

Renown ahead & Flora astern   at noon had an observation Lat. 38.56

Saturday 20th. July, the gale increas'd & the sea rose   the fleet a good deal scatter'd   the Como: off the Wr. Bow, the Flora astern, took in our fore topsail & Mizzon topsail   at 6 handed the Maintopsail & stood on under Courses till 10 when the night looking black & ugly the Ship was laid to under bare poles,   it Rain'd & lighten'd all night,   in the Morning the Wind Veer'd about to the Northwd. as P log – The fleet much dispersed in the gale, and we miss two or three ships this morning being able to count only 21 from the Masthd.   the Renown & flora both astern of us, some as far as we can see to leeward.   a Signal to come under my stern – at Noon had an Observation   Lat. 38.31

Sunday 21st. July   fair weather & little wind   the fleet drawing together again, lay to for the Renown to get ahead of us – the great difference betwixt our Lat. per accot. & observation, makes us conclude there is a strong current setting to the southward. the night clear, the sea fallen and a gentle breeze from the N.E.d the first fair wind since we left Halifax   in the morning the breeze freshens, the weather clear and moderately warm, – a strange sail fallen in wt. ye. fleet ahead. we now count 23 from masthead. The Flora spoke us, Sir Wm. Erskine ask'd for Majr. Grant say they hear bad accounts of some of our Transports but hopes it is not true.[20] At Noon had an observation   Lat. 38.21

Monday 22d. July   fair weather & warm, carrying steering sails to a fine breeze, the Renown a good way ahead leading the fleet, we astern with the Flora, our ship does not sail so well this passage as she did before, the Bristol a great way astern. the rest of the fleet 23 sail pretty close up; spoke the Experiment, Capt. McIntosh says the story about some of our Transports being taken is the same we hear'd at Halifax;   am afraid that some are fallen into the hands of the Yankies;   the Night clear and serene. steering sail taken in, in the morng the breeze fell off to very gentle, the fleet all in sight and ahead except one we take to be the Bristol who is very far astern,   the day warm, little wind & smooth water

3 steering sails out – the Recruits fired some powder. at Noon had an observation Lat. 39.45.

Tuesday 23d. July fair weather & moderately warm little wind & smooth water. the fleet all pretty close up except two astern, and we lag in the Rear – see a number of fish they call skips jacks, but they won't come near our bait – The night Calm clear, starry & moonshine, took the altitude of the some of the stars with ye Quadrant.

The morning foggy and very little wind, the Como: made a signal to ly to with starboard tack on board, during which time the Flora sent her boats on board the Renown & got some water; 21 sail seen from the Deck, & 2 more from the masthead far to the Eastward. at noon had an observation Review of Arms &ca. Lat. 39.48

Wednesday 24th. July fair weather & light winds the fleet close together spoke the Glencarin & the Mermaid Capt. Hunter reckons himself in Longi 72.50, he kept company with the Flora all the voyage; 3 weeks from Boston Bay last Saturday, they landed 60 men on Light H: island, & brot. off their colors and lanthorn – one of our sailors spear'd a skip jack. not a good fish. The fleet crowding under all sail; The Como: lay to[,] to put Capt. Brisbane (we suppose) on board the Flora after his dinner. saw a strange sail in the Eveng. to leeward – the night clear and a light breeze carrying steering sails, the morng clowdy, about 8 a hard shower it continued to rain for some time after, but clear'd about noon see 3 strange sail far to no:wd. – some of our sailors tho't they saw the land off the lee bow at Noon had an observation Lat. 40.00

Thursday 25th. July flying clowds but no rain little wind & smooth water, carrying all sail – The fleet close together 21 sail – spoke the York he says the Longi. 72.20. at Noon – the Renown & Flora hove to we suppose to sound; the water looks dark yett see a number of Porposes jumping very high – the night clear & moonshine, but very little wind. These two nights past took a Phillup [fillip] – the morning clear and the weather warm, slipping gently thro' the water, see a good many bottle noses two shot fired at them – 2 sail to leeward seen from the deck, the Flora bore away for them – at Noon had an observation Lat. 40.15

Friday 26th. July fair weather & warm, carrying all sail to a light breeze. – The Flora went down to the two sail to leeward & return'd towards the Renown soon after they both bore away, & the fleet followed, till we pick'd up the 2 sail who appear to be the Bristol & the Porter Snow, which makes the fleet now 23 sail. The Night Clowdy & warm but very little wind, it clear'd up towards morng –
See a strange sail to the N.E.ward the Como: hoisted his colours, answered by the frigate who soon after put about & stood to the Ewd. & at another signal tack'd again, the fleet pretty close hawling to the Westwd. at noon had an observation Lat. 40.30

Saturday 27th. July fair weather and little or no wind, the fleet pretty well together. The Flora standing towards the strange sail who appears to be a frigate coming down to us with all sail sett, the Eveng. turning calm she lay by at a good Distance – The night clear & serene, very little wind, towards morning cool & pleasant – In the morng. see the three man of war lying together but we don't know who this strange frigate is, about 6 A.M. she stood away to the Eastwd – spoke a ship with Hessians, they found bottom yesterday morning 70 fatm. – we sounded at noon but got no ground wt. 85 fatm. At Noon had an observation Lat. 40.19. –

Sunday 28th. July, fair Wr. & little wind, the fleet close up, the Como: made a signal to come under his stern, and bore soon away to the S.W.d – spoke the Bristol who informed us she had an engagmt. with a schooner privateer on Wednesday for about an hour, & beat her off with the loss of 1 sailor kill'd, his Mate wounded & 3 soldiers wod. they suppose the Prr. lost a good many men, the Porter Snow was along side the Bristol all the time the wod. soldrs. gone on board the Flora – in the Eveng. spoke the Peggy & Mermaid who inform'd us the Frigate that came into the fleet yesterday was the Liverpool 9 days out from N.York, that Genl. Howe was Encamp'd on Staten island, that Genl. Burgoyne was at Albany wt. 15,000 that they were in Ca: wt the Ocean & 5 or 6 more & left 7 on back of Long island 5 days ago, that we are now off Nantucket Shoals – several ships found bottom, some 40 fatm.[21] N:B: there must be a strong current setting to Ewd. – the last 24 hours clear and a fine breeze the fleet close together   the Como: hove to at Noon we suppose to sound, the Bristol a little astern   at Noon had an observation Lat. 40.5 –

Monday 29th. July   fair weather & a fine breeze   carrying steering sails   the fleet close up except the Bristol. spoke the Minerva and told them the news we heard yesterday & afterwards the Glasgow who sent us a young Pig which we haul'd aboard in a bag – the Night clear and the breeze steddy   the fleet crowding all sail – in the Morng fair Wr. & warm   the fleet close up except the Bristol; at 8 AM sounded & found bottom with 50 fatm. – the Como: lay to an hour & then took the Porter Snow in tow. the Frigate gone to bring up the Bristol   at Noon had an observation   Lat. 40.21

Tuesday 30th. July. fair weather & a fine breeze   carrying all sail. the fleet close up except the Bristol whom the Flora is gone for. spoke one of the Hessian Ships they think we are within 40 miles of ye land – at 7 PM. sounded 60 fathom, oazy bottom; being ahead reef'd the topsails. the fore part of the night clear & moonshine, but the breeze increased to close reef'd topsails, and towards morng came on hard rain. laid the ship to under bare poles, a high tumbling sea, and flying fog. sounded after 4 AM & found 50 fatm. as it clears up see most of the fleet count 21 sail   the como: not far off – about noon sounded again 45 fatm.   a signal to tack, about ship   at noon had an observation   Lat. 40.36

Wednesday 31st. July   fair weather and calm with a tumbling swell of a sea, the fleet lying tossing about in all directions – it was about 7 in evening we first observed an Eclipse of the Moon which became allmost total about 8 when Luna began again to emerge from under the shadow of the Earth, but clouds coming over when she was about half illumin'd we could not see the end or know the duration of it. the Morng. clear & a gentle air of wind, the body of the fleet at some distance from us to Eastwd. the water muddy like, and an appearance of a current – sounded on 49 fath: at Noon had an observation Lat. 40.25

Thursday 1st. Augt. fair weather & calm, the water smooth, sunk a bottle full of fresh water & well cork'd and it came up full of salt water the cork out. struck a shark with the little harpoon but he wriggled himself clear of it & twisted the prongs all manner of ways, – saw 2 or 3 guers. The Body of the fleet with the Como: at some distance from us S:E. in the Eveng. a gentle breeze sprung up, when we stood for the fleet. The Night clear as a bell – in the morng the fleet to windwd & astern crowding up, the Surprize a good way ahead has hoisted her colors. – see 3 sail ahead from the masthead. – a Review at Noon had an observation Lat. 40.21

Friday 2d. Augt. fair wr. & a fine breeze, three large sail ahead coming bowling down upon us, & prove to be 3 frigates viz. the Greyhound, the Orpheus and believe the Niger the last a small sloop in tow, they came under the Comos. stern sent boats aboard & lay to for about 2 hours, then 2 of them stood off and went down to a sail to leeward which we take to be the Flora see another sail wide of her and to leeward. The Night Clowdy the Fleet pretty close, the breeze freshens but veers to the Westwd – Single reef'd Topsails all night The Morng hazy the fleet pretty well up we the wr. most ship – see the land off the leebow, the leeward ships putting about, it must be Long island, count 22 sail the Flora close by us, one brig a good way ahead tacking. about 11 we put about & stood off to the So.wd. at Noon had an observation Lat. 40.36

Saturday 3d. Augt. fair weather & light winds, the fleet pretty close together the Como: & Flora ahead, the latter hoisted out her boat & went on board the Renown, they lay for some hours, the fleet got up – the land off the lee Bow, at 4 PM. tack'd P signal & stood towards the land again at night the wind came about to the No:wd. clear & shining towards morning came on a Squal of wind while clear & split our main topsail, at 2 coming near the land, put about at 4 tack'd again and made some westing, in the Morng. see the whole fleet ahead of us & to windwd. see the Neversunk & the coast of the Jerseys. the whole fleet turning to windwd to haul in with the Hook – one of the frigates (believe the Niger) tore away before the wind. Sounded 2 or 3 times about 10 fatm. at Noon took an observation Lat 40.22

Sunday 4th. Augt. light winds from the NWd. the fleet tacking and streetching along the Jersey shore, to endeavour to haul in with the Hook, in the Evening the Como: & Flora came to an anchor, we close by them, but as the water was pretty deep (14 or 15 fatm.) we stood off & on all night but by some mismanagement found ourselves to leeward in the morning & farthest from the land. – the men of war weighed & made sail but being almost calm made little or [no] way, they got out Boats ahead, see but few of the fleet, suppose a good many have got within the Hook – about eleven AM a breeze sprang up from the sea, which shut us in with the land, being the sternmost ship the Niger gave us a tow the breeze increasing went at a fine rate past the Hook

Sunday afternoon.[22] a fine breeze from the southwd. when within the Hook the Niger call'd to us to heave off the tow she stood in & came to anchor within the hook having a Pilot on board we stood up with all sail set the Renown & Flora ahead, got up to the watering place, Staten island where the fleet lay (above 200 sail) in the Eveng. – was in the boat to go ashore for orders but met Majr. McPherson with orders for us: to land in the morning, with little Baggage and 3 days Provision –

Monday morning 5th. Augt. prepared to land. first boat about 11, being a good dist from the shore & a strong wind & tide, it was late in the afternoon before we all got ashore, march'd in the eveng to Quarters in the country Peoples houses about 2 or 3 mile. few of the army Encamp'd almost the whole lodged in the farmers houses & barns Landed the whole co[mpan]y in good health after being above sixteen weeks on board of ship. N:B: the Bristol got up Monday afternoon.

Chapter II

'appointed Adjut . . . to the 4th. Battn of Grenadrs.'

White Plains, Newport, and New York City
16 October 1776 to 12 February 1777

Soon after John Peebles reached New York in August 1776, the British began an offensive designed to end the rebellion with a combination of force and persuasion. The British commanders, General William Howe and his brother Admiral Richard Lord Howe, had greatly superior forces; and they might well have broken the rebellion by trapping and destroying the rebels assembled against them at New York. But the Howes, clearly preferring reconciliation to conquest, decided to concentrate on manoeuvering the rebels out of New York rather than on trapping them there. By pressing the Americans to abandon their positions on Long Island, New York Island, and adjacent portions of New York and New Jersey, the Howes hoped to create the impression of British invincibility and encourage a negotiated peace. Thus, between August and December, they executed a series of turning movements, punctuated by limited and successful engagements, that forced the Americans to give up Long Island and New York City, withdraw into West Chester County, surrender the remainder of New York Island, and abandon much of New Jersey and Rhode Island. With each success the Howes made a fresh conciliatory gesture, and this combination of force and persuasion was threatening to break the rebellion when Washington surprised British forces at Trenton and Princeton. His victories, coming at the end of the campaign, inspired the rebels, blighted the Howes' hopes for reconciliation, and forced the British to give up all their posts in New Jersey except those around Brunswick and Amboy on the Raritan River.[1]

During the Howes' campaign of 1776 at New York and Rhode Island, John Peebles served as an adjutant to a battalion of British grenadiers.

In most British infantry regiments of this era, there were ten companies: eight of the line, one of grenadiers, and one of light infantry. All companies were expected to be able to march, manoeuver, and fire together in intricate and disciplined ways. The grenadier and light companies, made up of men specially chosen for their strength and skill, were expected to do more, to fight with greater independence and under looser tactical control on the fringes of the regiment or army. Peebles had come to America as one of three officers in the grenadier company of the 42nd Regiment. The day after he reached Staten Island, his company was withdrawn from the 42nd and assigned (with two other companies of grenadiers) to a special tactical unit, the 4th Battalion of Grenadiers. He was subsequently appointed adjutant to this battalion, probably in recognition of his strong education, prior administrative experience, and ability to express himself clearly.[2] He was expected to keep the battalion's records, to draft orders and instructions, and to see that assignments were distributed evenly among the officers and men.

The 4th Battalion of Grenadiers was, in turn, organized as a part of the 'Reserve' and assigned, at the beginning of the campaign of 1776, to the First Division of the army under the command of General Henry Clinton. Peebles and his battalion were among the advanced guard that turned the American flank on Long Island on 27 August and that led the British on to New York Island on 15 September.[3] In October the 4th Battalion of Grenadiers was disbanded and the 42nd Grenadiers were reassigned to the 3rd Battalion of Grenadiers. But the 3rd Battalion remained a part of Clinton's First Division and was in the advanced guard that landed in West Chester in October, pushed on to White Plains, returned in November to New York Island to join in capturing Fort Washington, and that went in December to occupy Rhode Island.[4]

Although Peebles' appointment as adjutant ended in October when the 4th Battalion of Grenadiers was disbanded, that appointment inspired his halting emergence as a diarist of the American War. As an adjutant, he had maintained a daily record of the general, divisional, and battalion orders that governed the 4th Battalion of Grenadiers – orders defining the organization and directing the movements of the army, establishing tactical procedures, praising or censuring the behavior of officers and men, convening military courts and ratifying their judgments, making routine assignments, and announcing promotions and appointments. For about a week after the 4th Battalion was disbanded, Peebles continued to record the orders affecting his company and its new tactical unit, the 3rd Battalion of Grenadiers. But in the middle of

October he began to embellish those orders with narrative accounts of the movements of the army and of its engagements with the rebels at such places as White Plains and Fort Washington. By the end of November, when he and the 3rd Battalion of Grenadiers embarked from New York for Rhode Island, Peebles was no longer recording orders; and his narrative embellishments had become a full and regular journal of his experiences in the American War – of the taking of Rhode Island, the social life of the British army in its winter quarters at Newport, and the redeployment of Peebles and his Battalion of Grenadiers from Rhode Island to New York and then to New Jersey.[5]

White Plains, Newport and New York City
16 October 1776 to 12 February 1777

Octr. 16th., 1776   N:B: March'd in the Night on order to Embark but it rain'd hard & the Troops return'd to their Ground.

Octr. 18th. the army march'd early in the morng. Genl. Clintons Division Embark'd at the place where we landed & went up a creek where we landed on the right hand shore, the rest cross'd near the head of the creek in the boats that carried us, except two Brigades left for a while on Frog Neck with Genl. Agnew. The Advanced Troops had a skirmish with the Enemy some kill'd & wounded, got that day to near East Chester. on the High road from N. York to Boston.[6]

Octr. 21st. NB march'd thro' N. Rochelle & turn'd to the left proceeded on the Albany road 3 or 4 miles & encamp'd on high Grounds to the right of the road, from whence we see several of the Enemys Camps to westwd.[7]

Octr. 23rd. N: Genl. Clinton went out with a Batt. of Light Infantry & some Chasseurs to reconoitre some Hills towards the enemys Encampments they had a small skirmish & returned in the Eveng.

[Octr. 25th.] Note The army march'd in above order to the westward across the Country 5 or 6 miles & came to Banks of the Brunx along which the Camp extended for 3 or 4 miles, the Enemy having a pretty large Camp on the opposite side, the Brunks or Brunse a Small River with steep banks, & high ground on each side, comes down from the northward thro' the Country for above 20 miles & empties itself into Harlem River near the mouth.

Octr. 27th. 1776   Note 'a Hessian Soldier stragled from camp & was taken by the Enemy, he was carried before Genl. Washington who sounded him with regard to the Hessians disposition for the service & told him they would get great encouragemt. if they wod come over to them, gave him a guinea &

dismissed him to go back to his Corps, when he returned he acquainted Genl. How with what happen'd who likewise gave him a guinea, but his own Genl. ordered him to be flogg'd. They have try'd more than once to seduce the foreigners.'

N: Capt. Cannons servt. & a Drum fired upon & chased by the rebels – within a mile or two of Camp.

[Octr. 28th.] Note   The Army march'd to the right No:wd. up the banks of the Brunse for a mile or two then turn'd more to the right, across the Country halting & reconoitring as we went along seeing marks of the Enemy in the way   about noon there was a skirmish in front with the light Infantry & some stragling parties of the Enemy we halted & fired some Cannon to clear a wood, then march'd on & came in sight of the Village of White Plains, on the heights about which the Enemy were Encamp'd & for-tifyed.   they drew out & fired some guns as we approached. The army drawn up with the Brunse & village of White Plains in front, a large body of the Enemy appeared on a hill on the opposite side of the Brunse to their Right of their works. After some time spent in reconoitring the Ground, a Cannonade began which came on to be very brisk on our side, then the 2d. Brigade of British and some Hessians were ordered to pass the Brunse at a ford in their front which the Enemy seemed disposed to defend, when our Troops moved down, the Enemy rush'd towards the highbanks of the Brunse in great numbers & began a very heavy fire upon them as they pass'd ye River which they kept up all the time they were forming & moving up the steep hill on t'other side but the steddiness & intrepidity of our Troops beat them from their strong grounds where they had taken the advantage of fences & stone walls, & made them retire back on the remaining body that was posted on the hill before mention'd who immediately turned tail with the fugitives & ran off in the greatest confusion to their works on the other hills.   in this attack we lost Lt. Colo: [Robert] Carr some other good offrs. & about 200 men killed & wounded: the Rebels suffered considerably both from our Cannon and Mus-ketry and exhibited to our whole army, (who were looking on) a recent proof of their inferiority in courage & discipline.

Octr. 30th. 1776 Note The Enemy busy at work on the Hills before us, they seem to have a great body of Troops here.

Novr. 2d. 1776 Note The Enemy are still busy at work on all the Hills. This Country is remarkably strong & very Hilly, & the Enemy have taken the advantage of it by posting themselves on the tops of the Highest hills which they are indefatiguable in fortifying. their sentries & ours firing at one another – a good deal of maroding going on, ye Guards &ca.

Novr. 3d. The Picqts. of the Reserve extend along the E road from White Plains towds. Rochelle see the Enemy in front who have nab'd some of stragling maroders. They say Genl. [Charles] Lee intended to get round our right flank. I Believe an attack upon the Enemys works on the Hill next to & above White Plains Village was intended two days ago, but they set fire to some Houses & went off in the night. They have still several Camps on the tops of high hills which they are busy fortifying. They have had a great part of their army here who seem to be Retreating into New England, & the Country here about is every where so strong & they so indefatiguable in working, that there is no prospect of a successfull attack witht losing a great number of men.

Novr. 5th. 1776 The army was put in motion early in the morng. from the left, & marched to the Southward, but owing to the great quantity of heavy loaded waggons & a rough Country they made but slow progress; in the afternoon the Rear of the army made several movemts. on the Hill where the action of the 28th. Octr. was & that to the left of it, the Enemy shewing themselves in small parties on the fortifyed hill opposite watching our motions. we lay on our arms on these hills all night owing I suppose to the impedement the Baggage & front of the army met with on the road, the night very cold & no covering.

Novr. 6th. we that remain'd on the ground last night march'd pretty early in the morng down the east side of the Brunse for 4 or 5 miles then turn'd short to the right & marched across a hilly rough Country for 5 or six miles to the North River at Dobbs ferry where the Army Encamped, on deversifyed ground along the East side of the River, the prettiest Encampment we had yet. Note   Some Frigates & victualers lying at Dobbs ferry – the Enemy have a Post & Battery on the opposite side. A good deal of clear Country but the weather foggy can't see far, the Encampment beautiful at night with the number of fires.

Novr. 7th. 76   Note. Genl. Kniphausen with a body of Hessians has taken Post some days ago on tother side Kingsbridge near the high grounds about Fort Washington.

Novr. 8th. 76   Note   The Battery on the Jersey Shore fired 10 or 12 rounds at Frigate & two ships lying near to the wharf Dobbs ferry and made some very good shots, distance about 2000 yards

Novr. 9th.   N: The Reserves did not move today, but one Battn. of the 42d. march'd up the Albany Road a few miles & took some Rebel Stores.

Novr. 12th.   The army put in motion early in the morng. which was clear & cold, but the arrangement of the Baggage & accidents happening to ye Waggons retarded us much in the forepart of the day. We the left Column march'd the road we came from White Plains as far as the Saw Mill Bridge which is about 1 1/2 miles, then turn'd short to the right & marched along the East bank of sd. River (in a fine Valley with high Grouns on each side) for 6 or 7 miles when we halted at a very good house, took our Tents &ca. out of the waggons & carried them 3 or 4 miles, thro bad road & a narrow pass which had been stop'd with a work lately made, Encamp'd on good ground within a few miles of Kings Bridge but don't know what Name they gave it, almost dark when we got to our ground & the waggons did not arrive for 3 hours after –

Novr. 13th. 1776   Note   The Baggage went off pretty early this morng. & the column march'd about nine, turn'd to the left across the country, pass'd the Encampments of some of the Brigades who have been there 10 or 12 days,   cross'd the Brunse at a Bridge where the Enemy had made some works, turn'd short to the right, crossed the Brunse again at Delancy's Mills & encamp'd about a mile below – Frog neck about a mile & a 1/2 off. Kings Bridge about 3 miles, and Morrisinia about 5 miles[8]

Novr. 14th. Reconoitred the Country about Kings Bridge & the east banks of Harlem River, at the former the eny. have had a great deal of Barracks & other buildings which they have burnt down, and left Ft. Independence standg. with all its Cannon, Genl. Kniphausen & his Corps have approach'd with yr. Battrys near the heights about Ft. Washington. The Enemy busy at work on the Hills across Harlem River

Novr. 16th. Attack of Ft. Washington

The Troops were under arms according to the orders of yesterday. We the Grenadrs. marched from our Encampment (leaving our Tents standg), an hour before day towards Kingsbridge when near that turn'd to the left & halted about sun rise in fields near Harlem River about a mile below Kingsbridge & out of sight of the Rebels works on t'other side Harlem River. Having a great train of artillery brought up to play against the Enemy, most of which was planted on the Eastern bank of Harlem River, a Cannonade began between six & seven in the morng. which increased as the day advanced from all our Guns & mortars on Harlem River and those in Genl. Kniphausens Quarter together with that of a Frigate lying in Hudsons River, and continue for several hours. The Light Infantry & Guards were early Embark'd in flat Boats about King's Bridge, that came round by the North River, & fell down towds. the high point of land opposite to where we halted, keeping themselves under cover of the westshore from few Guns the Enemy had on the high ground that was to be attack'd, against which our Guns and mortars kept a very brisk fire. it was near noon when a signal was made for Genl. Kniphausen to begin his attack upon the Enemy posted on the High Grounds to the Right nearest Hudson River. he proceeded with the Hessians under his Command thro the intermediate low-ground much retarded by Woods & fences to the foot of that hill where the Enemy were posted to oppose him, & sustain'd a very heavy irregular fire for above 20 minutes which he return'd as his

Situation wd. admit of gaining ground by degrees up the face of a steep hill render'd almost inaccessible by fallen Trees, the Hessians who are slow but steady Troops drove them at last from their stronghold & gain'd the summit of the hill. In the mean time the Light Infantry & Guards were landed at the foot of the high ground opposite to where we were, & dash'd up the Hill with alacrity, driving the Enemy before them. The Boats were immediately sent back for the Grenadrs who mounted the hill as they arrived without firing a shot. While these operations were going on to the northward of Ft. Washington, Lord Percy was advancing with his Troops from the Lines on New York Side, & the 42d. Regt. cross'd Harlem River near opposite to Colo: Morris's House which is 4 or 5 miles below King's bridge, where they were opposed by a considerable body of the Enemy Posted on those steep hills who began their fire upon them before they landed; notwithstanding every difficulty they push'd ashore unsupported, mounted the Hill & drove them quite across the island killing & taking a good many, & clear'd the way in a great measure for Lord Percy's Brigades to advance – by this time about 3 oclock in the afternoon all the different attacks had succeeded & we were in possession of all the High Grounds in the environs of Fort Washington, having taken & killed a good number between 3 & 400 of the Enemy & driven the rest into the Fort: Genl. Kniphausen proceeded with his Hessians to the very Barrier of the Fort which being surrounded on all quarars. they beat a parley & desired to Capitulate. The terms given them were to ground their arms and become Prisoners of War, which they did to the Number of about 2600 & the Fort was taken possession immediately by the light infantry & some Hessians. some of their best Troops were here & most them riffle men, Colo: [Robert] McGaw (an old acquaintance) Commanding offr. & one of the Cadwalladers Lt. Colo: The Fort which is an irregular Pentagon of Earth with a ditch, & abbatis de bois, is render'd strong from the ground arround it which is every where difficult of access by nature & render'd still more by their indifatiguable labour: it stands on the high bank of Hudson River about 12 or 13 miles from N. York has some out works & a strong battery at the water side; opposite is a fort on the Jersey shore. Most of the Troops returned to their former ground that night a good deal fatigued[9]

Novr. 17th. fine wr. & a day of rest   the 18th. we the 3d. Battn. Grenadrs. march'd to New York & Encamp'd on the Plains at the North end of the Town, some other Troops came there likewise – The Rebel Prisoners march'd into town. Things getting ready for a Secret expedition. We remain'd in this Camp about a week & then Embark'd for the Lord knows where – In the mean time Lord Cornwallis with the gros of the field army cross'd the North River & took Fort Lee and Constitution and proceeded into the Jersey.

On Monday 25th Novr. 3d. Battn. Grenadrs. Embark'd on board the Rachel & Mary & The Hunter Transports at New York, being part of the Troops for an Expedition the destination of which is not yet publickly known. 4 Line of Battle Ships 2 Frigates & about six thousand land troops British & Hessian make up the Force of this secret expedition, Lieut. Genl. Clinton & Sir Peter Parker the land & sea Commanders – Laid in stock & stores for a 3 or 4 weeks Voyage 12 officers in the Cabin, the 28th. Compy.   the 42d. (all but an officer & 20 detached on board the Rachel & Mary) the 54th. & the 57th. Compys on board the Hunter, an old ship & somewhat leaky John Hudson Master[10]

Tuesday 26th. Novr. employed in compleating our stores & laying in some warm cloathing for the men in winter. The Troops all Embark'd Genl. Howe in Town forwarding the Expedition, Lord Cornwallis gaining ground in the Jerseys

Wednesday 27th. Novr. a dirty rainy day with the wind at SW The men of war & some of the Transports fell down to red Hook some men from the Hospitals join'd the Compy.   wrote a few lines to Dick Marshall & appologized for a longer letter which I had not time to write sent him a riffle by Mr. Patk: Ried who goes for Glasgow first oppoy.   wrote likewise a short letter to AH directed to HN & a card to Miss Smith about her bror.

Thursday morng. 28th. Novr. in the morng. got orders to get under way and sail up the East River, which we did accordingly, the Master being somewhat acquainted with the navigation did not require a Pilot, the wind dying away came to anchor at the mouth of Newton Creek

Friday morng. 29th. got under way early, the Wind being North Easterly we took advantage of the flood tide & let the ship be carried up with the current, the rest of the Transports got also under way & followed us we drove up broad side formost managing the ship so with the sail as to keep her in the current & channel, near to Hell Gate an Agent Mr. Knowles come on board of us & tho' the wind was contrary meant to carry the ship thro' but we got into the Eddy at Hallets Cove & our stern touched upon the Rocks at the Point there, we then hauled into Hallets Cove & came to an anchor there as did likewise 9 or 10 more ships that came after us the rest of the fleet came too below Blackwells island – The mercury a Transport with Light Infantry struck just under the Fort at Hell Gate, got off again & touch'd on the upper end of Blackwells Island. they got her off there too, and came to an anchor in the Channel – some Horse Ships lying at Hallets Cove, took a walk ashore –

Saturday Novr. 30th. St. Andrew's day a Rainy morng. the wind about S:E: any thing that was; towards noon it clear'd up a little made several attempts to haul out into the Current in order to get up thro' Hell Gate but fail'd, we touch'd upon the point again, one ship got thro'; in the afternoon the wind came to the westward & blew pretty smartly but could not get the ships haul'd out into the stream. the kedge anchors would not hold, so gave it up for that day – and sat down to celebrate the day which is always kept with festivity & mirth by the wandering sons of St. Andrew, we had a good dinner, pour'd a libation to the saint, and did justice to his memory, with a hearty glass; may joy & good fellowship always preside at his feasts, & banish every foe to mirth & friendship –

Sunday 1st. Decr. the wind at West & fair weather made loose in the morng. & got into the stream when near the last of the

Ebb & had a fine breeze to stem the Current; the rest of the ships that were in Hallets Cove made loose also, & we all got safe thro Hell Gate & were followd by the rest of the fleet that were below, we sail'd up the East river & came to an anchor at Whitestone opposite to Frog point. the Mercury & another small man of war with us in all five or six & thirty sail, some not come up yet the large men of war gone out at Sandy Hook, we [word missing] our destination is for Rhode island & they will join us some where [word missing] being a fine day went ashore on Long Island & walk'd to flushing about 3 miles din'd with Mr. & Mrs. Colden, & return'd in the Eveng.[11]

Monday 2d. Decr. the wind about SW:W: sharp & cold the fleet in the same positions waiting for the remainder of the ships to come up fine weather some gone ashore to walk & shoot – killed a quail –

Tuesday 3d. Decr. a wet dirty morning wind about S:E: a signal from the agents ship for all masters, ours went on board & got some general directions & was told to go on board the Brune Commodore [William] Hothom, which he did & got a paper of signals for future observation The day clear'd up at intervals & about noon the wind came round to the southward & blew smartly. some of gentlen. gone ashore to walk and shoot a Scowry sort of a day, no more ships come up yet – they killed a brace of Quail and a wild Duck –

Wednesday 4th. Decr. it rain'd constantly the foregoing night & continues to do so still, little or no wind about SW. a good many more ships come up & two or three schooners come down the sound, the Fleet about 50 sail now – nothing new in the Comos. instructions, about noon a signal made for sailing on which the different ships got under way as soon as convenient & sailed to the Eastward with a fine breeeze at NW.[12] about 4 P.M. New Rochelle on the Larboard beam & I believe Oysty Bay on Starboard. – as the Evening came on the breeze freshen'd & the sky clear'd – a fine clear starry night & a smart gale the whole fleet close together going under easy sail 5 or 6 knots – in the morning Reef'd Topsails. about 6 AM a signal to lye to, as the day open'd saw 4 or five sail of large men of war lying at anchor near the middle of the sound – they must be those that sail'd from the Hook for our Convoy. We soon after haul'd in with the Coast of Conecticut and the whole fleet came to anchor in a kind of Bay we suppose not far from New London –

Thursday 5th. Decr. continued the fleet that is the Transport & frigates lying at Anchor in the mouth of this same Bay of which we don't yet know the Name. a Smart gale at WNW. The Capital ships of war lying at anchor to the south westward, near the middle of the Sound a boat from them about Noon gone on board one of the frigates our Como:, it does not yet seem clear where we are bound to, whether to land on the Continent or on Rhode Island – two signals from the Como. but I believe they do not concern us Transports, some small craft seen in the offing. perhaps Yanky Privateers – Signals from the agents for Masters of Transports, which they accordingly obey'd & got fresh seal'd orders not to be open'd but in case of separation & in presence of the Officer commanding the Troops on board, likewise a paper with the form of Sailing sign'd by Sir Peter Parker – in the afternoon the large men of war &ca. came up & join'd the rest of the fleet, who are now altogether & in number above 60 sail including some small sloops & schooners that attend the Fleet – no communication with the shore the wind blows off A fine clear starry night about seven was seen a meteor in the sky that left its tract for an considerable time for a great distance there was likewise one seen in the day time which was then taken for a Rocket.

Friday 6th. Decr. fine fair weather a little wind about East The men of war getting under way in the morng. & ar[e] follow'd by the transports, stand off to the southward till near the shore which I take to be Long island, then tack & stand over towards the Coast of N. England again, about ship & stand out to southwd. see a Town & Light House which we take to be New London at Noon bearing N about 3 leagues do

Form of Sailing

Chatham

Experiment   Lieut. Knowles's Transports   Asia

Lieut. Parry's Transports

Renown

Emerald   To repeat signals as command in 3d Past   Brune

Sphynx   Lieut. Dickinsons Transports   Centurion
          Lieut. Sutherlands ship

Preston

Friday 6th. continued the fleet all close together & getting into the order prescribed last page. in the harbour of New London see 6 or 7 sail one of them a pretty large square rigg'd Vessel, about Noon came into a strong current setting to the N.Ed. about 2 PM. the current slack'd & turn'd, on which Sir Peter made a signal to anchor, the signal repeated by the Preston, & soon after 3 Guns were fired off our Larboard Quarter on t'other side an island we take to be fishers island. The Fleet rather dilatory in obeying the signal it was repeated by the Commodore & soon after the whole came to anchor in above 20 fathom water. light wind about S.E. the middle of Fishers island bearing about N.E. 1 league New London about NBW, between 3 & 4 leagues distant, The East end of long island about south or SBE, 4 or 5 leagues off – just before we dropp'd anchor we ran foul of a ship of the 52d Regt. Colo: Campbell on board & tore her Foresail &ca. after a little altercation got clear & came to – a fine moderate Evening the whole fleet riding in the mouth of the Sound – the Night clear & the wind moderate –

Saturday 7th. Decr. about 4 in the morng. a signal was made

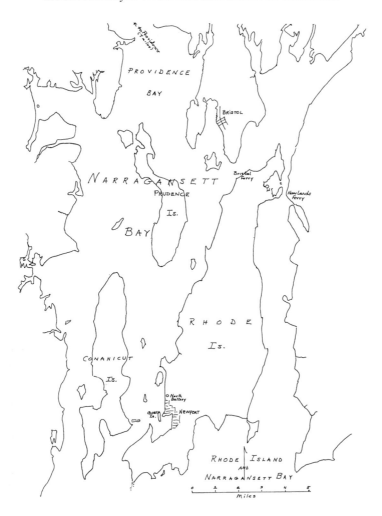

to weigh, but having a good deal of cable out it was some time
before the ships got up their anchors. the weather fair & clear &
the wind about WSW, made sail & steered EBN & ENE   at 8 an
island on the starboard bow which we take for Block Island about
3 leagues off, the Continent on our larboard all along [line miss-
ing] between 10 & 11 A.M. abreast with the East end of Block
island. the land to Port seems to be well inhabited, see some small

69

craft in shore – a fine steady breeze about W. or WSW going 3
or 4 knots with single reef'd Topsails, the Fleet pretty close up
together – a[t] Noon made Rhode Island, & the Islands thereabouts about 1 a signal from the Como: on which the Experiment
took the lead & the Asia folld., the Preston shot ahead, followd
by the Renown & the Transports crowded up, Soon after we
pass'd the Light House & saw the Town of New Port about 3
leagues off – Sail'd up a Channel Naraganset about a league
across, for five or 6 miles then haul'd up to S:E: we ran foul of
two ships & broke our Bowsprit, came to an anchor below the
Town as per signal about 4 P.M. & in the Eveng. recd. orders to
be ready to Land at day break caps on: no great appearance of
much opposition.   a pretty looking Country & well Cleared – saw
three large sail running off – Admiral Hopkins's fleet, gone to
Providence Colo: [James] Marsh took his leave in orders & gave
up the Comd. to Major [Charles] Stuart

Sunday 8th. Decr. got into the flat Boats early in the morng.
The Light Infantry & Grenadrs. & assembled under the stern of
the Experiment,   at a signal from the Como: & repeated by the
Experiment we pushed off to shore & landed without any opposition about 4 miles to the Northwd. of New Port,   we bent our
course towards the Town at first for about a mile or more, and
then turn'd back and marched towards the north end of the
Island, when about a Mile from Bristol ferry the Grenrs. were
order'd to lay down their Packs & load. (the light Infantry having
turn'd off to the right) we march'd towards the ferry and came
time enough to see the two last boats push off. the 15th. comy.
went down to the ferry house. The Rebels having a few Guns on
t'other side fired some round shot at us 9 12 & 18 pounders, but
did no hurt[13] – we lay upon our arms in a field about 3 or 400
yards from the ferry till eveng. & then went into the adjacent
Houses & barns some of which were inhabited and others not –
the Enemy have drove off as much of the live stock as they possibly could & many of the Inhabitants have left the Island either
from fear or disaffection. – they make a show of 3 or 400 men on
t'other side, have some works & are busy working still; the ferry
near a mile across, on this side of which is a fort not quite finished

intended for the deffence of this End of the Island – They have likewise a flag & some guns at another ferry to the Eastw Hollands ferry which seems to be much narrower, see some Vessels sailing about in that passage – Some Regts. gone to take possession of the Town, the rest of the Troops spread over the Country –

Monday 9th. Decr. The Troops Canton'd in Houses & Barns as most convenient some better & some worse, less moroding than usual only a few pigs &ca. suffer – orders on that head more strickly attended to on account of the Scarcity on the Island – The Enemy occupy a kind of fort on this Island on a Point of low ground opposite to Hollands ferry in which they have a few men –

Tuesday 10th. Decr. Cold weather. the wind at NW. The Battn. Parades at 10 in the field next the Wind Mill, the Light Infantry canton'd on the East Road the Grrs. on the West, a few straglers came towards the Light Infantry Quarters & fired some small arms at a great distance & ran off to the fort at the point probably to induce some of our people to follow within reach of their Guns.

Wednesday 11th. Decr. fine cold frosty weather some flagellations on account of irregularity, all quiet in Quarters, the Provincials still at work on t'other side the water, but seldom fire at us, the flag of the United Colonies constantly flying at both ferry's no communication with the Continent –

Thursday 12th. Decr. Clear wr. & hard frost some old offenders brot to the Post for the preservation of discipline & good order – In a house near us lyes a poor man out of his senses, propreitor of a good farm, & left by his bror. to the mercy of his Enemys – the people here about mostly Quakers, & whatever they think are willing to be quiet which I believe is the case with many others, the most violent & guilty have gone off, & some thro' fear: many of the Inhabitants of this Country are to be pitied

Friday 13th. Decr. Snow from the N.E. last night about 3 or 4 Inches, but the weather softned & it soon went off – A frigate &

71

2 50 Gun ships lying in the passage betwixt this & prudence Island. for some days past, one Gone up towards Providence & another lying betwixt Conanicut & the Main – burnt some houses on the low ground.

Saturday 14th. Decr. Soft weather but frost towards night. daily talks of our going to Town, some Regts. marching in, others changing their cantonments and so on – Returns sent to our respective Regts.

Sunday 15th. Decr. Clinking hard frost & very cold for the poor soldiers in the barn, several sick, an hospital form'd. all quiet in Quarters, NB a Picquet every night at the water side the Brigade next us gives a proportion

Monday 16th. Decr. fine clear frosty weather, orders for changing our cantonments tomorrow the 54th. & 63d. take up the Qrs. of the Light Infantry & Grenrs.

Tuesday 17th. Decr. March'd at 12 o'clock & Quarter'd along the west road from within 3 to one mile of New Port, pleasant frosty weather – Wednesday 18th. Decr. the Battn. assembled at the Qr. next the town about noon, & march'd into Town to the Quarter allotted for them. The men in uninhabited Houses, & some of the officers, others billited on families – in the forenoon a ship came into the Harbour under full sail, passed the Commore. & stood up, the men of war then fired at her to bring her too but she still continued her course, the Como: fired a good many shot both round & grape & two other ships. but she still went on, several boats push'd off after her & finding more men of war ahead in all the passages up to Providence, she threw up in the wind & pushed off her boat, but the men of wars boats being near they took the boat first and then the ship which proved to be a Transport taken by the provincials on her way from Cape Breton to N.York, they say four more were taken by the same privateer, & are to come in here for Providence This Town being situated on an Island and for some time past under apprehensions of a Visit from the British Troops, the Trade of the place has fallen to decay & most of the principal inhabitants left it, scarcely one third of the whole remaining & most of those very ill provided for the winter, it used to contain 10,000, a long scatter'd Town many good houses.[14]

Thursday 19th. Decr. employed in getting settled in Quarters & the Baggage from on board Ship, we hear'd yesterday the Grenr. Comys. of those Regts. with the Grand army are to go back to New York, which leaves us in suspense about our winter Qrs. – strange managment N.B. The Transports are all up in the Harbour of Newport some time ago & some have orders to clear out. The ships of war station'd to guard the Entrances – hard frost Began to breakfast with my Landlady Mrs. Wheatly an old fat widow about 3 score, civil body

Friday 20th. cold clear frosty wr. – in orders, a Detatchmt. of about 300 British & Hessians to embark on board of ships to go for fire wood, whh. is very scarce, & the 54th. Regt. to go over to Conanicut Island tomorrow. The Garrison Duty done by Nations, a great many Guards Vizt.[not enumerated] Orders for the visitation of the Qrs. a Capt. & Sub for the day-parade at 11 o'clock straw & a scanty allowance of fire wood issued out, the Inhabitants to give in their wood to the public magazine.

Saturday 21st. Decr. last night & this morng. a fall of snow from N.E. continued to snow almost the whole day. The Taylor gone to work to make up warm cloathing for the Company. flannel under Vests delivered out to the men, The Compy.[42nd grenadiers] all in one House at the South end of the Town – we live at Tavern 1/6 a head for dinner wine very high, yesterdays dinner 10/sterg. – had some Hessian Officers to dine with us to day, some of them spoke English, jovial companions

Sunday 22d. Decr. Divine Service, our Battn. did not go & had no Parade today, Last night frost, today clear wr. & pleasant the Country all around cover'd with snow – The Ships not yet sail'd that is to go for wood to Long Island –

Monday 23d. Decr. clear frosty weather. The Battalion in the field at eleven, the captains desired to manouvre their Companys for an hour or so as they thought proper. The Battn. to be at Exercise at 3 o'clock. the wr. rather too cold for field business; Orders for more frequent Visitation of the mens Quarters. a Subn. per Compy should at least visit the Barrack thereof 5 or 6 times a day to fullfill the orders; good exercise in cold weather – a Court martial, we try'd five Prisoners –

Tuesday 24th. Decr. fine clear cold weather, The streets very slippy, Creepers deliver'd out, for each Battn. 200. In orders a man condemned to suffer death for a Rape, but pardon'd at the intercession of the injured party; the second instance; tho' there have been other shocking abuses of that nature that have not come to public notice. The story of the poor old man & his daughter in Long Island was very bad indeed, hard is the fate of many who suffer indiscriminately in a civil war[15]

Wednesday 25th. Decr. Xmass clear frosty weather the wind about N. The Companys went to the Parade as usual when word came there was to be no General parade today, sent home the comys – went to Church & hear'd a very good sermon inculcating peace among men – a very neat Church wt, a handsome organ the Gift of Dr. Berkley Bishop of Cloyne, a good many Inhabitants in church some decent looking People & the women tolerably well dress'd for Yanky's – The Eveng. cloudy, visited the Barracks as usual, pretty quiet considering it is christmass – The ships sailed for Long Island last night for wood

Thursday 26th. Decr. cloudy morng. the wind at N.E. and came on to drizle & rain, at noon rain'd hard. yesterday bedding given out to the Troops some new some old, 42 beds Blankets & coverleds, a scanty allowance, no parade to day. clear'd up in the eveng. but no great frost –

Friday 27th. Decr. fine clear moderate weather Parade as usual, had some company to dine with us, my friend Willie, did pretty well at dinner, & came home with half a dozen in the Eveng. & completed the booze.

Saturday 28th. Decr. gentle frost – coals issued out for the

Garrison, a scanty allowance, only 2 bushels to each Barrack room – Capts. 3 & Subs 2. The old Houses & fences suffer – In the eveng. had a Battalion meeting to consult of a Club, only about a dozen present, agreed to meet twice a week, on Saturday Evenings. play cards & sup; & on Wednesdays to dine[;] afraid it wont hold – still believed that we shall go to NYork soon. Some fou & some foolish.

Sunday 29th. Decr. The Battalion went to Church inform our compy. dress'd in britches for the first time, what would Ld. E: say if saw us,[16] a Chaplain preach'd, the Church full some pretty looking Girls gentle frost & pleasant wr. – N: yesterday a boat came ashore from a privateer & was nab'd 10 hands, no more word of the Privateer

Monday 30th. Decr. the day somewhat cloudy but freezing had a field day at 12 oclock when we went into the Country & performed some manouvers of the majors on a plan of acting independently of any other Corps, the Battn. marching in column has an advance rear and flanking guards, & on whatever side attack'd the respective Guard keeps up a fire till the Battn. forms to that front. then retires to the Rear & joins the opposite Guard and makes a corps de reserve the other two guards form little Columns on the flanks of the Battn – we likewise march'd in square with these guards out – They answer'd very well being simple & easy, they are alwise the best judged things that are easiest performed – Visited the hospital things not as they should be – my man taken sick today, the old lady very kind to him –

Tuesday 31st. Decr. a fine clear frosty morning the wind to the North the day turned out cloudy & seem'd to thaw a little Parade at 11 oclock as usual – News come to Town that Genl. Lee is taken in Jersey – & there is a buzz of some action there[17] – went to buy some trimmings for a great Coat – the prices of everything in the shops immensely high here – charged a dollar & a half for a yard of glaz'd linen

Met with a Lady in the street well dress'd & had a very genteel appearance, & came afterwards into a shop where I was. upon enquiry I found this Miss Sal Leak whom I had often heard mention'd since we came here. She keeps a house of Pleasure & has done so for a good many years past in a more decent & reputable manner than common, & is spoke of by everybody in town in a favourable manner for one of her Profession, a well look'd girl about 30 – This Place must have arrived to a tollerable degree of modern luxury, when houses of that kind were publickly allowed of, & the manners of the people by no means rigid when subjects of that sort become family conversation – with this observation I conclude the year, God knows, if, how, or where we shall end the next.

Wednesday 1st. January 1777 –
A Happy New Year to all my friends, may those that are far asunder meet in good time & enjoy those pleasures that are best suited to ye mind.

> May peace & plenty crown this land
> and civil discord cease
> When Britain stretches forth her hand
> to give her children peace –

The day cloudy & soft the wind to the Southward, parade at 11 as usual did a few Manouvers in the field; today the Battn. should have dined together but a good many being previously engaged it is put off till tomorrow. We 42d. folks dined with Willie Dunlop on board his ship the Minerva had a very good Dinner & sat drinking till it was late. He gave some very good songs[18]

Thursday 2d. Janry. a fine clear morng. the weather quite mild & soft, & tho the wind is about N.W. not at all cold – it rain'd a good deal last night the grounds solf & the streets dirty – Parade at 11 as usual did a few Manouvres in the field – Yesterday a Frigate came in with two Brigs & a Schooner prizes, but have not hear'd the particulars – Today the Battn. had a dinner at Lawtons about 20 in Company, the Major absent, an ill contrived dinner & bad drink, club 3/6 – the Eveng. cold, freezing hard heard a good many Guns at a distance

Friday 3d. Janry. Keen frost with a sharp N.W. wind – a Vessel arrived from N:York last night which brings the confirmation of Lees being taken by Colo: [William] Harcourt in the Jerseys – a Red Ribbon come over for Genl. Howe, – Tis said, 900 Hessians are taken prisoners by the Rebels in the Jersey, & Colo [Johann Gottlieb] Rall kill'd in fighting his way thro' with a few men that stuck by him   a Concert to night[19]

Saturday 4th. Janry. 1777 The air quite mild & pleasant very little wind from N.W. They say it was a very good Concert last [night] & they had a dance after it about 20 ladies there some pretty well look'd Girls – This Concert is founded on a Subscription of a Guinea & a half each, they have already 80 Subscribers, is to continue once a week while the money lasts, always to conclude with a Dance. The ladies are furnish'd with tickets gratis which are distributed by Dr. Hallyburton
   in orders a ship to sail for England in a few days, & an opportunity to NYork, must write letters – A Battn. Club this Eveng., can't go –

Sunday 5th. Janry. clear frosty weather wind at NW Parade as usual the major not there – I came home & wrote letters   The Experiment & Asia they say are both going to England & to sail in a day or two – The Report of our Battns. going to N.York loses ground

Monday 6th. Janry. fine temperate frosty weather NW some ships arrived from New York victuales, confirm the news of Lees being taken, & the loss of the Hessians. The Experiment came down from her station, & the Renown came into Harbour –

Tuesday 7th. Janry. mild frosty wr. as usual wind NW   Some more arrivals from NYork with Stores & merchandise. The Packet for the Experiment closed, was too late with my letters must send them with the Asia, in whom goes Genl. Clinton and [Francis] Lord Rawdon I hear

Wednesday 8th. Janry. Pleasant frost & mild, wind NW   intended sending a bill home on the agents but heard this day on the parade that they do not draw the Subsiste. out of the Treasury, & Pay Masters Bills &ca. protested the business being transacted by a Pay Mr. Genl. in America. I am therefore dissappd. in orders Lord Rawdon will take letters to London dined wt. C Marsh a good [3 words illegible]

Thursday 9th. Janry. fine frosty weather as usual, yesterday the Experiment Capt. Wallace sail'd for England with the wind at N.W. the Asia to sail in a few days Short Parade the Major sick – Concert night

Friday 10th. Janry. Sharp cold day with a strong wind about West dust flying about very disagreeable – din'd on board the Glencairn Capt. Hunter the water being pretty rough & the wind right ahead going aboard, we got wet with the spray, very cold – fail'd in our first attempt owing to W Gs being frighten'd & not able to bear the cold wind – had a good enough dinner & plenty of drink, the Landlord & some of his Guests got fou, it was twelve before got ashore –

Saturday 11th. Clear frosty weather wind about N.W. call'd and saw the major & got the 10 guineas he borrowed from me at Staten Island (rather cavalierly) he complains of a pain in his breast, but probably its something else, an old Morbus Urethrae [perhaps gonorrhea]. – a great many Guns hear'd early this morng., which proved to be from a 4 Gun Battery newly errected on the Main, at the Cerberus frigate in the East Channel, which obliged her to quit her Station, she is gone out to sea, – they say some prizes are come in –

Sunday 12th. fine clear frosty Weather, wind NW. The Battn. went to Church, yesterday gave my letters to Lord Rawden who was very polite, one to my Father one to Dr. Fleeming & one to A.H. – In orders that Genl. Clinton with the Commander in Chiefs permission is going to England for the Winter, & the Command devolves on Lord Percy[20]

Monday 13th. Janry. N:B: Clear'd the Compy. to 24th. Octr. clear frosty weather wind about NW About day break 15 Guns from battery as a Salute to Gl. Clinton – The Asia saild this morng. for England (as Supra) The Preston Commodore Hotham saild for the Southwd. I believe Virginia & the Brune & another in consequence of orders from Lord Howe – yesterday arrived a flag of truce from Providence, a Capt. of one of their Vessels of war, about the Exchange of some Prisoners, An offr. of the 33d. who was taken lately in a ship with the Cloathing of eleven Regts. & some others, for some of theirs that have fallen into our hands since we have been here, about 30 I suppose – a Capt. of one of our Clyde fleet who has some letters from Colo. Campbell came with the flag[21]

Tuesday 14th. Janry. Very fine frosty Weather, wind N.W. A Genl. Court Martial sits this day for the tryal of a soldier of the 22d. Regt. for killing one Hessian & wounding another. the soldier was Safe Guard.

Wednesday 15th. Janry. cold & blowy from the Westwd. the dust flying about in the Streets very disagreeable – some arrivals from N.York brings an account of some engagement in the Jerseys wherein the 17th. Regt. in particular have suffer'd in making their way thro' a great Body of the Provincials – they say we are to go back to N.York – our Mess broke up for want of meat in ye market[22]

Thursday 16th. Janry. the morng. mild & pleasant Wind to S.W. came on to snow in the afternoon – The Genl. Court Martial Disolved – the soldier acquitted – In Orders, the Light Infantry[,] Grenads. & 3d. Brigade to hold themselves in readiness for immediate Embarkation, except the L:Infantry & Grenadrs. of the 54th. Regt. – The Officers of the Grenadrs. waited on Lord Percy in a body this forenoon Major Stuart not there; Sick – the Accounts from N.York does not seem to be favourable. Capt. [William] Leslie & Capt.Lt. [John] McPherson of the 17th. killed, Capt. Williams of 52d Grenrs. kill'd & Capt. [Erasmus John] Phillips 35th. & they say Genl. [James] Grant has lost some pieces of Cannon – Genl. [Hugh] Mercer of the Provincials woundd. & taken with a considerable loss on their side, but our losing ground

79

gives them spirits – This day recd. forrage money the Capts.
£20.12.6 the Subs £4.2.6, shamefull division A News Paper
came out today for the first time since we have been here printed
by one [John] Howe, nothing in it but what we heard before –
dined at Capt. [John] Cannons –

Friday 17th. Janry. a good deal of snow fell last night – this
morng. soft & pleasant, wind about S.W which veer'd to the
Northwd. in the course of ye day The Greyhound & Amazon
Frigates arrived from New York & a Transport with Recruits for
the 37th. all their accots. put together this affair in the Jersey
seems to terminate in our favour The Provincials have lost a
great number of men & we have suffer'd in some degree, but
there are so many different Accots. that it is difficult to reconcile
them. A flag arriv'd this day with Prisoners in consequence of a
Cartel Lt. Bragg of the Marines taken 27 Augt. & a good many
others – Memom. of orders Lord Percys complts. to the British &
Hessian officers of y. Garrison and begs their company to a Ball
tomorrow night – met Capt. Simmons of ye. Cerberus [one word
illegible] to dine wt. him tomorrow – din'd with [blank space]
today

Saturday 18th Janry. Hard frost & sharp N.W. wind This
being the Anniversary of the Queens Birthday (or the day that is
kept for it) A Detachmt. of 300 British fired 3 vollies on the
Parade at 12 oclock Preceded by 21 Guns from ye Battery & the
like number of Hessians on the Green behind the Church, at 1
oclock The Navy fired, each ship 21 Guns but a melancholly
accident happen'd from The Diamond Frigate who being lately
in action they had not taken sufficient care in drawing the shot, &
discharged a load of Grape into a Transport ship close by them &
killed 5 men & wounded 3, a round shot went likewise thro' a
Barrack room & broke a parcel of firelocks – Capt. Gr: & I went
off with Capt. Symons about 2 & had an exceeding good dinner
plenty of Drink & a kind welcome, talk'd of our old acquaintance
at Derry – The Cerberus had a good many shot thro' her at
Seconet had 3 men kill'd and several wounded – came ashore in
the Eveng. & dress'd for the Ball, went in at 8 & found them

Dancing in a long Room at the Crown Coffee House enlarged for the occasion, about 50 or 60 Women a few good looking Girls, some ugly old women the rest but middling, a genteel woman there a officer of Artillerys wife Mrs. Abbott who is just come in from having been 14 Months a prisoner with the yankees; – N:B: in coming in the vesel got aground, they wanted to get her ashore but she wd not stir till every man in the ship were first taken off, saying there lives were of service & hers was of none   I suppose there was above 150 Offrs. there the Rooms quite crowded – Tea coffee Punch negus wine & Plumb Cake, they Danced till past 12 & then broke up – I went to Coll. Campbells Mungo & Drank punch – [23]

Sunday 19th. hard frost wind N.W. orders last night for putting our heavy baggage on board this morng. The Eagle & Argo the 2 ships for the Grenadrs. the 15th. 33d. & 42d. in the former, the 28th. 37th. 46th. & 57th. in the latter.

More Cartel ships arriving every day with prisoners from Connecticut they all agree in reprobating the Yankee's, whose credulity & fears make them hope & tremble by turns. Dun: Campbell Ensn. & Qr.Mr. 26th. Arrived today with his family, from captivity, poor fellow he call'd to see me.   had company to dine wt. me today 2 water Capts. & our own folks, sat till 12

Monday 20th. Janry. the weather mild. wind to ye westwd. a guinea each for sea stores which they have made me undertake to lay out but it won't do – went down to Hodgesands & bespoke the articles – dined with Willie Dunlop & sat late as usual – a Concert to night

Tuesday 21st Janry. fine clear frosty wr. orders for Embarking tomorrow morng. repeated,   to parade at the usual place at 1/2 after 8. & at the Grand parade at 9 – a long & feeling farewell from Major Stuart in the orders. he seems to be hurt in losing the Grrs. – dined wt. Capt. Graham & some others. pack'd up in the Eveng. & returned to ym. sat till past 12 –

Wednesday 22nd. Cold Clinking frost wind at NW. sent my baggage down to the Minerva to go in her boat, went to the

Barrack & marched up the men to the parade where the rest were waiting for us, & Mr. Graham never thinking about the matter marched in Battn. to the Grand parade & from thence to the South Whaffs where we Embarked. 3 compys. the 15th. 33d. & 42d. on board the Eagle Capt. Noble, the 28th. 37th. 46th. & 57th. on board the Argo – The Light Infantry & 52d Regt. embark'd likewise in the morng. the 3 other Regts. in the afternoon, the wind now about North –

Clear'd with my Landlady this morng. & tho I over paid her she did not seem to be satisfyed, greedy & cunning like the rest of the Yankees

Thursday 23d. Janry. fine clear frosty weather wind at North talk of sailing today or to night a pity to lose this fine fair wind. allwise something coming aboard to the last. The Greyhound & Kingsfisher to be our Convoy. all on board & everything ready now. the wind fair but no orders for sailing yet – a Navy Court Martial sitting this [number unclear] days past, trying the Gunner of the Diamond for killing the men

Friday 24 Janry. last night the wind & weather changed & came on to blow fresh from the Southwd. with sleet & rain, the ship drifted half a mile in the night, & was near upon the Rocks. The day continues wet & blowy, no moving with this wind Sir Peter, – a dirty steerage & a Crowded Cabin. it continued to blow hard & rain till midnight

Saturday 25th. Janry. a fine soft morng. with the wind at S.W. mild & pleasant day, the ships drying their sails – seeing no prospect of sailing made a collection of another guinea to augment our Sea Stores – some Vessels came in from sea yesterday but have not hear'd yet what they are – got on board more wine Rum &ca. in Eveng. the wind came about to NW. we moved down to near our former station opposite the North Battery & near the end of Scape Goat Island –

Sunday 26th. Janry. fine clear weather wind about NW. not cold, this morng. two Frigates came in said to be the Orpheus & Daphne from N.York & a little sloop, but have not heard what news yet. The Diamond went up to her former station near Prudence Island & releaved the Emerald who came down about noon – went ashore on Scape Goat Island & took a walk for about an hour, there is an old Stone Battery there with above 30 Embrazures, the middle part of it Repair'd with Sod work & made a Fort of, call[ed] Fort Liberty by the Yankee's – the Navy people have a brewerie & forge there & repair their boats & sails – in the afternoon the ships that went to Long Island for wood arrived in port. The St. Lawrence Schooner & some Boats went out to meet them. – in the Eveng. got another weeks provision on board – let it not be told that they play Cards or flutes or fiddles on board this good ship on Sunday –

Monday 27th. Janry. a fine mild morng. wind about North but little of it – A Court Martial on Board the Argo for the tryal of some of Capt. Hamiltons Compy. for Sundry crimes & misdemeanors here's a fine fair wind and no word of our sailing – no Accounts from N.York that seems to be favourable – Jas. Graham died about 3 oclock this morng. of a putrid disorder, his wife sick –

Tuesday 28th. Janry. a Signal was made about 2 oclock in the morning for sailing on which the ships got up their anchors, & got under way by 3, with a gentle breeze from the Northward, mild weather & moon light, about 4 pass'd the light House & stood on about WBN going about 3 knots, as day light came made block Island, on larboard bow at 8 see fishers island ahead, & between 9 and 10 made the East end of Long island towards noon the wind fell away & came more to Westward, about one the man of war tack'd and stood in towards Fishers island as did soon after the rest of the Fleet and the whole came to anchor off Fishers island near the West end & about a mile or more from the shore in 17 fathom water, in all 20 sail vizt The Greyhound Frigate, the Kings Fisher & Merlin Sloops the St. Laurence Schooner & another & 2 small sloops & 14 sail of transports – see a Boat sailing between Long island & the Main – New London light House about NNW between 2 & 3 leagues distant. the evening fine, the night clear & moderate –

Wednesday 29th. Janry. between 7 & 8 in the morning weighed anchor & with a light air of wind & the assistance of the tide stood up through the Horse Race (a strong current that forms a Ripple across the Sound just above the west end of Fishers island) between 10 & 11 abreast with New London, see some vessels lying in the Harbour, partly unrigg'd and see likewise some works in form of Battery, the wind falling away & the tide young we dont get on much, the Argo came close on us, all well – as the day came on a gentle breeze sprung up from the SE & we slip thro' the water now at the rate 3 knots, the fleet all pretty close together, the two sloops of war farthest astern, the Merlin seems to be a dull sailer – see first one & then two more small sloops ahead, they seem to stand this way, the St. Laurence Schooner has set more sail & gone ahead. I suppose to see what they are, – the mildest weather I ever saw at this Season in this Country, no snow to be seen except a spot here & there, smooth water & pleasant sailing – The St. Laurence, spoke the first sloop which prov'd to be a small arm'd Cutter then put about & followed her along shore to the Eastwd., but the Commodore fired two shot & brot. her down to speak to him, after which he made a Signal & the Kings Fisher & the Sloop stood in to long island shore together & came to anchor, where we left them watching some small craft that had gone in thereabout – as the Eveng. came on the Wind freshen'd & look'd dirty, the Night Dark & came on to snow & sleet –

Thursday 30th. Janry. at 3 in the morng. it blew hard, reef'd topsls. by 4 the wind whisk'd about to N.E. & soon after to North and blew smartly with sleet & snow, close in with Long island shore, which being now the Lee shore obliged to claw off, as the morning came on it became more moderate & cleared up, the Country on both sides pretty deeply cover'd with Snow the Wind to the Westward of North cold & freezing, stood on up the Sound till about 10 oclock we came to anchor at City island where we found two sloops of war lying at Anchor, the Merlin & one of the Transports not in sight, about noon the Transport came up, – one of the Sloops of war got under way & went up the Sound, as did some of the small craft that were along with us – see the men of wars boats has communication with the Continent – the day cold & sharp & the wind too scant to get further up –

Friday 31st. Janry. A cold frosty morng., with a good deal of trouble got up our anchor about 9 oclock & set sail after the rest of the fleet who were under way before us (our ship is but weakly man'd & everything is frozen & ill to work) stood up about two or three miles & turn'd frog point the wind about NWBN came to an anchor very near the place where the fleet assembled when we came down, 1st. Decr. – The Adjut. & surgn. gone on board the Argo to Execute the Sentence of the Court Martial of 27th. – some of our lads gone ashore with their guns, cold & clear

About noon the fleet were furnish'd with Pilots that came from N.York and when the tide turn'd got under way again & dropped down as far as Hunts point about 5 miles & came to about dark – the Greyhound Capt. Dickson who was our Commodore from Rhode island has given up his charge of the fleet to the agents & Pilots with directions to get to N.York as soon as they can –

Saturday 1st. Febry. the weather changed to mild & soft the wind about S.S.W. Vessels sailing up the Sound – flying reports of some fighting in the Jerseys & about Kings Bridge – when the tide turn'd about 4 oclock weighed & got under way again & dropped down with the boats ahead below the Brothers near to Morrisinia, no wind, & came to near the Chester shore on the Main at Dusk – it seems the Rebels have burnt Montresor's house on that Island lately –

Sunday 2d Febry. a calm soft morng. any little air that is comes from the S.W.wd. so here we must remain till a favourable breeze comes to carry us thro Hell Gate which is about a mile or two from this some of our Cabin folks gone ashore on Long island to stretch their limbs No Ice in the River which is very extraordinary at this Season of ye year got some bread & eggs from Long island, rain in the afternoon –

Monday 3d. Febry. clear weather the wind about WNW pretty sharp, & too scant for us to go down, it blew pretty fresh in the night & we drove a little – the Capt. gone down to Hell Gate in the boat to see if there are any buoys on the Rocks or any marks sett up – between 11 and 12 A:M: the Juno Frigate passed us, bound to the eastward, but where we can't tell, She sail'd betwixt the Brors. & the Main which is the best channel; I am told there is water enough for any ship in the Navy in this East River, but it requires a fair wind & good Pilotage –

Tuesday 4th. Febry. fine clear weather mild & pleasant the Wind about S.W. Two of the Transports made loose this morning & got down thro Hell Gate with the assistance of boats, – went ashore with some others to take a walk on long island & get some fresh stock being quite out of all fresh meat we calld at several houses without being able to get any one thing but by going further into the Country we with difficulty procurr'd at several houses 7 young Cocks some Eggs & some bread, not a bit of Beeff Mutton or Veal to be got, & the few fowles they have left they keep for breed, they cost 2/York each & Eggs 2/ a dozen, – every thing here about was eat up by the army – all quiet here now; some of Rogers's Corps come over to Long island from Kingsbridge, they say the Rebels came & attack'd Fort Independence about 10 days ago, but were soon beat back with loss – almost dark before we got aboard, din'd on eggs and &ca.

Lts. [Harry] Gilchrist & Courtney went to New York today & to return as soon as they can –

Wednesday 5th. Febry. it rain'd a good deal last night & was likewise a wet night with some of our youths in the Cabin the morng. soft & something foggy the wind about S.W. four more of our fleet made loose this morning & got down thro Hell Gate, with this wind they can't venture more than a few each tide The St. Laurence Schooner likewise drop down with the latter end of ye tide – about 2 oclock P.M. a ship came up the River on which the Senegal Sloop (who has been lying here with us ever since we came down) made loose & went along with her up the Sound – The Greyhound Frigate still lying above the Brother islands – the afternoon clear fine weather small craft sailing up & down to & from N.York with wood &ca

Thursday 6th Febry. hard frost & a sharp NW wind blowing pretty hard some more of our fleet made loose and attempted to get down but could not make it out & were obliged to come too off Barren island, the Agents ship got aground, it blows too hard to make any further attempts today wind about N.N.W. our drink & fresh Provisions all out – Lts. Graham & Rawdon gone to New York & to return tomorrow – The Taylors complain of the cold & decline working

Friday 7th. Febry. last night moderate, the wind continues about the NW quarter & freezes hard, the Wr. clear & not so cold as yesterday no attempts made for getting down to day the wind too much to the Wd. Sent some men ashore for prog. – & a Serjt. to N.York with a letter to Gilchrist & Courtney to return immediately, he took a chance passage in a sloop got some bread Eggs & milk from the shore and, in the Evening Gilchrist & Courtney return'd, – There has been some skirmishing in the Jersey in which our Regt. has had a share, on the 1st. instant Major McPherson with 200 were out foraging, they met with some other foraging parties, they were attacked by a very superior number of the Rebels whom they beat off with considerable loss[24]

Saturday 8th. Febry. a mild morning little wind about NE when the Tide turn'd about 10 oclock we got under sail & stood towards Hell Gate as we came near which the wind dyed away, we got our boat & another ships boat a head, and got through this difficult passage very safely about eleven the tide carried down but the wind coming a head we were obliged to tack several times, got to New York & came to an anchor off the Fly Market about 2 o'clock, a good many of the Gentlen. went ashore – some little misunderstanding with the master of the ship, he wanted to come to at the upper end of the Town which we thought would not be so convenient & he did not like to be thwarted –

Sunday 9th. fine weather went ashore in the forenoon call'd & saw our Ladies & sick Gentlen. poor Mrs. G. still in that strange way, Chisholm better of his cough but has now got a fistulo in anno [anal fistula] poor fellow, Peter & McLeod recovering fast –

dined with Dick Colden by invitation of yesterday a large company & a genteel dinner, with plenty of good Madeira – we hear the 3d. Battalion is to be divided between the 1st. & second & that we are to go the jerseys immediately, the whole of us that came from Rhode island. – Spent the Eveng. & got abed in the House with Sick Officers

Monday 10th. Febry. fine frosty weather wind about NW Orders to land our heavy Baggage immediately & lodge it in Respective Regtal. Stores – met with several old acquaintances, among the rest Donald McLean who has been very ill used by the Rebels – met Mr: Geo: McCrea from Air he came out with Cargoe of Goods Value about £15000. belonging to himself, Mr MClure & Mr. Arthur but was unfortunately taken near St. Johns N foundland, & carried into Boston from whence he got to Halifax & from thence to N.York about 3 weeks ago, he brot me some letters which he had taken care to preserve, one from Tom Arthur on[e] from my Father & one from AH dated latter end of Aug

Monday dined with Mr. Crammond at a very good genteel mess of People of different Corps at a Mrs. Eyrys – made several enquerys about Dick Marshalls Brother but could hear nothing of him, but what I hear'd before that he was got into Delancy's Corps, & they are in Long Island – Met Capt. McKenzie in the street ask'd him about the Staff pay of the 4th. Battn. which he told me I wod. get at the Pay Mr. Gl. Mr. Barrows office. I accordingly called there & recd. about £13. for which I sign'd my name eight times – Walk'd out this forenoon to pay a Visit to Major Small but he was not at home – They have plays at N.York once a week by the offrs. & a Concert where the Hessian offrs. keep a Pharo Bank.

Tuesday 11th. Febry. a fall of snow this morning which still continues went to breakfast with Doctor McLean & had a long chat; could do nothing with the Baggage today – saw Major Small, he ask'd me to dine but I had promised to dine with our lads – went in the Eveng. to call for Mrs. McCrea at Mr. Reids they kept me there to supper, – I don't know yet what he intends to do –

Wednesday 12th. Febry. fine clear weather & frosty, went aboard and got our heavy Baggage ashore & lodged in the store, & meant to have got our cloathing aboard but Mr. Serjt. Stewart gets Drunk & neglects his business   Bot a Portmanteau & a pair of boots £7. filled the portmanteau with Campaign articles & left all the rest of my Baggage (except the Canteen Box & my Bedding.) vizt. 2 Trunks, Box with Bedsted, little Case, & tent &ca. in the Regtal. Store   took a snack with our lads & came aboard in the Eveng. to relieve Gilchrist who went ashore,   Mr. Wm. Gr never thinks of taking any share of this duty & as little of any other as he can help – slept aboard – was ask'd to dine by Capt. Mar of the Engineers but was so busy could not wait of him – call'd at the Coffee House & walk to meet Mr. McCrea but did not find him – met with Mr. John Allen of Philadelphia which he & many others were obliged to leave these troublesome times. – ask'd after old acquaintances, great alterations in that place both Natural & Political

Chapter III

'shabby ill managed occasions'

New Jersey
13 February to 6 July 1777

Defeats at Trenton and Princeton had a pervasive influence on Britain's conduct of the war in 1777. Sir William Howe, recognizing that he could no longer sustain posts on the Delaware, withdrew his forces from all of New Jersey except the easternmost portions of the Raritan River Valley between Amboy and Brunswick. This withdrawal not only removed British protection from most New Jersey Loyalists but also reduced sharply the support that the British could draw from the New Jersey countryside. Much of Howe's army was forced to spend the winter and spring of 1777 in crowded and sickly quarters (in transports docked in the Raritan or in the few buildings safely within British lines) and to skirmish endlessly with the rebels who attacked their camps and contested every foraging party.

Trenton and Princeton also affected Howe's plans for the summer of 1777 and his willingness to cooperate with other British commanders. Depressed by the failure of his conciliatory efforts and yet determined to show that his faith in the Loyalists of Pennsylvania was well founded, Howe planned an invasion of Pennsylvania by sea – an invasion that would gradually recover territory, gain the support of the loyal population, and promote a restoration of royal government. So intent was he on carrying out this plan that he refused to cooperate fully with a British army advancing south from Canada to isolate and conquer New England. He would promise little more than to send a detachment from New York to open the Highlands of the Hudson for the Canadian forces. But Howe did deviate briefly from his own plans before embarking for Pennsylvania. In June he expended nearly three weeks in a futile effort to lure Washington's army into a decisive battle in eastern New Jersey.[1]

John Peebles knew little of Howe's strategy; but he gained a vivid appreciation of living and fighting along the Raritan River during the winter and spring of 1777. From mid-February, when he and the 3rd Battalion of Grenadiers reached Perth Amboy, until late March, when his company was transferred to the 2nd Battalion of Grenadiers and posted at Brunswick, he experienced all too often the frustrations of living on crowded transports and foraging in the nearby countryside – of losing his men to 'ugly fevers' and 'shabby' little encounters with the rebels.[2] The weather and the quarters improved after he and the 42nd Grenadiers moved to Brunswick. The fevers and the fighting remained much the same until late May when substantial reinforcements began to arrive from New York and Rhode Island.[3] On 11 June General Howe reached Brunswick and promptly put his whole army in motion – advancing to Hillsborough, withdrawing to Amboy, and then advancing to Westfield and Rahway in vain efforts to provoke the rebels into a decisive battle. After more than two weeks of marching, countermarching, and skirmishing, the army crossed to Staten Island to embark for a summer's campaign in Pennsylvania.[4]

New Jersey
13 February to 6 July 1777

Thursday 13th Febry. Cloudy weather looks like rain or snow intended to have gone ashore to finish business & buy some things we want but got orders to get under way directly, & a Pilot came aboard to carry us to Amboy, a good many of the officers & men ashore no word of Serjt. Stewart with the cloathing, got under way about noon & went down to Red Hook below Governors island where the Agent & the Rest of the ships came to anchor those we left ashore coming aboard every opportunity, – being hurried away sooner than we expected were not at all provided with any thing to Eat & Drink so sent to Town & got a couple dozen wine & some cold meat whh was all they could get, in the afternoon cold & snowy –

Friday 14th. Febry. Hard frost & a sharp north wind got under way about 10 AM. & stood down thro' the Narrows, then giving the Bank to Starboard a wide birth hawled up to westward & stood up Rariton River or Bay a crooked channel & sometimes in 2 1/2 fathom, passed a man of war ye. Raven & a parcel of victualers lying at Princes Bay; the Mercury got aground there – about 2 P.M. came to anchor about a mile or more from Amboy the Tide turng about 8 most of the ships got under way again & turn'd up nearer to the Town, a Brig with the Horses aground at the point Staten island

Saturday 15th. Febry. hard frost & a cold N.W. wind in the forenoon warp'd up opposite to Amboy but it blew too hard to get near the Town, about 1 P.M. went ashore on Staten island to try to get some fresh stock being quite out, we made a range of 5 or 6 miles into the Country & got nothing but a few eggs & a little butter. din'd at the Sign of the Ship on hung beeff & Eggs & return'd to the ship about 9 oclock at night – The Commanders went ashore to Amboy & return'd in the Eveng. but no word of our landing nor where we are to go. Amboy and Brunswick & the villages between are occupied by our Troops but never move out except in large Parties, Elizabeth Town Woodbridge &ca are in

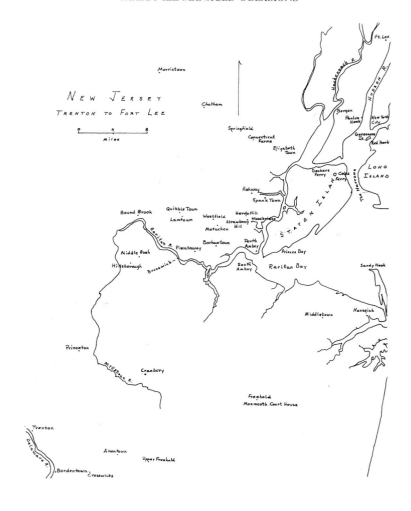

possession of the Rebels who take every opportunity to harrass our forraging Parties, but generally come off with the worst – Genl. Vaughan Commands here at Amboy, Lord Cornwallis at Brunswick &ca.[5] the Commander in Chief is expected here on Monday or Tuesday –

Sunday 16th. Febry. the Weather more mild got the ship hauled over to the Amboy side among the rest, – Capt. [Francis] Skelly & some of 71st. acquaintances came aboard to see us, two of their Battns are here the other a[t] Bonamtown with the 33d. the 42d. at Piscataway. they say everything is very scarce in the Country here & they live almost entirely on salt provision. – the afternoon turns cloudy, most of the Gentlen. gone ashore its going to snow, Snow & sleet in the afternoon –

Monday 17th. Febry. Clear weather & gentle frost wind NW no orders for landing yet. some of our men turning sick & no doctor to attend them our surgeon having left us at New York, sent for the Surgn. of the Light Infantry, who comes & visits them – Most of our Gentlen. gone ashore Eight of us aboard at dinner & had nothing but a little bit of salt pork. Reviewed the Mens arms & ammunition, they are compleated to 60 rounds P man & two spare flints. 4 firelocks wants some mending They have it ashore that Washington is drawing in his out posts & collecting his army in order to retire across the Delaware.[6]

Tuesday 18th. Febry. a cold sharp Northwind & frost got out the new cloathing & put it on the men, just as it is, having no time to get it fitted. it is in general too little for the men, set the Taylors to work to put on hooks & Eyes & turn up the corner of the skirt which is all that can be don[e] at present –

Wednesday 19th. Febry. hard frost & cold NW wind went ashore with some of our folks to take a walk & dine at the Tavern, sent Ms. Gennes to the Hospital, but they would not admit a sick Woman – They have thrown up 3 or 4 redouts with 2 pieces of Cannon in each, & have out lying picquets beyond these. – the British Regts. here (Vizt. the 4th. Brigade & 71th) are very weak in Numbers having lost a good many by the Enemy in that affair at Princetown and are very sickly, so that the duty of defence comes pretty hard – got but an indifferent dinner at the Tavern, the wine pretty good, club 18/ York – in the Evening according to custom some of the lads met at passdice & lost & win a few hundreds – General Howe arrived with his suite in the afternoon in a sloop from N.York & went to Genl. Vaughans who lodges at the Govrs. House. Mrs. Franklin still at home, her Husband prisoner in Connecticut[7] – Yesterday Colo [Charles] Mawhood went out with 800 on a foraging party when one Desaquilliers an officer of Ary. having gone before with two light horse men was wounded & taken prisoner,

Thursday 20 Febry. I believe last night was the hardest frost we have had this winter, a sharp NW wind, inclement Wr. for the out lying Picquets & sentries, the Genl. & his suite left this in the morng. for Brunswick Escorted by the Light Infantry & two Battns. the Troops from Bonam Town met them at the crossroads & took the Genl. under their charge, sometime after they parted, Those from Amboy in taking a turn in the Country fell in with some of the Rebels & drove them with a little firing in which we had two or three men wounded. the alarm came into Town on which the 35th. & the Waldeckers turn'd out & march'd a little way but they soon got notice that the affair was all over & they return'd, the whole came in soon after –

Friday 21st. Still hard frost & bitter cold, wind at NW in coming aboard last night from dining with Capt. Skelly I stepp'd into a little skiff that was so crank that with the least motion to one side she heel'd & I tumbled into the water, I scrambled out again & got aboard but it was devilish cold – went ashore & dined with Skelly today again, he & the Laird of McLeod in a mess, two fine young fellows – Capt. Duncan Campbell emigrants return'd from t'other side the Country where he had been with a flag to get his wife & family from Burlington but he was stopped by the way carried into PrinceTown blind folded & ordered to return by [Israel] Putnam – The Troops from Rhode Island took a walk ashore

Saturday 22d. Febry. the weather a little more moderate still cold & clear, a proportion of Bedding deliver'd out to the Troops on board, which looks like remaining there, sent to New York for our Grenr. Caps & some other articles, Serjt. Stewart gone for ours

Sunday 23d. Febry. a fine clear frosty morng. not so cold The Troops from Rhode Island went ashore early this morning – vizt 3d. Light Infantry & Grens. & the 3d. Brigade, & marched into the Country with a few field pieces & a train of waggons to bring forrage, the whole under the Command of Colo [Charles] Mawhood, when we had got a few miles beyond Woodbridge Colo: [Mungo] Campbell of the 52d. was detatch'd with 4 or 500 men to the left to make a Sweep into the Country, he got 4 Compys. of Grrs. with him, having ask'd for ours to be one of them, & I was order'd with 20 men to be the advance guard. – when we had marched about a mile & a half to the Westward, I discover'd a body of the Rebels on a hill which I acquainted Colo: Campbell of, Very well says he I'll manouvre them, he accordingly gave orders for the Detatchment to form & desir'd me to move on the edge of a wood in our front, as we came forward the Rebels disappeared, & I kept moving on thinking the whole detachment were coming after, but it seems they made a turn to the left while I went on in the tract of the Enemy, & soon after saw a body of them go into a wood where they halted, I sent a Corpl. to Colo: Campbell to acquaint him of their situation, but the detatchmt. being a good way off at this time he was long a coming back, – the Rebels seeing my small party drawn up & nobody near them sent out about 30 or 40 to bring us on to engage, I went up & met them & receiv'd their fire from behind a fence. I moved on to a fence in front & order'd my men to fire, which we continued to do at each other for a few minutes when they gave way. I believe at seeing the Detatchmt. coming up for I don't think we hit above 3 or 4 of them. I had two wounded: when the Detatchmt. came near I mov'd off to the left where a party of them were driving off some Cattle & sheep & some straglers firing at us, I then form'd & gave them a platoon & two or 3 rounds after, which made them take to their heels. Colo: Campbell sent up & order'd me to retire back to the detatchmt. which I accordingly did, they having withdrawn towards the left, he form'd his troops again in a field in the rear & to the left withall, & moving on still more to the left we saw another body of the Rebels coming down thro a Swamp & making straight for a wood, Colo: Campbell hurried us on, I suppose to get betwixt the wood & them, but they got into the wood before we could get within shot of them, he then order'd me up to a fence at the edge of the

wood with my little party which were reduced now to 14 or 15,
we went up to the fence under the beginning of their fire, we
posted ourselves there & kept up as much fire as we could two
Grenadr. compys 42d. & 28th. came up to our support but began
their fire at too great a distance; when they got up to the fence
they soon found themselves gall'd by a fire on their right, & those
in our front being all posted behind trees almost flank'd the 42d.
Compy. in this Situation the men are droping down fast when
they (the 2 Compys.) got orders to retire which I hear'd nothing
off. I remain'd at my post till I had not one man left near me,
except Jno. Carr lying wounded, & fired away all my Cartridges,
when seeing the Rascals coming pretty close up I took to my
heels & ran back to the Compy. under a heavy fire which thank
God I escaped, as I fortunately did all the rest of the day – in
this affair we had the worst of it for want of that support we had
reason to expect from the rear, where the 52d Regt. were drawn
up but did not move on tho' Colo Campbell says he left orders
for them so to do, but it seems in the interim Colo: Mawhood
had sent orders for them to retire or move to the right, however
they came down at last together with some others & gave a heavy
volley into the wood which cleared it of the Rebels, Colo:
Mawhoods division were drawn towards this scene of Action but
what they had to do in their thether [tether] I can't say – the
Rebels being now gone off we got the wounded brot. up to the
road taken some care of & put into Waggons. The Enemy seeing
a disposition to march back showed themselves again in our rear
which occasion'd a counter march to oppose them, but on our
facing them they retired with firing a few shot, we moved on
again, the men much fatigued & harrassed a great many of them
quite knock'd up; shortly after we got into the main road the
Rebels appear'd in our rear & rear flanks & harrass'd the Grenadrs. that form'd the rear guard very much. we were at last
obliged to halt & fire some Cannon amongst them which set them
a scampering, as we came near Woodbridge we found a large
body of them in a wood posted to oppose us in front. upon dis-
covering them we fired a few pieces of Cannon into the wood and
then formed a line in front which moved on to the wood & pour'd

in their fire, which made them the Rebels quicken their steps to their right, to which they began to move when this front line moved on to charge them. they fired some scattering shots in going off which did little hurt, we then got into the road again & moved on without further molestation & got into to Amboy between 7 & 8 oclock much fatigued –

Monday 24th. Febry. it came on to snow & blow last night, which it continues still to do very hard, the worst day of wr. we have seen this winter – In the affair of yesterday we have lost 69 killed & wounded & 6 missing, our Compy. has 2 Sergts. 1 Corpl. & 20 wounded & 1 killed, 2 Drrs. missing; went ashore in Eveng. & saw the wounded men several of them in a very dangerous way poor fellows, what pity it is to throw away such men as these on such shabby ill managed occasions. Capt. Gr[aham]: & I call'd on Colo McDonald to thank him for his civility & attention to the wounded men of our Compy. Colo: Campbell sent for Capt. Graham to speak to him, to talk over the affair of yesterday & to let him know where the fault lay of our not being supported

Tuesday 25th. Febry. the weather clear'd up, there has been a heavy fall of snow, – had a review of arms which are not in good order yet. the men much fatigued with Sunday Geo: Munro one of our wounded died this morng. – a sloop from N.York run ashore yesterday at South Amboy, some officers & men that were in her got over, but the Country people plunder'd the Vessel in which there was a good many things belongg. to the Genl. & a parcel of shoes for the 71st. –

Wednesday 26th. fine fair & mild weather, got our ship haul'd along side of the rest at the Wharf – went ashore & saw our wounded men dress'd, most of them very bad wounds indeed, Carr Wm. McIntosh & Miller & Srgt. McPherson I am afraid wont live – wrote to Colo [Thomas] Stirling a sketch of our Sundays affair, sent it by Lt. [John] Freeman who goes to Brunswick this night –

Thursday 27th. Febry. fine mild weather – Colo: Campbell

sent for Capt. Graham & I this morning to acquaint us that the
Genl. required some enquiry to be made why the Grenadrs. were
not supported in the affair of Sunday & to ask us all that we knew
concerning that, which can be very little, as it must be best known
to Colo: Campbell & Major Humphries what orders were given &
recd., it being pretty clear I think, that for want of that support
we expectd from the Column in the Rear we lost most of our
men & allowed the Rebels to escape better than they deserved –
The Battn. went ashore this morng. to stretch their limbs & to
get the ship clean'd, took a walk on the beach & came aboard
again, our arms in bad order still & a good many missing – I
hear a Court of Enquiry is sitting – By which it appears that
Major Humphries had received an order from Colo Mawhood not
to advance, but was not communicated to Colo Campbell till it
was too late – Wm. Millar died this morng.

Friday 28th. a fine clear frosty morng. The 3d. Light Infantry & Grrs. & 3d. Brigade went ashore at 9 o'clock to go a forraging we march'd soon after with two sixpounders & a train of
waggons, the whole under the command of Colo: [William]
Butler, went about 3 miles into the Country on the Bonam Town
road, where they loaded the Waggons with Hay & straw whilst
the Troops were posted all around to defend them, it was near
two o'clock before they had finish'd when we march'd into Town
again without seeing any of the Enemy –

Saturday 1st. March usher'd in with a snow storm N:B: we
hear'd from N.York two days ago that our frigates has taken part
of a fleet that got out from Philada. bound to France with Tobacco

Sunday 2nd. March fine clear cold weather – I went ashore &
visited the Hospital. several of the wounded men very bad, of
McIntosh & Carr I have very little hopes poor fellows, I never
saw men more patient & resign'd than they are – Din'd ashore at
the Tavern with a party made up of those who were most engaged
the 23d. Colo: Campbell Sir Jas. Murray, & the offrs. 28 & 42d.
Grenr. Compys. & talk'd over the affair of that day wherein it
was concluded that if the 52d. had advanced we would have made

a very handsome little affair of it, broke up in good spirits   club 3 dollars –

An order for the Troops as well those ashore as those on board be under Arms every morng. an hour before day & remain accoutred for 2 hours or so – by late intelligence an attack on some of our Posts by Mr. Washington is expected –

Monday 3d. March   cold frosty weather   The Troops were all under arms in the morng. according to orders; & about 12 oclock the Troops on board went ashore & those in Garrison turn'd out, & form'd at their alarm posts, occupying a line nearby in the sweep of the Redouts, the light Infantry & Grrs. in a second line within, to the right of the Barracks – Shore allowance of Provision

News – it has been reported for some days & generally believed that Genl. Carleton has come across lake Champlain & and taken Ticonderoga – & to day that the Randolph American Frigate is taken by the Pearl & a good many of her fleet, they say she fir'd after she struck & kill'd the Lt. that was going on board of her. filty Rascals

Tuesday 4th. March   The Light Infantry & Grenrs. went ashore at 10 o'clock   the 4th. Brigade & Waldeckers turn'd out, the whole to go on a forraging party, but it came on to snow & it was laid aside the Troops return'd to quarters & ships –

Wednesday 5th. March   The flank corps & 3d Brigade went ashore at 10 clock & when all things were ready Guns Waggons &ca. marched about 3 miles into the Country on the Bonam Town road & loaded the waggons with Salt Hay at the same place we were at last time, brot. in likewise some furniture of Judge Smiths, saw none of the Rebels to day – the 33d. & 37th. Compys. gone on board the Union Transport to make more room in the others & 6 or 7 offrs. –

Thursday 6th. March   Soft weather with sleet & snow. Cadet Potts came down from Brunswick to day on his way to N:York says alls well there & likewise with the Regt. our people had another skirmish with the Rebels lately, & killed a parcel of them – rec'd. a letter from Tom Ar: 5th. Novr.

Friday 7th. March fine warm mild day the Battn. went ashore at 1/2 after 10 o'clock & paraded on the Beach for an hour or two & came on board again which they are to do every fair day for the future, our men turning sickly our Compy. have 1/2 a dozen down with the flux; the Regtal: Surgeons ashore take it by turns to Visit the Grrs. – We hear the flank Corps are to go to Brunswick in a few days & join the Battns there –

Saturday 8th. March fine mild agreeable weather; The two Battns. of the 71st. & a Battn. of Hessians went out at 5 o'clock this morng. to cover the Boats that were taking in Salt Hay about 3 miles up the Rariton. The flank Corps, & 3d. Brigade went ashore at 10 o'clock & with two field pieces & some waggons went out to the last forraging place, The Grenadrs. & part of the Light Infantry were posted on the Woodbridge Road; we saw 3 or 400 of the Rebels go past our front to the left, they soon after fell in with part of the 52d. Regt. & Major Lamonds [Normand Lamont's] Battn. of the 71st from Bonam Town, and skirmish'd with them for above 2 hours, The 52d had 3 wounded & 3 missing the 71st. 5 or 6 killed & wounded. they drove the lurking rascals at last The Genl. arrived from Brunswick Escorted from Post to Post. & a Squadron of Light Dragoons who came out with us to meet his Exy. return'd to Amboy with him, while we staid to cover the Foragers, we came in about four

Sunday 9th. March fine weather & warm for the season. The Genl. set off this morng. for N:York by water, without any pomp or show, nothing new transpired – The Battns. went ashore at the usual hour of parade Staid about 2 hours, & got the ship a little cleaned which she had much need of for I never saw anything so dirty –

Monday 10th. March fine wr. & warm. The flank Corps & 3d. Brigade went ashore this morng. at 5 oclock & march'd with some field pieces in the former route but a little further on the Bonam Town road & filed off to the right & posted themselves on the Short Hills & high grounds near where about the Saturdays Skirmish was, where we staid a few hours covering the forraging party by Water. We return'd between one & 2 o'clock without seeing any of the Rebels, – An old man came into us who had been a Soldier formerly & lives in this Neighbourhood; he says the Rebels had upwards of 100 killed & wounded on the 23d. Febry. – Visited the Hospital The Wounded are all doing well except Wm. McIntosh who is just dying – Jno. Car holds it out surpizingly, all the rest are in a good way –

A Packet arrived at N.York the letters for the Jerseys are come to Amboy,   all peace & tranquility in Europe, –

Tuesday 11th. March Wm. McIntosh died this morning Remarkable fine wr. for the season Had the Battn. ashore for two or 3 hours on the beach & got the ship a little clean'd, our Compy very sickly, two men that were orderly in the Hospital on different days were taken suddenly ill, owing they think to the putrid stench in some of the rooms – our letters if there are any for us are gone to ye Regt.

Lt. Gil[christ]: gone to N:York on some important business of his own & to bring the Convalescents of the Battn. he'll not get drunk to be sure

Wednesday 12th. March it came on to rain last night about 10 oclock & rain'd hard all night, we had orders to land this morning for another forraging party but the rain prevented us, The Day however clear'd up, the men went ashore for about an hour, & the ship was clean'd

Thursday 13th. Another rainy morning which prevents our going ashore Southerly winds & warm weather, we hear there is another Pacquet arrived at New York. The wild Pidgions made their appearance to day in great flocks, which is much sooner than usual

Friday 14th. March fine clear & pleasant Weather the snow almost gone off the ground, the Battn. went ashore for two hours

Saturday 15th. March the Weather warm & Pleasant – after the Parade was over, Capts. G: & L: & I went over to Staten Island to take a walk, we wandered six or 7 Miles into the Country, dined at the Ship & came home about 8 o'clock, having walk'd 16 or 18 miles I daresay; about 10 we got orders to land at Midnight which we accordingly did and on Sunday 16th. about 1 o'clock in the morng. we march'd out above 2000 strong & 2 3 pounders with Genl. Vaughan at our head, before we got to Woodbridge he made a division of the Troops some went off to the left across the Country & some kept the Road to the Northward – just about day break we came upon some of the Enemys out Picquets' our Light Infantry exchanged a few shot with them & took some prisoners, the rest fled, The Divisions soon after join'd at Spank Town which was quite deserted, having all run off when they hear'd the first firing, we then came on to the Road and moved on homewards having taken in all 12 prisoners & killed 4 when we had got a few miles on, a parcel of the Rascals came on our Rear & kept up a scattered popping fire for a good while with the Light Bobs even till we got pass'd Woodbridge. Major [Henry] Johnston & two or 3 men wounded – we got into Amboy about nine a good deal fatigued the Roads & Country being very soft & deep – took some breakfast & went to bed – when I got up found a letter from A:H: dated 20 Octr come from the Regt.

Monday 17th. March usher'd in with St. Patricks day in the morng. at Reveilee beating, parade ashore at the usual hour, the Shamrogue mounted by the Hibernians, who dedicate the day to the Saint & the bottle or rather to St. for the sake of the bottle, we drank to his memory at dinner in the Cabin, but he was more amply sacrified to between decks – wrote A.H.

Tuesday 18th. March fine weather & warm – at 9 o'clock The flank Corps, 3d. Brigade[,] Waldeckers & a Battn. of Hessians with 4 six pounders march'd out in great haste having heard a party of the Rebels were betwixt this & Woodbridge, we moved on pretty briskly, having hear'd some firing in front which proved to be some of our light Horse skirmishing near Strawberry Hill, (1 Horse wounded) as we approach'd Strawberry hill saw a body of the Enemy drawn up on Herds Hill N.W. of Woodbridge who seem'd to make a stand & a larger Body were seen in the Wood

to the Eastwd. of the Hill, The Light Infantry had been detach'd
to the left some time ago & when we came to Woodbridge we
wheel'd up the Brunswick Road on which we Proceeded about a
1/4 of a mile & drew up our Guns facing Herds Hill & the Wood
to the right, in which direction they fired a few Rounds, on the
Commencemt. of which the Rebels on the Hill filed off by their
left to the Rear in pretty decent order & I believe without losing
a man, the Waldeckers & Hessians moved on in the Elizabeth
Town road while we the Grenadrs. moved forward from the
Guns & took possessn. of the Hill the Enemy had quitted, & saw
them retreating to the westward, we sent out & took in some
Cattle, & then return'd to Woodbridge where we halted a little,
at this time the Waldeckers fired some of their 3 pounders & some
small arms were hear'd in that direction we were ordered to
march up briskly to that quarter, but before we arrived the few
Rebels that made their appearance had walk'd off probably with
some loss as they did not come near us all the rest of the day,
we had 1 light Infantry man wounded, & returnd to Quarters
without further loss or Molestation with Drums beating to con-
vince the General of his Victory – Gilchrist return'd from
N.York – he brot. nothing with him but a Gon[orrhea]: Simplex

Wednesday 19th. March having got, orders last night to be
ashore at 7 o'clock this morng. we accordingly landed & march'd
up Town when we were told that we were to return on board of
the ship again – The Battn. went to the Parade, tryed and flogg'd
a prisoner of the 57th. & staid ashore till the ship was clean'd –
Note There is an ugly fever seized on a good many both in
Town & Transports of which several have died, & it seems to
spread, a ship appointed for an Hospital Ship, pretty full already,
Serjt. Stewart moved there yesterday, very ill –

Thursday 20th. March it rain'd almost all last night & continues to rain hard still no stiring out today. went ashore in the
Eveng. play'd Cards & sup'd

Friday 21st. March fine dry weather & a westerly wind the
Battn. went ashore to parade & get the ship clean'd, took a walk

round the out Sentry's – Sir Wm. Erskine came here to day from Brunswick by water, & his Major of Brigade on their way to N.York –

Saturday 22d. fine weather & wind at SW. Parade ashore as usual. Sr. Wm. gone to N.York by Staten Island Major [Archibald] Erskine by water Capt. Cathcart gone in the same sloop – a buz of something going on under Sr. Wm. We hear a little Expedition of 5 or 600 men under the Command of Colo. [John] Bird of the 15th. are gone from N:York believe up the North River wt. a frigate they went to Peekskill & destroyed a large magazine of the Rebels & return'd in about a week without any loss –

Sunday 23d. March fine pleasant weather – The flank Corps, 3d. Brigade went ashore before 5 oclock in the morng. & march'd together with the Waldeckers & a Battn. of the 71st. & 8 pieces of Cannon to cover Boats that went up to the Marshlands to the Eastwd. of Woodbridge to get Salt Hay, The Troops were disposed along the road beyond Woodbridge, down near the Church, & on Herds Hill, we staid about 2 hours, & march'd back; a few fellows made their appearance in our Rear which occasion'd a little firing betwixt the light Infantry & ym. 1 man wounded, some Horsemen appear'd on Strawberry Hill immediately after we pass'd it, at whom there was some cannon fired but I believe did not hit any of them, we march'd in Town with drums beating another Triumphall entry –

Monday 24th. March fine moderate weather – Got orders today to march to Brunswick & join the 1st. & 2d. Battns. of Grenadrs. & the 3d. Brigade are to go to Staten Island to Sail

Tuesday 25th. March the fine weather continues getting all ready to march tomorrow morng. – sent a man to N.York for stuff to make 2 pair trousers for each man of the Compy & to get some other articles –

Wednesday 26th. March the Light Infantry & Grenadiers disembark'd at 7 o'clock, Baggage & sick men put on bord 3 sloops we march'd between 8 & 9 o'clock with 6 waggons carrying our bedding pass'd thro' Bonam Town about 11 & thro Piscataway about an hour after they have been all quiet in their quarters for these 3 weeks past We went round by the Bridge & arrived at Brunswick about 2 oclock when the 3d. Battalions of Grenadrs. was divided between the 1st. & 2d. the 15th. 28th. 33d. & 37th. Compys. join'd the 1st. Battn. & the 42d. 46th. & 57th. join'd the 2d. Battn. The men Quarter'd in Store Houses & have got some bedding The Officers in Empty Dwelling Houses. This Place quite full of troops the duty easy & the Post quiet. Lord Cornwallis & Genl. [James] Grant commands

Thursday 27th. March a cold frosty morng. Parade at 1/2 after 8 o'clock the 2 Battalions of Grenadrs. make a respectable figure behind the Barracks, & the Hessian Grenrs. are formidable t'other side the road, but I hear those Troops are very sickly just now & their men dying very fast – went out to the bridge & din'd with our Light Subs

Friday 28th. March sharp frost – some deserters comg. in here almost every day, in consequence of the late Proclamation, by all accounts the Americans are becoming discontented with the service – wrote a letter to Colo: Stirling to get Gilchrist removed from the Grenrs. for in his absence I find I am the Eldest Lieut. in both Battns. – dined with the Marines –

Saturday 29th. March a Cloudy morng. & came on to snow in the forenoon which lasted for some hours. Capt. Graham & I walk'd out to Piscataway to speak to the Colo: about the Change of the Subns. of the Compy. found some difficulty in persuading him to Change Gilchrist, which I expected he would [have] done without hesitation when he saw the reasons I gave for his being removed, we are to get Saunders Grant in his place, but he would not agree to give another in place of Wm. Graham till his affair is settled; our lads all well & comfortable a good many of the men sick & some dying – din'd with our light Capt. & got fou with Claret

Sunday 30th. March fine mild warm day, but dirty walking

from yesterdays snow which is all gone – The man return'd from New York with the articles sent for, but we made a mistake about the Quantity of Canvas, so must send for more – Recd. a Cask of Bottled Port wine, a present from Dick Marshall betwixt Sandy Monro & I – Din'd with Lord Cornwallis, a genteel Table & moderate

Monday 31st. March   S.W. the day warm & pleasant   sent Corpl. Thompson to NYork for more Canvas for trowzers – 268 yards   sent also my man for some things – din'd with Major [William] Murray

Tuesday 1st. April   fine weather, nothing going on here, some deserters & blacks coming in to all the Posts & at N.York – dined with Genl. [James] Grant, the old fellow lives like a Prince – [8]

Wednesday 2d. April   fine spring weather – took a walk out to our Regt. & dined with the Buck Mess, they kept me all night – This day Colo: [William] Walcot went out with a flag of truce to negotiate about the Exchange of some prisoners the Rebels owes us, who it seems are above 2000 in our debt, but they don't like to give up the Hessians & Highlanders that are in their hands, gave him a Note of our two Drumrs. taken 23d Febry.

Thursday 3d. April   light rain with wind at S.W.   came home by the Bridge – Some waggons that went down the River to get forrage near where the arm'd Schooner lyes & under cover of her guns, had some shots fired at them by the Rebels but I believe did no mischief: four Companys of Light Infantry march'd that way early this morng. – din'd with my Capt. our little Mess is not yet form'd –

Friday 4th. April   pretty sharp frost last night & the air cold this morng. Bot. some things for the Mess – Lt. [Saunders] Grant joined ye. Company

Saturday 5th. April   a good deal of frost in the night.   the day pleasant   dined with Colo: Stirling, a feast day, prize Mada. – Corpl. Thompson & my man Return'd

Sunday 6th. April   fine day. Mounted Picquet. 1 Capt. & 2 Subs. & 60 at the left Redout,   the Capt. treats. – had a quiet picquet, saw nothing. Several people passing out & in[,] to & from the Country – deserters coming in every day.

Monday 7th. April   a smart frost last night. the day warm & pleasant, not much appearance of Spring yet in the vegetation – din'd wt. Major McPherson – Colo: Stirling came Today & look'd at the Grendr. Compy.   he said they looked very well Capt. Graham wanted a few changes but he wou'd not agree to any –

Tuesday 8th. fine weather & warm, numbers of deserters coming in daily, most of them Irish, who say all their Country men of whom there is a great many in the Rebel Army will all leave them, probably in consequence of Genl. Howe's Proclamation offering a reward & a passage home to such as choose to go to Great Britain or Ireland – 16 dollars to every man that comes in wt. Arms

Wednesday 9th. April   the weather uncommonly warm for the season & the Spring begins to appear in Vegetation – went out to dine wt. Majr. Billy [Grant] but by some mistake he did not expect us & we all dined at the Colos –

Thursday 10th. April, the weather exceedingly warm still. this day appointed by Lord Cornwallis for all the Absent Officers from this Quarter to join, they are coming from N.York cursing the Stupidity of the Place, yet all agree that there's nothing going on there but Luxury & dissipation, of all kinds. 70 Sail of Transports getting ready at N.York for some Expedition – Wrote letters to Marshall A.H. & my Fr. to go by Jno. Graham – recd. a letter from Dick dated 16th. Janry. they expect at Glasgow great things from us

Friday 11th. April   the weather temperately warm & pleasant. – dined with Major Grant, a large Compy. – he lodges with a Mr. Tyrells a Country Gentlen. who married a Daughter of Mr. Skinners a Genteel pretty woman.

Saturday 12th. April   cool & pleasant with the wind at N.W.

took a walk up the River the length of the yauger Posts about 3 miles from here, they have been in huts all winter & seem to be very alert – In the Eveng. an order came to Parade the 1st. Battn. Grenadrs. at 9 oclock, they march'd out by the Hessian Picquet preceeded by the 1st. Light Infantry to the N.Westward, the Yaugers & the Brigade t'other side of the river march'd some time after up the river toward Bound Brook, about break of day of Sunday the 13th. the Yawgers & some of the Light Infantry began to skirmish with the out Picquet of the Enemy near Bound Brook, & drove them with precipitation to the Village where the alarm was spread & they took to their heels as many as could get off – 3 officers & about 80 men were taken & 3 field pieces, 2 three's & 1 six pounder brass, and a great many stores were destroyed, the Number of the Enemy kill'd on this occasion is uncertain perhaps about 40, their Genl. [Benjamin] Lincoln escaped very narrowly,[9] The Troops return'd to their Quarters about 10 o'clock A.M. a good deal fatigued The Grenadrs. & Light Infantry had gone a great way round & cross'd the Rariton about a mile & half from Bound Brook, where they arrived just after the Yawgers had begun – The Troops at Piscataway & Bonam Town were likewise out & marched some miles towards Quibble Town, to take up the Enemys attention in that Qr. – the Prisoners were sent off to NYork in sloops with a Guard of 1 Sub & 20 from 2d. Bn. Grs.

Monday 14th April a cold NW wind – & Tuesday 15th. likewise cool this morng. about 3 oclock an attack was made on Bonam Town by about 600 of the Rebels under Genl. Cook they got within the sentrys' before the Post was alarm'd & began to fire on the Picquet. the 33d. & 71st turn'd out briskly, when Mr. Cook thought proper to walk off having taken 13 of the Picquet prisoners, & left 2 of their men wounded; this looks like tit for tat. The Rebels must have fired on one another & done mischief to themselves, between 30 & 40 firelocks were found next day. Supposed to be those of their killed & wounded –

Wednesday 16th. April warm & pleasant, was up at the Yauger Post, saw a parcel of the Rebels t'other side the water, they call'd turn out, turn out, the Covering Party for the Wood Cutters saw two parties of them on the Prince Town Road, they have always Scouting Parties out on all the Roads to our Posts –

Thursday 17th. cloudy with some rain – went to Piscaty. & got two abstracts from the Paymr. with the Balance up to 24th. Decr. 76 – a decently dress'd woman found dead this morng. in the field a little above the Town – Lt. [James] Campbell join'd the Comy. in room of Lt. Graham

Saturday foggy – on Picquet a Grr. of the 52d. deserted from his Post some Light Horse sent after him, 1 of them was killed

Thursday 24 April Nothing new for some days past, its said the fleet from New York is saild, 6 Regts. under the Command of Govr. Tryon Sr. Wm. Erskine & old [James] Agnew but where they are gone to is not yet known,[10] – din'd yesterday at Bonam Town wt. Capt. [Robert] Crane 33d., That Post has been alarm'd & fir'd at every night for this week past without doing any mischief – Note. Deserters are coming in every day in parties with their arms, – mostly Irishmen, they get 16 dollars each.

Monday 28th April, We hear the Expedition have landed at Stratford in Connecticut, near which is a large magazine which is probably their object
yesterday a Major Bear & a Capt. Yates of the Rebels came in from Princetown with a flag, to bring Capt. [William] Brereton of the 17th. Grs. at the request of Capt. [John] McPherson who is lying ill of his wounds there; they staid all night & took a look of our Parade this morng. after which they set off – a deserter came in this forenoon from a Serjts. Post about 1 1/2 miles from the Hessian Picquet on the Princetown road, they are Detach'd from a Post 6 miles from here – the Wind at N.W. & the weather cold this 2 days

Thursday 1st May a cold N.W. wind which checks the Vegetation – yesterday the Compy. was muster'd, from 25 Decr.-75 to 24 Decr.-76 by Mr Porter who went afterwards & muster'd the Regt. at Piscataway – Lord Cornwallis has recd. a

letter from Genl. Howe acquainting him with the success of the
Expedition to Connecticut, They have burn'd & destroyed a large
magazine at Danbury in which there was 4000 Barrels of Pork, a
great Quantity of flour, & many other articles, – They had a
Smart Engagement with the Rebels, killed or wounded two of
their Generals, [David] Worscester & [Gold] Sylliman, & broke
thro' them with charged Bayonets; on their return from Danbury
which is about 20 miles from Stratford, they found Genl. [Bened-
ict] Arnold had got betwixt them & their ships & was busy
throwing up works with 800 men, whom they attack'd & drove
off – the loss on our side amounts to 20 killed 80 wounded & 7
or 8 officers wod. amongst whom is Major [Henry] Hope of the
44th. & Capt. Rutherford of the 27th.[11]

Friday 2d. May Pleasant cool weather, – our Compy. & the
27th. went out on a covering Party with some waggons about 2
miles on the Cranberry Road – saw nobody – burn't two houses &
return'd about noon –

Nothing extraordinary for some days –

Saturday 10th. May The 42d. at Piscataway were attack'd in
the afternoon. – About 1500 or 2000 of the Rebels collected from
their different Quarters with an intention to cut off the 42d. –
About 4 o'clock in the afternoon they were discover'd with[in a]
Wood in front of their Post & fir'd upon, on which they
advanced & attack'd the Picquet and a heavy fire ensued – The
Company's turn'd out to their support & dash'd into the Wood
upon the Enemy – the Light Infantry Companys in that Qrs.
came up to their Assistance & the 28th. Regt. turn'd out briskly
to the support of the 42d. who had by this time broke thro' the
Rebels & put them to the Rout & pursued them to their Camp at
Metuchen Meeting house (about 4 miles) before they halted The
42d. suffered as follows Major McPherson slightly wounded in
the head by a Light Infantry Man – Lt. Stewart who had the
Picquet shot thro the thigh, bone brok. 3 Serjts. & 6 R & file
killed, 2 Serjts. & 15 wounded – of the Enemy about 30 found
dead in different places & 28 taken prisoners – deserters that have

come in since [word illegible] says they lost a great many, & a flag of truce that came this day the 12th. say they have 1 Major 2 Capts. & 70 missing, & begs we will bury their dead –

Deserters coming in fast from all Quarters, they say Washington intends to make a serious attack very soon, & that he is getting frequent Reinforcements from the Southern Provinces – May 12 Our Engineers have begun a Bridge across the River here, from the opposite side to the ferry slip, constructed of Piers made of Logs notched into one another, each pier about 12 foot by 8, & about 12 or 14 asunder, to be join'd by beams or sleepers, & cover'd with plank –

May the 16th. Orders for Encamping. The Tents pitch'd at 1 o'clock the Barrack bedding brot. up to Camp in place of straw – The Brigade on t'other side Encamp'd yesterday – The 37th. Regt. are come to Bonham Town & the 52d. to Piscataway where they are encamp'd, a Battn. of Hessian Grrs. are gone over to Encamp about a mile to the left of the 42d. together with 28th. Regt.

Saturday 17th. mounted Picquet yesterday & to day very high wind at W. a little after dark two soldiers one of the 64th. & one of the Marines deserted from their post on the left front of the Capts. Picquet, a Party went after them but saw nor heard nothing of them – it rain'd all night –

Monday 19th. May a good deal of rain these two nights past – yesterday a Lieut. [John?] Mallon came to join the 57th. Compy. Grrs. who is senior to me, advised to speak to Colo: [Henry] Monckton about it – instead of which I wrote him a letter setting forth my services & the hardship it would be to lose my chance of promotion in the flank Corps by an elder Lt. popping in now who declined serving in them before[12] – The Piers of the bridge all set down, about 30 in number? rain

Tuesday 20th. it rained hard all last night, the Camp overflowed, an extra gill of Rum given out to the men on account of the wet – The heavy Baggage of the Troops here all sent to New York this morng.

Wednesday 21st. fine day; Walked over to the Regt. & spoke to Colo: Stirling about a message he sent me to know if I wd give £50 to [Capt.Lt. Valentine] Chisholm in case I got the Capt. Ltcy. in consequence of his going out, I thought it was too much, and am of opinion that Mr. Chisholm should either sell or serve, that as he was no longer able to serve he could not expect promotion, if he sold the regulation price was as much as he could expect in the present situation of affairs, however to facilitate the matter & make it as well for poor Chisholm as we could, I agreed to give the £50, 20 of which Lts. [John] Rutherford & [Robert] Potts agreed to make up equally betwixt them on the above conditions & Ensn. [Gavin] Drummond gives £30, which with the regulation price from Ens. Campbell makes up 600 guineas to Chisholms if I suceed to this Captcy[13]

to day a parcel of the Rebels show'd themselves to the left of the Capts. Picquet, they fired a gun at them from the Ridout & they went off, probably they came to look at the new bridge

Friday 23d. May, This morng. at daybreak a scouting Party of the Rebels came in front of the Hessian Picquet which brought on a pretty fire for a few minutes, The Line turned out, the Hessians got up one of their Guns & fired a few rounds they soon disappeared, nobody hurt – Slept in Camp –

Saturday 24th. heard some firing about an hour before day in front of the Hessian Picquet, got up, but as it was only a few scatter'd shots lay down again, when about an hour after hear'd more firing in the Wood t'other side the 1 mile run, the men turn'd out, & accoutred but as the firing soon ceased they did not fall in – this firing proved to be from some Compys of the Light Infantry who went out at 2 in the morng. to way lay the Rebel Scouting parties, two of whom they saw, fired upon them & killed four, the rest got off – The Rebel Camp above Bound brook being struck to day Reconoitering parties of Light Horse, Yagers, & Light Infantry, went out to see if they could discover anything, they took one Light Horseman prisoner & 4 others, & killed one more that fired at & wounded Major [Turner] Strubenzee – nothing of any consequence discover'd by the prisoners, but by intelligence from Amboy they say Bonham Town is to be attack'd to night – The days warm, but the nights cold yet. The Bridge finish'd.

Sunday 25th. The Troops at Bonham Town & Piscataway were under arms last night in expectation of an attack, but nobody appear'd – We hear from York that there is an Expedition going on from there, 6 British Regts. vizt. The 4th. 15th. 27th. 23d. 44th. & 64th. & 2 Hessian Regts. are under orders to Embark They come to Jersey – the 63d. Regt. & 2 Hessian Batts. and some light Horsemen are arrived from Rhode Island

Monday 26th. May The 1st. Battn. Light Infantry with 2 field Pieces went out Early this morng. to Reconoiter the Enemy's situation at Bound Brook Lord Cornwallis & Genl. Grant went along with them. They found about 1000 there & heard some firing – they followed the Light Infantry all the way to within shot of the yager Post with 2 pieces of Cannon, where they exchanged some rounds in which Genl. Grant's Horse was killd – The Main Body of the Rebel army are supposed to be Encamp'd t'other side of the Mountain, They having left all the Villages near this

Sunday 1st June 1777 yesterday Eveng. the yagers perceived a scouting party of the Rebels near their Post. They sent out a Party after them, some on horse some on foot & killd & took the whole of them being 13 & an offr. One yager killed & one wounded – This morng. a detachmt. march'd from Piscataway before 1 o'clock Colo: [Mungo] Cambell & Major [William] Murray with part of the 42d. & 52d. Regt. they went thro' the Country as far as Lamtown & near to Quibletown without seeing a man in arms & return'd to their Camp about 7 o'clock Had letters today in answer to those I wrote in Rhode Island (7th. Febry. & 11 Mar my Father & Dr. F. & AH)

Tuesday 3d. June had another letter from AH 12 Janry. & one from Mr. Jamison 20 Mar. no news

Wednesday 4th. a fellow one Patoun taken up for corresponding with & giving information to Washington the Rascal undertook to fire the Magazine when the Enemy attack'd this Post – Some appearances of a movement soon –

Friday 6 June last night & to day wrote letters to my Father with the 2d. bill £40 – to AH & to Thos Arthur, Dick Marshall, & Mr. Jameson The Spy Patoun was hang'd today – Deserters coming in as usual & some Rascals are deserting from us. The 2d. Battn. Grrs. have lost 6 or 8 within this short time – A great number of ships arrived at New York lately with Foreigners & Recruits for the army – a good many Officers of the Guards to relieve a like number of those that serv'd last Campaign

Sunday 8 June the Sick of the different Battns. sent to New York, our Company very sickly for some weeks past, fluxes, & fevers, 10 sent to N.York this day, & 6 sick in Camp. N:B: Corpl. Davidson died 2d. June & fifer Steward the 3d. of fevers – 4 twelve Pounders & 20 flat Boats with their Carriages arrived

10 June A Genl. Court Martial for the tryal of some deserters that were apprehended by Country People

Wednesday 11 June The General arrived at Brunswick with his Suite – the 7th. & 26th. Regts. & the Remains of Ralls Brigade arrived in the afternoon & Encamp'd on the right of the Hessian Grrs.

Thursday 12 June the 33d. & 37th. arrived in the morng. all wet, & the Hessian Grenr. of Minirod. – the 42d. & 52d. arrived in the afternoon A Good many other Regts. come up & Encamp'd t'other side the River – Some works making for the Defense of this Place on both sides ye. River

June 13th. 1777 The army march'd from Brunswick at Night in two lines. The 1st. under the Command of Lieut. Genl. Earl Cornwallis & Major Genl. Grant consisting of the Hessian & Anspach Chasseurs Two Battns. Light Infantry (except 4 Compys. under Major [Peter] Craig to join Lt. Colo: [Thomas] Twisleton) 2 Medium 12 pounders, British Grenadrs. with their Battn. Guns, Brigade under Lt. Colo: [Thomas] Stirling (the

33d. & two Battns. 42d) with 2 Howitzers & 2 six pors. Brigade under Lt. Colo: Sir Henry Calder (the 5th. 49th. 52d. 37th.) with 4 six pors. Colo: [Carl Emil Kurt von] Donop with 3d. 2d. & 1st. Hessian Grenadrs., 16th. Dragoons leaving an offr. & 16 with Brr. Gl. [Edward] Mathew at Brunk Those Corps assembled & form'd in Columns of March by half Compys. on the Prince Town road at 11 oclock this night, the head of the Column at 1 mile run

The 2d. Division under the Command of his Exy. Lt. Genl. [Leopold Philip] D'Heister Major Genls. [Johann Daniel] Sterne[,] [John] Vaughan & [Charles] Gray Brigrs. Genls. [James] Agnew & [Alexander] Leslie to march by the left[14] – the 4 Compys. of Light Infantry wt Major Craig & Capt. [Patrick] Fergusons' [Rifle] Compy. to join the Light Infantry of the Guards under the Comd. of Lt. Colo: Twisleton – four Grasshoppers to be attached to this Corps – the Battn. of Guards wt. a Corps of Pioneers, 40th. & 23d. Regts. under the Comd. of Lt. Colo: [Henry] Trelawney to form the Advance Guard followg. Lt. Col: Twisletons Corps with 2 medium 12 pors. & two 6 pors. Maj. Genl. Sterne wt. the Hessian Brigade; Major Genl. Gray with the 2d. & 4 Brigades with 2 six pors. to each. Majr. Genl. Vaughan with 3d. & 1st. Brigade with 2 six pors. to each, 17th. Dragoons with their dismounted – Brigr. Genl. Leslie with ye Brigade of 71st. Regt. to assemble on the Prince Town road at 11 oclock in the rear of Ld. Cornwallis's Division & wait further orders. NB: The Baggage & women left at Brunswick wt. a Garrison Gl. Math[ews] 2 waggons to each Regt. to carry the offrs. canteens & provision. The first Division march'd to Hillsborrow the 2d. to Middle Bush, the light Troops had a little skirmishing in front of Hillsbw. in ye morng. of 14th. Capt. [Henry] Lysit 63d. wounded & a few men

The Enemy in a Strong Camp t'other side the mountains about 7 miles from here Hillsborrough to the Nod. 18 June 2 Subs. 55th. Grrs. taken prisoners by going wtout ye sent[rys]

June 19th. The Army under arms at 3 oclock morng. & march'd by the left back to Brunswick. the 2d. Battn. Grrs. being thrown in the rear had a few shots fir'd at them as they came near the 1 mile run, only 1 man wounded –

June 21st. The works at Brunswick demolish'd, & some Regts. march'd to Amboy wt. Genl. Vaughan

22d. June   The whole army quitted Brunswick in the morng. & cross'd over by Moncrieffs bridge.[15] The Grenadrs. & Light Infantry in the Rear, halted for a little on the heights on Eastside ye River when a body of about 1000 of the Rebels appeared on the upper ground near the Landing with 3 pieces of Cannon which they play'd for some time at a mile distance & did no harm, the Line moved on, when the Rear came to Piscataqua a Parcel of the Rebels fired on the Light Infantry from the Wood on the left where they continued skirmishing till two Battns. were sent up to the Edge of the Wood & pour'd in a heavy fire which sent them a scampering, before we got to Bonham Town another attack of the same kind was made on the rear which ended in the same manner   about twenty killed & wounded on our side   the loss of the Rebels not known, 1 Capt. taken

the Rear of the army arrived & encamp'd near Amboy about 4 P.M. the whole army (except a few Regts. gone to Staten island to Embark) encamped witht. the lines at Amboy, making a circular sweep from water to water –

25 June   The army struck Tents at 6 o'clock in the Eveng. & sent their Baggage within the lines, moved off their ground about 9 & put in line of march in two divisions on the Bonham Town & Woodbridge Roads where they lay on their arms till day break, when the whole march'd in two Columns, that on the right under Lord Cornwallis the left Genl. Vaughan,   under Genl. Howe about 8 o'clock morng. 26 [June] the Yagers & Light Infantry in front of the right Column began to skirmish & soon after fell in with a Body of the Rebels north of Metachy [Metuchen] M:House who had 4 pieces of Cannon, which they began to play on them The Light troops were supported by the British & Hessn. Grrs., killed a good many of the Rebels took 3 of their Cannon & about 150 Prisoners the 4th. Gun was found after in a thicket. The Rest

of the Rebels fled in confusion – The Course of the Columns was towd. Quible Town, when within 4 miles of it they turn'd to the right & join'd at Westfield where they halted for ye night.

June 27th. The Army marched in two Columns by the left to Raway, without meeting with any of the Enemy – in the Country we marched thro' these two days none of the men at home –

28 June the army return'd to their Camp at Amboy the Baggage gone over to Staten island, the Troops followg. fast – in the course of this excursion several men died from the excessive heat, fatigue & drinking water – about 20 kill'd & wounded the first day –

29th. June More Troops & Baggage crossing over to Staten island –

30 June The Remainder of the army crost over to Staten island & march'd to their several Encampments on the Roads leading to Cole's & Dykers ferries, it rained all last night & today – not a Rebel appear'd on leaving Amboy –

1st. July The Army march'd & Encamped on the heights about Coles ferry. The Genl. gone to N:Y: Ld. Cornwallis Comds. in Staten island.

orders for Embarkation. The Officers to lay in 3 weeks provision for the intended Voyage [illegible word] to Long island & N:York to buy stock & stores, laid out 8d Lt. Genl. Sir Henry Clinton arrived 5 July

6th. July our additional Compys. arrived 2 lts. & 170 NB wrote Dick M: & A 7th July inclos. the latter a Bill £3

Chapter IV

'the Rascals . . . hold out well'

Pennsylvania
8 July to 31 December 1777

The campaign of 1777 in Pennsylvania was extraordinarily frustrating for Sir William Howe. He was forced to abandon his preconceptions about the people of Pennsylvania, his strategy for ending the war, and, ultimately, his command of British forces in North America. He persisted in going to Pennsylvania even after being reminded that the ministry expected him to cooperate with British forces from Canada in a summer campaign against New England. Howe was determined to show that the people of Pennsylvania were loyal to the crown and would sustain his strategy of gradually recovering territory and promoting a reconciliation between Britain and America. Indeed, Howe sailed to Pennsylvania by way of the Chesapeake as if to ensure that he would be unable to take part in any operations against New England in 1777, that he would be free to pursue his own plans in Pennsylvania. But what he discovered on reaching the head of Chesapeake Bay forced an abrupt change in his strategy. Finding in late August that few of the inhabitants of Delaware and Pennsylvania were loyal to Britain, that the people could not be expected to support a gradual restoration of royal government, he decided to abandon his strategy of recovering territory and to try to end the rebellion by destroying the Continental army in a decisive battle. He did manage to engage and defeat Washington's army at the Battle of Brandywine on 11 September and to occupy Philadelphia two weeks later. But so far was he from destroying the Continental army that he was not able to open the Delaware to British shipping or to secure Philadelphia for another two months. Nor was he able to engage the Continental army to advantage – either when Washington attacked the British at Germantown in October or when Howe went looking for the rebels at Whitemarsh in early December. The failure of his hopes and plans was the more frustrating because while he devoted his army to Pennsylvania, British forces advancing south from Canada were isolated along the Hudson and forced to surrender at Saratoga. No wonder that when criticized by the ministry, Howe now asked to be relieved of his command.[1]

For John Peebles the campaign of 1777 in Pennsylvania brought nearly four months of continuous marching and fighting and an awakening respect for the strength of the rebellion. After nearly seven weeks on board a transport between New York and the head of Chesapeake Bay, Peebles and his comrades in the 2nd Battalion of Grenadiers were glad to disembark in the lush Maryland countryside.[2] But they soon found the inhabitants hostile and their recovery of Pennsylvania stubbornly contested. Defeating the Continental army at the Brandywine and occupying Philadelphia proved far easier than securing the city or feeding the troops that were to be posted there. Peebles and his battalion joined both in defending the northern or landward approaches to the city (they turned out to help repel Washington's attack on Germantown) and in opening the Delaware to British shipping (they joined in attacking the rebel forts and vessels that kept British ships from supplying Philadelphia).[3] Even after 2 November, when Peebles left the grenadiers to become captain lieutenant of a line company in his 42nd Regiment (a part of the 3rd Brigade of the army), his duty changed little; he still shuttled between the swampy banks of the Delaware and the dry, cold lines north of the city. By the time the British had opened the river but failed to destroy the Continental army in battle, Peebles was beginning to express his respect for the rebels and his impatience with Howe's efforts to defeat them.[4]

Pennsylvania
8 July to 31 December 1977

July the 8th & 9th   The Army Embark'd at Coles ferry, our Compy. on board ye America about a ton a half to a man. Genl. Clinton in absence of the Commander in Chief to command at New York & all reports to be made to him from Kings Bridge Staten island Rhode island &ca. – NB got abst. & money thro 13 to 24 June

16 July   The Fleet in the same Position off Staten island, some more ships coming down from N.York. & some arrivals from Europe. 200 addls. for the 71st. arrived yesterday –

18th. July   The Admiral [Lord Howe] came down to ye. fleet & was recd. by the ships of war maning the yards

19th. July   a signal for weighing but at ye. turn of the tide 8 AM: it fell quite calm so could not move   4 Frigates & some other ships arrived fr ye. Nod. 2 fr: Quebec –

Sunday 20th. July   a Signal made for sailing in the morng. when the fleet got under way; about one half of them turn'd down to the Hook wind S. & S.S.W.   the rest came too below the Narrows, about 260 sail in all besides 10 Men of War.

21st. July   the rest of the fleet except the large men of war came down to the Hook, wind variable

22d. Rain & little or no wind   nothing done.

Wednesday 23d. The wind being fair the large ships came down to the Hook early when the whole fleet got under way & stood out to sea with a fine breeze at NW
The Admiral stands to the Sod.   a frigate ahead men of war on the flanks & Rear. – in the afternoon the wind died away & came about the S.W.

24th. easy wr. & a light wind from N.W. see the land to starboard. Course about S.S.W. & SW.   in the Eveng. a signal for tacking & stood out all night to the Eastwd. with little or no wind –

Friday 25th. the fleet tack'd in morng. about 7 & stood in about S.S.W. – at noon Lat by Ob: 39.43 little wind the whole day in the afternoon see the land off the Starboard beam, course So: & S.S.W. light wind going from 1 1/2 to 2 1/2 knots. tack'd & stood out all night – [5]

Saturday 26th. July it blew a fresh breeze from the Sowd. & rais'd a little sea. The fleet stood out to the Eastwd. all day & tacked in the Eveng. when the wind fell away. – saw a frigate chase a small sloop, & brot her into the fleet –

Sunday 27 easy wr. & little wind we make very little way. at noon had an obn, Lat: 39.14. the afternoon almost calm –

Monday morng. a breeze from the S.E. the fleet stood in for the land, under easy sail but the wind fell away, in the Eveng. a thunder Gust the fleet lay too all night & made sail in the morng. of 29th at 3 the wind W.N.W Co: S.W. in the forenoon a sloop of war join'd the fleet – at noon had an ob: Lat 38.46 little wind at WSW

Wednesday 30th July made the land early in the morng. to the Sowd. of Cape Henlopen stood in with the wind about No: till near the Light House NB The Roebuck came out of Delawar Bay to us then tack'd, most of the fleet to leeward, stood off & on all night, light wind, –

Thursday 31st. see the land a good way off in the morng. almost calm, head to S.Ed. came a little breeze from the Sowd. course E.S.E at noon Lat 38.33 – several signals – stood E.S.E. till 4 P.M. then tack'd & stood to the Wwd. a fine breeze about 7 Eveng. tacked again & stood out S.E: & S.S.E all night wind about S.S.W & S.W. 2 1/2 knots

Friday 1st. Augt. Still standing on to the Ewd. of So. close haul'd at noon Lat 38.15. in the Eveng. the fleet tacked & stood to the Westwd. all night –

Saturday 2d. Augt. light wind at S.W. still, tack'd in the morng. & stood out S.S.E. at Noon Lat 38.14 tack'd in the Eveng. & stood in to the Wd. –

Sunday 3d. Augt. little wind & warm wr. tack'd in morng. & stood SBE at noon Lat. 38.11 Wind SWBS tack'd & stood westd in the Eveng. a Thunder Squal for 2 hours – lay too most of the night –

Monday 4 Augt. very little wind to Ed. of So – warm wr. lay about S.W. the fleet much scatter'd – Lat at Noon 38.8. – 24 fathoms water – supposed dist from the land 40 miles – eveng. Cloudy almost calm in the Night the wind Variable & Squally –

Tuesday 5th. Augt. easy wr. & light winds at S.W. & So: & S.S.W. stood out all the morng. about noon tak'd & lay up W.B.N. Lat 38.0 – some signals exchanged in the Eveng. from men of war farthest ahead tack'd & stood out again – in the night Lightening thunder & rain, the wind shifting about from W. to So –

Wednesday 6th. Augt cloudy with showers & almost calm wind about So:westly. standing to westwd. at noon every Quadrant made a difft. Lat fr: 38 – upwards tack'd & tack'd again the night showery did little

Thursday 7th. Augt. fair wr. & light winds the land seen about 11 A.M. ahead stood in till 4 P.M. 12 fm. water little wind S.S.E. 2 kts. tack'd & stood out East – Lat at Noon from 38.2. to 37.43 This Voyage proving longer than we expected sea stores runs short – about 25 leagues fr: Cape Henry

Friday 8th. The So:westerly winds still prevail light breezes at noon Lat 37.45. stood to Sod all night with a fine little breeze, warm

Saturday 9th. wind about west Co S.S.W all the morning at noon Lat 36.59. standg. S:BE in the Eveng. tack'd & stood in WNW & WBN part of the night

Sunday 10th. Augt. a hazy horizon wind WSW Co: So: all

the morng. at noon Lat 36.43. in the Eveng. tack'd & stood in about WBN. & WNW all night –

NB: got a supply of stores from a sloop 17 guineas

Monday 11th. Augt. the fleet still standing to ye Westd. at Noon Lat 36.52. expect to see the land tomorrow wind about SW. Co: WNW or so all night

Tuesday 12th. Augt. the wind more to west Co: NWBW some of the fleet about, at noon Lat 37.18 – in the afternoon made the land & stood in within 5 leagues then tack'd & stood out all night at So:B.E. – So: & SoBW

Wednesday 13th. still standg. about SBW. light wind at noon Lat 36.52. tack'd & stood in to the Westward the wind coming more to Sod: we lay up W. & WBS the land was made in the Eveng. by the ships ahead stood in all night but the wind westerd

Thursday 14th. tack'd early in the morng. & stood to the Sod. with a fine breeze. see land in the morng. at noon Lat: 36.54. about fleet & stood in WBS till near the Cape Henry & came to anchor about 8 P.M.

Friday 15th. a Signal for weighing about 5 or 6 am made a tack to the Sod. & put about a[t] 8. Cape Henry about WBN 4 leagues soon after the adml. made a signal for the fleet to make the best of their way in, there being little wind we did not get in till about 8 P.M. most of the fleet out.

Saturday 16th. lying at anchor Cape Henry So Cape Charles No. the rest of the fleet coming in, about noon a breeze sprung from NE which brot. in the fleet & those that were in before weighed anchor & got under way. in the Eveng. came to anchor about 10 leagues up the Bay – Squally night. lightning thunder & rain

Sunday 17. The fleet weighed & got under way in the morng. light wind at E. hazy & sultry stood up till the tide turn'd, about 12 then anchor'd about 5 or 6 leagues further up –

Monday 18th. The Fleet weighed anchor again in the morng.

about 6 & sail'd up the Bay wt. a SW breeze about 9 or 10 leagues further when the wind came to No: at the turn of the tide & the fleet came to anchor – NB: a galley seen on the larboard shore who fir'd some shot, two or three small men of war came too near where she was – The wind about No all the PM The fleet at anchor – a Packet arriv'd yesterday or the day before – got another supply of Mess stores yesterday – 11 or 12 Guineas –

Tuesday 19th. Augt. The fleet weighed again in the morng. & made a fine streech up the Bay – pass'd the mouth of Potowmack after which the Bay grows narrower, anchor'd in the Eveng. which look'd squally –

Wednesday 20th. Augt. The fleet weighed early in the morng. & stood up the Bay with a fine breeze at West & SW see the people on both sides the Bay the land to Port the appearance of being best cultivated & inhabited – made a good stretch of 12 or 15 leagues today & came to an anchor in the Eveng.

Thursday 21st. the fleet got under way early in the morng. wt. a fine breeze at SSW & stood up the Bay. at 8 AM abreast with Annapolis the Colours flyg. there, & at a work opposite. t'other side the Harbour – Sail'd up about 6 or 8 leagues above Annapolis & came to anchor in ye Eveng.

Friday 22nd. The signal being made early in morng. the fleet got under way with a gentle breeze of fair wind. warm wr. – The Channel growing more intricate The fleet dropp'd anchor & weighed several times. in the Eveng. the headmost ships up at Turky point – & I think near George Town – no appearance of an Enemy ashore
News – Ticonderoga taken by Genl. [John] Burgoyne 6th. July – Fort Geo: & Ft. Ann after – Capt. [John] Brisban[e] with the Flora retook the Fox Frigate 7th. July & Sir Geo Colier took the Hancock frigate –

Sa[t]urday 23d. the small craft in motion in the morng. & some ships getting into their stations which was all the movements of

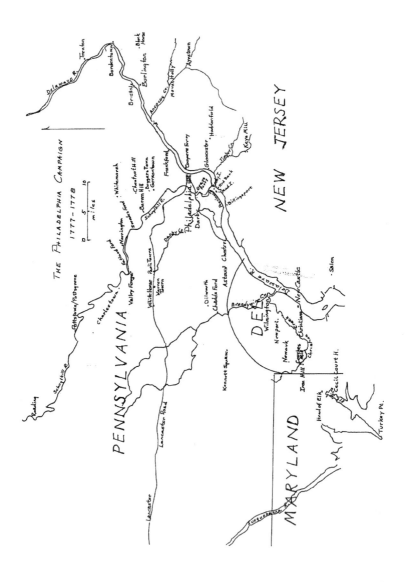

the day except some of the small arm'd vessels cruizing in shore both sides   one of them on the West side fir'd several shot

a man of some consequence came off from the shore to the Eagle & told the Great man that he was a friend to Govert. that there were no people in arms in this part of the Contry. tho' many ill affected. – some Report of Washington being entrenched at Willmington

Sunday 24th. Augt.   The fleet remaining in the same position The Adml. at Turky point & the Headmost ships at the Embouchuse of Elk River – Orders for dressing two days Provision – A Distribution made for the disembarkation   Light Infantry[,] Grenrs. & Yagers first wt. Lord Cornwallis & Donop. the rest as follows

2d. Debarkation	Hessian Grrs.
	Queens Rangers
	Guards. 4th. & 23d. Regts.
3d.	28. 49. 5. 10. & 27
	40. 55. 15. & 42
4th.	44. 17. 33. 37
	46. 71. & 64
5th.	Brigade of Sterne consisting of Du Corps,
	Donops Mirbach's, & Loo's

The Compys. to form as they land without attending to seniority or places – orders in the Eveng. to be ready to disembark at 3 in the morng. –

Monday 25th. Augt. the first Debarkation got into their flat Boats at 3 in the Morng. & arranged near the Roebuck, P signal & a little after day light the Boats row'd on P signal. – 2 frigates 2 sloops of war, the Vigilant & Gually [galley], along Starboard shore within us. The Roebuck & part of the fleet followed – we went up the Elk River as far as the ferry,   about 3 or 4 leagues The admls flag on board the Vigilant which went before,   we land'd about 9 o'clock a little above the ferry & march'd about 3 miles up the West side of the River   The inhabitants almost all gone off & carried everything with them they could, a pretty Country & plentifull Crops – the day exceedingly hot, & in the night a Thunder gust with a great deal of rain, – I believe the whole army are landed

Tuesday 26th. The Troops taking up their ground in their respective lines. – the light Dragoons Encamp'd on our left – orders for the followg. Corps to be in readiness to march from the right by 1/2 Compys. without beat of Drum tomorrow morning at 3 oclock in the followg. order – Infantry Yaugers, with an offr. & 12 mounted – two Bns. Br: Light Infantry with Queens Rangers & Ferguson Corps – Brit: Grenrs. 1st. Brig: Artillery – Hessian Grenrs., 2d Brig: Artillery, Foot Guards – 1st. & 2d. Brigades British – Baggage of the Genl. & staff offrs. – Hospital wagons & a waggon with Engineers tools – 3 Troops 16th. Dragoons with all their Dismounted – Mounted & Dismounted Yagers and the 3 Battns. of the 71st. – The Remaining Troops to continue here under Genl. Kniphausen till further orders – NB it rain'd hard all Night & early in the morng. the above order was Countermand'd

Wednesday 27th. Cloudy & Cool. The waggons & part of the Baggage sent for, & a Detachmt. for 3 days Bread & Rum it was late at Night before they returned. – Orders in the Eveng. for marching in the morng. agreeable to the orders of yesterday. – an allowance of fresh meat –

Thursday 28th. under arms at 3 in the morng. and march'd about day break in the order prescribed – got to the Head of Elk (a pretty Village) about 9, most of the inhabitants fled some of the Rebel troops had been there the night before, but went off in haste. Genl. Washington had been there 2 days before, they say he has taken Post with his Army about 9 or 10 miles from here towards the Delaware the Light Infantry posted on a Hill about 2 mile North of the Town the Grrs. to their right. Hessians in ye rear & so on. – a few shots in front a Dest. taken

Friday 29th. Augt. some firing at the Light Iny. Post in the morng. – The Camp Equipage & Baggage sent for & Provision to

1st. Septr, – the Baggage countermanded, & only the men's Tents came ashore   N.B. Moroding to shamefull degree, especially among the Hessians – above 40 soldiers of ye army missing, supposed to be taken or deserted – a Reward of a dollar for every head of Cattle & 1/2 a dollar for every sheep brot. to the Commissary – A considerable quy. of stores found in the Village & on board of small craft at the landing. Tobacco Wines Porter & necessaries, amt. £5000 – A Report that Genl. [John] Burgoyne has met with a Check, a Detachmt. of his army beat by Yanky Genl. [Benjamin] Lincoln. They say [Philip] Schyler & [Arthur] St. Clair has submitted – a Packet to sail soon wrote to AH & to my Fr.

Saturday 30th. all quiet, fine weather, warm days & cool nights some firing at the out Posts and more men Missing.

Sunday 31st. Augt. a Patrole of 200 fr: 1st. Br: fell in with some Rebels this morng. & had some firing, – 2 of the Rebel Light Horse came in, well mounted – Genl. Kniphausen with his Divisn. of the army has crossd the Elk at the ferry – all Baggage sent on board but the mens Tents offrs. to use soldiers tents. – wrote to my Fr.

Monday 1st. Septr. This morng. a party of Wynns Corps way laid a Scouting Party of the Rebels and to[ok] 2 offrs. & 3 men Prisoners & killed & wounded some – 2 men of 71st. found in the wood yesterday with their throats cut, & 2 Grrs. hang'd by the Rebels with their plunder on their backs – Kniphausen with his Column, near the front of our Camp. – Some News of Genl. Clintons giving a blow to the Rebels near Peakskill – a Declaration issued by Genl. Howe dated 27th. Augt. to encourage the Inhabitants to stay at home & pardon all that will come in, with some exceptions

Tuesday 2d. Two Genl Courts Marshall setting for the tryal of Mauroders – some straggling Rebels coming in. Orders to move tomorrow. Genl. Grant wt. about 4000 remains at head of Elk.

Wednesday 3d Septr. Camp at Coater's [Couchs's?] Mill Lord

Cornwallis. Qrrs. The Yaugers, 2 Battns. Light Infantry, Rangers & Riflemen[,] British Grenadrs[,] Hessian Grrs. 1st. Battn. Guards, a Brigade of British & the 16th Dragoons march'd at day break & proceeded along the Philada. road N:E:; about 8 the Yaugers fell in with a Body of the Rebels Posted near a Bridge & mill about 5 or 6 miles from Head of Elk, the Yaugers recd. a heavy fire from them, & made some difficulty in passing the Bridge, but the 2d Batt Light Infantry coming up dash'd over and drove the Rebels, with the loss of 1 kill'd & 10 wod. The Yaugers suffer'd about the same. The skirmishing continued in different parts of the wood first & last about an hour. The Rebels must have lost a good many, as five officers were found dead in the field. – The 2d. Grrs order'd to support the 2d. Light Infantry, they proceeded on the left of the Road about a mile & a 1/2 past ye Bridge & seeing nothing halted & came into the road when the whole march'd back to the Bridge & took up their ground near that for the night. The 1st. Batt Light Infantry struck off to the right in order to turn the Enemys left flank but met with a swamp which they could not get thro' – Kniphausen with his Coln. landed at Cecil Co: House got plenty of fresh Provn. in his Route & is now in our Rear about 2 miles, near Head Qrs. at Aikens farm. they consist of 3d. & 4th. Brigs. 1 Bat of 71st. & Hessian Brige.

Camp at Couchs's Mill thursday 4th. Septr. 1777   the Bridge at this mill crosses a rivulet or Creek that runs into Christine. The two Battns. Light Infy. & Hessian Yaugers on the East side, British & Hessian Grenadrs. on the west side; there are two roads from this Bridge to Head of Elk, & two on the other side that leads to New Castle & Wilmington   about 1/2 a mile in our Rear the Guards are Encamp'd on a high ground call'd Iron Hill from which there is a very extensive prospect of the Country all round, you see the Delaware below New Castle about 7 miles distant, about East, a long view of the Eastern Shore & Lower Counties, flat & woody. the Ground about Head of Elk & Chesapeake, & on the Wilmington road, you see the Village of Newark & the Ground about Christeen &ca. The Camp quiet, provisns. sent for, the mens Tents not to come up, recommended to the offrs. to send for liquor –

Camp at Couch's Mill & Bridge Aiken's Creek Friday 5th. Septr. quiet all round, the 1st Light Infy. went out reconoitering about 3 miles in front & saw nothing – in the afternoon a flag of truce came in with two letters one for Lord Howe & one for the Genl – a Light Horseman came in well mount'd & a foot soldier from Wilmington – 4 days Provision came up from Head of Elk –

Saturday 6th. Showery & sultry – The army in General healthy, some few of the men have a particular complaint of pains & swelling in their knees & ankles – Genl. [James] Grants Division come up from Head of Elk – Qr. Gd. a letter fr: H

Sunday 7th. a Detachmt. of the 2d. Light Infantry went out early this morng. as far as Newark about 3 or 4 miles & saw nothing, the village quite abandon'd – Several Deserters came in today among the rest an Ensign, who says that Washington has harrangd his army, thro' the Clergy, telling them that now is the time to defend their Country in General, & Philadelphia in particular, for if that falls all is gone, and that he is determin'd to stand & oppose us – Orders for moving at an hours notice, to march from the left in 3 Divisions. 1st. under Lord Cornwallis consisting of Infantry Yaugers. 1st & 2d. Light Infantry 1st. & 2d. Grenadrs. Hessian Grrs. – Yauger Infantry, 1st. & 2d. Guards, mounted Yaugers – 2d. Division under Genl. Grant – two Squadns. Queens Dragoons – 1st. Brigade of Artillery – 1st. & 2d. Brigades British 3d. Brigade Artillery 3d. & 4th. Brigades British, Baggage waggons & Provision train, 3d. Battn. 7th. to take the right flank of the Baggage – the Cattle Guard to follow in the rear of the Waggons – 3d. Division under General Kniphausen – Dismounted Yaugers, 2d. Brigade of Artillery – Brig: of Sterne, one Squadn. Queens Dragoons 40th. Regt. wt. 2 3 poundrs., 1st. & 2d. Battns. 71st. – Queens Rangers & British Rifflemen. Pioneers divided in 4 Divisions, – Br: Grrs. 1 & Artillery 3.

Monday 8th. Septr. The Army under arms by 3 oclock in the

morng. & we march about 5 from Couch's Mill about 7 pass thro Newark Villages quite deserted, from that to the cross roads, & proceeded on the Lancaster road beyond Nicholls's, which was Hd.Qrs. as we came to our ground saw a Column of dust rising out of the wood over the road in our front, which being reconoitred some of the Enemy were seen Horse & foot. The 44 & 42d. Comys. were sent down on which ye Enemy retired, a few skulking rascals came down in the Eveng. & fir'd at our sentrys which was smartly return'd & we were quiet there then for the Night –

Tuesday 9th. Septr. Hd.Qrs. at Nicholls's the army order'd to move at 1 oclock but was 4 or 5 before they got in motion & march'd about 3 miles by County road to the Eastwd. where the van took an ofr. of the Rebels, his party ran off. Encamp'd on a hill in the Dark, General Kniphausens division march'd by the Lancaster road to Kenets Square with all the Baggage & Provision train; Capt. [Duncan] Cambell of the emigts being sent from Hd.Qrs. towards Kenetts Square fell in with some of Fergusons rifflemen whom he took for Rebels in the night & advancing upon them was wounded

Wednesday 10th. Septr. Head Qrs. at Casket in the morng. & at Kenetts Square in the Eveng. – Lord Cornwallis division of the army moved about 6 this morng. back a piece of the road we came yesterday & then turn'd to the right & march'd to Kennetts Square where we found Kniphausens Division; we Encamp'd about 1/2 a mile to the Nod. of the Village. the whole 3 divisions collected here again – this change of our Route owing to the enemy's having retired from the heights of Newport & gone beyond the Brandywine

Thursday 11th. Septr. Kennetts Square in ye morng. the army put in motion by break of day – Genl. Kniphausens division (Reinforced with two Brigades British, 1st. & 2d.) moved on the lower or right hand road to Brandywine to Shades's ford with the spare Artillery & all the Baggage & Provision – The other division of the army march'd by the upper roads & crossed both branches of the Brandywine, by the road leading to Dilworth making two short halts[;] the 2d. Light Infantry had a skirmish in the morng. about 9 by the way, the last about a mile from Dilworth Village After having march'd, 15 or 16 miles; here the Genl. refresh'd & getting some recent intelligence of the Enemy he put the Troops in motion & made a quick disposition of those in front – The 1st. & 2d. Light Infantry & some Yaugers on the left the Guards on the right, 1st. Grrs. on the left of the Guards, 2d. Grrs. on the left of the 1st. & the 4th. Brigade on the left of the 2d. Grrs.; these moved on in Columns for near half a mile when the Rebels were discover'd drawn up on an advantageous ground forming an extensive line, with Cannon on several hills[.] The British Troops form'd their respective Corps & moved up to the Enemy under a heavy fire mostly from behind fences, & after giving them a few rounds charged ym. with such spirit that they immediately fled in confusion leaving several pieces of Cannon in the field & playing those that were more distant. Our Troops pursued the fugitives thro' the woods & over fences for about 3 miles, when they came upon a second & more extensive line of the Enemys best Troops drawn up & posted to great advantage, here they sustain'd a warm attack for some time & pour'd a heavy fire on the British Troops as they came up, who were by this time much fatigued with a long march & a rapid pursuit, notwithstanding these disadvantages we briskly attack'd ye enemy & after a close fire for some minutes charged them again & drove them into the woods in the greatest confusion; when the wearyness of the Troops & the night coming on prevented any further pursuit & saved thousands of the Rebels – Kniphausens Division about the time we began the attack (Vizt. between 4 & 5 o'clock in the afternoon) cross'd over the Brandywine after sustaining a Cannonade for several hours; The Queens Rangers & 4th. Regt. in front pass'd over & attack'd the Rebels briskly, driving them from their entrenchments & strong grounds, the 1st. Brigade & other Troops followed & attack'd the Enemy where ever they met them and drove them from every ground they possess'd untill the route became general & the Rebels fled in confusion from every quarter – In this days action the whole Rebel army were drawn out & posted to the greatest advantage, on all the high grounds from the North side Shades's ford to the westwd. of Dilworth Village (a space of 4 miles) being 20,000 strong & confident of Victory, but were beat & totally routed by about 5000 British Troops[6]

Friday 12th. Septr. Head Qrs. at Dilworth. – party's sent out to look for wounded & bury the dead: the loss on our side between 5 & 600 killed & wounded, that of the Rebels I suppose twice as much beside 4 or 500 prisoners & Deserters & 13 or 14 pieces of Cannon; an Hospital at Dilworth & houses adjacent[7] – Genl. Grant with 2 Brigades, moved about 3 miles on the Chester road & took post – – The Genls thanks to ye. army in genl. & advanced corps in particular for their Gallant & spirited behavior in the engagemt. of yesterday, by repeatedly charging & routing (under a very heavy fire) the Enemy posted to the greatest advantage

Saturday 13th. Septr.   The flank Corps & 1st. Brig. march'd at 6 in the morng. & came on to within 3 miles of Chester – the 71st gone to Wilmington – HeadQrs. near Dilworth still – The Enemy gone towards or over Schuylkill –

Sunday 14th. Septr. HQrrs. at Ashton Camp near Dilworth. A Patrol sent to Chester the place abandon'd by the Rebels – a Rebel frigate lying there – The Wounded escorted by Loos Battns. & the 71st. Regt. moved to Wilmington: all quiet in camp here – the Country for these two marches past mostly inhabited by Quakers who seem well disposed to Govt. Some Shameful instances of marauding yet

Monday 15th.[and 16th.] Septr. HeadQrs. at Ashton,   Lord Cornwallis with us 3 miles from Chester – The 2d. Light Infantry moved on in front about 1 1/2 miles towds. Chester – A Light Infantry man of the 5th. & a Grr. of the 28th. were Executed today at 11 o'clock in front of 1st. Grrs. for mauroding.   the 1st. Examples made, tho often threaten'd, & many deserved it –

Orders to march at 8 o'clock tonight by the left but it was 12 before we moved off the ground in the follg. order – 1st. Light Infy. 2d. Brig: 1st. Brig. 2d. Grrs. 1st. Grrs, Baggage of the army. 2d. Battn. Light Infy. the Genl. with Knip & the rest of the army to march in the morning in a separate Column, I have not heard yet what troops are gone to Wilmington [Mirback's] We turn'd off at the sign of the 7 stars into the Lancaster road, & march'd about 2 miles over very rough road & halted till day light, ye. 16th. when we moved on for 9 or 10 miles & made a halt. it came on rain – some of the Rebels being discover'd in front we moved on briskly for about 2 miles, the 1st. Light Infy. had a skirmish with them & killed 10 or 12 & took some prisoners who say that Washington with his army are close by us on their march to Lancaster. – it continued to rain hard all this time which probably prevented our moving on

The Troops ordered to pile their arms & make fires, but no shelter for a wieried soldier wet to the skin & under a heavy rain all night – Several deserters came in who give various accots.

Wednesday 17th. Septr. the rain ceas'd in ye morng. the men employ'd in drying their cloaths & cleaning their arms – the Troops put in motion between 3 & 4 oclock P.M. & moved forward about 3 miles to near the White Horse on the main road from Philada. to Lancaster, Genl. Kniphausens Column with whom is the Commander in Chief is to our left 2 or 3 miles.

Washington with his army was within a mile or two of us pointing to Lancaster –

Thursday 18th. Kniphausens division moved early in the morng. their van at the White Horse by daylight – Lord Cornwallis's division put in motion about 7 the whole army moved on together in the Philadelphia road for a few miles when Knip turn'd off to the left & took the road to Swede's ford, we kept the main road for 4 or 5 miles farther & then turn'd off to the left & fell in with the other division soon after who were halted. we moved on to the front – The whole Encamp'd in two lines on rising grounds in a large Valley about 6 or 7 miles from Swedes ford, 2 or 3 miles from Valley forge, & about a mile from the main road – Mr. Washington has turn'd tail & taken another Route, supposed to Reading

Friday 19th. the Advance Corps were in motion at 9 but

order'd to return to their ground & be ready to march at 4 P.M. –
fine wr. – Plenty of fresh meat but a scarcity of bread & rum –
two days due ye men
Note The offrs. get a quart of wine each –
The Light Infantry & Grenadrs. march'd in the afternoon
about 3 oclock to the Hill above the Valley forge which is near
the Skuylkill at the mouth of Valley Creek, Major [Peter] Craig
with some Compys. of Light Infy. having taken possession before.
at this place were found a great quantity of flour above 4000
Barrels, a good deal of Soap & Candles Camp Kettles Tomahawks
Spades Cannon Shot &ca. – Some Scouting partys of the Rebels
seen hovering about, they lit fires t'other side of the River, – a
fine Prospect from this Hill

Saturday 20th. Septr. Parties sent out to bring in Cattle – the
Light Infy. Yaugers at FatLand ford about 1 1/2 miles below this
they get a shot now & then at the Yankies on the opposite side –
some Rebels opposite to us who make a good many fires in the
night, some deserters come in, & some prisrs. taken today –

Sunday 21st. last night a Detachmt. consisting some Light
horse[,] the 2d. Batt: Light Infry[,] the 42d. and 44th. Regts. the
whole under the Command of Genl. [Charles] Gray march'd
about 9 or 10 o'clock and surpris'd a Body of the Rebels this
morng. about 1 o'clock somewhere between the Signs of Genl.
Paoli & Admiral Warren and put to death about 300 with their
Bayonets took about 110 prisoners, the rest about 1200 left their
arms & fled in the greatest terror & confusion with Genl. Wayne
at their head.[8]
some deserters come in who say that Washington with his army
is on the other side the Sckuylkill near Swedes ford Posted to
defend our Passage across the River.
The British & Hessian Brigades &ca. march'd today &
encamp'd on t'other side the creek extending two or 3 miles up
the River. we the flank Corps being now the Rear of the army
changed our front – a flag of truce sent out to desire Mr. Washington to bury those that were killed last night, & send surgeons
to the wounded – the flag came in upon Camp of theirs about 3

miles up & on t'other side the River where he supposes there
were about 3000 – They have a guard just opposite to us here
who ask'd for a truce for ye. day, which was agreed to by our
guard, & they chatted to one another

Monday 22d. Septr. HeadQrs at Charlestown The Commander in Chiefs thanks to Majr. Genl. Gray and his detatchmt.
for their steddiness in Bayonitting the Rebels without firing a
shot – the Hessian Chasseurs crossed the Sckuylkill in the Eveng.
about 4 miles above the Valley forge, & a detachmt. of the Guards
cross'd at Fatland ford – The Troops order'd to be under arms
by the rising of the moon which was between 8 & 9. The 1st. &
2d. Lt. Infy. Queens Dragoon & Rangers to lead the Column, the
Regts. to march by, & follow those on their right – British Grrs.[,]
Guards[,] 4 & 3 Brigs: Stern's Brig: Hessian Grrs. & Yagers 1st. &
2d. Brigades – Genl. Grant to give orders about the Baggage the
heavy Ary at the head of the 4th and 3d. Brigades – We march'd
between 1 & 2 oclock in the morng. of the 23d. & cross'd the
Sckuylkill at Fatland ford (up to a Grrs. breetches pockets) without seeing or hearing any of the Enemy, the Troops took up
ground as they arrived, made fires, & dryed themselves till about
7 or 8 oclock they were put in Motion again & march'd to the
Eastwd. HeadQrs. at Norrington, the advance Corps extending
two or 3 miles on a road leading to German Town – some pieces
of Iron Cannon taken today near Swedes ford, some Prisoners &
some deserters, who say Washington is at Pots Grove about 20
miles up the Sckuylkill – The Stores at Valley forge that could
not be brot. away were set on fire &ca.

Wednesday 24th. Septr. Hd.Qrs. at Norrington about 17 miles
from Philadelphia. orders for the Troops to be in readiness to march
in two columns by the right by break of day tomorrow, the right
Column under the Command of Lt. Genl. Earl Cornwallis to consist of – 1st. Light Infy. British Grenadrs.[,] Guards, 1st. & 2d. &
4th. Brigades British, one Squadron of Dragoons & Queens
Rangers, the Provision train Cattle &ca. – The Left Column under
the Command of His Exy. Lt. Genl. Kniphausen to consist of – 3d.
Brigade British, Brigade of Sterne[,] Hessian Grenrs., 2d. Light

Infy. one Squadn Dragoons[,] Yaugers & heavy Artillery; – The Baggage of each Column to march in front preceded by one Batn. of Infy. & one Squadron of Dragoons. –

N.B. The orders of yesterday for a distribution of wine & sugar, produced only 1 pound of Brown sugar for each officer –

Thursday 25th. Septr. The Troops put in motion at day break but it was 7 before we began to march in the Columns above directed – we march'd about 10 or 12 miles thro' a pretty strong Country, & came by Chesnut Hill to German Town, 6 miles from Philada. where the army halted – a rainy afternoon.

Friday 26th. Septr. The British & Hessian Grenrs. wt. Baggage & Guns two Squadrons of Dragoons 6 medium 12 s. & 4 Howitzers march'd about 9 oclock under the command of Lt. Genl. Earl Cornwallis to Philada the Qr.Mr.Genl. & a Dy.[,] the Commissy Genl. & a Depy. attend this Corps – The Troops march'd in about noon. the Streets crowded with Inhabitants who seem to rejoice on the occasion, tho' by all accounts many of them were publickly on the other side before our arrival, – The Congress went off the day before yesterday in great haste to Trenton & that way; the Rebels busy these two or three days past in removing every thing they could over to the Jersey, whether Public Stores or Torry property.

The 1st. Batn. Br: Grrs. Canton'd at the south end of the Town with some of the 12 s. & howitzers – The 2d. Bn & Hessian Grenrs. Lodged in the Bettering House a Capts. Main Guard at the State House, & other Guards in Town for Security, & preservation of good order. & a Subs. Guard at the Schuylkill ferry. an alarm of fire in the Eveng. but it was only a Chimney on fire by accident; the inhabitants afraid that the Rebels will set fire to the City – dined with Mr Guerney who has held out, on Parole; great Tyrany excercised by the Congress &ca. against those who would not join ym.

Saturday 27th. Septr. This morng. about nine two of the Rebel frigates & a Galley came up to the lower end of the Town when opposite to our Guns old Cleveland with 4, 12 s & 2 Hos [four twelve pounders and two howitzers] a Cannonade began which lasted for about 1/2 an hour, the Largest frigate (call'd the Delaware) struck, but the other got off – a Tender Schooner was likewise fired at & taken – the frigate taken possession by the marine Compy of Grs. & some sailors

Sunday 28th. Septr. 6 compys. 2d. Grrs. wt. Col. Mockn.[Henry Monckton] went down as far Darby to meet a detachmt. of sailors & return'd in the Eveng. without meeting them or seeing any People in Arms – The New Gaol full of Prisoners with the Provost – a skirmish up near German Town with Wynns's Corps & some Rebels –

Monday 29th. last night a Lt. & 50 sailors came up from Chester which with about 100 more collected in Town went on board the Delaware   the marine compy. came ashore leaving a Serjt. & 15
The 42d. & 10th. Regts. came down to Schuylkill ferry – I perambled the shops in Town for necessarys for the men but found very little   the shops almost empty   shoes 2 dollars

Tuesday 30th. Septr. The 10th. & 2d. Regts. cross'd the Sckuylkill & march'd to Chester where they Embark'd – our Battn. cross'd likewise at the middle ferry & march'd as far as Darby from whence a detachmt. of 2 compys went on about 3 miles farther & met the waggons that carried the Baggage of the 10th. & 42d.   we likewise cover'd a Commissary's party collecting Cattle,   stayed on the height above Darby all night, and return'd to the Bettering House by breakfast time next day, – came by the lower ferry – in Eveng. heard some firing which proved to be an attack made by a parcel of Rebel Row Galleys on the Roebuck & some of our ships lying above Chester, but they were soon beat off & sent up the River a piece where they have sunk some Chevaux de frize to stop the passage near Mudd Island, which is Fortified. & will stop our shipping for some time[9]

Wednesday 1st. Octr. 1777   we return'd to our Barrack as mentioned above by Breakfast – at one had a parade & a flogging match much drunkenness & irregularity among the men, which occasions frequent Courts Martial & Punishments; our folks keep out of the scrape pretty well –

Thursday 2d. Octr. Some cannonading heard below – The Delaware Frigate gone up the River – News about Burgoyne thot. to be favourable.

Friday 3d. Octr. we hear the 10th. & 42d. Regts wt. a Detachmt. of the 71st. went over to the Jersey side & took Possession of a Fort at Billingsport – on the main Guard in the State House – Magazines of Hay forming –

Saturday 4th. Octr. we were relieved off guard at six that the Battn. might go down towds. Chester but about that time we hear'd a firing at German Town, which grows very heavy and soon after we got an order to march thither in all haste, this proved to be an attack of the whole Rebel army on our Camp at German Town, they forced in the Picquets, & push'd the advanced Corps for some time, under a heavy fire & a thick fog, untill the Brigades got formed to support them, which took up some considerable time: most of the 40th. Regt. took possession of a large house which they defended & checked the progress of the Rebels, the different Regs. form'd as the ground or the attack of the enemy required, & charged or firmly opposed those by whom they were attacked, till they gave way & retreated, about which time we arrived to the front & pursued the fugitives for 10 miles without getting a shot at them but with our 6 pounders – In this attack which was the most spirited I believe they ever made on the British Troops, we have lost above 500 killed & wounded, tho' many of the latter very slight, among the former is Brig. [James] Agnew & Lt. Colo: [John] Bird, & Lt. Colo: [William] Walcot 'tis thot. wont live. – The Rebels must have suffer'd a good deal more, besides their loss in Prisoners, as one entire Regt. (the 9th. Virga) laid down their arms – we return'd in the Eveng. to Philada. after a march of 4 or 5 & 30 miles – the Rebels likewise attack'd the Guards at the ferries over Sckuylkill. the wounded brought into Town, & the Prisoners. between 5 &

600 prisoners, among whom are above 70 officers, shabby looking fellows[10]

Sunday 5th. Octr. the 10th. & 42d. return'd over from the Jersey side leaving a Detacthmt. of between 2 & 300 of the 71st. at Billingsport some Store Ships come to Chester from the fleet. a Chain of Ridouts making a little above the Town from River to River.

Monday 6th. the 10th. & 42d. came up from Chester with a number of waggons loaded with stores & provisions, & proceeded to German Town – some firing of canon down the River – Orders for some executions tomorrow – & a Genl. Court Martial to try some deserters catched among the Rebels
    some alterations made in position of the army about German Town – those in front further advanced –

Tuesday 7th. Octr. four Compys. of the 1st. Battn. Grrs. with a Field officer went to Province Island, I believe to make a Battery against Mud Island which last is Fortified & covers that part of the River where the Chevaux de frize is sunk – we hear that Lord Howe with the fleet is come into the River.

Wednesday 8th Octr. a two Gun Battery (12 pors.) made at the point where Sckuylkill falls into the Delaware, which was attacked by the Row Galleys but they made nothing of it, the intention of this Battery is to cover the mouth of Sckuylkill & protect the ferry to Province island – 2d. Batn. Grrs. went to the North end of the Town & encamp'd in hutts

Thursday 9th. a great deal of firing at the mouth of Schuylkill, from the Galleys & ye Battery, 300 British & Hessian Grrs. on duty there, call'd a working party with arms, relieved in the afternoon. – it rain'd hard all this Afternoon & Eveng. which prevented our going over to province island Boats brot. down on waggons to pass the ferry with –

Friday 10th Octr. 77 nothing done at the mouth of Schuylkill till the eveng. when a party went over with the Engineer, & carried some tools & matterials for making a Battery, some firing from the Row Galleys & our two Gun Battery at the Mouth of Sckuylkill – The Numbers for that duty augmented by a party from the 10th. Regt. who came into Town the 8th. – to assist in working at ye. Batterys &c

Saturday 11th. we were Rous'd this morng. an hour before day & soon after march'd with our Guns towards German Town, where it seems the Enemy were expected to make an attack, but when we were something more than 1/2 way we got orders to return to our ground. the men on duty at the Battery were likewise sent for, a great deal of firing at the mouth of Schuylkill this morng. – a Battery with two Embrazures finish'd last night – a man & a horse drown'd & a howitzer lost crossing the ferry to the island

The Galley's & floating Battery's &ca. kept up such a fire on our works on Province island, that those in the Battery were constrain'd to leave it, with some circumstances not much to their advantage. 2 offrs. & some men taken prisoners. – the duty very hard now, the men have not above one night in bed. Capt. [James] Moncrieff with 50 men retook the Battery from the Rebels

Sunday 12th. the 49th. Regt. came down from German Town to assist at the works on Province island, which are going forward under the fire of the Enemy's craft, & fort on Mudd Island – The Fleet we hear are come up to Chester, – The Roebuck & some others near the Chevaux de frize, – an addition to the working party sent down –

Monday 13th. last night or this morng. a fire vessel sent down by the Rebels, which was grapled by the Roebucks boats & sent adrift out of the line of the fleet, a heavy cannode betwixt the Roebuck & some of their ships. & some firing from their fort & Galleys on Province island, a place of arms made last night to cover 200 men –

Tuesday the 14th. Octr. busy these two days writing letters home as there is a Pacquet to sail soon – The works on province island go on but slowly – the land thereabout is all laid under water by the Rebels having cut openings in the Banks –

Wednesday 15th. the Battery's open'd today & threw some shot & shells among the Rebel fleet, which made them draw off a little higher up the River – they also fired at the Fort on Mudd Island but with little effect –

Thursday the 16th. A Genl. Court Martial sets today at the State House, Col [Robert] Prescot presidg. for the tryal of Major [John] Vattass & Capt. [Robert] Blackmore of the 10th. Regt. for misbehaving before the Enemy, in quitting the works on Province island the 11th.[11] – for duty at the Batterys 360, very little firing – The Transports not come up to Chester yet they say one is lost, belonging to the 64th

Friday 17th. on duty on Province island last night & today – at a Post by myself, distance from the Battery – very little firing on our side & less on t'other – I hear the Wounded are Embark'd at Wilmington to come up, – return'd to camp after 10

Saturday 18th. some firing as usual below – the News of Genl. Burgoynes success loses ground – Lord Rawdon arrived from Genl. Clinton with the News of his having taken Forts Montgomery & Constitution & opened the Hudsons River &c &c – they carried the works by storm ye. 6th. The 71st. & the convalescents arrived from Wilmington in Town in the Eveng., – Capt. Graham wt. them. The 3 Forts in the Highlands of N.York taken by storm. the loss on our side 150 killed & wod. among the killed is Colo. M[ungo]. Campbell, Maj. [Francis Bushill] Sill[,] Major Grant of the Yorkers, & Capt. Stuart 26th

Sunday 19th. Octr. yesterday a strong detatchmt. went out under Genl Grant for 7 or 8 miles & saw nothing – this day the army left German Town & came to within 2 miles of Philada. & Encamp'd nearly in the line of the Ridouts, the Light Infantry in front; some of the Rebel Light horse follow'd close to their rear & exchanged some shots with our Yager Light Infantry – very little firing at the Batterys today – Hd.Qrs. in Town

Monday 20th. This morng. the Picquets took a Capt. of Rebel light Horse: who says their army fir'd a feu de joy [feu de joie] for a victory over Burgoyne. & about 12 o'clock their fort & shipping at Mud Island began to fire, some say a feu de joy, but the Cannonade continued a long time, betwixt the Vigilant our Batterys & them. – Capt. Laird brot. up a Parcel of flat Boats last night thro' the Rebel fleet – This afternoon a Party of Rebels attack'd the Light Infantry Picquet & wounded some men

Tuesday 21st. the Hessian Chasseurs, Grenrs., & Regt. Des Corps, cross'd over to the Jersey side early this morng. at the upper end of the Town, under the comd of Colol. Donop – to take Red bank One third of the men off Duty at work on the Ridouts in front, relieved 3 times a day – The Grrs. gave some to the Batterys yesterday, – no firing at the Batterys today – Col. [William] M[urra]y. very ill –

Wednesday 22d. In consequence of an order late last night a detatchmt. of 1 Field officer 4 Capts. 8 Subs. & 200 Grenrs. were ready at six oclock this morng. for the purpose of storming Mud Island, but wind or tide did not answer & they did not march – 1/3 working at the Ridouts

Thursday 23rd. Octr. yesterday afternoon Colol. Donop with the Hessian Grrs. &ca after a march of 15 miles, attack'd the Enemys work at red bank, in which they were repulsed with considerable loss: Colo: Donop with abt 300 killed & wounded – In going up to the works they were gall'd on their flanks by a fire from the Enemys Vessels in the River & notwithstanding that & a heavy fire in front they perserver'd in the attack & carried some of the out works but the others were so high & surrounded with pallisades and frize that they could not get in, & were obliged to withdraw – the 1st. Bn. Light Infantry & 27th. Regt. were sent over this morng. to cover their Retreat, if need full. the whole return'd to this side, This Eveng. & in the night – Donop left in the field

Yesterday Eveng. the British & Hessian Regts. that were t'other side Schulkill came over to this side & broke down the temporary bridge after them, that was laid two days ago by Capt. [James] Moncrieffe

Early this morng. some of our ships of war moved up when a heavy cannonade began betwixt them & the Enemys Vessles & Fort which lasted for 4 or 5 hours. The Augusta a 64 got aground or on the Cheveaux de f[r]ieze, & soon after took fire she burn't for a longtime & then blew up, another ship thot to be y. Merlin likewise took fire & blew up – the firing ceased by degrees & all was quiet in the P.M.

The detachmt. of 200 Grrs. march'd down to the ferry & were in readiness to make the assault if the attack of the ships had not miscarried.

Friday 24th. all quiet down ye. River, the Ridouts in front going forward – The News concerning Genl. Burgoyne are various The Rebels say that he & his whole army are taken, for which Washington fired a feu de joy the 18th. – a Reading paper says that he has retreated to Ticonderoga; & we are of opinion that he found himself so hemm'd in that he was glad to get off.

Saturday 25th. Octr. very little firing below, 4 large men of war came up this morning near to Mud Island, but the tide turn'd & the wind died away before they got within shot of it & they dropp'd down a little again – the Rebels working at Red bank, the Galleys ly under it, the Rebel ship further up the River.

In orders, the Pacquet to go tomorrow, seal'd my letters & sent them in, for AH. T.A. & Dick M.

Sunday 26th. The works in front going on a good many Ridouts finish'd in ye. shape of ♍ I believe there is 10 or 12 in all – Capt. [Primrose] Kennedy 44th. arrived in 4 days from N:York, with the news of Genl. Vaughans having burn't Esopus & proceeding up the River – they had no particular accounts of Burgoyne but were uneasy about him, & Vaughan was gone up with 2000 to know how things were in that Quarter – Capt. Kennedy says there are about 4000 troops coming here from N:York the 7th. 26th. 63d. 17th. Dragoons & a number of recruits – a Parson came in today with a flag of truce, who persists in the story of Burgoynes defeat

Monday 27th. More promotions given out Major [Edward] Mitchel Lt. Colol. 52d. vice [Mungo] Campbell kill'd Major [Charles] Stuart Lt. Colol. 26th. vice [Dudley] Templer by purchase Capt. [George] Harris 5th. Major, & some others – The Dispatches not gone yet – dirty weather.

Tuesday 28th. The Storm increased it rain'd & blew hard all last night & today, at N.E. nothing going forward – the prices of every thing rising – their Market. Beeff 1/ Sterg. Butter a dollar per pound, – Salt provision comg up in small qutys. from the fleet by stealth by water to province island ferry, then by land –

Wednesday 29th. it still continues to blow & rain, the duty on Province island becomes very disagreeable, there is no getting to the Posts without wading up to the middle in water & mud for miles together & in the Battery's they are above the knee in water the whole time – went there today at 12

Thursday 30th. Octr. The wind came about to N.W. last night & the Weather clear'd up, nothing doing at the Battery's, which are full of water – Major [Cornelius] Cuyler with the dispatches for England sett out the day before yesterday – an express went down yesterday to Lord Howe – the relief came between 3 & 4 & we got home in good time, – got a plunge in the water –

Friday 31st. Octr. a long list of Promotions came out in whh. J. P. is mention'd as C. Lt. obtain'd with much difficulty after serving above nineteen years[12]

Saturday 1st. Novr. went to wait on Col: Stirling on this occasion, but he was out on duty saw the Major – prim – Strange alterans. in the Corps, hominem & mores

Sunday 2d. Novr. I took my leave of the Grenrs. & joined the Regt. & met with a welcome reception from some of my old friends, but some folks look shy
This Eveng. to our great loss & concern Colol. [William]

Murray died of a Fever   much lamented by all his acquaintances in general & by his friends in the 42d. in particular, where he had served as Capt. & Major for 20 years, with much merit & esteem. – Genl. Burgoyne's convention made public[13]

Monday 3d. more Battery's making on Province island, & floating Battery's constructing, for the attack of Mud island – at work today on the Ridouts at C[illegible]. poor Colol. Murray burried in the Eveng privately in Christs Church yard –

Tuesday 4th. Some necessaries for the offrs. came up from the shipping – but little firing at Mud island, our boats pass by them in the night.   a Gaudeamus with Dr. R

Wednesday 5th. Novr. a good deal of firing below today,   they say the Rebels have brot. some Guns to play on our shipping from the Jersey shore, – preparations going forward for a brisker attack on Mud island – went to thank the Genl. but found them all out –

Thursday 6th. it rain'd & blew hard all last night. – mounted Picquet an hour before day; this bad weather will retard our operations down the River –

Friday 7th. all quiet around, the works below going on slowly – Sat a Court Marl. –

Saturday 8th. went to Province island in the afternoon to work at the Battery – it came on to rain in the Eveng. I had a 100 men in the 6 Gun Battery & only 20 tools to work with, O ye Engrs. – the Battery unmask'd, but could not get the Guns in, the rain had soften'd the ground so much

Sunday 9th. it rained almost alnight & we left off work about 1 oclock in the morng.   the 6 Gun Battery was order'd to be open at 10 today but the wet weather last night prevented our getting in the Guns – return'd to Camp between 10 & 11, having dismiss'd my Party at the Genl. parade, but it seems I should have march'd them to the Brigade parade

Monday 10th. The 6 Gun Battery open'd today & kept up a

tollerable Cannonade together with some other guns. some shells, & pound balls thrown from a 13 inch Mortar – some of our light horse taken today by the Rebels in front of the Picquets: – the Rebels send strong Patroles of Light horse everyday close to our Picquets & out Posts, they have a Corps at Chesnuthill & Germantown Washington with the main body at White marsh

Tuesday 11th. Novr. very hard frost the firing below continues from our battery's the Enemy fire but seldom –

Wednesday 12th. Still firing away on Mud island. it is expected that there will be a practicable breach by tomorrow The Vigilant is to come up within shot of mudd island too – provision very scarce & dear. Beeff 2/ & 2/6 P lb. Sugar a dollar

Thursday 13th. the Siege of Mudd Island still going on the 6 Gun battery keeps up a pretty constant fire; The Grenrs. of the Guards in readiness to storm when practicable, to be supported by the 2 Regts. on Province island vizt. the 27th. & 28th. – these Rascals on Mudd Island hold out well, & fire a shot now & then too a floating Battery with two 32 pounders being ready was tow'd out of the mouth of the Sckuylkill & brought to anchor opposite Mud island, but it seems after some time firing they were obliged to quit their Battery and come ashore – Oh the Johns –

Friday the 14th. A Boat with 4 sailors & a marine came from the Enemy last night who say they are busy in removing everything from Mud island & preparing to leave it, the firing going on but slowly thro' the day, rather more in Eveng. & night – cold weather & westerly winds –

Saturday 15th. no firing below this Morng till 11 o'clock when there came on a smart & heavy Cannonade, mostly from our ships, The Vigilant & another has got very close to Mud island & some of the large ships Somerset & Isis within good shot they kept up a very heavy fire all day which together with our batterys silenced the Enemy's guns before evening

Sunday 16th. Novr. last night the Rebels in Mud Island burnt the Barracks &ca. & left it in a very shatter'd condition, it was to have been storm'd today by the Grrs. of the Guards supported by the 2d. Battn. Grrs.

The Generals thanks to the officers & men employed in the Reduction of Mud Island particularly the Artillery & Engineers. – The Fort taken possession of & some repairs making – wrote my Fr. by Mr. Dougl. Campbell

Monday 17th. last night Lord Cornwallis with a detachmt. of the army consisting of 1st. Light Infantry 1st. Grenrs. 27th. & 33d. Regts. & a Battn. of Hessians cross'd the Sckuylkill at the Brige about midnight & march'd to Chester, a party of Rebels in Darby fired on them as they went thro' & kill'd Serjt. Major of 33d. on which some troops rush'd in & kill'd about a dozen & took above 20 prisoners – this detachmt. is to be join'd by the Troops on board of ship come from New York, consisting of 7th. 26th. 63d. Regts. 17th. Dragoons Anspach Battns. & Recruits for the Army, the whole may amount to between 5 & 6000 men with which Lord Cornwallis is to land in the Jersey & take Red Bank as soon as he can –

Tuesday 18th. The Picquets of the Line drawn in nearer the Redouts, the 2d. Light Infantry come into the Ground of 1st Grrs. & 2d. Battn. 71st. to that of the 33d., so that all the troops are within the Line except some Yagers & the Picquets who have orders to come behind the Redouts on an alarm, – The Redouts all finish'd except some frizing, & the abbatis betwixt the Redouts all laid down –

Wednesday 19th. some firing down the River among the Shipping – an inlying Picquet from that Brigade ready to take possession of their respective Redouts on an alarm, the out Picquets to retire & the Quarter Guards to join their Regts – Orders for offrs & men belonging to N.York to embark –

Thursday 20 Novr. a Report that Redbank is Evacuated – some Rebels seen opposite the Town yesterday Eveng. – a Capts. Guard in Mud Island relieved every two days. Our Shipping trying to get up the Chevaux de frize –

Friday 21st. Orders came out last night for the Regts. to send to New York for their Cloathg & Baggage all offrs. & men; Lt. R: went off early this Morng. for the above purpose – N.B. sent to Mr. M.C. or Mr. Rd for some stores to come by same opportunity.

Early this morng. there was a good deal of firing in the River & a great Blaze seen down below, which proved to be the Rebel fleet on fire – finding they could not keep Red Bank & that our men of war would soon be up, they set fire to their large ships & blew ym up, the small craft came up the River & most of them escaped pass'd the Delaware Frigate as did some the night before. the Delaware fired a good deal this Morng. at their Galleys as they pass'd. –

Saturday 22d. fine mild Weather took a ride to see Mud Island, which is prodigiously shatter'd & torn to pieces & leaves a spectacle very much to the honor of those that defended it – some ships under sail to come up but the wind veer'd & stopp'd them for this tide. – they have found a passage thro' the Chevaux de frize & the Chain that was across the Channel just below Mud Island is cut so that the passage is open now with good pilotage for large ships – saw our people at work at Red bank but have not hear'd the particulars of Lord Cornwallis expedition – he is expected over soon –

Sunday 23d. very fine weather, a victualer & some sloops came up from the fleet; every thing excessively dear in Town, fresh meat 1/2 dollar P lb wine 10/ a bottle Rum from 3 to £4 a Gallon, butter above a dollar, & sugar 10 & 12/ P lb & every thing else in proportion – N.B. Settled the Accots to the Grrs. & paid Capt Graham the balance

Monday 24th. Novr. the fine weather continues some ships getting up thro' the Chevaux de frize Capt. D came up from Newcastle in his Boat, says a Transport run on the Chevaux de frize & sunk – Lord Cornwallis still about Redbank demollishing the works –

Tuesday 25th. smart frost in the night & moderate in the day, mounted Picquet in the morng. an attack was expected on the lines this morng. & a message sent to the Picquets to be on their guard; The Second Light Infantry & some Light Horse went out before day for some miles, but saw nothing, a Patrole of mounted Yagers went out at day light & fell in with a party of the Enemy & pop'd at each other for a while, but little harm done –

Wednesday 26th. a good many ships come up to Town & more followg some station'd at New Castle still with 8 weeks Provision – Transports going to Rhode Island to take in Genl. Burgoynes Army – Lord Cornwallis about Glocester – The 17th. Light Dragoons are come over –

Thursday 27th. Novr. The Yagers with Lord Cornwallis army had a skirmish yesterday over in ye Jersey they lost 30 kill'd & wound'd & drove the Rebels The Troops in the Jersey cross'd over today from Glocester, which they burnt, had some firing on their Rear. some of our ships of war cover'd their Embarkation – They have entirely demolish'd the works at Redbank in which the Rebels left a good many Cannon, some not spik'd, the place was made very strong & not to be carried by a Coup de main, but easily reduced by approaches – They have brought a large drove of Cattle from the Jerseys – the Qr.Mr. Genl. & his Deputys are making Arrangemt. for 12000 Troops in Town. –

Friday 28th. fine wr. & all quiet a report that Washington intends to attack us but I don't think he will be such a fool

Saturday 29th it came on a storm last night of wind & rain which still continues din'd with D. P. in Town & sup'd together a merry eveng.

Sunday 30th. Novr. cold hard frost in orders a Pacquet to sail for England the dispaches to go off this afternoon – wrote D.M. AH – a large party was to have din'd in Town & celebrate St. Andw. but it misgave for want of meat &ca. – din'd in Camp Pork & Glass of Port –

Monday 1st. Decr. still cold frosty wr. preparations making for a movement. pontoons rigging out on carriages &ca. &ca. – a pair of mitts given out to the men & blankets to those that wanted –

Tuesday 2d. Decr. nothing going on but the preparations for the intended movemt. frost & N.W. wind

Wednesday 3d. Decr. a good many Promotions in the orders these some days past – after orders Eveng. Gunfiring.[14]

Thursday 4th. Decr. An order came out late last night countermanding the former, & that the Troops were not to march till further orders, owing it is said to a Serjt. of Artilly having deserted with the orders. The troops desired to be in readiness to march at the shortest notice without baggage –

Friday 5th. Decr. orders came out late last night for the march of the Troops tonight in another position   Lord Cornwallis the Van Guard consisting of two Battns. Light Infantry, Chasseurs dismounted, British Grrs[,] Hessian Grenrs., 4th. Brigade British[,] two squadns. 16th. Dragoons 2 medium 12 s. & 2 Howitzers – Under the command of Genl. Kniphausen Regt. Du Corps, Regt. of Donop, 1st. Brig: British 2 Light 12 pors., Brigade of Guards 1 Squadn. 16th. Dragns. 5th. & 27th. Regts. 2 Light 12s. 26th. & 7th. Regts., 3d. Brig: British 2 Squadns. 17th. Dragoons, Hospital waggons Rum waggons, Empty waggons, 2d. Battn. 71st. Regt. mounted Chasseurs, 1 Squad: 16th. Dragoons, Queens Rangers on the right flank of the line of Baggage – no Baggage waggons allowed
The army march'd about 11 oclock at night from the left – at Germantown the advanced Corps had some firing & dislodged some of the Rebels from thence. then moved on & arrived at Chestnut hill about day light with some popping – soon after the 2d. Light Infantry supported by the 1st. got engaged with a body of the Rebels under the Comd. of Genl. [James] Irvine whom they routed after a smart fire for some minutes, & took their Gnl prisoner wound'd & some others kill'd a major and some men &ca. the army halted on the grounds shewn them, & the Great folks reconoitred – The Enemy Encamp'd on four strong hills

about two miles in front, where they have some Redouts & an abbattis –

Saturday 6th. Decr. very cold last night in hutts the men accoutred & their arms by them all quiet today, The Enemy seen making some movements, some think going off, but I believe its only altering position of some of their troops, much reconoitring & speculation, but nothing done today

NB had the honor of a visit from Lord Cathcart this morng. who delivered Lord E[glintoun]s compts. who he says had recomd. me to Sr. Thos. Sp Wilson for his aid de camp.[15]

Sunday 7th. Decr. Soft mild wr. The Troops put in motion last night about 11 & march'd by the right to Germantown where they turn'd off to the left & march'd about 6 or 7 miles where they divided, Genl. Gray with the 3d. Brigade Queens Rangers & all the Yagers struck off to the left & about a mile after came to a cross roads where they halted, the main body taking a larger sweep to the N.Ed. – about noon Genl. Grays division moved forwards & after advancing about a mile the Yagers had a skirmish with a body of the Rebels posted on a hill in front whom they soon routed having kill'd 8 or 10 & taken some prisoners, about this time & for a good while after heard a great deal of firing to our right which proved to be the advanced Corps of the main body meeting with different parties of the Rebels & driving them as they came on, in the Eveng. the 2 divisions made a junction & encamp'd on the high grounds about a mile & more from the Enemys hills, – The troops no provision today

Monday 8th. the weather foggy & very mild for the season, – all quiet about camp, the Generals & Engineers reconnoitring the hill in front which is very extensive & said to be fortifyed with Redouts abbattis &ca. and a Rivulet at the foot

About noon got orders to be in readiness to move & about 2 oclock we march'd off from the left in the face of the Enemy & returned to our lines at Philada. where we arrived about 9 oclock at night & took up our old ground. a small party of the Rebels show'd themselves in the rear about sunset occasioned some firing. NB the 71st had taken up our Camp burnt our wood & destroyed our boards & straw

Tuesday 9th. cold & frosty with some appearance of snow – The duty in the lines goes on as usual where I suppose we shall remain till hard wr. comes on or till Mr. Washington breaks up his Camp, which is too strongly fortifyed for an attack but too cold for him to remain with his army for ye winter

Wednesday 10th. Decr. gentle frost & all quiet

Thursday 11th. Sharp frost & cold NW wind orders in the Eveng. for a strong body of the army by detachment to be in readiness to march at 2 oclock in the morning – but it was altered –

Friday 12th. Early this morng. Ld. Cornwallis with the Light Infantry Grenadrs. & other Troops to the amount of above 4000 crossed over the Sckuylkill with a train of waggons to forage they bent their march up the river with an intention to break down Mr. Washingtons bridge near Swedes ford, but on their way fell in [with] the Potters Brigade whom they routed & drove over the bridge together with part of Washingtons army who had pass'd over, & who to secure their Retreat broke down the bridge and saved our people that trouble. Lord Cornwallis then made a sweep to the westward & sod. & came in by Hartford without meeting with any more of the Enemy

Saturday 13th. The Regt. recd. orders last night to be in readiness to march before day. accordingly we march'd (the morng. very cold hard frost) to Grays ferry where we found about 150 Waggons which we took under our Convoy & cross'd the Sckuylkill there on a Bridge of Pontoons, & moved on to the Blue Bell (about 6 miles from Town) where orders came from Ld. Cornwallis to move on we join'd his Troops about 3 miles beyond Darby towds. Hartford, the waggons dispers'd to get forage & the Troops divided along the Roads to cover ym. and in the Eveng. the whole return'd with a good hawl of forage, some cattle, & plunder, but old Grizly stop'd such cows as had been pick'd by the offrs & sent them along wt the public stock – a long string of Brevet promotions

Sunday 14th. mild wr. a Packet arrived lately had letter yesterday from AH & DM. & today another from AH by some private ship 22d. June & 27 July: The Brigade order hint at going into Town soon

Monday 15th. The weather remarkably mild for the season – busy all day writing letters to AH. AN. Dr. F. & D.M. to go by a ship to Glasgow dispatch'd by Mr. Blane
Recd. a letter from AH this morng. 27th. Augt.

Tuesday 16th soft & drizling rain all day The Qr. Masters of the different Brigades in Town getting Quarters for their respective Regts. – The Light Infantry goes into the Barracks, the Grenrs. into the House of Employment – a Guard House building in each Redout for a Capt. 2 Subs & 50 men

Wednesday 17th. Decr. mowzy weather a plentifull market in Town today Beeff & mutton from 1/ to 2/6 P lb
a work making at the middleferry Bridge on this side – the QrMasters busy about the Qrs. which will take some fitting up before we go into them –

Thursday 18th. soft mild weather – they say the Octr. Pacquet is arrived – an Hospital Court to sit for the examination of men unfit for service –

Friday 19th. it rained last night & the wind came to the NW & blew hard, & froze towards morng. – the day sharp & cold The Quarters look'd at by the Colol. & some arrangement made in his own way –

Saturday 20th. fine frosty weather saw some of our Qrs. today some good & some bad. & so on – a Proposal from the Coll. about messing with Norry this winter – subscribed by every body –

Sunday 21st. pleasant frosty weather went on a covering party for the wood cutters, but when on the Bridge we were sent back as there is no wood cutting today – preparing for a foraging party

Monday 22d. Decr. The Troops put in motion as by last nights orders & crost the Sckuylkill by the bridge at Grays ferry & moved on the Chester road till the front past Darby – the Light Infantry took post on the heights to the Sowd. of it & the Grrs. to Nod. The rest of the Troops posted all along the road from the ferry to Darby, while the waggons are employ'd in carrying forage to Town –

Tuesday 23d. Dec. fine moderate frosty weather, The Troops continue in the same position, & waggons in carrying forage, all quiet in & about camp –

Wednesday 24th. This morng. the Rebels catched 10 or 12 of our Light Dragoons, who were out on a scout, & fell in with a Party of the Rebels, who pursued them into a swamp. on Picqt. today – all quiet, – heard some firing at Philada. –

Thursday 25th. Xmass. Very pleasant weather for the season – 3 days provision come out from Town. The waggons still busy carrying home forage – this morng. the Light horse kill'd 3, wounded 2 & took 5 of the Rebels – some Battalions moved further down on the Chester road to cover the waggons below Darby Creek – The firing yesterday, was betwixt our lines & some Row Galleys that came down the River – Xmas not entirely forgot

Friday 26th. the fine weather still continues – Genl. Gray with 7 or 8 Battns. moved down the Chester road as far as the 10 mile stone to cover the foragers, we return'd in the Eveng. to our ground near the Blue Bell

Saturday 27th. Decr. a good deal of rain last night but not cold, the day moderate & fair – in the Eveng. got orders to change our ground in order to shorten the line, we moved just across the Creek at the Blue Bell and went down into the wood, but for want of waggons or by some mistake we did not get to our ground till near 10 oclock at night, when it was exceeding cold, with a sharp NW wind & not a bit of shelter for the men
orders to be ready to move in the morng.

Sunday 28th. it snowed all last night & was very cold, – The Troops march'd in the morng. & after seeing all the waggons over the Pontoon Bridge at Gray's ferry, the Bridge was taken up, & the troops with their Guns came by the Bridge at Middle ferry & return'd to their respective old ground at the lines – it snow'd all day & it was Eveng. before we got home – a small party of Rebels taken today Thus ended the long foraging party which continued a week, in which time it is supposed was carried into Town between 3 & 400 ton of Hay every day, which makes above 2000 ton, reckon'd to last the army four months

Monday 29th. cold NW & very keen frost – orders for the army to march into Quarters tomorrow the duty in the Redouts taken by Brigades a Sub & 30 in each during the day & a Capt. 2 Subs & 50 in the night –

Tuesday 30th. Decr. all or most of the Troops march'd into their Qrs. today – we don't go in till tomorrow The orders of yesterday respecting the duty of the Redouts altered in so far that the Capt. 2 Subs & 50 continue there day & night – the Redouts to be furnished as follows[16]

Wednesday 31st. we march'd into Quarters – the men employ'd all the morng. in carrying in the Matterials of their Hutts for firing & births [berths] in their Qrs. & at 2 oclock the Regt. march'd in & the Company's took possession of their respective Qurs. which in general are tollerably good – the House allotted for me the worst of the whole, but I got it chang'd –

Chapter V

'shoping wt ye ladies'

Philadelphia to New York
1 January to 5 July 1778

The surrender of a British army at Saratoga in October 1777 brought sweeping changes in the War for American Independence, especially in the British conduct of that war. The government of King George III tried at first merely to find a more aggressive commander for its forces (by replacing General Howe with Sir Henry Clinton) and to forestall foreign intervention (by sending a new commission to negotiate with the colonists). But after France announced that it had entered into treaties and an alliance with the United States – that it was willing to go to war to sustain the independence of the new nation – the British promptly altered their strategy to provide for a much wider war. To punish France and secure their own empire, the British decided to give up Philadelphia and possibly New York so as to free forces to attack the French West Indies and defend Florida, Canada, and the British Isles. To continue the war against the rebellious colonies – and to do so with fewer regular troops – the British would rely increasingly on their navy and on Loyalists. While raiding parties scoured the coasts of New England, regulars and Loyalists would restore royal government gradually from south to north, beginning in Georgia and the Carolinas. These decisions, made in February and March 1778, would shape British strategy for the remainder of the American War.

But while these decisions were being made and conveyed to America, British commanders were reluctant to act. The Howes, resenting the government's criticism of their conciliatory efforts and anticipating that they would be blamed for the loss of the Canadian army as well as the continuation of the rebellion, had resigned and were awaiting the government's response. So too was Sir Henry Clinton, General Howe's

second in command, who had asked to be recalled because he thought
he had been mistreated by Howe and was not eager to succeed him. All
three were, moreover, unsure how the loss of the Canadian army would
affect international relations and British strategy for the American War.
Such uncertainties discouraged offensive operations through most of the
winter and spring of 1778. Admiral Howe did order a blockade of American ports. Generals Howe and Clinton kept their forces largely on the
defensive at Philadelphia and New York. Only in late April and early
May did General Howe learn that he was to turn over his command to
Clinton and did Clinton and Admiral Howe learn that they were to carry
out the government's new strategy for a war with France and the rebellious colonies. Only then did the Howes and Clinton begin to act; and it
was mid-June before the British were ready to withdraw from Philadelphia in preparation for attacking the French West Indies and for reinfor-
cing Florida, Canada, and the British Isles.[1]

These sweeping changes of men and measures brought John Peebles
and his regiment a remarkably quiet winter and spring in Philadelphia.
Peebles did have regular duties to perform: taking his turn in the lines
north of the city, guarding prisoners at the new jail, and seeing that his
men were properly clothed, armed, and trained for field service.[2] He
also accompanied his regiment on occasional forays into the Pennsylvania and New Jersey countryside to gather forage, protect wood cutters,
or keep rebel patrols at bay.[3] But for nearly five months he had ample
time for diversions. He renewed friendships with colonists he had known
during his earlier service in America; he enjoyed a procession of ceremonial and casual dinners; he attended plays and balls; he shopped and
went to see David Rittenhouse's model of the solar system; he had his
portrait made probably as a gift for Anna Hamilton; and he took part in
the extravagant farewell, or mischianza, for Sir William Howe.[4] Indeed,
not until Howe had given up his command and Clinton had begun to
carry out the British government's new strategy, not until late May
1778, did Peebles and his regiment emerge from their winter routine.
In mid-June they were with the army when it abandoned Philadelphia
and marched across New Jersey for New York, stopping to repel an
attack at Monmouth Court House on 28 June and continuing on to
Sandy Hook where they embarked for Long Island on 5 July.[5]

Philadephia to New York
1 January to 5 July 1778

Thursday 1st. Janry. 1778 fine moderate frosty weather – mounted Picquet this morng. at daybreak in Redout No. 7 – but the orders of this day has chang'd the hour of mounting to 10 o'clock all quiet during the day & night – till at daybreak of

Friday 2d. Janry. seven deserters came into my out sentry's & laid down their arms – they came from their Hd.Qrs. at Valley forge last night having cross'd the Schuylkill on the Ice they say the Rebel army above 20000 are hutting there for the Winter, Mr. Washington having resolved to keep the field – dining at the tavern very expensive – generally 3 dollars

Saturday 3d. soft mild weather some ships coming up the River have got upon the Jersey shore lately & the Rebels have taken them a good deal of Cloathing & Baggage

Sunday 4th. the thaw continues a flag from Washington with some cattle & flour for the prisoners, sent by an offr. of rank in their artillery who gave himself some airs in talking

Monday 5th. fine moderate weather yesterday the Regimental Mess began with a plentifull dinner, but Norry's charges will be much above the agreement proposed by Coll. Stirling – dined today with the officers of the 3d. Battns. Grrs. at the Indian King, where a dinner had been bespoke to comemorate the Corps, 15 members present – had an Elegant dinner & good claret; club 50/⁶

Tuesday 6th. very gentle frost in the night, more waggons with flour for the Rebel prisoners – nothing at the Mess today but cold meat for want of wood, dined at ye Tavern
having been taken up with some other matters in duty, business, or pleasure, the little journal has been neglected for the remainder of the month of Janry. in which nothing very remarkable occurred. The weather in general was mild till about the 20th. when it came on a smart frost & stop'd the Navigation of the River which prevented a Pacquet & a man of war for New

York from sailg. till the latter end of the month – wrote by the Pacquet to AH & D.M. & T.A. & to Dr. McLean N.York.

In the course of this elapse the Playhouse open'd & play once or twice a Week for Charity to the Widows & Orphans of soldiers, The performers are gentlen. of army & navy & some kept mistresses – the gentlen. do their parts pretty well, but the Ladies are rather defficient – The City Tavern was likewise fitted up & open'd to receive compy. in the Style of Public Rooms, every Eveng. (except Sunda[y]) & a Ball every Thursday, the Expense defray'd first by a subscription of two days pay from every officer of the British & half a guinea for Ball Tickets; there is also a Pharo Bank kept by the Hessians –

There has been a good deal of forage brought in from about Frankfort under the Escort of Covering Parties of about 1000 strong – a Regt. every day at Dickinsons house & 200 Light Infantry on their left covering the wood cutters

Philada. Janry. 30th. 1778 – fine mild weather & sunshine today Coll. Stirling Inspected the 1st. Battn. with respect to arms accoutremts. & necessarys, – The arms in general not good order & wanting some repairs, the accoutrements bad. the necessaries compleated to at least 4 good Shirts 2 pr. Shoes & all the small articles – the new Coats have been on for sometime but not alter'd. – The Regt. to have white Breetches & blue long gaters, but they are not all made yet The new Bonnets are cock'd & on, – The men wear Philibegs [Kilts] yet, made of their old Plaids – The Inspection began at one & continued till 4 less strict towards the end being dinner time

Necessary Rolls & Returns of arms given in by each Company, accounting for defficiences & the mens assignment for yr. clearance to 24 Decr.

Saturday 31st. Janry. 78 – Rain'd all day & has been soft weather for some days past – the River open –

Sunday 1st Febry. Rain'd almost all last night – more letters collected yesterday for the Pacquet, which is expected to sail this day, the Wind West fair wr. & soft

Monday 2d. gentle frost & fine wr. I had the Redoubt today, it comes fast about – once in 8 days now – today we gave a Battn. to cover the wood cutters at Dickensons & Gurney's House – Coll. Grant 2 Capts. 4 Subs & 150 –

Tuesday 3d. the wr. suprisingly mild for the season, gentle frost at night & pleasantly warm in the day – today the party that went with money Cloathing & necessary's to our prisoners returned – they say they got a Passport from Washington to proceed & were beyond Lancaster, when they were orderd to return to that place, where they were confined for some days & then sent back here with most of the articles they carried out (some having taken out at Lancaster) The reason for their not being allowed to proceed 'tis said is owing to the Rebels being refused leave to purchase Cloathing &ca for their Prisoners here – 2 Serjts. 1 of the Light horse & 1 of the 42d. are missing Suppos'd to be killed or deserted about 45 miles from here – The contradictions in their orders indicates some distraction in their counsels, which I hope will increase – no communication allow'd with the Rebel prisoners here now, & if any of them are detected in making their escape they are to be put to death, – poor devils they suffer enough, & many of them are dying in Gaol – deserters coming in frequently & in parties – 12 Serjts. & 1 Corpl. of their artilly came in today who say their army at Valley forge are in great destress for want of Cloathing Shoes &ca. – and yesterday or today some country men brought in one of their militia Colls. prisoner, & some people from the Jerseys brought in a Committee-man – well done my lads keep it up –

Yesterday morng. died of a fever Mr. John Allen of this City an old acquaintance & a worthy man, he was Eldest son to Mr. Wm. Allen long chief judge of this Province & whose family is the most respectable in it, & John was the flower of the flock – he was much esteem'd by all who knew him & therefore much lamented

Let death attack us in the bed or field
All Ranks & ages to his force must yield

Happy the man who meets this foe unfear'd
For death or his Enemy never unprepar'd

Wednesday 4th. Febry. fine soft wr. & dirty roads, the waggons bring but small loads of wood, the horses weak & the roads
deep, the Garrison burn 800 Cord a week – The market more
reasonable now than it has been for these 3 months past –

Thursday 5th. the weather continues mild – the 2d. Battn. was
Inspected today   pretty much in same condition with the first –
The Coll. din'd with us today for the first time, we gave him his
[not legible] mirth & good humour presided – some people shines
at the table some in the field, some fills their purse & some the
Baton wield – But happy the man who sleeps at ease, nor stung
by conscience or yet bit by fleas[7]

Friday 6th. Febry. it rain'd almost all day – a flag of truce came
in with some Bullocks for the Prisoners –

Saturday 7th. continued to rain & snow all last night, with frost
towards morng.   the day clear & pretty cold – deserters coming
in daily

Sunday 8th. it came to snow in the forenoon & continued all
day. – went to church with the Ladies but was disappointed in
finding it occupied by Hessians   had compy. to dinner – Col:
Billy [Grant] &ca.

Monday 9th. fine clear frosty wr. a good deal of snow on the
ground,   a Play tonight – the Minor with Duke & no Duke,   very
well perform'd especially Mr. Phips of the Navy play'd the mock
Duke very well, – the House full   a good many Ladies – the
Genl. there[8]

Tuesday 10 Febry. fine sleighing I may say the first for the
season, mild wr. & looks like thaw –

Wednesday 11th. a day of rain   the streets all in a flood with
melted snow & rain – the 33d. Regt. went out this morng. to

163

cover some foragers but the badness of the weather render'd the jaunt fruitless –

Thursday 12th. frost & cold Westerly W I had the new Gaol Guard today, 28 Rebel officers in Charge of the Guard they are lodged in very good rooms on first floor & locked up every night, the Privates are upstairs, among whom there is a very bad putrid fever, of which they are dying very fast – our Grenadrs. dined with our mess today

Friday 13th. the frost continues foraging towards Frankford

Saturday 14th. Febry. hard frost & cold sharp N.W. wind, a large foraging party out beyond Frankford, brought in a good deal of forage & some prisoners
I walk'd out to Frankford today most of the people at home, no Rebels had been there for a week, when a party came down & cut the wheels of the mill
some rascals in the Country there about rob the people that are coming to & from the Market –

Sunday 15th. fine frosty weather went to Church, the Parson had a bad voice – call'd on Gurney – more cremonious than usual; his wife has been sick lately – they are uneasie about their farm –
Our Light Bobs din'd with us today & we got all hands very merry –

Monday 16th. frost continues at Hales in the Eveng.

Tuesday 17th. Febry. very cold weather a strong foraging party out today 6 miles beyond Frankford, brought in a good deal of forage & some prisoners, among the rest Lord Stirlings Aide de Camp Major Edwards[9] – din'd with [James] Cramond – a showy diner but not much drink – play'd dollar whist at the Rooms & won 8 –

Wednesday 18th. fine clear frosty weather

Thursday 19th. a strong foraging party out today their advance went 20 miles off & brought in some prisoners – a set of people call'd Refugees have taken up arms & make excursions, &

generally bring prisoners of some denomination or other, a good deal of forage brought in & Galloways furniture – dined at HeadQrs. – some shire of Air folks at our mess[10]

Friday 20th. Febry. it came on thaw yesterday, which continues with rain & sleet – one of our Battalions out today covering the wood cutters, out from Gun to Gun – the roads growing very dirty – a deserter came in to us from Valley forge   he says they live well enough there but are ill off for warm Cloathing –

Saturday 21st. fine mild weather frost in the night – call'd at Monsr. Sar & sat for the first time[11]

Sunday 22d. fine morng. after a gentle frost in the night, but came on to snow in the forenoon & continued all day & part of the night – had the Redoubt,   all quiet as usual –

Monday 23d. fine soft weather, a good deal of ice coming down the River which is expected will soon be clear   A Report flying about that there has be[en] some fighting about New York & Long Island, – Capt. Alexr. Campbell is taken up on suspicion of some Correspondence with the Enemy. not believed –

Tuesday 24th. Febry. fine clear weathr. gentle frost in the night – a Detachmt. of Dragoons went out last night, & some of the embodied Refugees along with them,   they went near 30 miles out to the nod. & took 130 head of Cattle that were going to the Enemys Camp at Valley forge, & brot them in with some prisoners this afternoon – A Genl. Court Martial sitting Lt. Coll. Musgrave Presidt. it is suppos'd Campbells tryal will come before ym.

Wednesday 25th. Febry. the weather remarkably mild & soft – last night the two Battalions of Light Infantry cross'd over to the Jersey – the 42d. & Simcoes Corps are to go tonight

Thursday 26th. Febry. the 42d. Regt. & the Queens Rangers cross'd the Delaware last night about 12 oclock & landed at Coopers island above the ferry house   we march'd immediately to the ferry Wharf where the Guns (4 three pors) were to land, but they held off some time on accot. of a few shot fir'd at them by a guard of militia that were at the ferry house and who ran off on our coming up these things being got ashore the Detachmt. proceeded with their Guns leaving a Field officers Guard to come up with the Waggons, we march'd to the Eastward thro' dirty road & arrived at Haddonfield about sunrise, where it was expected we should have fallen in with Genls. Wayne and Ellis who had a Detachmt collecting Cattle for the Rebel army, but they had got previous notice of our coming as they left Haddon-field last night about 11 o'clock & entirely evacuated the Village of troops which had been occupied by the Militia all the Winter, to keep the people from supplying the Philada Market, which the states have made felony by their Laws, the Village contains about 40 families mostly Quakers who seem to be heartily tired of this Contest – On finding the Rebels had gone so long before we came, & the day rainy Colol. Stirling order'd the men into barns & placed Guards about the Village. the offrs went in to the inhabitants houses, who seem'd well pleased at our coming –

Friday 27th. Febry. it rain'd much last night, the Compys. under arms at daylight some Detachmts. sent into the neighbourhood for waggons & forage, & forwarded to the ferry – sent in some live stock whh we buy here pretty reasonable – it rain'd & snow'd all day – some Rum taken by the Rangers at a house a few miles off – 2 or 3 Hogsheads – two of our men taken prisoners yesterday by some skulking militia –

Saturday 28 sharp frost last night The Rangers went this morng. to Timber Creek about 6 miles off foraging – a Field offrs. Detachmt. from the 4th. Brigade came over to Coopers ferry, to assist in covering the foragers –

Sunday 1st. March fine clear weather with gentle frost in the night – The Rangers went this morng. to Timber creek again & returned in the Eveng., a Detachmt. of ours went out to the NW to bring in forage Sir Wm. Erskine out here today reconoitg the Country & roads – The Light Infantry still in the Jersey down below about Billingsport or Salem – Pacquets arrived at Philada. down to Decr. –

Monday 2d. March   yesterday evening the Coll. got some intelligence of a great Body of the Enemy coming towards us & some shots being fired at the Rangers Picket across the Creek at Keys Mill   the Compys. order'd under arms, & soon after desir'd to go into the Barns & be ready to turn out at a moments warng. it then came on to snow;   about an hour or two after we were turn'd out again & march'd off by the left to Coopers ferry where we arrived about two oclock in morng.   exceeding cold, most of the men got under cover the rest made fires – the morng. was very stormy & boats could not get over,   about noon some of the Rebel light horse seen at the edge of the wood which occasion'd us to turn out – but they went off – however a few hours after a Body of Horse & foot came down & attack'd our Picquets on which we immediately stood to our arms & moved up to them, a short skirmish ensued and they ran off – 3 men of our & 3 or 4 of the Rangers wound'd   we pursued them a mile or two & returned to the ferry where we Embarked, cross'd & got to Quarters about 8 oclock – the Light Infantry return'd yesterday without seeing the Enemy

Tuesday 3d. March   a great fall of snow last night – N.B. received two letters yesterday from AH 28th. Septr. & 4 Novr. papers from London as late as 12th. Decr.

Wednesday 4th. March cold weather got a reading of Rivingtons paper to 14th. Febry. – high debates – [12]

Thursday 5th. hard frost – had Compy. to dine   took a pretty good Sederunt –

Friday 6th. notice in the orders yesterday that there are ships going home,   wrote some letters –

Saturday 7th. had the Redoubt,   dirty roads, the snow going away fast,   all quiet at the lines – last night a detachmt. of Light Horse & Infantry went out on the frankford road, made a sweep

167

to the left & came in on the back of Germantown where they routed a party of the Rebels, & took a Capt. & 17 prisoners –

Sunday 8th. fine clear weather & mild – sent my letters by Serjt. Cameron to AH. D.M. & my fr a number of Invalids goes home in this fleet & some deserters from the Rebels – they are to sail tomorrow if the wind & weather permits –

Monday 9th. dirty weather, snow & sleet, J[ohn] R[utherfurd] & I call'd on Mrs. Mc. & Mrs. Bt. for the first time & got a great dish of Chat, how some women talk – our mess din'd with Coll. Billy [Grant] today not much pleasure there Quand tous les deux etaient [one word not legible] –

Tuesday 10th. the dirty rainy wr. continues, we gave a Batton. today to cover the wood cutters. 1 F.O: 1 Capt. 3 Subs & 150. the C: went out at 7. The F.O. took his nap & his breakfast first – the roads very deep & no wood cut or haul'd, we got in by 4 oclock – Campbells tryal is finished, the Evidence a single woman who swears to the person positively charging her with letters to carry, – the defendant proves an alibi & makes a strong defense – we hear there [are] some Vessels taken below from N.York –

Wednesday 11th. Still dirty weather sat with Monsr. Sar. the last time il resemblez moi[13] – Capt. Campbell acquitted by the Court for want of Sufficient Evidence –

Thursday 12th. a foggy morng. which clear'd up & grew warm towards noon a Detachmt. of 3 Regts. the Queens Rangers & some others Embark'd on board of tranports with 12 days provision, to go down the River

Friday 13th. March fair wr. & very warm yesterday the Detachmt. sail'd down the River – & yesterday a fleet arrived from Rhode Island & some ships from New York under convoy of the Brune &ca. in their way up the River they Retook the Alert arm'd Schooner that had been taken by the Rebels about Wilmington together with two ships from New York Which they burn'd; a great many letters on board the Alert which were

thrown over board – the fleet from Rhode Island brings hay, chuffly, about 1000 ton.
Lt. [William] Stewart junr. of ours arrived. Poor Stewart who was wounded 10th. May at Piscataway is recover'd pretty well, but lost the use of his leg – A marriage last night of the most extraordinary kind I ever knew Strange infatuation, for a handsome young fellow of good Character & genteel family to persist against all friendly remonstrance to marry a Girl without the least share of beauty, fortune, sense or above Vulgar connexion –

Saturday 14th. March The Weather remarkably warm for the Season – Had the Redoubt Guard all quiet at the Lines a rub from the Coll. about plain coat some firing of Cannon down below – it appears from Rhode Island Papers & letters that the Transports were sent to Boston for Genl. Burgoynes army but that they were removed back from the Coast instead of sending them to Embark – a Genl. Court Martial sitting for the tryal of two officers of Allens Corps who they say intended to walk off –

Sunday 15th. Fair wr. & warm – had company to dine with us as usual the Mess live well just now having brought a good stock from the Jersey – the duty comes very quick about & makes it expensive for the Capts. – hard on the poor Capt. Lts.

Monday 16th. March foggy soft weather – we gave a Battalion to cover the wood cutters today – a Play tonight the Inconstant & L[etcher] pretty well done – Dr. Beaman of ye Hospl. Play'd the old man & Lord Chalkstone in ye farce very well – Ld. Cathcart play'd in both, with more propriety in speech than in some of the parts chosen – ridiculous in a man of his rank & fashion to play the part of a Valet & suffer the ceremony of being kick'd – The Play full of bawdy sentiments indelicate to a modest ear, but most women can bear a little either very Publickly or very privately – [14]

Tuesday 17th. St. Patricks day, the Hybernians mounted the Shamrogue & an Irish Grenadr. personated St. Patrick in a Procession thro' the Streets with a prodigious mob after him – the

169

friendly Brrs. & several other Irish Clubs dined together & dedicate the day to the St. & the Bottle –

Wednesday 18th. March fine weather the roads drying fast, the Regt. out today at Exercise twice, in divisions – look'd into the state of the Compy's. & shoes and find them very bad almost all worn out order'd a pair a man directly – last night or this morng. our scouting Party fell in with one of the Enemy's near Germantown & kill'd 4 & took 12 – deserters coming in daily a large party came in yesterday with the Shamrogue in their hats, to keep St. Patrick. – in the Eveng. paid a tea Visit to Mrs. Morgan wt. Mrs. & Miss Inglis found there Mrs. Archd. McCall & Miss Swift, an agreeable party of two hours.

Thursday 19th. fine weather & warm took home my little present for my little friend I wish it may get safe to her hand as I know she will esteem it much, & what signifies 9 or 10 to procure so rational a pleasure for one we love
had company to dine as usual which always ends in a hard drink, contrary to the primary intention of the Mess, – pass'd the Eveng. wt. Mr. & Mrs. R[utherfurd]: much cards and punch –

Friday the 20th. March the day as Clear & warm as you would expect in May had the Redoubt, all quiet in the Lines today a Party of Rebels were observ'd burning some houses & barns t'other side Sckuylkill on which a party of mounted Yagers scamper'd after ym & kill'd some & took some prisoners – Began Maredant today[15]

Saturday 21st. cold North wind a Pacquet to sail for England in a few days a deserter came in last night who said that there 800 Rebels at Germantown, had orders to be very alert – but hear'd nothing more of them – din'd with the Coll. today with the Ladies – not much fun there –

Sunday 22d. March clear cold weather I hear the Mail is to be sent home in the Price Frigate – no word of Coll. Mawhood & his Detachmt. yet –

Monday 23d. fine wr. less cold – saw the Comys. arms & necessaries today a good many things wanting – two soldiers executed today for desertion – one reprieved (at the intercession of Miss Franks) who had been guilty of a Rape on a girl 9 or 10 yr. old – a Genl. Court Martial sitting – Capt. Campbells accuser to be try'd in order to clear his Character, she having recanted her former evidence against him – look'd in at the Rooms in the Eveng. where saw much gambling going on as usual; a great deal of money lost & won this winter –

Tuesday 24th. fine wr. & warm took a Ride down the Neck – the people making up their fences, & publick inclosures making for Hay fields, the whole neck to be enclosed from River to River in a line below the House of Employment &ca.

Wednesday 25th. March fine weather & warm – went at one o'clock by appointment & saw the Orrery at the College made by one Rittenhausen on a new & more extensive construction than any was made before, the man was bred a watchmaker & had a turn for astronomy but never saw an Orrery in his life, notwithstanding he constructed one that stands errect which by the finest combination of wheels shews the Solar System to more perfection than any former ones, exhibiting the procession of the Equinox & every position of the planets from the earliest accounts to 5000 years in futurity – there is likewise a smaller machine of his constructing calculated for Eclipses & other Phenomena of this System which it is capable of shewing with the greatest exactness for any number of years to come; and in the same elegant case there is a side for the extension of jupiter & Saturn to their proper distances from the Sun, the wheels &ca. are there but not put together – the maker is now with the Rebels in some civil employment, treasurer for the State I believe – what pity it is so great a genius should not follow the track his talents design'd him for – [16]

Genl. [Charles] Lee arrived in Town today by land from N.York, and Mr. [Joshua] Loring Agent for Prisoners, a Cartel is to take place soon for a general exchange, in which Mr. Lee will be included – I went to the Play at night with a party of Ladies – King Henry IV & the mock Doctor Capt. [Thomas] Stanley of Dragoons the King Capt. Madden [Frederick Madan] of the

Guards, Falstaff, & Phips Percy all three very well done – & Dr. Beaumont shin'd in the mock Doctor[17]

Thursday 26th. March, rainy morng. had the New jail guard – 76 Rebel offrs. in Charge, the whole being in close confinement now on account of some having made their escape lately – A Pacquet ard.

Friday 27th. fine weather – the Papers full of News from home a great number of new levies raising The Spirit of the Nation seems to be rous'd had two letters from AH 13th. Decr & 2d. Janry.

Saturday 28th. fine wr. & warm a fleet from N:York arrived with Stores & Merchandize – The Regt. muster'd today, they look very well – a Review of Necessaries at 5 o'clock – din'd with Lord Cathcart, we sat till 1/2 past 8 at the Claret – his Lordships did not know I had got a Cap Ltcy. which was strange as he seems to affect my interest on accot of Lord E[glintoun]

Sunday 29th. March it came on a storm of wind & rain last night which continues all day – din'd wt. the Baron [Cathcart] recd. a letter last night from D. Marshall dated 21st. Septr. by a Mr. Welch –

Monday 30th. the weather not yet settled yesterday Coll. Mawhood & his Detachmt. return'd from down the River, they had a skirmish with the Rebels down in Jersey & kill'd about a score of them & took some prisoners – they have brought a good quantity of forage, & plenty of prog – A General [Daniel] Jones arrived here a few days ago, lately from England –

Tuesday 31st. had a booz last night with McPh & tete comme ca fine weather again; a General Court Marshall sitting, trying an offr. of Artillery for misbehaving – the Regt. out every good day at Excerscise with the Adjts.

Wednesday 1st. April Very fine warm weather, the roads almost dry again – took a long ride down the neck – Coll. [James] Patterson reviewing the new corps, Quarter'd on the Banks of the Schuylkill. – they are not near compleat yet, the Strongest are under 200[18] – Colls. [Charles] O'Hara & [Humphry] Stephens & Capt. [Richard] Fitzpatrick of the Guards are out at Germantown on the Cartel business – Lts. [Christian] Foster & Wilson of the 55th Grrs. come in on parole to be exchanged – and I hear Lt. Coll. [Archibald] Campbell 71st. is come to N.York from his long confinement in New England, where the Yankies used him very ill –

Thursday 2d. Cloudy wr. had the Redoubt; in the Eveng. came on a Violent Storm of wind & rain with Lightning and Thunder – & blew hard all night with heavy Showers – a fleet from NYork & a pacquet from England expected every day

Friday 3d. April blowy wr. cold the business of Cartel suspended on account of the Place being too near us

Saturday 4th. more moderate wr. Colo. [West] Hyde & Capt. [J. Wats. Todw.] Watson of the Guards quarrell'd about their people pulling down some old house, and fought, the former run thro' the arm – most quarrells rise from triffling causes –

Sunday 5th. fine wr. for the season last night a Detachmt. of Light Infantry & Rangers cross'd the Delaware at Glocester & march'd to Haddonfield, where they surprised part of a Detachmt of the Rebels & killed about 20 & took about 30 with a Major & some other officers – the Detachmt. return'd this morng. – had Company to dine – Sir Jas. Baird & Lt. Campbell came when dinner was almost over, & we can't find out who's guests they were –

Monday 6th. April fine wr. & warm the sentence of the Genl. Court Martial in orders. Lt. Wilson of the Artillery found guilty of quitting his post on the 27 Septr. 77 but on account of some favourable circumstances, he is only to be reprimanded – the Regt. out at Exercise – sat a Court Martial old Major Ms. din'd with us today –

Tuesday 7th. fine wr. – this morng. Detachments of Light Dragoons & Infy. & Hovendens Pensylvania Troop were out beyond Germantown in different roads & fell in with some of the Enemy

173

of whom they kill'd & took above 40 & the Light Bobs brought in about 30 Waggon load of leather from Germantown – the Hessians had a kind of Review in the Common today by Genl. Kniphausen

Wednesday 8th. April Blows hard a NW the story for yesterday did not happen till today –

Thursday 9th. fine warm weather we gave 300 to cover the Wood Cutters the 44th. were out likewise & the usual number of Light Infantry, on the Ridge road near 4 miles – all quiet in front, we got in at between 4 & 5 & din'd at the Cols. all hands but he himself din'd at Genl. Leslies. came home & join'd our folks & sat late –

Friday 10th. warm day – a Pacquet arrived yesterday evening, the letters came out today about one oclock, had one from my Dr. little friend date 19 Janry. acknowledging the receipt of mine of 30 Novr. – Letters by this packet mention the Death of Lady Eglintoun Sweet soul in the 21st. year of her age, She died suddenly, only 3 days illness and my Lord at London –

Saturday 11th. April rainy & warm some ships arrived from NYork Lord Howe expected every day he was at Sandy Hook when left it – a Pacquet to sail in a few days for England –

Sunday 12th. Showery & fine Spring weather. busy writing letters home –

Monday 13th. Cloudy growing weather the blosoms coming out, – had the New jail Guard today, 87 Rebel officers in charge –

Tuesday 14 soft weather continues, the Regt. had a field day with the Major a Frigate arrived with dispatches in 32 days from England, nothing transpired yet

Wednesday 15th. rainy we have 200 out coverg the wood Cutters to day – Lt. [John] Spens going home I gave him a Packet to Capt. Marshall inclosing a letter to FN with the trinket for AH. and a letter for my Father & one for T.A. I write to AH & Lord E – by the Pacquet which sails in a few days

Thursday 16th. April fine weather The frigate that came with the dispatches to the Genl. recd. them from an other man of war near the Coast, who went in to N.York to the Admiral – She has brought the Draught of a Bill declaring that Parliament will not impose any tax or assessment on America And another for appointing Commissioners to make up matters with the Americans & put them on the footing they were in 1763 &ca. &ca. &ca. these Bills brot in by Lord North with a conciliatory speech very humbling to Great Britain[19]
Genl. Jones gone to New York

Friday 17th. the Wind N.W & cool – Lts. Spens & Franklin saild today for Corke the former to join the Additionals & Recruit The latter on accot. of his health, they went in an arm'd Ship with a fleet for Corke some say the Genl. is recall'd last night a Detachmt. of Light Horse under the Command of Major [Fran. Edw.] Gwin went as far as Bristol (20 miles) and surprized a party of the Rebels, killed a few & took about 50 prisoners among are 2 Colls. a Major 27 or 8 other officers – some Light Infantry were near at hand to support them –

Saturday 18th. fine weather the wind about WNW out riding – the grass springing fast, & the early blossoms out, peach cherry &ca. – dined with our Grrs. today, a plentifull dinner a good dose of port – some Yagers out last night –

Sunday 19th. fine weather & warm the Spring coming on fast – some of the New Corps Encamp'd on the Banks of the Skuylkill – [Daniel] Astle din'd with us he has just sold out for 1600 guineas & is going home –

Monday 20th. April strong NW wind & dusty a number of Hessian officers came in to day from Captivity in order to be exchanged, but as the Cartel is broke off I don't know what will be done wt. ym. The Mail to be closed this Evening sent two letters one for Ld. E – conso[lin]g. & thanks & one for AH 8 pa[ge]s. – a field day in ye Eveng.

Tuesday 21st. fine spring wr. – the 3d. Brigade had the

covering of the wood Cutters, 100 from each Battn. – all quiet in front – staid out till past 5 oclock – The Covering parties augmented of late and employed in making facines – one each man. Sprain'd my leg –

Wednesday 22d. fine wr. wind Soly. – had the Redoubt – firing of Cannon in the River like a Salute – forgot to mention that about 8 or 10 days ago when the Light Infantry were out about Germantown, Serjt. McFarlane of ours who had the advance Guard fell in wt. a party of the Rebels, & kill'd 12 out of 15 –

Thursday 23d. April fine wr. wind W yesterday Lord Howe arriv'd with a fleet from N.York, of Victualers & Mercht. men – it blew very hard last night with rain all quiet at the lines – two of the 7th. deserted last night – St. Georges day

The Grenadrs. exhibited St George & made a procession thro' the Town – the Genl. gave them something to drink. – Mr. & Mrs. R[utherfurd]. dined with us to day Col. & Mrs. G[rant]. invited but were engaged

Friday 24th. The Wind NW & cool & dusty some New Works making in front of the lines, a working party of 400, under the direction of the field officer of the lines with an Engineer, a large Redoubt making on the Ridge road about 500 yards in front of that Barrier, & some smaller works to the right. & a Curtain work betwixt No. 7 & No. 8 – facines for this purpose have been making for some time past. – Capt. Geo: McIntosh of the Royl. Americans din'd with us today, he is about retiring – turning old & fat –

Saturday 25th. April blowy & dusty, at W The Pacquet nor fleet for Corke not sail'd yesterday being detain'd for Lord Howe's dispatches – Coll. Mawhood & some others gone home in the Pacquet – we hear that Genl. Burgoyne & his suite are gone home from Rhode Island, 'tis said they sail'd 9th. Aprl – Our Jersey stock being out, have recourse to the Market, which we find very dear – Butchers meat 3/ lb & upwards. Shed fish pretty plenty, & some herrings –

Sunday 26th. fine wr. took a ride this morng. a Detachmt. of Light Horse was out the length of White marsh, where they fell in with a party of the Rebels & cut down about a score of them & took 5 or 6 prisoners, Mr. Washington must have lost a great many men this winter, by desertion & the petit[e] guerre – he has just now given out a long order for lessening the Baggage of his army –

Monday 27. April fine warm wr. put the Garden seeds in the ground, – a walk in the Common with Ladies & saw a Horse Race, the Redouts going on in front one large one in shape of ♋

Tuesday 28th. the wind in the East The Royl. Artillery had a Review today in the Common, they went thro' the old fashion'd things in Battalion with 2 6 pors. on each flank; they look very well & are much improved since [James] Pattison came

Wednesday 29 cool Wind at N.E. we hear the Congress has resolved that the draught for a Bill is an insult on the American States, & they will not treat with Great Britain till the fleet & army are withdrawn from their Country & then perhaps they will enter into a treaty

Thursday 30 April cold & showery gave out a Clearance to the Company to the 24 April £182.10. –

Friday 1st. of May cold NW wind – The Public Rooms Closed last night with a Ball, pretty crowded – The Bank lost all they had on the Table, but I am told they have been considerable winners in the course of the Winter, some say 7000 many poor fellows have lost more than they can Afford, & some are selling out.

Last night a Detachmt. of Light dragoons mounted Light Infantry, Pensylvania Light Horse, & 14 Compys. of Light Infantry under the Command of Lt. Col. [Robert] Abercromby went out beyond the White Marsh and came upon a Body of Militia posted there, whom they attack'd early this morning, killed &

wounded about 100, & brought in 46 prisoners with some waggons & horses[20]

Saturday 2d. May   cool for ye season   had the Redoubt Guard
which is reduced now to a Capt. 1 Sub & 40,   the new made
works are occupied by the Grenadrs., in front of which, they are
making dams to stop the water to add to the strength of these
Posts

Sunday 3d. the weather warmer   our Regt. all out covering the
wood Cutters & making facines – the 55th. & 63d. Regts. cross'd
over to the Jersey side just opposite and a working party of 400,
to construct some works there, the working party to be relieved
every day –

Monday 4th. fair wr. & west wind   today the Commander in
Chief review'd all the Hessian Troops in the Common,   they
recd. the Genl. on the left march'd past & saluted & then went
off, they made a very good appearance – in marching past the
Genls. horse started at the Colours & his Ex: came down but was
not hurt, & quickly mounted again – Lord Howe was there too –
by this days paper we see that a Committee of Congress has taken
into consideration Lord Norths draught of a Bill, on Which they
have made some very shrew'd & haughty remarks, which the Congress have confirmed   it concludes with an article that they
should not treat with Great Britain 'till the fleet & army are withdrawn, or their Indipendency expressly declared –

Tuesday 5th. fine weather,   some deserters come who say
Washingtons army is reinforced – Another fleet to sail immediately for Cork – the last in which was Franklin & Spens only
sail'd a day or two ago, & the Pacquet not long before them –
Wrote to my Father yesterday & inclos'd a Bill on the Agents for
£30, gave the letter today to Capt. Geo: McIntosh to be put into
the Post Office at Corke,   a frank of Laurie's sent a News Paper
with the resolves of Congress to Ld. E. in a blank Cover, gave it
to [John] Cannon who has likewise sold out & going home, poor
fellow

Wednesday 6th. May warm wr. a fleet of arm'd transports arrived from Corke. 12 sail with provision & recruits they had 10 weeks passage, some ships a missing – din'd at Genl. Leslie's today a genteel little man, lives well & drinks good claret; Erskine has a snug birth of it there

Thursday 7th Allens & Clifton's Corps went over to the Jersey side to Join the 55th. & 63d. the whole under the Command of Genl. Leslie the works are finish'd. to the Eastward of Coopers ferry – yesterday Evening the 2d. Battn. Light Infantry embarked in flat Boats & went up the River with 3 gallies & an arm'd sloop – The Regt. had a field day in the Eveng Exercised & Manoeuvered by the Adjuts. neither of the Field officers there, – very strange indeed

Remember you had some words today at table which obliged you to take a step you did not like – A Great Ball at the Genls. tonight –

Friday the 8th. May fine weather a Field day in the morng. the Coll out & gave directions to the Adjt. how to go on Genl. Clinton arrived this morng. from New York, he is come to take the Command as Genl. Howe is expected to go home soon – arrived also the Porcupine Sloop of War in 5 Weeks from England, who brings account that France has publickly declared her espousal of the American Cause, & enter'd into a treaty of friendship & commerce which they are prepared to defend – The King has recall'd Lord Stormont his ambassador, & the Marquis De Noalles had set out for France, & a Declaration of War was expected every day – Went out & settled that affair better than I expected

The Regt. had a field day in the Evening again, Coll. Stirling out –

Saturday 9th. May fine Weather no Covering party out today our Brigade gives the Working party in front of the lines, I had it in the afternoon –

Sunday 10th. The Light Infantry &ca. return'd this morning they went up to BurdenTown & Burnt two fine Frigates a

Mercht. ship that were haul'd up & unriggd. & destroyed a good many Gallies & other craft they likewise burn't some houses, & were within 3 miles of Trentown – kill'd 4 or 5
a Pacquet to sail for England the Mail to be closed on Tuesday –

Monday 11th. warm wr. a field day in the Morning –

Tuesday 12th. May fine wr. wind NE. The mail for the Pacquet closed today according to the orders – wrote to my Father & enclosed a Bill ye 2d. on the Agents for £30 from the PayMr. dated 4th. May 30 days sight – and writ to my friend AH touching the trinket & the distant prospect – Great preparations going on for an entertainment to Sir Wm. Howe by a select No. of Field officers, in the Style of a Rigatto Fete Champitrass &ca. to be next week –
N.B. spoke to Colol. Stirling in the Eveng. about a Report of Long John Grants attemptg. to get into the Regt. in [Alexander] Donaldsons vacancy & he seems to be warmly inclined to prevent it, & to carry the step in the Regt. –

Wednesday 13th. May Cloudy Wind E. – Mrs. Grant (Minerva) died this morng. about 7 o'clock after a short illness, & slipt out of life with ease & unexpected, so suddenly – call'd on Coll. [William] Grant in the Eveng. he seems to be very much Affected –

Thursday the 14th. fine weather & warm Mrs. Grant buried at 6 oclock this morng. in Christ Church yard, the same Vault where Coll. Murray lies – had the Redoubt Guard today all quiet

Friday 15th. fine wr. in orders The heavy Baggage of the Army to [be] in readyness to Embark at the shortest notice, & it is recommended to the officers of the army to lighten their baggage for the field as much as possible – The Mail for England to be closed on tuesday next, – This I suppose is the same mail that was order'd to be closed last tuesday –

Saturday 16th. May warm wr. Employed yesterday & today in obtaining the exchange of Dick Marshalls Brother who was taken last Sunday in a boat going down to his ship, by a boat from the Jersey shore about timber creek – got one Potter a Yanky Skipper to go out & be releas'd in his Place – an arm'd ship called the Albion in 14 weeks from the Clyde is run upon the Cheveaux de frize, she beat off a strong Privateer in her way out – I hear of no letters yet – The Thames man of war with above 20 sail arrived from N:York

went to see the preparations for this Grand Entertainment which is call'd a Meschianza, which signifies a meddly. There is to be a Regato a Tournament a triumphal procession, & a fete Champitre [fête-champêtre] –

Sunday 17th. May the weather pleasant & cool, another ship arrived from Clyde in 8 weeks, called the Puttuxen, but I hear no news, 'tis strange I get no letters from my Friends there about – all the Regtal. waggon Horses to be delivered up to the Qr.Mr.Genl. departmt. had Company to dine as usual Mr. Welch – the Mess wine all out, we have drank 36 dozen since the Mess began vizt. 11th. Janry. 10 weeks made an attempt to go to the Meschianza house with some Ladies but it came on to rain & we were too late –

Monday 18th. cloudy & westwind – Recd. a letter from Father this morng. dated 13 Decr. acknowledging the receipt of the two Bills – & acquainting me that they are all well – Mr. Arthur had got mine of the 14/25 of Octr. – but I have not hear'd from him since – To day was the grand Entertainment called The Meschianza; – at 1/2 after three The Company assembled at the upper Wharf, where they Embark'd in barges & flat boats & on a signal made they set out preceeded by a Row Galley, the Vigilant man'd her yards at setting off and all the ships in at the wharves had their Ensigns at the Main top gallant masthead & other Colours out The Fanny (an Agents ship) lying in the stream was dress'd out with all kinds of Colours The Regatta proceeded down the River with musick, the Roebuck man'd her yards when they came near & gave them three Cheers in passing, & when past gave them a Salute, They landed at the lower most wharves & proceeded up to the ground where the Tournament was to be,

The Queens & Princesses & the other Ladies having taken their seats the Knights went round the Ground & saluted the ladies, then the Knights of the Blended Rose proclaim'd a Challenge by their Herald that the Ladies of Knights of the blended Rose were Superior to all the world for wit[,] beauty & accomplishments, which they wod maintain with arms, according to laws of ancient Chivalry, The Herald having proclaim'd at three different places, return'd to his station in front of his Champion, then the Herald of the Knights of the Burning Mountain advanced into the field and accepted the Challenge by asserting that their Ladies were not surpassed by any others in the world, on his return the two orders of Knights attended by yr. Squires came forward with their Chiefs at their head, when the White chief threw his Glove, & the Squire of the Black chief picked it up & return'd it, they then retired to their former stations & the trumpets sounding a charge, the whole rush'd on to the attack & meeting each other in middle ground broke their spears, they then charged twice with pistols, & as often with swords, when the two Chiefs singling out each other fought till the Marshall of the field came up & seperated them, on which they join'd troops & march'd in procession thro' the first triumphal arch, saluting the Ladies as they passed

The Knights then drew up on each side of the ground betwixt the two arches which was likewise lined with 1 officer & 20 men from each Regt. & their respective Colours, the Company then went in procession thro' the arches, all the musick playing about 100 instruments & the Knights & officers saluting as they pass'd, on the top of the 1st. Arch was the figure of Neptune, and in a line with the Capitals this motto, Laus illi, Debetur et a me Gratia Major; on the top of the other arch was the figure of Fame with this motto underneath: I bone quo virtus tua te vocat, I pede fausto[21] – The Company proceeded thro' the Garden up to the House where they turn'd & took a view of the Arches while the Candles were lighting, they then went into the several rooms of the House which were all very showly painted & adorn'd with looking glasses & branches, border'd with silks & ribbons of various colours, and here they drank tea coffee &ca. &ca,

after which they went to dancing and about 9 a handsome sett of fire works were played in the front of the arch next the House, in which Fame made a conspicuous figure – about 11 the Company went into the long room where Supper was laid, a room built for the occassion 100 feet long painted & decorated in a very showy manner with numbers of lights & looking glasses, here they sat down to a very Elegant Supper & a variety of the best wines, after supper they danced & drank till day light when the Company retired to their respective homes highly pleasd with the Entertainment tickets given by the Subscribers with a device of the setting sun & this motto arround: Lisceo descendens asseto Splendore Resurgans[22]

21 or 22 Subscribers Col. OHara one of the Principal Managers. Supper 900 guineas beside all the other expences, which I suppose will be about as much more –

it cost each subscriber £140 Sterg. – Col. Stirling one they had four tickets each to dispose of above 150 £

Tuesday 19th. May fine weather no covering party out today – A Play in the Eveng. Douglas by Major [Andrew] Gordon of the 26th. Lady Randolph by Mrs. Williams, who did very well[23]

Wednesday 20th. May last night in consequence of intelligence brought to Head Qrs. of a move in the Rebel army, The Light troops & Grenrs. were put in motion about 9 & several of the Brigades followed, they marched by different roads to the Northward, by White Marsh & Baron Hill &ca. and found by intelligence that a Body of about 2000 of the Rebels under Marquis de Fayette had cross'd the Sckuylkill & taken post near Baron Hill meeting house but upon the approach of our Troops they hastily decamp'd & cross'd the River again, – the 3d. Brigade & one of Hessians & 26th. Regt. all that were left in Town The troops return'd this Eveng. after a long march very much fatigued. there has been some little skirmish, in which a few of the Enemy were kill'd, among whom they say were two Indians – [24]

Thursday 21st. the fine weather Continues pretty warm,

the[y] say Admiral [James] Gambier is arrived in the River – orders to Embark the heavy Baggage   Compy. to dine as usual Majr. Capt. [Valentine] Gardner 16th. Dr Potts & Lt. [William] McPherson 16th. –

Friday 22d. pleasant wr. the Spring well advanced, the Vegetables of the season plenty in Market, meat very dear now – our Regt. had the coverg party & workg party in front of the Lines, & I had the Redout   Coll. Grant din'd with me, all quiet –

Saturday 23d. pack'd up my Baggage & Tent   the heavy part on board, made an assortment for the Field. 2 Coats 8 Shirts washing breetches & waist coats, trouzers, – They say we are going to leave this place altogether

Sunday 24 May   warm   busy in Embarking the Heavy Baggage Artillery, Stores, &ca. The Guns taken out of the Redoubts, but the working party at the New works still going on – many people of the Town very much distressed with the prospect of our going away – The Coll. call'd the offrs. of the 1st. Battn. together to propose messing with the Suttlers when it was agreed: to give 6/Ster P week & the Rations except half ye bread & all ye Rum to pay 2 dollars a Gall: for good Spirits & 2/6 Ster for bottle port, & to advance money to buy two horses & a waggon.
Genl. Howe Embark'd today about noon on which a salute was fired on shore – I hear he goes home in the Andromeda

Monday 25th. fine weather – The Merchts. have been told to pack up their goods, & such Inhabitants as choose to go from hence will be provided in Ships to carry them, – a trying circumstance to those concern'd & puzling to all – the troop beats at 6 & the Guards march off at 7 now –

Tuesday 26th. May   it rained hard last night & this morng. which was much wanted,   shoping wt. ye. Ladies – much speculation about this preparation for a movement   the works in front of the lines still going on –

Wednesday 27th. fine weather – The March Pacquet arrived today after a long passage, a great deal of vague News flying about – I had no letters, which I am surprized at, I hope my little friend is well

Thursday 28th. very cool – This morng. about 2 o'clock the two Battns. of Light Infantry a Detachmt. of Dragoons the 5th. one Bat: of the 42d. the 44th. went out the Barier and proceeded as far as Beggars Town where in consequence of intelligence we expected to find a Body of Rebels, but either the information was false or we were too late for there was nothing to be seen but a few light horse men towards Chestnut hill, we staid there till 9 & then march'd back to Town where we arrived about 11. – Genl. Clinton came out to us in the morng. about 8 –

Friday 29th. May, we had a field day this morng. at 5 o'clock, a very cold N.W. wind. The Additionals fired Ball – The Baggage Ships & others dropping down the River, they are to assemble at Reedy Island, our ships gone today

Saturday the 30th. cool wr. NW was to have gone to the Redoubt this morning but by some mistake of the Brigade Majors it was not our turn – The 7th. & 26th. Regts. gone over to Genl. Leslie on the Jersey side, our Brigade took their Redout last night – The Artillery are embarking some part of their stores & heavy cannon – the Merchts. buzy shipping their goods – The Qr.Mastrs. drawing what wood is due their Regts. out of the magazine & selling it in Town, some days past – Recd. Bat & forage money today £42.10

Sunday 31st. May Showery – The April Pacquet arrived this morng but no letter from Dear little friend, pray God all may be well, I rather hope they are miscarried than any other cause for this long silence – had a letter from D.M. 27th. March

Monday 1st. June 1778 rainy – had the New Gaol Guard today, several of the officers let out on Parole – no word of a french war yet, a talk of Commissioners coming out to negociate with the Americans, –

Tuesday 2d. June cloudy – W. easterly The 15th. Regt. gone over to the Jerseys to Billingsport a good many Waggons sent over & other things The Ships dropping down every day. & notwithstanding all this preparation the working party is still employed in front of the lines, in making Dams to stop the water in a hollow that runs along the front

Wednesday 3d. June cloudy N.E. – last eveng. some of the Rebel light Horse came near the lines & attempted to take off some of the working party, but fail'd; early this morng. the two Battns. Light Infantry the 17th. & 27th. Regts. went out on the GermanTown road where they met a few of the Rebels and took 4 light horse men, & return'd this forenoon

A Genl. Court Martial setting these some days past. some officers trying –

Thursday 4th. June a Royal Salute at one o'clock in honor of the day – had Compy. to dine sat late. – Potts – no illuminations at night – these things out of fashion in this Country now –

Friday 5th. warm wr. about 500 seaman from the different transports come up to man the flatboats – a return of Horses called for working at the Dams in front –

Saturday 6th. temperate, The Light Infantry 37th. & 1 Bat: 42d. went out this morng. at 3 oclock to Beggars Town & were followd at 5 by the 3d & 4th. Brigades, our advanced party had a little Skirmish with a party of the Rebels, in which they kill'd two & took two, we had 3 wounded Return'd to Qrs. about 1/2 after 10 –

This day Lord Cornwallis arrived from England, he came in the Trident man of war Commodore [John] Elliott, who brought likewise the Commissioners [Frederick Howard] Lord Car[l]isle Govr. [George] Johnson & Mr. Eadon [William Eden] – no French war when they came away – Jack Inglis came out acting Capt. to the Trident, and now gets the Senegal Sloop – one of the Row Gallies gone down to bring up the Commissioners –

The Greyhound arrived from New York & brought Genl. [James] Robertson, from thence & also Coll. [Cornelius] Cuyler and Major [Duncan] Drummond then came in Adml. Gambier who arrived lately at New York with 12 sail of Transports and

Victualers after a passage of 12 weeks – Little Dick Rutherford came likewise in the Greyhound he is a 1st. Lt. in the 21st. was wounded & taken prisoner in one of Burgoynes fights –

Sunday 7th. June much rain in the afternoon – The Commissioners arrived last night but a Salute of 21 Guns was fired for them this morng, they are lodged seperately in the best houses in Town, & officers Guards, & all Guards have orders to Salute & beat a March to them. Mr. [Adam] Ferguson Professor of Philosophy at Edinr. is come along with them, & some other Gentln. Mr. Eadon has brot. his wife –

Monday 8th. Pleasant wr. had the Redoubt – wrote a few lines last night to Col. Stirling about long Grant trying to come in to the Regt. in place of Capt. [George] McKenzie who is order'd home to take possession of his majority, hoping for his friendship & good offices & get the succession in our favour – The Comssrs. sent home ye offrs. guard, & keep only a Corpl. & 6
    The Anspachers order'd to embark & leave all Horses & waggons belonging to the QrMrGl. & yr. own horses under a guard

Tuesday 9th. June, cool last night today pleasantly warm – call'd on Col. Stirling but he was not at home, he came up afterwards to our house & taking me out he asked me if I had any objections to go to the Light Infantry. I said none but hoped he wod send me to the Grs. where there was an opening, but he wod not promise – he told me he had seen the Genl. & spoke to him about Rutherford & me succeeding in the Regt. & he told him he would always pay a proper attention to his recommendation, but that these vacancy's were not to be fill'd up yet – There are two or three applying to get in to the 42d. on this occasion but Col Stirling thinks we need not be uneasy –
    Covering party's for the Wood Cutters out today & yesterday. The Dams in front of the lines not yet finish'd – flags of truce passing to & fro – they say Mr. Ferguson is to go out tomorrow to speak with them if he can

Wednesday 10th. June warm a Flag came in to the Post over Sckuylkill early this morng. with two letters, soon after which

Mr. Ferguson went out in a Carriage & return'd in the afternoon what pass'd I have not heard, but I am told that everything but Independence is offer'd to the Americans; – Alas Britain how art thou fallen –

I ask'd Col: Stirling when I was to join the Light Infantry, when to my great surprize & astonishment he told me he thot. I had declined it as not convenient, & that he had spoke to Capt. Smith; very strange behaviour Mr. Stirling, I must say –

Thursday 11th. a warm day and produced nothing. we had a field day at 5 morng. & I had walk with little Cate in the Eveng. again who is always so agreeable that I wish I may not be too particular there

Friday 12th. June warm as usual the 46th. gone over to the Jerseys two days ago, – things sliping over by degrees had Company to dine Mr. Montgomery a son o Coldfields, come in from Virginia – & Capt. McKenzie who goes home in the Pacquet, to take possession of his Majority

Saturday 13th. warm & dry – much speculation about this treaty with the Americans, an answer is expected from Congress begining of next week – some of us dined wt. Mr. Montgomery at the Tavern –

Sunday 14th. various opinions about matters & things, every body surprized at our present Manouvres – had Company to dine & sat late, been almost fou these 3 days running – Mr. Montgomery & Capt. McGaghan –

Monday 15th. June moderate The Light Horse & Brigade of Hessians pass over today – and all the Bat Horses, what little Baggage we have is to go over to morrow morning – news from Rhode Island say the Genl. [Robert] Pigot on intelligence that the Enemy were making preparations for a descent on the Island, he cross'd over to the Main with 500 men attack'd the Guard on their Boats kill'd 40 or 50 & took a good many prisoners, and destroyed their flat Boats to the No. of 125, together with a great deal of artillery & stores – it is expected the mail will be closed this eveng.

Philada. 15th. June 1778 – a Regt. of Cavalry & a Brigade of Hessians cross'd over to the Jersey The Officers Bat Horses and all the Baggage they can spare likewise sent over – it is supposed we shall all soon follow –

Tuesday 16th. some deserters came in, and a great batch of prisoners sent out in cartel, some of the Rebel officers sent on board a ship a number of our prisoners expected in every day – and an answer from Congress relative to the proposals sent them is expected today or tomorrow – every thing going forward for an Evacuation of this Place –

Wednesday 17th. June very warm. orders to send every thing over the River but one blanket, & after orders for the Troops to be under arms at 6 in the Eveng. Provision to be drawn on the other side Nothing being now left on this side but the British Infantry, they march'd out in the Eveng. & lay at the lines, leaving the Town without the least disturbance with only the main & some other small Guards – &, the 33d. Regt.

Thursday 18th. at Break of day the Troops got under arms at the lines, and march'd by the Skirts of the Town down to Glocester point. (having evacuated the Redoubts & call'd in the Troops that were in Town) where they embark'd in flat boats & cross'd over to Glocester, by several trips the whole over in the forenoon, & two days provision being drawn there the Troops march'd to within 2 miles of Haddonfield where they Encamped in the usual manner, viz. Wigwams, – Strict orders against Plundering, & a Proclamation given out to encourage the People in the Jerseys to supply the army with fresh provision & forage, & remain at home
The Commissioners gone by sea – it is said that some officers & men staying too long behind in Philada. were catch'd by the Rebels who came into Town by 7 or 8 oclock in the morng. – a small party – the day very hot – Knip[hausen] at Haddond.

Friday 19th. The army marched by day light & proceeded thro' Haddonfield, forward to within 2 miles of Foster Town, the morng. showery & the day cool – we march'd I suppose about 10 miles, – The front near to foster Town the rear at Haddonfield The Troops occupying the best[?] grounds along the upper road to Mount Holly

Saturday 20th. June, The army, (the bulk of the Army) march'd this morng. at 4 o'clock & proceeded thro Foster Town Ayres Town, cross'd several branches of Nancokus Creek (the Bridges having been broke up & repair'd) & came to Mount Holly between 10 & 11 & Encamp'd mostly on that ground betwixt the Mount & to the No: of the Village, the morng. cool the afternoon rainy – about 800 of the Rebels left Mount holly yesterday morng. – Genl. Kniphausen with the Rear division of the Army I suppose march'd from Haddonfield this morning. the 15th. Regt. expected there from Billingsport to join them – The Course today various North & South of East, deep sandy road, more clear Country than yesterday The advanced Yagers had a little skirmish lost one man & took some prisoners among whom was a deserter from 28 Regt. – Norry's second dinner – no attendance & bad wine

Tuesday 21st. June a good deal of rain last night & this morng. – today hot & sultry – This part the front Division of the Army halted here at Mount Holly today & drew 2 day provision; Kniphausens division moved forward to Mount Holly – A Genl. Court Martial at 8 Lt. Col: Grant presidt for the tryal of some maroders & a prisoner taken by the Yagers who proves to be a deserter from 28th. light Company

Monday 22d. June rain in the night the army march'd according to the order prescrib'd & moved on to the Black Horse a small Village about 7 or 8 miles from Mount holly & Encamp'd in two lines facing NW – Genl. Kniphausen's Division on the left – the Queens Rangers on our Right, whose Piquet extending to the Right saw a few Rebel Light horse who fired on them at a great distance, – Maxwells Corps of Rebels left the Blackhorse this morng. – The Sentence of the Genl Court Martial in orders last night the Drumr. hang'd on the Road –

Tuesday 23d. The army march'd at 4 o'clock in three Divisions, the left under Genl. Leslie, Kniphausen's Division on the Right, we the middle division came by the Sign of the Rising Sun to Crosswicks about 6 miles.[25] The advanced Corps had a little skirmish at the Creek where a party of the Rebels had partly broke up the Bridge and made a little stand with some Cannon, but were soon drove off & pursued with a little loss – The Queens Rangers had a Captn. woundd The Van of the army, except the 1st Light Infantry recross'd the Creek & together with the rest of the middle Column Encamp'd in the Environs of the Village of Crosswick, – Genl. Kniphausens division on our Right about 3 miles – Genl. Leslies moved down towards BurdenTown where they had some cannonading in the Evening –

orders for Kniphausen to march at 4 our Column to be in readiness at 6 when Genl. Leslies division was expected to join. – pick'd up a tollerable good horse but the Coll. took him from me, spoke to him about it, but he said he wanted him for the waggons – paitresheen – he was taken from him again with another – tant mieux – dirty road today –

Wednesday 24th. June the weather these two or three days past cloudy & cool – few or none of the men Inhabitants at home & many houses deserted entirely Coll. Shrieves house (a Rebel Coll.) and Mr. Talmon's (a Congress man) burn't yesterday on the march contrary to orders and notwithstanding all the precautions taken, a good deal of plundering going on it was 8 o'clock this morng. before we got off the ground, march'd to Allens Town, 4 miles and Encamp'd on a very fine extensive piece of clear ground & almost level, to the N:Ed: of the Village, fronting the West in two lines – or NW – a pretty Country – A Remarkable great Eclipse of the sun today, but being cloudy could not see it till near & at its height, near 10 A:M: when it was almost total, as it went off the day clear'd up & grew hot – 11 1/2 digits[26]

Genl. Kniphausens Division on our Right a few miles, – Genl.

Leslie's in the Rear close up – N:B: The Cannon we hear'd last eveng. was the Rebels firing on Br Genl. Leslies Camp near BordenTown – our Regt. had the care of the Baggage today   one Battn. on the left flank   the other in the Rear

Thursday 25 June, yesterdays orders The Baggage to be loaded & the army ready to move at 4 o'clock tomorrow morng. – The First Division will march by half Compys. from the left in the followg. order – Brigr. Genl. Leslie's Corps consisting of the 5th. Brigade & Hovendents Dragoons – Pontons & Baggage – Cattle – 4th. Brigade – 3d. Brigade – Guards – Artillery – Hessian Grenrs. – British Grenrs. – Queens Dragoons – Light Infantry Queen's Rangers – Corps of Yagers – Allens Corps to flank the Baggage on the left – The army will receive one day fresh & one days salt provision & rum as soon as they come to their ground tomorrow   The army march'd at 4 o'clock this morng. according to the order above   Genl. Kniphausen's Division came in upon our road about 3 or 4 miles from Allens Town & moved on in our front proceeding on the road to Monmouth Court House, HeadQrs. at the Sign of the Sun in Upper Freehold, Knip with the Provision train 6 miles farther on – The road generally sandy & now & then a thick wood – a great many people left their houses & drove away their Cattle – a few of the enemy's Light Horse make their appearance at every Camp, they watch our motions & exchange a shot sometimes – the Weather very hot

Friday 26th. ready to march at 4 but it was 6 before we got off the ground march'd to the Eastwd. 8 or 10 miles & Encamp'd at Freehold or Monmouth Court House between 11 & 12 on a very fine extensive clearing facing to the Northwd. – Genl. Kniphausens Division came on to with[in] two miles of this yesterday & march'd from thence early this morng a Sandy soil & much Wood – hot with Thunder –

Saturday 27th June, The army halted & recd. one days fresh & one days Salt Provision – Here the two Columns join, and ly Encamp'd on a very fine extensive plain in the Environs of the little Village at Monmouth Court House making a line of about 4

miles the front about NW. The flanks facing outwd. with now &
then some little popping at the different out Guards, half a dozen
of the Sculking rascals taken this morng. The Genl. officers quarter'd in the village – many of the Hessians deserting & some of
the British, owing it is said to the prevailing opinion that we are
going to abandon this Country the foreigners to go home & some
of the British, the rest to different stations. – While Britain
mourns her fate – a dozen British Grrs. taken this afternoon washing in the rear of the Camp –

Sunday 28th June a fight – Genl Kniphausen with his Division & provision & Baggage train marched between 3 & 4 o'clock
on the road leading to Middletown   Our Division moved after 5
o'clock on the same road, observing the same order of march as
the two days past – Between 9 & 10 oclock when our Brigade was
about 4 miles advanced from the Village of Monmouth, (the Rear
of the Division I suppose about 2 miles behind) the Enemy made
their appearance in force near the Rear; the General rode back &
ordered the troops to face about and march back with all speed
to attack the Rebels; as our Troops approach'd their van, a Cannonade began about the East end of the Village, but the Enemy
soon retired to their more solid Column as the flank Corps moved
up, about 2 miles to the westwd. of the Village the Grrs.
attack'd, & the Light Infy. were sent to the righ[t]   The 1st.
Battn. Light Infantry & Queen Rangers were dispatch'd to the
right to try to gain the Enemys left flank, but meeting swamps &
much impediment in the Woods they did not get up in time,
mean while the Brigade of Guards & two Battalions of British
Grenrs. after a very quick march moved up briskly & attack'd the
Enemy in front receiving a heavy fire as they approach'd of both
cannon & musketry & when within a short distance they pour'd
in their fire & dashing forwards drove the foe before them for
some considerable time, killing many with their Bayonets but
seeing a fresh line of the Enemy strongly posted on t'other side a
Ravine & Swamp & well supplyed with Cannon & having suffer'd
much both from the fire of the Enemy & fatigue & heat of the
day, they were order'd to retire till more Troops came up to their

Support – The 3d. Brigade came up after a very quick & fatiguing march of six or 7 miles, and leaving their Packs at the edge of the wood on their right, they dash'd thro' that wood & a deep swamp, and came upon a Scatter'd Body of the Rebels whom the left of the 42d. drove before them, and coming to a rising ground saw the Enemy   in force on a hill about 7 or 800 yards in front playing a good many pieces of Cannon as Briskly as they could on everything within their reach, whilst our Cannon were playing upon them with I'm told tollerable success; while this Cannonade was going on, part of the 42d. cross'd a very deep swamp & took possession of a hill on their right, & were soon followed by the 44th. Regt. but seeing no appearance of the Enemy there they were order'd back to the Hill they left being Flank'd by the Enemys Cannon. These several maneuvers & rapid marches with the excessive heat & the difficult passes they met with had so fatigued & knock'd up the men yt. a great number of the several Corps died upon the Spot; while the 3d. Brigade halted a little while to breathe the 1st. Light Infantry & Queens Rangers came up on their right & finding themselves likewise much fatigd. & having drop'd a good many men, it was thought improper to advance any farther upon the Enemy who were strongly posted, & the Troops were accordingly order'd to retire to cover the Village of Monmouth where the Wounded & Sick were brought to in the Evening – where we remained till near 12 oclock at night, & leaving those of the wounded that were too ill to remove, with a Surgeon & flag we march'd forwards to join the other division of the Army whom we overtook near to Middletown about 9 o'clock of the morng. of the 29th.   in this action the Grenrs. suffer'd considerably having 13 officers killed & wounded and about 150 men killed wounded & missing Colo: Monckton among the slain – The Guards likewise lost above 40 – and the several other Corps that came up lost some men either by the Enemy or the heat & fatigue of the day, which was very distressing – The total of killed wounded & missing near 400 – 358 The line of Baggage was likewise attack'd by a small party about 10 or 12 miles from Monmouth, & had a few men kill'd & wounded   The last nights march about 14 miles NE thro' a thick wood & a sandy road almost the whole way, cross'd a creek about 5 miles from Middleton, march'd two miles further & halted till next morng. The face of the Country now changed from level to hilly – [27]

Monday 29th. June the weather still continues extremely hot – Genl. Kniphausens Division moved on to Middletown, with the Provision & baggage train – & wounded

Tuesday 30th. The 1st. Division (still so call'd tho' in the rear) march'd at day light thro' a hilly strong Country & came to Middleton about 3 miles, in the Environs of which the army Encamp'd – This little Village surrounded with hills is about two or 3 miles from Rariton Bay, and about 12 miles to the light house – from the Hills here about you have a fine view of the Bay, the Hook, the Fleet, Long Island, Staten Island & Amboy – In the afternoon the heavy division moved a few miles towards Neversink and about 10 o'clock at night the first Division followed, creeping & halting on a crooked road till 2 oclock of the morng. when we stopp'd & took a nap whh. was much wanted –

Wednesday 1st. July The army Encamp'd in a strong position, occupying the Hills from 2 to 4 miles eastward of Middleton & making a communication with the Bay in which the Fleet are lying within the Hook, our left extending towds. the Neversink, our right within less than two miles of the Village facing differently as the ground requires, or as the Enemy may be expected, who are still hovering about us, showing themselves in different places in our front & right, some popping shots, now & then – we hear the May Packet is arrived – no it is a Dispatch Boat with private Dispatches for The Adml. Genl. & Commisses. –

Thursday 2d. July – Employed in Embarking the stores & heavy Baggage of the army – The wounded & sick sent on board yesterday – The Camp quiet – 'tis said Washington has gone back with the bulk of his army –

Friday 3d. it rained some last night, and almost all this day, – mounted Piqt. this morng. at 1/2 past 2, no appearance of the Enemy – a man wod. by accident or design by his own piece –

The officers Baggage all sent off, except what their servts. can carry on their backs – The waggons & yr. horses gone –

Saturday 4th. the weather clear'd up towards noon – all the officers horses sent off – The waggon & train horses gone up to Long Island – great expedition this in Embarking our things so fast, – hear'd a great deal of firing in the Eveng. of Cannon & Small arms at a distance which we suppose is the Americans rejoicing on the anniversary of ye. Independence   The firing seems to be somewhere about Brunswick which I believe is the best Intelligence we have of where Mr. Washington is – orders to be ready to move at break of day –

Sunday 5th. July every thing being embark'd but the Troops & a few horses   The army march'd between 5 & 6 from yr. respective ground by different roads to the point of the Highland that joins the Hook, & there being a Gut of water across the low Sandy part next the main, a Bridge of flat boats was made for the Troops to pass some embark'd on board of flat boats & rode off to their ships but the greatest part of the army crossed at the Bridge & march'd along the Hook towards the Light House & went off in flat boats to their ships in the afternoon; it was night before the whole got on board. – a great number of horses on Sandy Hook yet not embark'd into the Vessels that are to carry ym. up – the day cool, march about 6 miles in the woods before we came to the point & about 3 or 4 miles on Sandy Hook, deep sand – provision drawn on board   a very irregular & ill managed Embarkation. This abrupt Reduction of the flanks Corps not relish'd

Chapter VI

'a sweep into the Country'

Long Island, Buzzards Bay, and New Jersey
6 July to 30 November 1778

Sir Henry Clinton and Admiral Lord Howe went to New York in June 1778 expecting that they would soon be able to send detachments to attack the French West Indies and to strengthen the defenses of Florida, Canada, and the British Isles. But their expectations were shattered when in early July a powerful French squadron arrived unexpectedly in North American waters. The French threatened to attack the British fleet at New York or to join with rebel forces in capturing the British garrison on Rhode Island. Until reinforced, Clinton and Howe could do little more than remain on the defensive at New York and, then, try to lure the French away from Rhode Island. When the French, having followed Howe to sea and suffered damage in a storm, decided to go to Boston for repairs, Howe had ships enough to pursue them while Clinton relieved Rhode Island. Even so, it would be November before the British had the forces to defend New York and Rhode Island and to send expeditions not only to attack the French West Indies island of St. Lucia but also to secure Florida, recover Georgia, and, perhaps, begin a restoration of royal government throughout the South.[1]

While Clinton and Howe concentrated on parrying the French, the British army at New York had little to do. John Peebles would be promoted during the summer and returned to the grenadiers, but in neither his old nor his new unit would he take part in more than minor operations. For nearly two months after the French arrived, he and the 42nd regiment remained encamped on Long Island, watching opposing warships come and go and awaiting news of actions offshore.[2] At the end of August he was promoted to captain of his former company, the Grenadier Company of the 42nd, and sent as a part of the 1st Battalion of

Grenadiers with some 4,000 troops to relieve the British garrison at Rhode Island. By the time that he reached Newport on 1 September, the French and Americans had withdrawn and the garrison was secure.[3] The 1st Grenadiers were, therefore, placed under the command of Major-General Charles Grey and ordered to destroy rebel shipping in Buzzards Bay and gather food on Martha's Vineyard. When they returned to Long Island on 19 September, they were promptly reembarked for New Jersey, where they spent another three weeks foraging between the Hackinsack and Hudson Rivers. In mid-October they were back on Long Island, preparing to go into winter quarters.[4]

Long Island, Buzzard Bay, and New Jersey
6 July to 30 November 1778

Monday 6th. July The Transports & some of the man of war got under way in the morng. & sail'd up the Bay, those destin'd for long island, come to at Gravesend the 1st. & 2d. Brigades at the Watering place the rest went up to New York, the horses on Sandy hook island to come up in the small craft – a fine fair breeze –

Tuesday 7th. The three Brigades vizt. the 3d. 4th. & 5th. Landed at Gravesend Bay in the forenoon, & in the afternoon got their tents ashore, the 3d. Brigade Encamp'd close by New Utrecht, the 4th. at Gravesend, & the 5th. at Flatland, their flank Compys with their fine dry ground, & the fields & the Country here about look as well as if nothing had happen'd – The Genls. gone to New York.[5] Lt. Colo. Stirling Commands the Brigade – no word of our horses yet – a fine place this for Sea bathing, within 1/4 mile of our Camp – a scrambling dinner of eggs at the public house

Wednesday 8th. July hot weather, but this Camp is open to the sea breezes whh. is very refreshing, – This part of the Country very ill water'd, no springs or running water here about, The Inhabitants obliged to dig deep, for water, 30 or 40 feet, we are supplied from their wells – milk & butter to be got & some fresh stock
  A great number of the Artillery horses arrived to day. The offrs. horses not come yet People appointed in the different districts to supply the Camp with fuel & forage –

Thursday 9th. July, hot & sultry hear'd a heavy Cannonade for above two hours this forenoon, supposed to be out at Sea – 'tis said a french fleet of 12 or 13 sail of the line & 6 frigates have made their appearance on this Coast, – the prize of one of our Cruising frigates came in yesterday with the account of their being seen pointing towards the Delaware or Chesapeak Bay – Lord Howe is gone down himself & order'd all the large ships to the

Hook – but all that he can collect will be no match for such a fleet. our horses did not arrive till this forenoon – an order for striking off the Capts. forage, from the Commissionary line –

Regtal. orders for a Review of arms accoutrements & Necessarys, a Return to be given in of the former, & the latter to be completed, & the Compys. to be clear'd to 24 June

Friday 10th. July a gentle breeze to cool the air – The Admiral & most of the men of war lying about halfway betwixt the Narrows & the Hook, more Accots. of the French fleet, The Maidstone Frigate is arrived who follow'd them all the way from Europe, says they seemed bound for Chesapeake & that Admiral Byron with 13 sail of the line & some Frigates had sail'd in pursuit of them – we hear that the Roebuck had a narrow escape but is come in to the Hook – The two Regts. of the Anspach, the 38th. Regt. & Col. Fannings Corps are Embark'd – supposed for Rhode Island – a Commissary come to camp to provide pasture for our horses, the Capts. allow'd as formerly – Mr. [James] Rivington sent me enclosed with a complet. a New Tragedy call'd the Battle of Hastings, by Cumberland. Thank you Mr. R.

Saturday 11th. July a smart Thunder gust just before day this morning, the day hot notwithstanding; some of the ships of war moving further down –

Sunday 12 July 1778 yesterday Evening the French Fleet came down to anchor outside of the Hook consisting of 12 or 13 sail of the line & 4 or 5 Frigates; see them this morng from our Camp very plain.

Lord Howe with all the ships he can muster lying within the Hook The Eagle, Ardent, Trident, Somerset, Nonesuch, 64's Preston, Isis Experiment, 50 Gun ships Roebuck & Phoenix 44's, Vigilant 18 24 pors. & some frigates. the Carcass & Strombolo The 15th. & 44th. Regs. gone down to Sandy Hook to make some works –

On notice given by Lord Howe that he wanted men, a thousand sailors from The Transports turn'd out Volunteers to go on board the fleet, some Masters & Mates, this was two days ago, & yesterday 60 more from the ships lying at the Watering place went on board the Vigilant – the Marine Grendr. Compy. gone on board the Eagle – and his Lordship tho' far inferiour to the French fleet is preparing to fight them should they dare enter the Harbour. I went to New York this morning for a few hours to find out if there was any Notifications of the Vacancies, nix saw Lord Balcaras, he is come in on parole in hopes of being exchanged, as likewise some other offrs. of that army.[6]

Dr. [Adam] Ferguson Professor of Moral Philoy. at Edinr. Secry. to Commissioners came down with me to see the fleet, he dined with us & return'd in the Eveng. a genteel well bred man, & you may be sure he is no fool, he was Chaplain the 42d. in flanders.

Monday 13th. July   cool The French fleet in the same position, Count D'Estaing Vice Admiral on board the Languedoc, 90 guns, they saild from Toulon about the 13th. April & have 1000 Land forces on board – 'tis said they have taken a Snow with Ammunition &ca. for the Carcass Bomb & the York sloop – two men of war the Raisonable & Centurion are expected from the Eastwd. if they arrive it is supposed that Lord Howe will attack. And Admiral Byron being above two months at sea may be expected every day now. Govr. Johnston on board ye. fleet.

The Comr. in chief went down yesterday & return'd last night or this morng. on his way up ran foul of a ship & had like to have been sunk, his Aid de Camp Capt. [William] Sutherland got his thigh hurt by an Anchor. – Head Quarters is now at Deny's Long Island, opposite the Narrows –

Lord Howe & Genl. Clintons letters to Congress with the Conciliatory Acts, in the York Papers, & the Congress's answer – Short & Insolent – and an account of the action at Monmouth from the Rebel Papers wherein they assume great merit & claim a Victory – the 17th. gone to cover HeadQrs.

Tuesday 14th. July   moderate wind at N: & N.E. these some days   The French fleet maneuvering a little, but keep pretty much the same station, about 2 or 3 leagues from the Light House, at the back of the Hook we can count 18. or 19 sail altogether. The Port complatly block'd up. and what I believe never was the case before a British Admiral block'd up in Harbour, by a French fleet – an old 74 fitting up at New York to join Lord Howe – Thre Compys. of Light Infantry & 3 of Grendrs. under the Commmand of Major [John] Maitland gone on board the fleet to act as Marines, The flank Compys. drew lots for it

Wednesday 15th July. The French Fleet still lying without the Hook about 2 leagues from the Light house, their numbers varry from 15 to 20 sail, beside small craft plying about among them – The Commisioners letter to Congress & copy of their Commission in the Papers & the Congress's Answer which is both insolent & insulting – and Washingtons account of the affair at Monmouth 28 June, our loss exaggerated, Lee in arrest[7]

Thursday 16th. hot – Col: [Duncan] McPherson & I took a ride to Jamaica & the plains, dined with Judge Ludlow where there was a great deal of Company came back to Jamaica in the Eveng. and staid there all night, supd at Bates's who keeps the house that old Combs did with a sign call'd Genl. Amherst stuck up the 16th Light Dragoons at Jamaica they expect to be drafted & sent home – [8]

Friday 17th. a breeze – set off from Jamaica about 8 in the Morng. & breakfasted with Genl. [Oliver] Delancy at the head of Flushing fly, where two of his Battns. are Encamp'd Cruger's & Ludlows saw Col: [Gabriel G.] Ludlow & Major [A.] Menzies left that between 10 & 11.[9] Stop'd a little at flat bush & got to camp about 2 oclock when I found a Card to dine with Lord Cornwallis at 3. Col. Stirling Capt. Chas. Graham & I there, ease & politeness Lord Balcarras & Capt. Campbell come down to see us

Saturday. 18th. July gentle breeze S.E. The french fleet lying in pretty much the same position, some firing hear'd off at sea yesterday, suppose they are taking some of our ships, 'tis said they have sent 30 sail into the Delaware already – we are afraid of the Corke fleet. Lord Howe still lying within the hook with a spring on their cables – the May Packet taken & carried into New London

Washington has cross'd the North River with his army & is somewhere about Fishkill, [Horatio] Gates near White plains

Sunday 19th. July warm   The Fleets below lying in the same situation, with some increase of small Vessels among the french fleet

a Packet announced in orders to sail in the course of the week, the mail to be closed tonight.   wrote a letter for Marshall, will add a P.S. before I send it off.

Monday 20th. cool & some rain can count 26 sail of Large & small without the Hook, the Large Ships make a line next the harbour the small ly off & Cruize about – our fleet in the same position –

Lord Bal[carra]s. & young [William] Finch went to York today, they have little hopes of being exchanged –

Tuesday 21st. a cool breeze from sea no alteration of the French fleet – The Leviathan an old 70 Gun ship gone down today to join Lord Howe   She is fitted out with upper deck Guns but I believe there is none in the lower tier   took a ride to the Camps of the 4 & 5th. Brigade at Gravesend & Flat land, the 46 Regt. gone down to the hook –

Wednesday 22d. July   cool & cloudy. The French fleet in motion today, stand. off & on, in the afternoon the whole a good deal further out, Lord Howe keeps his position – got abstracts and money today, the Compys. to 24 June –[10]

Thursday 23d. cool for the season   The French fleet have disappear'd; they went off in the night, but whether they are gone to some other port, or it is only a finesse, to bring out Lord Howe, is yet uncertain – three of our ships gone out & taken station where the french fleet lay –

had orders to move today but it was countermanded till tomorrow.

The offrs. paid as to 24 Augt. settled wt. McIntosh about my
little Bill –

Friday 24 July. not hot – The 2 Brigades viz the 3d & 4th.
march'd this morng. from their respective Encampments &
took up ground near to Bedford towards Bushwick the left of
the 3d. Brigade extending near to the Wallabacks facing about
east
   a Genl. Court Martial at Brooklyn Lt. Col Stirling prest. –
This Camp very ill off for water we have about a mile to go –

Saturday 25th. moderate a long string of prisoners to be
tried by the Genl. Court martial, a list of Black crimes, murder,
highway robbery, Rape, Ravishment, desertion &ca. &ca. – our
mess a mile from Camp on account of the distance of the
water which is only to be got at the wells of the farmers
houses –

Sunday 26th. July warm – sermon in Camp – took a ride to
see the field of action of the 27th. Augt. 1776, the troops to the
left came over a great variety of ground & would have met with
much more difficulty than they did if the right column had not
turn'd the enemys flank & frightened them with the prospect of
being all cut off, which made them retreat to their lines in the
greatest disorder & confusion –
   I hear the Renown is arrived from the West Indies, & saw the
french fleet off the Capes of Delaware – Lord Howe still lying
within the hook & 3 ships without.

Monday 27th. very warm – The Regt. was muster'd this
morng. at 8. – we muster'd on the spot 3 Serjts. 4 Corpls. & 1
Drr. & 68 private – NB I sign'd for an Effective Drumr. that I
knew nothing about, the Col: caused him to be inserted – [11]

Tuesday 28th. rainy warm & cool by turns – The Dispach is
arrived with some report of Adml. [John] Byron but it is kept
secret. – a large supply of water sent down to the hook –
   The markets rising both in Town & Country, butchers meat
from 1/6 to 2/6, poultry very high, butter 4/ bread very dear –

sent off a letter for Marshall yesterday to go by the Packet who was to sail yesterday. NB The Packet gone, my letter was too late

Wednesday 29th. July   warm wt. a breeze from the westward – Ld. Bal[carras]: & Majr. C[ampbell] come out to stay a while with us as it is uncertain whether they will be exchanged, or go back a good many officers of the Convention gone home in the Paquet.

Thursday 30th. very warm took a walk with fuzils round by Bushwick but saw nothing to shoot   we hear the Cornwall a 74 one of Adml. Byrons fleet is arrived at ye. Hook   the rest expected immediately, they say the fleet did not leave England till the 9th. June, what was the reason of that delay my Lord Sandwich – [12]

Friday 31st. a Thunder Gust this morng. early with a Great deal of rain. the day hot & sultry – took a ride to Newtown – the 5th. Brigade to march to Newtown tomorrow –
orders for the flank Corps to assemble at Bedford as soon as they can – Sutherlands Caledonian Volunteers to be incorporated into Lord Cathcarts legion –
the Raisonable & Centurion arrived two days ago – prenez garde [take care] Monsr. D'Estaing   if my Lord Howe gets another sight of you he'll make you break your word to your king.
Regtal. orders for a Review of necessarys knapsacks & overplus to be sent on board

Saturday 1st. Augt. hot weather some accounts of the french fleet having been seen steering to the N. Ed. no appearance of Adml. Byron yet. Review'd the Compy. only a few pairs of shoes wanting

Sunday 2d. Augt. hot wr. the flank Corps are assembling in our Neighboorhood.
we hear that Lord Howe is sail'd in quest of the french fleet, some think they are gone to Rhode Island –
The Col call'd the Comg. offrs. of Compys. together to ask

what is best to be done with the donation articles in store when it was agreed to have them on board ship, together –

Monday 3d. Augt. hot wt. Thunder Gusts About 1 o'clock this morng. a fire broke out in New York at the house of one Jones a Ship Chandler near the old slip which consumed between 60 & 70 Houses in that Neighbourhood, but was happily prevented from doing further mischief, & extinguish'd about 9 or 10 oclock, – from the best accots. that can be obtain'd concerning the cause of the fire, it appears to have been done by design, as Matches & combustibles were found in several places, a good many people are taken up on suspicion, some of them frenchmen –

Yesterday the June Pacquet arrived at the hook, the mail came up to N. York early this morng. – Col. Stuart & the Marquis of Lindsay came passengers.

high disputes in the Parlt. whh. was adjournd by a speech from the throne the 3d. June to 14 July the Nation was threatened with a french Invasion – Genl. Burgoyne not allow'd to see the King, but told his story to Parlt. – a board of Genl. offrs. ordered to inquire into his conduct but could not take congnizance of it as he is a prisoner – Lord Chatham dead – opposition still keeps up –

had a letter from my friend AH. dated 20th. May complaining of long silence, who I find had wrote regularly, but the letters must have miscarried, acknowledged mine of Janry: Lord Howe not sail'd yet, nor any word of Adml. Byron. I was in N. York for a few hours.

Tuesday 4th. Augt. hot & a good deal of Rain with Thunder – About 2 o'clock in the afternoon hear'd a great explosion amidst Thunder which proved to be the blast of 200 Barrels of Gun Powder in a Vessel lying in the stream opposite the Coffee house of N. York, but how it took fire is uncertain, some think it was lightning there was only one man on board & he & the vessel were blown to 10000 pieces the vast concussion of the air broke almost all the Windows in town & broke and unroof'd a great many houses.

I hear the Notifications of those officers appointed to the new
Rais'd Corps at home are come over by this Pacquet, if all those
we hear of in our Regt. are confirm'd it will make great promotion
among us.
only those of the Athol & Argyle Regts. are come. Jas.
Campbell & Lord Wm. Compys in the Athol & Jno. Campbell in
the Argyle

Wednesday 5th. Augt. hot wr. accots. in the Papers of a Col:
Butler wt. a party of Indians & Torys coming upon the Wyoming
Settlement on the Susquehanna, taking their Fort killing & scalp-
ing many & driving the rest away

Thursday 6th. hot weather some talk of moving from this
ground. The french fleet said to be at Rhode Island & the Rebels
to make a descent there in conjunction – some flying reports of
Adml. Byron being on the coast –

Friday 7th. the weather still continues hot – Lord Howe sail'd
yesterday with the fleet, steering Easterly, 'tis supposed for Rhode
Island – A report prevails that some of the french ships have
enter'd the harbour of Newport and met with a warm reception
from the Batteries & disabled some of them

Saturday 8th. Augt. hot still The wind fair for Rhode Island
these two days – a frigate & another ship of war, with 10 or 12
Transports went up the East River yesterday to go thro' Hell
Gate – we hear Lord Howe has fallen in wt. some of Adml.
Byron's fleet –
Paid the Qr.Mr. today £23.18.6. Br: Stirg. for sea provision for
the additionals, from Scotland to America

Sunday 9th. much rain with Thunder & Lightning, some
people struck at New York – Wind S.W. or there about the
15th. & 44th. Regts. are come from Sandy Hook & join'd the
Brigade, they made several works on the hook – a Packet to sail
in a few days. have wrote some, will finish tomorrow

Monday 10th. Augt. Cloudy & showery the wind to northward – finish'd two letters one for Dick M: & one for AH sent them to the Town Majors N. York.

Settled our Breakfast accot. from the time we left Philada. to this date – Innes owes me 19/3 Cury – abt. 40/ cash

Tuesday 11th. cool with the wind at N.E. & some rain, smart gale. – a flying Report said to come in by deserters that Lord Howe has defeated the french fleet – [13]

Wednesday 12th. it blew very hard last night at N.E. or there about, which still continues, cool & cloudy –

The Zebra is arrived who says she saw Lord Howe within 2 leagues of the french fleet off Rhode Island on Monday standing out

Much promotion in the orders these two days past no word of poor Gilchrist.

Thursday 13th. Augt. very blowy from N.E. to N.W. with showers. all anxious to hear from Lord Howe –

Friday 14th. a smart gale about E. something come in from Rhode island that says some of the french fleet had entered the Harbour & summon'd the place to surrender   Genl. Pigot return'd a short & spirited answer on which Monsr. D'Estaing brot up some of his ships against the Town & Batteries who met with such a warm reception that they were fain to haul off, & hearing of the British fleet approaching went out to sea as fast as possible & were seen within 2 leagues of each other near Block Island, steering S.W. but it thot by some that the late stormy weather wod. disperse them.

Colo: [William] Grants sale put a stop to again by some strange vindictive reasons of the comg. offr.

a showery eveng –

Saturday 15th. Showers & wet fog with the wind about N.E., a good deal of rain the overnight – The Pacquet sail'd yesterday with a good many Passengers – Stop'd at the Hook   some things come in from the fleet which brings pretty much the same accots. as the above – no action –

Sunday 16th. Augt. wet foggy wr. with the wind about East. – hear'd firing in the afternoon many promotions in the orders almost every day, – Col: Grants affair going on –

Monday 17th. warm wind about S:W a good deal of rain the overnight – a fleet arrived at the Hook of between 20 & 30 Sail supposed to be Lord Howe The late Stormy weather did a good deal of damage to both fleets & prevented General engagement, they had some single attacks

By a Yanky privateer run ashore on Long Island we hear that Rebels have landed 4000 men on Rhode Island & were to land 8000 men under cover of 3 french frigates left there by Monsr. D'Estaing

The July Pacquet arrived today

Tuesday 18th. Augt. hot with Gusts took a ride to the hill above flatbush see the fleet lying at anchor it seems that three of our ships have been engaged on Sunday last with three of the french, The Isis with a 74 La Caezar, the Preston with a 74 la Tonante, & the Renown attack'd the Languedoc which was disabled & 'tis thot. wod. have taken her if other ships had not come to her assistance on whh. the Renown sheer'd off –

Din'd with Lord Cornwallis saw the Papers to the beginning of July, Camps form'd in England, one at Foxheath of two Brigades of Regulars & 4 of Militia Comd. by Lt. Genl. [William] Keppel Major Genls. [William] Amherst & [Robert] Sloper[14] – Admiral [Augustus] Keppel watching the Brest fleet, two frigates taken from the french & one spoil'd, but no war declared yet – Got letters in the Eveng. one from H:N: dated 20 June acknowledging the recept of the trinket & enclosing one from A.H. of the 7th. & 9th. & one of the 18th. & 22d straight; one from my Fr. 22d. one from Dr. F. 25 & one from T.A. 24th. they wrote several by private ships – all these full of kindness & affection – we hear that more notifications are coming over concerning us –

Wednesday 19th. Augt. hot with Thunder & rain in the afternoon – memorial'd Coll. Stirling to be recommended for a Company; short facts & no flummery we hear the Monmouth another of Admiral Byrons fleet is come –

Thursday 20th. hot weather with Thunder showers almost every day for some time past. The Isis up at York repairing her rigging which was very much cut in the engagement with Le Caezar. The Apollo was dismasted in the storm Lord Howe carried his flag on board of her when he expected to engage D'Estaing the better to communicate his orders The French fleet is supposed to be off Little Egg Harbour refitting

Friday 21st. Augt. very hot. a Thunder Gust in the Eveng. – rode along the lines & to the Guanas with Capt. Lindsay –
A Genl. Court martial sitting at the ferry, they say Campbell the farrier is to be tryed for killing a parson at Jamaica –

Saturday 22d. cool & pleasant the Wind about N.E. went to York in the forenoon where I hear'd that the french fleet are gone back to Rhode Island that the Americans have landed 16000 men on the island, & the french have chased away Sir James Wallace who went there some days ago with 3 or 4 Ships, about 1 o'clock the Experiment arrived at N York having been chaced by the french down the Sound, he came thro' Hell Gate – the first of his size

Sunday 23d. cool & foggy wind Easterly; at Sermon A.M. we hear the whole of the french fleet are gone to Rhode Island, having tow'd some of their disabled ships – the Experiment gone down to the Hook. 'tis supposed Lord Howe w'd sail again as soon as possible no word of Adml. Byron yet which is very unaccountable

Monday 24th. warm with the wind to the Westward – Accots. from Rhode island say that all was well on friday last the Enemy had landed about 17000 & were making their approaches, and the french fleet were arrived – Lord Howe sail'd this afternoon, with the Cornwall, Monmouth 74s. Eagle, Somerset, Nonsuch, Ardent, Trident & Raisonable, 64s. Preston, Centurion, Renown & Experiment 50s. Roebuck, Rainbow & Phenix 40s.

frigates Bombs fireships & Gallies. The 15th. & 46th. Regts. order'd to Utrecht to Embark, – a Pacquet to sail in a few days letters to be given in tomorrow; must write the last Pacquet they say only sail'd from the Hook today – the 15th. & 46th. return'd

Tuesday 25th Augt. warm SW Lord Howe lying without the Hook   Report of a Cork fleet – to Flushing   in the Eveng. got orders to march 1st. Batt. Light Infantry 1st. Grenadrs. 3d. & 4 Brigades to march at 1/2 past 4

Wednesday 26th. march'd after 5. The morng. warm & the day very hot & severe on the men, could not make out Flushing, stop'd at the head of the Fly about 9 tenths of the men not up, some very ill & one or two died   the rear all up in the Eveng.

Thursday 27th. march'd at 1/2 past one & got to white stone between 4 & 5 where the troops Embark'd on board of Transports & were all on board by dinner in the Eveng. a Signal for sailing by the Carrysford, got under way about sunset Wind about N & little of it
join'd the 1st. Bn. Grs. this morng. vice C: Graham promoted. – had wrote a letter to AH but was too late in sending it off – [15]

Friday 28th. the wind coming more to the Eastward the fleet came to an anchor last night about 11 off City island; today the wind still contrary till the Eveng. when the fleet got under way with a light breeze about S.E. & saild about 4 leagues when the wind coming to East they came to, about midnight – got orders today for the manner of landing when we come to place of destination 1st. Light Iny. & Grrs. with 70 rounds to join the Enemy with points of Bayonets &ca. Genl. Clinton goes himself on board the Carrysford; & Genl. Gray, their suite on board a little sloop, 5 or 6 small ships of war wt us – we are on board the Esk. Capt. Mc.Donald wt. Col [William] Meadows & the 4th. & 5th. 15th. 40th. & 42d. Compys.

Saturday 29th Augt. cool with the wind about East. The fleet

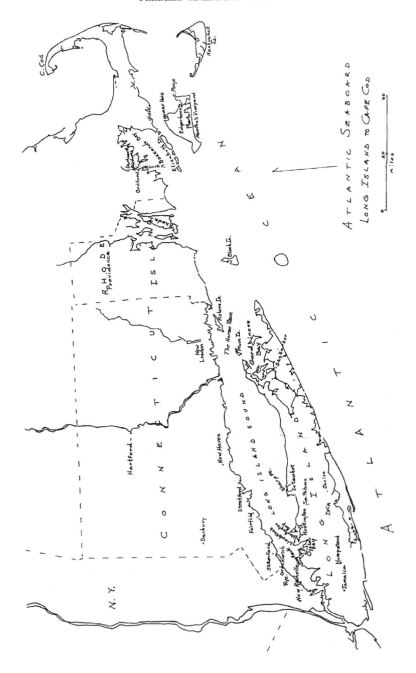

lying at anchor where they came to last night about opposite to
Rye & Hogneck –

Sunday 30th. the wind coming about to the Southwd. in the
morning the signal was made for getting under way when the
whole fleet got up their anchors & set sail about six steering East
about 32 sail of man of war & Transports & about 38 sail of small
craft. – a fine breeze going 5 & 6 knots with the fleet in good
order. The Light Infany on the right, Grenrs. on the left, Regts.
follow as they are Brigaded, men of war in front flanks & Rear –
about 1 o'clock P.M spoke the little sloop that carrys the Aid's
de Camp, & they told us that six of Adml. Byrons fleet with a
number of Vitualers were at the Hook the rest had join'd Lord
Howe

Monday 31st. Aug. The wind came abt. to E & N.E. early in
the morng. when near abreast with Fishers island, the fleet continued to work to windward till between 1 & 2 oclock when they
cast anchor off Block Island, in 12 & 15 fathom water, the middle
of the island bearing about SE 2 miles distant –

Tuesday 1st. Septr. The fleet got under way this morng. about
2 or 3 o'clock with a light wind from the So:ward, about 9 oclock
made Rhode Island, & see a large sail ahead, a frigate[,] soon after
see the Light House & the British Colours flying on a Hill East
of Town, as we approached the Harbours mouth some boats come
off from the shore and told us that the siege was raised & the
Rebels left the island the day before yesterday we got in to the
Harbour between one & two & came to anchor on the Conanicut
side the transports near the ferry. we find the Rebels had landed
to the amount of 18000 or upwards under [John] Sulivan & the
Marquis [La]Fayette & had made their approaches to with 500
yards of our works but on receiving intelligence of our Reinforcement comg: to the relief of Rhode island they raised the siege &
retired off the Island the 29th. Augt. by a Bridge at Howlands
ferry, Genl. Pigot sent a part of his army to attack yr. rear, which
they came up with & had a skirmish in which our people lost 200
kill'd, & wounded or more, & the Rebels carryd off all their

213

dead & wounded – no word of the Count D'Estaing they think here that he went off in dudgeon

Wednesday 2d. Septr. wind at East a party of our offrs. went ashore to Newport this morng. the Coll. & 6 or 7 more, & return'd to dinner, nothing new but suppos'd the Rebels are dispersed, being mostly militia that came to Rhode Island – in the forenoon a Signal for masters when the flat Boats were finish'd with 4 manlets [mantelets] each – in the Eveng. a Signal to weigh anchor when we all got under way & saild out of the harbour with the wind about N.E. & fine moonlight steering to the westward.

Thursday 3d Septr. The wind came to the north in the morng. & cold pass'd fishers island by 6 AM. the Horse Race between seven & 8, see New London on Lighthouse & haul well in with the Conecticut shore tack'd about 11, in order to gain the weather shore, & tack'd again & again at noon the Lighthouse of New London about N.E. 3 leagues, the fleet turning to windward & making for that port they seemed to be alarmed already by raising smoak's – In the Eveng. the fleet came to anchor off the Light House a mile or two distant but the wind being about North right off shore it was 10 oclock at night before some of the ship came to, The Vigilant got herself inbayd at Plumb island but got out in the Eveng. when the tide chang'd Genl. Clinton gone to N. York

Friday 4th. Septr. wind north & cool – The Fleet lying at anchor where they came to last night, see several works ashore on both sides the River & the Rebel Colours flying in each, that on the Hill east side of the River seems to be the largest, some Vessels in the Harbour, & some small craft crossing backward & forwards – Long & spirited orders this morng. by Major Genl. Grey relative to attacking the Enemy, ashore, boarding Privateers & preserving discipline, and a new set of Signals – some flat boats gone to Fishers Island to bring off Hay. – at Noon a signal for Adjutants on board the Surprize – only some addition to the orders against burning houses when we go ashore – in the afternoon the wind came about to W; & about 1/2 after 3 the Como:

made a Signal for the fleet to get under way, which was immediately comply'd with, we stood out to the So:ward toward the Gull islands and came across the Horse Race in the Eveng. when it was strong, the tide setting at the rate of 5 knots flood NWt – when the fleet were all thro' the horse race we bore away to the Eastwd. with a fine breeze from the west, and making various conjectures about our destination; a fine moon light night –

Saturday 5th. Septr. having stood to the Eastward all night we were this morng at day light within sight of the Light house on Conanicut island, with a light breeze at West, and soon after a fleet of large ships were seen off our starboard quarter crowding all sail & firing some Guns, we the Transports were first desired to make the best of our way into Rhode island, but soon after the fleet in chase were discover'd to be Lord Howe & his squadron consisting of 14 ships mostly double deckers – our Como: bore down to him with his convoy & when near hand show'd his Colours & soon after went on board the Adml. in his boat, about this time the Squadron tack'd & stood to the So:ward, & we continued before the wind, & soon parted, – our destination still a mystery, steering to the Eastward. – Lord Howe had been in Boston Bay for 2 or 3 days and look'd at the Count who drew up at Nantasket[,] about one o'clock abreast with the first of Elizabeth Islands 1 league distant the coast about 3 leagues off Steer'd about EN.E. and about 5 haul'd our wind & stood into a Bay call'd Clark's Cove in Buzards Bay where the troops were immediately landed on the East side and march'd about 3 miles to the Northward when coming to a Village call'd Bedford a Detachmt. was ordered to Burn all the Shipping lying there & part of the town suffer'd likewise, we then continued our march to the North, till we came to another Village Dartmouth & bridge about 4 miles & there burned some more Vessels & stores – here the Light Infantry & Grrs. took post on the heights to the west & Northwd. while the Battalions pass'd the Bridge & took a Road that turn'd to the Southward down the other side of the harbour, & 2 Regts. having cross'd below Bedford they took a Work that was just abandon'd by the Enemy & burn't a good many large Vessels &

some houses of a Village Fairhaven The Troops continued their march having met with only a few popping shots in the course of the night, kill'd some & took some prisoners and tho' led astray by the guide in the last part of the march arrived at a neck of land on the east side of the Entrance of the harbour. where our fleet lay & there Embark'd without any molestation all aboard between 9 & 10 A:M: of 6th. Septr. having burnt above 50 Vessels and a good deal of stores of different kinds 2 or three men wounded & a few missing The Troops march'd I suppose near 20 miles few or none of the Inhabitants at home the Yankies all fled for it, their guilty consciences not daring to trust to us

Sunday 6th. Septr. fine weather wind abt. South lying at anchor in the mouth of the Bay the innermost ships warping out from the shore; a few of the Rebels making their appearance the Gallies & Scorpion fir'd some Shots at them, the fire of last night not yet extinguished – some talk of going to Martha's Vineyard

Monday 7th. Septr. a light breeze from the westwd in the morng. a Signal for the fleet to get under way but after sailing out abt. a mile the wind dyed away & they came to again, a donation of about one days fresh meat to the Troops – about 1 o'clock two Row Gallies & some boats with Troops set off from the fleet, went ashore on the westside of Clark's Cove, or Rick-etsons Neck where they burn't a Sloop & 2 or 3 houses – a few Yankies came down to the shore & fired at them after they embark'd & the Row Gallies fired some shot at them –

Tuesday 8th. last night a Gally & Detatchmt. of Marines in boats went up to Bedford to burn the remainder of the shipping in the harbour where they met with some opposition – there was a good deal of firing between 12 & 2 of Canons & Small arms & I hear some kill'd & wound'd.

The morng. warm & calm – about noon a little breeze from the So:westward when the fleet got under way & stood out, about 5 PM. the Como: made a Signal to gather round him, the wind light & more to So:wd. Elizabeth Islands to windward covering the mouth of the Buzards Bay. The fleet tacking to get near the

Como: – yesterday a distribution of Provisions in order to make an average among the fleet 'tis suppos'd we have about a fortnights – use of water restricted –
I hear the 42d. left a Serjt. & 7 ashore that night we made the incursion –
killed wounded & missing perhaps above 30, most of them missing – the wind dying away come to anchor in the Eveng. – some of the ships not out of the Bay yet. – These islands not well laid down in the Waggoner, they are both more numerous & extensive than in ye Chart[16]

Wednesday 9th. Septr. the morng. cool with a light breeze from So: or S:S:E: ye. fleet got under way about 7 & tack'd to windwd about noon some ships got thro' betwixt the 2d. & 3d. of Eliza. islands counting from ye. West   the weather thick & raining – a dirty afternoon & towards Eveng. came on to blow when the fleet came to anchor some to the North & some to the south of Eliza. islands we came to about 3 leagues NB.E. from the west end of Martha's Vinyard the passage we came throw abt. 1 leag No

Thursday 10th. it blew hard all last night about N. & NN.E in the morng. a Signal to get under way about 7 with a moderate breeze at No: the rest of the fleet got throw the Gut betwixt the Islands & the fleet stretched up to the Eastward tacking as the wind serv'd – about noon see a fleet to the westward of about 20 sail standing after us
continued our course betwixt Marthas Vinyard & Eliza. Islands a strong tide setting to the westwd. see some of the headmost ships brot. to others astern   we got up about sun set when the fleet anchor'd in a Bay near the East end of Marthas Vinyard, a Signal for the Coms. offrs. of the flank Corps & 33d. –
The fleet astern of us are small Vessels from Rhode island come to take off what live stock we can get on this Island where we hear there is a great deal

Friday 11th. fine cool wr. wind No: & N.N.E. the 3d. & 4th. Brigades except the 33d. Regt. landed under the Command of Lt. Colol. Stirling to collect what stock they can & the rest of the

Troops are to go with Genl. Grey to Nantucket to destroy what Privateers or vessels they find there but no word of our moving yet this day at Noon – N:B: a flag of truce came from the Island yesterday Eveng: to know our business, & were told it was to get what stock of Cattle & Sheep was intended for the French fleet which if they would drive down to the shore & bring in their arms (for they Register here 500 militia) they would not be molested – This end of the Island seems to be well Inhabited & a good deal of wood on it, & this bay seems to be safe anchorage against So:ly & W:ly wind, nearly opposite is a pretty large Village – see the Horse Shoe Shoal from No: to N.E. & Cape poge about E. the bottom of this Bay So: NB: only 150 of each Regt. & 300 of the 42d. landed this morng. about 1200 in all, some advanced into the Country 5 or 6 miles. no word of our division moving yet – Drank the annniversary of Brandywine in a dozen of wine, got by handsome chance fr: Leonard

Saturday 12 Septr: pleasant cool wr. wind N:E:ly – The Brigade Major came along side about 10 to tell Col: Meadows yt. as many offrs. as he chose might go ashore for the day – went ashore accordingly & took a walk – the Inhabitants busy in driving down sheep & cattle to the shore & bringing in their arms – the island suppos'd to contain above 50,000 Sheep – 10,000 to be sent to Rhode island & some hundred Cattle, which will be embark'd today: the Troops ashore & on board got 2 days fresh meat – the island call'd 20 miles long & 6 broad, this Bay called Holms Hole, the principal Town 7 or 8 miles off called adgar [Edgartown] or old Town to the S:E: of this some Indians the aborigine of the island still inhabit here & have a Town – poor sandy soil, low scrubby woods, raise some Indian corn & rye sheep & Black Cattle, the former of a small, the latter a large breed – the people true Yankies The Rhode island fleet came out of the Bay in the Eveng. full of sheep & cattle –

Sunday 13th. Septr. cool wr. wind N:E: – The fleet with sheep for Rhode island sail'd this morng. at daybreak they carried above 6000 sheep, & are said to return for more – sent likewise to Lord Howe's fleet, 300 sheep & 150 Bullocks

The Inhabitants bring their arms but slowly, only 300 yet & say their stock of Sheep was not above 20,000 – a severe Reprimand in Genl. Grays orders today to the Troops ashore for their irregularity particularizing the 17th. 37. & 46. Regt.

had a walk ashore – a schooner arrived about noon we suppose with some orders – a signal for masters in ye afternoon who were told they are to take in as much live stock as they can –

no wine for some days past – Two days fresh Beeff to be issued to all the Troops

Monday 14th. Septr. very cool wr. & the wind continues between the No: & East – Embarking some sheep & some Cattle on board the Transports & making ready to leave this place; the Nantucket scheme we suppose will not take place. in the Eveng. a S:gnal for all Boats to be on board &ca.

Tuesday 15th. The wind & wr. continues in the Morng. a signal to get under way[,] those at the mouth of the Bay got out presently, but those that were within did not get out till the Eveng. The Como: & those that were out first, lay too for the rest of the fleet & when all pretty well up made sail about dusk & stood on to the westward, with a light breeze from N.E.

Genl. Grey's thanks to the Troops for their Behavior since under his Command & acquaints them of the intended Expedition to Nantucket which he is obliged to relinquish, in consequence of orders to return & join the army –

Wednesday 16th. made Rhode Island early this morng. between 7 & 8 a Signal to ly too when near the entrance of ye. harbour some flat Boats & small craft sent off to Rhode island, & about 1/2 after 9 AM. made sail again & stood to the westward with a light breeze from S:E all sail set at 10 Block island WBS. about 5 leagues at one abreast with Block island & soon after made Fishers island, towards eveng. the Breeze increased, at dusk the Como: lay to for the fleet to come up & then went on under easy sail showing a light about 9 it came on to blow at S:E: still and blew very hard all night, during whh. the fleet lay to, under small sail, very dark & rainy –

Thursday 17th. Septr. after day light the Gale moderated when the fleet made sail & stood up the Sound; some ships got inbay'd on Long island & came to an anchor, about Sharp point – the morng. rainy & foggy & as the day advanced the wind fell away the Como: & some others got up to Whitestone & anchor'd there, but the wind failing us we & some others brought to at Frog point about noon, & in the Eveng. when the tide turn'd got round the point and anchor'd with the Rest, where we Embark'd – [17]

Friday 18th. wind about South – orders to send the Baggage ashore & to be ready to Disembark tomorrow morng. at daylight – a long string of Promotions in Genl. orders, in which appointed Capt. 18 Augt. – one Campbell from 57th. put in on us, with I think great injustice to Rutherford who has only got the Capt. Ltcy.[18] – 8 or 9 Transports behind –

Saturday 19th. southerly wind & pleasant wr. – The Troops landed in the morng. & march'd soon after, in two divisions 1st. Battn. Grrs. took up their ground about 4 miles from Newtown towards Bedford about 2 o'clock on the right of the 2d. Battn. Grs.; the Light Infantry & the Brigades some where betwixt that & Bedford we have good ground facing about N.W. to Bushwick – we hear that Byron in arrived at last & that Lord Howe is to go home – a Detachmt. of 10 Regts to go to the West Indies under Genl. Grant, & some other divisions of the army in agitation – Strange manoeuvreing.

Sunday 20th. Septr. the ships that were left behind in the Gale of wind arrived at Whitestone last night & the Troops landed this morng. & march'd to their respective ground, a straggling rear. – wrote an addition to my letter of 25th. Augt. to AH: to go by this Pacquet or the man of war – the 10th. 45th. & 52d. Regts. are to be draughted in a day or two

Monday 21st. Septr. warm weather the 10th. Grr. Compy. left the Battn. this morng. to be drafted, those Regts. that are to be drafted go to make up those that are destin'd for the West

Indies – some excursion going on – the Light Infantry under orders of readiness, & 200 Light dragoons –

Tuesday 22d. got orders last night to march in the morng. by 3 o'clock – under arms at 3 & march'd off at 4 oclock to Red hook where we embark'd on board of Transports & flat Boats & landed at Paulus Hook [–] the four flank Corps 3d. & 4th. Brigades & some light horse[;] & flat boats went over to York island to bring some troops from thence – the Guards I believe – those from Long island march'd as they landed to the heights of Bergen where they halted & Cook'd – the Guns horses & Baggage &ca. getting ashore Lord Cornwallis Commands & has Genl. Grey with him – but don't know yet what this Expedition in the Jerseys is to be – the Battery at N:York fired a Royal Salute in Commemoration of the Day, & at 1 oclock the fleet did the same 7 or 8 double deckers & some frigates lying off N:York some ships of war lying off Staten Island & some at Sandy hook – the Eagle went down today to go home – wind about East – Adml. Gambier Commands at N York & Byron is gone to Rhode island – in the Eveng. the troops moved on to the Environs of Bergen where they hutted for the night. the people all at home – got a letter last night from T:A: dated 2d. June, by the Pembroke Capt. Boyd who I hear was kill'd in his passage out. –

Wednesday 23d. The Troops march'd this morng. day light to the No:ward, it came on rain in the morng. & continued to rain & blow all day long – pass'd thro' English Neighbourhood, at the head of which the Guards, & Brigades halted, the Grrs. on t'other side the mill & Liberty pole, & the Light Infantry Light horse & Lord Rawdons Corps, towards Newbridge, we got a compleat ducking today – a Picquet of the Rebels taken at Liberty pole by a few Light horse –

Thursday 24th. Septr. The weather clear'd up the Grrs. moved in the afternoon about a mile to higher & better ground, the Light Bobs at Newbridge they sent to Hackinsack today a few Compys. who met with nothing – two days fresh meat for all the offrs. of this army – we hear Genl. Kniphausen with a strong division has moved out from Kings Bridge while we make a sweep into the Country for the purpose of Collecting forage – [19]

Friday 25th. a fine day, took a walk to Newbridge 3 miles by the road but less in a line a pretty little Village with a Bridge over the Sackiny River to which the tide comes & is navigable for small craft; 2 miles down on the N:W side is Hackinsack, a larger Village we are making a work on the high ground about 1/2 mile north side of Newbridge, a square[,] the Grrs. give 200 of a Working party in ye. morng. the 15th. Regt. came up from Bergen & posted there – fresh meat to the men – went down to the Regt. to call on Colol. Stirling but he was out, saw him just as I was coming away – the lads all well – got 3 bottles port, & near 1/2 gallon Rum from Norrie – drink scarce in Camp –

Saturday 26th. some rain last night & this morng. – Genl. Clinton came to Camp last night & I hear is to stay some time, & that Washington has divided his Army, some at Peekskill & some in Connecticut – fresh meat – The Genl. went to Hackinsack with a reconnoitering party, & has taken up his Quarters at Newbridge – 100 Waggons come over to Collect the forage & some Commissarys to get Cattle – din'd with the Regt.

Sunday 27th. Septr. pleasant wr the 17th. Regt. went this morng. to cover HeadQurs. – The Genl. gone off today for New York He flies about like an apparition –
The work on t'other side Newbridge going on
In the eveng. got orders to be ready to march at 10 o'clock at night. –

Monday 28th. march'd last night at 10 Oclock, one Column under Lord Cornwallis consisting of the Guards[,] 1st. Battn. Grenadrs. & the 42d. moved from the Picquet ground in front the Liberty pole at 12 on the road to Tapawn where we arrived about sunrise & found the Village evacuated by about 500 militia who had got intelligence of our coming by two deserters, – another column under Genl. Grey consisting of the 2d. Battn. Light Infantry & Grenadrs. and 2 Regts. march'd by another road

222

to the northward and about an hour before day surprized a Cantonment of the Enemys Light horse of about 100 of whom they Bayoneted some 40 or 50 took between 30 & 40 prisoners the remaining few escaped, they were Lady Washingtons Light Dragoons The Col: (Bailer) & the Major both very badly wounded & taken – that Column likewise started a picquet of militia about sunrise near the Village of Tapon & took most of them prisoners – The 71st. Regt. & Simcoe's Corps cross'd the north river last night and appear'd at Tapawn soon after we arrived there but met with nothing in their way

The Troops halted their till the afternoon & then march'd back to yr. respective Encampments, & brought in some Cattle – pretty much fatigued, marching & halting far above 20 hours & little to eat or drink

Tuesday 29th. Septr. fine weather & warm, rested after yesterdays fatigue orders for clearing the Invalids to 24 instt & 2 months pay to be given to the offr who takes charge of them home to be ready 1st. Octr. our men to get credit for 5 pair hose 1/8[,] Bonnet 4 1/2d[,] Plaid 5/6 sent those wt the Genls. Coy.

A Party of 2 or 300 Rebels came down towards where we are making the work on north side of Newbridge & fired away at a great distance for above an hour when a party of Light Infantry dash'd out after them & drove them off –

Wednesday 30th. pleasant weather mounted picquet this morng. an hour before day, there was a good deal of firing in the night towards the Picquets of Lord Rawdons Corps –

Thursday 1st. Octr. 1778 came off Picquet this morng. all quiet. The two Redoubts on t'other side New Bridge are finish'd they are Squares with a platform for 1 Gun in each –

The foraging going on below by Vessels, – a large foraging party out yesterday in front for the use of the Garrison & rooting parties – The Guards cover'd –

This is the day appointed for all officers non Commisioned officers & invalids order'd home, to be ready to Embark –

Wrote to T:A: to go by some of those that are going home,

223

will send it to NYork tomorrow – sent by Bonton who put in ye. mail.

Friday 2d. Octr. another large foraging party out today towards Tapan, some Regts. from the Brigades cover, they bring the Hay down to the Mill about 5 miles below this in waggons & there put it on board Vessels – it will take a great while to lay in enough at this rate for the Winter – 5000 horses will eat a great deal of hay 1 1/2 tons each –
Adml. Byron arrived at New York & Genl. Pigot, – none of ships sail'd yet for Britain – a Detachmt. of 500 under Capt. [Patrick] Ferguson gone to Egg harbour

Saturday 3d. Octr. pleasant weather hear a good deal of firing of Cannon down about Staten island or Eliz: Town.
The Invalids &ca. to Embark tomorrow all those of the Grr. Compy. that were wounded in Hospital are discharged & recommended viz seven wounded at Monmouth – foraging going on in the Neck today   must write some letters

Sunday 4th. Octr. last night wet & blowy, today cold & rain – wrote to AH: & D:M: sent them to the Regt. to go to N.York by a Serjt.   they are to send there tomorrow –
put the stone & lost my sleeve button   Orders in the Eveng. to be under arms at 4 in the morng. –

Monday 5th. fine weather   two Battns. Light Infantry 1st. Grenadrs. one Battn. Guards, 33d. Regt. & 2d. Battn. 42d. all the Dragoons except an offr. & 20 & the Volunteers of Ireland – march'd this morng. & took post on the heights of Hackensack & about the Village while the Waggons were employed in carrying off the forage – staid there till the eveng. witht seeing any of the Enemy & return'd to our respective Encampments – they brot. off 240 waggon load of fine Hay.
A french Lt. of man of war come to NYork from Count D'Estaing about ye. exchange of prisoners, it seems they have taken the Thunder Bomb & Senegal Sloop, poor Inglis   two frigates arriv'd at the Hook –

Tuesday 6th. Octr. very fine wr. The 23d. Grenadr. Compy. Capt. [Thomas] Peters joined the Battn. this morng. –

Wednesday 7th. fine weather   The ships for Britain not sail'd yet, nor the Pacquet –

Thursday 8th. a large foraging Party out today towards Tapan I went out with a party for Vegetables of 105 file with arms which passes for a Picquet in this Battn. got plenty about 4 miles off – a great inclination to plunder & to be licentious among these Grenadrs. – confin'd two –
Came out with yesterdays Gazzette a Manifesto and Proclamation dated 3d. Octr. to the Congress, Assemblies &ca. &ca. from the Commissioners, making them an offer of peace & reconciliation on the most liberal terms & a free pardon to all Descriptions of people, to continue in force to the 11th. Novr. –
a Report of some Engagement of the fleets at home –

Friday 9th. fine mild weather   The Albion a 74 & the last of Byrons fleet arrived at the Hook in 30 days from Lisbon, being put in there dismasted   no war declared when she left Lisbon nor no word of any sea engagement – a Vessel from Halifax in 11 days all well there, – a fleet of Victualers from Corke come in – Adml Gambier at Rhode Island in the Colloden –

Saturday 10th. Octr. Showery & blowy in the forenoon & heavy rain in the afternoon from the N.E.

Sunday 11th. it blew & rain'd hard all last night & today, could not keep ourselves dry; lay in bed 18 hours

Monday 12th. fair weather & sunshine – The Savage Sloop of war arrived at N:York with account of an action between the British & french fleets on the 27th. July, the British had 133 killed & 373 wounded & kept the sea, the french loss not known, they form'd the line after that action in the Evening, but went off in the night –
Adml. Keppel had been refitted and gone to sea again; but no war declared. but orders to burn, sink, & destroy the french wherever we meet them – The Augt. Pacquet had sail'd before the

Savage came away – the west India expedition to go on – making ready to move –

Tuesday 13th. we (the troops in Jersey) march'd between 7 & 8 by the left & carried our straw with us to the ground betwixt the main road & Fort Lee the Grrs. occupied that ground where the Rebels were Hutted two years ago –

Wednesday 14th. we march'd again in the morning to the ground near Bergen & some cross'd over from Powlis hook – some desertion in the Battn. these two days past 8 gone off – NB New Bridge & the two Redoubts near that were destroyed the evening befor we march'd – Maxwell with about 700 at Aquackinack & the Lord Stirling with 2 Brigades at Pyrhymas [Paramus]

Thursday 15th. The troops crossing over all day from Powlis hook to Brooklyn we the Grrs. got over about 2 o'clock & march'd to our old ground, where we found our tents & pitch'd them, but no baggage came that day – the 23d Coys: gone to their Regt. again

Friday 16th. Octr. frosty morng. very cold last night, nothing but my Great Coat & a little straw – our Baggage arrived this afternoon. the officers horses not come over yet

Saturday 17th. fine clear wr. & frosty nights – orders for the flank Companies of the 4th. 5th. 15th. 27th. 28th. 35th. 40th. 46th. 49th. & 55th. to join their Regts. immediately – 165 days Bat & forage money to be issued to those 10 Regts. immediately, & to the rest of the army 1st. of next month – the offrs. going on the Expedition to give in their horses to the Qr.Mr.Genl. who will pay for ym.
Colo: Meadows in Battn. orders takes leave of the Grenadrs. with much Esteem Admiration & Respect – many promotions in the orders almost every day, much buying & selling, long prices & short services.

Sunday 18th. Octr. fine wr. – the 5th. 15th. & 27th. went this morng. to join their Regts. on Staten island, the other Coys. to join yr. Regts. tomorrow on York island a good deal of firing of Canon down about the Hook these two morngs. past

Adml. Byron there with part of his fleet, some lying without ye. Hook

Monday 19th. The Augt. Pacquet arrived yesterday, got letters today from AH. D.M. & my Fr. dated latter end of July. no remarkable public News as they sail'd before the Sloop of War that came last –

Admiral Byron sail'd yesterday from the Hook with 13 ships of the Line & some frigates. the fleet bound home & to Halifax sail'd along with him[,] he is to convoy them some distance off the Coast it was a large fleet altogether – probably he may fall in with D'Estaing.

Tuesday 20th. Octr. The fine weather continues – went to NYork about a little business, din'd with Lord Balcaras the Town a mere scene of confusion – The Expedition going forward but slowly – The 71st. under orders for Embarkation & some other Corps are likewise talk'd of to leave this – every thing wears the face of disorder, confusion, and undetermin'd councils at present. God knows how it will end –

Wednesday 21st. The 17th. 44th. & 57th. Regts. march'd this morng. to Fort Kniphausen to occupy the ground of the 71st. – tete comme ça & dined with us today, sat late

Thursday 22d. Charming wr. a Genl. Court Martial setting for the tryal of some officers & men – A pleasant ride to the Hill –

a Pacquet to sail the mail to be closed tonight Lord Rawdon says. Chas Grant dined wt. us – a talk of the troops here Hutting for the Winter –

Friday 23d. Octr. cool & pleasant sat a court martial at 10 o'clock after that wrote a letter to AH: & sent it express to New York to try for the Pacquet – put on board –

Saturday 24th. cloudy, a ride spoke to Coll. Stirling about the Brown donation cloth for trouzers to the men – we are to get our share –

The Genl. Court Martial trying today Lt [Robert] Jackson of the 57th. Grrs. for Disrespectful behavior to Lt. Coll. [Henry] Hope – a long charge of 6 pages given in against him

Sunday 25th. Octr. cloudy sent a state of the Grenrs. to the Regt. & recommended to be Corpls. Rod. McDonald John Forsyth & Alexr. Leslie
called on Mrs. Long John Grant I hope they are better match'd in temper than in size, he is 6 feet 6 Inches & she is a[s] little as AH: –
The Regs. for the Expedition Embark today, – a Royl. Salute at New York for the Accession –

Monday 26th. Cloudy wind E: & S:E wrote letters today to R:M. Dr.F. & Fr. to go by Capt. Munro, who I hear is to sail tomorrow for Clyde under convoy of a fleet of arm'd ships for Corke, the Pacquet goes at same time – Munro's & Crawfords notifications in the orders –

Tuesday 27th. cloudy wind S.E. a ride to Hell Gate, about 6 miles by our old camp near Newton, in 76[,] the 17th. Dragoons at Hell Gate & Newtown sent off my letters to Capt. Munro who recd. them –

Wednesday 28th. warm wr. a great number of prisoners arriv'd yesterday from the Rebels, mostly Hessians the 42d. got 44. more coming – poor creatures they have been often ill used & mostly in jails all the time – din'd at the Regt. wt. Capt. Grant stay'd late, – Drumr. McLeod that was taken 23d. Febry. 77 Return'd to ye. Comy. many promotions in the orders almost every day, – the Expe[di]tion Drop down to the Narrows, & the Cork Ships &ca. that are going home

Thursday 29th. Octr. cool wind S.E. Dull Camp – din'd alone – Sir Wm. Eskine has been out in the Country for some days past looking out for Cantonments for the Troops that are in Long Island

Friday 30th. fine wr. & warm got my Subsce. from the Paymrr. to the 24th. instt. £24.5. &ca. & my dinner but he never gives the offrs. an abstract with their pay, – called at R[utherfur]ds. in the Eveng. –

Saturday 31st. much Rain & wind from the N.E. cold & uncomfortable

The Regt. getting Brown trouzers of donation cloth, sent some of the Grrs. to get their measures taken yt. we may get our share – Capt. [Francis] G[raham] of the 37 Compy. & we club'd dinners today –

Sunday 1st. Novr. cold wind N:E. sent the Compy. to the Regt. to hear divine service –

Commandg. offrs. of Compys. called together by Colo: Hope to consult on best method of drawing & dividing the prize money for taking the Delaware frigate – agreed to sell the Bill tho' at some discount (4 P cent) & divide equally among the Survivors a Companys share £45. 13 – before the deduction of 4 P cent & we get only as a Compy. & a 1/2 which I don't think was fair – [20]

Monday 2d. Blew very hard last night & this morng. from the N:E: qr. & very cold – Genl. Grant & his Expedition sail'd on Saturday, their destination not known yet to us – built a Wigwam around my tent – On Saturday the 31st. ultio. the 16th. Light Dragoons were drafted, the 17th. got most of them – a Pacquet to sail in a few days – we hear the Septr. Pacquet is taken –

Tuesday 3d. Novr. frost last night the day pleasant & sunshine – orders for the flank corps to be form'd into one Battalion each, the Light Infantry under the Command of Lt. Colo: [Robert] Abercromby & the Grenadrs. of Lt. Colo: [Henry] Hope – more promotions & the Court martial dissolved – Colo [John] Yorke took his leave of the 1st. Battn. Grrs. in a verbal message by the Adjut. wishing us much happiness & Glory – Genl. Grant sailed from ye Hook

Wednesday 4th. Novr. pretty cold wind at N:W: – orders in the morng. to have the waggons loaded by 8 o'clock & to march at 9 – before 9 the 1st. Battn. got under arms & drew up on the right of the Parade when presently after the 2d. Battn. march'd from their Encampment by 1/2 Comys. to that of the 1st. who when they came near their left they presented arms & beat a march, the 2d. Battn. then form'd on their left & return'd the complet. & Colo Hope rode up & took the Command, they were then form'd into one Battalion, according to Seniority of Companies & march'd off by 1/2 Compys.

Right Wing.   Left Wing
7. 22. 26. 37. 43. 57. 64.   71.71. 63. 44: 42d. 33. 23. 17

arrived at Jamaica between 12 & one & Encamp'd at the West end near the English Church, the Light Infantry more to the east & back of the Town – the offrs. have to go into houses the best way they can till the Quarters are settled – The Town will be much crowded with the offrs. & the men will be obliged to hutt – we got a room in Doctr. Ogdens in the meantime, – old acquaintances –

Thursday 5th. blows very hard at N.W. sent off a letter for AH. by [Lt. Robert] Rollo to York to go in the Pacquet. – dated 3d. –

Friday 6th. moderate weather   nothing done about settling the Qrs. yet – we hear Colo: Hope is to go home & Colo: Yorke is to command the Battalion of British Grenadrs. – sent to Newton for more Cloth for trowzers

Saturday 7th. Cloudy, like to rain   a good deal of rain last night – a ride to the plains – Capt. Smith din'd with us, & Docr. Robison came in the Eveng. – sat late & drank too much.

Sunday 8th. very fine day a ride to the Bay, 3 or 4 miles off an Engineer & some workmen & tools came yesterday to give directions & assist in making Hutts for the men. The Qr.Mr. with some Inhabitants taking a list of houses for quarters for offrs.
Long orders of Coll. Hopes given out formerly to the 2d. Battn. about passes & Parades &ca. &ca. &ca.

Monday 9th. wet wr. in the morng. – din'd chez Monsr. Le

Coll. a very good dinner & claret   Lt. [Allan] McLean join'd the Company today

Tuesday 10th. fine wr. – The Ground for the hutts being mark'd out in the morng. on the So: side of the hill north of Town, the men with the few tools they had, broke ground & fell to work to make hutts for their abode in Winter, each hutt 24 feet by 12 to contain 12 men the wall partly dug in the face of the hill, & the rest made up of sod, the roof to be covered with cedar branches & straw or thin sod – they all front the South & are sheltered from the No: winds by the ridge –
on the parade in the Eveng. the offrs. drew for their Quarters, some good & some not – I've got Saml. Sacket above 2 miles off towards the ferry –
The Congress's Manifesto in the Papers, appealing to God for their conduct, & not only despising the threats of Great Britain but threatening in their turn, with much ostentation & vain glory – audacious wicked Rascals.

Wednesday 11th. Novr. a Storm of wind & rain – sent to New York for my Baggage & some stores, but the bad wr. prevented their coming today

Thursday 12th. fine weather   went to look at my Billet – a cold room in a Country house above two miles from here on the high road   2 Lts. in Town & one in the Country if we don't get some change made it will break up our little mess – The Hutts go on pretty well each of Sumach   Compys. have 4 hutts, the Highlanders 6 & 7   my Baggage & Stores arrived in the Eveng. –

Friday 13th. a good day for the work – a few days ago a fleet sail'd with the 71st. Regt. 2 Hessian Battns. & 4 or 5 of the new Raised Corps, the whole under the Comd. of Lt. Colo: [Archibald] Campbell 71st. secret expedition

Saturday 14th. Novr. cold & windy with frost at night; the Hutts come on but slowly this cold weather

Sunday 15th. cold N:W: wind   the 23d. Compy. joined yesterday – Some ships of war came in to N:York, who bring account the Monsr. D'Estaing has got out of Boston & given Mr. Byron the slip, who sail'd after him, but his fleet was dispersed by a storm, he with 9 or 10 sail has got into Rhode Island, & some into N:York but no word of the Comte –

Monday 16th. still blowy & cold   took a ride to the plains to see the Ludlow's, & din'd with the Coll. – cold working at the hutts – ask'd Capt. [Warren] Simondson in a note to change Billets, but he declined it –

Jamaica Long Island 17th Novr. 1778   fine weather for the Season, frosty nights   the men working at the hutts which go on tollerably well, –

Wednesday 18th. Novr. rain in the morng. & foggy – moved my Quarters & went to my Billet about 2 miles out of Town on the York road, at the house of Saml. Sacket, where I have a pretty good room & a bed closet of it, & a store room, the use of the Kitchen & a Stable. and they seem to be civil people – took a ride to Newtown & saw the Regts. hutts, they are more forward than we are

the Coll. not at home, told Robison I could not dine with him – Lord Cornwallis then looking at the hutts – came home to dinner, nothing but a little salt meat & greens – Mrs. McCraw taken possession of the Kitchen. – [21]

Thursday 19th. Novr. cold   The hutts coming on but slowly, it is almost time now for the men to be under better shelter than an old tent

Friday 20th. good Novr. wr.   ride up & see the hutts every day – & call on Lt. [Robert] Potts now & then who is sick   Docr. Robison & Lt. [Alexander] Innes din'd with us, or rather after us, tho' we waited some time for them –

Saturday 21st. hard frost last night   Lord Cornwallis looking at our hutts today – he is to go home with the Commissioners very soon –

Sunday 22d. clear frosty weather   a want of Nails for the

hutts – Capt. [John] Smith breakfasted in his way to N.York with letters to go by Capt. [Primrose] Kennedy, sent one by him for my Fr. with one inclosed in it to AH: dated 20th. – Capt. Smith & C: [James] Campbell came late to dinner, but we made it up in drink Lt. [Francis] Lea of ary. din'd with us too – We hear the Sommerset a 64 Gun Ship is castaway on Cape Cod, near 100 of her people lost, & the rest taken prisoners by the Yankies, – very bad indeed – every body apprehensive about Genl. Grants Expedition falling into the hands of Comte D'Estaing, no word of either of them yet; they sail'd about the same time   nor no certain accounts of the condition of Byrons fleet –

Monday 23d. cold NW. threaten'd snow in the morng. – the work at the Hutts at a stand for want of Nails & straw. all the waggons here about gone to the Eastward for boards to make doors, windows & Beds, which should have been provided before, but there seems to be a want of that care of & attention to the Troops that is necessary, & that we used to experience, matters & things seem to [be] conducted & carried on in a very unsteady manner, in this army.

Tuesday 24th. Novr. fine wr. took a walk to Newtown & dined wt. the Regt. – The Commissioners to Embark today or tomorrow, Lord Cornwallis & Genl. Grey goes home with them – Lt. Col Hope goes home for the winter, the Senior Capt. Command in the meantime till Lt. Col: York comes –

Wednesday 25 – fine frosty wr. got nails & some straw, going on wt. the Hutts –

Thursday 26th. a fine day, – went & dined wt. C: Rutherfurd & stayd till near 11 at night – a number of the Grrs. & L: Infantry offrs. out hunting a drag today – The Commander in Chief expected – The Expedition of the 71st. &ca. supposed to sail today –

Friday 27th. Novr. fine weather   sent to flushing fly for Thatch for the Hutts, no more straw to be had –

Saturday 28   likewise a very fine day   got all our Hutts cover'd

233

today, & are making up the births – had Col: Stirling Capt. & Mrs. Rutherfurd &ca. to dine, a pleasant party –

Sunday 29th. soft wr. & hazy – a Card from the Col: for us to come & keep St. Andrew with him but he was too late, we having ask'd some people to dine with us –

Monday 30th. Novr. 1778 rainy morng. sent the Compy. into their hutts in the forenoon, & gave out an order concerning their behaviour which I hope they will attend to – had four or 5 friends to dine with us, & being all honest fellows we pour'd a copious libation to the St. with mirth & good humour

Chapter VII

'dancing in the dirt'

Long Island
1 December 1778 to 28 May 1779

During the winter and spring of 1779, Sir Henry Clinton undertook few operations with the British army at New York – not just because that army had been depleted by recent detachments but also because Clinton, thinking he had been neglected by the British government, was temporarily preoccupied with getting larger forces and greater authority for conducting the war. In December he did make an abortive effort to liberate the British troops that had surrendered at Saratoga (he had learned that they were being transferred from New England to the middle colonies but was too late to intercept them when they crossed the Hudson River at King's Ferry). He also sent a detachment to raid the coast of New England, to comply in part with the government's new strategy of relying increasingly on the navy and Loyalists to continue the war against the rebels. But until late in the spring, Clinton was in no mood to do more. Having sent 8,000 troops to the West Indies and Georgia, being dissatisfied with the admiral who commanded the North American squadron, and doubting the viability of the government's strategy, he asked for more troops, a more energetic naval colleague, and more latitude in shaping strategy. If the government could not, or would not, satisfy his requests, he asked that he be permitted to resign. Not until May, until an energetic and congenial officer arrived to command the North American squadron, was Clinton willing to think once more of offensive operations, of a raid in the Chesapeake that would facilitate a thrust up the Hudson River and, perhaps, a decisive battle with the Continental army.[1]

Because Clinton was reluctant to undertake offensive operations and because the British grenadiers were assigned relatively secure quarters on the west end of Long Island, John Peebles and his men passed the winter and spring of 1779 more quietly than they had the previous winter in Philadelphia. Once they had taken part in the unsuccessful attempt to liberate the Canadian army at King's Ferry and settled into their quarters around Jamaica, they had few duties. Peebles occasionally served as officer of the day for his battalion – receiving and making routine reports, sending out patrols, and giving a dinner for other officers on duty. He also oversaw the discipline of the men in his company; inspected their arms, clothes, and equipment; and accompanied his men on the few occasions when they manoeuvered and fired with the battalion.[2] But there was rarely a day for more than five months when Peebles was not free for some informal diversion. There were many dinners with other officers and prominent Loyalists (occasionally, he dined 'very elegantly'), some evenings of cards and hard drinking, a few crude balls or country dances, and even an adventure or two with doxies from New York City.[3] And Long Island provided the security, as Pennsylvania had not, for such rural pleasures as hunting and sleighing.[4] Peebles' winter and spring of 1779 were, then, comparatively rustic but also quiet and agreeable.

Long Island
1 December 1778 to 28 May 1779

Decr. 1st. a day when most wandering Scotchmen have a head-ach – fine mild weather took a ride to expel the fumes of the port.

Wednesday 2d. a very fine day Still working at the hutts, trimming them in the inside & getting doors & windows made – one pane of glass to each hutt – bedding delivered out & some potts & axes –

Thursday 3d. roused this morng. early, the Battn. having got orders to march – The Light Infantry & Grenrs. march'd between 8 & 9 with their Guns to Brooklyn where they cross'd over to N:York & embark'd on board of transports lying in the N:River at the Hay Wharf – The Guards & some other troops having embark'd the Eveng. before & were lying up near Greenwich – as soon as we were on board we got under way directly & sailed up the North River as far as the Cheveaux de frize where we came to anchor at the turn of the tide – [5]

Friday 4th. got under way in the morning & stood up the River, when we were about Dob's ferry & Tarrytown saw a Column of our troops marching up the Country preceded by parties of Light horse, they Encamp'd, that night about TarryTown & we proceeded farther up the River & came too, near the Jersey shore about 5 miles below Kings ferry. our Ship stuck fast on the ground for a while but got off again with some assistance from the men of war – the Emerald frigate – the Commander in chief came up in her, but I believe went ashore at Tarry Town & join'd the troops there

Saturday 5th. up anchor early in the morng. & stood further up the River with the flood, the frigate, two Gallies & some transports ahead of us, when we got orders about 8 in the morng. that we the Grrs. & Light Infantry were to drop down to Tarrytown & should not have proceeded any further up that day. it being tide of flood we dropp'd anchor about 2 or 3 miles below Verplanks point   the Gallies being up that length fired some shot to shore on either side & soon after a body of men landed from the Transports on the Jersey shore, & having march'd a little way a Smoke arose that look'd very like the firing of small arms but believe it was only burning some houses tho' we saw about 200 of the Rebels at a house about a mile or two from thence   the troops staid ashore about an hour & Reembark'd again, & when the tide turn'd we all got under way down the River. the Master of our Ship (the Royl Scepter a Cork Victualer) seeing some of the Rebels near the shore & being fond of making a noise fired a parcel of his two pounders at them, but the chuckle head might as well have farted – we dropp'd down to near Tarry town that night

Sunday 6th. Decr. rain in the night   up anchor in the morng. & away down the River   the Troops ashore march'd early in the morng. back the same road again, we turn'd down with the tide as far as the Cheveaux de frize, near which our ship got a ground close in shore near the battery below Ft. Kniphausen but luckily we got her off again

Monday 7th. Decr. very fine wr.   got under way about 3 in the morng. & turn'd down with the tide as far as Greenwich 2 miles from N:York, where at the flood we drop'd anchor. and I sent an officer to York to receive orders, but soon after a boat came with a written order from Col [Robert] Abercromby to land the troops proceed to the Ship Yard, cross over to Brooklyn & march to Jamaica, which we accordingly did and arrived there about 3 oclock in the afternoon, – some Companies before us & some not yet arrived.

The purport of this Clintonian Expedition was to have intercepted Burgoynes people, whom the Rebels were marching to the Southward, but they cross'd the North River at Kings ferry two days before we got there, so we came back again

Tuesday 8th. Decr. rain in the night & a stormy day from the S:W: some more Company's arrived today

Wednesday 9th. better weather   more Compys. of Bobs & Grs. came up   I believe the whole are arrived now.

Thursday 10th. a wet storm – a letter from the Adjt. dated yesterday wrote by order of Col: York, containg. a Report of Capt. Lairds to Col: [John] York of the licentious & irregular behaviour of the Compys. that were on board the Royl. Scepter, & desiring another search to be made, – order'd the search, & wrote an answer to Col: York, vindicating my conduct & exposing the behaviour of that blackguard rascal the Master in terms more moderate than he deserved.[6]

Friday 11th. fair wr. & frost   Genl. Clintons letter to Lord George Germain of the 5 July in the paper of the 9th. instt., taken from a Rebel paper, giving account of the evacuation of Philada. his march thro' the Jersey, & the fight at Monmouth – better told than acted – Coll. Yorke spoke to me about the complaint of the Shipmaster & seems to be quite satisfyed with what I did, & advises me to go to N York to see how far the complaint is gone, as he was told it was Reported to the Comr. in Chief – [Capt. Jack] Hatfields Capt. complain'd too & we agreed to go to NYork together tomorrow –

Saturday 12th. fine frosty weather   sett off after breakfast Hatfield & I – got to Town 'tween 11 & 12 & found my chap at Capt. Lairds to whom I read the answer I had made to Coll. Yorke, which put the matter in another light; I Found he had been to Lord Rawdon with the complaint so I therefore went to his Lordship & show'd him the other side of the story and he was pleas'd to say that put the affair in quite another light, & assured me the Comr. in Chief did not know of it, so I made my bows and came off in the hopes of hearing no more of it. return'd in the Afternoon & dined with Jack Hatfield & Cuny

Lees account of the affair at Monmouth in todays Paper in vindication of himself, artfully drawn out, and well told, with praises on the Americans in general, & to the Yankys in particular, & some satirical wipes at Washington

Sunday 13th. Decr. bad wr. again no stirring out, a ship arrived in 10 weeks from Falmouth, no news transpir'd yet –

Monday 14th. clear frosty wr. a Review of the Compys. arms and Necessary's, some Shoes & Shirts wantg. the arms in pretty good order – The Light Infantry have got word that they are to march to the Eastward. went to Newtown to the Vendue of Gilchrists effects, & we din'd per engagement with the Major [Charles Graham] –

Tuesday 15th. a fine day – din'd with Capt. [Charles] McLean 43d. L[ight]:In[fantry]: prim'd – a Mercht. Ship arrived from England, above 11 weeks out – no war declared, nor no more engagements between the fleets at home, – they say D'Estaing is gone to [word faded]

Wednesday 16th. fine wr. & soft – we 42d. Grs. din'd with Capt. [George] Dalrymple & his officers, that Coy. is station'd at Newtown Creek, to cover Genl. Vaughans Quarters, & he has another Compy. of the 42d. on t'other side of the Creek close to his Qrs. – I came home in the Eveng, but some of the Boys got fou & played the fool – The 42d. Light Comy. came from N:Utrecht to Jamaica, to march with the Battn. when they go, –

Thursday 17th. wet wr. & S:W: wind some account in the papers of a Russian Squadron come to England –

Friday 18th. & Saturday 19th. pleasant weather, very gentle frost sat a Court Martial in the Offrs. Hutt –

Sunday 20th. Decr. vere fine soft wr. a ride to Newtown call'd on the R[utherfurd]s. – & the Major [Graham], & return'd to dine alone

Monday 21st. very fine mild & pleasant day – The Light Infantry march'd this morng. for the Eastend of the Island, where they are to cover the foraging for a month or six weeks. The Legion march'd a day or two ago for the same place – Hampton – out with my Gun in the marsh saw nothing but some Meadow

Larks – killed three – a hunt towards the Bay, but they lost the fox –

Tuesday 22d. it rained last night & then came on to snow & blow from the No: & freeze very hard, today clear & cold & the ground cover'd with snow   we hear the Octr. Pacquet is arrived at last –

Wednesday 23d. hard frost, & Snow in the afternoon, wind N: & N. E.   a Call from Colo: Ludlow, but he would not stay dinner. – The Pacquet left Falmouth 14 Octr.   great unanimity at home, – the British & french fleets at Sea – Russia & Spain mediators – Stocks rising & the Minority falling – a great number of the french West India men, & 3 of their East India men taken – Genl. Grant landed at Barbadoes.

in the eveng. a letter from AH: 20 Sepr. at Logan, Still anxious, had wrote by the Septr. Pacquet which was taken –

Thursday 24th: extreme cold   A Genl. Court Martial sitting at Jamaica today Lt. Col: Yorke Prest. for the tryal of some persons suspected of holding correspondence with the Enemy

Friday 25th. Decr. a great fall of Snow; had a wild Goose for Xmas   Dr.R[obison]: dined here, port wine & punch

Saturday 26th. it blew very hard at N: & N.E. & the snow drifted to such a degree that no person could stir out

Sunday 27th. Decr. very cold – The Roads shut up with banks of snow

Monday 28th. very cold Still wind N: on Duty at the Hutts, 1 Capt. 2 Lts. for 24 hours, the senior Lt. has the charge of the Qr.Guard, the Capt. seems to have nothing to do but to receive the Reports of the Companies send patroles & give a dinner and &ca. – 5 bottles

Tuesday 29th. more moderate   The Grenadrs. were muster'd at 11 o'clock   we had 70 private, 9 of which were on duty & 1 sick, 60 on the parade – a good many Ships at New York & thereabt. have suffer'd in the late storm

Wednesday 30th. Decr. moderate wr. inclin'd to thaw – a Report of Col: [Archibald] Campbells Expedition being landed in No:Carolina – finish'd a letter for AH: began 27th. to be sent off first oppy. –

Thursday 31st. a fine mild day and gentle frost, sent my letter to N:York by Lt. Dunbar, to go by the Paqt. or best conveyance –

Friday 1st. Janry. 1779 a very fine mild day & warm for the Season paid a Visit to the Ludlow's. we found the Judge & the Col: just going to dine with their Brother Daniel & they took us along with them, where dined very elegantly & spent the evening very agreably and came home with the judge – Major Graham & I –

Saturday 2d Janry. 1779 – a remarkable fine day – after breakfast & a dash of the judges entertaining conversation we bid him & his agreeable wife a good morng. the Col: gave us a convoy of a few miles, & a kind invitation to come and see him – got home between 12 & 1 Major Graham staid with us & Col: McP[herson]: & Capt. Grant came to dinner, took a moderate glass, & went in the eveng. by invitation of our Neighbour Mr. Betts to drink some warm Negus where we found a good many people & after a short ceremony the fiddle struck up & we all fell a dancing, the Newton Gentln. went away early, but we staid late

Sunday 3d. point de Nouvelles

Monday 4th moderate wr. – mounted at the Hutts; a Smoaky dark hole. 5 bottles call'd on Mrs. Cortland, & old Sally Combs

Tuesday 5th Janry. soft wr. & snow in the afternoon – Accounts from the Light Infantry that they have had a disagreeable cold march, and a good many men frost bit, but have got to plentifull Quarters at the Hamptons. 100 miles from here

Wednesday 6th. cold in the morng. but warm after – went to Newtown being sent for to get some Grenrs. got a Corpl. & 4, and to send the 3 Convalescents to the Regt. which makes us 77 R: & file to which the Compys. of the Regt. are levell'd exclusive of their prisoners. Return'd & din'd with Col: Yorke. easy & genteel –

Thursday 7th. fine soft wr. – went to the Regt. & got Abstracts & Money for the Comy, to 24 Decr. 78. Subsce. for myself to 23d Febry. & Bat & forage. – dined & spent the Eveng. wt. the Col: – Major [Archibald] Erskine there. Slept at Col: McP[herson]. he has got an appt. of 20/

Friday 8th. mild wr. we hear that the Corke fleet are arrived. – a Ball at Jamaica in the Eveng. about 16 Ladies, some of them from New York. danced till past 11, supp'd for an hour, & then danced for two more. danced & talked nonsense with Miss Ogden, a good piece, came home tween 3 & 4 in a sleigh, – post Voluptatem triste

Saturday 9th. sleet & rain – no stirring out today –

Sunday 10th. dirty weather & so was Monday, about 13 ships of the Corke fleet come in – we have been eating sower oatmeal for some time it is to be hop'd we will get some flour now –

Tuesday 12th went up to Town & saw my partner, being a fine day. They say this Stupid inelegant Ball will cost us £5. each, pox take 'em all.

Wednesday 13th. Janry. 1779 cold & frosty wr. – My Landlady for this fortnight past has almost every day shown some signs of insanity – She was some years ago confin'd in the Madhouse at Philada. –

Thursday 14th. clear & cold – on duty at the Hutts, 4 bottles in the usual style – a number of ships arrived from Halifax

Friday 15th. pleasant wr. dined at Colo: York's with Major Erskine, & staid supper, toute agreeable

Saturday 16th. fine wr. & cold Col: McP[herson]. Major Gr[aham]: & Capt. [Charles] Grant call'd in the forenoon & so did Maj. E[rskine] wanted them to stay dinner but they would not & insisted on my going with them – dined at the 2d. Battn.

mess & went to the Regtal. Club in the Eveng. lost money at Cards – much noise & little comfort Slept at Col: McP.

Sunday 17th a fine day – call'd on the R[utherfur]ds. & then on Capt. S[mith]: who is still confin'd within doors a dispute between him & Col: Stirling about the payment of his Company that were taken prisoners – The Commandg. offr. ought certainly to assist in recovering the Money he lost when taken, & then he will no doubt clear all the men – came home to dinner

Monday 18th. pretty cold looks like snow – The Queens Birth day a Ball to be at New York given by the General – A Ball at Jamaica anounced for friday next – the last cost us £4.7. – Cury. a take in –

Tuesday 19th. a fall of Snow from S:E: & So: some rain at night gave out clearance to the Compy. from 25 June to 24 Decr. 78 £259.8.7 1/4[,] Prize Money £66.15.11 1/4 – 18/9 each man –

Wednesday 20th. Jany. cold N.W. call'd on Col: Yorke – sent off Ball Cards to the Ludlow's – The offrs. to dine together on thursday 28th. N:B: in the Bag 120 guineas & 12 half Jo's £153.1s4. out of which I reckon myself in debt £140, or so – & I expect a balance from Major Gr[aham]: that will enable me to send home a little Bill of 40 or 50 –

Thursday 21st. clear & cold at NW up at the hutts in time but no parade – we din'd with Price today –

Friday 22d. moderately cold very fine Sleighing – Hatfield came & din'd with us – at the Ball in the Eveng. – no supper this time, – about a dozen Ladies, none of them handsome some old ugly & fat women, nothing very tempting to go above two miles & spend your money for amusemt. to others

Saturday 23 Jany. thaw with rain in the afternoon –

Sunday 24th. thaw & fog – on Duty at the Huts again 4 bottles – nothing extraordinary –

Monday 25th. rain last night and today, the snow almost all gone When I made my Report Col York told me the Pacquet was arrived, came home & found a letter from my Dr. little friend 20th. Octr. poor soul its anxious still about me; afraid some of my letters have miscarried – God grant us a happy meeting.

Tuesday 26th. snow from N.E

Wednesday 27th. fine wr. & warm sun went to Newtown to settle Accots. with Major Graham & Capt. Rutherfurd but the former was engaged, din'd at R[utherfur]ds.

Thursday 28th. Janry. Soft wr. a Battalion dinner at Polhemus's Genl. Vaughan was to have been there but he did not come – 31 at dinner Col: [Thomas] James & Col. [Archibald] Hamilton Guests a crouded room & not a good dinner we drank 6 doz: Claret 1 1/2 doz Mada. & 1 dozen port, beside porter & punch. much noise & little fun, staid till 10 & left them dancing in the dirt club 7 dollars

Friday 29th. soft thawing wr. a sober day at home –

Saturday 30th. rain'd all day a trio as usual –

Sunday 31st. the Snow almost all gone the roads very dirty – 11 Ships arrived from Corke – & some accots. from the Southward say that Col: Campbell is in Georgia

Monday 1st. Febry. 1779 fine day took the duty at the Hutts today for Capt. [William] Myers, nothing extra: there – 3 bottles – News from the West Indies that Adml. [Samuel] Barrington & Genl. Grant having taken possession of the Island of St. Lucia about the 12 or 13th. Decr. Monsr. D'Estaing made his appearance there with a Superior fleet & forces about the 16th. his troops landed on the 18th. & had a smart action in which they were repulsed & beat back by Brigr. Genl. [William] Meadows, with considerable loss – that they made another Attempt upon the Island on the 25th. with augmented force and were again repulsed by Genl. Meadows & drove back to their boats with

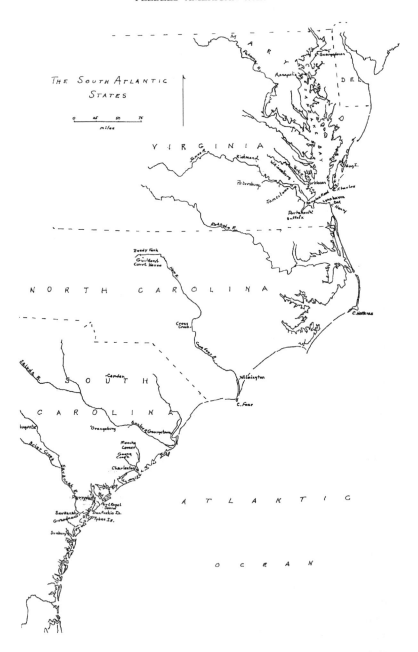

great Slaughter & made off with all haste to Martinico on hearing of Adml. Byron, who has them now Block'd up in Port Royale[7]

Tuesday 2d. Febry. foggy morng. but the day clear'd up & was warm the weather remarkably mild for the Season – went to Newtown & settled Accots. with Major Graham & Capt. Rutherfurd. the former in great dudgeon because I would not take orders on Gilchrists debts or wait till they were collected – din'd with Capt. Grant –

Wednesday 3d. fine mild wr. busy writing letters for the Pacquet that is to sail soon – Dispatches come from Col: Campbell who is in possession of Georgia – They took Savannah with very little loss on the 29th. Decr. – They landed at Girardots where about 50 Rebels fir'd upon the Light I: & ran off. kill'd Capt. [Charles] Cameron of the 71st. & a few of his Company, – about 800 made a Stand near the Town of Savanah with some Cannon but were soon routed by Sir Jas. Bairds Light Infantry; on the following days the Troops march'd further up the Country & chaced the Rebels into So: Carolina – Genl. [Augustine] Prevost from Florida took Sunbury 9th. Janry. & met Col: Campbell at Savanah[8] The Inhabitants were flocking to the Standard & taking the oaths of allegiance & the Troops preparing to proceed into So: Carolina –

Thursday 4th. fine wr. but dirty roads, wrote to my Fr. & to AH: gave the letters to the Adjt. to be forwarded by the Pacquet which is to sail next week inclosed a Bill of £50. to the old man.

Friday 5th. cold N:W: wind & frost went to Newtown to dine with Dr. Robertson a large Compy. & much wine, the Major not well pleas'd I see – came home at night & found the lads had not been idle there neither

Saturday 6 Febry. cold S:W: wind went to the Parade in the morng. took post on the Right Wing on account of the 38th. 54th. Companys having join'd the Battn. from Rhode Island two days ago, their light Compys. are come also & are to go to the east end – din'd at Newtown again today in order to be at the Club –

cros sick & out of humour, sat late & was tir'd of it in the Eveng.
it came on to snow & rain so I staid all night, Slept at the tavern.
An express from the Eastward two days ago, about the taking
a Rebel privateer of 16 guns, who ran ashore near Sagg harbour,
most of the crew escap'd in boats. – Major [Charles] Cochran
Legion

Sunday 7th. fine soft wr & warm very dirty roads the Snow
that fell last night melting away very fast, came home in the forenoon, & had a sober day –

Monday 8th. Febry. a fine day, the frost almost out of the
ground, the wr. remarkably soft & mild for the Season at the
parade, & paid some visits – din'd with C: [Thomas] Peter. came
home in the Eveng. & wrote a letter to T:A: acknowleding the
rect. of his of the 27th. April & 9th. Octr. –

Tuesday 9th. soft & foggy wind S:W: clear'd up towards noon,
took a walk & shot a large Squirel – very little sport here about,
a few quail but no getting a shot without a dog – sent T:As. letter
by Serjt. Smith who put in ye. mail had Company to dine, &
took a hearty glas

Wednesday 10th. the Wind S.W. & the wr. remarkably mild &
warm for the season Recd. letters from my Fr. & T:A: dated
6th. May 16th. June & 25 Octr. 1777 where they have been all
this time God knows a Frigate & some ships arrived from Halifax in 13 days

Thursday 11th. Febry. mild wr. Wind varriable like for snow
in the afternoon On Duty at the hutts – the Battalion took a walk
for an hour or so – Sat a Court Martial on one of the pioneers for
stealing – 5 at dinner, – 6 bottles –

Friday 12th. cloudy & raw Wind about So: –

Saturday 13th. S:W: winds & mild weather for the season –

Sunday 14th. rain in the morng but it clear'd up as the day
advanced The Company went to church – The Kings Speech to
Parliament on 26th. Novr. copied by Rivington from the Jersey

Gazzette – preparing for War, tho' he seems to wish for peace –
The Pacquet not sailed yet but some dispatches sent home in an
arm'd Vessel 8 or 10 days ago –

Monday 15th. pleasant wr. & warm   the Battalion manoeuvred
for an hour or so – took a ride to Newtown and call'd on the
happy little couple [the Rutherfurds], & promised to dine with
them tomorrow –

Tuesday 16th. this remarkbl fine wr. still continues. – Col:
Yorke march'd out the Battn. today Guns & all and we manoeuvred about in the fields for above 2 hours,   very warm – came
home & had an adventure with two Ladies from York – dress'd &
went to R[utherfurd]s. to dinner all three, where we stay'd till 8
o'clock – Mrs. R: shew'd me a letter from Sweet little Cate dated
9th. Jany.[9]

Wednesday 17th. foggy & rainy.   a Visit from my Landlady
who seems to be more compos'd of late –

Thursday 18th. & friday 19th. fine wr. the oldest people living
scarce remember so mild a season

Friday 20th. Febry. Wind West & pleasant wr. a fleet from
Corke arrived yesterday with News as late as 7th. Decr.   great
preparations making at home for a Vigorous exertion of the
Strength & Spirit of Great Britain   a great majority in Parliament – a fleet for Corke sail'd today   saw them out of the hook,
from the ridge   had the duty at the Hutts today   moderate – 3
bottles –

Sunday 21st. the fine weather still continues   wind So: & S.W.
hear'd the Decr. Pacquet is arrived so rode down to Newtown to
get my letters but found they were sent to Jamaica   ask'd a party
for dinner tomorrow.   came home & found 3 letters two from
AH: dated 20th. Novr. & 3d. Decr. the last ackg. mine of Sepr. &
Octr., had one from my Fr.

Monday 22d. Febry. Rainy foggy & warm; the wet day prevents
our friends from coming to see us.   some Expedition going on, I
believe the 42d. will be concern'd – the day clear'd up & the

Majr. [Graham] C:R[utherfur]d. & Dr. R[obison]. came after all to dinner – Col. Yorke & c: Peter sent apologies –

Tuesday 23d. fine wr. again the 42d. & 33d. made a move in the afternoon, but were countermanded & sent home again –

Wednesday 24th. fine wr. & westerly winds, went to N:York to stay a day or two & see their public amusements, but found there a Report that the Grrs. were to move, I staid but a little while in Town & came home to dinner, wrote a letter while I was in Town to AH: acknowledging the receipt of the two last & left it wt. Mr. Rivington to be forewordd the 33d. & 42d. Regts. march'd in the Afternoon & embark'd in flat boats about a mile S:W: of Brooklyn & after dark proceeded across the Bay

Thursday 25th. Febry. fine wr. a Sub: Serjt. & 24 men of the 42d. Gr. compy went to Genl. Vaughans as a guard till the 42d. Regt. return, we hear they are gone to the Jerseys some where about Elizabeth Town a good deal of firing hear'd thereabout this morng., rode to Newtown call'd on Mrs. R[utherfurd]

Friday 26th. much rain from S.W. The Troops that went to the Jerseys vizt. the 33d. & 42d Regts & Light Company of the Guards return'd yesterday evening – They landed near Elizabeth Town point by 2 or 3 o'clock of the morng. in marshy ground made a scatter'd broken march up to Elizh Town where they burnt the Barracks & some stores. Stayed some time in the place; in retiring they were closely follow'd by the Rebels who collected in numbers from the Neighborhood & fir'd upon our troops with their Cannon who had none to return so they made the best of their way to their boats with the loss of about 30 killed & wod – neither fun nor credit there –

Saturday 27th. a May day of wr. a long string of punishmts. & half the prisoners forgiven – a No. of the 43d sold yr. blankets[;] coming home after a ride met the happy little couple who came home & dined wt. us – An assembly last night at Jamaica – did not go –

Sunday 28th. encore le beau tems very warm went to Meeting

with the Company & heard a very decent sermon from Parson Burnet, whose wife was brought to bed lately a few months after marriage

Monday 1st. March St. David fine wr. still, we din'd with 23d Grs & celebrated St. Taffy with a copious libation – rote to R:M: & Fr. to go by Majr. [Norman] McLeod

Tuesday 2d. fine day wind So: Saw two ships go in to the hook – On duty at the hutts today 6 bottles this duty of the Capts. is to end tomorrow

Wednesday 3d. Rain from S:W: Battn. orders for a parade at sunset & the duty at the hutts reduced to a Subs Guard; we dined at Capt. Hatfields – Govr. Tryon made an excursion from Kingsbridge to Horseneck with 5 Battns. latter end of last week, kill'd a few Rebels took about 20 prisoners, & destroyed some salt works & 3 small Vessels –

Thursday 4th. fair wr. again NW a ride to the plains. some ships come in but have not heard what they are yet – our Parson din'd with us, – failing – [10]

Friday 5th. rained all last night & still continuous, clear'd up afternoon Genl. Vaughan having express'd a desire to dine with the Grenrs. (as the last invitation was misunderstood) a dinner was accordingly prepared & he came notwithstanding the badness of the day, was in good humour & staid till near 7 oclock – there was about 30 at Table, a plentifull dinner but ill laid down, a good deal of noisy mirth which is always the case on these occasions, came home about 8 oclock a good many staid till two or 3 in the morng & made a racket in the Village – £2.11.0

Saturday 6th. cold & raw with the Wind at E: & S:E: snow in the eveng

Sunday 7th. it snow'd all last night and some today, din'd at Genl. Vaughans with 1/2 doz more Grrs. got a neat little dinner & a dose of very good Claret, the little warrior in high good humour. lost the way coming home

Monday 8th. March fair weather & cool – took a pill last night
with an intention to live soberly for some time to try if that and
a few alter[n]atives &ca. will clear my face of the pimples – Mr.
Mc had 3 people to dine wt. him & they drank pretty well. –

Tuesday 9th. clear & cool. NW they say the sound is block'd
up by the Rebel Vessels & we have nothing here to drive them
away – Byron continues his blockade of the Count d'Estaing at
Port Royal Martinic as late as 20 Febry. or thereabout

Wednesday 10th. hard frost last night, cold with the wind at
NW Sent to N.York for stuff to make summer trouzers for the
Company Paid Norrie my mess accot. to 26th. of Augt. last
£6.17.8 – Sterg.

Thursday 11th. pretty cold Wind S.E. a talk of a french fleet
off the coast, if that were true the harbour of N:York would
become an easy conquest, nothing there but the Ardent – paid a
visit to Col Stirling, he is highly extoll'd in the Rebel papers for
his humane & genteel behavior at Elizabeth Town – they are right
to praise us for our linity –

Friday 12th. a good deal of rain last night today cold & blustery
from NW the Cork fleet sail'd today Major McLeod there, he
has my letters to my Fr. & to D:M: dated 1st. instt. sent the 2d.
Bill

Saturday 13th. a pleasant day I hear the adml. is sail'd with
the Ardent. & some transports are gone up the East River – something in the wind –

Sunday 14th. a fall of snow from the Eastward 1/2 a foot deep,
frost at night. –

Monday 15th. March the Sun melts the snow fast & makes
dirty roads Reviewd the Compys. arms, & set the Taylors to
work on the trowzers – we din'd at C: Hatfields Col Y[orke].
there two waggons with the Genls. baggage come from
N:York: & to be forwarded to the Eastwd. under escort of a Serjt.
15 Grrs.

Tuesday 16th. cold N:wind   one ship of the English fleet arrived   She part company about a month ago. Money & cloathing to come with them. some of the Genls aids de Camp came out to Jamaica this evening –

Wednesday 17th. clear & cold   the Comr. in chief came to Jamaica in the forenoon he staid about 1/2 an hour & he & his suite proceeded to the Eastward. The Sons of Hibernia celebrated St. Patrick without any mischief. I din'd wt. C: Hope

Thursday 18th. March pleasant day. The No: wind of the morng. came about to S:W: in the afternoon. – out shooting kill'd a Wood Cock & some small birds. The Wood Cocks come here in the Spring & Breed in this Country; but they are much smaller than those at home – The 42d. Regt. have orders to be in readiness at the shortest notice –

Friday 19th. a fall of snow last night & continu[e]s till noon 8 or 9 inches deep, but not cold – The Sons of St. Patrick give a dance tonight at Jamaica –

Saturday 20th. hard frost last night & cold No:wind today, but the influence of the Sun carries off the snow & makes all soft & dirty – a ride to Whitestone   14 large transports lying there ready to take in troops, but no men of war come there yet, The Adml. [Gambier] is expected in the sound.

Sunday 21st. March   cold Easterly wind; at the Presbyterian Church with the Company of Grs. that were sentenced by a Genl. Court Martial for maroding 1000 each, were forgiven

Monday 22d. rain & sleet from the N.Ed. with a gale of wind, clear'd up afternoon – the 23d. sent an apology on account of the wr. –

Tuesday 23d. fair wr. & Sun Shine, W:N:W: The 42d. & those Regts. that were under orders, are countermanded

Wednesday 24th. A Snow Storm last night & this morng. but moderated in the forenoon –   went to N:York to look at the Companys Caps & Arm Chest   the Caps almost all spoil'd by putting salt on them last year at Philada. the arm chest full but the Serjt. could not get at it, some new arms belonging to the Compy. Standing at the Corner next the door in bad condition, on account of their damp situation strange management to put Arms in a cellar

Thursday 25 March better weather but dirty streets, slept last night at Dr. McLeans in the Attic Story, & din'd with him yesterday on oysters. – din'd today wt. Col. McPherson – a fleet from Halifax arrived in 16 days with the flank Coys. of the 70th. 74th. & 82d. under the Convoy of Sir Geo. Collier one ship missing[11] – met at the Coffee house in the Eveng. my old acquaintance & chum Balnabie he is eldest Capt. & has the Light Compy. of the 74th. we spent the evening together with a party at Black Sams – N:B: yesterday arrived a Vessel from Georgia with public dispatches giving an account of a Victory obtain'd by Lt. Col: Prevost with about 900, over 2000 of the Rebels who had follow'd Col Campbells division from Augusta as far down as Briar Creek when a detour was made by a party of the British troops who came upon their rear & totally defeated them, about 400 taken 170 kill'd & many drown'd a Brigr. 2 Colls. & 23 other offrs. taken –

Friday 26th. fine wr. overhead yesterday & this morng. arrived a fleet from England under convoy of the Romolus with money, stores, provisions & merchandize, they left England beging. of Janry. were convoy'd part of the way by a fleet of 16 sail of the line 8 of whom return'd, & the rest went to the West Indies. The Commander in Chief returned to N:York today from the east end of this island, the expedition seems to be laid aside came home with Hatfield & din'd there, cuny sulky – Spruce Beer

Saturday 27th. fine day wind W: went to the parade & look at the Companys arms & dress which I believe is rather neglected by the Subs. – the young Gentlemen of the army at present are much fonder of their pleasure than their duty – went to Newtown to speak to the Col. about Knapsacks, not at home; – we met the happy little couple & brought them to dine with us

Sunday 28th. a little rain in the morng. we all 42d. Grs. din'd with Captn. [Stephen] Broomfield today & did not spare his wine –

Monday 29th. fine mild weather – out shooting, kill'd a parcel of Robins

Tuesday 30th. March pleasant day The Battn. march'd out a few miles to the eastwd. & manoeuvred –

Wednesday 31st. very warm for the season – the Missing Ship of the Halifax fleet we hear is lost on the Shoals off Egg Harbour almost all perish'd most of two flank Companies of the Hamilton Regt were on board; very bad lookout Mr. Sir Geo: Collier. –

Thursday 1st. April very fine day The Battn. out manoeuvring for 2 hours we hear Sir Jas. Baird is come from Georgia with the prisoners

Friday 2d. very warm – a ride to N: Utrecht to see Balnabie & to bring him up here for a few days but he can't come yet not being settled in Qrs. Saw Col: McGaw, who seem'd much inclin'd to renew our acquaintance & invited us to come & see him at Gravesend we express'd our mutual surprize at the political changes of this Country but he hop'd that political opinions would not interfere with personal friendships – [12]

Saturday 3d. April likewise very warm with a breeze from the So:wd. went to Newtown & spoke to the Coll. about our Cloathing which we are to get immediately – a fleet of Victualers arriv'd from Cork 9 sail yesterday Capt. S[mith]: & D[r] R[obison] din'd with us the former staid all night, we sat late

Sunday 4th. a Gust of Thunder & rain last night, today gentle rain & mild some men taken up last night of 38th. 57th. & 7th. Coys., they were out in the Country with arms no doubt for the purpose of mauroding

Monday 5th. April fine Spring weather, – a long punishmt. of some of those fellows that were out, the rest to follow – some of the rascals deserve to be shot –

Tuesday 6th. a little rain in the morng. – went to Town to see about the painted Knapsacks & bespeak a set of Tin Cartridge boxes for the Compy. – return'd in the eveng.

Wednesday 7th. fine mild wr. Adml. Gambier sail'd yesterday with 3 or 4 frigates for England, the command devolves on Sir Geo: Collier in the Rainbow. wrote a letter to be in readiness to go by the first oppoy. to my dr. AH:

Thursday 8th. warm & hazy – the Battn. out above 2 hours & 1/2 marching & manoeuvring in the fields – they talk of a fleet off the Hook – nix – got our Cloathing yesterday & the taylors have begun on it today – the coats only –

Friday 9th. April   pleasant wr. & westerly winds, the flowers & foliage spreading out fast, the spring in more forwardness than has been known these many years – shed fish come in –

Saturday 10th. aut Supra – went to Newtown in the Eveng. with R[utherfurd]: & staid all night, – happy little couple – sent my letter by Col: James who is to sail tomorrow for England – inclosed it to the Doctor, Kilmarnock

Sunday 11th. very warm. S.W. Lt. Col: McPh. came home with me & din'd with us – a Report of a Sea Engagement in the West Indies in which the French have lost 15 sail –

Monday 12th. mouzy wt. the wind E: & cool & raw.   din'd at Hatfields, with the doxies

Tuesday 13th. pleasant wr. wind S:W: out shooting, kill'd some small bird, only

Wednesday 14th. wind East & S:E: & fine wr. – The Battalion out and fired 10 rounds of Ball at mark – intented to have gone to Newtown, but Capt. [Ludovick] Colquhawn of the 74th. Grs. came & din'd wt. us – accots from Capt. [Thomas] Pitcairn 82d. Lt. [John] Snodgrass & about 100 men lost, the rest prisoners at Philada. –

Thursday 15th. Cloudy wind about S: afternoon clear – Lord Cathcart married to Miss Elliot NYork on Saturday last.[13]

Friday 16th. Thunder Showers in the morng. fine growing weather & warm all the vegetable world springing into life

Saturday 17th. fair wr. – a Number of Regts. under orders to Embark the 42d. one of them –

Sunday 18th. very cold N: Westward & frost – a message from Newtown to get money. call'd on the Coll. but he was Costive – got only £14. of a dividend of money arriving from the pay of Vacant non commission officers The Pay Mr. wod. have given me Subse. to 24 June but he was pleas'd to be testy & I left in a huff – din'd with the good little folks & wrote a P:S: to Miss I – s – [14]

Monday 19th. hard frost last night which has nip'd the early blossoms & will spoil much fruit –

Tuesday 20th. fine mild wr. again went to Town to buy some things for the Compy. (Russian Sheeting for waistcoats) & some things for the Mess – din'd wt. Mr. McCru & came home in the Eveng. –

Wednesday 21st pleasant wr. Six Battns. still under orders to move viz the 7th. 23d. 42d. 63d. & two of Hessians & Lord Rawdons Corps –

Thursday 22d. fine spring wr. & Friday 23d. celebrated at N:York by the Sons of St. George –

Saturday 24th. a Pacquet arrived at last she sail'd the latter end of Febry.

Sunday 25th. fine wr. went to Church This Pacquet brings the accots. of Adl. Keppels tryal who is acquitted wt. honour,[15] a Reinforcement of 12000 coming out early, vigourous preparations but no war declared – got two letters fr: AH. & one fr: Fr. all well Decr. & Janry. –

200 of the 42d. march'd this morng. to the narrows & embark'd

on board small craft to be join'd by Capt. [Patrick] Ferguson & the men under his command & some others for a little private expedition into Jersey –

Monday 26th. April   fine wr.   had a Review of Necessaries, &ca. only a few Prs. shoes wanting – a ride to the Regt. they still expect to move soon. had half a dozen people to dine with us

Tuesday 27th. Capt. Fergusons party returned from Jersey they went into Monmouth County in the prospect of being join'd by a number of friends to Government & destroying some magazines, but they were disappointed in both, had a skirmish with the Rebels, brot in about 30 prisrs. & some plunder – The 42d. have got orders to march & embark tomorrow at Brooklyn

Wednesday 28th. April 1779 – The followg. Troops Embark'd for some secret expedition vizt. four flank Companies of the Guards, the 42d. Regt., Lord Rawdons Corps, & two Hessian Batns. the Transports ly off red hook – in consequence of orders the over night I march'd from Jamaica to Genl. Vaughans Quarters there to remain till further orders. left a Serjt. & the Taylors at the Hutts – we din'd with the Genl. –

Thursday 29th. Warm wr. & So:ly winds   the Expedition not sail'd yet they have taken their tents & some Baggage enough for several months. – a Pacquet   din'd at the Gens. [Vaughan's] Genl. Tryon & his Suite the[re]

Friday 30th. cold & raw, a dull Stupid plan this, quarter'd at one Burtis's the com divided in the Qrs. of the two Coys. that were here

Saturday 1st. May   pleasant wr. a ride out with Mrs. R[utherfurd]. din'd with us. – tea Miss fish, – a letter from AH: 7th. Feby.

Sunday 2d. May   fine wr. & warm   put on our new coats & trouzers & sent them to hear Mr McL Preach gallis [Galatians?] at Newtown, – went to the English Church a very thin Congregation –

The Inhabitants of Newtown have presented & publish'd an address of thanks to Col: Stirling & the 42d. Regt. for their good behaviour while in winter Qrs.

Monday 3d. warm wind So:ly went [t]o N. York in the morng. & return'd to dinner, nobody pretends to know where this Expedition, is going, not sail'd yet
The Mail for a Pacquet to be closed this Evening, put in a letter for AH: dated 1st. & wrote a few lines to the Agents about wings to the Serjts. Coats –

Tuesday 4th hazy wind SE: a ride to Jamaica, a Genl. Court Martial setting there trying Col. [John Graves] Simcoe at the Complaint of Capt. Smith: Coll. York presdt.[16]

Wednesday 5th May cool Wind NW got a set of ten Cartridge boxes for the Coy. from N:York – Smith Kings Street – I hear the Expedition have sail'd out of the hook – Mrs. R: & Capt. S; din'd wt. us The troops commd. by M: Genl. [Edward] Mathews The Raisonable 64 Sir Geo: Collier the Rainbow & some other gone with the Expedition, supposed to Virginia[17]

Thursday 6th Strong NW wind Colo Stirlings answer to the address of the Inhabitants of Newton in yesterdays paper dated on board the Nestor May 1st.

Friday 7th. a cool steddy NWd. went to N:York in the morng. wt. Mrs. R. & return'd in the Eveng – din'd at Roubalets wt. my old friend Balnabie – nothing new in Town, all in the dark – a talk of a fleet off the hook

May 12th. 1779 The Light Infantry arrived at Jamaica from the Eastend, where they had been since beginning Janry. under the Command of Sir Wm. Er[s]kine who came up a few days ago & is going home next Pacquet – the Legion & two Companies of the 71st. Grrs. are coming by water – a few days after the troops left the eastend a Number of Vessels from Rhode Island came there for wood & were all taken by the Yankys.

14th. accots. from Georgia of an action about the 27th. ulto.

wherein Lt. Col. [John] Maitland, with 1500, defeated 2000 of the Rebels at Perrysburg under [Benjamin] Lincoln having kill'd & wod about 150 & taken 300 prisoners – [18]

Sunday 16th. May 1779 the 57th. Light Company march'd from Jamaica to join their Regt. for ill behavior & obstinate persevirance in it – din'd at Genl. Vaughans – 17th. May The Light Infantry Battn. march'd from Jamaica to Hell Gate & cross'd over to York Island & Encamp'd – had all our folk's here to dinner

Tuesday 18th. at York & turn'd the painted Knapsacks on the makers hands for being very ill done & bespoke a set from Davis came home to dinner – drank tea with the Ladies, – funny – the 63d. & 64th. in the Jersey covering Ferguson, who is gone on a scout to Pyrrhymus [Paramus]. The Grr. Compys. of the 70th. & 74th, march'd to Jamaica to join the Battalion, as did the Light Infantry embark to go to York Island. to theirs –

Wednesday 19th. rain & wind S:E: The 17th. Light Dragoons march'd to Hell gate to cross over, & the Queens Rangers came the length of Newtown

Accounts from Genl. Mathews dated 15th. They landed about the 10th at Portsmouth in Virginia, where there was a Fortification with upwards of 20 Guns, & a Major & 40 men who spik'd the Guns & ran off, they found a great manys ships & stores, & a great qaunty. of Tobacco, – The Guards went to Suffolk above 20 miles from Portsmouth & destroy'd 3000 barrels of Pork, with many other Stores & burn't the place; In the Country they were endeavouring to raise the Militia but they turn'd out very unwillingly. – much prize & plunder – [19]

Thursday 20th. May dirty wr. from S:E: a Cork fleet of about 12 sail arrived

Genl. Vaughan went to Jamaica to day to Inspect the Grenadrs. but the weather was so bad they did not turn out – Returns given in of those unfit for that service –

Friday 21st. the wet wr. still continues – orders for the Grenadrs. to be ready to march at the shortest notice

Saturday 22d. hazy & wet fog the wind still about the S:E: qr. The little Genl. sent for me this morng. to ask about the state of our tents, I told him they were wore out & I believe most Companies of the Battn. are in the same Situation. N:B: some burn't & some cut up. An Expedition going forwd. of some force but which way is yet a secret

Sunday 23d. May Whitesunday   clear & warm   sent our heavy baggage to the Regtal Store in York. – my two trunks & box with the bedsted – sent my Cap, Bonnet, broad sword, Rifle, & little Arthur case to Docr. McLeans, – for the field, Fly tent, bedding, Portmanteau, & canteen box – The whole Battn. sent theirs to their respective stores. Volunteer'd a dinner wt. the Genl. Vagn [Vaughan] very well received – Pondicherry taken 17 Octr.[20] dispatches sent off to Genl. Mathews –

Monday 24th. very warm,   a ride to Jamaica; order'd the taylors to join except two left with Capt. Colquhoun   evacuated the hutts & deliver'd up the bedding; Spoke to Col. Yorke about tents, he expects to get tents – Visited the Ogdens & bid them farewell; din'd with C: Hatfield, in the Eveng. with Ladies at Mrs. Rhs. much talk & some fun

Tuesday 25th. May   pleasant wr. went to NYork early with Mrs. Rutherfd. bot. some things for the Compy – we din'd with a party at Loorelys & Elms at Brooklyn & came home in the Eveng. The delaware Frigate going to Virginia with dispatches to Genl. Mathews. – Gave Mr. Saml. Sacket an order on Barrack Mr. Genl. for my fire wood money from 18th. Novr. to 27th. April & clear'd accots. with him –

Wednesday 26th. wet fog from S:E: orders for the Troops in Long island &ca. to move on the 27. 28. & 29 some by Hell Gate & some by Whitestone to form a Camp without the lines some where

Thursday 27th. fair – The 33d. Regt. & the Queens Rangers cross'd over to NYork Island at Hell Gate –

Friday 28th. the   Grenadrs.   march'd   from   Jamaica   to

Whitestone, where I join'd them about nine, found them divided into three divisions Commanded by the three senior Capts. [Stephen] Broomfield[,] [Charles] Lum, & Humis [or Harris?] under Col: York

Chapter VIII

'in a becalm'd & confus'd situation'

New York
29 May to 10 November 1779

Sir Henry Clinton began the campaign of 1779 hoping to end the rebellion in a single, climactic battle. Skeptical of the government's plan for relying increasingly on the royal navy and Loyalists to help restore royal government from south to north, he intended to lure or force Washington into a decisive engagement along the Hudson River. For a variety of reasons, he failed. In early June he captured Verplancks and Stony Point, interrupting American communications across the Hudson some thirty miles north of New York Island and threatening American control of the Highlands of the Hudson. Even so, Washington refused to risk a general action for these posts, and Clinton did not then have enough troops to impose battle on his unwilling enemy. While Clinton waited for reinforcements, Washington successfully attacked Stony Point and Paulus Hook; and a French squadron arrived to keep British troops who had gone to the West Indies in 1778 from returning to New York. The belated arrival of Admiral Marriot Arbuthnot and 3,500 sickly recruits on 25 August did little to improve Clinton's prospects. Arbuthnot proved an anxious, inconsistent colleague, and the whole of the British army at New York as well as much of the civilian population was soon struggling with a debilitating combination of aches, fevers, and diarrhoea. No wonder that when threatened by a French squadron, Clinton and Arbuthnot withdrew from Verplancks, Stony Point, and Rhode Island into fortified positions around New York City. They would not stir from New York until the coast of North America was clear of French warships.[1]

For John Peebles and the British grenadiers, for company grade officers and common soldiers who saw only belatedly and vaguely what

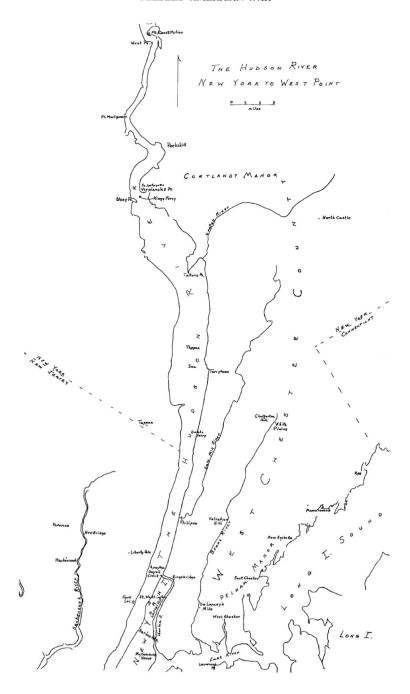

THE HUDSON RIVER
NEW YORK TO WEST POINT

0   1   2   3
miles

shaped Clinton's plans, the campaign of 1779 soon became stagnant and depressing. On leaving their winter quarters on Long Island, the grenadiers proceeded rapidly up the Hudson to help take and secure Verplancks Point.[2] But when Washington refused to risk a general engagement and Clinton decided to await reinforcements before going farther with his offensive, the grenadiers returned from Verplancks to spend July in a fortified camp near East Chester and the ensuing three months either in a camp on upper New York Island or on transports in the Hudson River.[3] Apart from occasional foraging expeditions and picquet duty, Peebles spent these months trying to keep his men from plundering and deserting and to combat the illness that from late August until November afflicted the whole army and left many of his grenadiers too weak to do any duty.[4] All of this inactivity, indiscipline, and illness eventually took its toll on Peebles' disposition. He became unusually critical of the conduct of the war, complaining by September that 'affairs have the appearance of being in a becalm'd & confus'd situation.' When subsequently Clinton withdrew from Verplancks and Stony Point as well as Rhode Island, Peebles was unsure what the purpose of the campaign had been or why the British had given up Rhode Island. His men were still ill when they entered their winter quarters at Jamaica, Long Island, in November.[5]

New York
29 May to 10 November 1779

Saturday 29th. The Yagers march'd from flushing & cross'd the East River from Laurences point to Wilkins's point near Westchester   the Grenadrs. follow'd them & march'd to East Chester near which they Encamp'd & found Regts. on the ground to their left,   the Queens Rangers & Legion in front, Genl. Vaughan Commands his Quarters in our Rear. – [6]

Sunday 30th. The Troops from Virginia return'd & came up the North River to Phillips's – in the Evening the troops that were Encamp'd marched to the left and Embark'd at Phillips on board of those Ships that came from Virginia & some small craft leaving their baggage behind in waggons got under way about midnight & sail'd up the River –

Monday 31st. Landed in the forenoon at the point above Croton River Taller's point & march'd up the Albany road to invest a fort on Verplanks point – the 17th. & 63d. & 64th. landed on the West side & took post on Rocky point – we creep'd on & halted & turn'd back till dark & lay down on the high grounds Cortland Manor[7]

Tuesday 1st. June   march'd at 3 AM up the Albany road past Verplanks point & halted for some time whilst from the other side of the River[,] Rocky point[,] & from the Gallies they threw some shot & shells into the little fort which surrender'd about noon   two kill'd & 1 wounded in the work, about 60 taken prisoners of war. the officers allow'd to wear their Swords – a Strong Redout with a Blockhouse in it, ditch, pallisade & abattis, with a 3 Gun battery towards the water – the troops took post on the ground about the fort late in the Evening 1/2 a mile facing N:E: – call'd Ft. Lafayette
The Troops on this Expedition are The 4 flank Companies of the Guards, the Light Infantry, British & Hessian Grenrs. the 17th. 33d. 42d. 63d. 64th. Regts., some Yagers, Regt. Prince

Charles, Volunteers of Ireland, Legion[,] Robertsons Corps & Fergusons –

Wednesday 2. June   halted, making some works on Stoney point for a Post

Thursday 3d. June   most of the Troops on this side march'd in the morng. to Peekskill where they halted for some time & saw a few Rebels on horseback – The Light Infantry & Fergusons people detach'd from thence to make a sweep into the Country for Cattle   the Ships moved up to Peekskill   two days provision issued out there, and we return'd to our ground late – warm flanking

Friday 4th. June   The Troops & ships fir'd in honour of the day, – we fir'd very ill – all the field offrs. dine with the Comm. in Chief   The troops from Virginia order'd on board to go down to the Lines to Philips's, & a Vessel sent for necessaries for those that remain here   The Light Infantry brought in some Cattle & Sheep this morng. after a long march – some of Fergusons men got a Shot at some Rebels on horse back & knocked down two[8]

Saturday 5th. warm weather   the works going forwd. on Stoney point   Genl. [James] Pattison commands there. –

Sunday 6th. June   Genl. Clinton gone down the River, the Command devolves on Genl. Vaughan – the 33d. Regt. to act as Light Iny. at Col: [James] Websters request – dined on board the Vulture Balnaby & I, she is the only man of war here, Sir Geo: Collier gone down – some desertion among the Grenadrs. – a Genl. Court Martial tomorrow to try one of the Irish Volunteers for a Rape, & some others for plundering; some sad dogs in this army –

Monday 7th. a Block house erecting on the hill on the right of the Grs. camp   it was framed before & brot. here from NYork   the Works on the other side going on briskly   several one Gun batterys on detach'd Collines, & one large on the highest part of the point with 24 pors. &ca. – Ferguson made a detour on the west side & brought hearsay intelligence of a brigade of the Enemy within 8 miles & Washingtons army about 20 miles off, in the Clove – The Light Infantry mov'd their ground this morng. near a mile to our left & face to the No:ward; the 33d. moved likewise & took up ground above the South bridge; the Yagers are at the No:bridge & the Legion within them, – this place which they call Verplanks point is almost an island form'd by two marshy Creeks, & is 4 or 5 miles round[;] from hence to Stoney point is called the King's ferry above 1/2 mile over, & is the principal communication the Rebels make use of to pass their troops & stores across the North River – they have a Strong Fort about 16 miles further up on West point called Fort deffiance where there is a large Magazine & Garrison –

Tuesday 8th. warm for some days past the block house getting up, here, and the Works going on t'other side – some shots at the Yager outpost.

Wednesday 9th. June warm & cloudy small craft with Sutlers plying from New York, & some Regts. have got their field baggage[;] ours is not come up yet owing to some mistake – about 2 or 300 of the Enemy seen on t'other side in front of their picquets but they disappear'd without doing any thing – nothing comes in from the Country, the Inhabitants have driven away their Cattle, & hold no communication with us –

Thursday 10th. a good deal of rain last night which wet us in our Wigwams – mounted picqt. this morng. a[t] day break a little in front of our Camp, a Sub: & 24 detach'd to the low ground at the side of the marsh, to which post a road comes in from the Country that seems to be the most accessable entrance for the Enemy. –
in the Papers – The Oliver Cromwell of 20 Guns taken by the Daphne – Reports of Genl. Prevost being in Successfull march towards Chastown [Charleston, S. C.] having a Strong body of Indians wt. his Army, a Speech of John Jay's in the papers to his Rebel brethren exorting them to raise men & money drawn up wt. specious art, address, & good language.

Col: Webster desires to be supported by six Companies of Grrs. in case of an attack on his post above the Church, but I don't see how they can get to him in less than an hour at least.

Friday 11th. cool with stong wind at N:W: all quiet round the Camp, & the works going forward – The Capts. of the Battn. went to Col: Yorke & represented to him the necessity of the three senior Capts. who command divisions taking their turn of duty as they know of no precedent that exempts them, Col Yorke represented it to Genl. Vaughan & they are to do duty till the Commander in Chief's pleasure is known, – when Capts. Command Regts. they take their duty in the line only – but these Capts. who command only a division of a Battalion of Grrs. were missing their turn of duty even in the line, –

Saturday 12th. cool & pleasant wr. The same number for work as usual, above 300 go from this side to Stoney point every Eveng. remain there for 24 hours, working only in the day time, with a long rest in the heat of the day, & double allowance of Rum the Grs. baggage Guns & women come up from below, ours safe, but there has been some roguery & embezzlement, – Genl. Pattison gone down in a Brig – he wanted the Vulture the only man of war here, but Genl. Vaughan told him he supos'd he was joking, – eh – the Rainbow comes up in the Eveng. – Reports from N:York say that Butler & Joseph has routed Maxwell & his brigade up the Susquehana somewhere, and that Genl. Prevost is in Chas.town, bravo *Nix* Drumr. McIntyre missing the Block-house here almost finish'd, – making fascines to improve the work round the Store house near Ft. la Fayette –

Sunday 13th. rain in the morng. – S:W: & showery all day – The Commandr. in chief came up this morng. in the Fanny, & a ship with ordnance, – his Ex: came ashore & look'd some of the Posts, – Lord Cathcart came about noon with some dispatches

Monday 14th. warm & dry wind S:W: Sir Henry gone down the River again in the Fanny, & the Vulture gone – Ferguson was out yesterday about 6 or 7 miles to the eastward & saw not a man in arms he drove in a few Cattle, – the works going on t'other side & they are going to erect another Blockhouse on this side within 100 yards or so of Ft. la fayette. A Pacquet to sail soon –

Tuesday the 15th. a good deal of Rain yesterday Eveng. & last night with thunder today warm & fair wind at NW –
wrote yesterday to A.H. & this morng. to my Father, enclosing the former, the letters go off for New York this Eveng. – some deserters coming in from the Rebels who say Washington has 7 Brigades in the clove of 1000 or 1200 each, – at work making a square Redoubt enclosing the last erected Blockhouse, parapet 15 feet, – 60 ft area Lozenge

Wednesday 16th. fair Wind Soly. all the baggage except what there is immediate use for sent on board of Sloops the two 71st Compys. excepted & those Corps who are supposed to remain here – a Work making round the Blockhouse on our right here too, & they are in haste to get them finish'd; rain in ye. Eveng.

Thursday 17th. Cloudy wind S.W: over at Stoney point, the Works there very near finish'd, a strong post – 12 pieces – the lozenge work round Blockhouse N. 2 finish'd, with a fleche towards the River and an abbatis round the whole
A new work traced out betwixt Fort La Fayette & the stone house, close to the bank, with an obtuse angle to the south bridge, where a gun may rake the passage of the beach – A fleche parapet covering two side of Blockhouse making an abbatis, a 6 por. put in the upper story

Friday 18th. warm wind Westerly two deserters come in from Washington who say the Rebels have defeated Genl. Prevost in So: Carolina – not true.

Saturday 19th. the same numbers at Work as usual – some few people from the Country venture in to the outposts with mutton, Veal, & butter to sell – Capt. McDonald comes up wt. the Coys. new knapsacks

Sunday 20th. on picket warm & dry wind S:W: Report of a fleet at the hook – and favourable Accots. from the So:wd. by the Solbay: dated 23d. May Savannah

Monday 21st. warm, no fleet, but a Ship from Whitehaven in
11 Weeks who brings us the first Copy of Genl. Grants letter
with the affair of St. Lucia –
Our Baggage Removed from Sloops to Transports, the L:
Infantry 3 & Grrs. 3[,] more works making to join the large flechs
with Blockhouse No. 2 & an abbatis along the front. the parapet
almost round B:house No. 1 finish'd, & the Abatis nearly
last night a party of the Rebels intended to surprise a party of
ours in front of the works on t'other side, but they having come
in in the eveng. being only a covering party the Rebels miss'd
their object & fired on some of their own people who were coming
a different way, kill'd or wounded an offr. & 2 or 3 more, as we
were informed by 10 deserters who left that party & came in,
most of them Burgoynes people – I hear Dr. McIntyre is with ye.
Rebels – The Genl. came up today & took a look, – these works
will cost Govermt. a Great deal of money, tho' not much laid out

Tuesday 22d June warm, wind S:W working still, Capt. [Alex-
ander] Mercer chief Engineer   make money my son –
Genl. Grants accot. of the affair at St. Lucia very well told,
but not particular we lost 2 Sergts. & 11 R: & file killed, 136
woundd the french lost 400 kill'd, 500 ill wod. & 600 slightly
well done little Meadows he lick'd ym. handsomly

Wednesday 23d. June very warm wind W: a flag of truce came
in yesterday to Stony point with some necessaries for their La
Fayette prisoners, & brot. with them a News paper, telling that
Prevost was beat the 23d. May, but we don't believe it yet. The
same numbers at work, which I think will not be finish'd these
some davs

N:B: The Country people bring in fresh meat to Col: Websters
post. &ca. by stealth

Thursday 24th. The works going on & a quty. of facines making for future use

Friday 25th. Very warm, at work in the morng – part of Robertsons Corps cross'd & landed about a league below, where they had some firing with the Militia but did no mischief they destroy'd some obstructions the Rebels had laid across the Road toward Bacon hill where the 33d were about a week ago & fired the Beacon – a thunder gust in the afternoon, three of the Hessian Grrs. hurt with lightning –

Saturday 26th. hot weather, the workg party comes off at 9, morng. & goes on at 3 P:M: – Lt. Col: Campbell of the Provincials who was taken going to Georgia, came in here today, & went down to N:York, being on parole he did not say anything of the Enemy – orders to move in the morng. – and they say a ship is arrived in 7 weeks who brings accounts of a prospect of a peace with France – The Country people have stop'd coming in being threatened by the Militia – 5 or 6 of Fergusons people deserted two days ago – yesterday a Scouting party of our Light horse from the Camp at Phillips's came up as far as Croton River & cut up some militia among whom were two deserters from L. Infantry

Sunday the 27th. June 1779 the troops Embark'd at Kings ferry, leaving the 17th. 33d, Fergusons men, & the two 71st. Grenrs. Comys. & Robertsons Corps, making in all about 1200, under the Command of Lt. Col: Webster, for the defense of both sides of the River, – the wind being contry. the Transports drop'd down with the tide a few miles & came to – on board the Robert, with the 54. 64. 70. & 74th. Col: York on board the Houstoun with the right division, the rest in small craft we got a ground two or three times about half way twixt Tallers point & Verplanks – the Vulture & a Galley left.

Monday 28th. The wind came fair about noon, N:W: got under way & stood down the River, most of the fleet a good way ahead, joined them at Phillips's about 4 when we all came to, landed in the Eveng. & march'd to our former ground the Grs. near East chester. – The Waggons & our Horses come to us at Phillips's we march'd from thence about 9 & got to our ground about mid-night 7 miles – The Royl. Brigade encamp'd 'twixt Phillips & Valentine hill – vizt. the 7th. 23d. & 42d. under Brigadier Stirling.

Tuesday 29th. June   our Baggage arrived early this morng. having left Phillips's about midnight, bad rough road but a fine moonshine night – The Weather very warm for some days past – the Compy. employ'd making hutts 3 of a side holding 12 each – we having not tents –
The Light Infantry on our right, the 17th. Dragoons on their right at East Chester, our Picquets advanced on the roads to New Rochelle & White Plains The Hessian Grs. on our left, Legion & Yagers in front &ca.

Wednesday 30th. June warm   the 7th. & 23d. Regts. under orders to Embark – three Regts. arrived from Rhode Island, the 54th. one of Anspach & Fannings Provincial – a little Refugee fleet cruising in the Sound commd. by Leonard, – The Refu-gees & Loyalists in Westchester County making excursions into Conecticut & retaliate on their enemies –

Thursday 1st. July   it rain'd a great deal last night & this morng. – a ride to the Regt. about 4 miles to our left, call'd on the Brgr. [Stirling] – got abstracts & money from the Paymr. for the Compy. to the 24 April two Musters, – Wrote to AH: to go by Capt. Anstruther's Bror. who goes with Sir Wm. Erskine in the Cork fleet, to sail in a few days – din'd with the Major [Graham] –

Friday 2d. July   cool after rain   an expedition going on under Genl. Tryon with those troops that came from Rhode Island with the addition of the 7th. & 23d. Regts.   the 63d. & 64th. fill up their place in Stirlings Brigade –
Lt. Col: Cornet [Banastre] Tarleton went out last night with a detachmt. of near 300 Cavalry to surprise something about Bedford near 30 miles off – but return'd without effecting it[9] – din'd with Brigr. Genl. Stirling – the Virginia prize money will turn out to be a very handsome sum.

3d. July warm, the 7th, & 23d. Regts. march'd to West Chester to embark – a ride to Kings bridge to see the works call'd at a Quaker farmers of the name of Hant, whose daughter Lydia a pretty Girl keeps a very distinct journal of the Sufferings of the family, & in the Neighborhood on Laurel hill a sort of Crown work closed, a Block house, & two little batteries, Redoubts on the high grounds without the Bridges – came home late to dinner found the Major & Capt R[utherfurd]: mellow to bed

Sunday 4th. July very warm – hear'd a firing of Cannons about noon to the Northwd. which we take to be the Rebels commemorating the anniversary of their Independance – A Report of a Sea Action off Brest in which the french fleet has been defeated by Adl. Mann – Nix
gave out a clearance to the Compy. to the 24th. April – a Genl. Court Martial sitting here Lt. Col: York presidt. –
The Country people bring things to sell; the Hessians have always a flesh market The Commander in chief gone to NYork – frequent excursions & depredations by small parties on both sides.

Monday 5 July very warm they say the Romolus with money & a fleet from Halifax is arrived & a ship from Georgia –

Tuesday 6th. July very hot indeed mounted Picquet at 3 morng. about a mile in front, all quiet, the Light Infy. Picquets & us din'd together – by the Ship from Georgia we learn the Genl. Prevost having no heavy Cannon, retir'd some miles further from Charlestown, where he waits for them –

Wednesday 7th. Cloudy & warm – yesterday Major Barrymore who heads a number of Mounted Refugees returned from a scout beyond White Plains 15 miles he had no fighting but drove in a quantity of Cattle sheep & horses, which they sell for their own benefit having no pay, but like Hussars serve for the plunder they take & to distress the Rebels – orders to receive Bat & forage money: & two deserters of the 38th. Grrs. to be executed on the 10th. – we hear Genl. Tryons expedition is saild to the Eastwd. – and we have orders to be in readiness to move –
a Letter to the Comr. in chief from Gl. Grant mentioning that

the 4th. 15th. 28th. 40th. & 55th. are Embark'd for No: America, the 5th. & 46th. gone on board the fleet & the 27th. 35th. & 49th. to be relieved by the Royl. Americans & returned here, Genls. Grant & Meadows gone home [Robert] Prescot comes with the five Regts. & Sir Harry Calder remains at St. Lucia with the three –
sent a Guard of 1 Serjt. 1 Corpl. & 12 to Genl. Vaughans at his request to take care of his baggage, obliged to him for his good opinion but would rather be excused –
The follg. Corps to march at 3 in the morng. in two Columns under Genl. Vaughans orders 17th. Dragoons, Queens Rangers, & Legion, ye. left L:Infantry, Br:Grrs. two Battns. Hessns. Grrs., Baggage & provision train & the 3d. Bn. Hessn. Grrs. Right Column

Thursday 8th. July warm, rain last night The Right Column march'd by Pells bridge & New Rochelle to mamaroneck where they arrived about 9 being 7 miles on the Boston road & 27 from N:York & Encamp'd on the heights about the Village the Grrs. to the No:westd L:I: to Eastwd. – most of the houses on the road abandon'd – the left Column took the road towards White plains, & are encamp'd about 3 miles on our left – A good deal of Cannon hear'd this morng. early to the Eastwd. – The Comr. in chief came up about noon – an invitation to dine with his Ex by Major [William] Crosbie; before dinner Sir Henry took occasion to ask me if I had hear'd from Lord E: & mention'd the death of her Ladyship, who he told me had recommended me to him before he left England last, & beg'd he wod. (he said) make himself acquainted with me, that is I suppose take some notice of me, His Excelly. was very complaisant, & I had the honor to sit next to him, But – these sort of [entry unfinished]

Friday 9th. July under arms at 3 & march'd at day break, with thunder Gust in the morng. much with heavy rain, moved on thro' Rye near Byrams Bridge and Encamp'd on the best Grounds, & I suppose the best position, saw the fleet in the Sound standing over to the Long Island shore we hear Genl. Tryon Burnt Fairfield & made another Landing on the Coast where he was repulsed, with some loss.[10] all quiet in Camp, no appearance of the enemy except a few horse men seen at the out Picquets, – maurading & desertion, for shame Grenrs. –

Saturday 10th. cold morng. moved at daybreak with the line of march reversed, & return'd to Mamaroneck where we took up the same ground we occupied two days ago Genl. Tyrons fleet lying over in Huntington Bay, Sir Geo: Collier come ashore & moved with the troops in a Phaeton, wt. Hansen on a Genl. Court Martial for the tryal of John Sutherland of the 64th. Regt. for desertion, he was taken this morng. near Rye, – a poor silly creature who tells a simple, & consistent story of his being in liquor & losing his way in the night, his greatest fault was in not returning, for it does not appear to me that he left his Regt. with an intention to desert. however he is condemn'd to suffer death by a mode of procedure in Court that I never saw or hear'd of before, & cannot reconcile to justice & humanity; a circumstance which I shall never forget, & now think in my own mind I should have protested against –

The Comr. in chief went to Phillipsburg in the afternoon; – they say Genl. Tryon has 50 men kill'd & wounded & some officers – I hear we are to remain here at Mamaroneck for 4 or 5 days

Sunday 11th. July a cool morng. & after 10 it rain'd all day – The 17th. Dragoons & legion & Simcoes moved last night somewhere to the Eastwd. – a great smoke seen this morng. about Stamford – out at the Camp where the left Column was, at one Griffin's, about 3 miles from White Plains, their baggage coming in here – The left Column return'd to their ground about noon they had been at Bedford about 18 miles off, to make another attempt to surprise Sheldons Regt. of Light horse, but they were gone, – they burnt the Village & returnd –

Monday 12th. very heavy rain yesterday Eveng. & all night, with Thunder the morng. cool & cloudy, but clear'd up in the afternoon – some rascals of Grrs. have been out plundering yesterday towards New Rochelle, two found out, but there were more concern'd, in taking

The Rolls to be call'd every hour in presence of an offr. pr. comy. & report to a Capt. of the day

Tuesday 13th. July, moderate wr. Complaints made to Genl. Vaughan that the Refugees in their excursions do not distinguish between friend & foe's – 3 days provision brot. up from New Rochelle wt. an escort of 1 Capt. & 100 – The Queens Rangers were out yesterday saw some Rebels but did not get at ym. a talk of some arrivals –

Wednesday 14th. warm – Genl. Tryon's fleet in motion turning up the Sound – a Cork fleet arrived a[t] York, & something from Ponobscot the Victualers left Cork 20 April – Saucy vain young man – [11]

Thursday 15th. very warm – 3 days more provision brought up from Rochelle – a Ride to the out Picquets of the left Column, within 5 miles of White Plains – din'd with Genl. Vaughan a Gust in the Eveng

Friday 16th. July moderate, wind NW hear'd a good deal of Cannon this morng. before & after day light, towards Verplanks point; And in the Eveng. we had the disagreeable News that Stony Point was taken by Assault on Thursday Night; and that Verplanks point was surrounded by the Rebels

Saturday 17th. Genl. Vaughans orders the over night for moving in the morng. which was accordingly done without any hurry, or the least appearance of the Enemy; marching in that order which the line always makes in retiring – at East Chester the Troops halted & form'd, for the Execution of two Grrs. of the 38th. for desertion, but as one was to be pardon'd, they drew lots, & he who drew the fatal billet was executed in sight of ye. Army at Noon – The troops then moved on & took possession of their former ground with orders not to stir out of Camp – The Troops under Genl. Tryon landed at Frogneck & march'd to &

Encamp'd on & about Valentines hill[12] – Stirlings Brigade
Embark'd to go up the River with the Comr. in Chief to see what
can be done for the Relief of Verplanks point the wind contrary
all day –

The affair at Stony Point not so mortal as we hear'd at first,
but by all accounts they have been surprized, & the Rebels have
gained a point, & perform'd an action, by which we have lost, &
they have gain'd, much credit – Col: Webster still holds out tho'
surrounded by great numbers, & his retreat cut off, a heavy fire
from Stony point, but only one man woundd

Sunday 18 July Genl. orders last night dated at Phillipsburg 9
o'clock for a genl. forage this morning at day break, at which time
all the Troops in this line march'd in two Columns – the Right
Column consisting of the Light Infantry, British Grrs. two
Battns. Hessian Grrs. the Baggage & the 3d. Battn. Hessian
Grenrs. – The left Column, the Yagers, flank Comys. of the
Guards, park of Artillery, 7th. 23d. & 54th. British the Hessian
Regt. Landgrave Prince Charles, & Boses, the King's American
Regt. Volunteers of Ireland, Baggage & provision train, the
Column to be closed by Emericks Chasseurs – Major Genl.
Vaughan will command the Right Column & will be attended by
Lt. Dursford A. D. Qr.Mr. Gl.[;] Majr. Genl. Mathews the left
with Lt. Rankin A. D. Qr.Mr. Genl. – a detachmt. of Pioneers
to march at head of each Column

The Light Compy. of the Royl. Highland Emigrants will fall
into the left Coln. in the rear of the flank Comys. of the Guards &
when the troops come to their ground will take the earliest
opporty. of joining the Corps of Light Infantry. – The Right
Column moved on toward Phillips's till they came to Saw Mill
Creek when they turn'd to the right & took the Valley road to
Dobbs's ferry where they arrived about 10 & encamp'd on the
high grounds above, the British Grrs. facing to the East, the
Hessn. Grs. to the North, the Light Infantry embark'd and went
up the River – the left Column march'd by the Riverside road
came after us & encamp'd on the high grounds to the So:ward of
us near a mile, & nearly opposite the ferry, facing outwards

The Comr. in Chief gone up the River in the afternoon with

the tide, to direct those Troops that are on the water, Viz Stirlings
Brigade & the Light Infantry, the wind Contrary – a fire from
Stony point on Verplanks in the afternoon – The Wounded of
Stony point Garrison gone down to N:York, the Prisoners, above
300 march'd into the Country –
N:B: the 17th. Light Dragoons Legion & Queens Rangers
march'd the 17th from Mamaroneck across the Country & took
post, the former at Croton bridge, the latter above tarrytown
The Rebels commanded by Genl. Wayne came against Stony
Point in great force 1400 & silence, & having surrounded the
Picquet attack'd the works on all sides   Capt. [Francis] Tew of
the 17th. the only offr. killed,   Capt. Campbell 71st. wounded &
got off   Lts. [Patrick] Cuming & [Archibald] McLean 71st.
wounded & sent to York

Monday 19th. July   very warm   The Columns halted, but no
appearance of foraging – the Picquets of the left Column being
ordered out with the Field offr of the day for the Execution of
Jno. Sutherland of the 64th. mentioned 10th. inst. Captn S—n &
I waited on Genl. Vaughan to ask his opinion of a case like that
which happen'd at the Court Martial which we found agreed with
ours, we then told him that there was an irregularity in the proceedings, or rather in giving sentence, which we could not reconcile to our judgement & conscience, and begged he would order
the Execution to be put off untill we could acquaint the Comr. in
chief with as much of the affair as the nature of our oath wod.
allow us, which he was very ready to do,   but on Enquiry he
found that the Comr. in Chief had left orders to pardon the
prisoner at the foot of the Gallows, which satisfied us with respect
to the safety of a mans life who was not regularly condemn'd.
The Ceremony was gone thro' & the poor man who behaved
very well and penitently at the approaching scenes of death,
fainted with joy when his pardon was pronounced – we hear the
Rebels have evacuated Stonny Point –
In the afternoon a letter from the Comr. in chief to Genl.
Vaughan acquainting him that the Rebels had left Stony Point
that morng. & that our troops were again in possession, that a

Galley in which they were carrying off the Guns & Stores &ca. was sunk by a shot from Verplankside. My servt. Jas. Sinclair taken ill yesterday wt. a coughing & spitting of Blood, in great quty.

Tuesday 20th. July a good deal of rain in the Night morng. foggy – Col: Wurmb & Emerick out foraging at day break, with all the waggons of the army, & the A.D.Q.M.Gs. The Light Horse Legion & Rangers came down from Croton & tarrytown, & encamp'd on the Hills east of the bridge over Saw Mill Creek –

The Light Infantry came down in the Evening from Stony Point which place they left early this Morng.

Stirlings Brigade left up the River but had not disembark'd –

Wednesday 21st. very warm – very little forage in this part of the Country, the Inhabitants having mostly left it the ground is overrun with weeds

The Light horse & Rangers brought a few Cattle & horses yesterday Capt. Rd. McK. of the Emts. an old 77r. dined with us & Capt. C.MZ: –

Thursday 22d. July Dobbs ferry Lord Cornwallis arrived yesterday at N:York in the Greyhound Frigate, & Col: Patterson & Lt. Col: Stuart, they sail'd ten or 12 days after the fleet, which they [say] is to bring us a Reinforcement of about 7000 –

Orders dated at 6 this Morng. for the Army to march at 9, back to their old ground betwixt Phillipse East Chester, – they march'd in two Columns as before, with the line reversed; the day hot & the road dusty, got to our ground about 3 o'clock – The Comr. in chief gone to New York –

Genl. Vaughan going home immediately, being no longer second in Command he was to have been Comr. in chief in case of accidents or remove, but the cards have taken another turn & so has Ld. Lisburn; I am sorry the little Warrior is going away

Friday 23d. July warm & dry – The Lt. Col: went to N:York this morng. & return'd in the Eveng. – Lord Cornwallis complets. to all his acquaintances & will be out to see the Army in a day or two His Examination before a Committee of the House published, concerning the conduct of the War under the Howes, in which he answers favorably as to facts, but gives no opinion; The Howes are much obliged to him, but the House is not much the wiser[13] – The Greyhound saild the 4th. June, Adml. Arbuthnots fleet 24th. May,

Sir Jas. Wallace has done something handsome on the coast of France

Saturday 24th. sent James early this morng. to Genl. Hospital N:York & wrote to Col: McPherson about him.

took Wm. Ross for my servant in the mean time, to whom Jas. delivered over my things yesterday as P inventory

Sunday 25th. July   Mounted Picquet before day at the former ground, the morng. cloudy & the day rainy, wind E & S:E: heard a salute – din'd at the house, 6 in Comy. a bottle each. The Light Infantry Picquet changed   The Capt. at the House on the Rochelle road

Monday 26th. another rainy day wt. the wind in the S:Ely. Qr. – we hear the Works at Stoney Point are making up again by the Brigade; – Fannings Corps went up there from Dobbs ferry –

Genl. Vaughan gone to N:York yesterday with his Baggage & a Serjt. & 4 of ours, a Corpl. & 6 return'd, – Genl. Mathews Commands in Camp – Qrs. at Babcocks – the 54th. Regt. gone somewhere to N:York

Tuesday 27th. July   Very warm   a ride to King's bridge & Ft. Kniphausen

Genl. Mathews orders for the army to march tomorrow morng. at 5 o'clock, and in the Eveng. countermanded

Wednesday 28th. cool wind Easterly   din'd with C:Col [quhoun]. – Major Barrymore of the Refugees out, was probably the reason we did not march this morng.

Orders again in the Eveng. for the army to march in the Morng at five, the Grrs. to go to McGowans, the Light Infantry to Horn's Hook. York Island –

Thursday 29th. Rainy morng. The orders for Marching Coun-

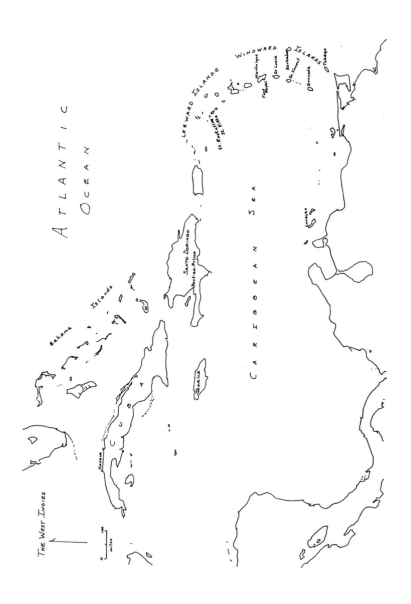

termanded again about 4 this morng. so pitch'd tents again & took another nap – much Desertion – a ship from Georgia in 7 days, says Sir Jas. Wallace is arrived there with 4 or 5 ships; that there has been an attack on Prevost at Stono ferry, & the Rebels repulsed with great loss. three from the Light Infantry deserted today, were pursued, one kill'd & two taken   two from the Grrs. went off & were taken up at New Rochelle by a young man call'd Vincent of East chester who march'd them into Camp, they were lodged in the Qr. Guard & in the Eveng. one of them (Bromker the 33d) cut his throat & dyed & was burried in the highway with a stake thro' his body. The Blonde frigate arrived from Halifax –

An officer from each of the Corps that were taken at Stoney Point come in for Necessaries, Lt. Grant of the 71st. Grrs. says that their two Companies had 50 killed & wounded, that the Garrison were alarm'd in good turn & the Works mann'd, that the attack on the right was twice repulsed, but that on the left succeeded by the negligence or mistake of Robtsons people, & the Work being open in the rear, The Rebels lost as many as we.

The Prisoners were march'd to Goshen & very well treated by Genl. Wayne who got a slight wound in the head; they have now left that & gone to Lancaster, the Country people very civil to them & seem to be well affected –

Butler within less than 20 miles of Goshen & had beat back all the Militia that were sent against him – [14]

Friday 30th. July moderate Wind about S:W: – The Grenville Pacquet arrived; sail'd from Falmouth 29th. May, – Sir Hugh Palliser acquitted. a fleet of 36 sail of the line under Sir Chas. Hardy to sail the latter end of June, a large french fleet at sea in May. we hear the french have taken Goree & Senegal in Africa, & St. Vincents in the West Indies M: la Mothe Picquets Squadron drove back to Isle of Aix with some loss   Yesterday Eveng. on the Parade the officers of the Battn. were called together by Lt.Col. Yorke, who said as Genl. Vaughan has always been polite & attentive to the Grrs., to any mark of respect we can show him have ye any objections – nem:con: – The little Warrior is going home, & wants to have the applause of the troops that served under him, to which he is very well entittled.

The particulars of the action at Stono ferry So: Carolina in the papers, with much credit to the 71st. –

A Schooner cut out of Boston harbour arrived at N:York by whom & other accots. the Yankies are making an expedition against Ponobscot, where Genl. [Francis] McLean with about 700 men have taken post – orders to march in the Morng. at 5, to the ground before mention'd –

Camp near McGowans York Island   Saturday 31st. July, a warm march of 13 miles, came to ground about noon[15] – The Papers full of English News & Parlimentary proceedings, a Committee of the Whole House on the Conduct of the War in No. America – The Island of Jersey attack'd by the French about the 1st. May. beat back with considerable loss

In the Eveng. got two letters from AH: dated 4th. & 18th. April acknowledging 20th. Novr. & 4th. & 24 Febr. but none betwixt; nor have I got any between the 7th. Febry. & these last, so that several have miscarried both going & coming   a Polite letter from Genl. Vaughan to the Grrs. in answer to their Compliment. we puff each other.

Sunday 1st. Augt. a hard Thunder Gust last night – Several Ships of War sail'd from New York gone to Ponobscot, Sir Geo. [Collier] in a funk –

Capt. S: gave us a batch of Scotch News & staid dinner, great revolution of property in the shire of Air –

Monday 2d. Augt. cloudy & showers   went over to Newtown Long island to see the little woman [Mrs. Rutherfurd] & the rest of acquaintances all well, – we hear the French have taken the Island of Granada & that there has been a sea fight in the West Indies.

Tuesday 3d. a ride to New York   a particular account of West Indies transactions in the papers by a Vessel who left St. Eustatia the 10th. ulto – matters are not going right there – Came home to Camp & din'd with Capt. S: who always drinks too much – Genl. Stirlings Brigade still at work on Stoney Point & the Rebels looking at ym. The Comr. in Chief & Lord Cornwallis has been up there t'other day – The field army are all now on York Island where I suppose we will remain till the fleet arrives. some say Genl. Clinton is to go home & Lord Cornwallis to Command, a little time will clear up these mysterious affairs.

Wednesday 4th. Augt. temperate nothing going on, some talk of transpts. getting ready for an expedition –

Thursday 5th. very warm the Rebel account of Stony point in the papers, & the resolves of Congress with thanks, & rewards for their gallant behaviour – had some of our friends the light bobs to dinner.

Friday 6th. warm writing to AH. to go by Genl. Vaughan a message from the little woman to breakfast tomorrow –

Saturday 7th. a Rainy storm from S:E: sent some arms to the Artillery forge New York to be mended – for the day in Camp ask'd to be one of a party to dine with Genl. Vaughan tomorrow at Hicks's N:York. The little Genl. wishes to part very good friends with the Grenrs. –

Sunday 8th. very warm indeed went to Newtown to breakfast, & from there to N:York where we had a little Turtle feast with Genl. Vaughan at Hicks's; only 8 in Company, took a very good dose of Claret, the little Warrior paid ye. Bill got some franks from the Genl. for my Father a Ship from Glasgow in 8 weeks no letters for me, nor do I hear any news

Monday 9th. the Grrs. changed their ground to the rear 2 miles, their right at the west side of the road near the 5 mile Stone, a pretty piece of green –

Tuesday 10th. Augt. very hot, wind W: a ship from Portugal who says there is a prospect of a Spanish War – some rain in the afternoon, din'd with J:S[Capt. John Smith?].

Wednesday 11th. very warm till the afternoon when came on to rain heavily, continued all night, & overflow'd the Camp, the ground being of a close clay soil bears the water on its surface for a long time –

Thursday 12th. Augt. very warm after the rain the ground still quite wet for whh. reason Col York applied for leave to change our ground, and we march'd at 5 P:M: about 3 miles to the northward & Encamp'd on a fine spot of ground where the action of 16th. Sepr. 1776 was we front a little to the eastwd. of North our left about 1/2 mile from the River. fine dry ground & pleasant prospects.

Friday 13th. Camp 8 miles from New York. The Compy. busy making hutts for ym. selves & some of them went down to the Creek at McGowan pass to look for thatch, where Hugh Fraser in bathing himself was unfortunately drowned without being perceived till it was too late,

Saturday 14th. Very hot weather & little or no wind, we hear the Yanky fleet intended against Ponobscot is dispers'd

Sunday 15th. Augt. still very hot wr. sent off my letters yesterday to AH: and my Fr. to Capt. Bell they are in a Frank of Genl. Vaughan's & dated 6 & 7th. they are to sail in a few days –
    a good deal of scalping on the frontiers of Pennsylvania; Genl. Sullivan conducting an Expedition against the Indians &ca. by Wyoming – [16]

Monday 16th. a good deal of rain in the night, today cool & pleasant, intended to go to Newtown, but my mare is missing tant mieux peut etre, – we were engaged to dine with our Light, but some on duty & some absent sent an apology –

Tuesday 17th. very warm weather & living, The Chisholm din'd with us, who never thinks of moving till he is drunk at which happy state he arrived between 9 & 10 & was carried off, ha ha ha

Wednesday 18th. Augt. very warm A fleet of ships come in from Georgia wt. rice & rum under convoy of the Perseus Capt. Elphinstone[17] who retook the June Pacquet near the Hook which had been just taken by 4 Privateers within 4 leagues of Sandy Hook N.W.B.N. she left falmouth 15 June, – The troops in Georgia in Summer Qrs. & most of Province has been overrun &

plundered in their absence by the Rebels & the unfortunate Inhabits. who took the oaths & protection of Governmt. are almost ruin'd – Govr. [Sir James] Wright arrived there in the Experiment, in order I suppose to reinstate civil govermt. there. his Daughter married to Sir Jas. Wallace at Savannah – The Govr. & those from home was surpris'd to find an Expedition had been undertaken against Chas. Town before the reinforcement arrived, where then did Mr. Prevost get his orders, they don't seem'd to be own'd here strange way of carrying on service this.

Thursday 19th. Augt. warm westerly w This morng. before day a party of the Rebels enter'd Powlis Hook without opposition (the Garrison being asleep) & took & carried off above 50 prisoners the Commandant Major [William] Sutherland got into an inclosed work with some Hessians & escap'd the fate of the rest. Col: Buskirks Corps of Provincials being out about English Neighbourhood 4 Companies of the Guards were sent early this Morng. to look after them.

Friday 20th. Showery wind S:E: The Guards & Buskirks Corps came in last night having taken a few prisoners, – the Rebels who took Powlis hook were comdd. by a Major [Henry] Lee, with about 100, retreated by Brown ferry – The Experiment Sir Jas. Wallace arrived at N York from Georgia
a Court of Enquiry order'd to examine into the circumstances of this affront at Powlis hook
Major Genl. Mathew Presidt. Brigrs. [Arthur George?] Martin & [George] Garth, Lt. Col: McPherson & [left blank] members – Din'd with Lord Cornwallis, with ease, elegance, & temperance, got wet coming home –

Saturday 21st. almost constant rain all last night & this morng. wind S:E: a Pacquet to sail in about a week. some Vessels come in from the West Indies whose accounts does not better our circumstances in that Quarter; Grenada & St.Vincents taken, & an engagement between Monsr. D'Estaing & Adml. Byron in which the British fleet were inferior in no. & tho they fought well, cannot deny but they had the worst of it. 21 Sail to 26.

Sunday 22d. Augt. the rainy wr. still continues & the wind about S:E: fair for the fleet. –

Monday 23d. much rain last night this morng. the wind came about to the N:W: & clear'd up – went over to Newtown to see my friend Rd. who is come down from Stony Point very ill, brought very low with a bilious complaint, but is now better; staid with the happy little Couple till the eveng. –
The 44th. Regt. going to Staten island suppos'd to be in place of the 26th. who are going to be drafted. The 17th. Dragoons went on Saturday from Newtown to Flushing to those a happy riddance, and to these unwelcome guests, – Capt. Deimar with his troop of Hussar's came over to York island today by Hell Gate; & some of the Light Infantry Baggage crossed over there this Eveng. the 57th. gone to town

Tuesday 24th. Augt. cloudy & cool wind from the northward – The Light Infantry Battalion cross'd over to Long Island this morng. they are going to take up ground near Denys's ferry probably on account of the mens health who were growing very sickly on that wet swampy ground about Horns hook. We hear that part of Adl. Arbuthnots fleet are arriv'd. – the Russel, a 74 Copper bottom'd, she has bro. the April Mail & some money, she left the fleet about 10 days ago, 100 leagues to the Eastwd –

Wednesday 25th. Strong wind S:E: Three letters from AH: of 21st. Febry. 5 & 21st. March, full of affection & anxiety poor soul, several letters missing yet. Jane arrived there 20 March, a joyous meeting
Adml. Arbuthnot in the Europa arrived with the fleet;[18] The Edn. Regt. McDonalds, part of the 82d. & a No. of Recruits for the different Regts. the troops very sickly having been above 5 months on board o'ship – Lt. Col: Hope & Majr. Drummond came in the Russel, the Robuste sent to Halifax, the Defiance to Quebec, with their respective Convoys.
we understand by the papers that the Rebels have made an attack on Genl. McLean at Ponobscot, have gain'd some points & been repuls'd in others –

Thursday 26th. cool No:westward went to Town, the Troops to land on Long Island & encamp at Bedford Bushwick &ca. – reced. a Letter R:M: 9th. March 3 others missing – Strange mismanagement of the Recruits at home, drafting them with great impropriety, & prejudice to the service, & the Regts. they belong to; Highland Recruits sent to other Regts. & those from English Regts. sent to the Highlanders, hurtfull to the Recruiting business, & productive of mutiny & desertion.

Friday 27th. Augt. pleasant & cool wind N:W: the Mail to be clos'd this evening, wrote & sent off a letter to AH: & one to R.M. I believe Genl. Vaughan did not sail till yesterday.

Saturday 28th. warm wind West went over in the Morng. to Newtown, to see the little couple, Capt. Rd. much better, staid dinner, & return'd in the eveng.
The Hessian Grenrs. gone into town to repair & make up some works, there are likewise some works making over at Brooklyn, for some time past –

Sunday 29th. warm wind S:W: the nights pretty cool now; They say the Battn. is to be divided into two, 1st. Hope's 2d. Yorke's – a Ship arrived from Glasgow N:B: recd. a letter yesterday from my Father dated 3d. March no mention of ye Bill all well, Jack & Charlie write – [19]

Monday 30th. Augt. warm wind S:O: a Compy. Review this morng. only a few pair of shoes wanting, some of their trowzers beginning to go already

Tuesday 31st. cool N:W: wind – struck tents & hutts to dry the ground
The Men growing very sickly within these few days, a general complaint over the whole army, they are mostly taken with headache & universal pain a chill & feverishness, which for the most part turns into a quotidien [quotidian] or tertian intermittent, & some few are taken with the flux.
I have 1 Sergt, & 11 sick today – six fellows down in the last 24 hours – The Country people here & in Long Island & likewise

very sickly: owing probably to the great deal of rainy wr. we had lately, more than any body remembers. with little or no thunder –

Wednesday 1st. Septr. warm wind Soy: more men falling down, 15 sick today the sick of the Battn (about 120) are lodged in two Barns, only one Surgn. to attend them, no nurses or utensils a great many officers are likewise falling sick of different Corps –

The 26th. & 44th. Companies left the Battn. today to join their Regts. on Staten island. The former to be drafted, the latter supposed to be going on some expedition as they are to be compleated to seventy 6 & and Lt. Col: Hope has join'd his Regt. – favourable reports of our affairs at Ponobscot, & of Joseph & his brethren about Wyoming –

something of consequence going on in the Cabinet, The Big wigs in deep consultation for some days past.

Emerich's Chasseurs dissolv'd –

Thursday 2d. Septr. warm in the day cool at night, wind southerly

The July Pacquet arrived last night a letter from AH: dated 26th. May Irvine happy among friends all well.

They say the Spaniards have join'd the french and War will be declared against them both very soon

Friday 3d. Showery all day with the wind about S:E: The Spaniards have publish'd manifesto's & their Ambassador the Count Almodavor has given in a rescript, acceding to the French Alliance with America, & complaining of some triffling grievances & injuries recd. from Great Britain; Ambassadors withdrawn & letters of Marque granted for making reprisals on the Spaniard the 26th. to be drafted today. the Officers to go to Newtown till further orders

Saturday 4th. a heavy constant rain last night, clear'd up in the morng. – went to Newtown to breakf. & staid dinner, The little man not so well again, a very sickly time everywhere, here about –

3 Sergts. & 23 today –

Sunday 5th. cool N:W: wind The number of sick increasing every day, in all the different Camps of the army, & nearly the same complaint vizt. a fever from Accumulated Bile more or less continued, according to the load or treatment of the patient & terminates in remissions, or intermissions with an ague – went to Bedford, to see Mr. McLean at his request, who has got the prevailing disorder, but is better. – The Parson very ill. My man better.

Monday 6th. Septr. warm with Southerly wind – for the day – visited the Battn. Hospital, about 200 Sick in three Barns, a Corpls. Guard & an orderly man at each, two Mates to attend them, & some comforts furnish'd from a Battn. fund that accrued from wood money last winter. – 50 Gus. – N:B: most of English & Irish recruits sent out for 42d. exchanged for Scotsmen from the 26th. –

Tuesday 7th. warm wind Soly. The Battn. muster'd this morng. by old Pitcher, we muster'd. 1 Capt. 2 Lts. 3 Sergts. 2 Corpls. & 34 private, the rest sick & on duty – at Town – nothing new – Affairs have the appearance of being in a becalm'd & confus'd situation. – Lord Rawdon has resign'd being Adjt. Genl – a letter from RM: 9 March a copy –
Wednesday 8th. Septr. warm S:W: sent to Town for Camp Equipage & got 14 tents 2 bell tents & 81 haversacks. The QMr. refused to deliver for the Establishmt. tho' I had settled that with him yesterday –
The number of Sick still increases today 2 Lts. 2 Serjts. & 33 R: & file –
Orders for paying the Hutt money £12 to each of the British Company's & 20 to the Hessians; spoke to Col Yorke to return us for 20 as a strong Compy.
The Light Infantry come to Brooklyn works making there –
The 44th, & two Hessian Battns. embark'd today – & Lt. Col: Hope in orders to take the Command of his Battn. of Grenrs.

Thursday 9th. a thunder gust this Morng. before day with a very heavy shower we have had no thunder for a long time –

Recd. £20 Hutt money, 5 guineas of it stop'd in the adjutants hands for an hospital fund to supply the sick with necessaries

Friday 10th. Septr. The Blonde frigate arrived from Ponobscot with accounts of the destruction of the Rebel fleet, the Siege rais'd, & the whole crew dispersed – they burn't 17 arm'd Vessels & above 20 sail of transports, our ships got two arm'd Vessels the Hunter & Hampden, this happen'd on the 13th. ulto. when the Rebels were preparing for a general attack by land & water, but the appearance of Sir Geo: Colliers squadron frightend them into a precipitate Retreat & destruction of their ships; they had besieged Genl. McLean for 3 weeks but with little prospect of success – [20]

a fleet of 8 sail of Cork Victualers arrived today they sail'd 11th. June – The 44th. & two Hessian Regts. sail'd under convoy of the Renown suppos'd for Quebec, Lum gone major to the 44th. Col. Hope come to the Grrs. –

Saturday 11th. Septr. a cool breeze from the S:W: went in the morng. to Newtown the little man has been thrown back a little with a jaunt to N:York to consult Mallet that muckworm – better today, from taking some laxative japonaceous pills, came home to dinner found the Battalion divided as follows 1st. Hopes consisting of 7th. 17th. 23d. 33d. 37th. 38th. 42d. & 43d. – 2d. York's, the 22d. 54th. 57th. 63d. 64th. 70th. & 74th. they chang'd ground & pitch'd accordingly[21] – Brigr. Stirling in N:York. come down from Stony point two or 3 days ago – Lt. Col: McPherson desir'd to join his Regt. some days ago in a very ungracious manner no other having come out Director Genl. of all the Hospitals British & foreign – much murmuring & complaint of Hd. Qrs. throughout – drank a bottle to the memory of the day[22]

Sunday 12th. Septr. warm wind S:W: 38 sick. only 7 men on the parade this morng. The Comr. in chief & Lord Cornwallis set off for Kings ferry; the wind came about to the No: suddenly & they return'd cool evening

Monday Septr. 13th. cool wind No: or N.N.E. the Experiment gone to Geoia. Brigr. Garth gone in her, supposed to command there vice Provost – Sir Geo Collier & some more ships come in from Ponobscot. we hear he has sent the Greyhound home – one of the Renowns fleet is come back to port having miss'd her Convoy. They sail'd in a very confused manner – a ride to Town. din'd at Hd. Qrs. major Crosbie, late. his Exy: did not sit long, & when he & Crosby were gone it was all noise & nonsense, how some people talk, – Shabby Bread & Cheese & a little punch in the Eveng. wt. the Brigr. Capts. Smith & McLachlan there slept in I:S: Qrs. got 9 men from the Regt. 7 of them Grrs. from the 26th. one of these in Genl. Hospital at N:York, & a letter from the Major recomending a Volr. (a Mr. Sutherland), to the Grrs. – the Delaware arrived fr: Rhode Island

Tuesday 14th. Septr. a cool N:Ed. came home to breakfast, & waited on the Col: – no. of sick still increasing – 41 club'd dinners with the 23d. Pork & fish. – The Blonde was to sail today. call'd on to be one of three to decide on a difference between two young gentlen. the one was more in the wrong than the other, but they were both to blame, whh. is generaly the case, in these affairs.

Wednesday 15th. cold & blowy wr. wind about N.E. this sudden change of the weather, marks the vicissitude of the climate in these provinces, which I believe is more in extreme than any other part of the world.

Thursday 16th. Septr. cool with the wind No: & N:N:E: intended to go to N:Town but the mare is amissing – Sick 44 –

Friday 17th. warm – a ride to Newtown & din'd with my little friends, he is better & she has got a touch of the ague –

Saturday 18th. Septr. warm day sat down to write letters, – in the Eveng. recd. one from AH: favour Lt. [John] Hathorn dated 11th. March – the 63d. Regt. order'd for embarkation in place of the 37th. who are very sickly

Sunday 19th. very warm went to Bedford to call on Mr. Hathorn but he was not at home, left a message – The 57th. Coy. gone to their Regt. much promotion in the orders –

Monday 20th. moderate some Regts. embarking. the 64th. come down to Spiten devil   the 63d. to NYork –

Tuesday 21st. went to Town to meet Mr. H: but he did not come – the 7th. & 23d. Gr. compys embark'd with their Regts. the 33d. come down   A fleet arrived at the Hook supposed to be Sr. Andw. Hammonds – consulting about Sea Stock

Wednesday 22d. Septr. cold No:Wind   wrote the Major in answer to his of 10th. Settled Mess accots. to this date   the lads in debt as P mess Book – got 6 months pay for myself yesterday from the Pay Mr. to 24 Octr. – 63 guineas & he is about selling out; gave my vote to Rutherfurd for being Paymr. – Sir Andw. Hammond with about 50 sail arrived, left Corke about 20 July The Parliament prorogued, & a prospect of more unanimity at home – about 1000 Hessian Recruits come in ye. fleet   The 33d. Comy. march'd this morng. to join their Regt. on board –

Thursday 23d. cool North wind at Town – The fleet drop'd down to the Hook   Lord Cornwallis to go on board this Eveng. this division consists of the 7th. 23d. 33d. & 54th. with their flank Comys. the Legion – & Volrs. of Ireland[23]   put in a letter into Post office for AH: Paid in ten guineas for the Mess on board being 28 days pay. collected by the Adjt. to be given to the Coll: to pay the Suttler – the 42d. continues at Stony Pt.

Friday 24th Septr. cold & raw NW with some rain in the after-noon – one of the transports of the 44th. Regt. turn'd, being dispers'd in a storm   the No. of sick still increasing – Lt. Grant gone to Jones's – new Embarkation Returns call'd for & an order for compleating the flank Coys.

Saturday 25th. warm wind Soly.   the fleet gone out of the Hook, supposed for Georgia or So: Carolina –

Sunday 26th. wind S:E: & came on rain in the forenoon which continued all day – went in the Morng. to Newtown the little Couple better – from thence to N:Y: call'd the Camp of the 80th. & saw Lt. Hathorn   din'd & staid all night in Town   a Report by a Privateer that d'Estaing's fleet was seen on the

Bahama Bank which has occasion'd Lord Cornwalliss fleet to
return into port – another ship of the 44th. come back – they are
putting Guns into the Batterys at N:York –

Monday 27th. Septr. fair wr. & cool westerly wind; came
home to dinner wrote to the Major about more Grrs. in compli-
ance with the order of 24th. part of Lord Cornwallis's fleet come
up to the Narrows; and a great no. of ships come from the North
River to the East River, & about 20 gone up thro' Hell Gate to
Whitestone – a letter from D:M: dated 23d. May by a Capt.
Lawrie wishing me to assist him in the sale of his Carronades[24]
I wish I could oblige you Dick but I don't know how – Saw Jack
Inglis & Richardson of the Guards in Town

Tuesday 28th. Septr. fine weather a walk to Laurel hill, the
works there still going forward, making a Communication from
thence to the work on the other ridge, by means of Redoubts of
different kinds & distances, joined by a line of Stockades – a
Scouting party out yesterday of a detachmt. of 64th. and Simcoes
as far as east Chester, expecting to fall in with part of Moylands &
Whiler Rebel dragoons, but miss'd them. Lord Cornwallis's fleet
at Staten island but they say his Lordship is on board the Russel
not yet come in – Various opinions about this french fleet & what
is to be done here. – The mail for the Pacquet to be closed this
evening – C. Hatfd din'd with me nobody else at home bottle
a piece to keep off the Ague –

Wednesday 29th. Septr. very fine wr. for the Season, the days
moderately warm & the nights cool – Genl. orders for the Troops
under Lord Cornwallis to land as soon as convenient the 7th. near
Brooklyn works, 23d. & 33d near Deny's – the 57th to go to
Sandy hook, the Queens Rangers to Richmond to relieve the 37th.
who go to Newtown on account of the very sickly state of that
Regt. the Volrs. of Ireland to be likewise landed on Staten
Island & to be station'd by Brigr. Patterson
  The Comys. of the 44th. that came back are to go to Paulis
hook – Lord Cornwallis's Corps will continue in readiness to
reembark on the shortest notice, so that their flank Compys. will

remain with them for the present. Lt. Coll. [John] Leland of the Guards to act as Brigr. – it seems Lord Cornwallis, & his Corps were destin'd for the Island of Jamaica

Thursday 30th. Septr. fine wr. wind No:ly I hope this weather will be of service to the sick & check the progress of the disease, which is still seizing on new subjects & but very few of the old recoving. the 37th. Regt. I am told have not 30 men fit for duty – [25]

Camp N:York Island Harlaem Heights near the North River and about 8 miles from Town, a very sickly Camp, tho the ground we [word illegible] is high & dry & looks to be as healthy a spot as any on the Island

Friday 1st. Octr. 1779 fair weather and warm, wind in the South

The Troops under Lord Cornwallis landed on Long & Staten Island agreeable to the order of the day before yesterday – no more word of this West India fleet. some disturbances at Philada. & remonstances from the Merchts. against the police –

The number of sick still increases, some few fluxes which has carried off some men; but the general complaint is an undistinct remitting & intermitting fever, with & without more or less of an ague which proves more lasting & obstinate as their great numbers does not admit of that care, treatment, & attention that is necessary only one Hospital Mate to attend 130 or 40 Sick, & few comforts –

Saturday 2d. Octr. fine wr. wind So:ly some more of the 44th. come in & we hear their fleet were entirely dispersed & some of them taken

a Party of the Inhabitants at work on Govrs. Island, & a proportion of the Militia of Long Island are required to work at Brooklyn, or furnish fascines, fraize &ca. we seem to be entirely on the defensive. & I hear that Rhode Island is be to evacuated Lt. Col: Stuart gone there some day ago on something of importance – being alone at home – din'd 43d. Lt. Ds

Sunday 3d. very hot, wind So:ly The Renown is come in with

two of the 44th. & one Hessian transport, of the rest they only know that one is taken, they suffer'd much in that Gale of wind that happen'd about the middle of last month. a Report that Monsr. La Mothe Picquet with the french fleet has call'd at Georgia & landed 5000 Troops; tant pis. Grant worse today –

Monday 4th. Octr. warm wind So:ly all the works still going fo[r]ward for the defense of these three Islands in case Monsr. should pay us a visit –

Genls. Phillips & Ridesel of the Non: army were at Eliza. Town together t'other day on their way in, but were recall'd by order of Congress & sent back to Chatham [26]

The No. of sick does not yet diminish here in Camp & what is somewhat strange those of the 44th. increased at sea.

Tuesday 5th. early in the morng. the wind came about to the North & NE & hazy rain in the forenoon & showery all day cold & raw – a bottle of port –

Wednesday 6th. cold with the wind from the No. & N:E: with rain – Col: Stuart is return'd from Rhode Island. no word of an evacuation of that Post which probably won't happen now as the french fleet is said to have gone back to the West Indies a Ship from Liverpool arriv'd at Rhode Island 22d. of September in 46 days, the Grand fleet had return'd to Torbay was reinforc'd & sail'd again with about 37 sail of the line & more getting ready, news as late as the 8th. of Augt. but no word of an engagement –

Thursday 7th. Cloudy & cool WNW went to Town & got waistcoat cloth for the Compy & a box of Soap – They say that Lord Cornwallis's Corps are to embark again, And that Stoney Point is invested. we must look before we leap –

Call'd on Major [John] Small – & din'd wt. the Brigr. [Stirling] tête a tête – consulted Dr. Morris & got a prescription for Grant. representing his case as a Rheumatic fever Rx Pilul: Plumm Ziij Sapon:Zi M fiat Pil: 48 Capiat No. 4 6ta quoque hora in haust: de infus: flor Chamom: cum gutt: xv ex Spt. Corn: Cerv: Zi & Lavin Z3 fs M – gave these to Dr. Muir to be administer'd by him – [27]

Friday 8th. Octr. cold & blowy at W: & W.N.W. a ship come in from West Indies in 18 days – Adml. Byron gone home the fleet at Barbados the fleet at Whitestone sailed to the Eastwd. in the Eveng. suppos'd to be ships going to bring the Troops from Rhode Island The eveng. more moderate – expected Capt. [Francis] Richn. of the Guards but he did not come –

Saturday 9th. fine mild day wind West took a walk with the Surgeon to look for a better hospital for the sick, we pitch'd upon the White Stable at Delancys burnt house for about 44, the House at the Creek side below McGowans for abt. 66, and the room of the house where they are at present for the remainder. 122 in hospital and above 20 in Camp, hope we shall get them moved tomorrow. McLean relaps'd into the Ague two days ago & went to Town today to stay till he is better – Grant no better. 2 Sergts. & 59 sick[28] petit[e] partie au soir chez monsr. L. Coll.

Sunday 10th. Octr. warm wind about west Accounts from Stoney point that the Rebels are making their approaches, & we have orders of being in readiness, & beside those that were order'd before, the 76th. 8oth. & 82d. if Mr. Washington should come there in force I'm afraid we shall have some difficulty in relieving that useless post, in the present sickly situation of the Army. I wish our people were handsomely quit of it – two ships gone up the River today.

cou'd not move the sick today for want of straw –

a letter yesterday from D:M: favr. Mr. Hastie dated 12 May acknowledging mine of 1st. March & recommending the bearer

Monday 11th. Octr. warm, wind everyway mostly So: small craft passing up & down ye. River, & three ships come up to take on board the Grrs. the Battns. under arms at 1 o'clock & march'd by the left to the beach below Jones's & embark'd on board the Joseph, Laurie, Eleanor on board the Joseph 17th. 37th. 38th. & 42d. Col Hope embarked a feeble Coy. of 3 Serjts. & 23 R: & file a good deal of firing & saluting below some privateers come in & another ship of the 44th. –

the 7th. 23d. & 33d. embark'd yesterday & the Volrs. of Ireland –

Tuesday 12th. Octr. strong Soly. wind. The Comr. in chief gone up to Stoney Pt. with the Fanny & some small craft,
A number of large vessels sunk at the entrance of the Hook to stop the passage in case the Monsr. should attempt to get in
our three ships mov'd up opposite the Camp ground, near the wreck of the Mercury. – the two Lt. Colls. stay ashore Lt. Grant gone to Town today in Commissary Grants Carriage, very weak

Wednesday 13th. cool wind in the North came ashore & took a ride to Town wt. Coll. Hope – a Spanish Pacquet from the Havanah taken & brought in by a privateer. another ship of hessians of that dispers'd fleet come in after being taken & retaken The Comr. in chief come down in the afternoon with the Fanny &ca.

Thursday 14th. Octr. cold & blowy from the North, no word of moving 8 of us in a mess on board. a Capt. & 2 Subs. to remain constantly on board the rest may come ashore in the daytime

Friday 15th. pleasant wr. wind No: I hear the pacquet sail'd some days ago went ashore & saw the Sick; some getting better, & some falling sick on board –
I understand it is left to Col. Hope to land the Grrs. when he thinks proper, but we are to remain on board a few days as there is less duty, & supposed to be more healthy The two Lt. Colls. at Jones's, where they have a picquet of a Corpl. & six from the Battns. alternately – The 7th. & 57th. & Vols. of Ireland are going to sea, the Grr. & Light Compys. to be left behind to join the flank Corps.
They say they are going to Halifax with Brigr. Stirling –

Saturday 16th. Octr. warm wind So: 7th. Grr: Coy. join'd today, & some recover'd men came on board – we are to get another large ship for a convalescent Hospital, & to remain on board on account of health – all quiet at Stoney Point & the 42d. expected down soon –

Sunday 17th. pretty cold at night & warm in the day, wind in the west, – came ashore & pitch'd my tent, – took a ride to New-town to visit the little Couple but the Capt. being not at home push'd on for New York, called on Hathorn not in Camp, gone into a house – came to Brooklyn just at 3 din'd at the ordinary with a very good sett of 12, cross'd the ferry in the eveng. & came home to camp –

Monday 18th. west & S:W: a ride to Town more works making for the defense of the place & guns prooving & getting ready to be mounted. Sir Jas. Wallace suppos'd to be taken by an 80 gun ship of the french fleet, off the Coast of Georgia after being dis-masted in the Gale, middle of Sepr. – & that the french have taken that province & made the troops prisoners

The Renown came up from the Hook having lost some masts, & some vessels come in – call'd on the Brigr. to bid him farewell, with some faint hopes, but as he did not, so I was resolved not to, touch on the subject –

call'd on Saunders Grant & found him better & on McLean but he was got out, it seems he has been applying to Genl. Stirling for leave to go home that young man will not do –

din'd on board – Capt. Hume dislocated his shoulder going up the ships side brot. the Surgn. & help to reduce it just before dinner

Tuesday 19th. cool, wind N.W. went on board in the morng. being for the day – 7 flat boats, a large ship & some small craft gone up the river, with an agent – it is reported that Adml. Parker with the fleet from the west Indies is on the coast – the Papers full of Congress business they have elected Saml. Huntingdon of Conecticut Presidt. vice John Jay who is going Ambassador to Spain, he goes with Monsr. Gerard who is relieved, addresses & answers to & from &ca.

Wednesday 20th Octr. warm, wind South sent ashore some of the recovered men that relaps'd again into the ague McNicol

died last night of the flux – those ashore recovering but slowly. a ride to Laurel Hill the works still going on, in joining that & the other ridge, Troops still without the bridge covering the workmen that are getting abbatis stuff, fraize &ca. for the works within. The Troops &ca. at Rhode Island were to be all embark'd today; but if Adl. Parker comes it may prevent the evacuation of that Place
I hear Stoney Point is to be evacuated immediately – another ship come up for the Grenrs.

Thursday 21st. fine warm wr. S.W. the Robuste arrived from Halifax a Stormy passage of 3 weeks – wrote a letter to Ld. C – t [Cathcart] begging the favour of him to recommend me to the Comr. in chief for a M:oB: – & spoke to Col: Hope about it, with whom I din'd today[29]

Friday 22d. Octr. foggy morng. warm weather & southerly wind – a ride to Spitten Devil see a number of ships & small craft coming down the River which we take to be the Troops &ca. from Stoney Point & Verplanks; I believe they have got off in good time, for the Rebels were certainly meditating something against that post. the taking & making of which, & the losing & taking & making again, has cost 7 or 800 men & seems to have been the whole business or object of the Campaign

Saturday 23d. a foggy morng. & a warm day, wind in the south, visited the Hospitals, our men getting better, on duty on board of ship where we continue to mess, 10 in number – a Pacquet arrived with the Augt. & Septr. mails, no Genl. sea action at home   The Ardent taken by 3 french 74s. The combin'd fleet too powerfull for the British 54 sail to 39 no match –

Sunday 24th. Octr. rain from the S.W. sent to Town for my letters & got them in the evening, no less than five from my little deary, vizt 14th. & 30th. June 16th. & 21st. July & 12th. Augt. – one from Dr. Fleeming 27th. July & one from my Fr. 23d. July acknowledging mine of the 15th. June, all well & happy & full of kindness & affection, for which God be prais'd & make us truely thankfull –

Monday 25th. cool N.W. wind a ride to Town to hear the news The french & Spanish fleets 60 sail lay off Plymouth 4 days in latter end of Augt. without attempting any thing, the British fleet being out at Sea miss'd them, but it was expected they would soon meet – the Spirit of the Nation very high fitting out more ships & raising more troops – The 42d. landed & encamp'd north of the Town, they are to take Town duty din'd with the Major & some more at Queens head staid till near 8 – club 3 dollars – call'd on Lord Cathcart who has had a relapse of this feverish disorder & looks very thin, he introduced me to his Lady a pretty woman & big with child – & then mention'd his having recd. my letter but that his illness prevented him from seeing the Genl. since, but he wod. take the first oppoy. of speaking to him or writing, & hop'd for the best, & seemed very willing to use his interest.

The 7th. Regt. are landed again on Staten Island, & its tho't Genl. Stirling is sail'd with the 57th. 4 compys. 82d. & the Volrs. of Ireland, for Halifax –

I hear the Grenrs. are to go to their old Hutts at Jamaica in a few days –

The Daphné to sail tomorrow for England & Col Stuart goes in her having got a new Regt. at home – finish'd a letter after I came home, but afraid I am too late –

Tuesday 26th. Octr. cool N.Wd. & clear Battn. orders for all the Baggage to be put on board tomorrow morng. & the ships to fall down with the tide & make the best of their way to Hallets Cove in the East River where the Grenrs. will disembark & proceed to Jamaica.

Wednesday 27th. clear & cold wind NW. The Transports got under way about 11 & drop'd down to New York, where we recd. orders to proceed to Brooklyn ferry & land there in the morng. –

The Rhode Island Garrison Arrived, having evacuated the place on [date not included] & left fuel & forage enough for the whole winter, a countermanding order had been sent to prevent their coming away, but it was taken – they had plenty of every thing, & the necessity of quitting that place does not yet appear –

got 20 men from the hospital t'other day & 6 of them are relapsed already –

Thursday 28th. Octr. fair & clear. The Grrs. landed at Brooklyn & march'd to Jamaica, & when the Baggage came up in the Eveng. Encamp'd on our old ground near the English Church, – Battn. Orders for the preservation of good behaviour read to the Compys. – officers to Sleep in Camp till the Hutts are repair'd & Qrs. arranged –

Friday 29th. Octr. pleasant wr. & warm wind in the Southerly Qr.
Battn. orders for occupying our former Hutts, & for making the necessary repairs immediately, no parades till that is done when application will be made for our going into them.
call'd & saw some old acquaintances who I believe are sorry to see the Grrs. return & that too so early into winter Quarters, for which indeed they have reason, for they suffer'd a good deal last winter from the depradation & tricks of some sad rascals
I find they have been as sickly here as any where, with the same kind of disorder

Saturday 30th. Octr. thick fogg in the morng. the day clear'd up & warm.
The men at work on the Hutts but no tools come yet – Brigr. Stirling come up from the Hook & tis said these troops will not sail.
The Rhode Island people to go to Huntington & Satawket – 54th. to New Town, Anspachers New York –
Wrote a long letter to AH: for the Pacquet that is announced – sup'd Major Cortlands

Sunday 31st. foggy morng. & warm day, a ride to Newtown to see the Paymr. but he was not there, wrote him a note by Dr. Robison, saw the little woman – came home to dinner – The Comr. in chief came here today on his way farther east & the Adml. with him –
Mr. McLean came here today to acquaint me of his intentions

of going home, he is to ask leave on accot. of his health & circumstances, but I fancy he has something else in view –

Monday 1st. Novr. cold nights in camp   Races at Hampstead today: The Genl. gone to Jericho – the few men that are well & off duty are working at the Hutts – dined alone & wrote more to AH –

Tuesday 2d. The Comr. in chief & the Admiral return'd to Town
Browns Corps march'd thro for Huntington, encore Solus –

Wednesday 3d. cold N.W. new thatching the Hutts, out shooting

Thursday 4th. cold wind NW went over to Newtown to breakfast with the little couple, & staid all day
the 43d. Regt. march'd thro' for Huntington – got a Bill from J:R: £50

Friday 5 cool & clear drew for Qrs. I Draw Abm. Ditmass only one little room, for me, & one without a fire place for 2 Subs.

Saturday 6th. pretty cold NW removed the sick into the Hutts, they are growing worse for want care & comfortable lodging –
The 57th. & a Hessian Regt march'd thro' for Flushing & the 38th. is come to the head of the fly

Sunday 7th. cool, wind westerly took a Sweep of a walk round south to look at the Qrs. have got the room at Creeds for one of the Subs. – had the 2 Lts. of the 76th. & 80th. to dine   Sent off my letters for the Pacquet one for AH: dated 30th. Octr. 1st. & 5 Novr. above 7 pages – & one for my Fa. with a Bill £50. on the Agents – varrious accots. about the state of Georgia

Monday 8th. mild wr. NW   The Light Infantry arrived to take possession of their former Qrs. had some to dine

Tuesday 9th. Novr. thick atmosphere & a cloudy uncommon Sky – got the rough work of our Hutts finish'd & reported to the

Lt. Coll. din'd at Rollo's his uncle there what a poor ugly creature the wife is

Wednesday 10th. cold N:W: wind   wrote to the Major about our donation articles &ca. – the Compy. struck tents at nine & went into their hutts   I sent my baggage to my Qrs. & went to see the Races on Hempstead Plains call'd on Judge Ludlow who went with me, but they were not worth seeing   din'd with the judge & came home in the Eveng. to my new Qrs. which I think will do very well if I get all for myself – the Landlord was formerly a Capt. in the Rebel Service I understand, but changed his mind – two french prisoners in the house

Chapter IX

'tossing & tumbling'

New York to South Carolina
11 November 1779 to 10 February 1780

During the summer of 1779, Sir Henry Clinton had begun to despair of ending the rebellion in a single, climactic battle along the Hudson River. As he did, he began to think of pursuing the British government's southern strategy – its preference for using Loyalists to assist the army in a gradual restoration of royal authority from Georgia northward through the Carolinas and Virginia. He eventually decided to undertake such a strategy not just because the British government preferred it and because he lacked the forces to gain a decisive victory in the north but also because he wanted to preserve the gains made by the detachment he had sent to Georgia in the fall of 1778, to protect that detachment and the Loyalists of Georgia from the attacks of rebels based in South Carolina. By late September 1779 he was preparing to sail for South Carolina. Before he could get underway, he learned that a French squadron had reached Georgia to join with the rebels in besieging Savannah. He decided, therefore, to postpone his expedition, to await the outcome of events at Savannah. Not until December was he sure that the siege had failed and that the French had returned to the West Indies. Only then was he willing to sail from New York, and he would be another seven weeks at sea before he could put his men ashore in South Carolina, before he could begin carrying out Britain's southern strategy.[1]

So it was that John Peebles and the British grenadiers were nearly three tedious months redeploying from New York to South Carolina. They had gone into winter quarters on Long Island in early November 1779. At first they found time for a variety of diversions – for the usual dinners, card parties, and ritualistic celebrations that emerged each time the army came to rest and even for several days of horse racing. But they were never able to settle into the predictable winter routine that they had known the previous year. They were too busy preparing for the impending expedition to South Carolina. Peebles now regularly inspected his men and their arms and ammunition, oversaw the storage of all heavy baggage, kept track of men who were ill or convalescing, and purchased food and drink – sea stores – for the voyage.[2] And once he and his men were at sea, they had to endure an exceptionally long and rough mid-winter passage. Strong winds and thick weather soon dispersed the more than one hundred square-rigged vessels that sailed from New York on 26 December. The transport carrying the 42nd grenadiers went on alone for five days and then in company with only one or two other ships until reaching the coast of Georgia. Contrary winds frequently kept Peebles and his shipmates lying to under close-reefed sails; the Gulf Stream retarded their progress; and heavy seas not only sank one of the small vessels in company but also threw them about their cabin, smashing their crockery as well as their shins.[3] They were at sea so much longer than they anticipated that they had to ration water and replenish their supply in Georgia before reaching South Carolina on 10 February 1780.[4]

New York to South Carolina
11 November 1779 to 10 February 1780

Thursday 11th. [November 1779] pleasant wr. for the season wind
N.W. visited the Hutts & Sick, the officers Hutt begun by Lt.
[Robert] Rollo, Grant sick in Town & [Lt. Allan] McLean I
understand has got leave to go home –
Capt. [James] G[raham]: 57, & [Robert] Potts call'd here &
din'd & propos'd messing, but I declin'd it, besides the distance
is too great –

Friday [12th.] sent Sergt. Smith & two men to NYork for the
Compys. donation cloth & the plaids & hose & my Baggage &ca.
went to Town to get that done & some other things, The 42d.
come into Town two days before, & busy settling in Qrs. got all
things over the ferry before dinner, took a Coffee room dinner at
Loosly & Elms's a trio 12/ cash & came home in the evening, but
for want of carriage left the Baggage at Brooklyn with the Sergt. &
3 men –

Saturday 13th. mild wr. rather warm W: & S:W: on duty for
the day – sent a Waggon for my Baggage whh. came up just
before dinner. – Solus – Sergt. Smith came up in the Eveng. with
the Plaids hose & 60 yard of the brown donation cloth –

Sunday 14th. rather warm call'd on the Col: [Hope] to report &
ask leave to go to N:York for a night but could not find him, so
proceeded without call'd on Capt Hathorn of the 80th. Sick:
Venerl Major [Charles] Graham & the Captains of the 42d. met
by appointment to consult about some Regimental money that is
lodged in Br. Genl. Stirlings hands when they were unanimously
of opinion that the Security is not sufficient & sign'd a paper
requesting Genl. Stirling to give a bond for the same & settle the
whole with the Paymr. before he goes to be deliver'd by Major
Graham who is empowered to settle the matter din'd at the
Queens Head Strachans & made a Sederunt till 1 o'clock of the
morng. – slept at Rutherfords

Monday 15th. blowy from west saw the parade 42d. Hessian

grrs. and Anspachers between 4 & 500 these last are fine looking fellows – made a fair visit & a noble call cross'd the ferry & came trotting home to dinner solus – The Taylors at work on brown cloth trowzers.

Tuesday 16th Novr. cold NW   The Sick recovering but slowly – all the men that are well & off duty at work on the officers Hutt every day   Got Col: Abercromby's permission for Mr Crue & partner to bring goods to Jamaica to sell during winter Balnabie came to me in the Eveng.

Wednesday 17th. Novr. wind NE & some snow – met with Lord Cathcart at Jamaica in his return from Huntington & took occasion to ask if he had spoke to his Exy. about that affair, not yet, but he wod. take the first oppoy. – Balnabie & Potts din'd with me the former stays

Thursday 18th. cold NW took a look at the hutts & made some calls –
Great news from Georgia of our having repulsed & defeated the combin'd attack of the french & Rebels at Savanah 3000 of the Enemy kill'd & wounded with very little loss on our side; the Particulars not yet come to hand. but the account authentic

Friday 19th. Novr. cold frosty morng. a more particular accont. of our success in Georgia in the papers it comes from St. Augustine by the Rosebud Privr. – the french landed 4000 men & were join'd by 5 or 6000 americans under Lincoln, they made a joint attack on Savanah 9th. Octr. headed by The Count DeEstaing when 1500 french were kill'd & wounded & as many Rebels D'Estaing himself wounded in two places, & Count [Casimir] Pulasky kill'd   the Rebels retreated to Carolina & the French to their ships
Accounts as late as 22d. Octr. from Savanah say that the french fleet were still on that coast –
The Army fired a few feu de Joy in the eveng. at their respective Qrs. & Cantonments on accot. of the above success

Saturday 20th. Novr. mild wr. & westerly wind – on duty for

the day – din'd at the tavern with Capt. Chas. McL[ean?]. & some more, he is going home some rain in the Eveng. – long orders about buying & selling & making Reports & returns & the Lord knows what all –

Articles Rec'd from the Regt. in consequence of the order of 2d. Novr. 6 pieces Russia drill, 38 Blankets 18 pieces 453 yds. Linnen 178 pairs of Shoes 178 prs Soles 118 yds brown Cloth 89 prs mitts 100 needles 2 1/2 lbs brown Thread 3 lbs white do. 1 thimble 6 pils. binding 89 doz: horn buttons 29 doz: shirt do. – recd. 17th. Novr.

a Letter in the Papers from Lt. Col: [Lewis Val.] Fuser of the Royl. Americans at St. Augustine to Genl. Clinton, with an Account of the Affair at Savannah, & one from Govr. [Patrick] Tonyn to the Adml –

Sunday 21st. Novr. Strong west & S:W: wind with wet fog The Sick recovering but slowly – 29 in the Doctors list, & 12 convalescents many relapses –

Monday 22d. blowy wr. westerly had a Review of Arms this morng. & found them in very bad order, all the men that are well & off duty are constantly at work, which is some excuse for themselves & their arms being dirty.

a man of the 74th. Grrs. found this morng. at Capt. Betts's Lt. [Christopher] Lysters, Qrs. almost dead, & some after expired, the cause is not yet known –

Tuesday 23rd. Novr. mild wr. writing letters to go by the fleet which they say is to sail in a few days to AH: my Fr. & Dr F

Wednesday 24th. cold frosty NW a Parade in the morng. for the purpose of inflicting punishment on some rascals that were out at night marodg. both Battns. Concern'd & flogg'd severly to put a stop to this infamous practice

went to N:York on business ask'd the Major by desire of Col Hope for an officer & some men to complete to the level of the Battn. compy. – both of which he declin'd giving, as he says they scarce of offrs. & the duty is hard on the men – complain'd to him of Qr.Mr. Smith having beat a man of the Grrs. & begg'd of him to speak to him about it which he said he would do – din'd with 2d. Battn. mess Geo:Dal[rymple]: at bed at R[utherfur]ds.

Thursday 25th. Novr. fine wr. no certain time fix'd for the fleet to sail for England – saw the Parade the 42d. Hessian Grrs. & Anspachers the Highlanders look very well, & in good clean order, the Hessian Grrs. dress'd up & powder'd, the Anspachers the finest looking troops & tallest, I ever saw, & in high discipline.

Major Crosbie ask'd Major Graham & me to dine at HeadQrs. tomorrow which detains me a day longer in town din'd today with the Major at the 1st. Batton. mess, things in tastey order

The Regt. in two messes, not well accomodated as to rooms, but may live very well as they are all rich with Virginia prize money – petit souper chaque soir, chez les petit[s] heureuze [Rutherfurds] ou jai couche et dejeune

Friday 26th. Novr. a fall of snow called on the Brigr: [Stirling] these two days past but did not see him at home – met him at Rivingtons Corner, dry in manner & displeas'd, I suppose on account of that paper sign'd by the Capts. spoke to him about Volr. Sutherd. but got no satisfactory answer, & he cut off – [5]

din'd at HeadQrs. 19 or 20 at table His Ex: complaisant & in good humour an extract of a letter from a Baltimore paper read giving an account of Adl. Parker having taken a man of war & 14 sail of Victualers bound for St. Domingo & a less certain account of his falling in with 6 or 7 sail of the line & 70 transports, broke up about 7 & went with a little party to the Queen Hd. –

Hints thrown out at Hd.Qrs. as if there was an expedition to take place soon – invited to St. Andw. there, tuesday next

Saturday 27th. Novr. clear frosty morng. & 3 or 4 inches of snow on the ground.

look'd at some men for Grrs. yesterday & today, but I believe won't get them yet a while – recd. abstracts & money from the Paymr. for the Comy. from 25th. April to 24 Octr. £352 &ca. left 300 guineas with him till next time I go to Town – show'd the mare at the Qr.Mr. Genls. office, for sale but they wod. not offer me any thing worth taking met his Lordship [Cathcart] there who very kindly & politely took occasion privately to tell me that he was going that day to speak to his Ex about my request, & ask'd me if I wod. take a 5/ P day in the Qr.Mr. Gl. department, which I declin'd,

bot. stuff for a Coat &ca. very high   crossd the ferry & got home thro' dirty road by 4, & din'd solus on salt pork, a sad falling off from yesterdays dinner –

Sunday 28th. Novr. soft wr. Drumr. McIntyre return'd from the Rebels, he says he was taken prisoner 11th. June, made his escape from a party that were conducting him to fairfield Gaol, lived among the Tory's ever since, & assisted by them to make his escape across the sound to Loyds Neck   Reported him to Col: Hope as above & he is forgiven. –

din'd at Capt. [Robert] Irvings with Rollo & his wife; very well – visited the hutts in the forenoon.

The Perseus Capt. Elphinstone come in from a cruise & brot. in a large prize of 24 Guns & 80 going to join the french fleet in Chesapeak where they are suppos'd to be by the last accounts,

18 sail of large french ships wt. stores & provision taken by Adml. Parker

Monday 29th. Novr. soft wr. a Genl. Court martial to set at Jamaica today for the tryal of Lt. Lyster 63d. for murder of that man of 74th. that was found dead at his Qrs. – adjourn'd till tomorrow

din'd wt Capt. Jas. Gr: at Mr. Smiths gave out to the Compy. a dollar a man & two to the Sergts. to keep St. Aw.

Tuesday 30th. fine wr. & gentle frost review'd the Compys. arms; pretty well a caution about good order &ca.

Went to Town to celebrate the day with his Ex: where the field offrs. & Capts. of the 42d. were invited, the Adml. [Arbuthnot] there the offrs. of the Royl. Highland emigrants & some others, about 24 in all. Major Small personated the St. who gave very good toasts & apropos for the occasion, The adml. very chatty & entertaining. Major [Adam] Hay sang some good songs & spouted a prologue very well a good dinner & drink till 10 oclock   a

numerous party of the Sons of St. Andw. din'd at Hicks's above
60, among whom were the Subs. of the 42d exchang'd a com-
plit. & some of our Compy. join'd them after we broke up, &
made a night of it –

Wednesday 1st. Decr. fine wr. & gentle frost in the night –
bot. some things & paid all accounts in Town – settle'd wt Mr.
McLean his mess accot. &ca. rather tardy in paymt. brot. home
Compys. money to 24th. Octr. – din'd solus, on ration
The fleet for England expected to sail on Sunday next –

Thursday 2d. rainy morng. sometimes sleet, & come on to blow
very hard about S:E: till the Eveng. when it shifted to W: &
NW & clear'd up wrote a letter to M: to go by the fleet –

Friday 3d. Decr. a hard gale at N:W: & W.N.W – walk'd up
Town & visited the Ladies & the hutts the no. of sick decreasing
Battn. orders to be in readiness to Embark on the shortest notice
with Camp Equipage & field Baggage only, the heavy Baggage to
be sent to store on further orders, no horses for the Capts. – I
hear the followg. Corps have got orders of readiness vizt Light
Infantry & Grenrs. 7th. 23d. 33d. 42d. 63d. 64th. Queens
Rangers & Legion Hessian Grrs. & two Hessn. Battns. – The
Transports named for the different Corps, the Grrs. have 3 ships
P Battn. 1st. Battn. The Margery, Thames & another

Saturday 4th. Decr. moderate weather, getting ready for
moving The mens brown trowzers are almost finish'd, the Taylors a cursed plague, – brought Balnabie Jas. Grm. & Potts home
to dinner, Sat pretty late the latter two went home Bal: staid

Sunday 5th. Decr. a cloudy cold morng. wind N.E: & came on
to snow in the forenoon which continued all day – with Coll Hope
in the morng. Settling about sea stock for our Ship, in which goes
the Coll. with the 17th. 37th. 38th. & 42d. & we club Six weeks
pay according to our rank to lay in Stock & Stores for the Voyage,
for which we are told we will be indemnify'd if the Expedition
does not go on.

Monday 6th. Decr. about 9 inches snow on the ground this

morng. clear & moderate wr. wind Noly. – doubtfull intelligence about the french fleets being in Chesapeak on which depends our motions – gave out 6 months clearance to the Coy. to 24th. Octr. din'd wt. Grm. & Potts –

Tuesday 7th. fine wr. & good Sleighing up in Town, – sent Camp Equipage on board o'ship with a man P Coy.
another consultn. with the Col. about the Sea Stores – have employ'd Corpl. McLeod of the 38th. to buy live stock & Vegetables, & I am to purchase the rest – din'd with Capt. [Warren] Simonds[on] a Sensible man with genteel manners a good officer & scholar, an old soldier & lives pretty freely, which most old soldiers do

Wednesday 8th. Decr. fine wr. wind in the NW. – our heavy baggage going into Store in York, scarce of carriage – had 1/2 a dozen to dine – Capt Dalpls. come to join the Light Intry. vice Smith who returns to the Regt. The Light Infantry to be divided into two Batts. Lt. Col: [Thomas] Dundas to have 2d. an order for the Barrack bedding to be taken on board with us – & offrs. horses intitled to forage to be recd. at the QMr. Gls. for the stated price

Thursday 9th. frost in the night & fine clear wr. – Sent my heavy baggage to Town – the Compys. articles very troublesome for want of package sent the mens blankets, having a new set of plaids, & they can't carry both compleated them in necessaries. went to N:York about the ship mess gave in a list to Mr. Gracie of what things we want in Town which he is to compleat in two or three days
Saw the Brigr. he thinks we wont go – dry – din'd chez les petits heureuze ou jai soupe & couche aussi – spoke to the Major about Sergt. McCr. & the men I am to get; no satisfactory answer The Qr.Mr. wod. not let the Baggage in because it came too late, spoke to him but he is harden'd; el deteriora Signor

Friday 10th. foggy with some rain The Roebuck come in from a cruise to Chesapeak – saw no french fleet took two prizes – a ship from Georgia in 14 days, all quiet there, the Blonde had

arrived with Genl. Leslie – Lt. Col Maitland dead & some
others – did some business left Town at noon din'd with C.
Hatd. & came home in Eveng.

Saturday 11th. Decr. frost & clear wr. visited the hutts &
scolded the Taylors – a rapsody wt. Potts
a journal of the Siege of Savanah in the Papers where Monsr. &
Jonathan are discomfitted –

Sunday 12th. rainy & warm with the wind in the southerly Qr.
wrote letters to AH: T:A. & my Fr. to go by the way of Clyde,
with one for R:M: – The 26th. Regt. invalids and women to
embark tomorrow

Monday 13th The storm of wind & rain continued till today at
noon when it clear'd up & moderated – a Compy. Review. The
arms not in good order, desir'd to see them again tomorrow –
they are compleated to 50 rounds of ammunition – 15 Sick & 10
convalescents – sent Sergt. Smith to Town to settle with the Qr.
Mr. about the last articles &ca.

Tuesday 14th. Decr. frost in the night & a hard Gale about
WNW cold & sharp –
The Compys. arms in better order today sent my letters to
Town to go by the fleet vizt. 1 to my Fr. with the 2d. of a Bill
£50, 1 to AH: & one to Dr: F: all inclos'd in a Frank to J.P. Gl.
Vaughan they are dated 23d. & 24th. Novr. &ca. to go by the way
of England. And one to R:M: 1 to T:A: 1 to AH: inclos'd to my
Fr. to go by Clyde, dated 12 Decr.

Wednesday 15th. cold sharp N.W. call'd on the Ladies din'd
with Major [Philip] Van Cortland, & drank tea with the Misses
at Dr. Hns. a smack from P—warhawkes – a letter from Col:
Hope the transports going to Whitestone tomorrow[6]

Thursday 16th. Decr. Snow from the S:W: went to York in
the morng. sent the mess stores on board & paid the Bills about
90 guineas, sent also my big trunk on board, The transports getting under way & going up the East River to Whitestone where
the troops from Long Island are to Embark, those at N:York

embark there, & those from Staten island come up in small craft. varrious opinions about this change of front, some think Rhode Island, some Boston is the object while others think it is only to be out of the way of the ice in No:River, the homeward bound fleet drops down to the hook today or tomorrow – came home with Col: Hope & din'd play cards & sup'd – lost 2 dollars gave 10 Guineas to Rollo from Major Gr[aham?]:

Friday 17th. Decr. cold & raw little wind from N:E: looks like snow a Battn Parade at 11 & to be every day – expect to embark as soon as the transport come to Whitestone. brought home a few friends to dine play'd cards till late, lost 4 1/2 dollars orders for sending our horses to Brooklyn to be dispos'd of the Qr.Mr. Genl.

Saturday 18th. a Storm of wind Rain & Sleet from the north – N:B: – sent the mare to Brooklyn by Sergt. McCraw who got ten guineas for her – din'd wt. Peter

Sunday 19th. a cold sharp N:W. wind & hard frost. Orders late last night to march this morng. to Brooklyn to Embark The Transports having returned to that place. I got the orders about midnight, & forgot it, till 9 when my man put me in mind that the Battn. was to march at 9 o'clock which hurried me – recd. this morng. the present of a Eor[e] from Miss O – with a note une [un] peu de tendre eh – [7]
Settled with Sergt. [Donald] McCraw for my washing, mess accot. & Cooking &ca. to this date; & left him & his family behind he having a hernia inguinalles [inguinal hernia] & his wife sick – got the Landlords Waggon to carry my baggage to the ferry & rode up to town, call'd & bid farewell at Major Cortlands & came to the parade just as the Battn. were marching off – bid farewell at the Doctors [Ogden], P[olly] a little affected The Troops that were under orders for this Expedition all in motion for Embarkation except the 42d. who are countermanded; those on Long Island to embark at Brooklyn, but it blew so hard we could not attempt it, the troops took shelter in Brooklyn Church. 23d. Hutts Bedford & other places near, for the night

Monday 20th. Decr. hard frost & strong wind at NW. The

Troops began to Embark in the forenoon & continued till night; very cold business, some men frostbit, & 2 or 3 drown'd   our Battn. all Embark'd but no baggage, got the men disposed of between decks which is very roomy, The offrs. lay on the cabin floor on a sail

Tuesday 21st. this cold NW wind still continues more troops embarking, but it is very tedious on account of the cold & strong wind   got some of our baggage on board, & some offrs. – & I got six men from the Regt. with their accots. to 24 Decr. a Copy of which I sign'd & sent back together with their arms, by the Sergt. who brought them – hear'd to day the Qr.Mr. Smith shot himself yesterday in the Store, tis supposed on account of some clandestine management on the Virginia expedition –

Wednesday 22d. the hard frost & cold wr. still continues, a good deal of ice in the Rivers   the fleet for England went down to the Hook the Remainder of the Troops & Baggage getting on board

Thursday 23d. Decr. very hard frost last night & much ice about the ships – the Romulus got under way at high water about 10 oclock & stood down to the Hook   the transports follow'd as they got ready being in danger from the ice & I hear six or 7 of them are drove ashore in the East River, we got down to near the hook in the afternoon & came to anchor The fleet for England sailed this morng. saw the rear out at sea – we found all the men of war lying at the hook with the adml. viz the Europe, Russel, Defiance Raisonable & Robuste line of Battle the Renown 50 Romolus & Roebuck 40, & two or 3 frigates   we hear the Comr. in Chief goes himself   wind about west all day & moderate

Friday 24th. clear & cold NW   The adml. with 6 large ships sail'd out & came to anchor without the hook   some more ships & vessels coming down

Saturday 25th. Decr. cold & cloudy with the wind about N:N:E.   the large men of war without are getting under way as the wr. does not admit of their riding there   a Signal from the

Europe for all masters when they got a paper of Instructions & signals sign'd by Capt. Swiney & a Paper with the ordr. of Sailing sign'd by the Adml. vizt.

Pereus [Perseus]

Europe

| Roebuck 1st. Grrs. | Principal agent | 1st. Lt.Infy. | Romolus |
| 2d. do. | | 2d. do. | |

Hessian Corps

| Hessn. Genl offrs. ships | wt. 2d. Agent | British General offrs. ships |

British Regts.

| Robust ordnance ships | wt. 3d. Agent | Engr Dept. | Defiance |

Victualers

Provincial Corps

| Renown | 4th Agent | Raisonable |

Russel

The Ships to keep their Stations within the men of war, & in tacking those on starboard to keep the wind   Xmas celebrated with mirth & moderation, 16 Gentln in the Cabin, a dozen of wine every day & a clumsy dinner, a Capt. & Subn. for the day a Regulation about the expenditure of water, having only 37 ton on board, & the daily consumption has been 1 1/2 tons, which is now lessened to about one –

Sunday 26th. clear & cold north wind   The large men of war without have made a stretch out & come in again near the shore outside the hook, a Signal for sailing the ships getting under way & sail'd out of the Hook about 2 o'clock in the Afternoon taking their stations according to the order of sailing, about 100 sail of square rigg'd Vessels beside Sloops & schooners steering to the So:d on duty for the day,

The Comr. in chief in the Romolus Lord Cornwallis in the Roebuck

Monday 27th. Decr. fair easy wr. & northerly wind, the fleet in good order & keeping a Southerly course the wind coming more to the Eastwd. & cloudy towards Eveng. a Man of the 38th. died last night

Tuesday 28th. this morng. about 4 or 5 oclock it came on to blow hard from the Eastward with rain, the fleet stretching away about S:W: in the afternoon the wind about S:E. & strong with constant rain & a high Sea a good deal of tossing & tumbling which affects the Stomachs of several in the Cabbin & many between decks   had a scrambling breakfast no dinner dress'd – N:B: we were alarm'd in morng. with a report of fire, which prov'd nothing

Wednesday 29th. Decr. last night very stormy, from S:E: & S:S:E with rain & a heavy sea, which still continues, & thick all round – the fleet much Scatter'd, see about 20 all lying to with our heads to the So:d in the course of the day the wr. clear'd & the wind moderated   we bore down to the leeward ships & coming under the Admirals Stern P signal took our station again in the fleet, who were all pretty well collected together by Eveng. when the wind came about to W: & NW see one ship has lost her main & mizen mast & some of the small craft missing – din'd at 6 PM   11 of our geese died last night in the coop

Thursday 30th. fine moderate weather & smooth water again the fleet sailing in good order & pretty compact, several signals made by the Adml. respecting the man of war one of which has taken the dismasted ship in tow; a Strange frigate come into the fleet, sent her boat on board the Adml. – at noon had an observation Lat: 35.50, Cape Hatteras suppos'd to be W. 1/2 S. dist. 50 leagues   in the afternoon the wind came more to the So:wd. &

we stretchd off shore – Spoke the Sukey, all well on duty for the day, made a thorough cleaning both above & below – & gave a bill of fare to the Cook – the Cow kill'd –

Friday 31st. Decr. it blew hard some part of last night about NW the morng. cloudy & dark with the wind at NW a fine steddy breeze Steering S.W.B.S. about 5 knots for the most part of the day, we are rather to leeward & a stern today – the fleet pretty well up & mostly going under courses & close reeffd TS cloudy at noon & could not see the sun – spoke the Resolution, well Lat by Reckg. 34.43. Long. 73.45

Saturday 1st. Janry. clear and moderate wr. wind about N:W: going better than 6 knots S:WB:S & SW – the fleet makes a long reach, under easy sail, not much sea & the water smoking i:e: a kind of smoak rising from the tops of the waves, owing to – at noon they had an observation Lat: 34.3. Long 75.39 the Capt. by which it would appear that we have been retarded by a Strong Current supposed to be the Gulfpt Stream din'd in good time & had a Concert & dance in the Eveng. when the wind came about Easterly –

Sunday 2d. Janry. 1780 it blew fresh last night from the East-ward & S:E: we steer'd about S:W: & SWBW at the rate of 4 5 & 6 knots, in the morng. the wind comes to the So:ward & SWd. & blows hard with rain & a high sea the fleet much scatter'd & the weather thick at noon very few to be seen – in the afternoon the wind came to west & NW & clear'd up & blew hard, wore ship & lay to under fore sail & balanced mizen a hard Gale –

Monday 3d. Janry. it blew hard all last night from N:W: which still continues with a rough sea, very few ships to be seen –
at Noon had an an observation the Capt. in Lat: 32.43. Long 75.19 the ship still lying to with her head about S:W: see the Resolution & Sukey off the lee bow & about 16 sail more in differ-ent quarters – continued to ly to the same way

Tuesday 4th. Janry. the ship lay to all last night with her hd about SW. but towards morng. wind abated about 6 oclock set double reeff'd topsails & courses & lay up W.S.W. the wr. clear the wind more moderate & less sea, only 4 or 5 ships to be seen – at Noon had an observation Lat 32.29 Long 75.43 – going 2 & 2 1/2 knots the Afternoon still moderate   we din'd at table, the wind coming more to the westard we fell off to S.W: & down to SBW towards Eveng. – the day cold

Wednesday 5th. Janry we had a pretty quiet night with a light wind going about S.S.W & SBW 2 knots or so in the morng about 6 oclock tack'd & stood to the northd wind about west course NNW or thereabout, an offrs watch upon deck during the night, saw five sail in the morng. but lost sight of them all but one by noon, the wind increas'd in the forenoon & came on to blow hard from west & raise the sea. the ship laid to under a fore sail & mizzen at noon when they had an observation Lat 32.19   as we are now separated from the fleet we must look to ourselves, there is seal'd instructions, for the master & Comg. offr. which being open'd enjoins to secrecy – Tybee a Regulation of water to take place tomorrow 2 quarts P man & some for Cooking at which rate we are suppos'd to have enough for 3 weeks   between 2 & 3 oclock P.M: we descried two large sail to leeward standing on the other tack, & about an hour after another sail – after 4 we bore down towards the Largest with our Ensign at the maintopmast head & found her to be a man of war but the dark came on before we were near enough to know her, we brought to on the same tack to windward of her about a mile that is the starboard takes on board the wind blowing very hard about west, & a high & heavy sea

Thursday 6th. Janry. it blew hard all last night, much tossing and tumbling; in the morng. the wind came to N:W: & grew cold, no ships to be seen today which is thick & stormy with showers of rain & hail

The Duty on board is a Capt. & 2 Subs, who take the three night watches; – the water began to be measur'd out – 2 pursers quarts P man P diem dismal weather no observation ships head about S:W: & S.W.BW. on which tack she continued to ly to all day under a reeff'd foresail & balanced Mizzen.

as the men were scarce of utensils to put their water in, they all agreed that their 2 quarts should be put into the Scuttle Butt altogether & drink as usual –

Friday 7th Janry. last night the wind continued to blow hard at N.W. tho' not quite so violent as yesterday fair, cloudy, & some stars; the morng. more moderate, set the mizzen staysail at 10 A:M: wore ship & laid her head to the Northward, with the same sail, viz: reeff'd foresail, Mizzen staysail, & balanced mizzen, wind about W.N.W & W.B.N. & a high sea at noon the Capt. had an observation which makes in Lat 30.21. as for Longitude he may guess at it but in my opinion we are above 100 leagues from the land – the day clear & no ship to be seen – saw some birds, viz a small woodcock some ducks, a little land bird like a Robin, some Gulls & mother Carys Chickens in the afternoon set the Mainsail wind NW: ships head about NBE 3 knots a tumbling sea

Saturday 8th. Janry. last night blowy & cloudy as of late with some spitting showers of rain or hail wind about N:W. lying from N.B.E in mid[?] & carrying courses 3 knots or better in the morng. see a sail off lee bow which we hail'd about 9 AM but could not hear each other a Schooner suppos'd to be one of the fleet; set close reeff'd fore TS this morng. whh. carried all day cloudy with more & less wind from the NW with Showers of rain & hail – at Noon had an imperfect observation Lat 31.14 see another sail of[f] the starboard bow but lose her again. Wind continues about NW course accordingly starbd. tacks 3 knots, plentifull dinner & drink

Sunday 9th. Janry. 1780 the wind & wr. during the last night continued to be blowy & showery from about N.W. in the morng. it came more to the Nod. & clear'd, at 6 AM veer'd ship & lay up W.B.S. & W.S.W. under courses going on the whole better than 2 1/2 knots a sail seen all this morng. of[f] the wr. beam –

at Noon They had a good observation Lat: 31:31 the wind less & the sea following Long in 73.29 – The Ship takes in some water at larboard portholes which being pump'd out runs down between decks & to the hold & wets our men & Baggage &ca. This Gale which has now lasted a week has stretch'd our rigging & loosen'd the supporters of the flatboat, & except living uncomfortably we have suffered no damage being a fine stout ship – in the afternoon & Eveng. the wind fell, & the sea also; going about 2 knots westerly.

Monday 10th. Janry. it was calm some part of last night & this morng. clear & mild wr. about 8. AM. a gentle breeze from the So:wd. sett TSs. a ship close by, bore down to her & found her to be the Peggy 2d. Battn. Grrs. ask'd them how the did, all well, gave them 3 cheers, they sent their boat on board for some Candles about 11 o'clock Capt. [George] Napier & Lt. [John] Steadman came in the boat & staid near an hour, they wrd. the Gale pretty well, ship leaky and pumps chock'd, – at Noon we had an observation Lat: 31.26. a fine breeze from the So:wd. going about 3 knots West, agreed to keep together, they saw above 50 sail 3 days ago, got up our mens bedding to try how it wod. stowe on the Qrs. in case of action. in the afternoon the Breeze increas'd & we went 5 & 6 knots West & WBN

Tuesday 11th. Janry. it blew very hard last night from S.W. & a high sea carried close reeff'd topsails till about midnight, in the morng. under courses, the Peggy carried a light till about 4 o'clock, but she dropping astern we put up one. as the daylight came on the wind came more to the westward with heavy showers towards noon it veer'd to NW & clear'd, see the Peggy 2 leagues to leeward both ships lying to under foresail & mizzen – head N.N.E at Noon they had a pretty good observation Lat 32.35, which looks as if we had got again within the influence of the Gulf Stream; twixt 12 & 1 bore down towards the Peggy under foresail   at 2 laid to[,] to Windwd. of her. both ships having veer'd, head about W.S.W. the Eveng. moderate, wind continuing about N.W. & WNW. courses & main topsail

Wednesday 12 Janry. last night clear, & moderate gale, lost sight of the Peggy & found her again at day light to So:wd. in the morng. the wind came to the westwd. & so:wd of west, wore ship about 9 and stood to the No:wd. a fresh gale under courses, head about N.N.W.

At noon they had a good observation Lat 32.17 The Peggy off the wr. Qr. a league at 2 o'clock made a Signal for her to come down to us which she obey'd – at dinner a heavy sea brought us & all that was on the Table down to leeward with a smash of Crockery some broken shins &ca. – the Eveng. blowy & cold

Thursday 13th. it blew hard all last night from the West to N.W. the ships continuing to ly to under courses with their heads to the No:wd. in the morng. NNE at 8: A:M: wore ship & lay up WSW cloudy & cold NW wind with showers of hail the Capt. had an imperfect observatn. which makes us in 32 & 1/2 the Peggy off the wr. Qr. near a mile the afternoon still cold & blowy & cloudy all round, uncommonly severe wr. for this Lattitude, head S.W.B.W. under courses 2 1/2 knots –

Friday 14th. Janry. the wind continues to blow betwixt the West & N.W. the ship lying to on the starboard tack all night, the Peggys light in view at day light made two sail to leeward one of them a man of war who made a signal for us to come under her stern which we did about 10 o'clock & found her to be the Raisonable with the Judith store ship under her care who seems to be in some kind of distress, the man of wars boat on board of her & the pumps going, the Peggy bore down likewise & we ly to under the mizzen with the larboard tack head about N.BW. blowing pretty fresh, cold & cloudy showers of hail at Noon we had an observation Lat: 31.48. – the Judiths boat out, & the man of wars boat made another trip to her, she looks as if she had sprung her main mast & a leak also. – The Boats went back & forwd. all the afternoon taking things out of the Judith to the man of war, who took her in tow at night; The Ships continue on the same tak driving to leeward

Saturday 15th. The Raisonable carried but a dim light in her poop last night which was pretty moderate the wind still in N.W. quarter cold & cloudy with showers of rain & hail, in the morng. boats plying 'twixt the man of war & Judith taking out Pontoons &ca. – spoke the Raisonable this morng. & told her our Situation with respect to water, but Capt. Evans did not promise any assistance he desir'd us to send our Boat to carry things from the Judith to the man of war & to bear down to the Peggy & tell her to do the same, which we did, our boat return'd afternoon & told us we were to take some of the Pontoons on board, they are preparing to abandon the Judith on account of her leak, at noon the Capt. had an imperfect observation Lat: 32.2, & we have certainly driven a good way to the Eastwd. so that I suppose we are six degrees of Longitude off the Land & the wind continues obstinately to blow more & less violently from the N.Wd. the air cold & raw, the sky cloudy, & spitting rain or hail, lying to, head to the No:d. the Judith evacuated in the Eveng. & suppos'd to go down about 7 o'clock

Sunday 16th. Janry. last night was clear & moderate, the wind westerly head to the No:wd. till about 2 in the morng. when the ships tack'd by Signal from the Raisonable who miss'd stay's & had very near run foul of us, going in the course of the night 2 & 2 1/2 knots in the morng. see the Judith lying on her beam ends to leeward of us 2 or 3 miles a[t] 9 AM tack'd & lay to the N.N.W. under reeff'd Topsails the wr. mild & the wind moderate about west, at noon we had an observation Lat: 32.12. ten or eleven of the 38th. ill of a fever supposed to be contracted from the wetness of their births, but it does not appear to be infectious – the 42d. only 5 sick. 3 of the flux & 2 of the ague, the men complain much for some time past of the water come thro' the deck upon them, the seams open from the workg. of the Boats the wind continues about west, with now & then a point to the So: head NNW 2 1/2 & 3 knots.

Monday 17th. Janry. some showers in the night, at 4 in the morng. tack'd by signal & stood to the Southward till 8 when the ships tack'd again & ly up NWBN & NW under close reef'd TS 3 & 4 knots the Peggy a good way astern the Raisonable shorten'd sail for her at 11 & so did we, she came up in about two hours, at noon had an observation Lat 33.0 – the weather clear & warm & a stiff breeze about WB.S. which raises a pretty high sea. in the afternoon the wind increas'd & blew hard towards night when the ships lay too, the Peggy ahead. up N.N.W. off No: it continued to blow hard all night about WNW. & a rough sea, lying too

Tuesday 18th. Janry. the wind more moderate in the morng. at 6. AM. wore ship & stood to the So:wd. with close reeff'd TS wind from west to WNW 2 & 2 1/2 knots The Raisonable about a league a head all the morng. Peggy close by. an observation at Noon Lat. 33.19 wr. cold & clear, wind & sea fallen, we ly between S.S.W. & S.W. jogging slowly on an inspection of water they suppose about 17 ton in the hold, which should last about as many days, but while this Westerly wind prevails we cannot haul in with coast.

between 2 & 3 P.M. made a signal to speak to the man of war, but i[t] being wrong at first it was 4 o'clock before she came down to us & ask'd for what we made that signal, when Col Hope told them that he wanted to acquaint Capt. Evans that we were scarce of water, & told him our exact situation, he answer'd that they were scarce likewise having less water & more men than their compliment but that he would stay by us & take care of us. – a rub to our Capt. about his rigging – & desired him to tell the Peggy to get up his topgallantmast as he expected a fair wind. – the Eveng. quite moderate course twixt S.W. & So 2 knots

Wednesday 19th. Janry. the fore part of the Night moderate & clear, towards morng. fresh breezes & cloudy, wore ship at midnight & stood NW & NNW. till 8 this morng. when we tack'd again & stood to the Southwd. wind about west going better than 3 knots close hauld at Noon an observation Lat. 33.08 – & they reckon themselves in Long 74.57 the Raisonable close by, the Peggy a stern blows fresh & the sea rising – in the afternoon & eveng. the wind increased at about W.N.W. with high tumbling sea lay to a while for the Peggy

Thursday 20th. Janry. a strong Gale all last night & a high sea carried courses & stood S.S.W. & SW 2 1/2 & 3 knots, the morng. rather more moderate & the wind more to the north, cold & raw with, small showers of hail, the Raisonable leading the Peggy just astern, an observation which makes us in Lat 31.56. by which we have gone more to the So:ward than the whole distance on the Logboard, by which it wod. appear that we are not only without the Gulf Stream but in a Current that setts to the So:ward

a cold N.W. wind, head WSW set close reeff'd main TS about 2 o'clock –

an order for the allowance of water to be reduced to 3 pints commencing tomorrow. in the eveng. the wind moderated & fell calm about 9, but a heavy Swell of a sea continued; – The Tables being all broke in the Cabin we din'd on the floor.

Friday 21st Janry. almost Calm & clear all last night in the morng. a light breeze from the So:wd. let out a reeff of the TS – see a Sail of[f] the wr. Bow in the forenoon the breeze increas'd about S.W.B.S. & S.S.W. going 5 & 6 knots West & W.B.N. the sail came down & join'd us she looks like one of our horse Sloops; the Peggy ahead all the morng. now both a little to windward at 3. P.M. & the sloop under the Raisonables stern: – a fine steddy breeze 5 knots W 1/2 N. three pursers pints of water P diem at which rate we are suppos'd to have enough for 19 days

The day being cloudy we had no observation. Lat: by reckong. 31.40 Long: 75.30, – in the eveng. ye wind fell with some rain, at 10 lay too

Saturday 22d. Janry. it blew strong some part of last night from the S.W. in the morng. it came to No:eastwd. in light breezes & thick wr. the sloop a missing. the Raisonable a league to windwd the Peggy close by, our head about NW about noon the Sloop hove in sight & came under the man of wars stern, after which she bore down to us with the signal to come under his stern, whh. we did about 2 P.M. & steer'd away W.S.W. with the wind about N.E. smooth water & thick wr. 4 knots we have lost 8 hours of a fair wind waiting for this sloop, which we suppose was sent to look out to the Northwd – or else trying to go away from us.

Light breezes & cloudy all the Eveng. slipping smoothly thro the water W.B.S. from 4 to 2 knots

Sunday 23d. Janry. last night was very quiet with a light wind from N.E. which came more to the No:wd. in the morng. from 2 till noon going 3 & 4 knots W.B.S. the sloop astern, shorten sail for her we find the two Transports go better than the man of war when the wind is large – The Compys divided into three watches, one of which are to be always on deck. the sky being cloudy these three days past we have had no observation; the wr. warm & clear horrizon today very little wind in afternoon and eveng. going about 2 knots S.W. & S.W.B.S. the ships close together, the Raisonable taken the sloop in tow & carrying all the sail that will draw. reduced our allowance of wine in the cabin to a pint each, at which rate we have about enough for 5 or 6 days only

Monday 24th. Janry. almost calm some part of last night & light airs from NW & W.N.W. with some rain the sky cloudy & the wr. warm, the morng. fine & clear the Raisonable to windwd. 2 mile the Peggy one [.] going on slowly about SWBS smooth water & little wind about WBN. An observation at Noon makes us in Lat: 30.56 which shews that we have not been obstructed by any current & must therefore be within the Gulf Stream & not far from Land, which I hope we will make soon, for the scarcity of water begins to be already felt by the men, some of whom like fools drink salt water. warm wr. with small showers going about W.B.S 2 & 3 knots as night came on the wind freshen'd to 4 & 5 knots W.S.W. it blew hard in the night & they reeff'd the topsails, the Raisonable & Peggy both astern

Tuesday 25th. Janry. blows fresh in the morng. & thick wr., towards noon it cleared up going from 3 to 5 knots abt. S.W.B.W. wind about NW & NWBW, 86 miles on the logboard, & the observation, at noon makes us in Lat. 29.56 the man of war just astern towing the sloop & the Peggy a little to leeward – cool & cloudy, wind less & not much sea – the water serv'd out to the men by messes – a number of flying fish seen today. we ly up

WBS. in the afternoon 4 knots & WBN in the eveng. with little wind calm most part of the night

Wednesday 26th. in the morng. the wind came to WNW TK'd. at 5 & stood to the SW till 8 see a strange sail to windward a Brig or a snow, she was coming down to us at first, but she haul'd her wind & stood & stood to the So.ward The Comor. made a Signal for her as friend, & made sail to get up with her but she went off lasking & soon disappear'd at Noon a clear observation of three Quadts. Lat: 30.21. by which there a differce. of 35 miles more to the Northwd. than by the dead reckoning, which can only be accounted for by the influence of a strong Current from the So:wd.

the wr. cold & clear wind mostly WNW & WBN from 12 to 4 stood to No:ward then TK'd. & stood the Sowd in the eveng. bore down to man of war, the Peggy to leeward blows pretty fresh 3 & 3 1/2 knots S.W.B.S. all night. some squalls with rain

Thursday 27th. Janry. clear & cold Morng wind W.N.W. the Peggy a missing for a while, the Raisonable bore down to leewd. & found her, we stand S.W.BS. 3 knots till noon wore ship & stand to the No:wd Lat by observation 30.7 which proves the certainty of Current from the So:wd. but not so strong as yesterday Course & distance S.S.W. 48 miles diff: of Lat: by observation 14 miles. continued to stand to the Nor:wd. till midnight when we tack'd by signal & stood S.W. it blew hard most part of the Night, & we had near ran foul of the sloop in tow of the Raison-able. – N.B. ye Como: spoke us in the Eveng. ask'd how our water held out & if all well pretty well

Friday 28th. Janry. clear & moderate, wind about N.W. & WNW Steering 'twixt S.W. & WS.W. 2, 3 & 4 knots the Peggy & man of war a head, out reeff's & set top Gallantsails at 11 at noon had a good observation Lat 31.15. which again ascertains a strong Current from the So:wd. – which must have likewise car-ried us greatly to the Eastwd. continued the same course all the afternoon, in the night lay up WBS & west 2 & 3 knots.

Saturday 29th. Janry. a fine clear morng. with little wind & smooth sea the man of war a head the Peggy close by on starboard beam, as the day advanc'd the wind came to the No: & eastwd. & increas'd from light to fresh breezes about 10 AM. we pass'd a ripple in the sea that look'd like the edge of a Current the Como: steers WBN & WNW at noon an Observation Lat 31.30 going 8 knots, wind about NNE in the afternoon haul'd up to NWBW the colours of the water changed & looks as if we were in soundings. –

about 4 P.M. the Raisonable made a signal for anchoring & soon after we saw two ships at anchor a great way ahead, & about sunset the Boatswain saw land off the larboard bow; stood in till 7 & the[n] tack'd, & stood about E.S.E. till midnight from 7 to 10 fathom water, tack'd at 12 & stood N.W. little wind & smooth water

Sunday 30th. Janry. light wind from the No:wd. tack'd at 6 & stood to the Ewd. see two man of war at anchor & see land which we take to be the Island of Tybee bearing NW, about noon the Raisonable desir'd us to make the best of our way in, while she stood away for the men of war, which we found were the Russel & Robuste, the former made the Signal to come under her stern, but as we thought it regarded the Raisonable only, we stood on by her directions till the water shoal'd when we put about & waited for a Pilot boat that we saw coming from the Russel, which boat boarded the Peggy & us & gave us Pilots each who carried us over the Bar but the tide turning we came to anchor about 1/2 league from the Light house at 4 P.M. within which we see 10 or 12 sail lying at anchor with the Vigilant, the first arrived about a fortnight ago a Hessian The Roebuck & Renown who arrived about 6 days ago sail'd again with the blonde frigate to ly off Charles Town Bar Lord Cornwallis went up to Savannah in a Brig the Roebuck took, from Chas Town bound to the West Indies this by information of the pilot who belongs to the Vigilant – the three men of war viz. the Russel Robuste & Raisonable ly at anchor in 10 fathom about East from the Beacon 9 or 10 miles off Lat by observation today 31.54. which agrees with that laid down for Tybee[8]

Monday 31st. Janry. fine mild wr. hazy horizon, see a ship aground to the Northward of the Bar, the Mr. of whom came aboard. She is a Private Victualler bound from England to St. Augustine out 14 weeks, she saw the Adml. & about 60 sail of the fleet yesterday about 8 or 10 leagues N.E. – at 10 AM we got under way & stood up to the harbour where we came to anchor about noon a little above the light house some more ships came up in the afternoon they are part of the Bulk of the fleet that continued with the Admiral who is come to below

Tuesday 1st. Febry. mild wr. & little wind, hazy, the nights cold the days pleasant & warm like October weather in New York A Number of Ships come up today with the Perseus & Tomkins The George & the Swan were abandoned at sea & the Troops taken out – The Defiance & some 10. or 12 Sail missing yet – men from the ships that were arrived go on Shore on Tybee Island & wash & take excercise, a Sandy island with Pine wood & some Cabbage Trees some wild deer & Hogs on the Island The Agent call'd for the Masters of Transports & told them they were not to deliver full allowance yet as this is not the port of destination –

Wednesday 2d. Febry. the mild hazy wr. continues more ships below ready to come up, but no word of the Defiance & those ships that are supposed to be with her.
Went up to Savanah in a Boat wt. Col: Hope set off about 2 o'clock & got there 1/2 after 5, about 18 or 20 miles the Banks & islands all the way up are low marshy ground, till you come to the Town which stands on a high bluff of sand, scatter'd buildings of Brick & wooden houses, the Town laid out in regular squares but not conected yet, call'd on [Capt. Francis] Skelly, sup'd at Genl. Leslies who is indispos'd – the 71st. in the Country The Genl. & Adml. went up today – two Hessians Regts. in Town & some provincials

Thursday 3d. Febry. hazy still sleep'd at Skelly's who is always kind & civil, took a ride before breakfast with him & saw the works made by [James] Moncreiff, & the those of the french during the Siege, the ground being quite sandy they are all tumbling again but those of Moncreiff do him great credit both for their number & position.

Walk'd out afterward & saw the ground by which Col: [Archibald] Campbell approach'd. – din'd at Genl. Leslies, & sup'd at the Lt. Governors Mr. [John] Graham –

Nothing to be got a[t] Savannah almost, except a little bread & very little very bad Beeff, wine two dollars a bottle, a kind of Tavern there, but very bad & extravagant. – a poor barren place

saw some Cherokees there who are come to offer their service & get some presents, above 200 of them 14 miles off

Friday 4th. Febry. fine weather & clearer than it has been lately – Breakfasted at the Lt. Govrs and set out about 9 Col Hope having got a passage for us with Capt. Elphinstone of the Perseus, we came down to the fleet at Tybee in two hours & a half no word of those missing ships yet two Negroes come in this Morng. from Charlestown

Saturday 5th. the Vigilant & two other ships went into D'Awfowsky Sound yesterday eveng – Most of the ships getting water in, they bring it with their long boats from 5 fathom hole. went ashore on Tybee & took a walk a good many men ashore taking exercise & all the women washing.

din'd wt. C. [Thomas] Peter on board the Thames late, – the wind off Shore for some days nothing coming in. The Legion & the sick sent to Savannah

Sunday 6th. Febry. clear & cool with the wind in the N.E. Qr. ashore on the island for a few hours a talk of sailing tomorrow, big ships go out, small ones by d'afousky – a ship come in about 3 o'clock. The Lord Mulgrave. 63d. Regt.

Bot. a Cask of Port from Moody [Master of the] Thames 40/ sterg. a doz: for few private members the Public Stock of wine all out today, & the fresh Provision all done 3 days ago, except one sick pig O the oyster party –

Monday 7th. Febry. it blew pretty hard last night from N.E. & this morng. it came about to the So:wd. thick & squally with rain & hail all day another ship arrived in the forenoon & we hear some heavy guns from sea which are answer'd by the Adml. in the Roebuck. The Line of Battle Ships went some days ago to try to get into Port Royal.

Margery Transport off Tybee 8th. Febry. 1780 – a strong cold westerly wind. a ship & two Brig's come down from Savannah The Transports getting water & provision we are compleated to 30 days, & have taken in our flat boat again. The Genls suite come down & gone on board the John. Agent Tomkins – a Signal from the flagship for everybody to be on board & from Agent Tompkins for all Masters; orders to sail tomorrow the Rendez-vous 20 Leagues alongshore The Commander in Chief come down Lord Cornwallis come down two days ago & goes in the Betsy & Polly his baggage ship

Wednesday 9th. Febry. a cold morng. with the wind in the north, The Agent made a signal for Masters & told them to get under way, the Adml. got underway in the Roebuck about 10 o'clock & stood out over the Bar & hove too, the rest of the ships follow'd as they got up their Anchors, wind westerly The Commander in Chief on board the John, Agent Tompkins. we are to take signals from Perseus.

No word of the Defiance & those ships suppos'd to be with her, 8 or 10, those two ships who came in last had left them 10 days, one of them a Victualer had only 4 days water when she came in. we weighed anchor about 3 P.M. with some other ships that could not get out sooner, & got over the Bar in the eveng. being calm we came to anchor about a league from the Light-house, the Bulk of the fleet East of us about a mile at ⚓

Thursday 10th. Febry. a fine mild morng. & almost calm, weighed & stood out to the Eastwd. with a light air passed the Russel, & Europe about noon lying at anchor 'tween 3 & 4 leagues from Tybee   The fleet steering E.B.N. with a light breeze from So: see the land to port off the larboard beam   at 1 going N.E. alongshore   The light breeze from the So:wd. continues & the fleet sail'd alongshore 3 & 4 knots smooth water, & clear wr –

Chapter X

'going on but slowly'

Charleston
11 February to 30 May 1780

When Sir Henry Clinton decided to go to Charleston, he was unsure how much of the British government's southern strategy he might be able to carry out. He hoped that he would, at least, be able to secure Georgia by dispersing the rebels in South Carolina. But on reaching Charleston in February 1780 he saw that he might do considerably more – perhaps win the kind of dramatic victory that would allow his forces to carry their offensive well beyond South Carolina and Georgia. Because the rebels seemed determined to defend Charleston and because Charleston occupied the tip of the peninsula formed by the Ashley and Cooper Rivers, Clinton saw an opportunity to trap and destroy the principal American army in the South. By early April he had cut off all land and water approaches to Charleston except those to the north by the Cooper River. The rebels still might have chosen to give up the town and save their army. They did not, and within three weeks, Clinton had cut their remaining line of retreat across the Cooper and was pressing his siege of Charleston relentlessly. On 12 May the rebels surrendered.

Clinton had won the greatest British victory of the war. He had captured some 6,000 soldiers and sailors, 300 cannon, and four warships as well as the most important town in the southern colonies. When subsequently his forces advanced into the interior of South Carolina, dispersing rebels and establishing armed camps, and when colonists came forward in 'gratifying numbers' to take oaths of allegiance and enlist in Loyalist units, Clinton concluded that South Carolina would soon be secure and that British forces would be free to go north, to enlist the support of Loyalists in restoring royal government to North Carolina and Virginia. He returned to New York in June, assuming his

335

victory at Charleston had changed the war in the South, had made feasible the government's strategy of relying on Loyalists to recover all of the southern colonies from Florida to Virginia.[1]

The soldiers and sailors who had captured Charleston – men like John Peebles and the British grenadiers – thought the campaign more pedestrian and less decisive than it appeared to their commander-in-chief. Peebles and his battalion worked for six weeks just to open a secure route through the coastal waterways, cross the Ashley River, and establish themselves on Charleston Neck.[2] They then had to struggle another six weeks to build and defend the system of trenches that spanned the peninsula and took their guns ever closer to the American lines at Charleston. Although they worked in rotation and at night, the sustained exertion and the fluctuations in weather as well as the strain of being under fire eventually eroded their health. Not until 1 May were they able to drain the wet ditch that guarded the rebel lines; and it was another week before they completed their third parallel which brought their cannon within 200 yards of the rebel abatis and which allowed them to bring overwhelming fire to bear on the American fortifications and town.[3] The siege, Peebles thought, had gone slowly; and when it was over, he was less optimistic about its significance than Sir Henry Clinton. He estimated that there were only 2,000 prisoners subject to exchange (the rest were militia to be released on parole); he could only hope that Clinton's proclamation encouraging the colonists 'to return to their loyalty . . . will have good effect'; and if a party of 25 Loyalists arrived from Orangeburg offering to serve against the rebels, he found most inhabitants in the countryside near Dorchester had given up prosperous estates rather than live under British rule.[4]

Charleston
11 February to 30 May 1780

Friday 11th. Febry. The fleet came to anchor by signal before one o'clock this morng. in 10 fathom water, at daylight see the land to the N.Wd. weighed about six & stood in with a light breeze from the N.E. about 9 see a Lighthouse to the northward which we take to be that of Charles Town bar, we stand in for an opening we see about 5 leagues to the So:wd. of the Lighthouse, the John leads The Adml. tack'd & stood off. about 11 the headmost ships got over the Bar 1/4 less 3 fathom steering N.W. and by noon the whole got into this harbour which we take to be No: Edisto a boat from the John gave chase to a boat near shore & took her up a creek, but the people escap'd. the fleet came to anchor about a mile within the entrance in 7 fathom, about 50 sail a signal from the Agents ship for all Adjutants & masters – orders for landing in two debarkations, the first this afternoon the second tomorrow morng. The Army Brigade as follows vizt: Light Infantry & Grenrs. under the Command of M Gl. Leslie (not yet come from Savannah) Hessian Grenadrs. under M.G. Gosport [Henrich Julian von Kospoth]. the whole under the Command of Lt. Genl. Earl Cornwallis, The 7th. & 23d. under the inspection of Lt. Col: [Alured?] Clarke, the 33d. 71st. & Yagers under the Inspection of Lt. Col: [James] Webster, the 63d. 64th. & Huyne's under the Command of M:Gl. [Johan Christoph von] Huyne a Transport of the 64th. Major McHroth join'd the fleet this morng.

Lord Cornwallis's division or The first debarkation got ashore in the Eveng. on the North side & march'd in the dark thro' very deep road & rain 3 or 4 miles, the head of the Column at Simons some went a stray in the night 2 Compys. of Light Infantry & 4 of Grenrs. lost their way with the Comr. in chief & Ld. Cornwallis, & after splashing thro' the mud & rain till near 10 o'clock we halted in a wood & made fires & staid there all night Johns Island So: Carolina

Saturday 12th. Febry. we march'd with the Genl. & Lord

Cornwallis in the morng. & join'd the Column at Simmons's where they had been all night living on plenty – The Light Infantry march'd forward about 8 miles, the Grens. about 2 miles to Rivers's the Rest of the Army landed and came up to Simmons's which is HeadQrs.

we found some sheep and a few Cattle here on Rivers's plantation which with Ld. Cornwallis's approbation were divided among the Grenrs., a very good Ration –

A Doctor who liv'd there run away. come back – Simmons a minor lives in England, his factor a Rebel, run off, a large Plantation & house and near 100 Negroes young & old on it. a light sandy soil flat woody Country the woods mostly pines, when cleared, produces corn & calavances.

This part of Johns Island reckon'd abt. 20 miles from Charles Town by Stono ferry & the Country here about is so intersected with creeks & water courses that they go several ways by water up to Chas. Town   no Baggage brot. ashore, only a second shirt some offrs. have been [in] soldiers tents –

Sunday 13th. Febry. rain last night again, the day cloudy – Col Webster with the 33d. & Yagers march'd past this morng. towards the Light Infantry. the 71st. not come yet   The Genl. & Lord Cornwallis with their suite having got horses of one kind & another went forward likewise. we dont march today, – caught a little horse & sent to the ships for Canteens &ca. in coming back he overset the whole & ran off – some things broke.

Monday 14th. Febry. cool & cloudy   The army march'd 'tween 6 & 7 o'clock in the order prescrib'd about 5 or 6 miles the Grrs. or front of the Column at Doctor Wells the rest in the rear along the road 2 miles Hd.Qrs. at Wilsons: the 33d. & Yagers gone on to Stono. the Light Infantry about 3 or 5 miles on the right 1st. Battn. at Fenwick sandy road, level country, pine wood & few houses – a Rebel Capt. & doctor taken yesterday, lately from Chas Town who say they mean to make a Vigorous defence

Capt. [James] Moncreiff & Major [Adam] Hay appointed Commissaries of Captures, all Negroes, Horses, & Cattle, to be delivered to them; some provision & Rum come up by water near to Stono meeting house, two days fresh meat to be issued.

More strict orders from Lord Cornwallis to the Comg. offrs. of Corps verbally against plundering & killing of Cattle. The Light Infantry have taken some sloops in Stono River with rice at Gibbs

Tuesday 15th. Febry. a good deal of rain last night which still continues, in showers against which we have no shelter but wigwams of pine bushes.

Battn. orders enforcing the Genl. orders in the delivery of Captures – & the Lt. Colls. & Captns. thanks to the Surgn. Muir for his care of the great no. of Sick last fall – a walk to the 1st. Battn. Lt. Infantry 3 miles they are lodged at Fenwick a large modern house with officies which holds them all & from which they see the Spires of Chas Town about 8 or 9 miles off to the northeastward. They have taken some Cattle & horses the latter very poor. The Column halted today

Wednesday 16th. Febry. fine wr. The Light Infantry moved to Stono ferry, the Grenrs. to Fenwicks & Gibs, the latter Ld. Cornwallis's Qrs. a good house on the bank of Stono River, the family at home

Genl. Leslie arrived & a Battn. of the 71st.

Thursday 17th. Febry. clear & warm The 1st. Light Infantry 33d. & Yagers have pass'd at Stono ferry & taken post on the other side – provision & stores getting forward by the inland navigation.

The Commander in Chief & his family come to Fenwicks & fix'd his Qrs. ask'd to dine there with some others but I was engaged to Col: Hope.

The Smyrna Galley arrived at Tybee some days, with the 63d. & 74th. Grrs. & the Defiance with 4 or 5 sail

Friday 18th. fine warm weather. we manoeuvre a little in the lawn before Fenwicks House HeadQrs. – they see a few Rebels near Stono but no firing – all quiet at the different posts din'd at Hd.Qrs. a good many there. – Secretary Phillips came after dinner with letters & accounts of the arrival of the ships at North Edisto that were with the defiance and of the Ceres from England with cloathing & stores at Tybee sail'd under convoy of the Richmond and Raleigh from Corke

Capt. Elphinstone who has the Command of our Galley's is in pursuit of the Rebel Galleys in the inland navigation which they think cannot escape him –

Saturday 19th. Febry. cloudy a walk to the 2d. Battn. Light Infantry at Chisholms 4 miles from here on the Bank of Stono River, 3 Compys. detach'd a little lower down, they see some Rebels sometimes on the other side being Jas. island some of our boats have pass'd up the River. they live in plenty there, & all quiet. it came on rain & got wet coming home no dry things to shift with; it rain'd till late at night from the eastward – we have fresh provision but nothing to drink except our allowance.

Sunday 20th. fine fair weather again a deserter came in last night, a German one of the Corps that was Pulaskys, they ly about 11 miles from Stono, only 32 in No.

Capt. [Peter] Trail who commands the Artilly. is come to Stono ferry with some Guns &ca. we are getting on but slowly –

Monday 21st. Febry The 2d. Battn. Light Infantry moved from their ground last night and arriv'd here at Fenwicks about 2 oclock in the morng.

the 1st. Battn. have repass'd Stono ferry & march'd to Fenwicks. The 7th. 23d. 33d. & Yagers are over Stono with Genl. Leslie it came on rain about noon & continued all day & most part of the night[;] some Boats came to Fenwicks landing to carry us across the River.

Tuesday 22d. clear'd up & the wind came about to the westward the Light Infy. expected to move but the tide or something did not answer. The reconoitering Galley fir'd some shots at people on Jas. island. & were mistaken in what they took for an encampment. uncertain yet where we shall land on James's Island.

Wednesday 23rd. Febry. it blew hard all last night at Westerly & was very cold which still continues – orders in the morng.

to march at 6. The 1st. Light Infy. march'd about 7, the 2d. about 2 hours after, to the River side where they embarked to cross, but it blows so hard that it is not yet practicable; we the Grs. are desir'd to pitch our tents again & remain, & send for Provisions to Gibbs.

we hear the Defiance is castaway off Tybee; very bad management Mr. Jacobs and that the Raleigh is arrived there from England with Genl. [James] Robertson. Engineers Stores & entrenching tools coming from Savannah – most part of the made up ammunition for the artillery was on board that ship the Russia Mercht. that was abandon'd at Sea; these blunders happen frequently in ordnance department.

din'd with Lord Cathcart at his Qrs. Mrs. Simmons call'd & saw Capts. Hathorne & Napier who are both sick there the first Lues in uvula [syphilis of soft palate] 2d. a fever his Lordship civil enough, but that is all I expect –

Thursday 24th. Febry. it blew so hard all day yesterday that the Light Infantry could not cross over to James Island, but this morng. being more moderate the 1st. Bat have got over & the 2d. are following, we were put in motion about 8 to go down to the Landing place but had not gone above 1/4 mile when we were turn'd back to our ground, there being no boats – hiss – the 2d. Battn Grrs. join'd us from Gibbs's just as we return'd – the 63d. take up their qrs. as a Cantonment being sickly – the Hessian Grrs. close by encampt & the 64th. & Huynes at Mathews – the two Battns. Grrs. march'd to Mathews's landing & embark'd in boats as they arrived & cross'd over to Hamiltons on James Island, the scarcity of boats made it night before they were all over, the 1st. Battn. moved on to Scots, where they found the Light Infantry.

The strong wind yesterday blew some ships off the coast

Friday 25th. Febry. James Island So: Caroa cold last night & a strong frost. The 2d. Battn. Light Infantry march'd at day light with the Comr. in Chief [and] Lord Cornwallis &ca. to Fort Johnson & reconoiter'd the Town and Harbour &ca. a good many shipping there with some frigates.

all the white men have left this Island & gone into Town, some have left their familys a thick settled Country & appearance of plenty, but they have drove off a great deal of the Stock – the Light Infy. return'd in P.M & brought some Cattle – The Hessian Grrs. cross'd over today & remain near Hamiltons. The 1st. Light Infantry 3 miles on, towards wapoo.

The Rebels have blown up the Lighthouse at Chas Town bar & spoil'd other marks for entring the harbour, & making other preparations for a serious defense. we can't properly invest the place unless the men of war get in & destroy their ships &c the day warm & pleasant, wind easterly.

Saturday 26th. Febry. fine mild weather. Genl. Leslie come over to his Command of Light Infantry & Grrs. the Regts. at Stono ferry remain there under the Comd. of Webster; all our provisions &ca. come round that way yet, & land now at Mrs. Pieryneaux near waupoo Cut which is Hd.Qrs. near 40 miles of inland navigation – The Light Infantry Picquets in view of the Town about 2 miles off. we had orders to move, but were countermd.

Sunday 27th. warm weather for ye. season The Adml. come up to Hd.Qrs. with Genl. Robertson who is come out to be Govr. of New York, & brot. Dispatches for the Comr. in Chief.

The Hessian Grrs. moved this morng to near Fort Johnston to which Place I took a ride to see what was to be seen there. 1st. a fine view of the Town about 3 miles off which looks well & something like New York several Batteries & Colours flying. a good many ships lying close by the Town & in both Rivers, some of them arm'd, three Rebel frigates lying off Sulivans island within shot of Fort Johnston, the largest above 30 Guns had a broad pendant, they fir'd 3 shot at us: Fort Johnston was destroy'd last year by the Rebels. Sulivans Island seems to be strongly fortifi'd & full of Embrazures towards the water. one 24 pounder one 12 por. & one 8 inch howitzer got up near Fort Johnston to be put into a battery there to try to make the Rebel frigates move. the 64th. at Hamiltons

The Generals & Adml. reconoitering

Monday 28th. Febry. warm wr. & easty. wind, some more ships arrived from Tybee, with a Battn. of the 71st. The 63d. & 74th. Grs. &ca. – a walk to the Light Infantry both Battns. at Perryneaux covering Hd.Qrs. some Ladies arrived there from Town by water to go into the Country, but are stop'd – a boat came in to the Lt. Infy. by wapoo from the Rebels last night with a Lt. of Marines & 6 sailors, the Lt. had been in our 17th. Dragoons, they deserted from an arm'd ship lying in Ashley River – The frigates opposite Fort Johnston seeing our people at work there, came nearer that shore after noon a little, & cannonaded them for two hours or more, the Hessian Grrs. being within reach of their shot were drawn back a little, one Artilly. man & two Hessn. Grrs. wounded, & one Negro killed, we fir'd a few shot from a Gun in the road, but I believe did no mischief. The frigates haul'd off again to the Sulivans island side. – The big wigs out that way again –

Tuesday 29th. Febry. warm wr. wind E:ly two 24 pors. en barbette at Ft. Johnston ready to play on the enemy's ships if within their reach, but at present they seem too far off.

The Adml. gone to the fleet with an intention to get some of his ships over the Bar & force a passage up the Harbour the first favorouble opportunity of wind & tide.

a Bridge making over waupoo near Perryno's, where there was one before some Rebels seen on the opposite side there; we hear the 7th. Regt. have had some men wounded near Stono ferry by small party of Pulasky's horse.

The 63d. & 74 Grrs. came up & join'd their Battn. they were long at sea, & on 1/2 allowance

Major [Thomas] Armstrong of the 17th. Regt. come here, left Cork in Decr. with Genl. Robt.son a fleet of Victualers &ca expected from thence every day – another demand for horses

Wednesday 1st. March rainy wr. on a Genl. Court martial for the tryal of 3 men of the 37th. Coy. for plundering. Lt Col: Abercromby Presidt. 3 Field offrs. & 10 Captns.

A Brig come to Perryno's with 8 32 pdrs. She came up Stono

River; they forgot some tackle a stormy night of cold rain & wind from S.W.

Thursday 2d. March clear & moderate wr. all quiet on this island; a bridge making over waupoo to the main, & the Bridge here over the New Cut repairing & making stronger

The Rebels have sent another ship down to Sulivans island, some Guns there about in the afternoon. A flag of truce came in to the Light Infantry & were sent back witht. an answer by his Ex:. matters going on but slowly. The Troops that were over Stono ferry come to Johns Island, leaving a post there with 100 men. some vessels come into Stono River by the inlet –

Friday 3d. fine clear wr. and cool nights wind N.W. some of the Transports came up to Hamiltons. The 7th. & 23d. Regts. come over to this Island & encamp near Perryneaux. The Engineers tools &ca. arrived, the Ships they were in went to Providence, being very leaky; had a barrel of limes & oranges sent me from thence by McQueen of the Garrison duty men there, formerly of the 42d. Grrs. & wounded at Brandywine. some suttling vessels come to Perryno's but every thing is very dear, Rum 4 dollars a gallon

Saturday 4th. March warm day and enclosed work with two embrazures making near Ft. Johnston out of the ruins of an Rebel work, & a small on the water side higher up – a Redout making round Perryno's house & two others on Waupoo for the defence of that post when the army moves. The Light Infantry Grenrs. 7th. & 23d. give the working party of 500. sent a present of oranges & limes to Lord Cornwallis Genl. Leslie & Col. Hope. din'd with Skelly, some Clergymen and people of this Country there[;] picked up a little Negro Boy for a fifer.[5]

Sunday 5th. warm wr. So:ly wind a Rebel Light horse man deserted & came in by the bridge at Waupoo, The Redoubts going forward there, & Guns & Stores landing. some of the ships come into Stono, the rest at No:Edisto, the men of war cruizing of[f] the Bar

Monday 6th. March rain from S.W. a Working party of 700 British twice a day, making these Redoubts. The Troops get fresh meat & Rice one day in three from the Comy. of Captures

we hear Genl. [James] Patterson with 1500 men is on his march from Georgia to join us

Tuesday 7th. close & sultry wr. The two Battalions of Light Infantry march'd last night over Waupoo Bridge to the main about 10 o'clock, & were conducted into the Country thro' very bad Roads above 12 miles about N.W. in order to get behind a Party of Rebels, whilst the 1st. Battalion of Grrs. march'd this Morng. at 5 o'clock & procceeded to the Bridge near Ashley ferry in order to intercept their Retreat; we arrived there 'tween 8 & 9 when two Companies pass'd the Bridge & fell in with a few straglers & fir'd on them, & took some prisoners, by whom we found the Party we were in search of had pass'd Ashley ferry yesterday & carried over great many Cattle

The Comr. in chief [,] Lord Cornwallis & Genl. Leslie were with the advanced Companies & went near the River side to reconoitre when the Rebels fir'd a 3 por from the other side several rounds but miss'd. we halted & mended the Bridge at the Church which had been broke down yesterday by the Rebels, & here the Light Infy. join'd us after a long & fatiguing march & having miss'd the Enemy they only took a few Country prisoners, among them a Mr. Loyd & a Mr. far.

A few Rebel Light Horse show'd themselves at the Church as we were coming off at whom the Battn. Guns were fir'd which set them a scampering, The Troops return'd to their respective Camps in the afternoon

I escorted the Genls. home thro' by ways near the River where they got a very good View of the Town & works from the nearest ground on this side Ashley River, not less than a mile; din'd at HeadQrs.

The Country as far as we went has the same uniform appearance, a dead flat intersected with swamps marshes & creeks the wood mostly pine & only clear'd about the Houses, several of which we saw that look'd very well, but all deserted; saw a good many Cattle, The Light Infantry drove in about 300 head

Wednesday 8th. March James Island the weather very warm for the season The Redoubts at & near HeadQrs. are finish'd – a good many Guns from the Rebel shipping today at people near the water side; The Admiral off the Bar

We are told that Genl. Robertson is going to New York in the Russel and will take letters, wrote to Rutherfurd a short sketch & sent it in to go by that opportunity.

Thursday 9th. rain in the morng. before & after daylight, we got orders at four to be ready to march at five, but for reasons best known to themselves we did not move; the day clear'd up Genl. Robertson & his aid de Camp set off for the Russel to proceed to New York, & I hear the 42d. are order'd to come here.

Friday 10th. March fine wr. & warm   The Light Infantry & Grrs. & 7th. & 23d. Regts. march in the forenoon by Wapoo bridge to the Main, taking the road to Ashley ferry for about 4 miles & turn'd to the right; & took up ground within 2 & 3 miles of Fenwicks point on Ashley River, The flank Corps facing outwards some heavy Guns coming by Waupoo Cutt; we are encamped in a thick wood mostly pine, flat & watery as usual

Lord Cornwallis & Genl. Leslie in houses near the River, we give two Companies to cover their Quarters –

The Queen of France & the other arm'd ship that were lying 'twixt the Town & the mouth of Waupoo are gone down to reinforce their little squadron at Sulivans Island; our ships at the Bar off & on

Saturday 11th. March rain in the night & sometime in the morng. but clear'd up in the forenoon when took a walk to the point which seems to be the nearest to the Town of any on this side & where I suppose a Battery will be made, but a too great distance to hurt the works at the Town. caught a horse

Sunday 12th. March fair wr. & cool a Party of 300, with arms went yesterday Eveng. & as many without went this morng. at 2 o'clock to make a Battery on the Point near the Wharff at the mouth of Waupoo, they compleat'd three embrazures & got in

two 32 pors. & an 8 inch Howitzer by day light, when two Rebel
Gallies in Ashley River took a position above the Battery, & fir'd
upon it for some time without doing any mischieff tho' they made
some very good shots with their 18 pors an arm'd Brig came
likewise to fire upon the Battery but as one Gun could point to
her, they gave her two or three shot which made her cut her
cable & go off & the Gallies finding they could make no hand of
it, went off likewise in the afternoon.

went on guard to the Battery at nine with 100 men, a Sub &
25 in the work the rest at little distance, helping forward the
matterials – His Ex: &ca &ca. came there just as the last Gally
went off, & reconoiter'd the Town & works for some time; Hd.
Qrs. still at Perryneaux. 200 men came in the Eveng. & finish'd
the Battery for 5 Guns & the howitzr by 10 o'clock – The Light
Infantry went out foraging this morng towards the Bridge at the
Church near Ashley ferry they got some bad Hay & saw a few
Light horse who fir'd at them & stood a return in grape shot but
no hurt done on either side – Skelly went to them with a flag of
truce to deliver some letters from Mr. Loyd & Far.

A Corke fleet arrived at Tybee under Convoy of the Richmond
the same that sail'd with the Rawleigh

Col. [Nesbitt] Balfour Col [Henry Edward] Fox & Majr.
[Thomas] Coore came passengers, & are come here to join the
Army, the two last join the Grenrs.[6] – a fleet from England are
likewise expected which sail'd before them – we hear that Genl.
Vaughan is arrived in the West Indies with Troops to make up
an army of 10000

The Charlestown folk turnout thick on their walls today to look
at us in our new Battery, & are workg just opposite to us, bout a
mile off

Monday 13th. March very cold last night & this morng. & a
strong wind at N.W. all quiet at the Battery   I was reliev'd at 6
o'clock in the morng. none of the Enemy's Vessels near us now,
the six largest ly down at Sulivans island, the rest are gone in
Cooper River

The wind will blow our ships off again, we have made a Battery on Light house island to prevent the Rebels from annoying our ships as they come over the Bar – The Margery being come up to Hd. Qrs. a party gone to see after the Baggage & get some things.

They are making the Battery an inclosed Work round the Barn, with Stockades & earth thrown up against them.

The dwelling house burnt yesterday & the Frenchmans furniture, as they had the small pox

Tuesday 14th. March cold again last night but clear & healthy weather, wind in North. A Field officers working party today finishing the work at the Battery & making a round Redoubt at the houses and a party taking up a 32 por. that was sunk in the Creek – Three Rebel Gallies came towards the mouth of Waupoo & fir'd some shot at the Battery but at too great a distance to do any harm – The Rebels are busy working on this side of the Town making up the intervals betwixt the former Batteries.

Wednesday 15th. fine wr. wind S.W. a working party last night hauling Guns and one this morng. of 600 making a 3 Gun Battery to the left of the former for the better clearing the River, & finishing the other works, we brot. this new Battery (which is made with Stockades instead of facines) so far forward that 300 may finish it tomorrow. The Rebels buzy at work just opposite to us, distance about a mile, covering every opening.

The 2d. Battn. Light Infantry out covering a forage, but they got very little. some more ships come up to Hd. Qrs. & a Brig from Glasgow with provision, out 13 weeks

Thursday 16th. March 1780 warm wr. & southerly wind – a Working party of 400 at the 3 Gun Battery & finishing the first, & the Rebels seem to be as busy as we, saw them Hanging somebody today on a Gallows without their works – some hundreds of hurdles made by the Light Infantry, probably for laying on the marshes to make them passable for troops – The Rebel Gallies all gone down to their ships at Sulivans island, no word of our Ships coming in yet.

Friday 17th. March Easterly & N:E clear & cool – a working

party of 200 finishing the Batteries – four days provision come out –

The Dr. has lost his Rump & dozen[7] – a Lieut of the Rebel horse & his bror. a Volr. came in last night –

Sent Sergt. Smith to the Shipping at Hd. Qrs. for soap for the Coy. got 68 lb at 2/Sterg. – he took 10 guineas out of the trunk & paid me the ballance viz £3.14 – at work in the afternoon, a cold dinner & punch – finish'd the works we hear that it was one Valentine a Mercht. that they hang'd yesterday for attempting to come out – & another man

Saturday 18th. rain in the night & till noon – Settled accots. wt. James & paid him for what he laid out for the mess &c something going to N:York soon

Sunday 19th. March 1780 rain in the morng. clear'd up in the forenoon got a sight of some Irish Newspapers of Novr. & Decr. they have got a free trade by threatening G: Britain in her distress.

Recd. a Letter from R. Marshall of the 12 July by Mr. [John] Ritchie Ensn. 44th. recommending that young Gentlen. he came in the last Corke fleet – din'd at Col: Hopes mess.

some Guns hauling up towards Genl. Leslies Qrs. Linings two Gallies in Waupoo near the landing

Monday 20th. clear & cool wind Easterly & high Spring tides. eight of our ships got over Chas. Town Bar this Morng. another to come, the double deckers were lightned but suppose will soon get in their Guns &ca. again & make an attack on the Rebel Ships if they dispute their passage up; two deserters came in last night from town, they reckon above 3000 in Garn. some manoeuvering among the Rebel fleet today in consequence of our ships having got in, all quiet in Camp & at the Batteries; see the Rebels still busy at their works in front of the Town

a Battn. order for a Review of Ammunition & to compleat to 50 rounds from the cartridge of the sick, – a good many of ours spoil'd from carelessness & bad accoutrements must be more attentive to that matter. we have not sick enough to compleat the rest.

Tuesday 21st. March fine weather   The Virginia frigate arrived from N.York & bring the Octr. Novr. & Decr. mails which arrived there 19th. Febry. in the Swift Pacquet – They have had a very hard winter at New York as ever was known. Staten Island was visited by Lord Stirling & 3000 but he did not feel bold enough to make any attack – Three several Detachments of our troops went out from King's bridge to white Plains, from Poulis hook to Newark, & from Staten Island to Elizabeth Town, and all succeeded in their attempts on the Enemy killing some and taking a great many prisoners – The Virginia came over the Bar, few letters come to hand yet, Lord Barrcidale come in her who is now Earl of Caithness, to purchase & go home

A letter from Chas. Grant to collect money for him, he says he is married to Miss Hunt. The Lord help him.

din'd with Peter, Mr. Ritchie there, he has join'd that Company in the meantime by desire of Col: Balfour to whom he is recommended

Wednesday 22d. March   fine wr. & warm, all the Rebel Ships that were lying at Sulivans Island are gone up into Cooper River, yesterday

The letters come up, I got no less than 8 from my little deary, vizt 20 Augt 4th. Sepr. & 23d. 3d. 12th. & 28th. Octr. 13th. & 25 Novr. all well & full of affection – they were enclosed by Rutherfurd who writes me of QrMr Smiths death & the conduct of the Regt. on clearing themselves &ca. &ca.   a letter from John Smith & a parcel of Newspapers, he is disappointed in getting the Majority of the 2d. Battalion   McIntosh was appointed & 'tis thot. Peter Graham will get it now, what luck some people have – a letter from my Father of 26th. Octr. all well, & a letter from Dd. Cunningham Lt. in the Grays better wrote than I expected – had Peter & Ritchie to dine & C: Cuningham

The Light Infantry, 33d. & Yagers march'd in the afternoon up the Country probably to meet Gen. Patterson – they did not march till the morng. of the 23d

Thursday 23d. March warm wr. wind in the So: The Admiral up here, the Ships in 5 fathom hole viz the Renown 50. Roebuck & Romulus 40s. Richmond, Blonde & Raleigh 32s, Perseus Camilla & Fowey 20s, are all ready to proceed up – the Rebels we are told by deserters are dismantling their ships & taking out their Guns to put into Batteries – we are making a little square Redoubt at the Creek near Genl. Leslies, Some Guns & howitzers come up there probably for embarkation.

some spies from Chas. Town skulking about us, these rascals have more impudence than any other people on earth two of them taken, Scot not found yet

Friday 24th. March fine wr. & little wind mounted Guard at 6 at the Batteries, 112[;] two of our Gallies at the wharff there all quiet, the Rebel ships lying t'other side the town in Cooper River. some ships arriv'd at Tybee from England under Convoy of the Iris & Hydra, they came by the West Indies – a good deal of thunder and lightning in the evening & rain in the night – something going to New York wrote to Rutherfurd to bring some stores &ca. in case it finds him there, & wrote a few lines to AH: inclosed to Dr. McLean to forward. Our Baggage put on board ye. Thames

Saturday 25th. clear & cool relieved in the morng – 3 men join'd from N:York I hear the Light Corps are about 5 or 6 miles off at a Bridge – Artillery & Stores getting up to the House where Genl. Leslie was, Linings[,] he is out with the Light Infantry, hurdles carrying down near that to make a passage on the marsh Hessn. Grrs. on the ground where the Lt. Infy. was

Sunday 26th. March fine cool wr. wind in the East – Genl. Patterson with his Brigade from Savannah come to Stono ferry – went to the Shipping at Hd.Qrs. to get some things for ourselves & the Coy. no Tobacco to be had except a little cut at 5/ Sterg. P lb – open'd my Trunk all safe, lent Capt. [Kenneth] McKenzie 37th. Grrs. 30 guineas, took out 20 for myself & gave the rest in care of Capt. [Donald] Moodie viz 80 – I hear we have 15 men of war in five fathom hole; the Iris ran ashore to the so:ward of Tybee – allmost all the Transports are up at Perryno's, the Margery gone to 5 fatm. hole to be made an arm'd ship – The

2d. Battn. 71st. come from Light house island, Majr. [Alexander?] McDonald to Hd.Qrs. the 63d. & 64th. there also, Majr. McCaren commands a Detachmt. at Ft. Johnston this week past. The Rebels burning houses &ca. withoutside their works

Monday 27th. March fair wind S.W. Artillery & Engineers stores collecting at the little Creek near Genl. Leslies late Qrs. Linings for some days past, near the little Redout

The 64th. Regt. march'd from Hd.Qrs. to the Battery's at the mouth of Waupoo, whh. is to be their Station for some time, The Iris got off, that fleet arrived at Tybee among whom is a ship with Cannon & powder, much wanted. we hear the Rebels are destroying some of their ships in Cooper River, – 2 men join'd from ye Ships

din'd with Lord Cornwallis. good things with temperance, & politeness is true Epicurism.

about 260 Sailors from the Europe & Raisonable come to man the flat Boats the boats are come to landing place near this, these two Men of War are lying in Beaufort River which they find to be an excellent harbour & easy navigation[8]

Tuesday 28th. March fine wr. wind Easterly The flat Boats pass'd out of Waupoo last night into Ashley River & up the little creek where the Artillery & Engrs. stores are collected – we have orders to be ready to march at 12 o'clock, we have five days provision in pork & flour the offrs. baggage to be left with the QrMr.

Genl. Pattersons Corps come near to where the Light Infantry are. [Lieutenant-Colonel Banastre] Tarleton with his dragoons had a skirmish with the Enemys t'other day –

a Col: [John] Hamilton of the Provincials & Dr. Smith of the Hospital taken prisrs 2 days ago, from Genl. Pattersons Corps

The British & Hessian Grrs. & two Fuzrs. Regts. march'd about 12 oclock by the bridge near Ashley ferry, & proceeded up the road about 3 miles further to Drayton Hall where we found the Light Infantry & took up ground near them for the night with orders to be ready to move at the shortest notice – the 1st. Battn. of the 71st. who came with Genl. Patterson took up ground in front of the Light Infantry & the Legion, the rest of that division betwixt Ashley ferry & our last Camp –

This Drayton Hall is on the south bank of Ashley River about 13 miles from Chas. Town & is one of the best houses I have seen in America, with handsome improvements Mr. Drayton who was a great Rebel is lately dead & left his fourth wife a widow who lives in the house with her children the old rascal was very rich, had 10 plantations & about 1000 Negros

Wednesday 29th. fine fair weather orders to march early in the morng. & the baggage to be sent to Ashley ferry – flat boats & ships long boats to the No. of 100 come up to Drayton Hall last night with some gun boats – The troops march'd about 8 oclock to the river side at the foot of Draytons Garden where they Embarkd; the jagers Light Infantry and Grrs. first trip & landed on the other side about a mile higher up without any opposition near Ben:Fullers – the boats return'd & brot: the Hessn. Grenrs. the fuzr. & 33d. Regts. the Genls offrs. Horses & some field pieces, & we moved on in the afternoon on the Chars Town road about 3 & 4 miles & took up ground near Bellingers, a friend to Got. just escap'd out of Town – This covers Ashley ferry for the passage of ye. baggage &ca.

Thursday 30th. March fair wr. wind So:ly The Baggage horses &ca being got over last night & this morng. the troops were put in motion about nine & march'd on the road to town about 6 or 7 miles where the yagers & Light Infantry met with a small party of the Enemy with whom they skirmish'd for hours, Lord Caithness while among the Comr. in Chiefs suite receiv'd a Shot in his belly, two yagers wounded [;] a small fleche in front of their works was taken possession of & left again, the firing ceas'd in the eveng. The troops took up their ground, yagers & Light Infantry in first line extending across the neck about 2 miles from town, Grenrs. British & Hessns. in a 2d. line about 7 or 800 yards in their rear the rest of the troops behind them some facing outwards Hd.Qrs. at Wms. on the right of the Grrs. flanking today thro' very bad swampy road – the other 1/2 of the Coy. driving in Cattle

Friday 31st. March cold & blowy at NW a hard Gale last night all quiet in front. Boats coming from the other side Ashley River with hurdles Engineers tools &ca. which are landed near the right of the first line Gibs's landing. a large foraging party out under the Command of Lt.Colo: Webster. They went near to Ashley ferry & got little or nothing. The Country near the Town swept pritty clean before we came. much reconoitering today.

Saturday 1st. April cool & pleasant wr. The troops got two day fresh provision more Engineers stores coming over & some artillery & provisions frames erecting on the road in front of the 1st. Lt. Infantry for the purpose of making works with expedition, they are faced with boards nail'd to right angled timbers parapet height, in divisions about 18 feet long

Sunday 2. April cool & pleasant wr. wind in the South – The Troops in Camp were under Arms at 4 oclock morng. the working party return'd at daylight they have made three large Redoubts within 7 & 800 yards of the Enemys works & with so much silence that they were not discover'd by the enemy. The two Battns. of Lt. Infantry occupy these Redouts for this day, and have made a trench of Communication betwixt them; the Rebels have a good many embrazures open to these Redouts but very few Guns in them. they fire a shot now & then mostly from one Gun, their works which are quite across the neck seem to be strong & well made with a very wide & deep wet ditch or canal from River to River, & a thick abbattis; they fire about 30 or 40 shot in the afternoon – we are busy in getting Artillery & stores from the other side and haul'd up from the Landing place, to the park, more frames errecting for Batteries [;] for duty in the Redouts tonight 800 B: & Hessn. Grenrs. Major Grahams Lt. Iy. & 200 of these to Cover a working party of 400 from the Reserve.

Monday 3d. April cloudy, wind N.E. not a shot fir'd last night, the working party made another work more advanced to the right, & return'd to Camp before day, the Grrs. occupy the Redouts today at which the enemy fire a good many shot, & have brought up some more Guns.

we have got a Gun into the right Redout. The Engineers & Artillery busy in their respective departments getting things forward – 16, 24 pors. come across, mostly Ship Guns; more frames & platforms getting ready.

The Rascals fir'd above 300 shot today & a few Shells in the Eveng. & did not hurt any body –

for the Redouts tonight 600, for work 500 the 33d. Regt. as Light troops make the Covering party. –

Genl. orders for the officers who hold Commissions in the Regular & provincial troops, to resign one & abide by the other

Tuesday 4th. April rain last night wind S.W. – was at work last night we carried out the frames from the Engrs. park for a Battery with 9 embrazures & set them down about 500 yards to the left of the left hand Redout, & within 600 yards of the Enemys works, where we broke ground & filled them up pretty well but not sufficiently to resist battering, towards morng. it rain'd hard & the men being much fatigued we left off about 4 & came to Camp; five Negroes came in to us having made their escape over the works The enemy did not fire a shot during the night, & we work'd in such silence that they did not discover us. after daylight they began to fire at that & the other works & about 8 o'clock one of their frigates a Brig & two Gallies came up near the left of the light Iny. Camp & fired broadsides till a 24 por. made them move off – our Camp Equipage come up, some things lost & some left behind –

din'd at Hd.Qrs. Majr. Crosbie. – a Bower[9] a fleet of 30 sail seen off the Bar

Wednesday 5th. April cool north wind The same numbers for the trenches last night as usual, finishing the 9 gun battery & the work on the right. The Enemy having found the range & direction fir'd a good many shot & some shells during the night. Lt. Grant on the Covering party was struck with a Cannon ball on the back part of the left shoulder which made a very large, but I hope not a dangerous wound, & a man of the 23d. Grrs. lost an arm – a Grenr. of the 7th. deserted & a man of that Regt. – a Hessn. Grr. detected in the march going off – two of the Rebel light horse

356

came in from goose creek, not so much firing from the Town today The fire increas'd in the Eveng. put Grant into a room in the Genl. Hospital

Thursday 6th. April cool with the wind about N.E. 1000 in the trenches last night & 500 at work, by detachmt. from the whole except the yagers, The Enemy fired a good deal in the eveng about relieving time, of both shot & shells, but our Batteries at Waupoo & two Gallies opening upon the Town, made them silent for the rest of the night and all this Morng. – a great many Boats seen crossing Coopers River yesterday & today loaded with people –

A New work made last night to the right of the two right hand Redouts, (place des arms)[10] some firing from the Enemy in the afternoon – for the trenches this Eveng. the same numbers as last night.

The offrs. & men of the Artillery who were taken out of the Russia Mercht. by one of our Privateers & carried to Bermuda, are come from thence in anor. Prr. & join'd their Corps

Friday 7th. April cool & clear wind N.E. a great deal of firing last night from the Enemy, & some from our side, Wapoo Batterys some Negroes come in from the Town who say they intended to have made a Sally.

ten or twelve Schooners & sloops came down Cooper River to the Town, suppos'd to be a supply or reinforcement; a good deal of firing from the enemy in the eveng. – The same numbers for the trenches as last night. The Rebels gave a cheer along their works in the eveng. & the Bells of the Town rang a peal

Saturday 8th. rain in the night wind about S.E. at work in the trenches widening the Communication between the Redouts, the enemy fir'd but little during the night, & this morng. – we hear their rejoicing was for a reinforcement of 750

Our ships in 5 fathom hole took the advantage of this strong breeze about S.E. to come past Sulivans Island, they got under way between 3 & 4 o'clock P.M. forming the line a head, when near 4 the Enemys Batteries open'd upon them and each ship when she came opposite to their embrazures fir'd a broadside which kept up a heavy Cannode for above an hour & a half, till they were all past, and soon after came to anchor in Rebellion Road, three double deckers & 6 frigates – The Eolus an arm'd ship who followed got aground. The Richmond lost her foretopmast the Adml. led in the Roebuck in a boat about sunset it came on rain & the wind shifted –

The same number for the trenches this night as usual

Sunday 9th. April cool & pleasant wind in the N.W. qr. The Enemy fir'd none in the night. The working party made a new Battery on the right for 12 Guns nearly finish'd, some sailors employ'd hauling up Guns for the Batteries, – some boats seen passing Coopers River with people & horses no firing today. Grant better. we hear that our fleet had 7 sailors kill'd & 14 wounded in passing Ft. Moultrie The same number for the trenches

Monday 10th. fine cool wr. wind NW a good deal of firing last night but no harm done, the two Rebel Ships that were up Coopers River a piece are come down to the Town where there seems to be only 4 in all that's rigg'd.

The Admiral come up to Hd.Qrs. & a consultation held at the Engrs. house rode to the Legion about 4 miles in the rear at the Quarter house, all quiet there my horse fell coming back & I hurt my breast & shoulder a little – in the Eveng. Major Crosbie carried in a Summons for the Town to surrender & the Garrison to become prisoners of war, they sent back a written answer, declining to accept of these terms & soon after began a smart fire.

a man of the 42d. Lt Infantry kill'd in one of the Redouts today. 18 pieces of Cannon mounted –

Tuesday 11th. April fine clear wr. wind in the S.W. qr. a good deal of firing last night, Mr. Fitzroy grazed in the shoulder, they expend a great deal of shot & shells to little purpose

a Pacquet arrived, but the mail is not come up yet. 6 weeks from Falmouth The same no. for the trenches & work, I go

Wednesday 12th. April 1780 fine wr. wind in the N.E. qr. On

Guard in the trenches at Battery No. 6 some firing about the time of relief & some very well thrown Shells, but luckily they did no harm, the rest of the night quiet & very few shot all day

our Batteries were ready this morng to open in concert with some ships that were to pass up Cooper River, but the wind did not answer, & we did not fire – The Battery on the right with 12 Guns is mann'd with sailors, The center one in front of no. 5 by Hessians has but 6 guns yet that on the left has 5, 24 pors. 1 of 12 & two 8 inch Howitzers – The working party last night made an approach from the middle Battery – The Enemy are busy strengthening their works & opening more embrazures, – 3 sloops came up to our fleet were fir'd at a good deal passing Sulivan island

The 33d. Regt. the Legion & Fergusons Corps are march'd back in the Country to scour our neighborhood –

The 23d. Regt. came over two days ago & the 64th. came today & takes up the ground of the 33d.

when I came home from the trenches I found 3 letters one from my Fr. dated 25 Jany. acknowledging the Bill of 3d. Novr. & one from AH: of the same date & one from T.A. of 27th. all well –

Sir Geo: Rodney has beat the Spanish fleet & raised the Siege of Gibraltar.[11]

Thursday 13th. April 1780. Siege of Charlestown continued After 12 days work in completing the first paralel which stands opposed the Enemy lines from six to eight hundred yards distance & which consists of six works number'd from the right, a Battery in front of No. 5 and a line of approach advanced from thence

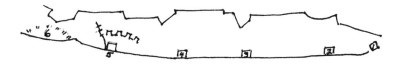

The three Batteries open'd this morning between 8 & 9 oclock with above 20 pieces of Cannon (mostly 24 pors.) 2 howitzers a

mortar & some cohorns & kept up a tolerable fire during the day, which brot a warm return from the Enemy, we set the Town on fire at three different times & places with Shells carcases or red hot shot, but they soon put it out again, & the Genl. gave orders himself to the Artillery offrs. not to set the Town on fire again, – This days firing has dismounted several of the Enemys Guns & toward eveng. they were almost silent – an artillery man lost an arm & an assistant kill'd by one of our own Guns hanging fire & going off when they put in the spunge, a man of the 37th. Light Infantry had his backside shot away looking for Balls –

The working party last night advanced the approach & made a traverse on it, but the moonlight increasing makes the nights very short for working – [12]

four & five deserters came in last night who say Mr. Lincoln is determined to defend the place to the last

Two Grenrs. deserted of 23d. & 38th.

Friday 14th. April 1780 the wind Easterly & N.E. these three days – & fair wr. a good deal of firing in the night mostly from us the working party made a piece of Intrenchmt. at the head of the approach within about 300 yards of Enemys abbattis.

The Legion & Fergusons Corps have surprized a Body of the Enemys horse about 20 miles in the Country, have kill'd 6 & taken about 70 prisoners, they & the 33d. are out still

Our Batteries began again early this morng. & kept up a pretty warm fire at the Enemys works who seem to have but few Guns to return it

The Yagers have got under cover within longshot & are popping at them with their riffles.

We have two Gun boats in the creek at the Brewery which communicates with Cooper Rr. they have two 6 pound carronades each. The 64th. Regt. are gone out to join Col Webster &ca.

Saturday 15 April cloudy, wind S.E. our Batteries fir'd a good deal last night and the working party got nearer the abattis but the enemy hearing them fir'd from their line with small arms & made them retire for a while, but they have thrown up a work very near the abattis 200 yds. & nobody hurt. & a Bomb battery made [;] a Rebel Galley come up near the Hospital & fir'd some Shots that way this morng.

Our Batteries do not fire so much today but there's a good deal of popping of small arms, twixt those in the advanced works & the Rebel lines –

we see a Rebel Camp on t'other side Cooper River – I hear Colonel Webster with his Detachmt. of about 1400 is to cross the River above 20 miles up & come down the other side.

a 13 inch mortar come from St. Augustine Rain in the afternoon & very little firing

Sunday 16th. April fair wr. & warm went to the trenches last night, & was sent to occupy the entrenchmt. at the head of the Sap with 130 men. a working party came there of 200 & lengthen'd the trench a good way to the left & carried out the Sap about 20 yards in front ending with a traverse, they left off about 3 oclock in morng. & went home, soon after 50 yagers came there who were posted along the banquet before day ready to take a shot when they could see, & we stood to our arms till near Sunrise – firing from both sides in the course of the night as usual, the Rebels throw their Shells better than we do, but did no harm; The night very light being almost full moon. When it was fair day light the Yagers began to fire at any body they could see about the enemys works, which are above 300 yards distant yet, they return'd the fire from some marksmen in a trench without their line of works but to very little purpose on both sides. The Yagers think they kill'd one, & the rebels kill'd one of our party a light Infantry man of the 16th. shot in ye. eye

Our Battery's kept up a superior fire all day, The Rebels having but a few Guns on their left that fire, & only two or three little mortars on their right. The Yagers went off in the Eveng. & I was relieved 'tween 8 & 9 – a Rebel Galley came in the afternoon near the Hospital & fir'd a good many shot, one of which went thro' the house but a small gun was brot down & drove her off –

We hear that Col Webster has cross'd the River above & is coming down t'otherside, the Rebels making works at Habeaw to defend themselves against him.

The Rebel prisoners that were taken by the Legion &ca. sent on board o ship they took likewise some Waggons & some letters from Lincoln to Col: Washington

Monday 17th. April warm wr. & little wind about N.E. a good deal of firing last night 4 or 5 wod. the working party carried out another sap in front of No. 2 about as far advanc'd as that to the left, the fire from the Batteries kept up as usual, we sent a dead 13 inch shell into the Town yesterday to let them see what we have, but the beds of the two large mortars are both insufficient

I hear the Navy have made a battery at the mouth of Wapoo from whence they fire into the Town when the fancy strikes ym.

some frigates & arm'd sloops are ready to come up Cooper River when the wind serves – two flag staff's set up at the foot of the Garden Lord Cornwallis Qrs. for Signals for them.

din'd with Lordship today, who is always very civil to me –

Tuesday 18th. April cool weather wind Northerly, The working party 100 less last night, they ran out another Sap betwixt No. 3 & 4 & part of a line of intrenchment to make the second paralel, a good deal of firing in the night on both sides & some grape from the Enemy –

our Batteries continue to fire during the day, with intervals of cessation. very few of the Rebels to be seen on their works – cold & rainy in the afternoon – for work in the evening. 400 a great many promotions in orders today

Wednesday 19th. cold wr. wind westerly The working party employ'd last night in improving the lines of approach & making traverses in the 2d parrallel as we find some of the Enemys Guns fairly infilade that intrenchment they fir'd a good deal on us, of round shot & grape & threw some shells a man of the 71st. kill'd & one wounded & a Hessian Grr. wounded – our Batteries kept up a superior fire during the night of both Shot & Shells but I suppose we do them but little mischief as they ly cover'd in their works – this parallel we are now on runs along the front of yr. middle works and I suppose about 200 yards distant from the

Abbattis, – we left off work about 3 o'clock in the morng. & came home

I hear the reinforcement from New York is arrived at Stono Bar & that the 42d. Regt. is there – arrived yesterday

The 23d. Regt. & a few Light Horse march'd yesterday, on Websters route. we see the Rebels making work at Habkaw it blows hard all day the Ships from NYork will not get up

Thursday 20th. April cool westerly wind – The working party last night push'd the sap a little farther, made a mortar Battery & improv'd the parallel, there were 3 kill'd & 4 or 5 wounded – a great deal of firing from the Ashley River side of the Town last night, which it seems was at our Gallies passing out of Wapoo to the Men of War, whom they join'd with the loss of 3 men kill'd & wound'd very little firing today on either side letters that is come by this fleet from NYork say that Adml. Rodney has taken 5, Spanish 70s. one blew up two lost, & 3 got into Cadiz much shatter'd

Friday 21st. April pleasant wr. & very little wind. The Ships from NYork have got up to Perryno's – There is the 42d. Regt. Hessian Regt. of Dilforth, the Queens Rangers, the Volrs. of Ireland & Browns Corps & some artillery –

There were two explosions in the Rebels works yesterday which is thought to be two small magazines of powder blown up with our Shells.

The Working party last night made a Barbette Battery with epaul[e]ments for two field pieces on the road leading to the Gate & about 300 yards distance, enlarg'd the Mortar battery & better'd the trench Balnabies man blown all to pieces with a shell & some few wounded.

The Sap going forward to a 3d parallel About noon the Enemy sent out a flag of truce with a letter to the Genl. & Adml. to signify that they were ready to treat upon honorable terms. The adml. was immediately sent for & the boat permitted to pass the town he arrived in the Eveng. when the Genls & he hark'd into council, the Rebels being anxious to get an answer sent another letter in the eveng. but the terms they demanded were too much to be granted & a refusal was sent out about nine & hostilities recommenced about ten with a good deal of firing from both sides which continued most part of the night. I understand they propos'd to deliver up the Town on the following terms. The Garrison to leave the Town with the honor of war viz 3 field pieces Drums Colours & baggage, & some days law to march into the Country. The inhabitants who chose it to follow with their Baggage but I believe the Genl. is determin'd to give them no other terms than to become Prisoners of war.

we see the Rebel Camp at Hobeau where they are still busy working & we suppose that Webster is not far from them watching their motions – but why not attack them Mr Webster –

Saturday 22d. April warm wr. wind about S.W. which is fair for our Ships to come into Cooper River but we are told that the Channel is block'd up & they can't find water enough with all the firing last night of Cannon Shells & small arms we had nobody hurt but Major Moncreiff who got a slight graze on the arm with a musquet ball.

The Queens Rangers, Volrs. of Ireland & the 42d. coming across Ashley River, they land at Gibbs landing, – but little firing all day

Sunday 23d. April 1780 warm – at work in the trenches last night where we were employed in carrying the sap forward from the 3d. parallel, on the left we got very near the wet ditch or canal & had only one man wounded, on the right they had 1 kill'd & 6 wounded with grape – firing from both sides now & then but most from ours of heavy shot & small shells, the Rebels threw no shells last night – the working party retir'd at 3 to the 1st. parallel, at 4 to the fleche where we staid till sunrise and came home to Camp –

The 42d. are encamp'd at present near the Engineers house, Simcoe's & Lord Rawdons gone to the rear, & will probably move out to reinforce Webster who we hear has taken a great quantity of stores &ca.

Monday 24th. April very warm wind about west – The Working party last night employed in improving the 3d. parallel & forwarding the sap – just after they had left off work & retired, the enemy made a sortir [sortie] upon the right, where they kill'd & wound 3 Yagers & carried off a Corporal & 9 Light Infantry much firing of small arms – two of the 38 Grrs. deserted last night –

Some more boats being got across from Ashley to Cooper River they were assembled at the Ship yard, where the Volrs. of Ireland embark'd & were carried over the River & were safely landed on the other side with Lord Cornwallis this morning before day, 'tis said they were to join Col. Websters Corps who were within a Short march of them, with intention to cut off the communication betwixt the Country & Garrison & prevent their Retreat. the boats in their return took a Sloop

Tuesday 25th. April warm wr. wind W about one o'clock this morng. the Rebels firing small arms on the working party they took it for a Sally & ran to their arms, when a smart or rather heavy firing commenced which lasted above 20 minutes

Ensn. [Duncan] McGregor 71st. kill'd Capt. N[orman]: McLeod & Lt. [John] Wilson wounded & tween 20 & 30 men in all kill'd & wounded.

The lines of Camp turn'd out & mov'd up a little way when by that time it was found the enemy had not come out, & the field officers at length got the firing put a stop to, which had been improperly carried to such a height without any real cause of alarm. The working party got the length of the first ditch & mar the Barrier Gate.

Lord Cornwallis still continues on t'other side

The advanced line of intrenchmt. makes now the 3d. parallel which extends from just opposite to the Enemys Barrier Gate on their right to that in their Center, from our left of which we are pushing a Sap towards their Batter. d'eau

The Rebels light up two fires out side their large Abbatis whh. burn all night & illuminate the Space betwixt us & them every night

Wednesday 26th. April warm but a fine breeze from S.W. some

Ships & Gallies were to have come up Cooper River today but the wind was rather scant at proper time of tide, some troops turn'd out to make a show of attack when they were passing the Town.

firing now & then as usual last night, the working party got on but slowly now being so near; combustibles ready to burn the abatis &ca. Lt. Beevor [Arthur Beaver] of the 33d. Grrs. wounded last night. The working party divided into two[:] one half in the Eveng. & one 1/2 in the morng. but little firing all day – for the trenches in the eveng.

Had a review of neccessaries found but little wanting, 8 pair of shoes & 4 or 5 shirts would serve us for two months to come, 46 linnen vests wanting to compleat to two each, & a whole set of trousers for the Summer, but our Coats are very ragged

Thursday 27th. April cool & cloudy wind in the East, & little rain

on Guard on the left of the 3d. parallel with 118 the working party carried the trench a little further to the left, & the sap a little nearer the Batter d'eau, & open'd two Embrazures of a Battery about the middle of this parallel, the platform not laid till the Morning. The Enemy kept up almost a constant fire of small arms on our left all night long, & fir'd a good deal of round, grape shot, & shells; 1 kill'd & 4 wounded in our part of the trench; they seem to be more suspicious of Barrier Gate on their right than that about the center, which we are quite close to, a Slack-fire kept up during the day, & the Yagers popping at their embrazures.

a good deal of firing on both sides at the time the relief came, about 8 o'clock

Friday 28th. April cool wind north we hear that Lord Cornwallis is in possession of Mount pleasant & that the Rebels have decamp'd from Hobeaw, a great deal of Smoke seen along that side today.

This seems to cut off their Retreat

The working party employ'd last night in thickening the parapet on the right of the 3d. parallel & sapping onwards to the dam on the left & carrying down stuff for platforms. the two Gun Battery mounted with twelves. The working party in the day time follow the former under cover, but little firing today

Saturday 29th. moderate. wind S.W. & more to the So: in the afternoon when some Ships & Gallies were expected up Cooper River in the afternoon. – a detachmt. sent by the Adml. in boats have taken 70 or 80 of the people from Hobeaw going to the Town yesterday morng. those at Mount pleasant retir'd to Sulivans Island

The working party last night were making a Battery for 5 Guns on the right of the 3d parallel which is close to their wet ditch & center Barrier Gate & still Sapping towards the dam & Barrier Gate on their right – some carrying matterials

The Sloop that was taken in Cooper is rigging out & arming at the Ship yard. but little firing at the works today. some men dropping down with sickness – mostly the ague or a lax [aches and fever or diarrhoea], if this business continues long, we shall feel it in that way. the men have but one night in bed. The Genl. Officers have but two. field offrs have five the rest of the offrs. of the army have 2 & 3 –

Sunday 30th. April a Strong wind at S.W. The working party going on with the Battery for 5 Guns very near the Ditch & opposite the Gate. there are likewise two others for two Guns each in the left part of the 3d. parallel – Sapping towards the Dam; 3 of the 63d. deserted.

a Man came in from the Enemy who left the Town about 10 days ago who had formerly been a Surveyor & was serving in their Militia   he gives a draught & discription of their works, & an account of their Strength & Stores &ca. by his accot. they must be scarce of provision

not much firing today on either side some of the platforms of the old Batteries are taking up for the new ones.

for the trenches in the Eveng. – a ship arrived from Clyde in 10 weeks

Monday 1st. May 1780 warm & a strong wind from S.W. which

makes it very disagreeable in the trenches which are all sand. The Working party last night going on with the Batteries & the sap towards the Dam and bringing up Guns & platform stuff.

The Enemy fir'd a great deal last night, above 300 rounds, & threw some shells. 6 Grenrs. kill'd & wounded, one yager kill'd this morng. & one lost his arm, all in the left of 3d parrallel

The Sappers being at last come to the Dam or Batter d'eau open'd it this afternoon & the water runs off freely, & will soon leave their wet ditch dry,

a good deal of popping of small arms all day, but not much Cannon, & we throw them a good many Shells some well & some ill as is generally the case on these occasions.

reliev'd by about 8 by Hessn. Grrs. – & I find that the 1st. parallel is now to be occupied by Picquets & the other two strengthen'd

Tuesday 2nd. May warm wr. & the wind continues in the S.W. Qr. tho' not so strong

The Batteries in 3d. parallel nearly finish'd & suppos'd to be ready tonight for 9 Guns – not so much firing last night & very little today – a deserter came in last night but these fellows know very little about the matter

We get on but slowly & hardly any of the impediments are remov'd yet which should be taken away before the place can be assaulted –

some of the men will get in liquor now & then notwithstanding all I can say to them – I knock'd down Nor: M.Kay on the parade not so much for being drunk as for swearing he was not, & tho' he deserved it I am sorry for it, for we should never punish a soldier in a passion –

Wednesday 3d. May 1780 very warm. several kill'd & wounded last night & this morng. – the Batteries not ready yet, a piece of Sap work making in front of the left of 3d Parallel for small arms.

The 64th. Regt. come over from Lord Cornwallis's detachmt. & brought 'tween 20 & 30 prisoners with them

The troops on t'other side Cooper have taken a great many stores of considerable Value, tobacco Indigo, dry goods, Liquors plate &ca & live in midst of plenty – above 300 Militia have deliver'd up their arms & return'd to their houses on parole. a great number of Women there who retir'd from the Town. Lord Cornwallis is about 10 miles from Scots ferry & has some detachments at [illegible] & Mount pleasant &ca.

Three White men & five Negros came in from the Town last night who says they are much harass'd & reduced to half allowance of meat – a man that deserted from the 7th. came back again.

The Legion have got a number of good horses & are better mounted now than ever they were before; Major Cochran has taken a good many Vessels some of them arm'd.

Thursday 4th. May a Cloudy morng. a great deal of firing last night of both Cannon & small arms, but I hear of nobody hurt – The working party employ'd in widening the trench & thickening the parapet of some parts of the 3d parallel & doing something towards making more Batteries in that line.

last night two boats with sailors boarded an unrigg'd ship lying at anchor in Cooper River a little above the Town & towed her up to the Ship yard, they tho't she was a prison ship, but she proves to be an hospital for the small pox, above 30 people in her

Rain with Lightning & thunder for about 4 hours in the middle of the day. & two in the Eveng.

two Sloops & two Schooners came over to the Shipyard Creek that were taken by the Legion –

Mr. [Edward] Rutledge a Bror. of the Rebel Govrs. & two officers, taken by some of Lord Cornwallis's division & brot. over yesterday [;] for the trenches this Eveng.

Friday 5th. May very cold last night & this morng., wind from the No. & NW found the trenches full of water & some parts fallen in from the excessive hard rain yesterday the working party did little or nothing last night, but some come in the morng. & repair'd the trenches. I was on the left of the 3d. parallel

The Enemy kept up a brisk fire of Canon & small arms all night long but to very little purpose & beat to arms about midnight & we made hardly any return except a shell now & then & a few small arms – but little firing of Cannon during the day the yagers & the Rebel marksmen popping at one another, one of the 17th. Grrs. shot thro' the body.

The water is still running off out of the ditch but it is not near dry yet

a Genl. Court Martial Sitting for the tryal of Capt. [Hayes] St. Leger of the 63d. for some difference 'twixt him & Major Wyms

Saturday 6th. May cool & pleasant The working party hauling more Guns down to the Batterys in the 3d. parallel last night. There are two field pieces 6 pors. in the 2d. parallel to be mounted in a little Battery on the left of that trench. a good deal of firing last night as usual

Sunday 7th. May pleasant wr. wind from So: & S.W. The Rebels kept up a warm fire of Canon & Musketry last night again, & beat to arms about an hour before day. They seem to be much afraid of an attack in the night – the deserters all agree that their provision is both scarce & bad.

our Miners are still working at the dam & draining the ditch.

we hear this Morng. that Sulivans Island is in our possession, being summoned by the Adml. last eveng. the Garrison surrender'd & about 200 became prisoners with Cannon Stores &ca. –

we are also inform'd that the troops on t'other side Cooper have had a dash at Col: [William] Washington & his Light Horse at a place called Santee ferry – This happen'd yesterday – it seems that Lt. [Lovett] Ash with the few mounted Light Infantry being out on a patrole was surrounded & taken by a body of the enemys Light horse, on hearing of which Lord Cornwallis sent Tarleton with the Legion to endeavor to surprise & get a blow at them, they accordingly came up with them at Santee ferry just as they were going to take boat & falling upon them suddenly they cut down about 20 took 32 & about 100 horses & drove the rest into a great Swamp. Lt. Ash being in a boat passing the River seeing how matters went, threw the Rebels that were in the boat with him over board & join'd Col: Tarleton.

The Genl. gone to see the Admiral & have a conference with him

Monday 8th. May warm & pleasant wind in the South.

On Picquet last night in No. 5 had a Detachmt. at No. 6 & one at the old Mortar Battery – a Picquet of 200 has for some nights past occupied the 1st. parallel & comes off in the Morng. about day light.

The Batteries in the 3d. parallel being ready the working party last night were mostly employ'd in carrying ammunition to them The Enemy fir'd less last night than for some nights before.

Things being in this State of readiness for a close attack the Genl. sent Major Crosbie early this morng. with a flag to Summons the place to surrender & caution them against the consequence of an assault, on which they ask'd till 12 o'clock to consider of it, at which time they return'd an answer agreeing to the first & most important articles & stipulating for terms & circumstances regarding property & individuals, for which purpose the truce continued till the evening, & again prolong'd till the morng. at 8 o'clock. The Admiral sent for. –

The sentence of the Genl. Court M. in orders, Capt. St. Leger being try'd for Mutinous & disrespectfull behaviour to Major Wyms as his Commanding officer is acquitted of the first part & found guilty of the last, for which he is to be reprimanded by the D.A. Genl. at the head of his Regt. tomorrow morng.

it is worse than ridiculous to accuse a man of more than you can make appear

Tuesday 9th. May 1780 warm with a pleasant breeze from the S.E. – The truce still continues, & the treaty going on; which spun out till 8 o'clock eveng. by these Rascals increasing their demands untill they were no longer Allowable & hostilities began again about 9 with great violence on both sides & kept up a warm fire all night –

& today the 10th. [May 1780] the fire continues pretty brisk, we have dismounted & silenced some of their Guns on their left, & one of our 12 pors. is hurt 10 or 12 men kill'd & wounded & 3 officers wod –

The working party or rather Miners first, are pushing forward by sap from two places on the Right of the 3d. parallel.

By an intercepted letter from one Smith an offr. of some Rank in Town to his wife in the Country dated 30th. April it appears that they have given up all hopes of keeping the place, or of getting away, now that their retreat is cut off by Lord Cornwallis & must soon surrender for want of provision, which corresponds with the information of deserters.

The above letter is very well wrote, is full of love, politics, & desponding intelligence to his dear Sally –

The Admiral gone down to the Ships and as it is probable the Town must surrender for want of Provision in less than a week I suppose they will put off the Assault to some days –

Thursday 11th. May 1780 warm we kept up a superior fire last night of both Canon & small arms and this morng. befor day the Town was set on fire in two or three places whh. still continues to burn – but little firing in the day – two deserters come in last night who confirm the Scarcity of pron.

I hear Lord Rawden & Coll. [William] Dalrymple the Qr.Mr. Genl. are arrived from New York, in the Iris, a short passage a flag from the Enemy about 2 o'clock P:M: which I believe offers to surrender the Place upon the terms the Genl. granted before in the mean time there is a cessation of hostilities –

Friday 12th. May 1780 warm & windy from the eastwd.

The terms of Capitulation being settled last night, the Army were under Arms this morng. agreeable to the after orders but several delays on the part of the Enemy made it past 2 oclock before the two Compys. of Grrs. took possession of the Gate & Horn Work when soon after the Continental troops & some of their militia march'd out & drew up in the ground betwixt the two abbatis where they laid down their Arms & Colours, the British flag was immediately hoisted at the Gate as the Rebels march'd out & a Salute fir'd of 21 Guns The Genl. Leslie with three British Regts. took possession of the Town & the prisoners were put into the Barracks & other places under a Guard, the offrs. at liberty to walk about with their side arms

They are ragged dirty looking set of People as usual, but more appearance of discipline than what we have seen formerly & some of their officers decent looking men most of the Army were drawn up near the wet ditch during this ceremony which lasted till Eveng. The 7th. 42d. & 63d went into Town the rest return'd to Camp.

[13th. May] went this forenoon to see the Town & the prisoners, all disorder & confusion there yet – many very good houses in town some hurt with shot & some burnt & those burnt near two years ago are not rebuilt. The streets are all sand except here & there a piece of brick pavement as the sides.

They talk of 6 or 7000 prisoners of one kind & another but I don't suppose there will be above 2000 of these subject to exchange, as all the Militia &ca. get their parole & the inhabitants of the Town their property – met with Coll. [Nathaniel] Gist of the Virgns. an old acquaintance –

Wrote to R.M. a Sketch of the Expedition, & intended to write some other long letters, but was call'd upon for duty which obliged me to curtail his letter & write a few lines to my little friend AH: least the dispatches should be sent away before I come off, as I am told the Perseus is to sail tomorrow with [Thomas] Lord Lincoln & [John] Lord Caithness & Capt. [Henry] Broderick –

Sunday 14th. May easterly wind & showers last night & today – on duty in the lines, & have detachmts. on the left of all the three parallels taking care of the Batteries & guarding the Gate at the dam on the right of the Rebel works – not reliev'd till past nine, – the detail much neglected –

they are busy in Town putting things into order, nobody allow'd to go in yet but who are pass'd by a field officer except the Light Infantry who are under orders of readiness to march, they are allow'd to go by parties & see the Town – sent my two letters to Lord Caithness who promises to take care of them and expects to go tomorrow morning

Monday 15th. May rain last night wind in the East.
The Light Infantry are countermanded & the 71st. march'd this morng. & I hear have cross'd the River Cooper.
a Report going about of a french fleet expected on the Coast –

the intelligence of their sailing from france brought by the Pearl to New York, & forwarded here by the Iris, but their destination was not known; a fleet was sent after them from England

A melancholly accident happened between one & 2 o'clock by the blowing up of a Magazine in Town, which the Artillery were examining & storing up arms in   Capt. [Robert] Collins & Lt. [John William] Gordon of the Arty. kill'd Lt. [Alexander] McLeod 42d. & others kill'd & wounded in a shocking manner, the Town set on fire & continues burning & another magazine in danger, being near the fire   The fire was got out by the activity of the Militia inhabitants & Negroes before evening, having burnt a Barrack, the gaol, & house of Correction, in which were good many people, The principle Magazine was not far off with about 500 barrels of powder in it. The occasion of the blast was suppos'd to be owing to some of the firelocks (which were all loaded) going off by accident near some powder.

Very Strange Management to Store up loaded Arms in a Magazine, of Powder

Tuesday 16th. May cloudy & showers They still busy in Town taking an account of the prisoners & other things which business seems to be but little understood by the different departments & therefore ill managed

The two Hessian Regts. of Ditforth & Huyne went into Town yesterday as part of the Garrison. Lord Cornwallis who came over yesterday is gone back again to his command on t'other side Cooper, The great quantity of valuable Stores found there, turns out to be an object worthy of attention for the Army.

The Rebel officers going over to Mount pleasant – our ships coming round from Stono – din'd with the Major   the Regt. still in Town without baggage. only 150 go to the trenches now –

Wednesday 17th. May. close weather & warm with showers of rain

a Meeting of the field officers of the Army to consult & agree upon the Manner in which the prize money shall be divided 'twixt the Navy & Army –   they appoint a Committee from each. The Perseus sail'd, Sr. Andw. Hamond went in her too

The Articles of Capitulation publish'd & the correspondence concerning it.

Thursday 18th. May, warm weather & easterly winds, which is against the Perseus & the Ships coming round –
The Genl. went in form to wait on the adml. who has taken up his Qrs. in Town – I din'd at Hd.Qrs. which is still here at Williams's. The Light Infantry, 42d. & Queens Rangers have got orders of readiness to march at the shortest notice –

Friday 19th. the same kind of wr. I went into Town to see it more particularly & took a look from the top of high Steeple which gives a very fine view of the Town the Rivers, & the Country, see a great many very good Houses & all of them very elegantly furnish'd, whh. gives an idea of style of living & luxury –
dined with the Regt. who hold their mess at a handsome house belonging to Genl. [William] Moltrie they expect to march in the Morng. N.B. I have made two or three requests to the Major, concerning the Compy. all of which he refuses, – many men change their minds with their condition and there is no help in us
People coming from the other side Cooper in great Numbers to Town & the Rebel Militia going out – The Continental officers going over to the Barracks at Mount pleasant.
The Navy & Army do not agree so well about dividing the spoil as in taking the place – Lord Cornwallis still on t'other side at Silkhope, peace & plenty there, they say there is about 1000 Rebels near Santee ferry; probably covering the removal of their Stores & valuable things

Saturday 20th. May 1780. warm with the wind in S.W. qr. the Transports getting over the Bar and up to Town. a walk to Quarter house where the Queens Rangers are, they have generally 2 or 3 Compys. from 6 to 10 miles advanced few or no Inhabitants in all that space & the Country quite bare of everything. The Militia going out in numbers to the Country on parole.
We have orders to be in readiness to Embark at the shortest notice. a Pacquet announced in the orders to sail in a few days for England.

The Light Infantry march'd in the Evening, & the 42d. Regt; out to the northward.

Lt. Col: [Alured] Clarke going to Savanah to Command there with the Rank of Brigr.

Sunday 21st. May 1780 very warm with a little wind in the South. The Queens Rangers have likewise march'd out into the Country. a great many ships come up to Town, The Transports to water immediately Those allotted for the 1st. Battn. are

The Nestor 348 tons.	17th. 37th. & 76th. Compys.
The Thames 306 tons.	7th. 23d. & 33d. & Surgn.
The Houston 250 tons.	43d & 38th.
The Jno. & Jane 150 tons.	42d. field officers. & M: of B
an Agents ship of 378 tons	

put on our new trouzers today – writing letters for the Pacquet – AH:

Monday 22d. May very warm, & little wind we have orders to be ready to march in the Eveng. & leave our tents heavy baggage behind. finish'd my Letter to AH: inclos'd Rollo's Bill £21 & gave it in, least [that is, lest] the Pacquet should sail before we return – sent a Sergt. to Capt. Moodie settled accots. & recd. the remainder of my cash £46.10 – The Transports watering at the Brewery – The Triton arrived from England a few days ago with dispatches & sail'd last night or this morng. for New York with Major Crosbie a Detachmt. of 150 Grenrs. going to Sulivans Island to relieve Fergusons people who are going to move out – & I hear Lord Cornwallis is in motion towards Santee & George Town.

proclamation spreading about in the Country to encourage the Inhabitants to return to their Loyalty & restore order & good Government in the Provinces of So: & No: Carolina which I hope will have good effect.

The British & Hessian Grenrs. & yagers with Genl. Kospoth march'd in the Eveng. about 8 & halted in the wood near Bellingers about 11 o'clock having march'd I suppose about 7 miles

Tuesday 23d. May, was a very hot day we mov'd early in the morng. & took up ground with our right just above Bellingers house, our rear to Ashley River, facing about N.E. made shades & rested, & we hear we are to remain here for some days; 9 miles from Town   The Light Infantry & 42d. about Monks Corner, Queens Rangers somewhere betwixt this & that – the purpose of all these movements, we suppose, is to Collect Stores, fresh Provisions, & open the Country communication with the Town (& kept idlers out of Town – while the Ships are getting ready)

Wednesday 24th. May much Thunder last night, & a little rain, today cool & pleasant, wind about S.E. a ride to Ben Fulers where we landed, about 3 miles

I see Hessians send their servts. & horses about 15 miles up the Country & get plenty of fresh stock – they're fendy folk –

a Party of 25 men with arms & horses arrived here in the evening on their way to Hd.Qrs., they are come from Orangeburgh to acquaint the Genl. that they and a great many more friends to government are ready to shew their loyalty by their services against the Rebels by whom they have been persecuted & wish to take revenge. – they are in a hunting dress mostly riffle shirts, arm'd with riffles & travel on horseback, & are call'd Carolina Crackers.

Camp at Bellingers near Ashley ferry Thursday 25th. May 1780, British & Hessian Grenrs. & Yagers under Genl. Kospoth.

A Party of a Capt. 2 Subs. & 42 R: & file march'd this morng. about 1 o'clock to Dorchester &ca. to collect fresh stock in that neighborhood for the offrs. of the two Battns. B. Grs. which is to be divided by those Compys. who send money to purchase it; they sent in 6 Bullocks some Calves Sheep & pigs & 5 or 6 dozen of Poultry in the evening, from Dorchester a Village on Ashley River about 20 miles from Charlestown – every house has the appearance (tho' deserted) of the Inhabitants having lived in affluence & luxury, but this wanton Rebellion has broke in upon their pleasures, & their comforts too, & reduced many wealthy people to shifting circumtances, & the poor negroes to a starving condition in many places hereabout –

The Queens Rangers come to Dorchester   The Light Infantry & 42d. continue at Monks Corner –

Friday 26th. May warm with light showers & some thunder. an arm'd Vessel come from N:York wt. dispatches &ca. but nothing of their purport has come this length yet.

The Party that went for fresh stock returned in the eveng., having made a tour by Goose Creek but were not so successfull there as about Dorchester – they met many genteel Inhabitants (ladies) who were civil & polite

The Rolls call'd frequently during the day to prevent stragling & of course doing mischief in the Country, notwithstanding there are several complaints among us but the Hessians plunder methodically to a great distance in the Country.

Saturday 27th. May cloudy, wind S.W. The Hessian Grenrs. order'd to return back near the town or probably to Embark for their irregularity in the Country. they march'd in the forenoon –

Sunday 28th. May 1780 warm   The two Battns. B. Grrs. march'd this morng about 4 o'clock & took their former ground near Hd.Qrs. at Wms. without tents.

The Hessns. in their old ground also. The Light Infantry & 42d. march this Eveng on their return, having had nothing to do but to receive submission & give paroles a plentifull Country about Monks Corner

Another proclamation come out dated Hd.Qrs. Charles Town 22d. May calling upon the Inhabitants to peace & Government, promising countenance & protection, and threatening the delinquents with confiscation of their Estates &ca. &ca. &ca.

Went to Town & got a Packet of letters brot. from New York by Capt. [David] Anstruther 42d. they came from Scotland by the Ruby on whom Ensn. [James] Spens has taken his passage but he got a Ltcy. in the 2d. Battn. Enclos'd by H.N.: recommending Mr. Spens two from my little friend & one from my Father in Decr. –

Monday 29th. May 1780 Rain last night and almost all day,

very bad for the men who have no shelter – the Grenrs. get leave
to go in & see the Town by parties –
Orders for Embarkation: The Yagers tomorrow morng. the
Br: & Hessn. Grrs. on Wednesday morng. & the remainder for
this embarkation on Thursday – The Light Infantry & 42 came
in the eveng. to their old ground, tents They have got something
to eat & drink &ca. and a little indeed –
din'd with Genl. Leslie – who had now almost got rid of this
troublesome task of settling the affairs of the Town, & is to be
succeeded by Genl. Patterson as Commandant.
I hear Lord Cornwallis has been at George Town, & is now on
the March to Camden, other Smaller parties traversing the Country under the Command of Lt. Col: Balfour: Major Ferguson
&ca. have particular instructions to conciliate the minds of the
people & establish peace & good order in the back Country

Friday 30th. May 1780, some rain in the night & morng.,
cloudy day, wind N.E. in town & on board of ships buying
things for the Compy. & for the mess on board the John & Jane –
The Merchts. have not yet got Permission to land their goods,
but they are getting some things ashore, & in a few days the Town
will be well stor'd with all kinds of Goods, tho' the prices are
very high
din'd in Town at a house of entertainment with 1/2 doz of our
Regt. a Veal dinner for a dollar a head, bad Mada wine 6/Sterg.
P bottle   Port wine sells for 40/: P dozen   porter 14/ Rum 2
dollars, sugar 1/2 a dollar P lb. & so on
They are about settling the market prices of goods for the use
of the Army, & the Merchts. Report is to be laid before a Committee of field officers

Chapter XI

'we march & manoeuvre . . . when it is not too hot'

New York
31 May to 15 November 1780

Notwithstanding his success in South Carolina and the British government's preference for an offensive in the South, Clinton returned to New York in June 1780 hoping to end the rebellion in a single decisive battle. So intent was he on such a strategy that he assembled nearly three-fourths of his army at New York. Yet for all his apparent resolve, he was soon distracted by the arrival of a French squadron, by disagreements with his naval counterpart, Admiral Marriot Arbuthnot, and by the prospect of capturing West Point. His initial plan – of returning from South Carolina to surprise Washington in New Jersey – was spoiled when subordinates who were ignorant of the plan invaded New Jersey prematurely and when news arrived that a French squadron was bound for Rhode Island. To meet the French threat, Clinton proposed that he and Arbuthnot join forces – in reoccupying Rhode Island to deny the French a base or in attacking the French as soon as they arrived. After Arbuthnot rejected his proposals and the French reached Newport, Clinton embarked a part of his army and went as far as Huntington Bay, Long Island, before learning that Arbuthnot was still unwilling to cooperate in an attack on the French. In August Arbuthnot proposed a conference to plan a joint attack, but when Clinton went to the east end of Long Island for the meeting, Arbuthnot had gone to sea. Infuriated, Clinton turned down further proposals for attacking the French and tried unsuccessfully to exploit Benedict Arnold's offer to betray the American post at West Point. So it was that in five months at New York, Clinton and his army of 20,000 managed little more than a skirmish with their enemies.[1]

Indeed, John Peebles and the British grenadiers did less campaigning in the summer of 1780 than in any previous summer of the war. On returning from South Carolina they stopped only long enough on Staten Island for Clinton to learn that he had little prospect of engaging Washington in New Jersey. They then sailed up the Hudson to pass a month camped in West Chester, foraging and skirmishing until they embarked for an attack on the French at Rhode Island. When Arbuthnot refused to support that attack, they disembarked on Long Island to await further orders.[2] They marched and manoeuvred, paraded, and built huts for the winter; they visited friends, caught up on correspondence, and sent barrels of apples and seedlings to Scotland. But because Clinton and Arbuthnot could not agree on a plan for attacking Rhode Island and because Clinton's plan for getting control of West Point miscarried, the troops on Long Island did no further campaigning in 1780.[3]

New York
31 May to 15 November 1780

Wednesday 31st. May 1780 warm & clear   The B: & Hessn. Grenrs. Embark'd early this morng. – the Adml. & some more men of war dropping down –

Got abstracts & money from the Paymr. for two musters for the compy. from 25 Octr. to 23d. Febry. last; & a Bill of £50. on the Agent, dated 30th. on accot. of my own Subsistce. for which the little man takes the usual premium of 2d. in the dollar, which is not fair as the exchange stands at present.

Busy buying stores for the mess on board Lt. Colls. Hope & Fox Major Brigade Scot & us – a months pay to each – wrote to my Fa. & sent a Bill of £21 to my Sister & one of £50 to be added to the rest

Thursday 1st. June warm weather but generally a breeze from the sea some part of the day – The Light Infantry & 42d. Regt. & Queens Rangers embark'd this morning, which I believe makes nearly the whole of this Embarkation – numbers of people coming in from the back Country to show their loyalty – Lord Cornwallis's Corps after making various movements in Country, to George Town & up the Santee River, receiving submissions & grant paroles &ca. Lt. Coll. Tarleton was detach'd with all the Legion mounted who made a forced march of near 100 miles in 24 hours, came up with a body of the Enemy a good way beyond Camden, cut down about 170 & took their Cannon, Colours & baggage with the loss of about 24 kill'd & wounded among the former are two officers.

Friday 2d. June warm as usual. getting everything aboard, The transports being compleated with water & provision for 70 days are ordered to drop down tomw.

din'd ashore with a party at Stricklands where we had a batch of tollerable good Claret but it was 9/Sterg. a bottle – on board at 8

The news of our Success in the back Country publish'd in hand bills – I hear Lord Cornwallis remains here   The Comr. in Chief [Sir Henry Clinton] goes with us suppos'd for New York –

Saturday 3d. June a breeze from So: The Transports got under way in the morng. but the wind being contrary they did not get far down some to Rebellion road & some near Sulivans Island The men of war getting over the Bar. haul'd the Seine on Jas. Island just above Fort Johnson & got plenty of fish –

Sunday 4th. June aut supra – The Transports &ca. got under way about the turn of the tide about 8 o'clock & moved down to 5 fathom hole, two or three got a ground below Sulivans Island, went ashore on that island as we came by to see The Fortifications, vizt. Fort Moultrie an irregular Square with 4 Bastions, all made of the Palmeto or Cabbage tree the best kind of wood for resisting shot, about 30 embrazures open to the Channel, a 15 Gun battery a little above of the same matterials, of which they make all their strong works in this Country   a row of pallisades set obliquely outwards all round the Fort, some places double, Barracks in the inside for 4 or 500 Men; a Bridge of communication from the Island to the Main above 1000 yards long made of the Cabbage tree   They have a large barrack on Hadrils point near Mount pleasant, where the Rebel offrs. are just now lodged, – Lincoln I hear goes by land to Philada. & a cartel ship going there

This being the Anniversary of the Kings birthday the Town fir'd at 12 & the men of war at 1 o'clock   see some large ships joining the adml. [Marriot Arbuthnot] without the Bar suppos'd to be the Europe & Raisonable, and likewise a number of Vessels coming in – from Savannah – The Rainbow gone out to sea, they say for New York – The Bonita Sloop of War come in from Savannah

June 5th. cloudy a little wind about N.E. which won't do to go over the Bar, so we remain in 5 fathom hole   The Admirals flag on board the Europe again –

Tuesday 6th. June warm with a breeze from the sea which prevents our getting over the Bar today. The Snow Pacquet got out, & came to near the Adml: She has got the Mail on board, & Col Bruce & Mr. Fitzroy

Wednesday 7th. warmer at night than in the day – a light breeze from S.W. in the morng. made the Transports get under way from 5 fatm. hole, & by noon about one half of them got over the Bar when the wind failing the rest came to anchor within side, our ship touch'd in coming over tho' we had Pilot. so here we ly, above 50 sail without, & above 40 sail within, – Wind S.E:

Thursday 8th. June 1780 a fine breeze about S.W. brought the rest of the ships over the Bar this morng. about 9 or 10 Clock When the Adml. made a Signal to get under way, which was repeated by the John Capt. Tomkins & obey'd accordingly at Noon Charles Town Steeple bears W.N.W. 7 leagues distance – The masters call'd & acquainted of the order of sailing in their stations as last voyage – & that if the men of war should meet with & engage the Enemy the Transports are to disperse & take care of themselves. we steer E.B.N. 4 & 5 knots –

	Europe	
Roebuck		Romolus
Grenadrs.		Light Infantry
Richmond	Yagers and Hessian Grrs.	Blonde
Camilla	42d. Regt.	Bonita
Raisonable	Queens Rangers	Renown

Gave out Money to clear the Compy from 24th. Octr. 79 to 24th. Febry. 1780 amount of Balances present £136

10 sick of the ague got a fine [few?] medicines from the Doctor but they will soon be expended

an ordinance Store Ship Sprung her Mzn mast in the Eveng. & the Roebuck took her in tow the head most ships lay to a while for the Rear

Friday 9th. June the wind about No: & NNE all last night & this morng. the fleet pretty well together steering to the Eastward with a strong breeze under reeff'd topsails – the day cloudy & cool

At Noon an observation Lat: 32.25 – one of the Large men of war has sprung her main top mast. The Raisonable or Renown. the fleet a good deal scatter'd in the course of The day [;] the Adml. bore down in the Eveng. & collected them

Saturday 10th. June a good deal of wind & sea last night, we continued to stand out to Eastward 2 & 3 knots till 5 in the morng. when the fleet tack'd & stood in about N.N.W. & N.W. the wind & the sea both fell; at Noon Lat 32.45 by observation. – see Dolphin & flying fish – supposed to be in the Gulf stream – 30 leagues from land

Sunday 11th. June 1780 easy weather with the wind from N:E: qr. going 3 & 4 knots about N.N.E. or so The fleet pretty well together about Noon the Adml. made a Signal for the Transports to go ahead while he lay by as if seeing a strang[e] sail, on which the John took the lead & steer'd N.N.E. but soon after the Adml. made sail again & hauled up to E.N.E. a light wind 2 1/2 knots the Lat: by observation at noon 33.31 No. to the East of Cape Fear about 44 miles smooth water – 19 fathom water at 10 Some that were sick with the ague have got quit of it & others are seized with it

In the Eveng. the Richmond made a Signal for ships to come under her stern & another for the Sternmost Ships to make sail, The Adml. made a private Signal & crowded all sail ahead followed by the Roebuck, he struck his flag & went a head of the fleet which we suppose was bidding us adieu & leaving the Convoy under care of Capt. Hudson of the Richmond being the Senr. Capt. here, & he took the lead accordingly – fair wr. little wind, & smooth water

Monday 12 June 1780 warm wr. & light breezes from the Southward & S.W. carrying all sail 2 & 3 knots – The Adml. Raisonable & Roebuck have left the fleet last night. the Pacquet gone two days ago –

Lat observd at Noon 34.05 Long. 75.30 a Boat from the Peggy

Navy Hospital Ship for a Supply of water, having come away with very little,

The Commodore lay to & made the Signal to come under his stern about 3 oclock P.M. The Rear closed up with a fine light breeze from the South, & in the eveng. were in close order & very compact carrying all sail & going better than 4 knots, fine clear wr.

Tuesday 13th. June 1780, pleasant wr. & light breezes from the So:wd. & westwd. the fleet in pretty good order steering N.E. 3 & 4 knots. Lat: observ'd 35.29 by which it appears that we are in the Gulf Stream & have been in it great part of the night Dist: sail'd Course Correct Long in 73.41 [;] about 1 o'clock steer'd North with fine fresh breeze at S.W. 5 knots, which continues, the fleet crowding all sail & pretty well up – the Camilla having in tow & Snow astern – some people hear'd firing a head –

Wednesday 14th. a damp hazy morng. but the wind still continues fair, going 4 & 5 knots all night due North, & sometimes 6 this morng. – by noon it clear'd up when we had an observation Lat 37.28 dist:run 117 miles Long: in 73.49. The fleet close up with the Commodore, who goes under more or less of his three topsails as he finds they can keep up see a great number of porpoises & two whales above 50 feet long

about the same number sick but mostly new ones, & the medicine all expended This ague which has now gone thro' the whole of the Company, & some repeatedly, is still lurking in the Constitutions & shows itself irregularly without any apparent reason how to account for it, in some every day & some every second day more & less violent in the Eveng. it fell calm for a while with fog the night variable winds & sometimes foggy, making but little way

Thursday 15th. June cloudy & damp wind from the N.E. qr. & but little of it the fleet pretty wide of the Comor: steering NNW Lat by observn. 37.58 course cor: North 30 miles

at 2 o'clock P.M. see two strange sail off the lee bow, they seem to be large. & standing towards us, in the eveng. they came into the fleet, one of them a 20 Gun Ship the Galatea who went along side the Richmond & sent a boat aboard, the other was one of our transports – a ship of the Light Infantry & was chased by the Galatea we are going 2 & 3 knots north with the wind about E.NE. & east, cold & raw

Friday 16th. June 1780 cool & cloudy wind about East steering to the north 2 & 3 knots, the fleet in close order, crowding all sail to a gentle breeze & smooth water at noon had an observation Lat 38.45 N. Sounded in 25 fathom water Long: 74.21. Cape Henlopen west 24 leagues about 3 P.M. the Bonita spoke us & told to make all sail possible as there was a fleet to windward, the man in a passion seem'd befrightnd from the mast head we see 10 sail mostly small Vessels about S.W. from us

in the Eveng. the Richmond hove to, & the Bonita fir'd 2 Guns & made the Signal to come under her stern, & we were told to follow her, the rest of the men of war staid to bring up the rear, except the Romolus who made sail a head all day. a fine breeze & smooth water wind S.E. course No: & NB.E. 3 & 4 knots –

Saturday 17th. June 1780, cloudy morng. & rain at 8 & 9 after which it clear'd up with a fine breeze about S.W. made the land this morng. suppos'd to be about Barnegat had 16 fathom water, & steer'd along shore at Noon see the Highlands of Navesink at N. 1/2 W. dist about 7 leagues Lat: obsd. 40.2. The fleet make a very long line some far astern the whole crowding all sail with the prospect of getting in; in the afternoon the breeze increas'd & we went 6 & 7 knots which brought us in with the Hook between 4 & 5 when it was foggy; we got a clear blink of the Light House & stood up but it grew so thick that not above one half of the fleet got in, & of those that did get up some ran aground near the narrows & foul of one another, we came to below the Narrows & below the Crowd in the evening it clear'd up when the Ships got under way & came to anchor at the Watering place; where the Admiral was lying ye Europa

Sunday 18th. June 1780 a Strong wind about W.S.W. most of

the fleet got in today, & the Raisonable who had been aground on the east bank at the Hook came up & join'd the Adml. nine sail come in likewise from the West Indies, who were the fleet we saw the 16th.

Genl. Knyphausen is in the Jerseys with 6 or 7000 men, they had a Skirmish beyond Elizabeth Town with some of Mr. Washingtons people in which the 22d Regt. & Anspach Yagers have suffer'd a good deal. The Rebel Army have increas'd their numbers & come down from the Mountains so that Knip is rather in a hobble at present, Encamp'd between Elizabeth Town & the Point

Br. Genl. Stirling was wounded near Elizabeth Town at their first going over by some skulking rascal from behind a house; his thigh bone broke, & very ill   Orders for Landing on Staten Island but it blows so hard that we can't get ashore today – Col: Fox gone to join his Regt.

A Pacquet arrived about a fortnight ago, she was chased ashore on Long Island but saved the Mail –

Monday 19th. June Strong westerly wind & cold. The Troops Landed this Morning on Staten Island, & march'd into Cantonmts. The Light Infantry about Deckers ferry British Grenrs. at & near Richmond Hessian Grenrs. on the South road, 42d. Regt. from Coles to Deckers, Queens Rangers in the Fort at Richmond –

It is suppos'd that Mr. Washington is on the Move, & that we shall not have occasion to go over to Knyphausens Assistance

got 4 letters this Morng. from my little Anne, dated. 7th. & 20th. Febry. & 5th. & 19th. March anxious still about thee, thou art all I prize

Richmond Staten Island Tuesday 20th. June 1780 fine cool weather they have had an excessive cold winter here, a very late Spring, & the Summer is not come in yet, The Country looks well tho' & you could hardly suppose that this Island had been almost laid waste four years ago –

all quiet over in the Jersey side & we have no word of moving –

I am Quarter'd at Louis De Bois's house the Compy. in the
Barn –
The Admiral with the Ships of War gone down to the Hook

Wednesday 21st. June some warm showers which will do the
ground a great deal of good being much in want of rain   on duty
for the day – had a long Court Martial for the trial of drunke-
ness & irregularity of which there are a good many instances, &
some too of the 42d. –
We have three small Picquets out at Night on the Crossroads
to the South which the Capt. of the day visits in the course of
the night, & orders frequent Patroles as may seem necessary –
Genl. Orders for the Troops in Staten Island to be under the
Command of Genl. Knyphausen as the times may not admit of
Application to Genl. Leslie – Lord Cathcart appointed to do duty
as Major to the 1st. Battn. Grenrs –

Thursday 22. very warm   a ride to Pillion's – offrs. who have
business at N:York get leave to go there   sent a letter to Sergt.
McCraw to bring trowzer cloth shoes &ca.
Lord Cathcart join'd the Grenrs. & begg'd off the Prisoners
that were just going to be flog'd   two of the 42d. by that means
escap'd   ask'd to dine with him at the Cols Mess but I was
engaged to C: Colquhoun   but I din'd with [Warren] Simondson
as Colqn. went to N:York   while at dinner we got orders to march
at 5 oclock to Coles ferry & Embark, all the Troops from So:
Carolina
1st. Grrs. march'd at six & arrived at Coles in 2 1/2 hours
after, where we found that most of the Transports were gone up
to Town, but were order'd down again to take us in; those
Embark'd whose ships were there, the rest lay on the ground for
the night –

Friday 23d. June the remainder of the Chas Town Troops
(except the Queens Rangers who are gone to the Jerseys)
Embark'd this morng. & when the tide servd about noon they got
under way & stood up the North River with a light breeze from

the Southward, which carried us up to, & near to Phillips's where we came to anchor –

hear'd a good deal of firing in the Jerseys about Elizabeth Town &ca. we suppose that Knyphausen is in motion forward & we are going to make a diversion in his favour, eh harry[4]

Saturday 24th. June that part of the Army that was in New Jersey made a move yesterday into the Country towards Connecticut farms & Springfield & meeting with some of the Enemy they had a skirmishing fight in which we had 50 or 60 men killed & wounded, & return'd to their Camp near Elizabeth Town And this Morng. they all left the Jersey, the Bridge was broke up the 22d. Regt. went to Staten Island the 43d. to NYork the rest of the Troops came up in Vessels & join'd us at Phillips's where we continue to ly at Anchor   a Sloop of war & another ship up in the Tapan Sea reconoitering

Sunday 25th. June 1780 very warm The Troops landed this morng. from their Transports & Vessels with 3 days provision and when all ashore they march'd & took up the ground the Army occupied last year, the right at East Chester the left at Phillips's; The Camp Equipage & field Baggage to be sent after us when Waggons come to carry it –

Monday 26th. the Baggage come to Camp, & we have orders to provide the men with necessaries as the Army will probably remain on this ground for several days, officers therefore get leave to go to Town –

Camp near East Chester Tuesday 27th. June 1780 – A Packet arrived yesterday at NYork in 6 weeks from Falmouth, which brings account that the french fleet expected on this Coast had not sail'd when she left England – The Genls letter of 9th. March James Island, in the London Gazette of 26. Aprl. Got three letters today from AH: of the 3d. 16th. & 30th. April, very anxious & uneasy about us, having had no accots.

The Guards come to the ground the Hessian Grrs. were on last year. Genl. Mathew at Babcocks. Genl. Leslie at East Chester. Commanding the Light Infantry & Grrs. The line to be under the Command of Genl. Knyphausen who takes up his Quarters at Phillips's a number of offrs. gone to Town some on business some on pleasure –

Wednesday 28th. June 1780 Rainy day. dined wt. Capt. [Walter] Home G:S: Vine

The West Chester Refugees make excursions into the Country & bring in horses Cattle & some prisoners as usual

Things for market full as dear as last year, the Country being constantly drain'd –

Genl. Knyphausen dates his orders at Phillipsburg.

Thursday 29th. June the Commander in Chief come up to Phillipss which makes Genl. Knyphausen move his Qrs. to Babcocks – Bought a Bay Mare 14 guineas

a Pacquet going home, & a fleet to sail soon for England, Genls. Tryon, Mathew, & Pattison going home &c &c

Friday 30th. June very warm   Mounted Picquet at day light at the usual place about a mile in front, all quiet there, the Light Infantry Picquet on the right, the Guards on the left the Refugees of West Chester &ca. went out above 200 strong on horseback to take Cattle & make depredations on the Enemy

Saturday 1st. July warm wr. Wrote to my little friend to go by the Pacquet as they say the mail is to be closed tomorrow eveng.

Sunday 2d. July. the Refugees return'd having got a licking from the Yankies a call in General Orders for Mowers & hay makers, they are to be paid by the Comry.

Went to N.York in the Eveng., left Camp at six & got there about 10 oclock Slept at Rutherfurds, the little Couple both sick with the Ague, & she is big with Child –

Monday 3d. July very warm put in my letter at the post office they expect the mail to be closed this eveng. but perhaps not for some days it is not a Pacquet but a Small Brig with 4 Guns, which the Capt. of the Carteret Pacquet Bought to carry him home, having lost his own Ship on Long Island – din'd with my friend

Dond. McLean & his Wife &ca. he was married last Thursday to
Capt. McDonalds daughter of the Emigrants –
    presented Sergt. McCraw to the board of Physicians & got him
Invalided. he fought well last winter in suppressing a gang of
Robbers at Jamaica, he killed one & wounded two, & recd. two
wounds

Tuesday 4th. July cloudy & cool no less than three sleep at
Rutherfurds the Major, Saunders Grant & I the little happy pair
are ever good and obliging
    Went over to Long Island today with Capt. Home to see our
old acquaintances about Jamaica I din'd at Doctor Ogdens where
they were all very glad to see me, & the old Lady insists on my
sleeping there, Miss Polly sick, I believe they think I have a little
tendre there call'd at Major Smalls but he was not at home, saw
Sergt. McCraw & his wife & child told them to get ready to go
home in the fleet, & gave the Boy 2 guineas – Spent the Eveng.
at Major Cortlands where I got a very kind reception from that
happy family[5]

Wednesday 5th. July a good deal of rain last night. the day
cloudy having Slept & breakfasted at the Doctors, & had a flirtation with the Girls, I call'd on Capt. Home at Laferts & we went
to Town in the forenoon
    The Country looks very well tho' the season has been late; the
farmers do not like Govr. Robertsons proclamation requiring
them to give in two thirds of their Hay to the public Magazine –
    din'd with a party at Smiths Tavern club 3 dollars & nothing
good for it –
    Call'd on Col: Geo: Clarke who has just given up the Barrack
officer favor of Major Crosbie; the former has made a good deal
of money by it, & I suppose so will the latter – two men of war
arrd. fr: Halifax[6]

Thursday 6th. July very warm finish'd my business & left
Town about 11 o'clock, it being excessive hot it took me near 5
hours to get to Camp, N.B. I don't think much of my mare; bot.

a Saddle &ca. for her that cost me 6 guineas   Receiv'd 13 guineas
from Lt. Grant in part payment of his mess accot. –
left the little Couple a good deal better, & I hear Genl. Stirling
is doing well.
The Commander in Chief in Town. The Admiral at the Hook
with the large men of war vizt. the Europe, Robuste, Raisonable,
Renown, Roebuck &ca. – a talk of three Regts. going to the West
Indies, they even go so far as to name the 22d. 43d. & 57th. for
that purpose – the 44th. left this 22d. May for Canada, Major
Lum staid behind & is going home, which occasions a differce.
twixt him & Col Hope

Friday 7th. July Still very warm   The Mowers & Haymakers
are working some miles in front, & are covered by a party of 300
from the flank Corps & Brigades by turns –
a Corpl. & 9 of Diemars deserted with as many of the best
horses –
orders for the Invalids to be clear'd to this date, & eight weeks
pay to be sent to Lt. Willington; sent Sergt McDonald with Sergt.
McCraws accot. & money to go by the way of Jamaica, as our people
of the Regt. would not give themselves any trouble about the matter.

Saturday 8th. July very warm a good many of the men falling
down with the ague, which took such a strong hold of their constitutions last year, that they are very subject to a relapse this

Sunday 9th. July warm as usual mounted Picquet a[t] day
break, & soon after hear'd that my Tent was rob'd in the night
of all the loose articles that was under the bed, vizt. six or seven
bottles of wine & Rum, one pr. new Shoes two do. of my ser-
vants & some new linnen for shirts of his, &ca. there are some
sad rascals in this Battn. who are wicked enough to do anything, &
have cunning enough to escape in general.
We are now told for certain that a fleet of 9 sail of the line
some frigates & about 40 transports are arrived off the Delaware
from France, The Guadaloupe fell in with them in the nighttime
near these Capes;

all quiet at the Picquet where the Young gentlen. have plenty of time to make love to Jemimy, Hannah, & Sibby – our Commandant laid up with some thing he calls the goute [gout].

Monday 10th. July very warm   This Report of the French fleet does not seem to be confirm'd – The Army to be muster'd begining on the left

Tuesday 11th. July very warm still   The Haymakers busy all round; a fine grass Country this; the small fruit ripe & plenty

Wednesday 12th. a breeze of wind which makes it something cooler today, nothing stirring but varrious accots. of this fleet –

Thursday 13th. not so very hot – A Ship of war from the West Indies brings account of an Engagement there at sea in which both fleets have suffer'd a good deal in men but no ships taken on either side, after a warm conflict they withdrew to their respective harbours.

Camp near East Chester friday 14th. July warm weather still – We hear a fleet of English Men of War are arrived at the Hook under Admiral [Thomas] Graves.
Saturday 15th. moderately warm Adml. Graves's fleet consists of 6 ships of the Line the London of 90 Guns, 3 of 74 & two of 64.[7] Adml. Arbuthnot joins him with his force & they are to sail immediately in quest of the french fleet.

Sunday 16th. cloudy & warm Adml. Arbuthnot has got 5 or 600 Volr. Sailors to serve with him on this occasion in the prospect of having a knock at the french. he has now under his Command 9 Ships of the Line one of 50 guns 3 of 40 & 11 or 12 frigates & 20 Gun Ships.
din'd with our Regt. the Light Capt. & I & I.G. & paid a visit to Mrs. C. Grant who is in Camp   She looks well, & may turn out something.

Monday 17th. July very warm   The Grenrs. were mustered this morng. 1st. Battn. at 6, after which we manouvered a little in front,

Tuesday 18th. a Strong breeze from the N.W. which makes the heat more tollerable – mounted Picquet this morng. at day light there was a great dance at the Regent house last night & this morning; today the little Girl of 2 year old fell into the well (20 feet) but was taken up in a few minutes & recover'd

Had a conversation with Capt. [Robert] Irving about Rollo, to advise him against quitting the Army &ca. –

Wednesday 19th. moderately warm After orders last night to have no more Baggage in Camp than what the Battalion waggons can carry, & to send the rest to N:York, & for the Queens Rangers to march this Morng. to Frogs neck. our waggons distributed by the Lt. Col: we get one. We hear the french fleet have got into Rhode Island –

Orders to have our superflous baggage ready to be sent off tomorrow.

a Genl. Court Martial from the flank Corps to sit tomorrow morng. at East Chester. Lt. Col: Abercromby Prest.

Thursday 20th. July a cool breeze a letter in the Papers from Sir Geo: Rodney to Admiral Arbuthnot dated St. Lucia 18. June from which appears that they had a General action on the 17th. April & two Encounters since & tho' the french fleet are Superior to ours yet they gave way, & avoid fighting.

for this day I command the Battn. there being the Lt. Col. & 3 Capts. on Genl. Court Martial, 1 Major & 4 Capts. sick, 1 Capt. on Picquet.

The Genl. Court Martial trying a deserter of the 38th. Light Infy. catch'd by two Refugees near Byram Bridge, The Lt. Infry. have lost 10 men by desertion from this ground

Friday 21st. July moderately warm The superflous Baggage & the sick sent off yesterday evening for N.York I sent nothing as I think the Waggon will carry all we have –

a field offrs. party from the flank Corps & Guards went out at daybreak to cover the Hay makers, in front.

hear a good deal of firing of Cannon this forenoon to the Southward

The Romolus, Camilla & some other cruizers have taken great part of a fleet of Tobacco ships –

The 42d. Regt. the Anspach troops & some Hessian Corps Embark'd at Phillips   the 57th. & two Hessian Regts. gone within the lines of Kings bridge   The Admiral & the fleet sail'd two days

Saturday 22d. July a cool breeze   the firing yesterday morng. was at a Blockhouse near Fort Lee occupied by a Corps of about 70 Refugees, they were attack'd by a strong body of Rebels under Genl. Wain [Wayne] with 6 pieces of Cannon but the Refugees Repuls'd them with considerable loss.

we hear the Adml. has sent back word that he was join'd 30 leagues at sea by the Roebuck who had look'd in at Rhode Island & counted 11 Pendants flying in the Harbour, & to hurry the Embarkation of the troops destin'd to follow.

The Camp Equipage sent to Kingsbridge & the troops here order'd to march in the morng., those in the north River drop down   Rode out to see Lydia about 5 miles in the Rear, & got from them a Memorial to be presented to the Comr. in chief of their sufferings & cruel treatment by Col: Emerick[8]   din'd with Light Bobs & the Boys got fou

Sunday 23d July 1780   The Light Infantry & Grrs. of the Line & those of the Guards march'd this morng. at five to frogs neck, & the 37th. & 38th. Regts. & Hessn. Grrs. in order to Embark but the ships are not come to Whitestone yet.

The 1st. Grrs. embark as follow vizt.

The New Blessing	7th., 37th. the Comg. offrs. & Majr. of B.
The Polly	38th., 23d., 33d. Capt. Millet
The Thomas	43d., 76th. Capt. Hatfield, a Surgeon
The Union	17th., 42d. Capt. Peebles, Artillery & a Surgeon

These troops take up ground on frogs Neck according to the line of march & make Shades –

That man of the 38th. Light Infantry who was tried at East Chester for desertion was executed today after the troops came to their ground, hung on a tree at the road side

Monday 24th. July very warm being for the day yesterday I Reported to Col Hope the irregularity of the 37th. Comy. as reported to me by Sergt. Wooff, on which occassion Lt. Cook acted very improperly, & I told him so.

The troops were put in motion at 10 o'clock & the Light Infantry & British & Hessn. Grenrs. Embark'd; a good many Ships not come up yet, & some got ashore at Hell Gate – sent our horses & batmen to Kingsbridge

We hear that Admiral Arbuthnot has arrived off Rhode Island & block'd up the french fleet there – A large french East India Man that was taken by Adml. Graves's fleet, is come in to New York valued at £100,000 –

Tuesday 25th. July on board the Union Transport – Giles master old & worn out in the service, wind in the East

gave evidence at a Court Martial on Sergt. Woof, as well to justify myself, as to show that Mr. Cook was in the wrong.

some more ships getting up thro' Hell Gate – the 43d. here at Whitestone Capt. [George Philip] Hook of the 17th. Coy. come to join –

Wednesday 26th. July close & sultry, call'd on Col: Hope on board New Blessing about Cook, and we went ashore with some others on Long Island, din'd with Col. (Archy) Hamilton at Flushing, where we had a very genteel dinner & exceeding good wine, of which we took a tollerable quantum & came home to our ships in good spirits.[9]

We hear the Blonde frigate is aground at Hell Gate, more ships coming thro' – The Commander in Chief come up.

Thursday 27th. July warm wind S.W. Mr. Cook made me an appology in a very awkward & absurd manner, the Sergt. broke. the rest of the ships & Vessels being come up the remainder of the troops Embark'd.

The [space left blank] frigate & the Camilla come up to the

fleet by way of Convoy the Genl. on board the Grand Duke   the Qr.Mr. Genl. Major Crosbie & some more come up from York A Signal at six P.M. to get underway

Friday 28th. July wind westerly   The fleet got under way yesterday Eveng. with a fair breeze, consisting of above 70 Sail, with two or three of the small men of war, we sail'd to the Eastward as far as Huntington Bay where we came to Anchor in the Morng. and about 9 or 10 o'clock two of the men of war left the fleet & set all sail to the Eastward. soon after a signal from the Grand Duke for all Masters, who were told to send ashore & compleat their water; a good many of the ships were those intended to go home & had only 70 days Provision & water for 40 men, which when divided amongst our Present numbers on board, do's not make more than from 10 to 18 days allowance   This halt with a fair Wind occasions various conjectures.

Saturday 29th. July wind still West   Ships boats going ashore for Water, whh. is a good way off. The fleet continues here at Anchor in the Mouth of Huntington Bay, in which lyes an old India Man & a Galley by way of Guard, they both got under way in the Afternoon & anchor'd among the fleet
little or nothing to be got from the shore, the Inhabitants seem to have but little to spare, & that little they don't seem willing to part with –

Sunday 30th. July cool with the wind at N.E. a fresh breeze   a man of war join'd the fleet this morng about seven from the Eastward. she looks like the Galatea – Signals from the Grand Duke from one to 2 oclock of four different pendants suppos'd to be for Commanding offrs. &ca. The wind moderated & Veer'd to the east in the afternoon.

Monday 31st. July 1780 a Signal in the Morng. to get under way, on which the Ships got up their anchors & made sail to the westward, with a fine breeze from the S.E. which brought us up to Whitestone by noon where the fleet came to anchor again
Orders to send for the Camp Equipage & the troops to land when it arrives.

The Commander in Chief went to Town.

We hear that the reason for our Returning was, in consequence of information from the Adml. that Rhode Island was in too strong a state of defence for us to attempt anything there, the Rebels having reinforced the french with a great number of men from the continent.

The french fleet in the Harbour of Newport and our fleet cruising betwixt that and Block Island

Tuesday 1st. Augt. Whitestone harbour   The Camp Equipage that was at Kingsbridge come down by Frogs Neck & pass'd over to Long Island in the afternoon.

A Sloop of War & the Admirals Tender came up the Sound & pass'd on towards N:York – a walk ashore – I hear my mare is lost

Wednesday 2d. Augt. very warm   The Light Infry. B: Grenrs. & Yagers landed this Mning. with 3 days provision on Long Island, & took up ground about a mile S.E. of Flushing near where the 57th. Regt. built Hutts last winter.

Orders against breaking of fences and hurting the Corn &ca. as usual.

A fleet arrived from Charles Town, & something from the West Indies that says Adml. Rowley has taken a fleet of Spanish transports with about 5000 troops on board   Ensn. [John] Ritchie of the 44th. appointed by the Col: to do duty with 42d. comy. till further orders

Thursday 3d. Augt. warm very warm wind about So: The 2d. Battn. Lt. Infry. mov'd a little way in front & we got orders to be in readiness to move at a moments warning, but did not stir –

We hear Mr. Washington has cross'd the north River with his Army, at Verplanks point, with an intention to look at Kingsbridge. Genl. [John] Lelands Brigade Landed & Encamp'd 'twixt Whitestone & Flushing. – The Guards & 42d. Encamp'd at Whitestone

Friday 4th. very hot – Still under orders to be ready to move

399

at a minutes notice, wrote to Rivington to insert an advertisemt. about the Mare –

The Comr. in Chief at Flushing

Saturday 5th. Still very hot had a long Court Martial on some notorious offenders of which there are a good many in this Battn.

Sunday 6th. Augt. Very hot thunder & rain in the afternoon – The Grenrs. march'd this Morng. at Revielie [Reveille] beating & march'd about a mile S.E. & took up ground where water is more plenty; The Light Infry. & Grrs Battns are set down in different spots as most convenient for wood & water, about 3 miles from Jamaica & near 2 from flushing.

Mr. Rivington has publish'd a Gazette extra; with Sir Geo: Rodneys letter to the Admiralty, by which it appears he had an action with the french fleet in the West Indies on the 17th. April, and beat them, tho' it would appear he was not well supported by some of the Ships of his fleet, his loss 120 killed 253 wod.

Monday 7th. Still very hot   On a Genl. Court Martial compos'd of the flank Corps for the tryal of a Grr. of the 43d for insolent & Mutinous expressions to Lieut. McDonald in the execution of his duty. 'tis very odd how people will differ in opinion about these matters –

Tuesday 8th. Augt. very warm & the musquito's have now made their appearn.

a Pacquet being anounced in orders sat down & wrote to my little friend AH: & I dined with Hathorn & made him fou

Wednesday 9th. much Thunder & rain – wrote a long letter to my Fr. & inclos'd the 3d. of the Bills that I sent from So: Carolina

Thursday 10th. hot & sultry went to Jamaica & paid a visit to the Ogden Family, the poor old Doctor very ill with a Hydrocele, miss dress'd out, & looks with an eye to some want of attention, eh –

din'd with our Light Bobs – Major Delancey is return'd from the Adml. whom he left cruising off Rhode Island   some of the Regts. are making facines[10]

Friday 11th. not so hot a Ride to the Regt. at Whitestone to speak to the Major about Mr Ritchie purchasing Rollo's Lieutcy. but as he was not at home & beg'd of Capt. Smith to represent it which he did & got his consent –
called on the little Couple at a house near their Camp –

Saturday 12th. Augt. black & cloudy with showers – an officer of man of war came from the Adml. who had sent in a flag of truce to the french & by that means saw their strength & situation they say there are none but french there

Sunday 13th. clear & very warm. Capt. Savage come from the fleet, had been reconoitering about Rhode Island.
Talk of a move, – The Adml. is sending a frigate home which will take letters –

Monday 14th. very hot They say the great folks are holding a Council of War at N:York
The 17th. Dragoons march'd to the Eastward they go to Bethpeg tonight –

Tuesday 15th. Augt. very hot Genl. Mathew gone in the Galatea to the Admiral probably with the result of the Council of War. our fleet off the East end of Long Island. – The Comr. in Chief gone to the Eastward, at Hampstead tonight

Wednesday 16th. hotter still. some thunder & a little rain in the evening The Light Infantry are to move Eastward The Qr.Mr. Genls. waggons gone there

Thursday 17th. Augt. the wr. still hot no stirring out except in the Evengs. & Morngs. some more Troops going to Staten Island –

Friday 18th. Augt. Camp in the Widow Fields orchard who won't make much Cyder this year.
The Light Infantry march'd yesterday Eveng. to the Eastward, they got to Smith Town
a ride to Jamiaca, very hot, call'd on the O[gden]s gave Major Gordon an advertesmt. about my mare –

Saturday 19th. Augt. hot wr. with Soy & S.W. winds – we hear the June Pacquet is taken & carried into Philada. Major Cochran who sail'd t'other day in a little Vessel for home, was attack'd by a parcel of boats, & return'd –

Sunday 20th: cool with the wind in the North. the first tollerably cool day we have had these three weeks a walk to Flushing & some Peaches at Prince's Garden, who has the greatest variety & best fruit in this Country, & raises a great number of all kinds of fruit Trees, & some others, for sale, he used formerly to make £1000 a year of his Garden & Nursery.

Monday 21st. cool & pleasant Cochran & his Vessel forced ashore by some privateers near Huntington –
The Lt. Coll. tells us in orders that he has given out some general Rules for manouvering the Battn. of which we are to get a Copy[11] – We march & manoeuvre through the adjoining fields every evening and morning, when it is not too hot. –

Tuesday 22d. Augt. cool & pleasant weather wind S.W. took a Ride to see the Ludlow's about 7 miles, neither of them at home The Coll. with his Battn. at Loyds Neck, The Judge at Jamaica sitting as Super Intendant of the Police of Long Island to which he has been lately appointed by Govr. Robertson with the Comr. in Chiefs approbation, an office that was much wanted, & he is very capable to fill it. saw the Ladies who were very civil as usual & Mrs. Geo: Ludlow always very kind. She ask'd me to stay dinner but I declin'd it as the judge would not be at home.
we hear the Commander in Chief is return'd to N:York. having offer'd the Admiral any number of men he pleases, to assist in attacking the french but I believe they have given up thoughts of it for the present, as we must take care of what we have.
Mr. Washington is increasing his Numbers & strengthening his Army by new Levies, & a proportion of the Militia from each province, who seem to be more ready to furnish their quota, than for some time past; this french Reinforcemt. has given them new life & spirits again, but how it may turn out, time only can let us know.

Wednesday 23d. Augt. moderate Thursday [24th. Augt.] very hot again. The June Pacquet taken & carried into Philada. Capt. [Colin] Campbell of the 44th. & several other officers passengers – There has been a serious Mob in London just before the Pacquet sailed

Friday 25th. Augt. very warm a Large party of us dined at Jamaica[;] club 50/ about 1/2 came home.

Saturday 26th. Still very warm The flank Companies of the Guards & the 42d Regt. march'd this Morng. from Whitestone to go by hell gate to the Horns hook – a Capt. Command from the British and Hessian Grrs. gone to Huntington with a Convoy of provisions. the Lt. Infy. at Smith Town still

we hear Mr. Washington is taking up posts on the west side of Hudsons River & fortifying at Fort Lee, Hoebuck, & the heights of Bergen

Sunday 27th. Augt. moderate, a breeze from the So:ward hear a good deal of firing of Cannon about New York. diné aux voisins

Monday 28th. The firing was 'tween Powles hook & Bergen. The Rebels have withdrawn after burning some houses & destroying the forage in that Neighbourhood –

Tuesday 29th. warm no word of our moving but some Corps are getting ready to Embark.

we hear from So: Carolina that Lord Cornwallis with the greatest part of the Army has gone up towards Cambden to oppose Mr. Gates & keep the Country in awe. Gates who has got the Command of Rebel Army to the Southward is said to have 2000 & gathering what more he can in No: & So: Carolina

Wednesday 30th. Augt. cool after the rain last night – Went to New York early in the morng. to get some Money. The homeward bound fleet to sail on Saturday or Sunday.

The 42d. Encamped a[t] Greenwich The Guards under orders to Embark & the few of the 82d. & 84th. that are here, a Regt. of the Hessians & the Queens Rangers

Thursday 31st. warm   employ'd all the Morng. writing letters to go by the fleet; wrote to AH: to my Far. to R:M: to go by Capt. Muir bound for the Clyde: din'd with the Regt. who mess in Comry. Grants house   The Major not there but left a message for me to carry to Col: Hope about Mr. Ritchies chusing a purchase in the 43d. in which I think he has acted very improperly

Friday 1st. Septr. cool & showery left Town about noon & got to Camp to dinner, paid 20/ for a horse from Brooklyn

Saturday 2d. cool & cloudy with showers of rain from N.E. very heavily all the forenoon.   we hear the July Pacquet is arrived & that all was quiet in England again the Parliment prorogued,   the Fleet sailed,   the Nation more united, & in high spirits with Charlestown News which arrived the 15th. June.

Sunday 3d. a good deal of rain last night & this Morng. & it pours down heavily all the forenoon, the Country was much in want of it, for this has been the hottest & dryest summer anybody remembers
din'd chez Coll. the afternoon fair in the evening got four letters sent me enclos'd by Rutherfurd, three from AH: of the 21st. May 5th. June & 23d. do. very anxious & uneasy till they got the Charles Town News. one from Dr. F. of 24th. June all well & happy

Monday 4th. Septr. warm   went to Jamaica to see the Taylors who at work in one of the Hutts on the Coats. hear'd that Docr. Ogden died last night call'd & saw the family who are in great grief & distress –

Tuesday 5th. Septr. cloudy & showers   The fleet for England sailed yesterday under Convoy of the Renown &ca. Genls: Tryon, Mathew & Pattison   Lord Cathcart & a good many more officers gone home. – went over to funeral   a Report from the Jersey's that Lord Cornwallis, has beat Gates, killed 800 & taken 6 pieces canon

Wednesday 6th. Septr. cool & pleasant   The news from So: Carolina of Lord Cornwallis having defeated Mr Gates comes

from several hands thro' the Rebel Country & is believed.[12]   we
hear that Admiral Rodney has had another engagement with the
Count De Guichen & beat him again

Mr. Washington now occupies the ground 'twixt English
Neighbourhood & Paramus; in the Dumps I suppose with this
news from the Southward.

Thursday 7th. Septr. cool much talk of this good news – An
Expedition going forward, the follg. Corps are under orders of
Embarkation   The Guards the 76th. & 8oth. the detachments of
the 82d. & 84th. two Hessian Regts. the Queens Rangers & Fannings Corps. – Suppos'd to be destin'd for the Southward   Lt.
Ritchie in orders vice Rollo who Retires   had a few friends to
dine, sat late.

Friday 8th. Septr. warm a walk to the Hutts to see how the
Taylors goes on, about 1/2 the Coats done – the Act. of Gates's
defeat in the Rebel Papers of the 6th. inst. & printed in hand Bills
at N:York today. they Acknowledge the loss of 1000 Continentals & more than that number of Militia, & 8 pieces Cannon.

The severest blow they have got this war – prandium solus
[dined alone]

Saturday 9th. pleasant wr. a Pacquet being announced in the
orders to sail in few days, wrote a piece of a letter to AH: –   din'd
wt. Col: Fox & made a party for Monday at Jamaica

Rivingtons paper full of this News from the Southward, & we
hear the Genl. has got a Copy of Gates's letter to Congress

Sunday 10th. Southerly wind & a great many Muskito's   a
Ride with Hatfield, called at Major Cortlands the family still too
much afflicted, & I call'd on my old Landlord Ditmass, miss
grown coarse, his [son] Abm. left him about a month ago & gone
to the Rebels, he says without his knowledge, but I can hardly
believe him –

The Pacquet not to sail till friday

Monday 11th. Cool & pleasant to what it has been, but the
Musquito's plague us – The little agreeable party who came

together from Chas. Town met to dine at Jamaica on the Remains of a little mess fund in my hands; we had a plentifull dinner & tollerable good Madeira of which we drank about two bottles each, nor did we forget the Memory of the day which was likewise celebrated by another party from our Battn. in the same house die natis – [13]

Tuesday 12th. Septr. cool & cloudy a walk to Flushing call'd on Col Hamilton. Mrs. Hamilton has been ill, is now better, eat fruit at Princes. Rain in ye. Eveng

The Country people very sickly especially about Jamaica, & a good many dying. The Army keep their health better than last year, the Grenadrs. Battns. have about 60 or 70 sick each, mostly an indistinct remitting or intermitting fever, sometimes with a ague. bilious, bile at bottom   at present I have but six or 7 & last year at this time had above 50 –

Wednesday 13th. cool   sent to the Store to get the Waistcoat Cloth &ca. and some Coats changed, which are too small, they are less this year than usual.

Thursday 14th. thunder & a gale of wind from the So: wrote a long letter to my AH: to go by the Pacquet which they say to be closed tomorrow

Friday 15th cool nights & warm days a walk to Jamaica & call'd on the Ogden & Cortland families the Major very sick & some of the Children   the old lady still very low, the girls better.   call'd on Capt. Home who is in sick Qrs. din'd with Capt. Mc:K: aux voisins

Sent my letter this morng. enclos'd to Rutherfurd to send by the Pacquet & told him in part.

We hear Sir George Rodney is at the Hook with ten sail of the line 'tis said that he is in search of Monsr. Bougainville who left the West Indies with nine sail of the line the rest of the fleets gone into port there – or somewhere else (arrived yesterday[)]

Saturday 16th. cool & pleasant   Papers found on board a Spanish Ship taken & carried into Bermuda says there is a Revolt of the Spanish Provinces in So: America

Sunday 17th. cool & rawish with a very strong gale from the So:ward which brought warm wr. in ye Eveng. Buried Dun: McKenzie who died yesterday in the Battn. Hospital to a putrid fever in five days – we hear four of Sir Geo: Rodneys fleet are gone to join Adml. Arbuthnot. & the Expedition that was going forward is put a stop to for a while –

Monday 18th. warm & So:ly wind   had a Review of Necessaries only 13 prs. Shoes & 7 Shirts wanting. the Coats nearly finished & the Westcoat Cloth come up

Tuesday 19th. warm day wind in the S:W: – a Schooner arrived yesterday from Charles Town with dispatches from Lord Cornwallis   She brings the Chas Town Gazzette of the 31st. Augt. with an account of the action of the 16th. 7 or 8 miles from Camden wherein Mr. Gates is compleately defeated with the loss of 'tween 7 & 800 kill'd, & above 900 prisoners, many of whom are wounded, & 8 pieces of Cannon taken, which was all they had, and all their baggage Colours &ca. ca. and likewise of another action on the 18th. at the Hanging Rock about 40 miles above Camden, in which Lt. Col: Tarleton with the Legion & Light Infantry killed 150, took 300 prisoners, & 2 pieces of Cannon, & put the rest to flight, a Corps of 12 or 1400 men under Col [Thomas] Sumpter, who ran off & left their arms, baggage, & a number of prisoners & waggons they had taken a few days before. our loss in both Actions about 300 kill'd & wounded, including 10 offrs. 3 kill'd & 7 wounded, in the former Capt. [Alexander] Malcolm of the 33d. & Capt. Chas. Campbell of 71st.

Letters & papers taken the 16th. discovers a dangerous Conspiracy of a number of the Inhabitants of Chas. Town, who if Gates had been successfull were to have set fire to the Town, released the prisoners, & destroy'd the Garrison; most of them were apprehended & sent on board an arm'd ship; this & many other cases plainly shews that they are villains in grain, & never to be trusted –

Wednesday the 20th. Septr. cool   Gates's letter to Congress in the papers, by which it appears he ran away among foremost with

the Militia, & left the Continentals to make the best of it & get
out of the Scrape as well as they could, he is in dolefull plight, &
deserves every infamy & disgrace that can happen to him; he
had 6000 men, which was above three times the number of Lord
Cornwallis's army The handsomest & most compleat affair that
has been done this War. – Capt. [Alexander] Ross gone home in
the Providence frigate with Lord Cornwallis's dispatches –

Three more of Sir Geo: Rodneys Ships gone to Adml.
Arbuthnot, & talk of an expedition that way – call'd on D[anie]l.
Ludlow

The Watt Letter of Marque Capt. Coulthand that brave fellow,
lost on the East end of Long Island, a few of the hands saved –

The Country very sickly, & the Troops falling down with a
bilious fever –

Thursday 21st. Septr. heavy dews & warm days, unhealthy
kind of weather. We manoeuvr'd for about an hour to [John] Lord
Dalrymple & Major [George] Damer of the 87th. Lord Chewtons
Regt. who are on board Sir Geo Rodneys fleet.

din'd with Col Hope with an agreeable party, Major [Thomas]
Coore there, who was taken going to the West Indies by
DeTernays fleet, carried to Rhode Island & come in on Parole,
he has gone thro' a variety of Misfortunes since he was appointed
Major the 28th. near 2 years ago

Friday 22d. very warm for ye. season southerly winds & numbers of Muskito's The sick list increasing, above 100 in this Battn.
we keep up well yet, 8 in Battn. Hospital & 2 in the Genl Hosl,
a good many offrs. down. the 37th. Regt. almost all sick. had a
little party to dine, – The Light Infantry are order'd to march to
Jamaica – The Genls orders announce the Victory in So:
Carolina for whh. a feu de joy is to be fir'd at N:York this Eveng.
And the fleet & Garrison fir'd a rejoicing to day for the Corron-
ation –

Saturday 23d. Septr. warm wind in the south. a walk to
Jamaica & visited the sick there who are getting better.

a Brig from Chas.Town, a frigate going there immediately, & the former Expedition to go on –

Sunday 24th. warm & So – for the day in Camp, visited the Hospls. above 120 sick in this Battn. mostly of that remitting fever –

Monday 25th. cool nights and warm days, with heavy dews at night din'd with Mr. Danl. Ludlow about 2 miles from Camp; his Wife not at home; he has one of mine for a Safe guard. a good dinner & good madiera, he is a sharp keen hand – very fine peaches from old Cramlyn's at the Plains – [14]

Tuesday 26th. Septr. cool wind N. went to York in the Boat from flushing got there 1/2 after 9, did some business, & din'd chez les petit[s], – some of those Corps are order'd to Embark on thursday –

Wednesday 27th. cool with rain in the afternoon – To our great surprise & astonishment Genl. [Benedict] Arnold came in today from West Point, having deserted the Rebel Service, And Major [John] André who went up there to Negotiate this secret business is taken prisoner & will be in danger of his life.

This affair it seems has been transacting for some time past, in which Arnold was to have given up West Point, where he Commanded, or allowed us to take it. at which time he was to have join'd us with as many as he could bring, we wod. have taken the rest prisoners & all their magazines, whh. wod. have been a great coup.

Thursday 28th. Septr. cool wr. paid 3 guineas for a pair of Boots & a pair of Shoes – finish'd my business got Money from the Pay Mr. & came off in the Boat a little after 3, having taken a Beeff Steak at Strachans we came to flushing Bay in 2 hours but it being low water we were obliged to land on Lawrences point & walk to Camp, above 6 miles; Lt. Grant being recover'd of his wound came up with me – The Battn. to march tomorrow into Cantonments in & about Newtown; on Accot. of their sickly

state 'tis thought that this Expedition that was so much talk'd [of]
will not take place it being suppos'd to have been only a blind for
a dash up the north River to fullfill the plan laid with Arnold.
The Sandwich come up opposite ye. Town in the No: River –

Friday 29th. Septr. 1780 – pleasant wr. for the season – The
Grenrs. march'd this Morning at 7 from their Encampments at
the fresh Meadows, to Newtown, where they went into Cantonments, the Men into Barns the officers in houses. I drew John
Leveridge & Jno. Moore Senr. two large Barns for the Compy.
but not good Qrs. for the Offrs. –
din'd at my Qrs. & began a Compy. mess of Lt. Grant Lt.
Ritchie & me –
Some more of Adml. Rodneys fleet gone to join Arbuthnot.
two frigates come from the West Indies & taken 4 or 5 Rebel
prirs. by the way, & the Blond came in yesterday from a Cruise &
brought in very pretty Rebel privateer Ship of 24 guns taken near
Bermuda –

Saturday 30th. Septr. warm   The Battn. parades at 9 in a field
near the Village; we have about a mile to go. a small guard at each
Quarter – a Capt. of the day to Visit ye. Hospitals three in
number, about 90 sick –

Sunday 1st. Octr. warm days went to church where there was
a very thin Congregation, not above a dozen of the Parish & about
as many offrs. to whom the School Mr. read the Service & a
Sermon
some Messages to & from the Rebels about Major André –

Monday 2d. Octr. fine weather   Genl. Robertson, the Lt.
Govr., & Mr. Smith gone out with a flag to the Rebels, to try if
they can by any arguments or persuasion save Major André's life,
who is condemn'd by a Board of Genl. Officers to be hang'd as a
Spy.

Tuesday 3d. Octr. a storm of wind & rain from the N.E. – The
sentry at the next House fired several shots last night at some
fellows who attempted to take off a Cow.

Wednesday 4th. cool & cloudy   The 37th. March today to Denys's the 38th. to Brooklyn the 43d. & Queens Rangers go over to Staten Island.

A fleet arrived from Halifax & some ships from the West Indies on Monday last.

Had Mr. McDowal of the Sandwich[,] Cunningham & Peter to dine, sat late.

some of Sir Geo: Rodneys Ships out cruising, no word from Arbuthnot.

Thursday 5th. wet & blowy we din'd with the 76th. next house. no parade on Rainy days but when the wr. permits a genl. parade at 1/2 after 9 in the morng. & a Compy. parade at Qrs. in the Eveng.

Friday 6th. Octr. fine weather   This day we hear the melancholly story of poor Major André's death, whom the Rebels hang'd last monday on the supposition of being a spy. we are told that he behaved through the whole of his tryal, confinement & execution with great fortitude &, Manly Spirit; he wrote to the Comr. in Chief, begging his Commission might be sold for the benefit of his sisters, as his last request. the Genl. much afflicted & the whole army sorry for the untimely death of that promising young man

Saturday 7th. Genl. Arnold published an Address to the Inhabitants of America assigning his reasons for joining the British Arms & reprobating the conduct & tyranny of the Usurpers, tempora mutantur. rain in the Afternoon a Battn. Club in the Eveng. at Rapalje's   Several people are taken up at N:York by the Prevost on suspicion of holding communication & giving intelligence to the Rebels –

Sunday 8th. Octr. fine wr. & warm   yesterday the Refugee post at Bergen was attack'd by the Rebels, who were repulsed –

Monday 9th. Genl. Leslies expedition is Embark'd some days consisting of the Guards the Detachmts. of the 82d. & 84th with their flank Companies, a Regt. of Hessians Watsons Corps made up of the 17th. & some provincials, and Fannings Corps.

They are order'd to receive their winters forage money –

The Comr. in Chief anounces and Laments Major André's death in yesterdays orders, & Arnold appointd Coll. of a Regt. with the Rank of Brigr. Genl. –

Tuesday 10th. Octr. Lord Dalrymple of 87th. appointed aid de Camp, & Major Delancey to act as Dy. Adjt. Genl. till further orders

a Ship from Cork in 8 weeks & one from England, the Cork fleet sailed 14th. Augt. & the English before

Wednesday 11th. fine weather & warm for the season We hear that we are to Hutt for the Winter at our present Quarters The Light Infantry come to Bedford the 42d. into Town –

Thursday 12th. rain from S.E. The Expedition not sail'd yet & some think they won't go at all –

a french Vessel got into Rhode Island from which springs various Reports of De Ternay to quit that Place, & a Cessation of Arms &ca. &ca.

Friday 13th. rain in the morng. The Augt. Pacquet arrived yesterday she had a long passage having lost a Mast in a Gale of wind, our letters not come out yet –

The Pearl has taken a french frigate loaded with Indigo & sugar and sent her into N:York – we hear Mr. [Henry] Laurens last Presidt. of Congress is taken on his way to Europe with all his dispatches, –

A Ship arrived from the Clyde in 7 weeks, who says every thing looks like a peace with Spain –

Saturday 14th. warm wr. not much news transpir'd, 22 sail of Russian & Swedish men of war arrived in Plymouth Sound

at the Club in the Eveng. where sat late & drank a great deal of punch – got my letters by the Pacquet two from AH: 7th. 21st. July & one from J.B. 28 July surprised I have not hear'd from my Father –

412

Sunday 15th. Octr. warm wr. wind Southerly & S.E. We muster'd strong on the parade today having [George] Lord Chewton & some of his officers to look at us – took a ride to the hill
where we saw a fleet at the Hook which we take to be that from
home. The Pacquet sail'd yesterday –

Monday 16th. cool wr. we are told at the parade to begin our
Hutts with such tools as we can borrow in the Neighbourhood,
till we get others from N:York no parades till the Hutts are finished, so we came home & fell to work; I shall make three Hutts
of two Rooms, each 14 feet Square, 24 men in each hutt. The
fleet that arrived yesterday was from England with Stores
Recruits &ca &ca. they fell in with Adml. Arbuthnot who convoy'd them to the Hook & went again to sea no word of the
Corke fleet which sail'd the 14 Augt. hope Monsr. De Ternay
will not fall in with them –
Recd. a letter from Dr. F. date 22d. Augt by favour of a Mr.
Hutchinson whom he recommends, he came by the Patty from
Clyde all friends well.

Tuesday 17th. cold, wind at N.W. working at the Hutts all
hands. –
Genl. [Charles] O'Hara Capt. [William] Brereton & some other
offrs. came passengers in the fleet,[15] but no word of poor McLean
whom we now give up all hopes of & must have been lost in their
way home last winter –

Wednesday 18th. Octr. cold nights The Troops commanded
by Genl. Leslie are sail'd under Convoy of the Romolus & two
frigates bound to the Southward about 3 or 4 & twenty hundred – [16]

Thursday 19th. White frost this morng. Those Regts. that were
not provided before march today to their respective Qrs. for the
Winter. 7 Regts. in New York. The Resolution a 74 commanded
by Sir Challoner Ogle arrived today from a Cruise. & saluted the
Adml.

Friday 20th. warm The Light Infantry cross'd over yesterday & are Encamp'd near Bedford till their Hutts are repaired, we got some tools & nails today & are going on with the Hutts pretty well

Saturday 21st. Octr. cool wr. nothing Sunday [22 Octr.] a holiday from work, at Church Recd. a letter from my Fr. dated 4th. Augt. acknowledging the receipt of the Bills sent from Chas. Town. it came by Mr. Jno. Boyd Carlungs son in the Patty from Clyde, he & Mr. Hutcheson came here today to consult about what is best to be done, Boyd talks of going into the Army, & Hutcheson wants a Mateship –

Monday 23. fine weather went to N:York call'd by the way on Col: Fox about the Mate, but found he was provided spoke to Dr. Nooth & Dr Veal about Hutcheson they advise him to go to Bermuda as Mate to the Garrison Battn. & Surgn. to the Garrison 8/a day, so do I –
A Party of us din'd at the Queens Head & took a boose of Claret to bid Peter farewell, he is going to So Carolina to Command the Regt. asked to dine at HeadQrs. tomorrow

Tuesday 24th. Octr. fine wr. yesterday was brought to town a Rebel Mail taken on the road to Hartford, containing many letters expressive of their despondencey
Spoke to Mr Cunningham about Mr. Boyd & we find upon the whole he had better go into business than the Army –
The Comr. in chief gone to Long Island & does not return till late in the Eveng. & I don't dine there; dine at the mess wt. I.S.

Wednesday 25th. pleasant wr. finish'd my business & left Town about noon & came home to dinner –
Arnold has publish'd a proclamation to encourage deserters from the Rebel Army to come in & serve in his Regts. & some wipes at the Congress &ca.
a Pacquet to sail in a few days

Thursday 26th. writing letters a fleet to sail for Chas. Town soon with the Recruits &ca. &ca. when the Court Martial is over that is now setting on board the Resolution trying Capt. Bateman for misbehaviour in the West Indies

Friday 27th. cloudy & warm the Hutts going on pretty well – an old Hutt at New Town burnt & a Corpl. of the 43d. in it

Saturday 28th. Octr. a rainy day finish'd my letters & sent them off to go by the Pacquet which is to sail tomorrow vizt one to J:B: one R:M: & one to my little friend, N:B: sent off a letter when I was in Town for Lt. Maxwell which came inclos'd from his uncle, A Cartel is at last agreed on & the Commissary's of Prisoners are now met to settle the detail, Mr. Loring told me he expected the prisoners from Lancaster in soon – Major Genl. Phillips & Major Genl Riedesel of the Convention Troops are Exchanged, & in full activity of Service, & all the offrs. of this & the Northern Army who were on parole at New York are also exchang'd

Sunday 29th. Octr. fair wr. again a ride to Jamaica & call'd on our frds. a Report that Major Ferguson who Comd. a Detachmt. of Militia back in So: Carolina is kill'd & most of the party taken[17] – Major Genl. Phillips appointed to Command of the Light Infantry, British Grenrs. & 42d Regt. –

Monday 30th. fair wr. & warm We have orders to apply to our Regts. to be compleated or levelled –
The Plays begin tonight at N:York for the benefit of Soldiers Widows & Orphans

Tuesday 31st. cloudy & showery The Col: came round the Qrs. to see the progress of our hutts, & told us the Genl. Phillips was coming to see the Battn. tomorrow – Wrote to the Major for 3 or 4 men –

Wednesday 1st. Novr. 1780 a Storm of Wind & Snow & truely winter like, prevents Genl. Phillips from coming
Offrs. belonging to the Southard are ordered to join, and all the Recruits & Stores & Baggage belonging to the Regts. in So: Carolina & Georgia are to Embark on friday the 3d. instt. at Brooklyn –

Thursday 2d. cold wind NW The late bad wr. retards our Hutts & this cold wr. makes it necessary to get them finish'd soon, the 43d. are in a week ago.

I am to get no Men from the Regt. at present, the Major continues to refuse every request I make

Friday 3d. The Recruits &ca. for the Southward are Embarking today.

The Pacquet I am told did not sail till yesterday; – some more of these intercepted letters publish'd –

Saturday 4th. Novr. 1780 – cold weather, frosty nights. The Hutts cover'd in, next week will finish the inside work

Sunday 5th. fine healthy wr. a long walk by Hellgate to work off the fumes of Saturday night; these Clubs exceed all rules & moderation.

we din'd with the Coll. today Colin Campbell there just came in from Captivity

Monday 6th. & Tuesday 7th. cold frosty weather – The Ships for the Southward sail'd Capt. Hatfield 43d. Grrs. appointed Govr. of Sulivans Island

Wednesday 8th. cold westerly wind took a ride to Jamaica, called on the Ogdens who have been very ill treated by a Hessn. Capt. of Grenrs. Qrr'd. there from thence went to Mr. Danl. Ludlows to dine we were rather late, but it turned out very well after all, very kind & civil

Wrote a letter to [Capt. George] Beckwith about the behaviour of that Hessn. Offr –

Thursday 9th. Novr. sent two men to the Hospital Board with Epileptick fits, A: McDond. & Jas. Campbell

The Yarmouth Capt. Lutwedge a 74 going home with a fleet, expect to saild on Sunday – busy writing letters

Friday 10th. cold & cloudy Sent off 3 Barrels of Apples & a doz. of trees to go home in Aldersley Capt. Steward for the Clyde, one for Ld. Eglintoune, one for Marshall & one for T:A: & the trees sent off in the afternoon my letters viz J.B. Esqr. R:M: Esqr Dr. F. Mr. T:A: my Fr. & AH:, all these things forwarded by Mr. Geo: Mc.

The Corke fleet arrived, they came by Chas Town – 60 sail

Saturday 11th. I hear Col: Hope goes home in the Yarmouth, sorry he is going to leave us, a good officer & polite man –

Sunday 12th. fine weather went to Town to bid Col: Hope farewell, met him in the Eveng. & sup'd together with a few others at Strachans –

Monday 13th. cloudy with some rain There was to have been horse races today at the flatlands, but the bad weather prevented them, came home to dinner on a horse I have for tryal, they ask 20 gs.

Col: Hope takes leave of the Battn. in orders, vide the next page – an express from Genl. Leslie having landed in Virginia & taken Post at Portsmouth they have taken several ships & a good deal of tobacco & other things – great sickness & mortality in So: Carolina

Tuesday 14th. Novr. rainy morng. Adml. Rodney together with the fleet for So: Carolina, & that for England making ready to sail altogether –

Wednesday 15th. fine wr. The fleet sail'd today. The Company went into their Hutts today & got their Barrack bedding & utensils mount a Guard of a Corpl. & 6 and gave them a Caution with respect to yr. behaviour

Visited the Hospital & reported to Lt. Col: [John] Yorke who is appointed to the Comd. of the 1st. Battn. 10th. Novr. & Lt. Col Fox to the 2d. Lord Winchelsea Majr. to the 1st & Major Damer (both of the 87th.) to the 2d. – the 22d. Comys. change with the 38th. Compy.[18]

Chapter XII

'obstinate & malevolent'

Long Island
16 November 1780 to 13 June 1781

By the end of the campaign of 1780 Sir Henry Clinton had begun to think once again of the war in the southern colonies. He did not intend to shift the focus of the war from the middle colonies to the South. He did wish to satisfy the British government which remained committed to attacking the rebellion from south to north, to support Lord Cornwallis who commanded British forces in Georgia and the Carolinas, and to offset the redeployment of French and American forces. Thus between October 1780 and May 1781 he sent four separate detachments from New York to the southern colonies. The first two were to establish posts in the Chesapeake, destroy rebel magazines, and act in favor of Cornwallis. The third and fourth were to sustain the troops already in the Chesapeake against increasingly formidable French and American forces in Virginia and North Carolina. Altogether, in seven months he redeployed nearly 9,000 men from New York to the Chesapeake and Carolinas. By the spring of 1781 he had three-fifths of his entire army in the South, but he still did not plan to make his principal offensive there. He expected that many of the men he had sent to the Chesapeake would rejoin him for a summer's campaign in Maryland and Pennsylvania.[1]

So it was that much of the British army was in motion during the winter and spring of 1781. Even John Peebles and the British grenadiers who remained on Long Island found little rest in their winter quarters. They did have time for an occasional dinner, ball, play, or concert in New York City and for a walk, ride, or even fishing, golf, or bathing on Long Island.[2] But they never really settled into the social life of New York or Long Island. In December, February, and April they expected to be included in detachments being sent to the Chesapeake.[3] In January they went to Staten Island to spend two weeks in barns waiting to exploit, if possible, a mutiny in the Continental army.[4] And from November until June they prepared, more intensively than in any previous winter or spring, for active service: marching long distances, firing at targets, practicing tactical manoeuvres, and standing inspections.[5]

The winter was particularly disquieting for John Peebles. In addition to being unsure what the grenadiers would do, he was unable to shape his own future. In early December he tried to sell his commission and resign from the army. Although he found what he thought a qualified buyer and a satisfactory price, his colonel – Thomas Stirling of the 42nd Regiment – refused to approve the transaction. Peebles tried reasoning; he became angry (so angry that he later thought it prudent to destroy what he had written in his diary); and he appealed his case to the Commander-in-Chief.[6] All to no avail. Stirling was 'obstinate & malevolent,' and not even Sir Henry Clinton was willing to overturn his decision. By late February Peebles had accepted his fate: he would continue to serve in the 42nd until he could find a replacement whom Stirling would approve.[7]

Long Island
16 November 1780 to 13 June 1781

Thursday 16th. The fleet gone out a ride to Jamaica & talk'd with Major Cortland about that Hessn. Capt. who is not yet removed, he must be a mean dirty fellow – Chas. Grant din'd with us his wife was to have come; but her cloaths not come

Friday 17th. Novr. fair & soft a long walk & paid Visits – a ship arrived from Liverpool in 11 weeks nothing new – The married pair din'd ws[with us] today tho'

Saturday 18th. blowy wr. call'd on Col: Yorke, Capt. Sn. & I went to Jamaica & din'd with Major Cortland according to promise very civil & kind always –
That rude Hessn. Capt. denies the whole story, what a sad fellow he must be

Sunday 19th. rain in the morng no church today –

Monday 20th. fine wr. – we begin to draw forage from the 12th. instt. a Ration of 14 lb hay (half fresh half salt) & 6 lb oats or 5 lb Indian Corn & we begin this day to be supplied with firewood by the Inhabitants under the direction of the Capt. of militia at the rate of 3 feet of a Cord for each Room –

Tuesday 21st. Novr. 1780 they talk of a fleet going home under Convoy of the Thames frigate

Wednesday 22d. rain last night & this Morng. bad for the Ball the 64th. dined with us –

Thursday 23d. fine weather The Refugees went over to the Jersey yesterday & had a good deal of firing

Friday 24th. cloudy with rain in the Eveng. from the So: & SW –
The Light Infantry march'd to Denys's in order to cross over to Staten Island we hear the Marquis La Fayette is about Elizabeth Town with the Rebel light Infantry &ca. with some design

upon Staten Island – it was a false alarm occasion'd by some of the Refugees on Bergen point

Saturday 25 Novr. a very rainy day! The Light Infantry return'd to their Qrs. without crossing over –
Genl. Phillips was to have come up in order to see us tomorrow but the bad wr. prevented him –

Sunday 26th. fine day no genl. parade as was expected this Northern Genl. is out of luck with respect to wr. on the days he appoints

Monday 27th. fine wr. The killing of Cattle among the Grrs. is become notorious Alexr. McDonald & Peter Barby were absent last night, & it was found out this Morng. that they had been at Cornelius Rapelje's about a Mile off attempting to take a Cow, in which infamous business that rascal McDond. was, made prisoners by two Negro's and Barbey was shot dead on the spot

Tuesday 28th. Novr. fine wr. a Card from the Commander in Chief to dine with him on St. Andrew's day
officers of the 17th. Regt. & others that were prisoners coming in daily in consequence of the Cartel –

Wednesday 29th. mild wr. sat a long Court Martial yesterday on various offenders, – orders for a Genl. parade tomorrow

Thursday 30th. mild a General Parade at 10 The Battn. looks well all in new Cloathing – orders for a Genl. Parade every day the wr. will permit
went to Town din'd at HeadQrs. about 30 in Company, sat till 9 then went to the Regts. Mess & was merry till 3 o'clock in the Morng. – The Subs had two parties & celebrated the day with claret, one party sent a deputation very ill managed
The Medea frigate arrived from England in 33 days with dispatches for Sir Geo: Rodney & the General[;] a New Parliment – the Queen brought to bed of a son; some changes in the sea Commanders, Geary & Barrington have struck the flags, Darby Commands ye. fleet Some Ships arrived from Hallifax, Capt. Dunlop one, saw him & some Cork Victualers from Chas. Town

An embarkation to take place in a few day vizt the Light Infantry 1st. Bn. B: Grrs. Hessian Grrs. 42d. Regt. Yaegers & Simcoes Corps –

Letters from Genl. Leslies Detachmt. who were again Embark'd & ready to sail – suppos'd to Carolina – Lt. Coll. [Harry] Johnson & some of the 17th. Regt. come in –

Friday 1st. Decr. 1780 cold northerly wind Recd. Subsce. for the Company to the 24th. Octr. & came home in order to clear them before the Embarkation – A Genl. Court Martial to sit tomorrow to try this rascal McDonald, wrote a few lines to Col: Fox who is Presidt. to get him turned over to the Navy or somewhere else

The Battn. under orders to hold themselves in readiness to Embark at Moments notice – with little baggage, no Women or horses

saw Lt. Maxwel in Town & spoke to him about purchasing a Company but this Expedition puts a stop to that plan for the present

Saturday 2d. very hard frost last night & today – orders for 165 days forage money – and the 80th. Regt. and Robinsons Corps added to the No. of troops for Embarkation – & 2d. Battn. Grrs.

Sunday 3d. Decr. 1780 a storm of Snow last night & this morng. no parade one of our hutts catched fire in the top of the Chimney, the consequence of a great mistake in the fabrication, they being top'd with Gabion work plaster'd with cut Straw & Clay, which we now find is subject to take fire, so may expect more accidents of that kind, & perhaps be entirely burnt out before winter is over; some of the Mens own faults who advised this kind of tops to the Chimneys –

Monday 4th. Decr. clear & cold frosty weather; a Battn. parade –

Tuesday 5th. fine weather no more word of moving – Wednesday had the 17th. & some more to dinner Thursday we din'd with Col York & with Light Bobs on friday –

Friday 8th. Decr. mild wr. & soft wind S.E. – after dinner went to Town in the Eveng. a Ship from the West Indies who brings an account of a furious hurricane about the 8th. Octr. which has done a great deal of damage to many of the Islands. in Barbadoes 1500 people have perish'd & several Ships lost –

The Expedition is changed, & now only the 80th. Regt. Queens Rangers & Robinsons Corps with some Hessians the whole under the Comd. of Arnold to Embark in a few days –

a Pacquet to sail in a Week accounts from So: Carolina that Lord Cornwallis is well again & with the army at Camden who are growing stronger[8]

[January 2, 1781] a Genl. Court Martial sitting for tryal of Lt. Col: Johnson for suffering the Post of Stonny point to fall into the hands of the Enemy – Major Genl. Phillips presidt.

Wednesday 3d. soft weather & mild intended to call on Stirling to ask his reasons for this kind of conduct, but I thought it might make the matter worse therefore left Town to let it work a little din'd with Balnabie & staid all night & in the Morng. of the 4th. Janry. orders came dated the 3d. for the flank Corps & the 42d. Regt. to be ready to march at the shortest notice, with 2 days provision ready drest, – came home in ye. forenoon got my forage money from Cooke & paid 5 dollars Subscription for an Assembly

Friday 5th. Janry. 1781 Recd. orders at 4 oclock this morng to march immediately – The Battn. assembled at Rapalje's Tavern & march'd at day light got to Flatbush about 10 o'clock where we halted till night, when we were again put in Motion about 9 & march'd to Denys's ferry where we cross'd over after the Light Infry. to Staten Island, some Companys got under cover & some lay in the fields till morng. – the 42d. Regt. countermanded

Saturday 6th. Janry. soft wr. order'd to draw provision at Ryarsons but did not, march'd about noon into Cantonments the Light Infantry to the westward of Richmond, British & Hessian Grenadrs., 'twixt that & Coles ferry. The occasion of the Movement is I believe on account of a Mutiny or Revolt in the Rebel Army; where the Pensylvania Line and some others insist on being paid up their arrears in hard money & discharg'd agreeable to their terms of inlistment, which being refused, they seiz'd a Magazine of provn. spik'd some Cannon, took some with them & march'd off towards Princtown, near which they have taken post –

Sunday 7th. a Rainy day The Battn. parades at Richmond we went by mistake, no parade today, Genl. Phillips Qrs. at the tavern there, we are at Hilyers a mile off

Monday 8th. clear cold frosty wr. Parade at 11, – Genl. Phillips's orders about the disposition of the Troops & artillery and pointing out the alarm posts with our Right to the Fort above Richmond, & the line extending along the Ridge to the left the 37th. in readiness to move with us

Tuesday 9th. Janry. 1781 frost I chang'd Qrs. yesterday Eveng. to Egberts – Parade at 11 & draw provision, no word of the Revolters having any design to come over to us, Tho' I believe offers have been sent to them – 12 men brought over from the Jersey by Lt. Stuart of Provenl. Cavaly

Wednesday 10th. rain last night & a wet foggy day, remarkably mild wr. for the season; no parade today.
The Hessian Grenrs. march'd to Coles's yesterday & embark'd in small craft, suppos'd to return. 'tis said the Revolters are gone into Monmouth County.

Thursday 11th. clear & gentle frost, The Light Infantry were under orders to march but were countermanded –

Friday 12th. fine mild weather The Light Infantry with two 3 pors. march'd this morng. to Billops point opposite to Amboy staid there some hours & return'd in the Eveng. they saw a few Rebels in [entry incomplete]

Temporary Cantonments in & about Richmond Staten Island 17th. Janry. 1781 clear cold frosty weather wind about N:W: & rather too cold for the men to ly in Barns
The Comr. in chief with his suite having returned to New York, Genl. Phillips Commands in Staten Island: there being no

further Accots. of the Revolters 'tis supposed they are making up matters again –

Thursday 18th. moderate frost   The Major Genl. gives a dinner to the Comg. officers, on the Queens birthday –

Friday 19th. black frost   we got orders about midnight to march at half after 7 in the morng. & assemble at ⚇ The Major Genls Orders for the Troops to march to Coles ferry, pass over to Long Island & return to their former Quarters   The 2d. Battalion Grenadrs. leading – The Grenadrs. march'd about 9 oclock & were all cross'd over to Denys's by one when they march'd from thence & got to their Quarters at Newtown by 6 o'clock. The Light Infantry did not march today they come tomorrow –

A Party of Rebels cross'd over from the Jersey last night, & came upon a Picquet of the Light Infantry, took off the Sergt. & 1 man & wounded one & carried off 12 firelocks, they had hold of the officer but he got loose from them in the scuffle –

Saturday 20th. Janry. 1781 very fine mild weather – The Light Infantry cross'd over from Staten to Long Island & came to their Qrs. at Bedford   The Major Genls Orders to Report the arrival of the Troops & no officer to leave Qrs. till that report is answer'd –

Sunday 21st. Janry. 1781   Rain last night & this morning – no more Accot. of the Revolters, 'tis supposed the Congress are making it up wt. them.

Monday 22d. cold & raw   had a Parade at 11 o'clock – Col Yorke gone to Town to the Court Martial which sits again today on Col Johnston – I ask'd leave of Capt. Home & went to Town to see if anything can be done in my affair,   spoke to the Adjt. Genl. who says he can't mention it any more to the Genl. unless Stirlings objections are removed as everything of that kind must come thro' him when he is on the spot, I then went to Stirling & ask'd him if would agree to it & forward a Meml. but he is obstinate & malevolent.

Tuesday 23d. There was a very violent storm of wind, rain, &

snow last night & this Morng which blew down large trees & unroof'd some houses; 4 women kill'd

The Invalids Embark today & the Mail to be closed this Eveng. – I put in a letter for my little friend AH: dated 17th. & 22d. with an account of my design & disappointment[9]

Wednesday 24th. Janry. moderate I took Lt. [Alexander] McGregor to Stirling & talk over the affair he offers 1800 guineas as soon he gets his affairs settled at home, & the jew says it is a very handsome offer, & that he will keep it open for him till he writes from home

Thursday 25th. Intelligence came to Town last night that the Jersey Brigade had likewise Revolted & come to Elizabeth Town – Genl. Robertson gone over to Staten Island to see what is best to be done –

I left Town about noon & came home to dinner, brot. Lt. Maxwell with me & told him of the objections & the stop Stirling had put to his getting the Company & advised him to close in with an offer of one in the 76th. Regt. – Capt. Cunningham & he goes to Kingsbridge tomorrow about it, & settle with Capt. McDonald if they can

We all went to the Assembly in the Eveng at Rapalje's – about a dozen Women there I danced & staid till past one but they did not break up till past three –

Friday 26th. Janry. 1781 cloudy & drizzling no parade – Recd. a letter from the Paymr. with a set of Bills of Exchange on the Agent for £50 dated 25th. to be sent to my Fr. He says the brigr: is going home in the Spring –

Saturday 27th. cloudy & sleet wrote to my Fr. & sent the 1st. of the Bills inclos'd to Rutherfurd who will send it by the fleet who drop down tomorrow or next day –

Sunday 28th. Capt. R gave my letter to Col McPherson of the Guards who goes home in the Brilliant of 36 Guns he promis'd to cover it with a frank when he gets to London. Orders ashuring the men who came in from the Troops of Convention that all possible care will be taken to settle & adjust their claims of pay & Cloathing, to give in yr. Accots to Capt. Campbell 24th. Rt.

Thursday 1st. Febry. 1781 The fleet for Britain & Ireland sail'd from the Hook under convoy of the Clinton & the Briliant – a ship from Virginia brings news of Arnolds success –

13th Febry. a Pacquet sail soon   Wrote to my Fr. & sent the 2d. of the Bill for 50 & wrote to my little friend AH: mentioning my reasons for wishing to retire. –
A schooner from Chas. Town says Tarleton has been defeated – The Chas Town frigate from the Chesapeak with prizes taken there –

Thursday 15th. Febry. The Pacquet with the Decr. Mail is arrived & the Hallifax arm'd ship from Chas Town with the Novr. Mail which was brought there by a Pacquet which return'd from thence – This Last ship brings also dispatches from Lord Cornwallis with an account of Tarletons being defeated by Morgan the 7th. & one Battn. of the 71st. all kill'd wounded or taken – [10]

Friday 16th. Febry. 1781 at Qrs. – Recd. the Letter of decr. Mail two from AH: of the 6th. & 19th. Novr. & one from J:B: of the 27th. Octr. & 1st. Decr. The Novr. Mail not open'd yet
din'd with the 64th. where was Col: York Major Damer & the MOB [major of brigade] –
Capt. Chads Royl. Navy being appointed to succeed Capt. Laird, all applications in that department to be made to him – Agent of Transports

HeadQrs. New York 17th. Febry. 1781 – The British Light Infantry the British & Hessian Grenrs. the 42d. Regt. & 76 Regt. will hold themselves in readiness to Embark at the shortest notice – The above Corps are to give in Embarkation Returns immediately to the Adjutt. Genls office –
Sent Lt. Maxwell a letter that came inclosed from his Uncle about the purchase of a Compy. in the 76th. but that was dispos'd

of before the Pacquets arrived & sent my horse for him to come up tomorrow

Sunday 18th. Febry. 1781. frost Recd. my Letters by the Novr. Mail vizt. 2 from AH: of 8th. & 21st. Octr. one from my Father of 26th. Oct. all well, & one from J:B: 27th. of Octr. about Maxwell & Cunningham but they were too late, Needham has got Donaldsons Majorcy The Brigr. has got letters also about Maxwell & sent for him, & talk'd about his purchasing & mention'd one or two in the 22d. Regt. – had Cuningham & Maxwell to dine & talk'd about what was best to be done in the present affair – & a letter from R:M: 27th. Octr.

Monday 19th. fine mild wr. a long list of Promotions from the War Office. Major Genl. Jno. Campbell to be Colonel of the 57th. Regt. vice Sir John Irvine removed to 3d. Horse, & brevit promotions of Colls.[,] Lt. Colls. & Majors a great number –
din'd with Major Damer, a very genteel Man, a son of Lord Miltons, much accomplish'd & seems to like good eating & drinking

Tuesday 20th. Febry. 1781 'tis doubtful yet whether the Grrs. Embark on this occasion, & likewise uncertain where the Expedition is going some talk of the So:ward, Arnold is Block'd up in Virginia by some french Men of War, & they say there is some movement among the french at Rhode Island – Major [Alexander] Robertson is sent by the Genl. to the Admiral to concert measures
Wrote again to my friend acknowledging the rect. of the letters by the Novr. & Decr. mails, & to likewise to J:B: in answer to his –

Wednesday 21st. Febry. fine wr. a Walk to the Hill, see two ships without ye. Hook din'd alone, glad to get a sober day now & then something come in from Virginia & that says one of the french Ships are aground in Chesapeak & Capt. Symons was preparing to attack them

Thursday 22d. Snow & rain last night today clear & soft – hum

428

drum – sent two invalids to the Regt. & wrote the Major for men to compleat

Friday 23d. Febry. 1781 – mild weather, as indeed has been the whole winter season hitherto – orders for the flank Corps to practise firing of Ball –

Saturday 24th. Blowy from the West Coll. Johnson's Court Martial finish'd The Light Infantry & 76th. Regt. are said to Embark soon, their Ships are lying off Brooklyn –

Sunday 25th. very fine weather Major Robertson return'd from the Admiral but we don't hear what is the result, I am affraid there is not a good understanding between our sea & land Commanders –

had party to dine, & as is constantly the custom now, we drank too much, above two bottles of Madera or port is generally the quantity that most people carry off

Monday 26th. Febry. 1781. a strong wind about S.W. – The Battalion assembled at the Quarters of the 37th. Company at flushing Bay & fired 8 rounds of Ball at Targets by Single Man, by files, & by Companies –

a Ship from Jamaica says Sir Samuel Hood with 5 or 6 Ships of the Line & as many thousand Troops are arrived in the West Indies

Tuesday 27th. gentle frost last night the day mild & clear. Col York gave the Battn. a walk across the Country for 4 or 5 miles, after which I went to Town to see about getting some men, & to speak to Mr. Maxwell about a Company in the 22d. din'd with the Major who agrees to give the men, & a promotion of a Sergt. & Corpl. in the Comy. sup'd & slept at the happy little Couples who are still kinder; Chas. G[rant] & his wife there but ah me what a difference –

Wednesday 28th. Febry. tipsy last night a very fine day & warm – pitched on 3 men for Grenrs. – I could not find Maxwell today, but I am told he is engaged in terms of agreement with Capt. McDonald of the 76th. –

a Ship from St. Lucia in a month nothing new in the West Indies, Potts had a letter from his Bror. who is well –

Brigr. Stirling has got a touch of a fever these two or three days which he is afraid of

asked by Capt. Nat: Phillips to dine at HeadQrs. on friday.

Thursday 1st. March some snow   The Battn. fired 8 rounds of Ball yesterday at the same place,

Friday 2d. March rain – went to Town & din'd at HeadQrs. The Genl. so much involved in business & papers that he did not come down to dinner – Orders for the Light Iny. 76th. & Regt. Hereditaire to Embark tomorrow morng. countermanded at night, bad wr.

Saturday 3d. March 1781 very fine warm day but blows very hard at W – a Ship come in from Glasgow in 13 weeks. but no letters for us – I din'd with the Major [George] Sweetthenham there, who is exchanged, & goes home in a few days, ask'd to write me from Derry which he promis'd to do –

Sunday 4th. fine mild wr. The Light Infantry Embark'd this morng early & the Regt. Hereditaire, the 76th. on their march to Town to Embark, the 57th. go to Kings Bridge & Linsings Grrs. take up their Quarters –

a Report that the Romolus is taken – a Rebel Lt. Col came in yesterday, he says the Congress have call upon the Inhabitants to give in their plate, but they have refused – came home & pass'd the day and Eveng. solus –

The Embarkation very carelessly managed no orders about Baggage or provision – another Messenger gone to the Adml. – no convoy for these troops

Monday 5th. March 1781   a stormy day of wind & rain, at home solus

Major Genl. Phillips to command this Expedition, suppos'd for Virginia

Tuesday 6th. fine weather again   The Rebel Newspapers say that Lord Cornwallis has pass'd the Roanoke & got into Virginia having chased Mr. Green all the way before him[11] The Bonita Sloop arrived yesterday from Chesapeak in four days, brings account that Arnold is strongly posted at Portsmouth, & has a fortified Post at the great Bridge about 10 miles from thence, they had heard of Lord Cornwallis's progress & were preparing to make a diversion to facilitate his march towards Petersburgh –

Orders from the War office ascertaining the establishment of the Army in America, the old Regts. to 56 P Company except the 42d. the Convention Regts. to 30 P Compy. the young Regts. of 100 to 85 P Compy. except that 76th with the usual Commission & non Commission officers

Wednesday 7th. March rainy got three men to the Company from the Regt. yesterday with their accots. & clearance to 23d. Febry. want 18 to compleat – Snow in afternoon

General Orders of the 5th. for clearing the Mens accots. to 24 Febry. & Reporting it – The Lt. Col: recommends it to us to buy our summer things before this clearance is made, & express'd a wish to see the Battn. uniform in their dress about the legs & thighs Vizt: Linnen breetches, & black Cloth gaiters.

Friday 9th. March 1781. rainy & blowy weather The Transports to drop down to the Narrows, no Convoy yet – a long string of promotions in this days Orders, all of the Convention Army. –

Saturday 10th. Snow & rain &ca. Sunday fine Weather but dirty roads. The Grenadrs. have been talking for some days past of giving a Ball at New York – a ride to Jamaica to visit the Ladies –

Monday the 12th. fine weather part of a fleet from Charles Town come in some days ago, who bring accounts to 24 Febry. all well there, some Troops arrived from home & a pacquet from Falmouth –

Tuesday 13th. March 1781 cold N.W. wind The Expedition lying at the hook were said to have sail'd today under convoy of the Chatham from Chas Town Roebuck from Hallifax & 1 or 2 frigates – The Admiral expected at the hook, but that I suppose depends on the motions of the french at Rhode Island, of which there are varrious accounts

A Schooner arrived yesterday in 48 hours from Chesapeak Bay, with dispatches from Arnold who is strongly fortified at Portsmouth & had made a foraging excursion, in which he had a skirmish with the Rebels, kill'd 16 took 20 or 30 – Lt. Stwart of the 80th. kill'd.

We had a Meeting today to concert measures for the dance, subscription 8 guineas a field officer 5 a Capt. & 3 a Subn.

Wednesday 14th. blowy & rainy caput purganti pro me refrigerans – amico meo ad ientaculum – some Arrivals at New York[12]

Thursday 15th. March 1781 fine wr. A Ship from the West Indies & one from London bring account of Letters of reprisals granted, & Hostilities commenced against the Dutch. the former says Sir Geo: Rodney has taken St. Eustatia & 150 sail of Vessels there & was going against Curacao, The Ship from London saw a french fleet about 50 leagues off the Capes of Virginia, & likewise fell in with Admiral Arbuthnots fleet 20 leagues nearer the land, so it is probable old Mariot will have a knock at Monsr. D'Astouche whom he has been watching so long; it is supposed the french have taken all their Troops from Rhode Island – 1500 troops in the Men of War[13]

Friday 16th. March 1781 fine wr. Having bought the summer dress for the Company (Vizt. Linnen breetches of Russia Sheeting, & black cloth long gaters) gave out their clearance to 23d. Febry. inclusive. some thing arrived from Virginia who saw a fleet of Men of war under British Colors near the Capes on Tuesday last – wrote a letter to my AH: to go by the buckskin hero

Saturday 17 March St. Patricks fine warm wr. several men drunk on the parade this morning no keeping them sober when get money –

Reported to Col: Yorke that the Company was clear'd according to general orders Went to Town & settled accots. with the Paymr. recd. my own ballance to 24th. April left the balance of

the two last absts. of the Comy. vizt. to Decr. & to 23d. Febry.
in the Paymrs. hands – abt. £107 –

Sunday 18th. March 1781. Very fine weather & warm for the
season wind about S.W. these two days
we are told that fleet sail'd from the hook yesterday vizt The
Light Infantry 76th. Regt. & a Regt. of Hessians under Convoy
of the Chatham Roebuck & 2 or 3 frigates Yesterday a ship or
two came in from Charles Town one of them a Pacquet from
thence with Col: Bruce who arrived there in the Assurance [;]
nothing matterial transpired yet. A Brig from the Clyde arrived
yesterday too
came home today, the subs. all absent – din'd with the 76th. –
The fleet they say are put back to the hook by contrary winds –

Monday 19th. March 1781. fine weather wind in the west –

Tuesday 20th. a strong gale WNW or there about – the fleet
sail'd this morning again, from the hook

Wednesday 21st. it continues to blow hard to the northward of
West, & N.W.

Thursday 22d. fine moderate wr. & cool; after the parade all
those who subscribed to the Ball went to Town, I din'd with a
Party at Roubalets at 5, Company being expected at 7 –
All things having been previously settled & adjusted for this
Grenadier Ball Capts. Oakes & Dalrymple the Managers, The
Company began to meet a little after 7, in an hour there was an
elegant show of above 40 Ladies & I suppose above 100 Gentlen.
The Commander in chief [Sir Henry Clinton] [,] Genl. Robertson Genl. Leland, Genl. Birch with yr. suite, all the heads of
Dipartments & many others both from Public & private invitation; Genl. Knyphausen was ask'd but did not come After a few
minuets, we began Country dances which continued till 1
o'clock & then sat down to the most elegant Supper ever I saw in
this Country, The Comr. in Chief & Genl. Robertson went away
before Supper The Ladies were all away by 3 o'clock when the
Gentlen. closed their files & drank & sang till past 8 o'clock when

the remaining few retired to another room & got breakfast after which some went to bed, some to visit their partners, & some to the bawdy house.

Friday 23d. rainy day, lay down for about 4 hours, din'd avec mes amis, & was perswaded to stay the eveng. – a Vessel come in from Chesapeak who says they saw a fleet there under British Colours – a doubt tho whether they are french or ours

Saturday 24th. March 1781 fine weather after a gentle frost – intelligence come to Town that Monsr. Le Marquis Lafayette coming down the Chesapeak from Head of Elk with a body of Troops to Attack Genl. Arnold, was met by two Arm'd Vessels & obliged to put into Annapolis, – and also that Lord Cornwallis had taken Genl. Greens Cannon & baggage some where near the Roanoke – call'd & saw Janet Shaw – din'd at Mr. [Edward] Goolds a Mercht. in Hanover Square of whom I had bot. some Wine, & found there a very genteel Company & elegant dinner, Coll: [Roger] Morris's family whose daughters are very handsome, Isaac Lowe & his fat frow who I'am told gives very good dinners too, play'd Cards & spent the eveng. all in Style.

Bot. two Lottery tickets viz No. 6618 & No. 6625 of the 2d. class of Refugee & other poor Lottery 3 dollars each – we Suppose the fleet that sail'd from the hook on Tuesday are got to Virginia –

Sunday 25th. March 1781 – pretty hard frost last night the day cold with the wind W.N.W – The Parade which is very showy & much attended to, is still at 11 o'clock; nothing new, cross'd the ferry & came home by two a Docr. Clepham din'd with us, I believe he is principal of the Navy hospital –

Monday 26th. cold & blowy   The Battn. fired Ball at Flushing Bay   a Board met today at New York consisting of Genl. Robertson Genl. Leland Genl. Birch Col: Yorke & Major Graham but for what purpose have not hear'd – prize money

Last night a Midshipman arrived express from Adml. Arbuthnot with an account of an action fought on the 16th instt between the British & french fleets off the Chesapeak, which has not been decisive nor a ship taken on either side – accot. dated 21st. They descried each other early in the morng. & manoeuvred till 2 o'clock when a scatter'd engagement began in rough sea, in half an hour it was pretty general & at 3 oclock the Enemys line was broke but three of our ships the Robust Prudent & Europe being disabled in the action they could not pursue the french, so the British Squadron steer'd for the Chesapeak where they arrived next Eveng. & came to anchor in Lynhaven Bay with the loss of 1 Lt. 2 Midshipmen & 40 Seamen kill'd & about 80 wounded in all They were repairing their damage and would be ready to sail in quest of the foe on the 22d. I wish our fleet that sail'd from the hook on the 20th. may not fall in with the french –

Arnolds Troops in high spirits being freed from this formidable attack of the french the Marquis Lafayette & the Militia who were to have acted in concert –

Tuesday 27th. March 1781. a Strong NW wind & pretty cold

Wednesday 28th. Snow & Sleet all day from the N.E. winter like again –

Thursday 29th. a hard Gale at N:W: & cold; I hear'd the Pacquet & the Buckskin hero were to sail today or tomorrow, the latter being bound for the Clyde, sat down & wrote a long letter to my little friend, in which I enclosed the former of the 17th. instt – wrote also to my Father & inclosed these together with the 3d. of Bill of 50, sent them off to Town with my servant in the afternoon to the care of Mr. Walker Mercht. –

Friday 30th. cold Strong N:W: wind fir'd Ball three deep, 12 rounds News from the West Indies that a dutch Adml. & 27 Sail of Ships are taken by Adl. Rodney –

Saturday 31st. March 1781. a very fine day, warm in the mid hours play'd Golf in the manoeruvering ground, broke two Clubs at 10/ a piece –

Sunday 1st. April a cloudy morning, rain in the afternoon a ride to Jamaica after the parade – we had a few friends to dine with us & as usual took a booze.

I hear the Packet & the Buckskin hero sail'd on friday. they both carry letters to my Father & to AH: – Another Rebel Mail taken & brought in the contents not transpir'd yet.

Monday 2d. April we were to have had a field day with Ball, but the bad weather prevented it – A board of field officers setting on the subject of prize Money, the shares will be very small I imagine, & hardly worth the officers accepting

Tuesday 3d. April 1781. a showery day which again prevented our firing Ball – A Report come thro' the Rebel Country that Lord Cornwallis has defeated Gen. Green somewhere near the Roanoake

Wednesday 4th. April the above news gains belief & further say the Rebels left 700 men dead on the field at Guilford Court House –

Thursday 5th. fine warm wr. The Battalion fire'd Ball at Flushing Bay

Rivington has publish'd a Gazette extra: with two letters from Mr. Green giving an account of his defeat at Guilford Court house on the 15th. March, wherein he only Returns 229 kill'd wounded & missing; but it seems to be a dress'd up story to impose on the people.[14] Genl. Phillips arrived at Portsmouth in Virginia in 5 days

a long list of promotions in this days orders – Capt. & Mrs. R & the Dr. din'd wt. us

Friday 6th. April 1781 fine wr. had a great Match at Cat & drank the losings in the Eveng. at the Tavern

Saturday 7th. a hazy morng. but it clear'd up – The two Battalions had a field day with Ball near Jamaica Bay, & did several manoeuvres conjuntctly. we were out 8 hours –

Sunday 8th. blowy at west The 1st. Battn. paraded in the large field & did some things over again that we did wrong yesterday, very simple when properly directed a talk of our embarking when the ships come from Chesapeak to take us there. it came on to blow very hard in the Eveng.

Monday 9th. it blew hard all last night at N.W. today moderate with the wind at So: took a ride to the hill, from whence see a fleet of 9 sail off the Hook Standing in suppos'd to be Adml. Arbuthnot from Virginia.
The Rebels have publish'd a fuller account of their loss in the action at Guilford Court house in No: Carolina 1307 killed, wounded, & missing

Tuesday 10th. April 1781 a Brig in 33 days from St. Kitts brings the particulars of taking St. Eustatius 5th. Febry. by Adml. Rodney & Genl. Vaughan, with near 200 Sail of Vessels in the harbour & one frigate. & likewise a fleet who had sail'd from thence the day before of a Dutch Adml. with 25 sail of rich laden ships under his Convoy, the Adml. killed & the whole fleet brot. back to 'Statia. immense riches taken both ashore & on the water, the Captors will make their fortunes.

Wednesday 11th. April 1781. The Adml. & his fleet come within the hook he has brought a Number of empty transports from Virginia who are order'd to wood & Water immediately –
a long walk with Capt. S: lent him 30 guineas   paid

Thursday 12th. fine weather Various accounts of the late sea action off the Chesapeak, some accuse old Mariot of want of spirit & conduct, & some make reflections on the behaviour of other ships.

Friday 13th. clear & cool N.W. some of the Men of War come up – a Visit from Capt. & Mrs. R: who mean to stay a few days – Lt. Ritchie in Town for some days about purchasing a Company, probably in the 37th. –

Saturday 14th. cold N.W. wind   The Capt. went to Town early to a Genl. Court Martial, & return'd to dinner, Madam & I took a ride out in their new Chair

Sunday 15th. April 1781 – we march'd about & manoeuver'd

for an hour after parade – fine wr. but rather cool for the time o year, this is reckon'd a late Spring, tho' we had a very mild winter. –

din'd at 3 as the happy little couple were to go home in the evening, they set out about five –

Monday 16th. coolish & rawish   The Battn. assembled at 9 at Col: York's with the Guns, we march'd along the York road two or 3 miles join'd the 2d. Batt & we march'd & manoeuver'd together over the hills into the Jamaica road, from thence home by the middle road –

I went to see the Races down near & beyond flatbush, a great crowd of people there a little after 2 o'clock six horses started for a plate of £100 Cury. the best two of three heats of 3 miles each heat, it was a very pretty race, but easily won by a Bay horse belonging to one Jones from Satacut who went the heat in 4 minutes; we came off immediately after that Race & got home 1/2 after 5, 12 miles from here. These races are to last a week –

A Major & Subaltern of the Brunswick Troops who were quarter'd at Guana's near yellow hook, were carried off last night by a boat from the Jersey's with all their Money said to be 500 guineas

Three people taken up lately at Flushing who call'd themselves refugees but prove to be rebel officers from New England they were reconoitering several Quarters of this Cantonment about flushing Bay & are now lodged in the Prevost [provost] –

Tuesday 17th. April clear & cool wind NW   The french account of the sea engagement in the Papers of this day, in which they acknowledge yt. the intent of their expedition was frustrated, by being prevented from going into Chesapeak, but they don't own being beat, tho' our fleet was superior.

Wednesday 18th. April 1781 fine wr. after a short field day took a ride to Jamaica all well – a Vessel arrived from No: Carolina but I hear no news – Ritchie come home disappointed of his purchase. some prizes arrived at N:York of Goodriches   A Vessel call'd the prosperity to sail in a day or two with the Mail for England –

Thursday 19th. April cloudy wt. showers wind in the South & S.E. some Ships arrived hear them Saluting this morning, one came in yesterday from Lisbon in 6 weeks but brings no news – Genl. Robertson came out this morning to see the British Grenrs. which being previously known every body was out that was able, & well dressed, The two Battalions met on our parade ground, the Genl. walk'd along the front & was Saluted, after which we were put in motion & did several manoeuvres together, but it coming on rain we were soon dismiss'd Adml. Arbuthnot came out & din'd with Col: Yorke. he talk'd of the engagement with D'Astouche, giving himself credit, & blaming some other Ships for breaking the line – Cuffs Corps order'd on board the fleet as Marines, they will embark 400.

The sick of the fleet landed on Long Island about 700 –

Friday 20th. April cloudy & some rain we were to have had a field day the same as yesterday, but the weather prevented it.

Saturday 21st. fine weathr wind N.W. The 2d Battn. fired Ball at flushing bay – a ride to the Hill to look for a Pacquet. saw a ship without the hook tacking & turning to windward –

a Card to dine with the Sons of St. George on Monday 23d.

Sunday 22d. fir'd 12 rounds of Ball. a Pacquet arrived, & a fleet off supposed to be from Chas. Town

Monday 23d. April 1781 fine wr. The Janry. Mail come in a Sloop of War call'd the Cormorant. She was long detain'd in Torbay after the mail was aboard, all the letters are therefore of an old date The french had made an attack on the Island of Guernsey & were repulsed –

The fleet from Chas. Town brings accounts from Lord Cornwallis, his Victory over Mr. Green at Guilford Court House cost him dear, 5, or 600 kill'd & wounded, Col: Webster dead of his wounds &ca. Lord Cornwallis's Army retired to Cross Creeks

for Supplies, he himself was at Wilmington – Letters from Chesapeak mention that Genl. Phillips was embark'd in ships & flat Boats for an expedition –
'tis reported that the pensionary of Amsterdam was torn to pieces by the populace for being the occasion of bringing on this Rupture between Britain & Holland – nix
The Sons of St. George in the two Battns. of Grenadrs. din'd together at Rapalje's tavern in commemoration of the day, only three guests there, I was the presidents right hand supporter as being a son of St. Andrew, and Capt. Lyset on his left for St. Patrick. 18 in Company a very good dinner & plenty of drink, mirth & good humour, I staid till near eleven, & came home sober expecting to find my letters by the Pacquet but the Serjt. was not come home –

Tuesday 24th. April rainy day Recd. two letters this morng. one from AH: dated 27th. Decr all well & kind as ever one from R:M: very friendly, one inclosed from my Fr. I think there should have been another from my little friend according to custom, & I expected one from J.B. in answer to mine of the 28th. Octr. –
made a present privately.
Genl. & Battn. Orders about the Captured provision in So: Carolina, to a asertain the quantity & Stoppages

[Wednesday 25th. April] Yesterday or the day before arrived a fleet of 30 or 40 sail from Chas. Town under convoy of the Assurance of 44 Guns & some others

[Saturday 28th. April] An Embarkation to take place in a few days I hear; of the two Anspach Regts. the 43d. & 17th. supposed for Virginia. – 'tis said the Pacquet will sail in a day or two wrote a letter to my little friend AH: & sent it off to be put in the mail

Newtow[n] Long Island Sunday 29th. April 1781 we hear that Coll. Yorke is going to the Southward to join the 33d. by particular request of Lord Cornwallis

Monday 30th. April The 17th. 43d. Anspachers & Cuffs Corps embark'd today. The Men of War getting ready for sea, some ships for this Port taken off the hook t'other day tho' there are above 20 pendants flying in the harbour, ofy [that is, o fie] Marriot –

went to Town to see the play, din'd with the Major, [Thomas Otway's] Venice preserv'd pretty well done –

Tuesday 1st. May fine warm wr.   two Battalions of Hessian Grrs. went to New York in place of the Anspachers & the 2d. Battn. B: Grrs. went to Jamaica in their room, some Hessians gone to Denys's

Staid in Town & din'd with my little friends & went with them to the Concert

Wednesday 2d. May fine weather   The Transports drop down to the Narrows, some of the Men of War in the East River, some in the North, & some down below – The wind has been in the Easterly quarter for this week past & no arrivals –

bid Col: Yorke farewell & left Town about noon, he goes in the Richmond to Carolina to join Lord Cornwallis & so does Lord Chewton, but will sail with the fleet – The Pacquet not gone yet, & 'tis supposed wont go till the fleet sails –

Thursday 3d. May 1781 pleasant weather wind in the west – a Ride to Jamaica & call'd on some of the 2d. Battn. &ca.   a Report that the french fleet are out – the Medea gone to see –

Friday 4th. May warm, wind So: Colol. Marsh expected to join. – Capt. Todd come to join the 43d. Company.

Saturday 5th. fine wr. went afishing   The Men of War dropping down – Capt. Ch:G[rant]: din'd with us, his wife was to have come but cod. not get a chair. tant mieux

Sunday 6th. a blowy day at South a Ship from the West indies, says the french have very little force in that quarter, & that some of our ship & troops are comig from thence here, The Dutch Islands of Berbicia & Demarera taken by privateers

We din'd with the 76th. at Leferts   Call'd on the Ogden family –

Monday 7th. May 1781 – a Storm of wind & rain from the S:E. which continued all day –

Tuesday 8th. cloudy with showers a Rebel frigate call'd the Protector sent in to NYork on Sunday. taken by the Roebuck or Medea, she mounts 26 Guns bound from Port au Prince to Boston – The french fleet still in Rhode Island

Wednesday 9th. fine weather again a Ride to the Hill nothing to be seen. The fleet nor Pacquet sailed yet. a ship from the Clyde in 12 weeks Lt. Ritchie in orders for the Compy. 37th Regt 28 Aprl

Thursday 10th. The Richmond frigate sail'd yesterday with Lord Chewton Col: Yorke & dispatches for Lord Cornwallis –

Friday 11th. fine weather Col: [James] Marsh come to join the Battalion[15] The two Battalions give a guard alternately to Flushing of a Sub; & 30 –

Saturday 12th. May 1781 – The fleet at the hook expected to sail today –
This day being the anniversary of the taking of Charlestown, by a proposal which originated at HeadQrs. a large party of those who were there, dined at Roubalets, there were 98 in all, the Comr. in chief [Sir Henry Clinton] & his Suite Genl. Knyphausen Genl. Gospoth & Genl. HakenBerg &c. &c. I staid till about 11 & came home with Rutherfurd – club £4 –
Wrote a letter to R:M: as I hear the Pacquet is to sail tomorrow, a number of passengers going, gave it to young Capt. Robertson 71st. – applied to the Major for two officers but I suppose I shall get but one –

Sunday 13th. warm Came home & had a party to dine the 76th. & J:R: 300 Rebels landed near Loyds Neck –

Monday 14th. May 1781 The 2d Battn. Grrs. got orders yesterday Eveng to be in readiness to march in a minutes warning, supposed to the Eastward to drive off the Rebels landed there –

Tuesday 15th. Still warm wr. the 2d Battn. did not move, I

442

suppose the vagabonds are gone off – we hear the fleet & Pacquet sailed today – no not yet –

Two Ships arrived lately from England who sail'd the beginning of March, they bring account that the Grand fleet had sail'd to the relief of Gibraltar and that Lord North had express'd a prospect of a reconciliation among the Belligerent powers – the Pacquet that sail'd from here 31st. Janry. arrived 22d. Febry. & the fleet soon after

Wednesday 16th. May warm with rain in the afternoon – went over to Jamaica by appointment & had a great match at Cat for a dinner they beat us. £4 –

the Arm'd Brig Genl. Monk arrived with dispatches from Virginia with an account of Genl. Phillips's movements up James River & destroying a great quantity of Tobacco & stores at Petersburg & thereabouts, & beating a Body of the Rebels under Genl. Mulhenburg &ca. Genl. Phillips sick

Thursday 17th. very warm for ye. season. NB the above dispatches did not arrive till today & the particulars printed in a hand Bill by Rivington –

Had a party to dine – I expected the Major but he holds off

The Battn. Parades at 8 o'clock now & must go by the road which makes it above 2 miles to us –

Friday 18th. May 1781 The Refugee Post near Fort Lee was attack'd this morng. The 54th. Regt. order'd to support. have not hear'd the issue yet –

They repulsed [the] Rebels & drove them out of English Neighbourhood –

Saturday 19th. warm Genl. Robertsons Baggage Embark'd in the Amphitrite, suppose he is going to Virginia to take the Command of the troops as Genl. Phillips was very ill –

Sunday 20th. warm in the forenoon with the wind in the south, rain in afternoon. something arrived from Carolina with a Report of Green having attacked Cambden & repulsed by Lord Rawdon – we din'd with the 76th. in doubt –

Lord Rawdons thanks in the papers to the officers & men for that well fought Action – 'tis said the 64. Regt. & Watsons Corps arrived at Camden the day after

New Town 21st. May 1781 – The Battn. is to parade on Thursday next at 5 o'clock. 'tis expected that every body that is well will be under arms –

They say the Rebels are meditating another attack on the Refugee post at Fort Lee, & we are going to Support –

Genl. Robertson saild down to the hook in the Amphitrite for the Chesapeak.

Tuesday 22d. May   a great deal of rain last night. The Yagers came to Jamaica this Morng. but we have no orders to move yet –

we hear that Adml. Arbuthnot & his fleet are gone to Gardners Bay again to watch the Motions of Monsr. D'Astouch   The Yagers are return'd to yr. Qrs. and we hear that the Refugees are with drawn & the post abandon'd –

New Town Long island   Wednesday 23d. May 1781   a Pacquet arrived with the February mail which came by the way of Chas. Town, nothing new of that date. In the Eveng. I recd. three Letters from my little friend AH: viz 12th Decr. 11th. & 23d. Janry. all well & well pleased, with my letters &ca. of the 9th. & 10th Novr. –

Thursday 24th. cloudy & showers   The field day was put off – took a ride to Town where I got a letter from my Father of the 29th. Janry. to which was anex'd three from my little Nephews John, Charles, & David.   all in good health & coming on pretty well

a Vessel from Chas Town which call'd in at Virginia & brought Accots.   They say Genl. Phillips is dead.

The Amphitrite & the Pacquet are both at the Hook yet –

Friday 25th. May 1781.   a Storm of wind & rain from the N.E.

Saturday 26th. it cleared up   Lt. Dixon [William Dickson] join'd the Company

Sunday 27th. fine wr. & warm a Ride to Jamaica to call on Judge Ludlows family who are come there to live, both for safety & convenience found them all well, ask'd to dine there tomorrow, –
Our Mess din'd today with Colol. Marsh & Major Scott, the 23d there too I hear today some accounts of Lt. McLean & those who were supposed to be drown'd in the ship with him, that went from here in Decr. 1779, the Report says that they were taken up at sea just as the ship was sinking by a Portuguese Vessel & carried to the Brasils from whence they are return'd to Lisbon –

Monday 28th. May 1781. warm wr. with the wind in the South a fleet of man of war at the hook but nobody here or in Town knows what they are, some say Arbuthnot, some say Rodney some say the[y] are french –
din'd at the Superintendants, Col Fox & some of the 2d Battn. there –

Tuesday 29th. oak boughs & firing for the restoration – The fleet at the hook is old Arbuthnots, who has allowed the french at Rhode Island to get supplies from Philada.
a Report of a sea fight in the West Indies betwixt Sir Saml. Hoods Squadron & the french fleet from Europe, 12 sail to 22 was no match, therefore Mr. Hood was glad to get off with some damaged ships – something arrived from Virginia Lt. Noble which brings certain accots. of Genl. Phillips's death, & that Arnold has join'd Lord Cornwallis; Genl. Robertson the last detachmt. arrd. in Chesapeak come back

Wednesday 30th. May 1781. fine warm weather & a very favourable season for the Country hitherto. the Pacquet sail'd at last –

Thursday 31st. pleasant wr. The Battn. paraded this Morng. at five with wooden forms in their pieces. The Col. manoeuverd us for about two hours for the first time; God knows he is no conjurer at the trade –
din'd at Jamaica with Simondson P engagement. – old Oliver gives a dinner

Friday 1st. June 1781. cool went into the Water for the first time this season, but it is too far off to go every day. The young people of this Island have a practice of going into the sea about this time of year in great parties; they go from hence to Rockaway beach, where the young men & women wade into the sea together in great numbers untill they are thoroughly drench'd, & then come out & put on dry cloaths & make a frolic of it – Comodore [Edmund] Affleck remains in York to Command, the Fleet gone to the Eastward, the Royal Oak to Halifax to be repair'd

Saturday 2d. June cool & pleasant a ship from Jamaica mentions nothing of an engagement in the West Indies – a Report that the March Pacquet is taken

By all the latest Accounts from Europe the Emperor & Czarina are mediating a peace among the Belligerent powers.

Sunday 3d. June warm a good many people in Church to-day & Parson Moore gave us a very good Discourse on Love, joy, & peace. –

ask'd by Mr. Wilkens to dine, but expecting company at home I excused myself when lo & behold we were disappointed, after providing for 5 or 6 strangers which the Doctor gave us reason to expect, none came nor send an apology. – Report of a fleet at the Hook.

Monday 4th. June 1781 Newton Long Island very warm The day Celebrated at New York with firing & feasting, & a feu de joy in the Eveng by the Militia – Orders to give in Returns for the Summer Bat & forage by the 7th. instt.

A homeward bound fleet getting ready to sail under Convoy of the Confederate. I wish the April Pacquet would arrive first

Tuesday 5th. cool & cloudy. an invitation for the mess to dine with the 76th. but I excused myself, being resolved to write so sat down & wrote to my Father in answer to his of the 29th. Janry., & a long letter to my sister in answer to the Boys, on the Subject of Education

Wednesday 6th. rainy from the East bad wr. for the Races at Ascot Heath –

Another Rebel mail brought in, but the contents are not transpir'd. some promotions in Orders.

Thursday 7th. June 1781. a great deal of rain last night din'd alone, the Subs taking their pleasure, & the Doctor sick.

Friday 8th. Showery a long walk with Cuningham who din'd with us, his letters says the Apples were very good –

Saturday 9th. clear & pleasant a ride to the Ridge, see five sail off the Hook, wind about west, or W.N.W. some of the letters that were taken in the Rebel Mail publish'd, mostly on the Subject of their depreciated money, & they expect a Reinforcement from France – sent to ask the Major & the happy couple to dine tomorrow,

Sunday 10th. pleasant weather my little friends came but the Major excused himself, I believe he has an affaire of Gallantry on hand. Genl. Arnold arrived from Virginia with some of his Corps mounted – Arnold has brought his own Corps & Robinsons Corps along with him both very weak from desertion.

an express boat gone to Virginia with dispatches for Lord Cornwallis by Lt. Nairn 71st. – Col Marsh fell & hurt himself a Number of promotions in orders yesterday & to day, And Orders for the following Corps to prepare to Encamp immediately, they will deliver their Barrack bedding & utensils on Tuesday next to the Bk. Masters of their respective districts – 17th. Dragoons, British Grenadrs. 38th. 42d. Jagers, Hessian Grenrs. Regt. Du Corps. Losburgh junr. Combin'd Battns. 3d. Delancy's 4th. Skinners & Loyl Americans.

closed my letters in the Eveng. one for my Father to go by a Glasgow Ship & one for AH: to go by the Pacquet or fleet

Monday 11th. June 1781. warm sent off my letters early this morng. to Capt Rutherfurd to be forwarded as mention'd which he promises to do –

Tuesday 12th. very warm. a Ride to Town. The fleet & Pacquet are still at the Hook, with some arm'd Vessels bound for Virginia, & Adml. Arbuthnot with his fleet in the offing –

Orders for the Troops to Encamp on Thursday as follows 17th. Dragoons Jericho British Grenrs. near Bedford, 38th. near Harlaem, 42d. Greenwich; Hessians Grrs Bowery &ca. – din'd with my little friends & came home in the evening – Barrack bedding given in & like fools we did not keep good blankets

Wednesday 13th. Busy packing up, & making ready for Camp; & clearing accots. in Quarters. having made no Acquaintance in this place, have no occasion to take leave. orders to assemble at the Church at 1/2 after 5 tomorrow morning in marching order

Chapter XIII

'pointed to the Chesapeak'

Long Island to the Virginia Capes
14 June to 28 October 1781

Although three-fifths of his forces were in the South by May 1781, Sir Henry Clinton planned to recall some of those forces for a summer offensive in Pennsylvania and Maryland. He intended first to raid Philadelphia and then to occupy the Eastern shore of Maryland as a refuge for Loyalists and a base for British forces operating in the Delaware and Chesapeake Bays. But an impetuous subordinate and a French fleet gradually overturned his plans and made Virginia the setting for the decisive campaign of the American War. In late May Clinton was 'forced to believe' that Lord Cornwallis had unexpectedly reached Virginia. Clinton was furious with his subordinate – not just for deciding to go to Virginia without consulting him but especially for refusing, subsequently, to cooperate with his plans for the summer. Yet, knowing that the British government preferred an offensive from south to north and that the Royal Navy wanted a base in the Chesapeake, Clinton temporarily put aside his own plans and authorized Cornwallis to establish a base in the Chesapeake. By the time that Clinton had received reinforcements enough to consider more than the defense of New York, by mid-August, Cornwallis had begun to fortify Yorktown, and French and American forces were assembling against him there. A French squadron had sailed from the West Indies for the Chesapeake, the combined armies of France and the United States were marching south from New York to Virginia, and another French squadron would soon sail from Rhode Island for the Chesapeake. Clinton and the commander of British naval forces in North America, Admiral Thomas Graves, understood the threat to Cornwallis. On 31 August Graves sailed for the Chesapeake, and two days later, Clinton embarked 4,000 troops to follow

Graves as soon as the seas were clear. But Graves was never able to open the way for a relief of Cornwallis. After engaging the French inconclusively off the Chesapeake on 5 September, Graves was unable to keep the much more powerful French fleet from resuming its blockade of Yorktown. Graves returned to New York, repaired his ships, embarked Clinton and 4,000 men, and made a final, half-hearted attempt to rescue Cornwallis. He was too late. Cornwallis surrendered on 19 October.[1]

When Clinton postponed his offensive in the middle colonies, when he allowed Virginia to become the seat of the war, his forces at New York became spectators to the climactic events of 1781. Early that summer the troops at New York – including John Peebles and the British grenadiers who were then camped near Bedford, Long Island – worked on improving the fortifications that would protect the city when Clinton went on the offensive in Pennsylvania and Maryland.[2] Once Clinton put aside that offensive, once he began to concentrate on resisting the Franco-American forces gathering against him and Cornwallis, Peebles and the grenadiers came closer to an active role in the campaign. In mid and late August they prepared to embark for attacks on the French squadron at Rhode Island, attacks that were in each case cancelled. On 6 September they did embark for the Chesapeake, but they did not sail because Admiral Graves could not give them a safe passage.[3] Finally, in mid-October they went with Clinton and Graves in their belated effort to rescue Cornwallis. Arriving after Cornwallis surrendered, they got no closer to combat than distant glimpses of French warships.[4] Their campaign was over.

The campaign of 1781 gradually eroded Peebles' patience with the conduct of the war and with his own continued service in the army. He had been bitterly disappointed when during the previous winter he had been unable to sell his commission and resign from the army. But he made no further effort to sell out until in late June he received a very sympathetic letter from Anna Hamilton, sharing his disappointment and 'wishing for a happy meeting soon.' Encouraged by her letter, he tried and failed once again to find an acceptable buyer for his company.[5] Such a renewal of his personal frustration, coming at a time when he and his battalion were little more than spectators to the war, may have made him less charitable in judging his superiors. At least, by September he was unusually harsh and skeptical in describing events. When Benedict Arnold sacked New London, Peebles said he was 'throwing away mens lives to very little purpose.' In October when he heard that Cornwallis was 'under no apprehensions,' he added only 'hum.' And when Admiral

Graves took a month preparing his ships to relieve the beleaguered Cornwallis, Peebles observed that the navy 'does not seem to be in a hurry on this occasion.'[6] By the time he knew that Cornwallis had surrendered, Peebles' patience with the war and the army was exhausted. He was ready to go home.

Long Island to the Virginia Capes
14 June to 28 October 1781

Thursday 14th. June 1781. Newton Long Island   The Battn.
assembled at New Town Churches & marched from thence about
6 o'clock. The Country people furnishd us with as many Waggons
as we wanted, as well to get quit of us, as to part with a good
grace   came to our ground about 9 oclock about a mile to the
NW of Bedford, where the Light Infantry were Encamp'd, about
which time the 2d. Battn. arrived likewise & drew up on our left
facing the Town of N:York; which Genl. Riedesel perceiving, said
it might probably strike the Genl. that we should face outwards
to the Enemy, and desired we might come to the right about,
which was immediately done, but it made an awkward Camp, as
the 2d. Battn. were on the right, & the wings were changed.   got
new Camp Equipage – we have very good dry airy ground but
very near a mile to go for water & not a bush to make a shade
near hand –

Friday 15th. June   Camp near Bedford Long Island 1781   rain
last night & this morng. Coll. Marsh being confin'd to his bed in
NYork with a hurt on his knee since Sunday,   Capt. [Walter]
Home Commands the Battn.
I hear the homeward bound fleet & Pacquet are sail'd & that
Adml. gave them a Convoy off the Land – sent by them in a ship
for the Clyde a letter to my Father & sister dated the 9th., & by
the Pacquet one to AH: of the 10th. –

Saturday 16th.   fair weather   having had a Card yesterday
from Mr. Foxcroft an old acquaintance, I call'd on him today   he
lives here in the Wallabach with his wife   gave him a safe guard,
ask'd to dine tomorrow[7]   a walk to Town, – Report of a fleet
being arrived at Chas Town from Cork with provisions &
troops, & that the french have got a Reinforcement to Bostn. of
600 men & that Rhode Island is dismantled, some of the Troops
gone on board, some to join Washington

Sunday 17th. June 1781   pleasant weather, took a ride to the

hill see Adml. Arbuthnots fleet at the hook nine sail large ships, &
some small far off.

Capt. Home & I dined with Mr. Foxcroft the PostMr: Genl.
there was Govr. Franklin & Mr. Chew Major Rooke, & Parson
Odell, very good dinner & drink, Mrs. Foxcroft a well bred
woman

Battn. Orders to change our ground tomorrow morning –

Monday 18th. cloudy & cool The Tents struck at Revielie
[Reveille] beating & the Battn. march'd soon after about a mile to
the rear, to a very good piece of ground where water is at hand,
within the old Rebel Lines; we face about east, with our left to
the head of the Wallabach marsh – The Men employed in making
Bowers before their Tents – The officers looking for houses to
dine in, we've got a room & a Kitchen close by in a waste house
said to belong to Capt. Binson of NYork Rangers – The Ships
bound for Virginia at the hook yet

Tuesday 19th. June 1781 – A Brig arrived from Corke in 7
weeks who says the fleet from thence with 4000 &ca. &ca. sail'd
a Month before she did – & by corresponding accounts they went
to Charles Town & are arrived at Chesapeak   The April Pacquet
is supposed to have taken the same route, all which must gave
chagrin at Hd.Qrs. She likewise brings favourable accounts of the
Meeting held at Vienna, – she also brings accounts of a Revolt in
Corsica which may make a diversion for the french   These things
publish'd in a Mercury extraordinary by H: Gaine together with
intelligence thro' the Rebels of our Grand fleet having relieved
Gibralter & had an action with the Combin'd fleet in which we
took 6 or 7 sail of the line destroyed some others & beat the rest
into port in a shatter'd condition – ce [c'est] bon si vrai –

Recd. our Bat & forage money today, went to Town & paid
some debts – Got the Compys. Coats, on which the Taylors go
to work tomorrow

Camp at the Wallabach 20th. June 1781 fine weather & a pleasant Camp not much above a Mile from the ferry   The 42d. Regt.
in consequence of orders late last night embark'd this morning &

went down to the Narrows, 200 of the 54th. & some troops from Denys's. Suppos'd they are gone into the Jerseys to destroy some Boats & craft in the Rariton River under the direction of Br. Genl. Skinner[8]

Thursday 21st. June warm wr. The Detachmt. under Skinner cross'd over Rariton Bay to the Jersey shore, pointing towards Middleton –

Friday 22d. The Detachmt. return'd from the Jerseys. They landed yesterday morning about 4 miles to the westward of Middletown & made a sweep thro' pleasant Valley in order to drive in a quantity of Cattle for the use of the Navy & Hospitals, but they were so delatory in their motions that the Inhabitants had time to drive almost the whole away, & the Militia collected to defend & protect the Country, & hung upon their Rear most of the way, they Return'd by Sandy hook with, a few Cattle & some sheep & the loss 10 or 12 men; having had a long March in a Warm day to very little purpose

Saturday 23d. June 1781. warm   The Admiral & his fleet still at the hook, the fleet from Corke by the way of Chas Town are said to be in the offing –

din'd with Major Genl. De Riedesel who Commands in this Island & lives near Brooklyn, he has a Wife & four young Daughters   He Commanded the foreign troops in Genl. Burgoynes Army, & was a long time prisoner together with his family, he is a genteel polite man, & esteem'd a good officer & Speaks English tollerably well, as does likewise Madam la Baroness, who is very fat, but a good looking, cheerful, affable, well bred Woman – he dines at 3 o'clock in conformity to our Customs, & is very civil to the Grenadrs., & very good dinner & wine enough[9]

Sunday 24th. June 1781 – Went to Town & walk'd out to the Regts. Camp near Greenwich, very few of the Officers at home. They lost 4 or 5 men in the Jerseys either taken or deserted & Ensn. Sutherland got a scratch in the thigh some way or other; a stupid affair altogether.

din'd with Foxcroft who has a snug party every Sunday, very

civil to me. We hear the French & Rebels intend forming a Camp at White Plains –

Monday 25th. pretty warm & pleasant weather for the season, took a ride round by Flatbush, Utrecht, & Denys's & came home by the Guana's; – The fleet still lying without the Hook, the Adml. gone down; pasquinades flying about reflecting on his conduct, whh. by all accounts is blameable in many points the Ships for Virga. sail'd Lt. Maxwell went with them

Tuesday 26th. June 1781 Showery The fleet that was expected from Corke arrived today having been at Chas. Town where they landed three Regts. vizt. the 3d. 19th. & 30th. & some Recruits, they likewise call'd in at Virginia & left stores, provision &ca. & brought the remainder here with 400 Recruits, & the Earl of Lincoln & Major Loyd passengers & some other officers Lt. Col: Watson of the Guards came with them from Chas Town, with dispatches from Lord Rawden – [10]

Wednesday 27th. two Pacquets arrd We hear by these Pacquets that old Mariot is recall'd, & that Adml. Digby is coming out to Command in this Station, & brings Prince William with him, [11] it is also reported that the french have receded from the convention at Vienna, which will prolong the war. The Dutch mustering up a fleet, & the Neutral Powers increasing their Navy.

Hyder Ally with an immense Army in the french interest has defeated our forces under Colls. Bailie & Fletcher in the East Indies –

Thursday 28th. June 1781 – Went to Town in the Morning to get my letters by the Pacquets which are those of April & May, the March Pacquet being taken & carried into Havre de Grace mail & all Got three letters from my little friend of the 18th. March 4th. & 22d. April, one from T:A: of the 29th. March, & one from my Fr. of 24th. April all well; the little woman very anxious and uneasy at my disappointment, & the vexation it gave me, but like me was getting the better of it. & wishing for a happy meeting soon. din'd with my little friends, a party there, they wish'd me to stay the Eveng., but I came home to Camp to read my letters over again.

Orders for a Working party of 200 Grenadrs. tomorrow morng. 'tis well I came home as I am for that duty. Cuffs Corps come ashore & go to the ground about McGowans pass under the Command of Capt. [Colin] Campbell of the 44th.

The Big Mess give a dance in the Barn tonight to the Miss Vanhorns Miss Franks Miss Moores &ca.

Friday 29th. June 1781. thick wet fog in the Morning, clear'd away in the forenoon Went on the Working party before six. 100 employed taking down the top of the Spiral Redoubt, which is to be lower'd a good deal & level'd, 50 employ'd in the ditch of the Fort, & the other 50 making fascines, we left off at noon & came to Camp to rest & dine, & began again at 4 & wrought till sunset. brought the officers that were on duty with men to dine at 1/2 after two –

Saturday 30th. warm wr. S.W. we hear the Adml. is going home immediately in the Roebuck, the fleet still lying off the Hook. The General & Admirals letters in the Papers, on the Subject of the Virginia expedition they seem not to coincide in their ideas of that Business –

Sunday 1st. July warm a Rebel 20 Gun ship come in prize to the Medea & we hear the Marquis Lafayette Store Ship is taken & carried into Halifax – din'd with Geo: McC.

I hear a party of 50 Rebels from New England landed on Long Island t'other night & came within two miles of Jamaica with an intent to Rob & plunder, but being misled by their guides they return'd witht. doing any mischief –

Monday 2d. July. very warm sat down to write letters by the Pacquet but I hear she will not sail for a week yet.

last night that notorious scoundrel Alexr. McDonald went to Newtown Kills & kill'd a hog at Widow Hallets, was pursued & taken by the people of the house & in the scuffle he wounded one Adolf Humpherys in the head with a tomahawk, of this they sent me notice in the morning, & I sent a Corpl. & a file of men for &

lodged him in the Qr. Guard & applied to the Commanding officer to have him tried by a Genl. Court Martial. – [12]
had our friends the 76th. & Capt. Ritchie to dine with us, did pretty well.

Tuesday 3d. hot wr. a party of Rebels 800 they say, came down near to the Kings bridge had a Skirmish with a patrole of Yagers kill'd two or 3[,] wounded the Capt. & some others, & drove in the pickets but were chas'd off by some troops that went out – this seems to indicate their approach and intention of having a force near our lines to prevent our getting forage, & making detachments, as well as to harrass when they can – we hear the Light Infantry & Anspach Battns. are expected from Virginia soon.
we had the Major & Capt. & Mrs. R to dine with us, a pleasant party.

Wednesday 4th. July 1781 very warm   Genl. Riedesels orders for the Brunswickers to furnish 24 of the working, they are to parade for the future at 4 oclock every Morng. without the Bridge of the New Fort, except the 50 for fascines –

Thursday 5th. July Adml. Arbuthnot sailed in the Roebuck for home   Part of the Garrison of Pensacola arrived in transports from the Havanna, they Surrender'd the 10th. May to Don Galvez the Spanish Genl. who had 16 ships of the line & 8000 land troops, in all a force of 23000, against 1100, who obtain'd an honorable Capitulation after being 9 weeks invested

Friday 6th. July 1781 – some more of the Pensacola people come in, Genl. Campbell not yet arrived[13] – Yesterday a Vessel arrived from Virginia by whom we learn that Lord Cornwallis was at Williamsburg & Genl. Leslie at Portsmouth all well & pleanty of provisions &ca.   a Report that Genl. Lee is come in there.
went to Town & spoke to Col. Marsh & Major Graham about the prisoner McDonald   agreed to send him to the provost & let him take his chance at the first Genl. Co: Martial   din'd at Rds. where was a party.

Saturday 7th. very warm weather at work at 4 in the Morng. on the Fort & the Spiral Redoubt, came off at 9 & went again at 4 in the Afternoon till 7 – had old Major McDonald to dine who gave us part of the history of the Siege of Pensacola

I hear the ship Gen Arnold will sail on wednesday next for the Clyde, will send my letters in her by Mr. King –

Sunday 8th. July 1781. very hot wr. We got orders to march to Hell Gate & cross over to Horans hook, but was countermanded: a Report of a Sea Action in the West Indies in which Sir George has trim'd Monsr. du Grasse had a party to dine –

Monday 9th. another hot day – a Vessel come in from Virginia who says the Enemy are gathering strength in that province & will have a strong force under Fayette. Col: Simcoe has had a Skirmish with a very superior number, & came off with eclat.

din'd with the Major, a good many strangers, got to the ferry just time enough to get over

Tuesday 10th. heavy rain last night Writing letters to go by Mr. King in the Genl. Arnold for Glasgow. he expects to sail in a few days, no word of the Pacquets going

Wednesday 11th. cool & pleasant din'd in Town with my little friends who had a pleasant party. – came home in the eveng. & was muster'd by Mr. Porter at 7 o'clock 47 private present 30 on duty –

Thursday 12th. July 1781 – cool We hear a great deal of firing of Canon this Morng. at a great distance up the sound a Ride out by flatlands & flatBush a pretty Country, & appearance of plenty. brought Capt. C: home to dinner where I found Mr. Menzies, & had a long talk about his affairs

Friday 13th. moderate heat The firing yesterday was at Loyds Neck which it seems was attackd by some small french men of war & other arm'd Vessels & they Landed about 400 Men chiefly french & made a shew of attack on the Fort occupied by the Refugees under Col: Upham who fir'd some grape shot at them on which they walk'd off & embark'd with very little loss & sett sail to the Eastward –

finish'd my Letters & gave them to Mr. King vizt. one to my Fr. inclosing a Bill of £60. a long one to AH: dated 2d. 7th. & 13th. & one to R:M: of the 10th. & 13th. about Maxwell, whose purchase I hear will be concluded very soon –

The Medea frigate & Savage sloop came up from the hook in order to pass up through Hell Gate to the Sound for the relief of Loyds Neck – more of the Cartel Ships with the Pensacola Garrison arrived,

we are told that Mr. Washington with his Army has taken up ground near Dobs ferry & the french on his left on the eastside of Mill creek –

Saturday 14th. July went to work at 4 in the Morng. but it come on rain about 7 & sent us home wet, & was showery likewise in the afternoon & we did not go – something arrived from Virginia Genl. Campbell arrived from havana.

Sunday 15th. warm wind So: & S.W. By a Dispatch Boat that arrived yesterday from Virginia with letters from Lord Cornwallis we learn that his Lordship after destroying a great many public stores & much tobacco & trying in vain to bring the Marquis La fayette to Action, he went from Williamsburg to cross over James River at James Town, & when half of his army had got over, his rear was Attack'd, on which the remainder were form'd into two lines, the Light Infantry the first, the 43d 76th. & 80th. the 2d. the former being opposed to Militia drove them immediately but the 2d. meeting with the Pensylvania line & a detachmt. of La Fayettes continentals with 2 six pors. a smart action insued for some minutes, when the Enemy gave way & abandon'd their cannon, & night coming on prevented any further pursuit. The Loss of the Enemy suppos'd to be between two & 300, ours not mention'd, this happen'd on the 6th. instt. – His Lordship gone to Portsmouth.[14] The Light Infantry & Anspachers expected here soon – We hear Tabago is taken & that the french have a Superior fleet in the West Indies 27 Sail of the line to 21 –

Monday 16th. July very warm & Sultry – went to Town to prosecute McDonald at a Genl. Court Martial that was to have sat today but it was put off – The News from Virginia publish'd in a hand Bill by Rivington

Tuesday 17th. July 1781. warm Soly. wind The Pearl & Iris frigates come in with some prizes. & a large ship from Jamaica. a ride to the hill near Flatbush saw these ships coming in, & Adml. Greaves's fleet still lying without the Hook 7 sail of the Line; the adamant at the Narrows, the Warwick in the No: River opposite the Town – Lt. Dickson wants to bring on a transaction but I am afraid it won't do I hear the Genl. Arnold sailed today, but Mr. King did not go in her being taken sick

Wednesday 18th. warm Ships getting ready to go to Canada & Halifax to take every body that belongs to these districts, the Brunswickers to embark in a day or two. Brigr. Genl. Patterson appointed to Commd. the Grenrs. some days ago, & is to come to Long island as soon as Genl. Redeisel goes 'tis said the Pacquet will sail latter end of the week.

Thursday 19th. July 1781 a great deal of rain – the Savage sloop & Genl. Monk who were up in the Tapan sea came down, & got a peppering on the way from a battery made by the rebels our mess din'd in Town with Mr. Wardrop

Friday the 20th Writing letters to my Fr. & AH: to go by the Pacquet that is to sail in a few days. The Hornet Sloop of war arrived from England with dispatches for the Admiral only, & which are kept a profound secret.

Saturday 21st. pleasant & cool went with a party to Jamaica, din'd, went in the eveng. to the plains, return'd to Jamaica sup'd & staid all night at Rochforts, where we got exceeding good entertainment. Ludlow's Battalion Encamp'd at Jamaica which are the best looking Provincials I have seen & near 400 strong, call'd on the Colol. & the judge but the former was not at home

Sunday 22. July 1781 hear'd a great deal of firing about Kingsbridge this morning our Party left Jamaica about noon & came as we went by the south road through flatbush din'd at our Mess, & they went to Town in the Eveng. very well pleas'd with the jaunt.

the firing this Morng. was the whole french & Rebel army came down & fir'd a few shot at the [word illegible] & attack'd the Refugees about Delancy's Mills & took post there about 8000[15] – I hear the Adml. has slip'd his Cables & gone to Sea –

Wrote to the Agent dated the 21st. instt. to buy me a ticket in the State Lottery

Monday 23. The Orpheus frigate arrived yesterday from Virginia, Major Damer passenger, who comes to join the Grrs. again. he gives a high & pleasant account of Lord Cornwallis & his operations in that Country, but the troops call'd from thence, & which are dayly expected, will put it out of his Power to do anything more in that quarter this season

Tuesday 24th. July 1781 The Enemy went off yesterday Eveng. & retired to their former ground near Chatterton Hill, the refugees follow'd their rear & pick'd up a few stragglers –

gave my letters to Mr. Foxcroft to put in the mail, one to my Fr. dated the 20th. inclosing the 2d. of the Bill for £60. Major Fraser on Oglivie. one for AH: to the care of my Sister: And one to the Agent to buy me a lottery ticket – The Troops for Canada & Halifax embark'd under the Command of Genl. DeRiedesel who takes his cordial leave in orders

Wednesday 25th. very warm a few days ago last sunday a Party of Refugees from Loyds Neck went over to conecticut & surpris'd a Methodist congregation, & brought off the Preacher & all the Men 50 in No. & about 40 horses, the prisoners went over to Town today, – The Transports for Halifax & St. Laurence dropping down, to be convoy'd by the Warwick & Garland

a Battn. of Hessian Grenrs. moved out to Cover HeadQrs in the Country, where the Genl. generally dines

Thursday 26th. July 1781. N:E: foggy The Mail to be closed this Eveng. – how they always detain the Pacquets now beyond the time given out – a ride to Flatbush in the Eveng. carried to visit a house full of Ladies, some very handsome & some very smart, some with teeth & some with none, bad teeth or the loss of them very early in life, is a misfortune the women of this Country are very subject to.

Friday 27th. went to work at 4 o'clock in the morng. on the Spiral Redoubt, we left off at 8 & begin again at 5 P:M: – a Sloop of War arrived from the West Indies, on secret business.
a Gazette extra: publish'd by H. Gaine wt. Greens letter to Congress giving an Account of his Siege, assault, & Repulse at Ninety Six in So: Carolina, wherein he says 57 kill'd & 70 wounded The last ship of the Pensacola Garrison arrived, she was taken by the Rebels, & retaken.

Saturday 28th. July 1781 This Vessel from the West indies says all was well there, Sir George, at Barbadoes, part of the Squadron at St. Lucia; The french fleet at Martinique, taking in wood & water being superior to ours, their designs doubtfull
a Ride to the Hill near flatbush to see three or four sail standing in for the Hook. The Northern fleet lying at the hook

Sunday 29th. very warm a promotion of Major Generals come out vizt. Patterson, Stirling [,] OHara. Goold & somebody else, Dalrymple, I don't think any of them will ever make a figure in history – a Patrole of the Enemy came down near Kings bridge yesterday eveng. – Major Genl. Patterson come to command in Long Island
Monday 30th. July 1781 – hot wr. went to Town to attend the Genl. Court Martial but they put off the tryal of McDonald for another week after Summoning the Evidence for this day – a Ship arrived from Liverpool, after a long passage. company at the Mess. The fleet for Halifax & Canada sail'd under Convoy of the Warwick, & the Speedy Pacquet for England

Tuesday 31st. July warm A Vessel come in from Virginia who says the troops we expected here were lying in Hampton road a Vessel from Charles Town says Mr. Greene has retired over the Saluda that Lord Rawdon has demolish'd 96 & taken post at Orangeburg. that Lee & Washington with a strong body of horse

had attack'd the 19th. Regt. at Monks Corner but were repulsed
3 times. –
Adml. Greaves with the fleet is said to be cruising off Rhode
Island, or thereabout. Genl. Pattersons Orders for Reports
Returns &ca. & in case of alarm to turn out & wait for orders –

Wednesday 1st. Augt. 1781. a breeze N.E. Genl. Pattersons
orders for the Guards to mount at Sunset. & the 2d. Battn. to
take ym. by turns din'd again at Foxcrofts

Thursday 2d. very warm The Solebay arrived from Chesapeak
the Troops expected here were still on board of ship but it is
doubtfull whether they are coming here
'tis reported that some Men of War are gone up the Delaware
the Grrs. Light Infantry 22d. 38th. 54th. & 57th. Regts. to be
compleated with Recruits tomorrow we get none

Friday 3d. very warm a Ship from the Clyde in 7 weeks & 3
days call'd the Alexander, nothing extraordinary Adml. Darby
had return'd, & Adml. Digby was cruising with 10 Sail of the line.
Genl. Goddart [Thomas Goddard] had taken Basan [Bassein] in
the East Indies –
Din'd with Mr. Goold, a party there Saturday very hot, went
out with an intention to Shoot plever but saw none. The June
Pacquet Arrived –

Sunday 5th. Augt. 1781 very Warm Went to work this Morng.
in place of Oaks who is sick; after breakfast got my letters vizt.
two from my dear little Anne of the 9th. & 24th. May, acknowledging four of mine, all well, one from my Fr. of 24 May, & one
from R.M. of the 1st. June no great news by this Pacquet, the
convention for peace not likely to take place, some troops to come
out soon.

Monday 6th. hot weather a shower in the afternoon which
cool'd the air for a little went & din'd with the Major. [Capt.
William] Tod, Grant & I

Tuesday 7th. warm very warm Races to be next friday at

Ascotheath, the officers horses of the Grrs. & none but offrs. to ride a talk of our moving soon

Wednesday 8th. Augt. 1781 warm   The detail for work alter'd, the Garrison Battn. & Pioneers give a proportion   this Oval Battery will soon be finish'd now

between 2 & 3 oclock P:M: There was a very hard squal of wind & rain accompanied with Thunder & lighting, which cold the air a little – The Refugees from Loyds Neck make depradations on the coast of Conecticut

Thursday 9th. warm still Lord Cornwallis's Letters relative to his open operations in Carolina's & the Signal Victory he obtain'd at Guilford Court House, in the papers which shows the Sufferings & Merit of that little Army in very strong Colours, & much praise is due to his Lordships good conduct & spirited behaviour on such trying occasions.

A Court of Enquiry from the Grenrs. to sit tomorrow at Brooklyn. I am for it –

Friday 10th. Augt. 1781 cool in the morng. but hot in the afternoon. confin'd all the forenoon by this Court of Enquiry, at the complaint of a Tavern keeper for being confin'd by the Officer of the Guard. – which he deserv'd.

went to the Race ground about 3 o'clock where found them all at dinner. The Saddle had been won by Tods horse, mine only third. there had been two or three other very good races, & we had several in the Evening, one of which was won by Strawberry for 5 guineas. more matches made for next week –

orders for the remainder of the Recruits to be distributed to the 17th. 23d. & 43d Regts. tomorrow an officer from each of these Grenr. Companies to take charge of, & remain with them at the 6 mile stone N:York island –

Saturday 11th. pretty cool, a ride to the Hill see a fleet coming up. we went from there to New Utrecht & din'd on bacon & eggs & Spatchcock got a bottle of good port & came Galloping home.[16]

the Major Genls. thanks for the accuracy of the Court

Sunday 12th. Augt. cool with the wind about East – the fleet that arrived yesterday are from Bremalee [Bremerlehe] with German troops, mostly Recruits, about 2900 in all a Pacquet announced to sail tuesday. The Rebel frigate Turnbull taken & sent in here by the Iris – also the state ship Bellisarius & another above 20 guns some deserters coming & going twixt the two Armies, mostly hussars from the french – The frigates cruising off Delaware have fallen in with a fleet bound from Philada. to Havana mostly laden with flour & captured & good many of them. a Report arrived that a 40 gun Ship of ours has taken 8 Sail of transports with french troops in the Bay of Boston. nix & another Report says that Washington has issued a Proclamation anouncing his designs against N.York & advising the inhabitants to remain quiet or to come out to him it came on rain [in] the afternoon & continues

Mr. Foxcroft sent for me in the eveng. to see an old acquaintance where I found Mr. Baynton a young gentlen. of Philada. who came in to my guard a night or two before Brandywine, he is now a Lt. in Allens Corps & is to get a Company soon, this young man behaved with great spirit in Pensacola particularly at the Attack of Mobile, he is a very pretty lad & seems to be a young man of spirit & genius –

Monday 13th. Augt. it rain'd hard & incessantly all last night & still continues busy writing letters as we are told the mail is to be closed tonight. wrote a short letter to my Fr. inclosing the 3d. of Bill of £60 & also a letter to AH: for Bess to forward wrote to RM: in answer to his two & a few lines to the Agent to buy me a lottery ticket, letters were all collected & sent to Town by a Sergt. in the eveng. to be put in the Mail it clear'd up in the afternoon

Tuesday 14th. Augt. 1781 cool The German troops landed at Brooklyn & go to Flushing & Newtown Genl. Leslie arrived yesterday in the Blonde he left Chesapeak in the Carrysford bound to Charlestown, but changed into the Blonde at Sea & put in here – a Vessel came in last night from Chesapeak in 50 hours who says that Lord Cornwallis had taken post at York Town, having left Genl. O'Hara with the Guards & some others at Portsmouth, & that the Marquis de la Fayette was at Williamsburg – went to Town with Major & Mrs. Cortland & din'd there en famille, an agreeable familly. I am sorry to find that Rd. finds some difficulty in getting leave to go home, things goes more by favour than by right, here.

they have as usual deceived us about the Pacquet which won't sail for some time yet

Thursday 16th. cool weather a fleet of Men of War come in Supposed to be Adml. Greaves, they are come to anchor within the Hook –

The Major Genl. [Paterson] came to Eveng. parade without the least previous notice & look'd at the Battn. who did a few Manoeuvres & were dismiss'd, this he calls a general inspection. Steddy – well appointed

Friday 17th. Augt. 1781 Showery   The Major Genls. orders against depradation, & for restoring order & discipline to the army & women –

We had Races today again at Ascot heath; Strawberry won his match easily   we had also a fox Chase, the first ever I was at, but I can't say I enjoy'd it much – Spent the eveng at Foxcrofts where we had a pool at Quadrille, did not get the orders for marching till 9 o'clock

Saturday 18th. we march'd at five o'clock & came to our ground about eight, none of the Qr.Mr. Genls. people to shew us our ground, we Encamp betwixt Laurences & Hallets Cove facing about N.E: The Hessian Grenrs. march'd today also & are come just opposite to us on t'other side of the Water at Horans hook & McGowans pass   The 54th. Regt. cross'd over from Powles hook & go to Kings bridge. The troops of Anhalt Zerbst take their post, they are cloathed in white faced with red & wear boots & they say Emerick has got the Command of that Post. another instance of favour ill bestow'd

Sunday 19th. Augt. Camp near Hallets Cove   Cool weather for some days past   The Two Battns. Encamp'd in a line with a little space between for the QrMr. & Suttlers, on pleasant dry ground, water convenient & wood for Bowers &c

a Ride to Newtown & Jamaica to call on our old acquaintances & with a party of 7 din'd at Rapaljies – a squal of wind & rain in the afternoon – came home to Camp about nine

Monday 20th. the Hessian Greanrs. are at work making up the Fort at Hell Gate for the defence of that passage from the Sound Genl. orders for each Corps to send a Non Commission officer to the Genl. Hospital twice a week to take away the recover'd men –

Tuesday 21st. August. 1781 Camp near Hallets Cove – cross'd over to York island & took a ride to the lines on which I see no alteration, the Yagers & Refugees are Encamp'd without the lines, & No. 8 occupied by a Capts. Guard of 80

Washington we are told has moved from White Plains & retired to North Castle, or some think to Peekskill –

Wednesday 22d. The Swallow Sloop of war coming with dispatches from Adml. Rodney to Adml. Greaves was chaced ashore by 4 Rebel Privateers near the hook, on the 16th. instt. the Vessel & dispatches lost, the crew sav'd

Thursday 23. Augt. 1781. Various accounts of the motions of the Rebels & the french, some think the latter have gone for Rhode Island, others think they are both cross'd the North River –

Friday 24th. cool & pleasant weather we ride about Newtown & see old aquaintances & procure something for the Mess, which is ill to be got hereabout, & obliges us to send to Town We got orders in the Eveng. to march in the morng. to Bedford –

Saturday 25th. Augt. Tents struck at five & the two Battalions march'd at six, & a little after eight we met A Dy.Qr.G Armstrong who shewd us ground just on the North side of Bedford, where we Encamp facing about East. NB the Waggons in the Battn. does not carry above half our Baggage great part left behind, to be brought up tomorrow

Camp at Bedford Sunday 26th. Augt. 1781   The 57th. Regt.
gone to Staten Island & the Hessian Grenadrs. cross'd over to
Brooklyn yesterday & are gone to Deny's ferry.

The Report now is that Mr. Washington with his army & part
of the french are at Chatham in the Jersey's supposed to have a
design on Staten Island –

Monday 27th. warm had a review of the Company, few nes-
sary's wanting – went to Town din'd with the Regt. J:S: we are
to receive abstts. & money to the 24th. Augt. – Slept at Rds.
Madam not well of a cold & troublesome cough, & pregnant their
scheme of going home can't take place just now –

Tuesday 28th. Augt. a Small fleet going to the Southward. the
Blonde with Genl. Leslie to Charlestown & some ships to Virginia
with Recruits &ca. wrote to Peter, & gave it to Majr. Brereton

Arrived at the Hook in 17 days from the West Indies, Sir
Samuel Hood with 13 Ships of the line & 4 frigates & the 40th. &
69 Regts.[17] – we got orders to be in readiness to march at the
shortest notice, & in the evening orders to march a[t] 6 in the
morng. leaving The Tents & heavy baggage behind

Wednesday 29th. Augt. 1781 The Grenrs. were ready to march
this morng. when a Countermand came dated last night at 10
o'clock, on which we pitched our tents again on the same ground.
The Hessian Grenrs. the 42d. 54th. & 37th. Regts. were also
under orders. 'tis supposed we were going to Rhode Island to take
that & the french fleet but it seems they have got intelligence that
the french fleet left Rhode Island on Thursday last – went to
Town & recd. the Compys. Abstracts to 24th. Augt. left 300
guineas with Rutherfurd for a few days till the mens Accots. are
settled[.] settled my own accot. to 24th. Octr. & recd. the balance
din'd avec mes amis Docr. Clark there &ca

Thursday 30th. Augt. 1781   very warm these two days – The
fleet getting ready for sea, there will be 19 sail of the line under
Adml. Greaves   The Robuste & Prudent repairing at N:York
Report of a french fleet from the West Indies being on the coast
a Vessel from the Chesapeak who left Lord Cornwallis's Army all

well in Summer Quarters in & about York Town several officers come passengers. The ships bound for Virginia & Chas. Town not sail'd yet. sent Hathorn a letter inclosed in a few lines & gave it to Dr. Clark.

Lieut. Crammond died this morning at 5 o'clock of a bilious fever, six days ill. & was interr'd at 6 in the eveng. in St. Pauls Church yard with the usual form, & a very long procession of officers of the Army. he was a very much accomplish'd young man but had a pride a Vanity & a temper that prevented his being liked in the Regt. or esteem'd in the army he was Aid de Camp to Genl. Knyphausen eldest Lt in the 42d. aged 26

Friday 31st. Augt. The 40th. Regt. landed & go into New York in place of the 37th. who ma[r]ch to Mc.Gowans the 40th very weak not above 250, but they are order'd to get all their Recruits that were drafted into other Regts. – Races at ascot heath again

Saturday 1st. Septr. had a long Court Marital tryed 10 prisoners most of them for being out at night.

Sunday 2d. The fleet gone to Sea 18 Ships of the Line two 50s & 10 frigates.[18]

an Expedition going on Under Arnold supposed against Connecticut. The 40th. 54th. & 38th. Regts., Robinson & Buskirks Provincial Corps all assemble at Newtown this day, & Embark tomorrow at Whitestone. went with a party to Jamaica & had a turtle feast club £3.

Monday 3d. Septr. 1781 The Pegassus frigate arrived from the West Indies. she had five or six ships under convoy but fell in with a french fleet in L:38 who took all her convoy, they were 12 sail of the line & a number of transports about 60 leagues off the coast steering S:W: it is to be hoped that our fleet will fall in with them – A Genl. Court Martial sits down today at N:York Col: Fox Presidt. Went to Town & got money to clear the Company to 24th. June & gave it out £150.6.7 left 180 guineas in Rutherfurds Box. clear'd Accots. with Mr. Marchinton to this date; came home with H[.] & din'd wt. him

469

'tis Reported that the french fleet that were at Rhode Island have got into Chesapeak, & that Washington is going to the Southward.

Col: Marsh orders the Coys. to be clear'd to 24 Augt. The 17th. Dragoons, Jagers, British & Hessian Grenrs. 37th. & 42d. Regts. du Corps Prince Charles & Bernau are order'd to hold themselves in readiness to Embark at the shortest notice –

Tuesday 4th. Septr. S:W: winds 3 days The Pearl frigate come in from looking out for the fleet – and some of the ships that were under convoy of the Pegassus having made their escape, the rest expected

Genl. Arnolds fleet sail'd this morng. from Whitestone with a fair wind for New England, about 2000 supposed against New London two Vessels arrived from Virginia who bring accounts that a french fleet were in the Chesapeak of 23 Sail, a 64 & 2 frigates in York River the rest in Lynhaven Bay – supposed to be the french fleet from the West Indies – Mr. Washington with his combin'd army reckoned above 6000 had embark'd at Trenton to go to New Castle & cross over to Head of Elk to embark'd down the Chesapeak to join & cooperate with this grand design to save Virginia

The Corps that were yesterday order'd to be [in] readiness to Embark at the shortest notice were to send Embarkation Returns precisely at 10 o'clock tomorrow morng. – more arrivals from the Chesapeak who say the french had 4 ships in York River & our fleet were in with the Capes – Battn. orders for the Companys to Embark as formerly ordered –

Wednesday 5 Septr. 1781 Another Rebel mail taken by the Refugees went to Town about a little business of my own & some for the Mess on board o ship bespoke sea stores for our ship the Apollo in which goes Col Marsh[,] the Brigade Majr[,and] The 7th. 22d. 37th. & 42d. Companys, the other four Companys on board the Esther. came home to dinner, club'd Mess's –

a Melancholly incident happen'd in the Eveng Lt Curry of the 22d. Compy. was found on the Jamiaca road about 2 1/2 miles from Camp, just expiring, his horse standing by him, & without showing any other signs of life than breathing he was quite gone in half an hour after he was brought to Camp in a chair & when examin'd no appearance of any hurt was to be found about him he had lost the faculty of retention & the feces had come away involuntary when found, about 1/2 after 8 oclock by a Corpl. of the 7th. He was an exceeding good young man of an amiable temper & disposition & much lik'd in the Corps

Thursday 6th. Septr. 1781   The Grenrs. march'd from their Camp at Bedford before 6 oclock & got to Denys's between 8 & 9 where they found the Hessian Grenrs. Embarking, & when they were all on board the Batteaux were employ'd in Embarking us, the whole on board by Noon   The 37th. 42d. & Hessian Regts. Embark at New York –

The Zebra Sloop of war arrived this morning from England via the West Indies in nine weeks with dispatches   She saw a french fleet suppos'd to be Mr. Barras 60 leagues from the Capes of Virginia & by the last accounts our fleet were in Lat. 38 in Soundings, so it is to be hoped they will get between them[19] – A Rebel privateer Brig of 18 Guns went past about 1 oclock prize to the Medea

Friday 7th. Septr. 1781 arrived the ship Fox from Corke in Six weeks, & from Glasgow in eight weeks & a letter of Marque Ship from Bristol   they bring Como: Johnstons letter dated 30th. April in Port Praya in St. Jago with an accot. of the action of the 16th. do. in which the french with a Superior Squadron attack'd his while at anchor, & were repulsed. Genl. Meadows with his usual Spirit & humour went with the Comore. on board the Hero during the fight. Capt. Sutton of the Isis misbehaved & was put under arrest.[20] Capt. Paisley of the Jupiter much praised

The Dundas Galley arrived from Chesapeak with dispatches from Lord Cornwallis.   she left York Town on Monday says there are two of the line & two frigates in York River the rest of the french fleet consisting of 17 Sail of the Line were in James River, & at the tail of the horse shoe[;] those in Jas. River were supposed to be disembarking troops, to join the Rebel army under Fayette, our Ships of war the Charon   Guadalope   Bonetta &

Vulcano fire ship were lying near the Batterys at Yorktown on which & on the opposite side at Glocester were mounted 150 pieces of Cannon – Tarleton had taken 20 Rebel pilots intended for the french fleet

Genl. orders for 20 days forage for the Horses that are Embark'd & those left behind belonging officers who are intitled to draw forage are desired to draw it at the nearest Magazine left mine with Dr. Charlton New York by Capt. McKenzies recommend, & sent him a note to draw forage a Rebel privateer Brig went past yesterday, prize to the Medea – We are laying Stock & Stores in proportion to the Public forage, & every body supposes we are going to Virginia, but will not sail until accounts from the fleet & Chesapeak, makes it safe & expedient The ships with the Troops up at the Town cannot drop down till Arnold returns as most of their sailors are with him

Apollo Saturday 8th. Septr. 1781 cool N.W. The Prudent a 64 being repair'd dropp'd down to the hook & also the Hussar Sloop, the Robuste not yet ready[;] some of the letters that were taken in the Rebel Mail published big with the prospect of great events this whole force & attention pointed to the Chesapeak, which likewise draw ours thither, & make Virginia & Maryland the theatre of war

Recd. a letter from Dr. Fleeming dated 7 July came by the Fox, Capt. Montgomery, all friends well at home, his son Tom had come home from Jamaica in a bad State of health but was recovering –

Apollo off Deny's Sunday 9th. Septr. 1781 took a walk ashore with intention to dine at New Utrecht, but in three public houses they could not muster up a dinner for 3 of us bought some wild pidgeons & came aboard The Colonel nor Brigade Major not come aboard yet, we hear that Arnold has burn't New London &ca. &ca.[21] fine weather the accounts from Arnold say that he landed at New London on thursday morning & attack'd the Works on both sides the River, he himself with the 38th. Regt. & Provincials attacked the Town & carried it with little opposition or loss, but the 40th. & 54th. under the command of Lt. Colol.

Eyre found a very obstinate resistance from the Works on the East side of the harbour in which were 35 pieces of Cannon & about 200 men mostly Sailors & 3 months men.

These two Regts. moved & were led on with great spirit & gallantry to the Assault of that strong Redoubt, & notwithstanding the difficultys & obstructions they met with[,] the want of Scaling ladders or any preparations for an Attack of that kind, & a brisk fire kept up from the work, they persver'd in their endeavors to get in, & at length carried the place with the loss of about 210 kill'd & wounded, five officers of the 40th. with Major Montgomery at their head were kill'd & five officers of the 54th. with Col. Eyre at their head were wounded – The Rebels were all either kill'd or wounded except a few who hid themselves & were afterwards made prisoner

The Town was then burn't Stores Magazines wharves &ca. & all the Shipping in the harbour except a few who escap'd up the River When this Business was finish'd the Troops were Embark'd that evening & the fleet sail'd over to Gardners Bay or there about from Whence Mr. Arnold sent Lord Dalrymple & Capt. Beckwith (who were sent with him[)] to Report to HeadQrs. The Magazine at Fort Cressal was not burnt, nor the Church & some houses on New London side. upon the whole this affair is judged to have been fool hardy in Mr. Arnold & throwing away mens lives to very little purpose –

Monday 10th. Septr. 1781. two frigates from sea came to anchor at the Hook, & some other Vessels seen without, the Prudent got under way & join'd them & they all made sail to the Southward, we suppose to join the fleet –

Arnolds expedition return'd yesterday the 40th. & 54th. quarter'd in New York, the 22d. order'd to Embark in place of the 54th. – The lively Sloop of war arrived from England in 6 weeks, Adml. Digby sail'd 10 days before with 3 or 4 ships for this place & the Prince

Tuesday 11th. Septr. 1781 no news or arrivals from the Southward & of course no word of sailing – having a good stock on board we live very well 12 in No.; drank the Memory of the day   The Men go ashore by turns to wash, the 2d. Battn. go by Companies with their arms

Wednesday 12th. Showery, with variable winds, mostly from the south these two or 3 days

Thursday 13th. fine weather   The Pegassus frigate arrived from the fleet with dispatches to the Comr. in chief, by which we find that the french Fleet from Rhode Island had not join'd Monsr. de Grasse in the Chesapeak who on the approach of Adml. Graves they slip'd the Cables & came out with 24 sail of the line, that a partial engagement ensued, in which the Shrewsburry & Intrepid were particularly concern'd & suffer'd a good deal

The Pegassus left them on Monday last within a league of each other & tho' we have only 19 sail of the line to 24 the french avoided coming to action. they left one 64 & 3 frigates in Chesapeak, & had landed about 3000 men on So:side James River

Lord Cornwallis will soon be surrounded by a formidable army –

Friday 14th. Septr. 1781 fine weather   went ashore on Staten Island to see the works at the flag staff where the 57th. & a Battn of Skinners are, they are enlarging & strengthening the principal work & making other improvements – some of the transports are dropping down to the narrows – a council of war held last night on the subject of the news by the Pegassus of the Comr. in Chief & Lt. Genls. –

Saturday 15th. more of the transports coming down. The few men of 16th. Regt. to be drafted on Monday into the 40th. went ashore on long Island & took a long walk, for without excercise the digestive powers grow weak

Apollo off Denys's Sunday 16th. Septr. 1781 warm wr. All the Transports with the 22d. 37th. & 42d. & the three Hessian Regts. are come down & ly near the Watering place   The Battn. landed this morng. by orders of the Major, our Compys. took a walk, those of the Esther clean'd their arms & accoutremts. & came on

board again 'tween 10 & 11. The Guard Ship at the hook moved
into the entrance of the harbour, the Robuste getting ready for
sea –

Monday 17th. Septr. warm & Soly. winds[22] a Gazette extraordinary publish'd by Rivington with B: Genl. Arnolds Letter to
the Comr. in chief dated off Plumb Island the 8th. instt sent by
Lord Dalrymple with an account of his expedition which is very
well told, but it appears that he was both mistaken & misinform'd
with regard to the Strength of Fort Griswold on the Grotton
side & had sent orders to Col. Eyre to prevent the Assault of the
place, but they came too late & these fine fellows were sacrificed.
Lt. Coll. Eyre being wounded & Major Montgomery kill'd in the
attack, the Command then devolved on Major Broomfield of the
54th. who behaved with great spirit on the occasion
On the New London side where Arnold was himself Capt.
Millet with 4 Compys. of the 30th. took Fort Trumbull (which
was an open work) with the loss of 4 or 5 files only & the people
that were in it made their escape & got over to Fort Griswald
which encouraged them to stand a Storm tho' the place was summon'd a Col: Ledyard Commanded who was Kill'd with most of
his officers, & 85 were found dead, & 60 wounded, the rest were
made prisoners, about 70, the Barracks & Magazine in Ft. Griswold was order'd to be burn't by Capt. Lemoine of the artillery
but by some mistake or neglect of his it was not done the reason
of which he is to account for –
a Pilot Boat came in express from Virginia, She left the Chesapeak on tuesday & Reports that Lord Cornwallis had nearly finished his Works of Defense at York Town & Glocester & the
Army on York side were Encamp'd without the Works were in
great health & spirits & had plenty of provision, 4 months
a ride on Long Island, & went to Gravesend Bay & saw some
of our lads haul the Seine they got about 400 herrings & a few
other fish. A Man of War came into the hook
Tuesday 18th. it come on to blow yesterday eveng. about So: &
S.S.E. & continued all night, this forenoon it veer'd to the S.W. &
blew hard with showers, in the afternoon it clear'd up with a

N.W. – a prize brig came in, & several Pilot Boats went up the eveng. clear & moderate

Wednesday 19th. Septr. 1781 cool & pleasant after the Gale, wind about west a Sloop of War arrived in the Morng. & went up to Town; a[t] 9 A:M: a Signal on Staten Island for a fleet of Men of War which proved to be Admiral Graves with his fleet. The french fleet having got into Chesapeak again, & our fleet being in want of repair he is come here to water & refit. The Terrible a 74, was so leaky that they were obliged to abandon & burn her at sea[;] some frigates, Victualers, & small craft gone down to the hook, with water & supplies. in consequence of orders our Transports moved over to the Staten island side & came to anchor off Coles ferry among the rest. Orders for the Troops to land in the morning & Encamp on Staten Island near Coles ferry, where a D QrMr Genl will point out the ground.

Thursday 20th. Septr. 1781 a blowy Morning at N.W. which prevented the Troops from landing. The fleet working into the Hook

Friday 21st. more moderate & cool The Troops disembark'd this Morning & Encamp'd in the Neighbourhood of Coles ferry the Br: Grrs. on the high Ground behind Ryersons, just where they were in 77 before they Embark'd for the Chesapeak, the Hessian Grenrs. & Regts. Du Corps & Prince Charles form a line in their Rear, the 42d. close by the ferry, the 22d & 37th. about 1/2 a mile out on the Richmond road, the jagers in their front

Camp Staten Island Saturday 22d. Septr. 1781 sent for all our things from on board of Ship as we hear the Transports are going down to water the Fleet. Lodged two Casks containing 6 doz port & a 5 gall Keg of Brandy at Mr. Drumonds near the Watering place, untill we move –

This being the Anniversary of the Kings Coronation the Battery at New York fir'd at 12 o'clock, & the fleet at the hook & the ships up at Town fir'd at one o'clock a Royal Salute – din'd with the Major at their Mess which they have set a-going as formerly drank too much as usual on these occasions Promotions in orders

Sunday 23d. Septr. 1781 warm took a long walk by Deckers ferry and towards Richmond, came home late & din'd with Todd & them – the wind being favourable the fleet moved up from the hook, the Ships that wanted most repair went up to Town, the rest came to anchor off Coles ferry, where they are water[ed] immediately.

They talk varriously of their engagement off the Capes of Virginia, the west India Squadron say that restraining Signals prevented them from cutting off & taking 4 or 5 of the Enemys Ships & the Gravites give themselves great credit for manuvering & offering Battle to Superior fleet for 5 or 6 days –

Camp Staten Island 24th. Septr. 1781 The fleet busy watering at the diferent runs & springs on this end of the Island The London & 8 or 9 more are up at Town the Barfleur & the remainder here. a frigate arrived from Sea. The Perseverance from England with Adml. Digby & 3 Sail of the Line who are off the Hook –

Tuesday 25th. Septr. we see Adml. Digby off the hook but the wind being about west he can't get in Prince William the Kings third son is with him.

A Vessel arrived from Virginia who says the french have now 34 sail of the line in Chesapeak having brought 27 from the West Indies & are now join'd by the 7 who were at Rhode Island, they have taken the Iris & Richmond who were foolishly sent in to reconoitre; the Charon burnd this Vessel bring accounts from Lord Cornwallis that he has two months provisions & his little army in good health & spirits –

Adml. Digby brought the July mail some of the letters come down from Town in the Evening, got one from my Dr. little Ann dated 27th. June 1st. & 3d. July acknowledging mine of the 28 April, all well but still very anxious for some happy event to bring us together

Wednesday 26th. Septr. 1781, N:W: we are told a Pacquet is to Sail immediately & also the lively Sloop of War – wrote to AH: of our situation & in answer to the last – The young Prince came

up in the lively Brig & landed at N:York under a Royal Salute
from the Battery. Adml.

Digby still without the hook where we see two other ships have
join'd him   The fleet busy Watering, Victualing & refitting, &
they are going to fit up some fire ships

Camp Staten Island 27th. Septr. 1781. Adml. Digby's Ships
come up & the Warwick & Pearl, the two last have been cruising
Wrote a long letter to R:M: with a Sketch of Affairs since the
last, & hearing the Mail was to be closed this Eveng. sent them
off to the care of J:R: –

Friday 28th. very warm   The Prince George went up to Town
yesterday Eveng. – and this Morng. the Admirals exchanged a
Salute. The Warwick, & Pearl arrived –

Genl. Leslie sent a Message last night that he would be down
here today to meet the Commanding Officers of Corps, but he
being detain'd by a council of war, he sent his Aid de Camp Capt.
Skelly with a paper expressive of the business which was to let
them know that the Troops were to Embark on board of Men of
War & to take as little Baggage as possible   Embarkation Returns
call'd for

Saturday 29th. Septr. 1781 rain in the night & this Morning
from the East   The Govr. council & Inhabitants of N:York write
an Address to the Prince –

Sunday 30th. Septr. The Pacquet sail'd yesterday.   din'd on
board the Princessa with Lieut. McDowal   she suffer'd but little
in the late engagement & will soon be ready, but some others
won't be ready these 10 days – N:B: Lt. Wilkinson [who has been
permitted to purchase a Captaincy in the 64th. Regt.] has been
only 4 months a Lt. & gives 2400 guineas to Russel who has been
only 3 years Capt. has 10/ a day for being a Secretary, & has a
post of 20/ a day in So: Carolina; another shamefull abuse of
favour Mr. Clinton –

[Tuesday 2d. Octr.] N:B: we did not receive this order of Mr.

Gospoths [for the British Grenrs. to march to Billops Point at
10:00 AM] till past ten. The provisions were not yet divided, the
heavy Baggage was to be sent on board o'ship, & waggons to be
procur'd to carry our field Baggage, in which the Hessians had
taken the Start of us, & tho' they march'd two hours before us,
we got to Richmond before them, & as the Camp Equipage could
not be up to night the Battns. were canton'd along the road to
the westward of Richmond.

Sent my Trunk & bedsted on board Baggage Ship, reserving
in the field as usual my Tent portmanteau Bedding & Canteen –

Staten Island 3d. Octr. 1781 cold morng. The Grrs. March'd
in the Morng. the shore road by the Blazing Star, & took up
ground near Dessessois, which is two miles short of Billops Point.
the Baggage did not come up till after dark; a cold bleak hill   see
the Town of Amboy about two miles off which seems to be almost
quite deserted. a few militia men show themselves opposite the
jagers.

Camp West end of Staten Island 4th. Octr. 1781   cold NW
wind, The Men employed in pitching their tents & cleaning their
arms &ca.

The cause of this Movement is yet unknown some thinks we
are going into Jersey to get fresh stock, some think it is to let the
Prince see the Island & the troops both, & others are of opinion
that it is only to divide the troops more equally on the Island –
i:e: that inhabitants may share the burthen of the mischief occasion'd by the Soldiery.

Friday 5th. Octr. 1781 a cold night & frost Major of Brigade
Losach came to Camp last night with the distribution of ships for
the Grrs. Vizt. the London, Prince George, Barfleur, & Bedford,
Majr. Genl. Patterson goes in the Bedford   And Col: Marsh &
Col Fox has settled it that the 1st. Battn. go on board the
London & Barfleur & the 2d. on board the Prince George &
Bedford.   The 7th. 37th. 42d. & 43d. Compys. go on board the
London the 17th. 22d. 23d. & 33d. the Barfleur & we hear the

Comr. in chief has order'd the Comissy. Genl. to furnish the offrs. with fresh Stocks, & they are to lay in for themselves some Wine tea, & sugar.

Accounts recd. from Lord Cornwallis that he has four Months provision is well fortified, his Army in good spirits, & in no Apprehensions. so we were told

Octr. 6th. The Fleet are busy making the necessary repairs, & compleating their water and provision, and are expected to be ready about the 12th. instt., when the Troops will embark on board the Ships of War agreeable to a distribution given out for that purpose, in order to make a Spirited exertion for the relief of Lord Cornwallis, & on which probably depends the fate of America, & the Superiority of the Sea. The french are said to have four & thirty Sail of the Line in Chesapeak Bay, & we have only six & twenty here, including three fifties, two are expected from the West Indies, & one more from the Northward. By the last accounts from Virginia The Army at York Town were in good health & spirits, had four months provisions, were well fortified, & under no apprehensions. hum

Major Cochran gone in a small Vessel to try to get to Lord Cornwallis with dispatches from the Comr. in chief – [23]

Camp Westend of Staten Island Some of the Rebel Militia come out at Night in boats from Woodbridge creek, & reconoitre our out posts & sentries & sometimes take a shot. we have sentries all along the shore from Dessessois to the Blazing Star &ca.

A fleet of Victualers from Corke arrived at the hook of above 40 Sail under convoy of a frigate, 12 weeks out, & a ship from London also the Carrysfort with a prize, a mast ship intended for the french fleet –

A List of Promotions from the War office & leave of absence; in orders the 4th. instt. And Orders by the Comr. in chief. The 37th. Regt. the Regt. du Corps & Prince Chas. to be under the command of Major Genl. Wormb till further orders, & Major Brigade Wynard is attach'd to this Brigade. The 22d. & 42d. Regts. to be under the Command of Brigadier Genl. the Earl of Lincoln, & Major of Brigade Phillips to be attach'd to this Brigade till further orders. All officers & men belonging to absent Corps to be under the Command of Major Darby of the 7th. & to do Duty at Brooklyn fort

Camp near Dessesois Westend of Staten Island Sunday 7th. Octr. 1781 a hard Gale about N.N.W. & No: – most of Corke fleet got up yesterday eveng. a few lying at the hook
No provisions come to Princess Bay, we are therefore obliged to send to Coles ferry, which makes us one day without provision –

Monday 8th. Octr. pleasant weather The remainder of the Corke fleet coming up, The Gardens Potatoe fields &ca. in the Neighbourhood suffer a little by the Soldiers, if they would Stop there in moderation, I would excuse them, but to kill & take their poultry, pigs, & cattle, can not be overlook'd or forgiven, tho' it is often done with impunity as it cannot be found out who did it.

Camp West end of Staten Island 9th. Octr. 81 In consequence of orders recd. in the night, The Jagers, British & Hessian Grenadiers march'd back to their respective Camps near Coles ferry. a warm day & the road very dusty some of the Waggons broke down; – what an amazing quantity of baggage the Hessians have, see a Ship going up that looks like a Pacquet. we din'd with the Regt. & got a booze.
N:B: my horse lame from a kick obliged to have him led all the way Camp near Coles ferry Staten Island

Wednesday 10th. Octr. 1781 – The Augt. Pacquet arrived yesterday, got three letters this morng from my little friend AH: dated 10th. June 14th. & 29th. July, all well & full of Affection, & wishing & praying.

Camp near Coles ferry Staten Island 11th. Octr 1781 a large man war at the hook supposed to be one of those from the West Indies.
gave my horse to Lt. Loraine of our Regt. to keep or sell for me, as he is left behind convalescent, & a certificate to draw forage for him

[12th. Octr. 1781] The Camp was struck at 1/2 after 7 oclock &

481

the Baggage loaded in waggons & sent down to Coles ferry, when we were told the troops order of Embarkation were to march past the Prince & Salute as they went to their Boats   The Morng. very warm & we did not march off till 'tween ten & eleven. The Prince being arriv'd he was posted near the beach on the ground where the 42d. were Encamp'd, and the Troops according to their order in line, march'd past by half Company's & the Officers Saluted the Young Prince who was accompanied by Adml. Digby & the Dy. Adjt. Genl. &ca. &ca. he seems & is said to be a very fine young man, smart & sensible for his years, & sufficiently well grown, a strong likeness of the King, & a handsome Address, he was in a plain Midshipman uniform, look'd chearful, & took off his hat with a good grace. The troops then march'd to their boats & were Embark'd on board their respective Transports in a few hours.

About Noon two Ships of the line came up & anchor'd among the fleet, Vizt. the Torbay & Prince William from the West Indies. These will want water &ca. and by all accounts the fleet will not be ready to drop down & fit for sea these some five or six days yet and I understand we are to remain on board of Transports untill the Ships of the line are at the hook or over the Bar, when they are to take the troops on board according to their distribution

On board the Esther Transport off Staten Island Saturday 13th. Octr. 81 busy as usual after Embarkation in putting a lumber'd ship in order, & getting on board stock & stores for sea –

about 11 o'clock it came on a sudden & violent Squal of wind from the N.W. & continued to blow hard all day, with some rain, the Men of War struck their top masts & lower'd the fore & main yards, some passage Boats lost 'twixt this & York, & the Alcide ran foul of the Shrewsbury & broke her bowsprit & fore yard –

Sunday 14th. moderate & cool wrote a piece of a letter to my AH: to go by the Pacquet – in the afternoon the Men of war that lay here in the narrows went down to the hook, 11 of the line.

Monday 15th. fine wr. & warm finish'd my letter & sent it up to Town to the care of Mrs. R: to put in the mail a party of us went ashore on Long Island & took a walk & bot. some butter two sentences of Genl. Courts martial in orders. Lt. Hislop of Skinners Corps is honorably acquitted. Ensn. Sutherland of the 42d. is acquitted but the conduct of the Subns. in prosecuting was justifiable & proper –

Tuesday 16th. Octr. The Prince George & some other of the big ships came down to Staten Island. The Centaur got a ground above this & on the Jersey side near low water, & got off again with the flood without any damage –

An express from Lord Cornwallis who finds himself hardly press'd & wants assistance, the Enemy broke ground about the 1st. instt. The Navy people does not seem to be in a hurry on this occasion –

The Col: & all hands come on board. got our forage money for 163 days – a large frigate & some prizes went up some say the Magicienne from Halifax

Esther Transport off Staten Island 17th. Octr. 81 The London & I believe all the remainder of the Line of Battleships except 3 come down in the forenoon with a strong breeze at N.W. & came to below the Narrows; it is to be hop'd they will embrace this favourable wind & spring tides to get over the Bar about noon the Transports got underway & came down to the hook & anchor'd among the fleet, the London &ca. came down in the Evening. The Princessa went over the Bar

Thursday 18th. Octr. 1781 cool at N.W. a Signal being made at 7 this morng. for the Transports to come along side of the respective ships of war that were to take their troops on board, we got under way & came to along side the London & by means of a rope from each end haul'd close to her, & the troops went on board by seniority of Companys, & were dispos'd of on the middle and lower decks, 6 to a mess between the Guns

Appartments made for the officers on the middle deck before the Wardroom, of canvass curtains, & Cotts slung betwixt the Guns. The Comr. in Chief & his suite & Col: Marsh in the

Admirals appartments on the upper deck, & mess there. the rest of the officers eat in the Wardroom where all the Gentlemen seem to be very civil about 20 at table a very good dinner, and plenty of Wine, with freedom & ease.

Friday 19th. Octr. the N.W. wind continues The fleet got under way in the morning about 7 we got over the Bar about 8 with 4 fathom water which is nothing to spare, see a fleet in the offing the rest followd in course & the whole was over by noon, & all the Troops Embark'd, – a great many Signals made for Boats officers & ships, & the Capt. of the Pacquet came on board for the admirals & Generals dispatches, I took that opportunity to write to R.M. of our motions so far – The fleet got under way about 3 P.M. when the wind fell & came round to the Southward we stood out to Sea all night about S.E.

London at Sea Saturday 20th. Octr. 1781. a Strong wind about S.S.W. the fleet standg out from the Land close haul'd, till noon when the whole tak'd by Signal & stood to the westward, 40 fathom water –

N:B: The fleet we saw yesterday was from England above 60 Sail under Convoy of the Centurion, Lord Dalrymple went on board in the Perseverance & return'd with the dispatches

The wind increas'd all the afternoon & blew hard in the night from the Southward the fleet tack'd at midnight, & stood out again The Amphion join'd from a Cruise took two rich prizes & saw two frigates & a 64 off the Capes of Virginia –

Sunday the 21st. moderate but the wind still in the Southerly Qr. – see a Ship has carried away her maintopmast, bore down to collect the leeward ships, it proves to be the Alcide about ten have out a signal for the fleet to form in the Order of Sailing – In the afternoon the wind veer'd about to West & WNW & we haul'd up to S.SW & SW. along shore in Soundings 'tween 20 & 30 fm.

London at Sea Monday 22d. Octr. 1781 Moderate wr. all last night going 4 & 5 knots about S.W. the day clear & cool keeping S.W.B.W. 3 & 4 knots under reef'd topsails some of the Ships a

great way astern   The Alcide has got a maintopmast up   The Drum beat to Quarters yesterday, when the Soldiers were Appointed to their Stations along with the Sailors at the great Guns. The 7th. 37th. & 42d. on the lower deck, 7 to each Gun officers included, the 43d. to have small arms our firelocks are put down below in the Breadroom –
At noon had an observation Lat: 38.40 suppose to be near abreast with the Delaware about 15 leagues off the land. Some dispatches sent off to go by a Whaleboat to be tow'd in shore by a Pilot boat in the evening little wind & hazy   The Ships Company muster'd at Quarters

London at Sea tuesday 23d. Octr. 1781   the wind came about to the so:wd. in the night which was very warm; the Morning almost calm, the fleet pretty close up, sliding on under topgallantsails 1 1/2 knots S.W. & S.W.B.W. all the forenoon, Made Signals for Ships to send Boats for letters that came by the Centurion   At noon they had an Observation Lat 38.0 about 20 fathom water, gravel & small shells Admiral Digby came on board, The fleet tack'd in the Eveng & stood out with a light wind about S.B.W. & hazy –

Wednesday 24th. Octr. The fleet tack'd in the morning at 4 & stood in at WBS. & W 1/2 S. 3 & 4 knots till noon when the frigate ahead made the land, & the fleet tack'd & stood out to the Eastward having 15 fathom water.   The fleet close up going under easy sail, they say two strange ships join'd the fleet   This Morning one of the Pilot Boats brought on board two people from Virginia which they found on Cape Charles, One of them a Negro Pilot says he escaped from York Town on Thursday last, 18th. instt. when there had been a cessation of hostilities, for the purpose of making a Capitulation & supposes the place surrendered next day   in the evening it blew hard at S.W. & soon after came round to N.W. a Gale of wind; we lay too under a fore sail mizen & mizen staysail

Thursday 25th. Octr. 178[1] cool with the Wind at North, stretching along shore. see the land off the Starboard beam   this

morning the Nymph came alongside & sent on board Genl. Dalrymple Major St. George & Capt. Lewis of the 64th: they came
in the fleet from England; they left N:York last Sunday & say
there had arrived a dispatch from Lord Cornwallis of the 15th.
when he had given up all hopes & said it was too late to risk
anything to save them

at Noon supposed to be about 7 leagues from Cape Charles, a
light wind at North, the fleet close up, the Carrysford about 4
miles off the Starboard bow, looking out

The Adjt. Genl. spoke to me today & told me Genl. Stirling
was going home & gave me some hopes of making a bargain with
Lt. Gordon when we return to New York

The Fleet tack'd in the Eveng. & stood out to the Eastward –
Genl. Leslie came on board & had a long conference with his Ex:
[Sir Henry Clinton] we suppose on the Subject of his going to
Charlestown to take the Command &ca. &ca.

Friday 26th. Octr. a strong southly. wind & hazy, standing
off & on, in the Eveng. the wind came about to the North & blew
hard all night, clear & cool, the fleet veer'd twice

London at Sea Saturday 27th. Octr. 1781 a Strong wind at
north, the fleet standg: in under clos'd reef'd topsails & courses
W.NW. 20 fathom water, at 8 A.M. the Warwick & Nymph sent
a head about 11 they make a Signal for Land, which proves to be
Cape Charles WBN 4 or 5 leagues, one of our small Schooners
that had been sent in shore 3 days ago, join'd us at Noon Cape
Charles W.B.N. 8 miles the fleet all a stern & pretty well up The
Nymph & Warwick having bore away about S.W. for Cape
Henry, we Starboard our helm a little after 12 & followed them
The land which the pilot took for Cape Charles proves to be Hog
Island, we see Cape Chas. in the Eveng after which we tack &
stand off the land again

Sunday 28th. moderate wind about NNE The fleet tack'd at
2 in the Morng. & stood in for the Capes, which we made about
eight Capt. Elphinston came on board & told he counted 46 sail

of Vessels great & small at anchor in Chesapeak near the horse Shoe, at 10 see a ship standing out whh. we take to be friend[24]

The fleet stood in till noon when Cape Henry was about 3 & Cape Charles about 2 leagues distanced the fleet tack'd & lay to, head to S.E. we see the french fleet from the tops 'tween 30 & 40 Sail The ship we see betwixt the Capes lyes to & makes Signals, suppose her to be a french frigate reconoitering our fleet, & reporting by signals The Warwick & Nymph stand in towards him a Whale boat came in board from Smiths Island at one, she is one of ours that was sent off a few days ago, has taken a brig which lyes at anchor off Cape Chas. –

Genl. Leslie came on board in the afternoon & got his orders & instructions for Chas town & went on board the Carrysford, the Blonde & she made sail to the Southward in the Eveng

The french fleet by all the Reports ly at anchor across the Bay twixt the Horse Shoe & Middle Ground 35 or 37 Sail three or four came out & looked at us at a distance, The Warwick & Nymph return'd to the fleet & reported as above the fleet tack'd & stood out

Chapter XIV

'bring us together in peace, love & safety'

Long Island
29 October 1781 to 2 March 1782

When Sir Henry Clinton returned to New York at the beginning of November 1781, he could not have known that Lord Cornwallis's surrender at Yorktown would mark the end of major operations in the War for American Independence, but he certainly could have expected that he would be blamed for the loss of such a large part of his army. No wonder then that he sought both to protect the remaining British posts in the southern colonies and to exculpate himself for Cornwallis's surrender. He authorized Lieutenant-General Alexander Leslie, who now commanded British forces in the South, to give up Savannah if necessary to secure Charleston; he promised Leslie an additional 2,000 men should he be threatened by a French squadron; and he sent reinforcements to East Florida and the Bahamas. But what consumed Clinton during the last months of his command were Cornwallis's charges that Clinton was responsible for the disaster at Yorktown, charges that Cornwallis made in his official correspondence immediately after surrendering. Clinton denied that he had required Cornwallis to establish a base at Yorktown and to remain there even at the risk of losing his army. He also argued that if Cornwallis had properly fortified Yorktown, he would have been able to hold out until well into November, until Clinton could have come to his aid. Clinton made these arguments repeatedly – in his correspondence, in a pamphlet he prepared for publication in London, and in conversations with anyone who would listen. But he was never able to gain the initiative in the debate. Cornwallis managed to state his position first and to arrive home months before Clinton; and the British public tended to believe Cornwallis. So it was that after Yorktown, Clinton was more successful in protecting what remained of British forces in America than in securing his own reputation.[1]

John Peebles was well aware of the Clinton-Cornwallis controversy, but after Yorktown, he was far more concerned with his own future than with the conduct of the American War. Even while en route to the Chesapeake in late October, he had talked with Clinton's adjutant-general about selling his commission and resigning from the army. The adjutant-general encouraged him to think he might soon be permitted to sell. But on returning to New York, he found the major of his regiment indifferent and the colonel positively hostile. Not even the intervention of a prominent naval officer could dissolve the colonel's 'rancour & malevolence.' Peebles appealed to the adjutant-general who told him that nothing could be done until the colonel either went home or changed his mind.[2] Finally, in late December the colonel departed and the adjutant-general agreed to support Peebles' selling to any lieutenant 'proper for the Regt.' and able to pay the price. It took another six weeks to complete the transaction – to get the major of the 42nd to approve Lieutenant William Dickson, to allow Dickson to meet the purchase price, and to secure the final approval of the commander-in-chief.[3] By 8 February Peebles was saying farewell to his company. He then booked passage on a ship that was bound for Glasgow, said goodbye to American and British friends, and sailed on 2 March. Peebles' American War was over. He would be home in time for a late May wedding.[4]

Long Island
29 October 1781 to 2 March 1782

London at Sea Monday 29th. Octr. 1781 we stood out about S:E:
till 4. A.M. when tack'd & stood in & made the land to the So:
ward of Cape Henry wind W: course N.N.W till ten when the
wind came to N.W. & we lay along shore under easy sail, about
noon the Nymph was sent off for N:York with Lord Dalrymple &
Major Robertson & in the afternoon the Rattlesnake was dis-
patched for England wrote a few lines to AH: inclosed to my Fr:
wind N.NW., we stand away N.E. & I suppose are bound for
NYork again having what they call offer'd the Enemy Battle   see
a Strang[e] Sail to windward between us & the Land which we
take to be a french frigate watching our Motions –

Tuesday 30th. clear & cold NNW fresh we stood on about NE
all night under easy sail & continue so this Morng. at 11 AM.
see two Strange Sail in N.E Qr. NB Lt. Sharp gone with Genl.
Leslie Aid de Camp   at Noon had an observation Lat 37.10 –
wind NW. Co:NNE. 2 & 3 knots – The two Strange Sail prove
to be the Amphion from N:York & the little Brig that was taken
by the whaleboat – Capt. Beazley came on board, but I hear no
news – The Prince Wm. order'd to take charge of the fire Ships
&ca. & bring them on to N:York   The fleet stood on under easy
sail some ships a good way to leeward & astern

Wednesday 31st. Octr. The wind shifted about to the Southward in the night, the fleet standing No: under very little sail,
two of the fireships a missing the Warwick & Adamant order'd to
look for them & bring them on   a Signal made for the Capt. of
the Amphion who came on board about 11 & got his orders from
the Admiral, & went astern and also a Signal for an officer from
the Prince George who came on board & got a Pacquet – we then
made Sail & steer'd North, going above 6 knots, at Noon in Lat
38.18 by observation; top Gallant Sails   The fleet continued at
this rate till night when steer'd at N.N.E

Thursday 1st. Novr. 1781   the wind came to S.E. after midnight & we had rain in the morning which continued with little intervals all day, with a strong wind in the Easterly qr. & very heavey squalls one of which about 1 P.M. carried away our Mainsail, the foot rope broke & it blew all to shreds, they cleared the remnants & bent a new one in half an hour, & laid the ship to under a fore sail close reef'd Maintopsail & Mizen. the fleet a stern, most of them out of sight being thick weather; The Gale took off at night, which was lucky for us, for if it had continued all night we should have drift'd near the Shore, & the wind come to about S.S.W. & we went away N.E. & N.N.E

about 9 see a Sail to the westward, who soon after shew'd two lights, which not being well understood we got the Qr.deck Guns prim'd the Upper deck Guns shotted, & the middle deck Guns clear'd, but the Signal was found to be that of a friend which we answer'd by triangular lights at the Mizenpeek & she approach'd us being one of our own fleet, the rest all astern out of sight

Friday 2d. Novr. 1781 see the land in the morning both Navesink & Long Island the formr about W.S.W. 6 or 7 leagues, little or no wind & a great Swell only 5 Ships near us see the rest of fleet about 2 leagues to the Southward in the afternoon the wind came to N.E. when we stood in towards the hook & came to anchor in the Evening about 2 leagues from the Light house, the Swell not yet fallen so could not attempt to go in, neither had we a Pilot –

London off Sandy Hook Saturday 3d. Novr. cool & cloudy, wind about N.N.W. Pilots came aboard in the Morning, but they seem to be of opinion that we can't get in with this wind, – The Transports coming out – a Signal for all flag officers, who came aboard about 10, & were recd. by an officers Guard of Marines, then a Signal for an officer from each ship who came on board & got orders to put the Troops on board the transports with care & safety, the Transports anchor'd near their respective ships & after 12 when the men had got their dinner they began to shift the troops with the long boats & flat boats, towed by the Men of wars barges we bid the officers of the London farewel to whom we are much obliged for their polite & civil treatment all the time we were on board; the wind being pretty strong & the sea rough I don't think the troops will be all Shifted today, we got all on board the Esther by 3 oclock P.M

Col: Abercromby came on board the London in the morng to wait on the Comr. in chief having come from Virginia in the Bonita Sloop of War Capt. Dundas, agreeable to an article of the Capitulation which took place the 19th. the particulars of which are in the New[s] Papers copied from the Pensylva. journal, Lord Cornwallis Surrender'd on much the same terms we gave Lincoln at Charlestown, the troops to be Quarter'd in Virginia, Maryland, & Pensylvania a few officers to be left with them the rest get leave to come in on Parole. The Enemy had about 20000 Troops & about 90 pieces of Artillery, they lost between 7 & 800 & we about 600, vide the last page the Genl. went up in the Eveng. in a schooner, was saluted by the London 13 guns

We hear they have been in fear & trembling at N:York in our absence, they hear'd or took it into their heads that we were beat & the french coming here, they had ships ready to sink &ca. &ca.

Esther Transport off Sandy hook 3d Novr. Strong wind about WN.W. we got under way in the evening with the flood tide & made a tack or two but lost ground so came to anchor again in 17 fathom water about 5 miles from the Light house

Sunday 4th. Novr. 1781 The wind still continues in the N.W.Qr. & blows fresh, some of the transports try to turn it in, but they make no head of it so here we ly at anchor waiting a more favourable opportunity to get into the Hook, & up to Denys's, where the Troops are to land & encamp in the vicinity of that, till further orders. N:B: The wind continued about N.W. all the week, & frequently blew very hard we got under way every flood & gain'd more & less, but did not get to Denys's till Saturday 10th. Novr. when we landed in the Eveng.

Saturday 10th. Novr. 1781 The Troops as they arrived at Denys's land & go into Cantonments from that to Bedford, 9 or 10 Ships not yet come up, our four Companies move on beyond New Utrecht & take up Qrs. for the night, the Baggage landed –

Sunday 11th. Novr. we march in the Morng. to Bedford & go into Cantonments there, & on the road to Newton 3 or 4 miles, Our Baggage came up in the Eveng. Col: Fox with part of the 2d. Battn. we hear are not yet come up.

The Winter Quarters for the Army is out in Orders, the British Grenrs. Jamaica but I understand we are to remain here till the Hutts are repair'd by the Country people – we are at the two Duree's in Bushwick – the other troops that are come up go over to York –

Monday 12th. Novr. Snow & sleet from N.E. got orders after 9 at Night to parade tomorrow morng at our old Encampment & press Waggons at our Qrs. a stupid order, as it might on this occasion have express'd the purpose of the march & route for waggons

Tuesday 13th. Novr. 1781 The Companies assembled at their old Encampment near Bedford between 7 & 8 & march'd to Jamaica where they went into Cantonments the 1st. Battn. in the East end of the Village the 2d. in the west, untill the Hutts are repaired & some more made – NB we 42d march'd 6 miles about

We hear the London sail'd for the West Indies Jamaica on Saturday the 10th. & Sir Saml. Hood with 19 Sail of the Line sail'd on Sunday for the windward Islands we suppose; the rest of the fleet to remain on this station except the Robuste & Europe who are to go home with the Convoy from hence, – no cordiality among the Admirals –

Wednesday 14th. Novr. fine weather I went to Town to get some warm Cloathing for the Compy. for Winter & to see my friends the Rds. Madam brot. to bed of a boy about a week ago, both doing well found the two brors. at home Dick who is 1st. Lt. of the Prince Wm. much emaciated with the Gout din'd there with the Major, Chambre Madam, Beeff Stakes & Claret, a happy little meeting –

Thursday 15th. Novr. 1781 fine weather a Vessel arrived from Virginia with some of the Prisoners, the rest with Lord

493

Cornwallis had sail'd for this Port before them, except the offrs. of two Corps who were to come by land. The men & officers that were to remain had gone to their different districts in Virginia Marryland & Pensylva. according to the terms

a Pacquet sail'd for England today which I did not know of till it was too late for writing din'd wt. Dr. McLean who has lately been very ill & had a narrow escape – Spoke to Major about my affair & mention'd Gordon, but he does not seem to listen with that attention I could wish or expect – the fleet some say will sail in a fortnight, & I wish to go – Bot. gray cloth for trowzers the same as the Regt. & got the waistcoat cloth out of store – Capt. Douglas of the Chatham married to Miss Burges last night

Friday 16th. Novr. 1781 fine wr. an order for getting our Baggage & Cloathing out of Store to Qrs. by Col: Marsh, boats & Waggons to be furnish'd by the Qr.Mr. Genl. Depmt. I hear Mr. Breun resigns his Dy.QMr. Genlship, suppose he has made his fortune & wants to be off – Comry. Wier died the other day worth a great deal of money.

The Men of war come up from the Hook two days ago, Adml. Digby's flag on board the Lion in the No:River. houses clearing out for the Prince & him – din'd at Mr. Goolds a large party. – Genl. orders 15th. Novr. for the Recruits of the 17th & 43rd. to be drafted to the 40th. 54th. & 57th. & the offrs. of the Corps in Virga. who are not Prisoners to be quartered at Flat Lands & New Lotts Capt Willington of the 57th. sold out – NB an advertisement at Rivingtons for a Majority of an old Corps to be sold, odd a Survey of Barrack furniture to be the 19th. – a flag from Virga. with some of ye. prisoners

Saturday 17th. Novr. 1781 cloudy & came on to rain from the Easterly Qr. notwithstanding which I cross'd over & came home – find the Qrs. not settled yet –

Jamaica Sunday 18th: Novr. 1781 wr. being informed that Judge Ludlow was to have an officer, & that he said he would rather have me, I call'd there to know, but I find he expects to be

exempted, so I chose the Dy Assistt. Barrack masters Qrs. they being thot. to good for him – din'd with the judge
some of the Gentlen. of the London came up to dine with us, but they have mistaken the day –

Monday 19th. The Battn. parades in the field below the Hutts at 10 o'clock, The hutts drawn for by lot we have drawn four tollerable good which will hold 18 men each, 3 Companys will have to make entirely – that little assistt. Bk. Mr. has complain'd & got leave to keep his Qrs. so I shall remain where I am at the Widow Distmas's
Lord Cornwallis & several other officers are arrived, two more ships with officers sailed before them –

Jamaica Tuesday the 20th. Novr. 1781 look'd at the hutts & gave directions for the Repairs the Inhabitants are slow in bringg. up the Matterials –
Lt. Dickson having mention'd his desire to purchase some months ago & having told me that his friend Capt. Elphinston had spoke to Genl. Stirling who, he said, had no objections I therefore spoke to Mr. Dickson about the price which he does not object to, so I wrote to Stirling

Sir
    Being desirous to quit the Army & go home for the same reasons I mention'd to you last year, I hope you will have no objection to Lieut: Dicksons purchasing my Company, he being the only Lt. in the Regt. that I know of for purchase

& sent it by Mr. Dickson –

Wednesday 21st. cold & a little snow The three gentlen. of the London Morris, Ammons, & the Parson, were to have din'd with us today at Rochfords, but they have sent an apology a Note from Rd. acquainting me that his youngest Boy is dead, & that they have turn'd their minds on going home in the fleet

Mr. Dickson brings me a Verbal answer from Stirling, who still holds up the same objections, that of McGregor, & I understood his objections had been withdrawn at Capt. Elphinstons request to oblige him, or I never would have ask'd him again

Thursday 22d. Novr. 1781   cold & clear   the hut business goes on but slowly – we din'd at the Doctors Qrs. today for the first time, where we are to mess for the Winter being most centrical; but I have yet some hopes of getting home

Friday & Saturday good wr. for the season   Spoke to the Col: about the A.Dy.Bk.Mr.   I hear Rd. has got leave to go home & wants to see me. Lord Cornwalliss letter in the papers

Sunday 25th Novr. fine morng.   went to Town, to see Rd. & to try if anything could be done at present in my affairs,   put the Company into their Hutts.   spoke to the Adjt. Genl. who says it can't be carried on till Stirling is gone, or his objections removed, but I find his rancour & malevolence still continues, so I must wait – din'd with my little friends who have taken a passage in the Walter for Glasgow & wish I was going with them so do I, they expect to embark about the 1st. Decr. – rain in the afternoon

Monday 26th. Novr. 1781   all the ships from Virginia with prisrs. come in except one, the Lord Mulgrave in which are above 100 officers of the Light Infantry, 17th. 23d. 33d. & 43d. 71st. &ca. they sail'd about the 2nd. inst & had 4 weeks provision,   all concern'd are very uneasy about them – The Amphion come in from a Cruise
spoke to Dickson & desir'd him to fix his credit with Capt. Elphinston before he goes away, as when Stirling is gone I shall open a transaction

Tuesday 27th. Novr. 1781   fine wr.   bot. some wine & left Town, a great deal of it broke[;] Mr. Gracie you must make it good, din'd with the 76th. & came home in the eveng. & found a Card to dine at Hd.Qrs. St. Andrews day & with Judge Ludlow on thursday

Wednesday 28th. Snow & Sleet no parade, this weather against the hutters

Thursday 29th. cold & blowy at north din'd at the Judges, a great party there the two Lt. Colls. were to have been there too but Lord Chewton & Col Yorke are with them today,
borrow'd 20 guineas to give the Comy. for St. Andrew –
wrote some letters to go by friend Rutherfurd

Friday 30th. Novr. 1781. fine wr. Call'd at the Colls. & got a letter to Genl. Delancey about the A.Dy.B.Mr. which I deliver'd to him & told him the Story & got a letter from him to Col: Crosbie which I left at his house
After I got to Town look'd about for a Lodging which is very ill to be got, then call'd on the little couple who don't expect to Embark till next week –
having dress'd & mounted a St. Andrews X went to Hd. Qrs. about four, found the Prince there, with his green Ribbon & Star on, he was recd. by a Captns. Guard of the 42d. with Colours &ca. The Company were near an hour in collecting & it was past five before we sat down to dinner, Genl. Campbell in the Chair as St. Andrew, Major Murray 84th. his Croupier, the Prince on the left hand of the Saint & Adml. Digby on his right the Comr. in chief next the Prince & Genl. Robertson next to ye Adml. Genl. Stirling & Capt. Gayton opposite to Capt. Elphin-ston & Genl. Hamilton, after that every body sat down as they happened to come in, about 45 in number the table in form of ⊢, a very good dinner with Several Scotch dishes such as Sheepshead broth, cocky licky, a Haggies &ca.
after dinner a course of General toasts were given for the occa-sion, & a number of sentiments, the Band of Musick & the Pipes of the 42d. play'd alternately, & the little Prince being highly pleas'd with the Piper gave him a bumper after every tune, & behaved himself so properly that he was admired by every body there – The Comr. in chief's family din'd at Roubalets & sent a deputation by Majr. Hanger which was returned by Capt. Scot, we sat & drank moderately till near 11 o'clock when the Croupier having given a round of our Brother Saints summ'd up the Senti-

497

ments with – May our Royal Master be serv'd, as well as he is lov'd, by all the Sons of those Saints we have given; to which the whole Company Stood up & drank a bumper The Prince was then ask'd for a Lady, & he gave the Dutchess of Devonshire, & his Carriage being come he went off with Adml. & ye. Company broke up went to Roubalets & Sup'd, where got a very indifferent bed & no conveniences –

Saturday 1st. Decr. 1781 a Ship from Glasgow (the Ruby) arrived at the hook two days ago but not yet come up – seal'd my letters & gave them to [John] R[utherfur]d. vizt. 1 to AH. enclos'd to my Father, one Dotr. Fleeming, one to R:M: & one to Lord Eglintoun with a doz: young Pippen trees & [to] Dick R[utherfur]d. a letter for Potts, Barbadoes he had lik'd to have miss his Passage, the Prince William went down this morng for the West Indies; & the Warrick gone to sea Recd. 30 guineas from Mr. Goold in part of 180 left in his hand by Rd. my balance & came home to dinner

Sunday 2d. Decr. fine weather & so was Monday

Tuesday 4th. Decr. 1781 cold & cloudy, rain in the Evening sent my Batman to Town with some poultry for the little couple, they talk of the fleet dropping down Thursday or Friday

Wednesday 5th. Decr. snow in the morning, which prevented me from going to Town

Thursday 6th. went to Town to bid my little friends farewell din'd at Roubalets with the Major & a party club 48/ had Rivingtons Claret the best I ever drank in this country 14/ a bottle, – sup'd at the Coffee house & slepd at Mrs. Brandons a lodging house 5/ a night –

Friday 7th. all passingers &ca. going on board, the fleet lying in the North River ready to drop down, about 100 Sail bid my little friends farewell they went on board in the Eveng – I went out to Greenwich & with the Major & got fou The Octr. Pacquet arrived in 45 days the Septr. Pacquet sail'd 3 weeks before her & also a fleet for this Country with Lord Dunmore to go to Virga. &

take possession of his Government again. got three letters in the Eveng. one from my Fr. dated 24 Septr. acknowledging mine of the 10th. & 20th. July inclosing the Bill of 60 one from my little friend dated at Logan 21st. Septr. in answer to mine of 23 July all well & happy with her couzins – One from the Agent in answer to mine of 21st. July & 13 Augt. he has purchased a lottery ticket for me No. 33139 cost £14.9.6

Saturday 8th. Decr. fine weather took a long walk with the Major &ca. along the Quarters of the Regt. which extends from Greenwich to Jones's house about 6 miles the officers very well lodged, but the men not & much scatter'd – came back to dinner & staid another night with them some of the fleet drop'd down to ye. narrows

Sunday 9th. Decr. 1781 a Storm of Snow – Came into Town & intended to go home but the weather so bad that I staid & din'd with Mr. McCree, reter'd to my lodging in the eveng. & wrote a letter to my AH: in answer to her last of 21st. Sepr.

Monday 10th. some snow in the Morng. but the day clear'd up, finish'd my letter & gave to a man at whiteHall who was just going down to the Robust with the last dispatches – cross'd the ferry about 1 o'clock with Todd & came home together, & I din'd with him at the opposite Mess; pretty well I thank you –

Tuesday 11th. The fleet all down at Staten Island. some say the young Prince is going home, Lord Cornwallis goes in the Robust. Major Brodrick appointed to 1st. B:Grrs.
Jamaica Wednesday 12 Decr. 1781 – fine clear cold frosty weather. a Vessel arrived from Charlestown in 10 days who bring word that the Lord Mulgrave had arrived there all safe & were to leave that soon for this place. that Genl. Greene was within 24 miles of Chas.Town, but Major Craig & all the other troops from the outposts being come in, the Garrison was near 8000 strong which will [bid] defiance to Mr. Greene

Thursday 13th. some more arrivals from ChasTown, the

Camel they say, & we are told that the Septr. Pacquet was to call at ChasTown.

N.B. there was a very ungentleman like altercation at our Mess last night. I hope they will settle it properly –

Friday 14th. fine cold wr. still   sent to Town for some necessaries for ye. Coy. & the New Coats,   our New Major come to join the fleet still at the Narrows

Saturday 15th. Decr. 1781   The Homeward bound fleet sail'd today under convoy of the Robust & Janus   Lord Cornwallis Genl. Arnold Col York Col Dundas & Col Tarleton & some others gone in the Robust, Mrs. Arnold gone in a private ship – at a Club in the eveng at Rochforts to be every Saturday night –

Jamaica Long Island Sunday 16th. Decr. put on our New Cloathing   fine wr. went to church & heard Mr. Bowden (formerly a Lt. in the 46th. Regt.[)] preach a Philosophical Sermon on the Subject of future rewards & punishments which he thinks perfectly agreeable to the justice of God –
The Camel arrived from ChasTown   all well there, part of the Army in the Country 20 Miles, but Mr. Greene makes them keep a Sharp look out –

Jamaica Monday 17th. Decr. 1781   Clear frosty weather & NW wind

Tuesday & Wednesday nothing extra   The officers of Lord Cornwallis's army that left Virginia in the Lord Mulgrave & put into Chas.Town are arrived in three ships except a few who staid behind on account of their health

Thursday 20th. Decr. rainy morning the snow all gone –

Friday 21st. hard frost & clear   Went to Town & spoke to the Adjt. Genl. about getting my affair brought forward he seems to be Willing & spoke also to the Major who has no objections if Drumond does not hold out the regulation.   return'd to dinner with intention to go to the Assembly but I found it was carried on by a few in their own way that I wod. not go –

Saturday 22d. Decr. 1781 Jamaica went to Town again in the morning to the Adjt. Genl. but he was so busy expediting the ChasTown fleet that I could not see him this fleet carries thither all absent offrs. & odd men that belong to the Southward under convoy of the Charles Town din'd & spent the Eveng. at Mr. Foxcrofts

Sunday 23d. went with the Major to the Adjt. Genl. who agree to the transaction with any one Lt. that we can find proper for the Regt. & that will give the price. Drummond is off & I believe Dickson will get it, if Capt. Elphinston arrives in time to indorse his Bills din'd with the Major at his Qrs. where we bung'd our eye as usual there & staid all night – The Charlestown fleet sail'd – the Europe expected to sail on Sunday next

Monday 24th. Decr. 1781 blows hard & it came on to snow about noon cross'd the ferry when it was very rough a boat overset just before & a sailor drown'd we got safe over but it was near enough had a very disagreeable ride home with the wind & snow right in my face

Tuesday 25th. Xmass The ground cover'd with snow as usual at this Season of mirth & festivity, & the sleighs flying about. Our Mess being engaged to dine with the Mess over the way, we met at the usual hour vizt. 4 o'clock sat down to a good dinner and took hearty drink, which is to be repeated at our Mess on New Years day. with some intermediate drinks with other people, in this manner we live & go on, trying to procure pleasure at the expense of the constitution

Jamaica Wednesday 26th. Decr. 1781 a drunken parade – call'd at the Ludlows & Ogdens to bid them the Complets. of the Season, & din'd at the Judges en famille Dickson gone to Town to push forward this affair of purchase, the Warwick is come in from a cruize –

Thursday 27th. had the lads of the 40th. to dine

Friday 28th. thaw & rain a sober day at home, intend for Town tomorrow

Saturday 29th. frost again a melancholly accident happened last night – some young Gentlen. din'd at Capt. [Gilbert] Afflects of the 63d. about a mile west from the Village, among whom was Lt. Stedman of the 64th. they drank hard after dinner, & 'tween 8 & 9 o'clock took it into their head to go to New York[5]

New York 31st. Decr. 1781. thaw & rain in the Morning – waited for Mr. Dickson till 1/2 past one, tho' he promised to be in at ten & I met him a[t] Brooklyn about 2 o'clock. he went over to show his letters to Capt. E: & I came home to dinner, very dirty roads

poor Stedman was burried yesterday it did not appear on examination that there were any mark of violence sufficient to have caused his death, it was supposed the horse drag'd him for some way as his Cloaths were much torn – he like Lt. Curry had had an involuntary stool, or perhaps after death when the retentive faculty is gone, the contents of the intestines come away – he is about £200 in debt & his Father not well able to pay it is another distressing circumstance to the family –

The Pandora arrived from Quebec in about 6 weeks, all well there a Schooner from ChasTown in 14 days all quiet Mr. Greene retiring, may be to Savanah a ship from Jamaica in 11 weeks

Jamaica Long Island 1st. Janry. 1782. May this year be propitious to our wishes my dear little woman, & bring us together in peace, love, & safety. having engaged our Neighbours over the way to dine with us, we had a very good dinner, plenty of wine, with mirth & good humour, till some were fou & then we parted about midnight – the fleet I hear is sail'd

Wednesday 2d. Janry. it blew very hard last night & still continues abt. N.W. with frost

Thursday 3d. Janry. mild wr. a great Party gone to Town to a Ball by subscription at Roubalets

Friday 4th. fine mild soft weather & dirty roads, took a ride

down south with Capt. Cr. who came home to dinner with us –
N.B. a number of the Men of the Compy. got the itch put them
under cure – we then went out to Greenwich & din'd with Dr.
Robertson, pretty well to [word illegible] Slept at the Majors –
The Bonita Sloop of war that the french took a[t] Yorktown
Virga. arrived at New York today prize to the Amphion wt. 120
french soldiers on board bound to the west Indies –

Thursday 10th. Janry. 1782 soft got 2 musters Cash for the
Compy. to the 24th. Decr. from Ensn. Rose two days ago &
Subce. for myself to 23d. Febry. & lodged the money with Mr.
Goold, I took up today 220 guineas & came home with this to
clear the Company – nobody at the Mess but the Docr. & me
things does not go on so well there. I find we are to be muster'd
tomorrow & I find that every body here knows more of intentions
than I imagined
   A Detachment of about 200 consisting of 100 Light from
Powles hook under the Command of Capt. Ball, 50 from the 40th
Regt. & 50 from the 42d. the whole under the Command of Capt.
Beckwith Aid de Camp to Genl. Kniphausen set off yesterday in
the new constructed boats about one o'clock; they drop'd down
to Denys's in the afternoon and in the night went up the Rariton
as far as Brunswick with an intention of burning some boats that
were said to be getting ready there for hostile purposes they got
to brunswick a little before day & were fir'd on by the Guard and
wod. Capt. Ball & another officer & kill'd & wound'd 8 or 10 men
of the party, who however went into Brunswick, destroy'd 2 or 3
boats & return'd today[6]

Monday 21st. Janry. 1782 clear & cold our mess were
engaged to dine with the 54th. Regt. at Flushing, where they had
a great Cockfight, & 1st. Febry. there is to be a Horse Race, a
sack race, & a grinning match all in the Regt. – I staid till past
nine & left them at it

Tuesday 22d. hard frost & very cold & came on snow in the
afternoon din'd at Judge Ludlows where there was a great party,

well chosen   I sent my Negro Boy there, to remain or not as we might agree,   I ask 16 guineas for him, which is near about what he has cost me since I had him.

I hear the Pacquet goes on thursday   I must therefore go to Town tomorrow to try if I can get my affair settled & go with her, tho' it is expensive

Wednesday 23d Janry. 1782   a Snow Storm all night which still continues, so that there is no travelling today nor even stirring out –

Thursday 24th. a good deal of Snow on the ground which has drifted & stopped up the roads, therefore staid at home all day again – The Judge sent back my Negro Boy having discover'd that he had the Itch

Friday 25th. very cold with the wind to the Southward of West – I went to the ferry in a Sleigh, where I found there was a good deal of Ice in the River & very bad crossing, however I got over with some difficulty, & I call'd on the Adjt. Genl. who told [me] the Memol. wt. some others were still before the Genl. not yet decided upon nor can't be till the Pacquet is gone, which is to Sail tomorrow the Mail to be closed tonight   I put in my letter at the Post office to AH: telling her how far the Matter was carried, together with my reasons & intentions

I spoke to the Major & ask'd him to come to our Assembly, but he declin'd it for want of Cloaths & not time to see the Commandant, which I was sorry for, as I brought a Sleigh on purpose to bring him up & had provided a dinner – I cross'd the ferry again about 2 oclock easier than before, & took up Col Marsh who was at a loss for a Conveyance.   being disappointed of my Company I din'd with Cunningham & went together to the Assembly in the Eveng, which was more numerous than usual, 17 Ladies young & old, they all danced tho' few of them handsome, Polly McIvers bears the Bell, She is really a pretty Girl with face like Eloisa's –

Saturday 26th. Janry. 1782   had a head ach all day which I don't know the cause of, & is new to me – I took a long walk thro' the Snow & din'd with Major Scott at Col: Marsh's Mess where my head ach went off by degrees   They live in a style & drink Claret

Sunday 27th. thaw & some rain   I din'd with Col: Marsh where there was a pretty large party, who went to cards about 8 o'clock & I came home. they play too deep for me.

Monday 28th. wet & slopy in the morng. with a cold S.W. wind, which came to W in the afternoon & froze hard   din'd with Capt. Dalrymple at Major Brownlow's, they two live together & give claret to their friends,   'tis out of my power to give equal returns to this manner of feasting. as we have no Mess I live by myself.

Tuesday 29th. Janry. 1782. very hard frost, & cold sharp wind to the Northd. of west. I hear the Pacquet sail'd yesterday with a fair wind. 20 passengers
the Boy Edmondston came & din'd wt. me he is recommended to succeed Dickson

Wednesday 30th. last night & today the hardest frost, & coldest weather that has been known here these 20 years   a good fire & a bottle of Port helped to keep out the cold, had the above two to dine &ca.

Thursday 31st. moderate wr. I hear the North River is froze over below Greenwich, & the East River almost closed at the ferry – sat a Court Martial at the Hutts in the Officers guardroom. din'd alone, & read Cardinal DeRetz Memoires,[7] who exposes the intrigues of a court in Odious but true colours

Friday 1st. Febry. 1782   had a parade & a punishment after which rode out for a few miles on the York road, cold & raw din'd alone, drink my pint of port & read my book & walk about the room till nine, then take a draught of grog & a little bread & cheese & go to bed about ten; as our Mess is broke up, I can't think of forming or going into another till I see the issue of this affair at Hd.Qrs. & then take my measures accordingly.

Saturday 2d. Febry. clear & cold a ride down south after parade call'd at the Judges & got the History of Phillip 2d. din'd & spent the Eveng solus, aut supra, for Grant is seldom at home, & Dickson lives wt. his whore –
I hear the Kings Speech is come to Philada. which they say is in the usual Style, of Carrying on the war with Vigour

Sunday 3d. Febry. 1782 a great fall of Snow, but not cold; kept the house all day –

Monday 4th. clear mild weather & fine sleighing – The Coll. Major & a great many of our officers in Town by which means I find I command the Battn. in which there is nothing to do at present but to dismiss the parade & receive the Reports.
Capt. Simmondson call'd to get a Copy of my Memol. he being determined to sell out for reasons which I think with him are very good, we took a ride together & I din'd with him. he is a Sensible & honest man, & good old Soldier character

Tuesday 5th. Febry. 1782 – very fine mild weather & excellent sleighing – rode out till two din'd alone; scribbled & mus'd

Wednesday 6th. the fine wr. continues – I went to N:York in the Morng. saw Col: Delancey in the street who told me the Comr. in chief had agreed to my affair & that it would be out in orders in a day or two on which I made my bows & thank'd him, & ask'd when I could see the Genl. to thank him & take my leave[;] today or tomorrow he said or any morng. I pleas'd – I hear'd of a Brig going to Liverpool, but upon Enquiry find she is fill'd up & there is no room, she is very Small & can only take three passengers – saw the Major & told him what the Adjt. Genl. said, ask'd him to come up on Friday, but he says he is engaged he proposes my coming to his Qrs. & making up a Mess there –
took up 20 guineas from Mr. Goold left Town about two & came home to dinner, a very warm ride –

Thursday 7th. Febry. very warm call'd on Mrs. Judge Ludlow & got a book took a long walk & spent the rest of the day & Eveng. at home solus. Capt. Home call'd & left a message for me to dine with him today, but I am not in Spirits to go anywhere, Col Fox ask'd me for tomorrow –

Friday 8th. like for snow or rain having ordered the Company to parade at my Quarters at 1/2 after ten   I sent for Lts. Grant & Dickson to come to breakfast that they might be present, when I spoke to the Company about my leaving them. Dickson came but Grant did not – The Company having come at the time appointed we went out & look'd at them & found them very clean,   I then order'd the Ranks to close & spoke to them as follows vizt.

Royal Highland Grenadiers   I am sorry that I am going soon to leave you – in doing which I very much regret my leaving so respectable a Regt. & Corps as that to which I belong, & the Company I have the honour to Command, with whom I have served so long with satisfaction & pleasure to myself   If any of you has any claims or demands on me as your Captain I shall remain here for some days yet & will readily listen to them & satisfy them with justice & as I intend to take the first opportunity of going home to Scotland, if you have any letters to send, or anything that I can do for you there I will do it with pleasure; And Gentlemen, I earnestly hope that you will always preserve that good name you are so justly possess'd of whether in Qrs. or the field, And in all your future services I sincerely wish you all, that honour, Success, & happiness which your merit & good behaviour so well deserves –

I could hardly make an end of this little speech, my voice faulter'd, and my knees shook under me. I was glad to get into my room where my heart swell'd at the thoughts of it. I saw the poor fellows were affected too – I order'd them five gallons of Rum to make a drink of grog in the Eveng.

din'd with Col: Fox & went from them to the Assembly which was pretty crowdd.   danced with Mrs. Judge Ludlow   staid till 12 o'clock & came home to bed.   it was both raining freezing

Jamaica Saturday 9th. Febry. 1782   it froze hard last night & blows cold at NW   call'd on the Ladies at the Judges, who are nothing the worse of their dancing –

Sunday 9th [10th][8] a cold raw wind from S.W. din'd with a party at Drury's, where we drank upwards of 2 bottles of Madeira each, with good humour & friendship. I am sensible of these peoples kindness for me & shall feel the want of such society by & by.

Monday 10th [11th] a mild day took a long walk, din'd at home alone, & drank no wine –

Tuesday 11th.[12th] pretty cold several people call'd, Dickson staid to dine he says our affair is in Orders –

Wednesday 12th.[13th] Febry. 1782. thaw I hear there is a 20 Gun Ship arrived from England in 8 weeks – The Narcissus Capt. Edwards with dispatches – The Kings Speech 27 Nov. in the same steady strain of carrying on the war – Sir Geo: Rodney gone to the West Indies with 10 sail of the line, & Adml. Kempenfelt out with 12 or 13 sail of 3 deckers –

Thursday 14th. Febry. 1782 a Ride to the Plains with Judge Ludlow whose conversation is both instructing & entertaining on all Subjects; we call'd at the Colls. & Dor. Laurences &ca. – din'd with Capt. Home where there was a great party: & drank hard as usual

Friday [15th] a fine warm day, took a long walk, din'd alone, & read Montesquieu Persian Letters[9] – must go to Town tomorrow to see about the Ruby who I hear is to sail soon & pave the way for my departure

Saturday 16th. Febry. 1782 thaw went to Town in the Morng. & bespoke a passage in the Ruby for Glasgow, they expect to be ready to sail on thursday next went to Hd.Qrs. to wait on the General but he was so busy I could not see him ask'd to dine there on tuesday. din'd with Major Cortland, when I told Mrs. Cortland that I expected to go in a few days for Scotland, she burst out a crying, – came home in the eveng. very dirty roads indeed

Sunday 17th. fine mild weather. went about taking leave of my friends & leaving cards where I don't find ym. at home

Monday 18th. soft wr. still & warm. had a great many visits to bid farewell

Tuesday 19th. Febry. 1782 a Snowy day but not cold call'd on Judge Ludlows family & bid them farewell, agreed to correspond with the judge – set off for Town & left orders for my Baggage to come tomorrow din'd at HeadQrs. his Ex: did not come in from playing ball till past 5 a 1/4

Wednesday 20th. cold got my Baggage & horse over; lodge at Mrs. Brandons maiden lane at 5/ a night 3 in a hole of a room din'd at Strahans with a party of the Regt. drank claret; went to an oyster house

Thursday 21st. cold, went out to the [42d] Regt. for a few days – din'd with the Major today & staid there all night, comme il faut

Friday 22d. with Dr. Robison & Saturday 23d. with Capt. Smith, having a set of bedding carrying about –
A Number of promotions in the Genl. Orders today, which clears me of the service

Sunday 24th. Febry. 1782 din'd wt. Mr. Goold who is always very civil, on Monday with the Major & a party at Strahans & went in the Eving. to the play vizt. [Sir John Vanbrugh's] the provok'd wife, rather overdone a Miss something sung the very well – called on the Secretary for my blank Ensigncy,

Tuesday 26th. din'd at Hd.Qrs. his Ex. very facetious, I took an oppoy. after dinner to make my bows & thank him which was very graciously recd. & desir'd to see me before I go

Wednesday 27th. Din'd with Col Abercromby, in great taste

Thursday 28th. Capt. Campbell of the 74th. beg'd of me if I went to Edinn. to speak to his Man of business about raising money to purchase Thompsons Majority – he ask'd me to dine at Genl. Gunnings & Majors Graham & Fraser

Friday 1st. March 1782 NYork   Saw the Genl. [Sir Henry Clinton] on the parade who asked when I was to go on board & told him tomorrow at 11 o'clock & he desir'd he might see me din'd with Mr. Foxcroft   There is great news current in Town today of Sir Saml. Hoods having beat the french fleet in the West Indies about the 27th. Janry. & that the french troops in their attacks on brimstonehill St: Kitts were repulsed with the loss of 800 & moreover there is also a Report of Adml. Rodney having arrived at Barbadoes with 10 ships of the line & also that Admiral Kempenfeld had taken 10 Ships of the line in the Channel, all this News comes thro the Rebel Country – put all our Baggage stock stores &ca. on board, as we expect to sail tomorrow Morning –

Saturday 2d. March 1782   cold with a little snow wind NNW The Ruby made a signal for sailing in the Morning; busy taking up letters & bidding farewell.   met the Generals Secretary Capt. Smith in the Street who told me that his Ex: wanted to see me at 1/2 after ten, I accordingly went & after waiting some time Major Montgomery & I were introduced into a private room where we found his Ex busy en deshabille just finishing some letters – he then open'd a conversation addressing himself to Major Montgomery & me relative to the letters betwixt him & Lord Cornwallis on the Affairs of the Chesapeak, some of which letters had been seen by the public others not but all printed – he wish'd us to understand that his conduct & instructions to Lord Cornwallis about taking post in Virga. was not so subject to blame as[10]

Saturday Morning 2d. March   I met with the Generals Secry. Capt. Smith in the Street who told me that his Excellency wanted to see me at half after 10 o'clock. I accordingly went to Hd.Quarters and after waiting a little time was introduced into a private room where I found his Exy. busy en deshabille just finishing some Letters, he then open'd a conversation relative to the Letters betwixt him & Lord Cornwallis on the affairs of the Chesapeak, some of which letters had been seen by the publick others not. he wish'd me to understand that his conduct and Instructions to Lord Cornwallis about taking post in Virginia was not so subject to blame as might be implied from his Lordships Letter of the 20th. Octr. And that the delay in coming to his relief was not his fault, nor had he given him positive assurances of doing so, as it depended on the Fleet. & a great deal more in order to make it appear that the taking post at York & Glocester was more Lord Cornwallis's own choice than his pointing out – Ordering at the same time Capt. Smith to read the respective letters on that Subject, which he had printed in a Pamphlet, His Excy. also told me that he had expressed to Lord Cornwallis after he came to New York, both in conversation & by letter, that he wished him to alter that part of his letter of the 20th. Octr. which might bear the implication of its being the Commander in Chiefs orders & not his own choice the taking post at York & Glocester in Virginia. and a great deal more on that Subject to exculpate himself from all blame in the Choice of that Post & Surrender of the Troops.

He then gave me a Pamphet containing his conduct & correspondence with Sir Peter Parker in Carolina in 1776, & in it also some letters to & from Admiral Arbuthnot which had not been publish'd – he also mentioned the circumstance of Engineers tools which his Lordship complained of the want of, he said he sent 2000 at one time, & 400 at another, he also express'd his hope that Lord Cornwallis would in his place in the House of Lords do away all matter of blame imputed to him in his letter of the 20th. Octr., he then wish'd me well & a happy Voyage, I bowed & took leave, – Got the dispatches from the Secretary who saw me to wharf but having miss'd our own boat he got one on which I went on board at 12 oclock the ship lying to below the battery

Appendix A

Biographical Notes

This appendix contains biographical sketches of the individuals who appear most frequently and prominently in John Peebles' diary. Although Peebles usually referred to colleagues and acquaintances by their surnames, he sometimes used initials for his family and closest friends. Here is a list of regularly used abbreviations.

TA	Tom Arthur
Ld E	Archibald Montgomerie, Earl of Eglintoun
Fr	John Peebles' father, John Peebles
Dr F	Dr Charles Fleeming
Col Billy	Lieutenant-Colonel William Grant
AH	Anna Hamilton
DM/RM	Dick Marshall
R,Rd.	John Rutherfurd

Abercromby, Robert (1740–1827). Abercromby, who had served with distinction in North America during the Seven Years' War, became lieutenant-colonel of the 37th Regiment in 1773 and commander of the 1st Battalion of Light Infantry in October 1776. He proved an aggressive and successful leader during the Philadelphia, Charleston, and Yorktown campaigns. He further distinguished himself in India and died the oldest general in the army.

Arbuthnot, Marriot (1711–94). Having commanded at Halifax at the beginning of the American War, Rear-Admiral Arbuthnot became commander-in-chief of the North American squadron in August 1779. During the next two years, he proved incapable both of cooperating with the British army and of acting vigorously on his own. He frustrated Sir Henry Clinton during the siege of Charleston and the ensuing summer at New York (allowing the French to take Newport), and he fought the French inconclusively off the Chesapeake in March 1781. He was recalled in June 1781.

Arnold, Benedict (1741–1801). An inspiring but reckless commander of men, Arnold served the American cause effectively in 1776 and 1777. When his plot to betray the American post at West Point was exposed in 1780, he fled to New York and served the British as a brigadier-general in command of detachments in the Chesapeake and on Long Island Sound. After the war he became a merchant in England.

Arthur, Tom. Arthur, of Irvine, Ayrshire, invested in cargoes shipped to New York and corresponded regularly with John Peebles during the American War.

Burgoyne, John (1722–92). When the War for American Independence began, Burgoyne was a major-general, member of Parliament, and playwright. Although he had served in the War of the Austrian Succession and the Seven Years' War, he had had little experience as a commander. He was at Boston in 1775 and in Canada in 1776 in supporting roles. Each winter he went home to criticize his superiors and to suggest that he could do better, that he would be a determined and victorious commander. When at last he got his chance – leading an army from Canada south across Lake Champlain in 1777 – he proved far too determined for his own good. Without adequate cooperation from New York and without a secure source of supply (he gave up his communications with Canada in a country that could not feed his army), he persisted in trying to reach Albany – to live up to his own boastful rhetoric. Blocked and held along the upper Hudson River, he was forced to surrender at Saratoga in October 1777. His defeat brought France into the war and seriously reduced Britain's prospects of success. He did not serve again in America.

Byron, John (1723–86). Vice-Admiral Byron appeared only briefly and ineffectively in the War for American Independence. In the spring of 1778 he was ordered to North America in pursuit of a French squadron under Admiral d'Estaing. But delayed in leaving Britain and battered by a storm in the Atlantic, Byron was unable to assemble his ships in America until mid-October, three months after d'Estaing had reached New York. Byron eventually followed d'Estaing to the West Indies where in July 1779 he attacked him inadvisedly and unsuccessfully. That October Byron went home, ill.

Campbell, John. A veteran of the Seven Years' War in North America, Campbell entered the American War as lieutenant-colonel of the 37th Regiment. He commanded British troops on Staten Island in 1777–8 and in West Florida, 1779–81 (with the local rank of major-general). He surrendered Pensacola to a large Spanish force in May 1781, was paroled to New York, and promoted to lieutenant-general.

Campbell, Mungo. As lieutenant-colonel of 52nd Regiment, Campbell commanded foraging parties in New Jersey during the winter of 1777 (failing on February 23 to support John Peebles' company). He was killed during Clinton's attack on the Highlands of the Hudson in the autumn of 1777.

Cathcart, William, Lord (1755–1843). After studying law, Cathcart bought a commission in the 7th Dragoons and entered the American War as a volunteer with Clinton in 1777. He became a captain in the 17th Dragoons and served at Philadelphia and Monmouth in 1778, raised a force of Scottish volunteers (Cathcart's British Legion), and went with his Legion to

Charleston in 1780. Ill, he returned to command the 38th Regiment in New Jersey and then to go home in October 1780. He served in the wars of the French Revolution and Napoleon and represented Britain as ambassador to Russia and at the Congress of Vienna.

Clinton, Sir Henry (1730–95). A veteran of the Seven Years' War in Germany and a member of Parliament, Clinton served in the American War as third in command to Thomas Gage (1775) and second to Sir William Howe (1775–8). From May 1778 until May 1782 he was commander-in-chief. He was a learned and able tactician, but he lacked the confidence to be an effective general officer, to advocate his ideas forcefully with superiors or to impose them firmly on subordinates. He succeeded in evacuating Philadelphia and in securing New York and Rhode Island in 1778; and he took Charleston by siege in 1780. Otherwise, he failed to engage Washington in a general action, to cooperate with the British navy in attacking the French at Rhode Island, to keep Lord Cornwallis from invading Virginia, and to relieve him once he had been trapped at Yorktown.

Collier, Sir George (1738–95), entered the American War in 1775 as captain of the frigate *Rainbow*. He soon demonstrated his energy and skill – both in supporting the army at New York in 1776 and in commanding the few ships stationed at Halifax, 1776–8. For four months in 1779, while acting commander-in-chief of the North American squadron, he was remarkably successful in cooperating with the army in raiding Virginia and Connecticut, capturing Stony and Verplancks Points, and relieving Penobscot. Rather than serve under Arbuthnot, he went home to command a ship of the line and to enter Parliament. He served briefly as an admiral in the wars of the French Revolution.

Cornwallis, Charles, Earl (1738–1805). A student of European warfare and a veteran of the Seven Years' War in Germany, Cornwallis volunteered to serve in the American War out of a sense of duty (he had opposed taxing the colonists). He commanded portions of the army under Sir William Howe and Sir Henry Clinton in the campaigns of 1776–8 in the middle colonies. After the British captured Charleston in May 1780, Cornwallis remained to command in the southern colonies. He won battles and marched after the rebels, but he did not have the patience or, perhaps, the forces to carry out Clinton's plan for a gradual restoration of British authority in the South. After a pyrrhic victory at Guilford Court House in March 1781, Cornwallis took his army to Virginia where he was trapped and forced to surrender at Yorktown. He, nevertheless, emerged from the American War with a reputation for energetic leadership and went on to distinguish himself as governor-general of British India.

Crosbie, William, who was a major in the 7th Regiment (October 1778) and lieutenant-colonel in the 60th (August 1780) and in the 22nd (June 1781), served on Sir Henry Clinton's staff as barrack-master-general.

Dalrymple, William (d. 1807). Having served as lieutenant-colonel of the 14th

Regiment at Boston before the War for American Independence, he commanded the garrison on Staten Island during the New York campaign of 1776 and, possibly, the 79th Regiment in the West Indies in 1778 and 1779. By May 1780 Dalrymple had returned to the army in North America as quartermaster-general and as Sir Henry Clinton's emissary and advisor during the last months of the war.

DeGrasse, François Joseph Paul, Comte (1722–88), was an able, experienced naval officer who served as a division commander of French fleets in Europe and North America during the opening years of the War for American Independence. In 1781, when promoted to rear-admiral and sent with a squadron of warships to the West Indies, he used his discretionary power to leave the West Indies and join a Franco-American army in besieging Lord Cornwallis at Yorktown, Virginia. He kept the British North American squadron at bay until Cornwallis surrendered. Although captured in the West Indies the following April, he helped while a prisoner to negotiate the treaty that ended the war.

DeLancey, Oliver (1718–85). A veteran of provincial service in the Seven Years' War and a successful New York merchant and politician, DeLancey raised a brigade of 1500 Loyalists, DeLancey's New York Volunteers, at the beginning of the War for American Independence. Two of the three battalions in this brigade eventually served in the southern colonies; the third remained with DeLancey on Long Island. He left New York with the British in 1783 and died in exile.

DeLancey, Oliver (1749–1822). Born in New York but educated in England, DeLancey made his career in the British army. He served throughout the War for American Independence in North America – with his regiment in the New York, New Jersey, and Pennsylvania campaigns of 1776–8 and then successively as deputy quartermaster-general, deputy adjutant-general, and adjutant-general of the army under Sir Henry Clinton. After the war, he returned to England, became a member of Parliament, and rose to the rank of general in the British army.

Digby, Robert (1732–1814), who had been promoted to rear-admiral in 1779 and served as second in command of the Channel fleet, reached New York in September 1781 to replace Thomas Graves as commander-in-chief of the North American squadron. Because Graves was preparing to sail to relieve Cornwallis, Digby did not assume command until after the relief expedition had failed. He soon went home, ending his service at sea.

Eglintoun, Archibald Montgomerie, Earl of (1726–96), raised the 62nd (later the 77th) Regiment in 1757 and commanded it in North America during the Seven Years' War. By 1776 he was colonel of the 51st Regiment, a major-general in the army, and a representative peer for Scotland. He tried to use his influence to advance the career of John Peebles who had served in his regiment and was an Ayrshire neighbor.

Elphinstone, Hon. George Keith (1746–1823), served in North American waters from 1776 to 1780, convoying transports, enforcing a blockade of rebel ports, and taking part in the siege of Charleston. He went home in 1780, assumed command of the *Warwick*, and after distinguishing himself by capturing a Dutch warship, returned to America for the remainder of the war. During the wars of the French Revolution and Napoleon, he had many successful commands – ending his service as Admiral Lord Keith.

Erskine, Sir William (1728–95). Having served with distinction during Seven Years' War in Germany, he sailed for America in the spring of 1776 and was soon appointed brigadier-general in command of the three battalions of the 71st Regiment. He became quartermaster-general of the army at New York in October 1776 but continued to lead troops in battle. He resigned his posts and went home in the summer of 1779.

Estaing, Charles Hector Théodat Comte d' (1729–94), commanded a French expeditionary force in North America and the West Indies during the campaigns of 1778 and 1779. Although he thoroughly disrupted British operations, he did not achieve what he or the Americans hoped he would. He reached New York in July 1778, too late to intercept the British who were withdrawing from Philadelphia. He subsequently decided not to attack the British fleet at New York or, after his ships had suffered damage in a hurricane, to join the Americans in besieging the British garrison at Rhode Island. In the autumn of 1778 he went to the West Indies where he captured and held St. Vincent and Grenada. But when he returned to North America in September 1779, he was again unsuccessful in cooperating with the Americans. The combined Franco-American attack on Savannah failed; and d'Estaing, severely wounded, returned to France.

Ferguson, Patrick (1744–80). At the beginning of the War for American Independence, Ferguson invented a breech-loading rifle and raised a band of riflemen in his regiment, the 70th. He led that band at the Battle of Brandywine (1777) and in a raid on Little Egg Harbor, New Jersey (1780). Appointed major in the 71st Regiment, he created an even larger irregular force of 300 men which he commanded at Charleston in the spring of 1780 and in the Carolinas until his death at the Battle of King's Mountain in October 1780. He was a principled, creative professional soldier who became mired in destructive partisan warfare.

Fleeming, Dr Charles. To judge exclusively from John Peebles' correspondence and diary, Fleeming seems to have been a physician of Irvine, Ayrshire. It is possible that Peebles got some of his early training in pharmacy and medicine with Fleeming. It is clear that the two were friends from the era of the Seven Years' War and that they remained close friends – and corresponded regularly – throughout the War for American Independence.

Fox, Henry Edward (1755–1811), served in North America from the beginning of the War for American Independence. The son of a former secretary at war and leader of the House of Commons, he had the money, connections, and ability to rise very rapidly in the army. By October 1778, at the age of twenty-three, he was lieutenant-colonel of the 38th Regiment; and in November 1780 he was appointed to command the 2nd Battalion of British Grenadiers. He remained in America until 1782. During the ensuing wars with the French, he held high military and diplomatic posts.

Foxcroft, John, served jointly with Benjamin Franklin as postmaster general of British North America from 1761 until the eve of the American Revolution. Foxcroft then became a leading Loyalist, living on Long Island and entertaining his 'old acquaintance' John Peebles during the last years of the American War.

Gambier, James (1723–89). Rear-Admiral Gambier was able to use his friendship with the first lord of the admiralty to gain appointment as second in command of the North American squadron in 1778. But he was such a foolish man and an incompetent officer that neither Admiral Lord Howe nor General Sir Henry Clinton would entrust him with any responsibility or cooperate with him. Gambier did succeed to the command in America during the winter of 1778–9, but he was promptly recalled and went home in April 1779.

Graham, Charles. Captain Charles Graham was appointed to command the grenadier company of the Black Watch in August 1776. In August 1778 he was promoted to major in the Black Watch and may also have been serving by then as major in the 2nd Battalion of British Grenadiers. He and John Peebles frequently worked and dined together.

Grant, Charles, became a captain and company commander in the Black Watch in March 1776. In 1780 he married a Miss Hunt, but he remained in the Black Watch and a good friend of John Peebles throughout the American War.

Grant, James (1720–1806), served with the 77th in North America during the Seven Years' War and as governor of Florida, 1764–71. When the War for American Independence began, he became a brigadier-general and brigade commander in the British army in the middle colonies. Contemptuous of the rebels, he performed carelessly in the Trenton-Princeton campaign of 1776 and at the Battle of Monmouth in 1778. He then led a detachment that took and held the French West Indies island of St. Lucia. He went home in August 1779.

Grant, William, commanded the grenadier company of the Black Watch when the regiment sailed for America in 1776. He was already a major in the army and became a major of the second battalion of the Black Watch in August 1776. The following August he was promoted to lieutenant-colonel in the army. But after his wife died (May 1778), he seems to have sold his commission and retired from the army.

Graves, Thomas (1725–1802), who entered the American War in 1780 as second in command to Admiral Arbuthnot, became commander-in-chief of the North American squadron in July 1781. When Admiral DeGrasse arrived with the French West Indies squadron to trap Cornwallis at Yorktown,

Graves tried to help. But after fighting DeGrasse inconclusively off the Chesapeake on 5 September, he retired to New York and was so slow repairing his ships that he did not again reach the Chesapeake until Cornwallis had surrendered. Graves escaped blame for this disaster and served again during the wars of the French Revolution.

Grey, Charles (1729–1807), who had served courageously in Europe during the Seven Years' War, came to America in 1776 to command a brigade under Sir William Howe. In the campaigns of 1777 and 1778 he led highly successful attacks on rebel forces at Paoli (Pennsylvania), Tappan (New York), and Bedford (Massachusetts). He then went home – not to serve again until the French Revolution.

Greene, Nathanael (1742–86). Next to George Washington, Nathanael Greene was the most important American general of the War for Independence. A Rhode Island merchant who somehow won appointment as major-general in 1776, he led brigades effectively in the campaigns of 1776 and 1777, served doggedly as quartermaster-general from 1778 to 1780, and came into his own as commander of American forces in the southern colonies, 1780–3. With a small, ragged force of Continentals and militia, he gradually forced the British to give up all of their posts in the South except two ports – proving himself a remarkably able strategist, battlefield commander, and revolutionary leader.

Hamilton, Anna (1741–1812) (Anne or Ann), was the daughter of Charles Hamilton and Isobella McDowall Hamilton of Craighlaw, Wigtownshire. Her father was the collector of the customs in Irvine, Ayrshire, where, it seems likely, she met John Peebles. She and Peebles were well acquainted before the American War and corresponded regularly while he was in America. They married as soon as he returned to Scotland in 1782.

Hamilton, Archibald, a retired British army officer who had married a daughter of Lieutenant-Governor Cadwallader Colden of New York, became a Loyalist during the American Revolution. He was appointed colonel, commanding, of the Queens County, New York, militia and aide-de-camp to Governor William Tryon. For several years he had great power over civil, military, and judicial affairs in Queens County; but he abused his power and created resistance among the people of Queens County to him and to British government.

Heister, Leopold Philip von (1707–77), commanded the first contingent of Hessians to enter the American War. Arriving at New York in July 1776, he took part in the battles of Long Island and White Plains. He was recalled after he had disagreed with Sir William Howe and the Hessians had been defeated at Trenton.

Hood, Sir Samuel (1724–1816), entered the American War in 1780 when he went to the West Indies as second in command to Admiral Rodney. In July 1781 he was sent to North America with fourteen ships of the line to reinforce and serve under Admiral Thomas Graves. An able officer, Hood was not responsible for naval failures in the Yorktown campaign. After Cornwallis' surrender, Hood returned to the West Indies where he distinguished himself in the last year of the war. He commanded briefly in the Mediterranean in the wars of the French Revolution.

Howe, Richard, Lord (1726–99), had established himself before the War for American Independence as a talented, aggressive naval officer and a critic of British policies toward the colonies. In 1776 he sailed for America as a peace commissioner and commander-in-chief of the North American squadron. For at least six months he clearly put greater emphasis on negotiating peace than on destroying the rebellion. Spurned by the colonists and criticized by the British government, he concentrated increasingly in 1777 and 1778 on breaking the rebellion. When the government persisted in criticizing him and his brother (Sir William Howe), he asked to be relieved. He remained in America only long enough to parry a French squadron off New York and Rhode Island in the summer of 1778. He went home to command with great success in the last year of the American War and the opening campaigns of the wars of the French Revolution.

Howe, Sir William (1729–1814), had distinguished himself in North America during the Seven Years' War. When the War for American Independence began, he went to Boston as second in command and led the British attack on Bunker Hill in June 1775. That autumn he became commander-in-chief. Although he commanded at a time when the rebels were inexperienced and without overt foreign aid, he never found a way to end the rebellion. He wavered between destroying the Continental army in battle (so as to restore royal government) and recovering the colonies piecemeal (so as to promote a negotiated settlement). Such an inconsistent prosecution of the war gave the rebels just the opportunities they needed to avoid a crushing defeat and to build a viable army. Thus he captured New York, Rhode Island, and parts of New Jersey in 1776 without destroying the Continental army or breaking the rebellion. In 1777 he took Philadelphia while the rebels managed to isolate and capture another British army advancing south from Canada – managed to win a victory at Saratoga that brought France into the war. Howe, knowing that his policies had failed and that he was coming under increasing criticism, resigned. The British government chose Sir Henry Clinton the new commander-in-chief.

Knyphausen, Wilhelm Baron von (1716–1800), arrived in America with the second contingent of Hessians in October 1776. When his superior, General von Heister, was recalled in early 1777, Knyphausen became commander-in-chief of German troops in America. He led a wing of the British army at the Battle of Brandywine in September 1777, but thereafter, he commanded mainly garrisons and foraging parties. He retired in 1782.

Lafayette, Marquis de (1757–1834), came to America in the summer of 1777 a twenty-year-old nobleman and army officer offering to serve as a volunteer without pay in the rebel forces. Washington soon found him a brave, effective leader who could be trusted with independent commands and who could help secure greater French support for the rebellion. In 1781 Lafayette not only parried Cornwallis in Virginia but also commanded a division of the Franco-American army that forced him to surrender at Yorktown.

Leslie, Alexander (c. 1740–94), was a lieutenant-colonel of the 64th Regiment when the War for American Independence began. After serving at Boston, he went to New York where he commanded a battalion of light infantry and a brigade in the campaign of 1776. His most conspicuous service came in the southern colonies in the last years of the war. He took a detachment to the Chesapeake in late 1780, joined Cornwallis for his invasion of North Carolina that winter, and when Cornwallis invaded Virginia, remained behind to command at Charleston. After Cornwallis' surrender, Leslie presided over the British withdrawal from the remainder of the South.

Lincoln, Benjamin (1733–1810). At the beginning of the War for American Independence Lincoln rose from a lieutenant-colonel of Massachusetts militia to major-general of the Continental army. A sound, tactful administrator, he organized militia for the defense of New York against a British army advancing from Canada in 1777. After recovering from a wound suffered at Saratoga, he was appointed to command American forces at Charleston, South Carolina, and was captured there with his garrison in May 1780. He was subsequently exchanged in time to command American troops under Washington in the Yorktown campaign.

Lincoln, Thomas Pelham Clinton, Earl of (1752–95), the spoiled son of a duke who was an officer in the 1st Regiment of Foot Guards and a member of Parliament, went to America in 1777 to serve with his father's cousin, Sir Henry Clinton. When Clinton became commander-in-chief, he made Lincoln one of his aides-de-camp, his emissary to the government, and eventually a brigade commander. Although Lincoln became more responsible during his service in America, he was often disparaged by fellow officers.

Ludlow, Gabriel G., brother of George Duncan Ludlow, was lieutenant-colonel of the 3rd Battalion of DeLancey's New York Volunteers. He and his battalion, which John Peebles thought the 'best looking Provincials I have seen & near 400 strong,' were posted on Long Island for much of the American War.

Ludlow, George Duncan. A justice of the New York Supreme Court before the American Revolution, Ludlow became a prominent Loyalist. In 1780 the British appointed him superintendent of the Court of Police on Long Island, a post with considerable administrative and judicial power. Those who resented his power accused him of enriching himself. John Peebles found Ludlow an educated and congenial friend. His brother was Lieutenant-Colonel Gabriel G. Ludlow qv.

Marshall, Dick. To judge exclusively by John Peebles' diary (none of his correspondence with Marshall seems to have survived), Dick Marshall was one of Peebles' closest Ayrshire friends. Peebles corresponded regularly with

Marshall during the American War, looked after Marshall's brother who served in Oliver DeLancey's corps and was captured during the Philadelphia campaign of 1778, and sent Marshall presents of a rifle, wine, and apples. Marshall, in turn, wrote faithfully to Peebles and may have asked him to help promote his business interests. Yet for all of their correspondence and apparent friendship, Marshall remained a shadowy presence in Peebles' diary – someone who was too close to need or receive an introduction.

Mathew, Edward (1729–1805), entered the American War in the summer of 1776 as a brigadier-general commanding a brigade of guards. He took part in the landings on New York Island in September and the capture of Fort Washington in November 1776. In 1779 he and Sir George Collier led an unusually successful raid on rebel shipping and stores in the Chesapeake. He returned to England in 1780.

Moncrieff, James (1744–93), who had been trained as an engineer at the Royal Military Academy at Woolwich, served effectively under Sir William Howe in the opening campaigns of the American War in New Jersey and Pennsylvania. But he especially distinguished himself in the southern colonies, preparing the defenses of Savannah that withstood the Franco-American attack of 1779 and helping direct the successful siege of Charleston in 1780.

Ogden, Dr. Peebles may have known Dr Ogden of Jamaica, Long Island, before the American War began. (When assigned to live in Ogden's house in November 1778, Peebles described him as an 'old Acquaintance.') Whenever they met, their acquaintance blossomed into a friendship during the American War. Peebles frequently called on the Ogdens, danced and flirted with their daughter Polly, grieved with the family when the doctor died, and protected his widow and daughter from Hessians quartered nearby. Peebles continued to see the Ogdens until he resigned his commission and went home.

O'Hara, Charles (c. 1740–1802), an officer of the Coldstream Guards who had served in Germany during the Seven Years' War, helped organize the defenses of New York against Admiral d'Estaing's fleet in the summer of 1778. Although Sir Henry Clinton was not impressed with him, O'Hara did well while serving under Cornwallis in North Carolina and Virginia during the final campaigns of the war.

Paterson, James, who was lieutenant-colonel and then colonel of the 63rd Regiment, served as adjutant-general of the British army in America from June 1776 until June 1778. After nearly a year's leave in Britain, he returned to command detachments in the capture of Stony Point (June 1779) and Charleston (May 1780) and in defense of Staten Island (1781).

Peebles, John (1739–1823). Lieutenant John Peebles of the Black Watch sailed with his regiment for North America in April 1776. On reaching New York, he and his company were assigned first to the 4th and then to the 3rd Battalion of British Grenadiers. After taking part in the campaign of

1776 at New York and Rhode Island, he and the grenadiers spent the winter and spring of 1777 in New Jersey (from March 26 as the 2nd Battalion) and the summer and early autumn capturing Philadelphia. In October 1777 Peebles was promoted to captain-lieutenant and returned to duty with the Black Watch, serving through the ensuing winter and spring at Philadelphia and withdrawing with the rest of the army to New York in June 1778. On August 18 he was again promoted – to captain in the grenadier company of the Black Watch which was then with the 1st Battalion of British Grenadiers and which took part in raids on Massachusetts and New Jersey before going into winter quarters on Long Island. Peebles would spend the remainder of the war with the British grenadiers, campaigning along the Hudson in the summer of 1779, going south to take Charleston by siege in the winter and spring of 1780, returning to New York to prepare for a variety of aborted missions, and becoming ever more discouraged with the progress of the war and ever more eager to sell his commission and leave the army. Finally, after Cornwallis had surrendered at Yorktown, he was able to sell out, go home, and marry his beloved Anna Hamilton.

Percy, Hugh, Lord (1742–1817), a veteran of the Seven Years' War in Germany, went to Boston in 1774 as a brigadier-general. He led the relief column at the Battle of Lexington and Concord, accompanied the army to New York in 1776, and commanded divisions in the Battles of Long Island and Fort Washington. He went with Sir Henry Clinton to capture Rhode Island that December and remained to command the garrison there. In June 1777 he resigned out of frustration with Sir William Howe.

Phillips, William (1731–81). Trained as an officer of artillery, Phillips distinguished himself in Germany during the Seven Years' War. In 1776 he went to Canada to serve as a brigadier and then major-general with the army that was to invade the rebellious colonies. The next autumn he was taken prisoner at Saratoga and remained in rebel hands until paroled in November 1779. When finally exchanged, he commanded British forces in the Chesapeake during the spring of 1781. That May he died of a fever, esteemed as an aggressive, innovative artillerist.

Prescott, Richard (1725–88), went to Canada on the eve of the War for American Independence. Captured at Montreal in November 1775, and exchanged in September 1776, he joined the detachment that took Rhode Island in December 1776. He was now a brigadier and assumed command at Newport after Lord Percy went home. But he was again captured by the rebels and did not gain his release until May 1778 or resume command until just before the British withdrew from Rhode Island in October 1779.

Prescott, Robert (1725–1816), who had served in Europe and North America during the Seven Years' War, entered the War for American Independence as lieutenant-colonel of the 28th Regiment. After taking part in the campaigns of 1776 at New York and 1777 in Pennsylvania, he returned to New York in 1778 and embarked with the expeditionary force that captured the

French West Indies island of St. Lucia. He was a major-general by the end of the American War.

Prevost, Augustine (1723–86), served in North America during the Seven Years' War. He entered the War for American Independence as a colonel commanding British forces in East Florida. In December 1778 he invaded Georgia, captured Sunbury, and then, in October 1779, withstood a siege at Savannah by a French fleet and army. Soon thereafter he went home.

Rawdon, Francis, Lord (1754–1826), came to America in 1774 with his regiment, fought gallantly at Bunker Hill, and took part in the campaigns of 1776 and 1777 in the middle colonies. In June 1778 he was promoted to lieutenant-colonel and made adjutant-general, a post he did not like or hold long. In April 1780 he joined Sir Henry Clinton at Charleston, bringing with him his newly raised provincial regiment, the Volunteers of Ireland. He remained in the South, distinguishing himself first under Cornwallis and subsequently on his own. When Cornwallis advanced into North Carolina and Virginia, Rawdon defended South Carolina with great skill until forced by illness to resign his command and go home in July 1781.

Riedesel, Baron Friedrich Adolphus (1738–1800), who had served as aide-de-camp to Prince Ferdinand of Brunswick during the Seven Years' War, commanded the first contingent of Brunswickers to enter the War for American Independence. In 1777 he and his men were with the British army that surrendered at Saratoga. After three years as prisoner of war, he was exchanged in October 1780 and given command of British forces on Long Island. He returned to Canada in late 1781 and went home in the summer of 1783.

Rodney, George Brydges (1719–92), became famous and wealthy for his victories at sea during the War of the Austrian Succession. But he spent his fortune on Parliamentary elections and was living in France when the War for American Independence began – to escape his creditors. His debts paid by a French nobleman, he returned home and gained command of the Leeward Islands squadron in late 1779. In 1780 he relieved Gibraltar en route to the West Indies, fought the French inconclusively off Martinique, and pursued them, he thought, to North America (the French had gone to Europe). He returned to the West Indies in November 1780, captured the Dutch port of St. Eustatius, and became so preoccupied with prize money that he failed to concentrate his forces against the French. When in August 1781 he went home ill, the French were able to sail to the Chesapeake and join in trapping Cornwallis at Yorktown. Rodney did return to the West Indies the following year to win a final, great victory over the French at the Battle of the Saints (April 1782).

Rutherfurd, John, went to America in the spring of 1776 as a lieutenant in the Black Watch. He remained in the Black Watch through the war, rising to captain-lieutenant in August 1778 and captain in February 1781 and serving, for a time at least, as adjutant to the second battalion of the regiment.

Rutherfurd and his wife were John Peebles' closest friends during the war.

Simcoe, John Graves (1752–1806), served with his regiment at Boston and in the middle colonies in the opening campaigns of the War for American Independence. In October 1777 he became commander of the Queen's Rangers, a unit of Loyalist infantry and cavalry. He led the Queen's Rangers from Monmouth (June 1778) and Stony Point (June 1779) to the Chesapeake where he served under Benedict Arnold and Lord Cornwallis. After being captured at Yorktown, he was promoted to colonel and went home.

Stirling, Thomas, commanded the Black Watch in the War for American Independence from June 1776 to December 1781. Although only lieutenant-colonel of his regiment, he was soon acting as a brigadier-general in the army. He led brigades in New Jersey during the spring of 1777, in Pennsylvania that autumn, and in New Jersey again in June 1780 (where he was wounded). A difficult and undistinguished officer, he left the Black Watch in December 1781 to become colonel of the 71st regiment.

Tarleton, Banastre (1754–1833), volunteered for service in the War for American Independence and first saw action with the 16th Dragoons at New York in 1776. By late 1778 he had become lieutenant-colonel commandant of the British Legion. He took the Legion south in 1780 and remained after the siege of Charleston to distinguish himself as an aggressive and ruthless cavalry officer. Except for a humiliating defeat at Cowpens in January 1781, he was remarkably successful in the Carolinas and Virginia. He was captured with Cornwallis at Yorktown and paroled to England.

Tryon, William (1729–88), entered the British army in 1751 but shifted to imperial administration after the Seven Years' War – as lieutenant-governor and governor of North Carolina and then as governor of New York. After the War for American Independence began, he got permission to command Loyalists and led a series of raids along the coasts of Connecticut and in the Hudson River Valley. In September 1780 he went home, ill.

Vaughan, John (d. 1795), who had served with the British army in Germany, North America, and the West Indies during the Seven Years' War, entered the War for American Independence as a colonel with a local rank of brigadier-general. He commanded the British grenadiers in the Battles of Long Island and White Plains in 1776. After a winter in England to recover from a wound, he returned to New York to serve as a major-general under Sir Henry Clinton in campaigns along the Hudson River in October 1777 and June 1779. Late in 1779 he went home, was appointed commander-in-chief in the Leeward Islands, and spent the remainder of the war in the West Indies.

Washington, George (1732–99). When the War for American Independence began, Washington was a member of the Continental Congress. Fellow delegates saw him as a man well suited to lead their forces – a man so successful in his private life, so satisfied with his accomplishments, and so committed to a republican revolution that he could be trusted with power. He did not disappoint his colleagues or his countrymen. In the opening campaigns of the war – around New York City and Philadelphia in 1776 and 1777 – he fought often and well enough to preserve the spirit of the revolution and the morale of the Continental Army. By 1778 that army was able to fight the British to a draw in a formal European engagement. Thereafter, George Washington kept the army together until the British gave him a chance to join the French in striking a decisive blow – to trap and capture Cornwallis' army at Yorktown. He had been just the persistent, upright, and deferential leader that the revolutionary leaders needed to win their independence and establish the new United States.

Yorke, John, entered the American War as major of the 33rd Regiment. He served with his regiment and the 1st Battalion of Grenadiers in New York, New Jersey, and Pennsylvania until the autumn of 1778 when he became lieutenant-colonel of the 22nd Foot. In November 1780 he returned to command the 1st Grenadiers at New York. When Lieutenant-Colonel James Webster of the 33rd Regiment was killed at Guilford Court House in March 1781, Yorke took command of his old regiment and served with Cornwallis through the Yorktown campaign.

Appendix B

Glossary of Military and Nautical Terms

Abatis. A barricade created by felling mature trees, stripping them of leaves, and placing their sharpened, intertwined branches toward the enemy. Abatis were used to strengthen field works or other fortifications.

Battalion. During the War for American Independence, the British used the term battalion to describe at least two types of infantry units. When the British augmented an existing regiment (the 42nd, 60th, or 71st, for examples), they did so by creating battalions within the regiment. Each of these new battalions had the same size and organization as the parent regiment (roughly 500 men, organized in ten companies); hence an enlarged regiment of two battalions had about 1,000 men. The British also created battalions of grenadiers and light infantrymen by taking the grenadier and light infantry companies from their parent regiments and organizing them into tactical units called battalions. Thus John Peebles' grenadier company from the 42nd Regiment was at one time or another a part of the 4th, 3rd, 2nd, and 1st Battalions of British Grenadiers; and those battalions seem to have been of considerably different size – from as few as 150 to 300 or more men.

Brigade. The British organized regiments or battalions of infantry into tactical units called brigades. During the American War, brigades usually contained four regiments (but sometimes as few as three or as many as five). Brigades came under the command of a brigadier-general or a senior colonel.

Carrying courses. See *Courses.*

Claw off. To tack or sail to windward from a lee-shore so as to escape shipwreck.

Clew up. To draw up the lower corners of a sail – the clews – to a yard arm on a square-rigged ship; that is, to reduce the area of a sail exposed to the wind.

Company. The company was the basic infantry unit in the British army during the American War. The size of companies varied, but in ordinary regiments of the line, a company had 3 officers, 6 noncommissioned officers, and 38 privates. There were 10 companies in a regiment: 8 of the line, 1 of grenadiers and another of light infantry. The company of grenadiers that John Peebles commanded had more than 80 noncommissioned officers and privates because it contained all of the grenadiers in a regiment that had been augmented from roughly 500 to 1000 men for the American War – that is, his company was twice the size of an ordinary company of grenadiers from a line regiment.

COMPASS CARD

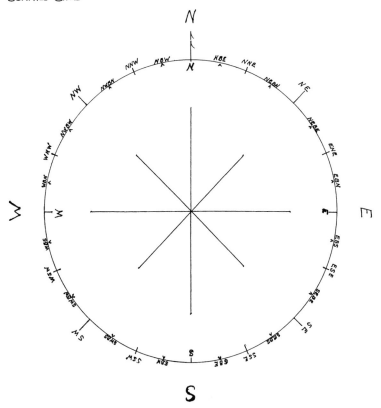

Courses. The name given to the principal sails of a square-rigged ship, usually the mainsail, foresail, and mizzen sail but sometimes the main and fore stay-sails as well. The courses of all brigs and schooners (fore-and-aft rigged vessels) were the main staysails. A ship said to have been 'carrying courses' had only its courses or lowest sails set. See also *Sail*.

Double-decker. The British used the term double-decker or two-decked ship to describe larger frigates and smaller ships of the line – that is, ships carrying from 40 to 74 guns arranged on two decks.

Embrasure. A narrow opening in the wall of a fortification or in the breastwork of a battery (wider within than without) through which a gun was fired.

Fascine. A long, thin bundle of branches (6 to 10 inches in diameter and 9 to 16 feet long) tied securely together with twigs and used to hold up the sides of trenches or to make the walls of batteries.

Fleche. A detached, arrowhead-shaped fortification placed so as to point toward the enemy and to defend the approaches to a larger fortification or position.

Fraise. A palisade of sharpened poles placed in the ground and inclined toward the enemy to strengthen earthworks or fortifications. See *Palisade*.

Frigate. During the War for American Independence, the British used the word frigate to describe intermediate size, square-rigged warships that carried as few as 20 guns and 150 men and as many as 50 guns and 370 men. Frigates, smaller than ships of the line and larger than armed ships, schooners, and sloops, were most often used in convoying transports and supply ships, blockading ports and patrolling the coasts of the rebellious colonies, and supporting the British army in its operations along rivers and bays.

Hand. To take in or furl a sail.

Hurdle. A bundle of branches or twigs (about 5 or 6 feet long and 3 or 3 1/2 feet wide) closely interwoven and covered with earth to screen soldiers or to fill in marshy ground or trenches.

Larboard. The left or port side of a vessel – opposite of starboard.

Lask. To sail with the wind on the quarter or abaft the beam – that is, to sail not directly with or into the wind.

League. A measure of distance usually estimated in English usage to be about 3 miles or 3 nautical miles. Peebles used the word league primarily in a nautical sense.

Light Bob. A light infantryman.

Palisades. A row of stout stakes (about 9 feet long) buried 3 feet in the ground and placed 6 inches apart so as to strengthen the defense of a fieldwork or a fortification.

Place of arms (or place d'armes). A securely fortified place where troops assembled to protect against a surprise attack – especially, a place where, during a siege, the attackers assembled troops to guard their working parties against sallies by the defenders.

Platoon. A unit of infantry, smaller than a company but not of fixed size (a 'few files,' according to Thomas Simes). Some colonels divided their regiments into platoons in order to gain greater control over the regiment's musket fire. Peebles rarely used the word 'platoon' in his diary.

Pounder. A term was used to describe the size of a gun; that is, a six-pounder fired a shot weighing approximately six pounds.

Redoubt. A square defensive work of stone or earth, surrounded by a ditch, to protect detached guards outside fortifications, a camp, or a line of trenches. The sides of a redoubt were usually from 60 to 120 feet long and 9 or 10 feet thick.

Reef. To reduce the area of sail exposed to the wind (to lower and fold a square-rigged sail).

Regiment. The word regiment had a variety of meanings in the British army during the American War. Most often it described an infantry unit of roughly 500 men organized in 10 companies (8 of the line, 1 of grenadiers, and 1 of light infantry). Some regiments were doubled or quadrupled in size for service in America; thus the 42nd was expanded from 500 to 1,000 men, organized in 2 battalions of 10 companies each (each battalion had its own set of roughly 30 officers). The term regiment was also applied to the only two cavalry units employed in North America, the 16th and 17th Light Dragoons (but cavalry units were usually only about half the size of an infantry regiment).

Sail. All sails were named after the mast, yard, or stay on which they were set. Thus: d was the mainsail; e, the main topsail; f, the main-topgallant sail; g, the foresail; h, the fore topsail; i, the fore-topgallant sail; k, the mizzen sail; l, the mizzen topsail; m, the mizzen-topgallant sail; o, the main staysail; p, the main-topmast staysail; q, the main-topgallant staysail; t, the fore staysail; x, the jib; and y, the spritsail.

Schooner. The British used the word to describe a relatively small, fore-and-aft rigged warship carrying about 6 guns and 30 to 40 men.

Ship of the line. The largest warship in the British North American squadron, 1775–82 – two-decked, square-rigged vessels carrying 64 to 74 guns and 500 to 617 men.

Sloop. In the British navy during the American War, a small warship carrying 8 to 18 guns and 80 to 125 men.

Wear ship (past tense *wore*). To change from one tack to the other by turning away from the wind – to present one's stern to the wind while changing tacks.

Weather bow/quarter. That side of a ship's bow/quarter that is toward the wind.

Appendix C

Catalogue of Omissions

This is a catalogue of the various orders, lists, accounts, and excerpts that have been omitted from this edition of Peebles' diary. The catalogue offers a brief summary of each document or group of documents that has been omitted, showing where each may be found in the manuscript notebooks (by notebook and nearest diary entry). Although these documents do not add substantially to an understanding or appreciation of Peebles' diary, they may be of use to historians with specialized interests in the War for American Independence.

Notebook 1 (Peebles Diary, GD 21/492, 1, SRO)
5 August 1776.
   'Instructions, Signals . . . ,' n.d., issued to the masters of transports sailing from Greenock, Scotland, to North America in the spring of 1776 under the command of Captain John Brisbane of the *Flora*.

Notebook 2 (Peebles Diary, GD 21/492, 2, SRO)
Prior to 16 October 1776.
   General orders for the British army at New York, 30 June, 1 August to 24 September 1776. These seventy-eight general orders provide instructions for the army under General William Howe while it assembled at New York, fought the Battle of Long Island, crossed the East River at Kip's Bay, and captured New York City. They warn the army against plundering, plan the embarking and disembarking of troops, prescribe tactics, report the results of courts martial, appoint working parties, announce promotions and assignments of officers, establish the order of battle, require mustering, distribute recruits and replacements, ask for the return of items lost or stolen, assign units to picquet duty, distribute provisions, enjoin cleanliness, praise the performance of officers and men, establish values for various currencies, require accounts, seek stragglers, assign posts and quarters for various units of the army, ask for returns of casualties, require making fascines, announce the departure or arrival of mail, regulate the distribution of horses, wagons, and fodder, and provide for the wounded and sick.
   Regimental orders for the Black Watch, 8 August, 23, 24 September 1776. These orders announce the appointment and assignment of officers within the regiment.

Battalion orders for the 4th Battalion of British Grenadiers, 18 August to 14 September 1776. Thirty-seven orders assigning men for various duties, requiring cleaning and bathing, forbidding plundering, and appointing courts martial.

Division orders for the First Division of the army at New York, 1 August to 18 September 1776. Thirty-five orders making assignments for picquets and other duties (includes a strength report of 18 September 1776).

Interspersed among diary entries, 16 October–17 November 1776.

General orders for the British army in West Chester County and at New York, 17 October–15 November 1776. These twenty-six orders provide mainly for the movements of the British army against the Continental army from Frog's Neck to White Plains and Fort Washington. They are much like the general orders issued from 30 June to 16 October 1776 but they also include a definition of the relative seniority of regular and provincial officers, a statement of the benefits to be paid for officers and men killed or wounded in action, and injunctions against too much baggage.

At the opposite end of this notebook are various orders, notices, and duty lists issued between 25 August 1776 and 24 June 1777, including a summary of casualties at the Battle of Long Island and British orders of battle for the campaigns of 1776 and 1777.

Notebook 3 (Peebles Diary, GD 21/492, 3, SRO)
6, 24 December 1776 and 13 June 1777.

Peter Parker's order of 2 December 1776 for entering Newport harbor; amounts of firewood to be issued British officers at Rhode Island, winter 1776–1777; and a catalogue of Captain Moyle's library.

Notebook 4 (Peebles Diary, GD 21/492, 4, SRO)
3–22 December 1777 and after 6 January 1778.

General orders for marching against the rebels and for foraging (total of four orders of early and mid-December 1777) and a state of the grenadier company of the Black Watch 24 October 1777. At the end of the notebook (after 6 January 1778): a list of Peebles' loans; a roll, state, and account of the grenadier company of the 42nd of 25 April, 10, 13 June, and 19 July 1777; and summaries of casualties at the Battles of Brandywine and Germantown.

Notebook 5 (Peebles Diary, GD 21/492, 5, SRO)
Prior to 30 January and 11 May, 28 December 1778 and 24 February 1779.

Excerpts from books on trees and love; General Howe's farewell and King George III's thanks for the army's performance at the Battle of Monmouth; and an excerpt from a book [by Rousseau?] on the social man and the savage.

Notebook 6 (Peebles Diary, GD 21/492, 6, SRO)
21 June, 5, 7, 8, 18 July, 2, 16 November 1778.

With the exception of copies of letters to and from Henry Laurens of 10 July (with diary entry of 18 July), these are five of Sir Henry Clinton's general orders directing the march of his army through New Jersey and its posting around New York City.

Post 16 November 1778.

Return of casualties at the Battle of Monmouth; state of Lord John Murray's company of the 42nd Regiment on 29 May, 18 June, 2 July, 1 August, 2, 25 October 1778; roll of the 42nd grenadiers June, 27 August 1778; return of 42nd grenadiers 31 August 1778; accounts of provisions drawn by Lord John Murray's company 24 February to 27 August 1778; and Major-General Charles Grey's orders of 4, 7, 8, 13, 15 September 1778 for operations against Bedford and Martha's Vineyard.

Notebook 7 (Peebles Diary, GD 21/492, 7, SRO)
17, 30 September 1779.

General orders of 16 September ordering various units to prepare to embark at New York; state of 42nd grenadiers on 30 September 1779.

At the end of notebook.

List of men joining the 42nd grenadiers from the 26th Regiment, n. d.; list of debts owed to Peebles, n. d.; and roll of the 42nd grenadiers, n. d.

Notebook 8 (Peebles Diary, GD 21/492, 8, SRO)
27 October 1779.

General orders 25 October 1779 ordering troops to disembark from ships in the Hudson River and designating winter quarters for the army at New York.

Notebook 9 (Peebles Diary, GD 21/492, 9, SRO)
12, 13 February, 1 April 1780.

General orders issued to the British army approaching and beginning the siege of Charleston, South Carolina.

Post 12 April 1780 and on the endleaf of the notebook.

Peebles' record of three cash transactions 14, 26 March and 17 July 1780.

Notebook 10 (Peebles Diary GD 21/492, 10, SRO)
Before 13 April 1780.

Passage in Latin dated 1 January 1780.

11, 12 May 1780.

General and battalion orders for receiving the surrender of Charleston, South Carolina; Sir Henry Clinton's thanks to his troops.

21, 26 June 1780.

Excerpt from [David] Hume; state of the 42nd grenadiers, n. d.

Notebook 11 (Peebles Diary, GD 21/492, 11, SRO)
Before 27 June 1780.

Extract from the works of [Edward] Gibbon.

27 July, 22 August, and 13 November 1780.

General orders for an expedition against Rhode Island; 'rules for manoeuvering the battalion,' c. 21 August 1780; battalion orders announcing a change of command.

Inside rear leaf of notebook.

Provision receipts for 42nd grenadiers 15 February to 2 June 1780.

Notebook 12 (Peebles Diary, GD 21/492, 12, SRO)
28 January to 5 October 1781.

General orders (a total of twenty-four interspersed among diary entries) for the British army at New York: reporting on the progress of operations in the Chesapeake and the Carolinas, announcing the results of courts martial, listing promotions and appointments of officers, calling for returns, and directing various units to prepare to embark for Virginia.

5 October 1781.

A list of the fleet at New York 5 October 1781; excerpt from *Dictionaire des Anecdotes*.

Notebook 13 (Peebles Diary, 21/492, 13, SRO)
6 October to 14 November 1781.

General orders (total of six) directing the army at New York to embark for the Chesapeake and, after its return, assigning winter quarters. Battalion orders (three) for carrying out the general orders.

13 February 1782 and separate sheet inside cover of notebook.

General order 12 February 1782 for making fascines; return of Franco-American forces besieging Yorktown, October 1781; invitation for John Peebles to dine with Sir Henry Clinton, 26 November 1781.

Appendix D

Guide to the Manuscript of John Peebles' Diary

John Peebles kept his diary for the American War in thirteen small leatherbound notebooks that are now a part of the Cunninghame of Thorntoun Papers in the Scottish Record Office (GD21/492, 1-13). Because Peebles did not fill his notebooks in a strictly sequential way, it can be difficult to find the original manuscript text for a particular part of his diary. This guide is designed to link each of the chapters in this edition to the manuscript notebooks in the Scottish Record Office.

Chapter	Dates in Diary	Manuscript volume in GD21/492
I	12 April to 5 August 1776	1
II	18 October to 17 November 1776	2
	25 November 1776 to 12 February 1777	3
III	13 February to 12 June 1777	3
	13 June to 6 July 1777	4
IV	8 July to 31 December 1777	4
V	1-6 January 1778	4
	30 January to 15 June 1778	5
	15 June to 5 July 1778	6
VI	6 July to 16 November 1778	6
	17-30 November 1778	5
VII	1 December 1778 to 27 April 1779	5
	28 April to 28 May 1779	7
VIII	29 May to 30 September 1779	7
	30 September to 10 November 1779	8
IX	11 November 1779 to 7 February 1780	8
	8-10 February 1780	9
X	11 February to 12 April 1780	9
	13 April to 30 May 1780	10
XI	31 May to 26 June 1780	10

Notes

Publication details of all books mentioned in the Notes are given in the Bibliography.

Notes to Introduction

1 See bibliography.
2 Clinton kept his diary at Charleston, 8 February–28 March 1780; Pattison, at Philadelphia and New York, 17 June 1777–29 December 1779; Montresor, in New Jersey, Pennsylvania, and New York, 1 January 1777–24 December 1778; Mackenzie, at Boston, New York, and Rhode Island, January 1775–December 1778 and January–November 1781 (only patches of his diary have survived); Barker, at Boston and Halifax, 15 November 1774–31 May 1776; and Bamford, at Boston, Halifax, and New York, 8 January–31 December 1776.
3 Major-General Robert Cuninghame's return of the annual review of the 42nd at Waterford, Ireland, 30 May 1775, reported that 28 of 30 officers and all 378 of the rank and file in the regiment were Scots. Other regiments reviewed at the same time – that is, some 47 other regiments of foot reviewed between 1774 and 1777, had much more balanced representations of Englishmen, Irishmen, and Scots among both officers and men. See returns of annual reviews, 1774–7, War Office Papers, Class 27, Vols. 30, 32, 34–6, Public Record Office, Kew, England. Cunninghame's return is in WO 27/35.
4 Peebles was baptized 2 September 1739, the son of John Peebles and Mary Reoch, OPR 595/1 from 119, General Register Office (Scotland). John Blair to John Peebles, 1 June 1758, Archibald Montgomery to John Peebles, 15 August 1759, and Jeffery Amherst to John Peebles, 23 August 1763. Cunninghame of Thorntoun Papers, GD 21/674, 675, 676, Scottish Record Office, Edinburgh. Cited hereafter as Cunninghame of Thorntoun Papers, GD 21/674, SRO.
5 Compare Cunninghame's return of the 42nd, 30 May 1775, WO 27/35, and J. A. Houlding, *Fit for Service The Training of the British Army, 1715–1795*, pp. 109–10 (tables 1–3). George III to John Peebles, 31 March 1770,

and William Howe to John Peebles, 5 October 1777, Cunninghame of
Thorntoun Papers, GD 21/678, 681, SRO.

6 Ira D. Gruber, 'On the Road to Poonamalle: An Irish Officer's View of the
   War for American Independence,' *The American Magazine and Historical
   Chronicle* (1988), p. 2; Houlding, *Fit for Service*, p. 109.

7 John Peebles, 'Return of Bread, Coals . . . ', 23 June–30 September 1772,
   GD 21/490, SRO; John Peebles' Diary, 31 January, 2 February 1782, 25
   March, 12 July 1778, Cunninghame of Thorntoun Papers, GD 21/492, 1–
   13, SRO. Cited hereafter as Peebles Diary. Appendix D shows where entries in Peebles Diary are to be found in the thirteen manuscript notebooks
   in the SRO.

8 24, 25 June, 3 July 1776; 29 January, 12 February, 26 September 1777,
   Peebles Diary. John Peebles to Dear Sir, 20 September 1762, and Ja Dalyell
   to Major Zobel, 14 June 1763, Cunninghame of Thorntoun Papers, GD
   21/487, 488, SRO.

9 16 November 1776, 12 February 1777, 3 February 1778, 2 April 1779, 13
   May 1780, Peebles Diary.

10 24 June, 3 July 1776; 12 February, 26 September 1777, Peebles Diary.
    Captain Peebles Location in Cumberland, 22 July 1762, Cunninghame of
    Thorntoun Papers, GD 21/699, SRO.

11 2 August 1776, 9 March 1778, 18 August 1780, Peebles Diary.

12 11 September 1777, 28 June 1778, *ibid.*

13 16 November 1776, 2 April–12 May 1780, *ibid.*

14 23 February–1 June, 31 August–28 September, 10 November–25
    December 1777; 2 March–6 June, 5–8, 28 September *passim*; and 6, 16
    March, 10 May 1777, *ibid.* See also Howard H. Peckham, ed., *The Toll of
    Independence Engagements & Battle Casualties of the American Revolution*
    for casualties that the British suffered while skirmishing.

15 23–24 February 1777, Peebles Diary.

16 1 August, 13 September 1776, 4 September 1778; 24, 27 February, 2 March
    1777, 8 March 1781, *ibid.*

17 23, 30 December 1776, 31 March, 7 May 1778, 15–16 February, 30 March,
    8, 14 April 1779, 26 February, 30 March, 7, 8, 16 April, 31 May 1781,
    ibid.

18 30 December 1776, 21 August 1780, *ibid.*

19 29 August, 2, 14 September 1777, 1 March, 26 May 1780, *ibid.*

20 6 June, 29–30 August, 6 October 1777, 27 June, 14 October 1778, 9, 29
    July 1779, 7, 20 July 1780, *ibid.*

21 15 September, 22 December 1777, 23 March, 24 June 1778, 21 March, 4,
    5 April, 7 July, 29 October, 24 November 1779, 23 July, 18 August, 27
    November 1780, *ibid.*

22 8 October 1781, *ibid.*

23 12, 18 December 1776, 14 September 1777, 26 February 1778, *ibid.*

24 12 June 1776, 19, 22 January 1777, *ibid.*

25 26 September, 4 October 1777, 4 May, 13 July, 10 November 1778, 23 March 1780, *ibid.*
26 13, 22 November 1777, 12, 19 May, 22 August 1780, *ibid.*
27 16 April, 10 June, 28 October 1778, 26 February, 17 July, 2, 22 October 1779, *ibid.*
28 8 September 1780; but 24, 25 June, 9 September, 6, 16 October 1781, *ibid.*
29 6 December 1777, 28 March 1778, 8 July 1779, 4 March 1780, 1 December 1781, *ibid.* Peebles did cultivate friendships with gifts – of oranges and limes for Cornwallis and of apples and trees for Eglintoun (4 March 1780, 1 December 1781).
30 30 March, 1, 5 April 1777, 21 March, 6 May, 17 July 1778, 6 January, 7 March, 8 July, 7, 8, 20 August, 26 November 1779, 7, 27, 29 March 1780, 2 March 1781, 19, 26 February 1782, *ibid.*
31 17 July 1778, 20 August 1779, 27 March 1780, *ibid.*
32 23 June 1781, *ibid.*
33 19 February 1782, 26 November 1779, 26 February 1782, 2 March 1781, 2 March 1782, *ibid.*
34 Ira D. Gruber, 'For King and Country: The Limits of Loyalty of British Officers in the War for American Independence,' in Edgar Denton III, ed., *Limits of Loyalty*, pp. 23–40; Ira D. Gruber, 'George III Chooses a Commander in Chief,' in Ronald Hoffman and Peter J. Albert, eds., *Arms and Independence The Military Character of the American Revolution*, pp. 166–90.
35 5 June 1776, 18 January 1777, 4 June 1779, 1780, 1781; 22 September 1778, 1780, 1781, 25 October 1778, 29 May 1781, Peebles Diary.
36 4 June 1779, 1780, 1781, 18 January 1777, 1779, 26 September, 12 October 1781, *ibid.*
37 Returns of annual reviews, forty-eight regiments of infantry, 1774–1777, WO 27/30, 32, 34–36.
38 23 April 1778, 1779, 1781, 17 March 1778, 1779, 1 March 1779, 30 November 1776, 1779, 1780, 29 November 1778, 1781, Peebles Diary.
39 30 November 1781, *ibid.*
40 14 May 1778, 25 December 1776, 1777, 1778, 1779, 1781, 1, 2 January 1777, 1 January 1782, *ibid.*
41 22 September 1780; 11 September 1778, 1779, 1780, 1781, 12 May 1781; 5 January 1778, 28 January, 5 May 1779, 20–1 February 1782, 7 June, 18 May 1778, *ibid.*
42 12 April, 9 December 1779; 14 November 1781, 2 February 1782; 27 December 1776, 28 November 1778, 2, 16 January 1779, 1 April 1781; 28 December 1776, 6 December 1781, *ibid.*
43 28 January 1782; 25 March 1779, 2 September, 14 November 1781, *ibid.*
44 10 January 1777, 15 February, 19 March, 14 June 1778, 25 February 1781; 28 January 1779; 1, 5, 9 February 1782, *ibid.*

45 26 January 1777, 2, 8 January 1779, 1 January 1780, 25 January, 28 June 1781, 8 February 1782, *ibid*.

46 17 February, 19 March 1778; 19 February 1777; 1 February 1782, *ibid*.

47 6 April 1781, 1 February, 27 January 1782; and quoting 2 January 1779, 17 February 1778, 16 May 1781, *ibid*.

48 7–29 January 1778, 4 January 1777, 1 May, 21 December 1781, 25 January 1782; 13, 22 March 1781, 3 January 1782; 23 March, 1 May 1778, *ibid*.

49 10 February 1777, 7–29 January, 9 February, 16, 28 March, 19 May 1778, 30 October 1780, 30 April 1781, *ibid*.

50 12, 22 January 1779, 24 February 1782, *ibid*.

51 15 March, 26 January, 4 February 1777, 5 November 1780, 15 September 1781, 15 February 1782, 5 February 1780, *ibid*.

52 2, 3 December 1776, 21 December 1778, 9 February, 18, 29 March 1779, 3, 17 August 1781, 26 November 1778, *ibid*.

53 7 July 1778, 1 June 1781; 10 February 1778, 22 January 1779, 4, 5 February 1782; 2–3 February, 6 July 1780, 1 April 1781, *ibid*.

54 4 October 1778, 31 March 1781; 10 November 1779, 16 April, 6 June, 7, 10 August 1781, *ibid*.

55 21 May 1777, 7, 8 May 1778, 19 November, 13 December 1781; 30 August 1781 (quoted); 28 July 1778, 14, 26 November 1779, 22 January, 14 August, 20, 21, 25 November 1781, *ibid*.

56 24, 26 February, 2, 10, 11 March 1777, 3, 4 July 1780; 2 May 1780, 24 February 1777, 9 September 1781; 24, 25, 27 July 1780; 18 November 1778, 19 December 1779; 2 February 1782, *ibid*.

57 8 March 1779; 9 October 1779, 12 September 1780. On three other occasions – the winter and spring of 1777, the spring of 1780, and September 1780 – he complained that his men were sickly; but on none of these occasions did he have more than sixteen of his eighty men confined to bed. 17 February, 7, 11, 19 March, 8 June 1777; 11, 14 June, 8 July 1780; 12, 22 September 1780; 9 October 1779, 12 September 1780, *ibid*.

58 19 March, 8 June 1777; 24 August–13 December 1779 *passim*; 12, 17, 20, 22 September 1780, *ibid*.

59 Sylvia Frey, *The British Soldier in America: A Social History of Military Life in the Revolutionary Period*, pp. 51–2; Fred Anderson, *A People's Army Massachusetts Soldiers and Society in the Seven Years' War*, pp. 90–107.

60 John Rutherfurd to John Peebles, 26 July 1801, and John Peebles to his father, 27 January 1781, Cunninghame of Thorntoun Papers, GD 21/417 (no. 13), 489, SRO. 9 March 1778, 26 November 1778, 22, 25 February 1779, 2 July 1780, 13–15 April, 13 May 1781, Peebles Diary.

61 21 May 1777, 28 January, 3 September, 7 December 1781, 27 February 1779, Peebles Diary.

62 John Rutherfurd to John Peebles, 2 February 1790, 22 December 1804, 20 July 1806, 16 April 1812, Cunninghame of Thorntoun Papers, GD 21/417 (nos. 2, 9, 7, 1), SRO.

NOTES

63 12 February, 26 September 1777, 3 February 1778, 2 April 1779, 13 May 1780, Peebles Diary.

64 1 December 1776, 9 February 1777, 17 July 1778, 22, 26 July 1780, 24 March, 16 June 1781, 24 February 1782, *ibid.*

65 16 July 1778, *ibid.*; Joseph S. Tiedemann, 'Patriots by Default: Queens County, New York, and the British Army, 1776–1783,' *William and Mary Quarterly* (1986), pp. 59–62.

66 16 July, 16 November 1778, 10 November 1779, 27 May, 26 December 1781, 14, 2, 7, 8, 19 February 1782; 25 September 1780, 29 November 1781, 22 January 1782, Peebles Diary.

67 21 July 1781 (quoted), 1 January 1779, 25 September (quoted), 8 November 1780, *ibid.*

68 4 November 1778, 8 January, 19 December 1779, 4 July, 10 August, 4, 5, 15 September, 8, 16 November 1780, 26 December 1781, *ibid.*

69 4 January, 19 December 1779, 13 May, 10, 15 September, 18 November 1780, 14 August 1781, 16 February 1782 (quoted), *ibid.*

70 16, 17 June, 12 August, 22 December 1781, 1 March 1782, *ibid.*

71 10 February 1777, 16 May 1778, 25 January, 28 February, 13 June 1781, *ibid.*

72 26 June 1776; 5 May 1778, 19 March, 15 April, 12 May 1778; 10 November 1780, *ibid.*

73 18 August 1778, 25 January, 25 August, 24 October 1779, 22 March, 19 June, 3 September 1780, 28 June 1781 (quoted), *ibid.* Peebles was flattered by the attentions of Loyalist women, but he never let their attentions go beyond flirtations.

74 3, 22, 24, 25 January, 13 February, 28 June 1781, *ibid.*

75 25, 26 November, 21, 23 December 1781, 8 February 1782, *ibid.*

76 Marriage contract, John Peebles and Ann Hamilton, 20 May 1782, inscriptions Hamilton family burial vault, John Peebles' monthly fees as surveyor for the Port of Irvine, October 1792–July 1809, Cunninghame of Thorntoun Papers, GD 21/159, 698, 191, SRO.

77 John Peebles' account book, estate of Dr William Hamilton, 8 September 1798–25 June 1810, inscriptions Hamilton family burial vault, George III to John Peebles 12 December 1798 and 28 June 1803, Cunninghame of Thorntoun Papers, GD 21/227, 698, 689, 690, SRO.

78 John Peebles to Thomas Adair, 24 July 1804, marriage contract between Lieutenant-Colonel John Cuningham of Caddel and Sarah Peebles, August 9, 1804, John Rutherfurd to John Peebles, 2 October 1805, Archibald Cuningham petition to be examined as an advocate, 4 March 1834, Cunninghame of Thorntoun Papers, GD 21/214/2, 215, 417 (no. 5), 251, SRO.

79 David Hay to John Peebles, 7 April 1804, John Peebles' monthly fees as surveyor for the Port of Irvine, October 1792–July 1809, David Stewart to John Peebles, 16 May 1818, and John Rutherfurd to John Peebles, 16 April

1812, Cunninghame of Thorntoun Papers, GD 21/416 (no. 6), 191, 500, 417 (no. 1), SRO.

80 Inscriptions Hamilton family burial vault, receipts for discharges of legacies, 27 June 1825, Cunninghame of Thorntoun Papers, GD 21/698, 249, SRO.

Notes to Chapter I

1 25 January 1779, Peebles Diary.

2 John Peebles to his father, Halifax, 29 June 1776, Cunninghame of Thorntoun Papers, GD 21/491, SRO.

3 William Howe to the Earl of Dartmouth, 26 November 1775, Lord George Germain to Howe, 5 January 1776, Colonial Office Papers, Class 5, Vols 92, 93, Public Record Office, Kew.

4 William Howe to Dartmouth, 21 March 1776 (received 2 May 1776) and to Germain, 7 June 1776, CO 5/93. R. Arthur Bowler, *Logistics and the Failure of the British Army in America 1775–1783*, pp. 107–9.

5 11 June, 5 August 1776, Peebles Diary. Altogether, from the time that he embarked for America in 1776 until he returned to Scotland in 1782, Peebles would be aboard a transport or warship fourteen times and would spend cumulatively about sixty-six weeks afloat in just over six years service in the American War.

6 Frasers Regiment, the 71st, was being augmented to two battalions for service in America. After reaching New York, the 42nd would also be expanded to two battalions or from roughly 477 to nearly 1,000 men. See battalion and regiment in Appendix B Glossary of Military and Nautical Terms.

7 The officers commanding the 42nd when it sailed for America were: Lieutenant-Colonel Thomas Stirling, Majors William Murray, William Grant, and James McPherson and Captains George Mackenzie, Charles Graham, Archibald Erskine, John Smith, Charles Grant. The colonel of the regiment, General Lord John Murray, did not serve in America. See Appendix A Biographical Notes for sketches of Stirling, Graham, Charles and William Grant.

8 For wind and course directions see Mariner's Compass Card in Appendix B Glossary of Military and Nautical Terms. 'Elsa' was Ailsa; see map of The British Isles p. 20. Peebles has adopted the nautical day in his journal of the voyage to America; that is his entry for 29 April begins at noon on the civil date of 28 April. (Afternoons and evenings precede mornings and noons in his diary.) Peebles and the grenadier company of the 42nd were embarked on the *Thames* transport, James Moodie, the master.

9 See sail plan for a square rigged vessel in Appendix B Glossary.

10 By 'Western Islands' he probably meant the Hebrides.

11 The word that follows 'to load &' is not clear; it may be 'cock' – meaning to light the match that would be needed to fire the 'two guns.'

12 The king's birthday was celebrated on 4 June (civil date), which was the 'fore part' of Peebles' nautical day, 5 June.

13 While at Boston, Peebles seemed to slip into civil dating; he reverted to the nautical day on 15 June.

14 Admiral Lord Howe had sailed from England on 11 May to assume command of the British North American squadron and to join his brother, General William Howe, in a peace commission. He went to Halifax, found that his brother was no longer there, and put back to sea – on 22 June – en route to New York. See sketches of the Howes in Appendix A Biographical Notes.

15 See Appendix A Biographical Notes for sketches of Dick Marshall and Anna Hamilton.

16 Entries for 27, 28 June suggest Peebles has adopted the civil day once more; he would return to the nautical day on 4 July.

17 Robert McConnell Hatch, *Thrust for Canada*, describes Carleton's success in driving the Americans from Canada. Arnold escaped to build a squadron that kept the British from advancing south across Lake Champlain until October 1776, when winter was upon them.

18 Peebles is, as he said, again using the nautical day.

19 McVea appears to be the master of the York. See the remainder of this entry and that of 25 July 1776.

20 See Appendix A Biographical Notes for Sir William Erskine.

21 General Howe was at New York, but Burgoyne was not at Albany (the Canadian army would get no farther than Lake Champlain in 1776 or Saratoga in 1777).

22 Here Peebles shifted from nautical to civil time.

Notes to Chapter II

1 Ira D. Gruber, *The Howe Brothers and the American Revolution*, pp. 72–157.

2 General Orders, 6, 16 August 1776, Cunninghame of Thorntoun Papers, GD 21/492/2, SRO.

3 General Orders, 20, 26 August, 14 September 1776, *ibid*.

4 General Orders, 8, 11, 21, 24, 25, 28 October 1776, *ibid*. 5, 6, 16, 25 November, 8 December 1776, Peebles Diary.

5 Order Book 4th Battalion Grenadiers, 6 August–8 October 1776, John Peebles diary, 16 October 1776–12 February 1777, Cunninghame of Thorntoun Papers, GD 21/492/2, 3, SRO.

6 Clinton's division was leading the way from Frog's Neck into West Chester County. James Agnew, Lieutenant-Colonel in the 44th Foot, was serving as a Brigadier-General and brigade commander. He would be killed at the Battle of Germantown in October 1777. For a sketch of Clinton see Appendix A Biographical Notes.

7 For the British army's advance to White Plains and then to Dobbs Ferry and Kingsbridge see map, 'The Hudson River New York to West Point,' p. 264.

8 For these marches see map, 'Staten Is., New York Is. and S. W. Long Island' back endpaper.

9 For excellent scholarly accounts of the Battles of White Plains and Fort Washington see Christopher Ward, *The War of the Revolution*, pp. 253–74. For sketches of Knyphausen and Percy see Appendix A Biographical Notes; for abbatis see Appendix B Glossary.

10 Sir Peter Parker (1721–1811), who shared the command of the expedition with Clinton, had also been with him on the abortive attack on Charleston in the spring of 1776. Parker would command at Jamaica from 1779–81.

11 This was Dick Colden (see 1 December 1776, Peebles Diary), possibly Richard Nicholls Colden whose wife Henrietta was a native of Scotland. Gregory Palmer, *Biographical Sketches of Loyalists of the American Revolution*, pp. 165–6.

12 For voyage to Rhode Island see map, 'Atlantic Seaboard Long Island to Cape Cod,' p. 212.

13 For 'pounders' see Appendix B Glossary.

14 For an excellent map of Newport and other principal American towns in the Revolutionary era see Lester J. Cappon, ed., *Atlas of Early American History The Revolutionary Era, 1760–1790*.

15 A table showing quantities of firewood and candles to be issued for the winter has been omitted; part of the table is missing.

16 'Ld. E:' is Peebles' patron, Lord Eglintoun. See Appendix A Biographical Notes.

17 Peebles reports the capture of Charles Lee (1731–82), a former British army officer who had moved to America before the Revolution and was serving as a major-general in the Continental Army. Lee would be exchanged in time to serve at the Battle of Monmouth in 1778, where he did not perform well. He was subsequently tried, suspended, and, eventually, dismissed.

18 Since Willie Dunlop is not listed as an army officer and since the *Minerva* was not a warship, Dunlop was probably master of a transport and, possibly, an Ayrshireman.

19 Peebles has heard that General Howe has been knighted and that a detachment of Hessians has been overrun at Trenton. The American victory was far more important than Peebles could have known – important in restoring the morale of the rebels after a succession of defeats.

20 For sketches of Rawdon and Dr Fleeming see Appendix A Biographical Notes.

21 Peebles may be referring to Lieutenant-Colonel Archibald Campbell (1739–91), who had been captured en route to North America and would remain a prisoner until May 1778.

22 Peebles has heard of the British defeat at Princeton, which further encouraged the rebels and was more important than the British were then saying.

23 Peebles means to say he has gone to Lieutenant-Colonel Mungo Campbell's to drink punch. See Appendix A Biographical Notes.

24 By 'our Regt.' Peebles meant the 42nd; James McPherson seems to have commanded the foraging party.

Notes to Chapter III

1 Gruber, *Howe Brothers*, pp. 158–233.

2 22–4 February, 7, 19 March 1777, Peebles Diary.

3 26 March, 7 April, 25 May, 8, 11, 12 June 1777, *ibid.*

4 13, 19, 22, 25–9 June 1777, *ibid.*

5 For Vaughan and Cornwallis see Appendix A Biographical Notes.

6 Peebles' first mention of George Washington, the commander-in-chief of the Continental Army. See Appendix A Biographical Notes. Washington was not, as the British suspected, planning to retire across the Delaware.

7 Governor William Franklin (1731–1813) would remain in prison in Connecticut until October 1778. Unlike his famous father (Benjamin Franklin), Governor Franklin was a staunch Loyalist and would go to England in 1782. His wife died while he was in prison.

8 Grant in Appendix A Biographical Notes.

9 Benjamin Lincoln in Appendix A Biographical Notes.

10 For Governor William Tryon see Appendix A Biographical Notes. For report on Danbury raid see 1 May 1777, Peebles Diary.

11 For Arnold see Appendix A Biographical Notes; for Danbury raid, Ward, *War of Revolution*, pp. 492–495.

12 Peebles wrote to Lieutenant-Colonel Monckton who commanded the 2nd battalion of British Grenadiers – possibly with success. Mallon became a captain in the 63rd that September; Monckton was killed at Monmouth.

13 This transaction shows the web of conventions and expectations that shaped the system of purchasing commissions. Peebles clearly wanted to be promoted, but he was offended by the price until he found a way to shift

some of the cost to others in the regiment who would benefit eventually by Chisholm's selling out. For a sketch of Peebles' friend, John Rutherfurd, see Appendix A Biographical Notes.

14 For sketches of DeHeister (von Heister), Vaughan, Grey, and Leslie see Appendix A Biographical Notes.

15 Bridge seems to have been built by Captain James Moncrieffe (1744–93).

Notes to Chapter IV

1 Gruber, *Howe Brothers*, pp. 224–67.

2 8 July, 24, 25 August 1777, Peebles Diary.

3 11, 12, 26 September, 4, 8, 16, 17, 29, 30 October 1777, *ibid*.

4 31 October, 2, 3, 16, 8, 9, 13, 22 November, 7–8 December 1777, *ibid*. See also 21 May 1777, 16 November 1778 for additional information.

5 Peebles has kept to the civil day while at sea. This voyage may be followed on the map, 'British North America, Virginia to Newfoundland,' front endpaper.

6 For a more detailed account of the British victory at the Battle of Brandywine see Ward, *War of Revolution*, pp. 341–59. Scholars give Washington only 11,000 to oppose a slightly larger British force (Cornwallis' and Knyphausen's forces combined), Peckham, *Toll of Independence*, p. 40. Peebles' account makes clear that the British were too tired and had too little daylight to exploit their victory.

7 Peebles estimates of casualties are close to twentieth-century figures; see Peckham, *Toll of Independence*, p. 40.

8 For a more extensive account of what the rebels called the Paoli Massacre see Ward, *War of Revolution*, pp. 358–9.

9 Gruber, *Howe Brothers*, pp. 244–60 describes British efforts to open the Delaware to their shipping.

10 Ward, *War of Revolution*, pp. 362–71 gives a full account of the Battle of Germantown. As Peebles noted, the Americans were unusually aggressive at Germantown.

11 For Colonel Prescot see Appendix A Biographical Notes.

12 Peebles records his having been promoted to Captain Lieutenant in the Black Watch. To accept this promotion he has had to leave the grenadiers and rejoin his regiment in a line company. In saying he has served 'above nineteen years,' he is counting his service as a surgeon's mate.

13 That is, Burgoyne's surrender at Saratoga – his having signed a convention – has been 'made public.' By the terms of the convention, his army was to return home and not to serve again in America during the war. Congress, fearing that Burgoyne's army would merely release other troops for service in the colonies found reasons to keep the Convention Army prisoners in the United States. See 14 March 1778, Peebles Diary.

14 Orders deleted; see entries for 4, 5 December.

15 William Lord Cathcart has brought the Earl of Eglintoun's compliments; for both see Appendix A Biographical Notes.

16 Entry not completed.

Notes to Chapter V

1 Gruber, *Howe Brothers*, 268–303; William B. Willcox, *Portrait of a General Sir Henry Clinton in the War of Independence*, pp. 197–237.

2 1 January, 2 February, 20 March, 22 April, 14 May, 8 June; 12 February; 30 January, 7, 8, 11 May 1778, Peebles Diary.

3 26 February–2 March, 10 March, 9, 21 April, 3, 28 May, 7 June 1778, *ibid.*

4 5 January, 3, 5 February, 11, 18, 19, 25 March, 15 April, 18, 19, 26 May 1778, *ibid.*

5 18–28 June, 5 July 1778, *ibid.*

6 Norry seems to have been an agent who agreed to provide meals for the officers of the Black Watch. See also 20 December 1777, 20 June 1778, *ibid.*

7 For this entry John Peebles seems to have adapted several lines from Jonathan Swift's 'A Rhapsody.'

8 Peebles has attended two plays: *The Minor*, author unknown, and *Duke & no Duke* by Nahum Tate.

9 William Alexander, Lord Stirling (1726–83), was born in America but claimed to be the Earl of Stirling (and he was called Lord Stirling by Americans). Wealthy and prominent by the time of the Revolution, he became a major-general in the Continental Army and served with merit throughout the war – primarily in the mid-Atlantic states.

10 Probably Joseph Galloway's furniture. Galloway, a leading Pennsylvanian and Loyalist, was head of civil government in Philadelphia during the British occupation. (He had a country home.) He eventually withdrew to England and was not permitted to return to the new United States.

11 Peebles was having a portrait done for Anna Hamilton. See 11, 19 March, 15 April, 12 May, 18 August 1778, Peebles Diary. The artist was Pierre Eugene du Simitière (1734–84); see Paul Ginsburg Sifton, 'Pierre Eugene du Simitière . . . Collector in Revolutionary America' (PhD thesis, University of Pennsylvania, 1960), pp. 427–9. I owe special thanks to Dr Ellen G. Miles, who made me aware of the connection between Peebles and du Simitière.

12 Probably *Rivington's New York Loyal Gazette*, which may have been the first daily newspaper in North America. James Rivington had been a successful bookseller in Philadelphia, New York, and Boston before the Revolution. After withdrawing to England in January 1776, he returned to

New York and began publishing his newspaper in October 1777. He remained in the United States after the war but was forced out of business.

13 Peebles seems to be trying to say that he finds the portrait a good likeness.

14 Peebles has again seen two plays: *The Inconstant* by George Farquhar and *Letcher*, author unknown.

15 Maredant was a medication sold in New York during the Revolution as a cure for rheumatism, inflamed eyes, and disorders of the blood. See Oscar Barck, *New York City during the War for Independence with Special Reference to the Period of British Occupation*, p. 95.

16 David Rittenhouse (1732–1796), the foremost observational astronomer in British North America, had worked as a surveyor and clockmaker. He built his orrery, or moveable model of the solar system, in 1767. After serving in the government of Pennsylvania during the war, he became first director of the United States mint and president of the American Philosophical Society.

17 The plays were: William Shakespeare's *Henry IV* and Henry Fielding's *The Mock Doctor*.

18 See Appendix A Biographical Notes for a sketch of Colonel James Patterson.

19 Frederick Lord North was the principal minister in the House of Commons 1770–82. Although he was not a strong advocate of coercive measures, he presided over the ministry throughout the American War – perhaps out of a sense of obligation to the king. The peace overture of 1778 had been conceived as a measure that might forestall French intervention. Adopted belatedly, it had no prospect of success – either in keeping France out of the war or in reconciling the colonists. See 4 May 1778, Peebles Diary.

20 For Abercrombie see Appendix A Biographical Notes.

21 The first motto – or tribute to Sir William Howe – may be translated: 'I owe him praise and greater thanks'; the second, 'Go, good man, where your virtue calls you and go with good fortune.'

22 The motto on the tickets: 'gradually setting and rising with accustomed splendor.'

23 Major Gordon and Mrs. Williams have had, it seems, the principal roles in John Home's *Douglas*.

24 For the action at Barren Hill see Ward, *War of Revolution*, pp. 562–567; for Lafayette, Appendix A Biographical Notes.

25 The remainder of the march through New Jersey may be followed on the map 'New Jersey Trenton to Fort Lee,' p. 93.

26 Peebles estimated the eclipse to be of 11 1/2 digit magnitude (of a possible 12).

27 Monmouth, the last great battle of the war in the middle colonies, marked the emergence of the Continental Army as an effective fighting force – a

force sufficiently disciplined & skilled to overcome the flight of its advanced units and to fight an experienced British army to a draw. For tactical details see Ward, *War of Revolution*, pp. 576–86.

Notes to Chapter VI

1 Gruber, *Howe Brothers*, pp. 304–24; Willcox, *Portrait of a General*, pp. 225–55; Ira D. Gruber, 'Britain's Southern Strategy,' in W. Robert Higgins, ed., *The Revolutionary War in the South: Power, Conflict, and Leadership*, pp. 217–21.

2 7, 12, 23 July, 7, 17, 24 August 1778, Peebles Diary.

3 27, 28 August, 1 September 1778, *ibid.*

4 5–6, 10–15, 19, 22 September–15 October, 4, 10, 30 November 1778, *ibid.*

5 Peebles' movements on Long Island may be followed on the map, 'Staten Island, New York Island and S. W. Long Island,' back endpaper.

6 Alexander Earl of Balcarras had been taken prisoner at Saratoga; he was now a part of the Convention army seeking exchange.

7 Peebles reports the complete failure of the Carlisle Peace Commission's overtures to Congress. Nothing short of the recognition of the independence of the United States would now have drawn Congress into a negotiation.

8 This is the first mention of George Duncan Ludlow who was to be one of Peebles' closest friends among the Loyalists; see Appendix A Biographical Notes.

9 For DeLancey and Ludlow see Appendix A Biographical Notes.

10 The British feared an attack this day because the French had favorable winds and tides for crossing the bar at Sandy Hook. But by evening the French were gone.

11 Stirling was, Peebles suspected, expanding his rolls with phantom men so as to increase the income he received from the government. Alan J. Guy, *Oeconomy and Discipline 1714–1763*, chapter 4, did not find the practice very common by the mid-eighteenth century.

12 Peebles was more critical of ministers than of generals – here of the first Lord of the Admiralty, the Earl of Sandwich.

13 A tropical storm or hurricane – to judge by the direction of the wind – had struck Long Island and the opposing fleets as they were about to engage off Rhode Island. Both fleets suffered from the storm and some isolated engagements.

14 Although Peebles wrote Foxheath in his diary, he seems to have been referring to the camp at Coxheath. See Houlding, *Fit for Service*, pp. 328–30. John Bartholomew, ed., *Gazetteer of the British Isles* does not list a Foxheath.

15 Peebles has been promoted to captain of the grenadier company of the Black Watch – his old company which was serving as a part of the 1st battalion of British Grenadiers. His new company had a strength of eighty common soldiers and fourteen nco's, drummers, and fifers.

16 Waggoner is a corruption of the name of a Dutch hydrographer, Lucas Jansz Waghenaer (1533–1606). The British used 'Wagoner' loosely to denote any book of charts.

17 Once again, the map, 'Staten Island, New York Island and S. W. Long Island', back endpaper, covers Peebles' progress.

18 Peebles reports the announcement of his promotion to captain (18 August 1778) and his frustration that Sir Henry Clinton has decided to appoint an officer from another regiment to a captaincy in the Black Watch, that an outsider has been preferred to his friend John Rutherfurd.

19 These movements may be followed on the map, 'The Hudson River New York to West Point,' p. 264.

20 Peebles seems to be saying he thinks his company of grenadiers should receive more than 1 1/2 of a company's share of prize money because his company is nearly twice the size of a regular line company.

21 Mrs. McCraw was the wife of Sergeant Donald McCraw of the grenadier company of the Black Watch. She and her husband looked after the details of Peebles' housekeeping (preparing his food, keeping his accounts, looking after his horse) until McCraw was wounded and sent home in the summer of 1780.

Notes to Chapter VII

1 Willcox, *Portrait of a General*, pp. 256–75.

2 3–7, 28 December 1778; 24 January, 11, 16, 20 February, 2, 27, 30 March, 1, 8, 14 April 1779, Peebles Diary.

3 23 December 1778, 1, 2, 8, 12, 16, 22, 28 January, 16 February, 5, 7 March, 12 April 1779, *ibid.*

4 21 December 1778, 22 January, 9 February, 18, 29 March, 13 April 1779, *ibid.*

5 This expedition may be followed on the map, 'The Hudson River New York to West Point,' p. 264.

6 Peebles clearly thought the captain of the transport that had carried his company to King's Ferry was making a false claim – presumably so that he might be reimbursed for damages. See 5 December 1778, Peebles Diary.

7 See map, 'The West Indies,' p. 282.

8 For Prevost see Appendix A Biographical Notes. For a twentieth-century account that is remarkably similiar to what Peebles heard, see Douglas W.

Marshall and Howard H. Peckham, *Campaigns of the American Revolution An Atlas of Manuscript Maps*, pp. 76–9.

9 While in Philadelphia, Peebles had found Cate most agreeable; see 11 January 1778, Peebles Diary.

10 James MacLogan had been chaplain of the Black Watch since June 1764.

11 For Collier see Appendix A Biographical Notes.

12 Colonel Robert Magaw had commanded rebel forces defending Fort Washington in November 1776. He had been taken prisoner and may well have been on parole, awaiting exchange.

13 Cathcart married Elizabeth Elliot, daughter of Andrew Elliot, a Loyalist who had been a customs official in New York and who would soon be lieutenant-governor of the colony (1780–83).

14 Miss Inglis may have been the agreeable 'Cate' with whom Mrs Rutherfurd corresponded. See 11 January, 18 March 1778; 16 February 1779, Peebles Diary.

15 Admiral Augustus Keppel had commanded the British fleet against the French in the summer of 1778. After an inconclusive engagement off Ushant, Keppel's friends criticized his third in command, Sir Hugh Palliser, for failure to obey orders. Palliser, who was also a Lord of the Admiralty and a political opponent of Keppel, promptly charged Keppel with misconduct and neglect of duty. A court martial subsequently acquitted Keppel in a most public and political trial. The verdict touched off riotous celebrations.

16 For Simcoe see Appendix A Biographical Notes.

17 The ensuing expedition to the Chesapeake was one of the most successful British raids of the war. See Gruber, 'Britain's Southern Strategy,' pp. 222–3.

18 Lincoln see Appendix A Biographical Notes.

19 See map, 'The South Atlantic States,' p. 246.

20 When the war spread to India, the British were able to gain control of the seas and to capture the French trading port at Pondicherry (Piers Mackesy, *The War for America, 1775–1783*, p. 380).

Notes to Chapter VIII

1 Willcox, *Portrait of a General*, pp. 273–93.

2 30 May, 1, 7, 14, 27 June 1779, Peebles Diary.

3 28 June, 31 July, 12 August, 15, 28 October 1779, *ibid.*

4 9 July, 31 August, 1–30 September, 4–27 October, 1, 6 November 1779, *ibid.*

5 7 September (quoted), 22, 27 October, 1 November 1779, *ibid.*

6 These movements may best be seen on the map of 'The Hudson River New York to West Point,' p. 264.

7 At first, Peebles called Stony Point, 'Rocky point'; but by 2 June he was using the accepted name, 'Stony Point.'

8 Patrick Ferguson's men carried rifles and were capable of killing their enemies at much greater ranges than soldiers in line regiments who had smooth bore muskets.

9 See sketch of Tarleton in Appendix A Biographical Notes.

10 Operations in Long Island Sound may be followed in map of 'Atlantic Seaboard Long Island to Cape Cod,' p. 212.

11 A cryptic and prudential entry: Peebles did not make clear who was 'saucy' and 'vain.'

12 See once again map of 'The Hudson River New York to West Point,' p. 264.

13 Peebles' summary of Cornwallis' testimony before the House of Commons was accurate and astute. See Gruber, *Howe Brothers*, pp. 342–3.

14 See August 1779.

15 For camp at McGowans see map of 'Staten Island, New York Island and S. W. Long Island,' back endpaper.

16 Peebles has heard of John Sullivan's punitive expedition against the Loyalists and Indians of western New York – an expedition mounted after the Loyalists and Indians, led by John and Walter Butler, had ravaged the frontiers of Pennsylvania and New York in 1778. Sullivan systematically destroyed Indian towns during the summer and autumn of 1779. See map of 'British North America Virginia to Newfoundland,' front end paper.

17 George Keith Elphinstone, see Appendix A Biographical Notes.

18 Marriot Arbuthnot, see Appendix A Biographical Notes.

19 Jack and Charlie were Peebles' nephews, children of his sister, Elizabeth Fraser. After the war, he would try to help his nephews gain appointments in the army and the customs service. See 24 May, 5 June 1781, Peebles Diary.

20 For an account of Collier's successful relief of Penobscot, Maine, see Mark Mayo Boatner, *Encyclopedia of the American Revolution*, pp. 851–2.

21 Although the grenadiers have been reorganized into two battalions, Peebles' company (the grenadier company of the 42nd), remains in the 1st battalion – now under Lieutenant-Colonel Henry Hope.

22 11 September is a double anniversary for Peebles: of his birth and of the British victory in the Battle of Brandywine.

23 Cornwallis was embarking with 4,000 men to relieve Jamaica, which was thought to be threatened by a French fleet. Cornwallis would sail on 24 September and return on 27 September, after having learned that the French had bypassed Jamaica and were en route to North America. See Gruber, 'Britain's Southern Strategy,' pp. 225–6, and 26, 27, 29 September 1779, Peebles Diary.

24 It is not quite clear what Peebles meant by 'carronades.' It is possible that Marshall had invested in the manufacture of the new naval cannon or carronade that was especially designed to fire a large, low velocity solid shot that would shatter the hull of a warship and inflict more damage on the enemy's crew than the shot fired by a conventional naval gun. If so, Marshall might have asked Peebles to promote his new gun which was being manufactured at the Carron iron works near Falkirk, Scotland. It is also possible that Marshall was using the word facetiously and asking Peebles to help him sell a set of pistols. The British used carronades during the siege of Charleston. See 17 April 1780, Peebles Diary.

25 That is, only 30 of perhaps 300 men were fit for duty.

26 Major-General William Phillips and Baron Friedrich Adolphus Riedesel had served with the Canadian army in 1777 and, after being captured at Saratoga, had remained with the Convention army. See Appendix A Biographical Notes.

27 Worth Estes, MD, of Boston University suggests the following translation of Dr Morris's prescription: 3 drachms [8 drachms to the ounce] of Plummer's Pills mixed with 1 drachm of soap and made into 48 pills. Take 2 every 6 hours in a draught made of an infusion of chamomile flowers with 15 drops of a mixture of 1 ounce of smelling salts & 1½ ounces of Lavender.

28 Peebles seems to be saying that sixty-one men in his company – or roughly two-thirds of the whole – were ill. At no other time during his service in the American War did he record such widespread illness among his men.

29 Peebles has been asking various friends to recommend him for appointment as major of brigade. He was not, it seems, able to ask his colonel, Brigadier-General Thomas Stirling. See 18, 25 October 1779.

Notes to Chapter IX

1 Willcox, *Portrait of a General*, pp. 289–302; Gruber, 'Britain's Southern Strategy,' 224–6.

2 14, 22, 24–6, 30 November, 3, 13, 7 December 1779, Peebles Diary.

3 20, 26 December 1779, 5, 10, 12, 14, 15, 20 January 1780, *ibid*.

4 12 January, 5, 10 February 1780, *ibid*.

5 For the captains' petition that so displeased Stirling, see 14 November 1779, Peebles Diary.

6 It is not at all clear what Peebles meant by 'a smack from P—warhawkes'; but that is what he confided to his diary.

7 Miss Polly Ogden has sent Peebles a parting gift, but the manuscript is illegible just where he has named the gift.

8 For Tybee Island see map of 'The South Atlantic States,' p. 246.

Notes to Chapter X

1 Willcox, *Portrait of a General*, pp. 302–22; Gruber, 'Britain's Southern Strategy,' pp. 226–8; 8, 28 April 1780, Peebles Diary. See map of the siege of Charleston p. 336. I am indebted to Richard Groening for his expert help in locating many of the plantations along the British line of march.

2 11 February, 4, 12, 29 March, 2 April 1780, Peebles Diary.

3 4, 5, 10, 11, 16, 19, 21, 23, 27, 29 April, 1, 8, 11 May 1780, *ibid.*

4 13, 22 (quoted), 24 May 1780, *ibid.*

5 Somehow Peebles managed to keep young Ned, then about nine, with him for nearly two years. In January 1782 he tried to sell Ned to George Duncan Ludlow. Ludlow refused to buy Ned because he had 'the Itch,' but he did indenture him to Peebles. It is not clear what became of Ned. Indenture for Ned, 19 February 1782, Cunninghame of Thorntoun Papers, GD 21/158, SRO; 22, 24 January 1782, Peebles Diary.

6 See Appendix A Biographical Notes for a sketch of Fox.

7 It is not clear who has lost what.

8 Beaufort River flows into Port Royal Sound; see 'The South Atlantic States,' p. 246.

9 It is not quite clear what Peebles is saying – perhaps that Crosbie or the dinner at headquarters was a little too formal for Peebles' taste or, alternatively, too boorish. He does not seem to have enjoyed the meal.

10 See Appendix B Glossary for place of arms or place d'armes.

11 Rodney had relieved Gibraltar on his way to the West Indies. See sketch in Appendix A Biographical Notes.

12 The siege of Charleston was one of the few times in the War for American Independence when either side conducted a regular siege – Yorktown was another. In the more densely populated parts of western Europe where nations were able to build fortresses to protect their frontiers, sieges were quite common from the late seventeenth until the mid-eighteenth century. Europeans relied on engineers to capture a fortress by digging their way to within a few hundred yards of the defenders' walls and erecting batteries that could either breech the walls or pound the defenders into submission. In North America there were only three or four places that were so well fortified as to invite a siege. For a discussion of fortifications and siegecraft see Reginald Blomfield, *Sebastièn le Prestre de Vauban, 1633–1707*, and Christopher Duffy, *The Fortress in the Age of Vauban and Frederick the Great, 1660–1789*.
The siege of Charleston was very systematically and cautiously done. The British sought to capture the town and its garrison with a minimum of risks and casualties. They succeeded, constructing three parallels and displacing their batteries forward until able to force the rebels to surrender.

Notes to Chapter XI

1 Gruber, 'Britain's Southern Strategy,' pp. 231–2; Willcox, *Portrait of a General*, pp. 322–46; William B. Willcox, ed., *The American Rebellion Sir Henry Clinton's Narrative of His Campaigns, 1775–1782*, pp. 188–218.

2 19–23, 25 June, 11, 24 July, 2 August 1780, Peebles Diary.

3 21, 22 August, 21, 25, 28, 29, 30 September, 5, 16 October, 8, 10, 15 November, *ibid.*

4 See maps of 'New Jersey Trenton to Fort Lee,' p. 93 and 'The Hudson River New York to West Point,' p. 264.

5 See introduction for Peebles' friendships with the Ogdens and Cortlands.

6 For Crosbie see Appendix A Biographical Notes.

7 For a sketch of Graves see Appendix A Biographical Notes.

8 Peebles visited Lydia Hant and her family in the summer of 1779. He knew that she kept a journal of their sufferings during the war, and he now sought to protect the Hants from Andreas Emmerich, a lieutenant-colonel of provincial forces. See 3 July 1779, Peebles Diary.

9 For Hamilton see Appendix A Biographical Notes. For ensuing movements of the British fleet and army on and around Long Island see map of 'Atlantic Seaboard Long Island to Cape Cod,' p. 212.

10 For DeLancey's career see Appendix A Biographical Notes.

11 Peebles copied these lengthy 'Rules for Manouvering the Battn.' into his journal; they may be seen in Cunninghame of Thorntoun Papers, GD 21/492, 11, SRO.

12 Cornwallis had won a decisive, if illusory, victory over Gates at Camden, South Carolina, on 16 August 1780. He destroyed the rebel army but was unable to use his victory to restore Loyalists to power in the Carolinas.

13 A triple celebration: of victories at Charleston and at Brandywine and of Peebles' birthday.

14 Daniel Ludlow was a brother of Gabriel and George Duncan Ludlow who are described in Appendix A Biographical Notes and the Introduction.

15 For O'Hara see Appendix A Biographical Notes.

16 Leslie's departure marked the beginning of a gradual (and not clearly intentional) redeployment of British forces from New York to the Chesapeake. See Gruber, 'Britain's Southern Strategy,' pp. 232–3.

17 Peebles first acknowledges that Cornwallis' efforts to restore Loyalists to power in the Carolinas were not going well. Patrick Ferguson had been killed and his 1,000 Loyalists overwhelmed at King's Mountain, South Carolina, on 7 October 1780.

18 For a sketch of Yorke see Appendix A Biographical Notes.

Notes to Chapter XII

1 Willcox, *Portrait of a General*, pp. 342–391; Willcox, ed., *American Rebellion*, pp. 219–298; Gruber, 'Britain's Southern Strategy,' pp. 230–7.

2   17, 22 November 1780, 21 February, 22, 25, 31 March, 30 April, 1, 5 May, 1, 9 June 1781, Peebles Diary.

3   30 November, 8 December 1780, 17, 20 February, 8 April 1781, *ibid.*

4   5, 6, 17, 19 January 1781, *ibid.*

5   30 November, 4 December 1780, 26, 27 February, 1, 26, 30 March, 5, 7–8, 15, 16, 19, 21–2 April, 17, 31 May 1781, *ibid.*

6   1 December 1780, 3, 22, 24, 25 January 1781 (8 December 1780–1 January 1781 have been cut out), *ibid.*

7   22 (quoted), 28 January, 13 February 1781, *ibid.*

8   Entries for 9 December 1780 to 1 January 1781 have been cut out of Peebles' notebook. He seems to have decided it would be prudent to destroy what he had said in frustration and anger at being denied permission to sell his commission.

9   Anna Hamilton was clearly sympathetic with Peebles' efforts to sell out; see 28 June 1781, Peebles Diary.

10 Peebles has just heard about Tarleton's defeat at Cowpens, South Carolina, on 17 January. Tarleton attacked a smaller force of rebels that were skillfully placed and managed by Daniel Morgan, losing 110 killed, 200 wounded, and 527 captured out of about 1,100 cavalry and infantry. This stinging defeat provoked Cornwallis to burn his baggage and pursue Morgan and Nathanael Greene into North Carolina where in March he would nearly lose his own army at the Battle of Guilford Court House. Britain's strategy for recovering the South was unravelling. For a sketch of Greene see Appendix A Biographical Notes.

11 See map 'The South Atlantic States,' p. 246.

12 Although the Latin is difficult to understand, Peebles seems to have been ill, perhaps as a result of having had too much to drink. He told his friend at breakfast that he had been chilling his head and purging himself.

13 Rodney had captured St. Eustatius, but he had become so preoccupied with plunder that he cancelled the attack on Curaçao, Mackesy, *War for America*, p. 417. Arbuthnot's opponent was Charles René Dominique Gochet Destouches, who would give up his command in May 1781.

14 At Guilford Court House on 15 March, the British did force the American forces to withdraw. But in gaining control of the ground, the British suffered such heavy casualties that they could not remain in the piedmont of North Carolina to exploit their victory – to rally the Loyalists. Cornwallis withdrew to Wilmington and went from there to Virginia, leaving Greene free to recover the hinterlands of the Carolinas during the spring and summer of 1781. No one at New York could as yet know the outcome of the Battle of Guilford Court House. See 23 April 1781, Peebles Diary.

15 James Marsh, lieutenant-colonel of the 43rd who had previously served with the grenadiers, was replacing Yorke as commanding officer of the first battalion of grenadiers.

Notes to Chapter XIII

1 Willcox, *Portrait of a General*, pp. 381–444 (quoting p. 389); Willcox, ed., *American Rebellion*, pp. 282–350; Gruber, 'Britain's Southern Strategy,' pp. 235–8; Franklin and Mary Wickwire, *Cornwallis the American Adventure*, pp. 311–88.

2 14, 29 June 1781, Peebles Diary.

3 18, 25, 28, 29 August, 3, 6, 7, 19 September, *ibid.*

4 28 September, 12, 18, 28 October 1781, *ibid.*

5 28 June (quoted), 17 July 1781, *ibid.*

6 9 September (quoted), 6 (quoted), 16 (quoted), 25, 29 October 1781, *ibid.*

7 See Foxcroft in Appendix A Biographical Notes.

8 See map, 'New Jersey Trenton to Fort Lee,' p. 93.

9 Marvin L. Brown, Jr., ed., *Baroness von Riedesel and the American Revolution Journal and Correspondence of a Tour of Duty, 1776–1783*, pp. 108–10, provides a glimpse of the Riedesels' life on Long Island when Peebles dined with them.

10 See Appendix A Biographical Notes for a sketch of Lincoln.

11 Sir Henry Clinton had at last succeeded in having Arbuthnot recalled, but Digby would not arrive until September or exercise his command for long (see Appendix A Biographical Notes).

12 Alexr. McDonald may be the same man who was captured while trying to steal a cow on 27 November 1780 (Peebles Diary).

13 See Appendix A Biographical Notes for John Campbell.

14 Map of 'The South Atlantic States' (p. 246) helps place Cornwallis' movements.

15 The movements of the armies about New York may be followed on maps of 'The Hudson River New York to West Point,' p. 264, and 'Staten Island, New York Island and S. W. Long Island', back endpaper.

16 Spatchcock: an Irish dish prepared in an emergency; that is 'a fowl split open & grilled after being killed, plucked, and dressed in a summary fashion' (OED).

17 See Hood in Appendix A Biographical Notes.

18 Graves was en route to the Virginia capes, where on 5 September he would engage the French West Indies fleet commanded by Admiral DeGrasse (Appendix A Biographical Notes). That inconclusive action would allow the French to keep control of the Chesapeake and, somewhat reinforced, support the successful Franco-American siege of Lord Cornwallis' army at Yorktown, Virginia.

19 Barras did manage to elude Graves' fleet and join DeGrasse in the Chesapeake, increasing DeGrasse's superiority over Graves and providing the siege guns that would be used at Yorktown.

20 For an account of this action in the Cape Verde Islands see Mackesy, *War for America*, p. 390.

21 Peebles had two separate entries in his diary for 9 September 1781. The first ended here; the second, with the redundant date eliminated, began with the following paragraph.

22 For Peebles' account of Arnold's raid on New London see Map 'Atlantic Seaboard Long Island to Cape Cod,' p. 212, and Marshall and Peckham, *Campaigns*, p. 123.

23 Again, Peebles had two entries for a single date, 6 October 1781. The first, which seems to have been an official pronouncement with the addition of one or two of Peebles' comments, ended at this point; the second began with the following paragraph. The date on the second has been eliminated.

24 Two entries for 28 October 1781: the first ended here; the second began with the next paragraph. The date on the second entry has been deleted.

Notes to Chapter XIV

1 Willcox, *Portrait of a General*, pp. 440–63; Willcox, ed., *American Rebellion*, pp. 332–50.

2 25 October, 15, 20, 21, 25, 26 November 1781, Peebles Diary.

3 That Stirling departed is an assumption. *A List of the General and Field Officers, as They Rank in the Army; of the Officers in the Several Regiments of Horse, Dragoons, and Foot, on the British and Irish Establishments . . . for 1783* (London, [1783]) shows that Stirling became colonel of the 71st regiment in February 1782; and Peebles' diary makes clear that Stirling's opposition to his selling out ended abruptly in late December 1781. It seems likely, therefore, that Stirling left the Black Watch, went home, and assumed command of his new regiment in early 1782. 21, 23, 26, 31 December 1781, 25 January, 1 February 1782, Peebles Diary.

4 8, 16 February, 2 March 1782, *ibid*; marriage contract between John Peebles and Ann Hamilton, Irvine, Ayrshire, 20 May 1782, Cunninghame of Thorntoun Papers, GD 21/159, SRO.

5 Peebles cut out the page for 30 December 1781 – perhaps because he once again vented his frustration over selling out, perhaps because he said something indiscreet about Stedman's death.

6 Peebles again cut out pages from his notebook – entries from 11 to 20 January 1782.

7 Jean François Paul de Gondi, Cardinal de Retz (1614–79) was a French ecclesiastical and political leader of the mid-seventeenth century. His *Mémoires*, written in retirement, describe contemporary court life.

8 Peebles misdated this and the next three entries – hence the corrected date in brackets.

9 Peebles was reading Charles de Secondat, Baron de la Brède et de Monte-

squieu's best known work, *Persian Letters*, which provided a clever criticism of early eighteenth-century French society.

10 Peebles made two entries for this his last day in America. Although the entries begin in much the same words, they are different enough to warrant being considered together. Each is complete as Peebles wrote it.

Bibliography

Manuscript Sources

William L. Clements Library, Ann Arbor, Michigan
Clinton Papers (Sir Henry Clinton's extensive correspondence for his service during the American War).
Germain Papers.
Howe Papers.

Library of Congress, Washington, D.C.
Map Division (especially, 'Plan or Part of the river DELAWARE from Chester to Philadelphia . . . 15 November 1777').

John Rylands University Library of Manchester, Manchester
Lord John Murray Papers (Murray's correspondence as colonel of the Black Watch).
Clinton Papers (Sir Henry Clinton's manuscript notebooks, especially numbers 6 and 7 which contain his journal kept during the siege of Charleston, 8 February to 28 March 1780).

Public Record Office, Kew
Admiralty, Class 51 (captains' logs for ships serving in America).
Colonial Office Papers, Class 5, Volumes 91–104 (correspondence between the secretaries of state for America and the commanders-in-chief in North America).
MPH 225 (Bernard Ratzen's 'Plan of the City of New York' with manuscript annotations post 21 September 1776).
War Office Papers, Class 17 (monthly returns for regiments – volume 152 for the 42nd); Class 27 (regimental reviews – volume 35 for the 42nd).

Scottish Record Office, Edinburgh
Cunninghame of Thorntoun Papers (GD 21/492, 1–13 for the manuscript note-books containing John Peebles' diary for the American War; GD 21/153–724 for other documents relating to Peebles' service, life, and family).

Diaries and Journals of British Officers

André, John, *Major André's Journal . . .* , ed., H. C. Lodge (New York, 1968).

Anon., 'A Contemporary British Account of General Sir William Howe's Military Operations in 1777,' ed., Robert Frances Seybolt, the American Antiquarian Society, *Proceedings* (1930), pp. 69–92.

Bamford, William, 'Bamford's diary: the Revolutionary Diary of a British Officer,' *Maryland Historical Magazine* (1932), pp. 240–59, 296–314 (1933), pp. 9–26.

Barker, John, *The British in Boston Being the Diary of Lieutenant John Barker*, ed., Elizabeth Ellery Dana (Cambridge, 1924).

Digby, William, *The British Invasion from the North: Digby's Journal*, ed., James Phinney Baxter (Albany, 1887).

Downman, Francis, *Services of Lieutenant Colonel Francis Downman*, ed., F. A. Whinyates (Woolwich, 1898).

Enys, John, *The American Journals of Lt John Enys*, ed., Elizabeth Cometti (Syracuse, 1976).

Hadden, James M., *Hadden's Journal and Orderly Book*, ed., Horatio Rogers (Albany, 1884).

Hamilton, Henry, *Henry Hamilton and George Rogers Clark in the American Revolution with the Unpublished Journal of Henry Hamilton*, ed., John D. Barnhart (Craufordsville, 1951).

Harris, George, *The Life and Services of General Lord Harris*, by Stephen R. Lushington (London, 1840).

Haslewood, John, 'Journal of a British Officer during the American Revolution,' ed., Louise P. Kellogg, *Mississippi Valley Historical Review* (1920), pp. 51–8.

Hughes, Thomas, *The Journal of Thomas Hughes*, ed., E. A. Benians (Cambridge, 1947).

Kemble, Stephen, *The Kemble Papers* (*Collections* of the New-York Historical Society) 2 vols. (New York, 1884–1885).

Mackenzie, Frederick, *Diary of Frederick Mackenzie*, 2 vols. (Cambridge, Massachusetts, 1930).

Montresor, John, *Montresor's Journal*, ed., G. D. Scull (*Collections* of the New-York Historical Society) (New York, 1882).

Pattison, James, 'A New York Diary of the Revolutionary War,' ed., Carson I. A. Ritchie, *New York Historcial Society Quarterly* (1966), pp. 221–80, 401–46.

Robertson, Archibald, *Archibald Robertson Lieutenant General Royal Engineers His Diaries and Sketches in America 1762–1780*, ed., Harry Miller Lydenberg (New York, 1930).

Russell, Peter, 'The Siege of Charleston: the Journal of Captain Peter Russell, December 25, 1779 to May 2, 1780,' ed., James Bain, Jr., *The American Historical Review* (1899), pp. 478–501.

Simcoe, John Graves, *Simcoe's Military Journal A History of the Operations of a Partisan Corps called the Queen's Rangers* (New York, 1844).

Stirke, Henry, 'A British Officer's Revolutionary War Journal, 1776–1778,' ed., S. Sydney Bradford, *Maryland Historical Magazine* (1961), pp. 150–75.

Atlases, Gazetteers and Maps

Adams, James Truslow, ed., *Atlas of American History* (New York, 1943).

Bartholomew, John, ed., *Gazetteer of the British Isles* (Edinburgh, 1963).

The Times Atlas of the World, 5 vols. (London, 1955–1959).

Boatner, Mark M. III, *Landmarks of the American Revolution* (Harrisburg, 1973).

Cappon, Lester J., ed., *Atlas of Early American History: The Revolutionary Era 1760–1790* (Princeton, 1976).

Faden, William, 'Boston its Environs and Harbour . . . from the Observations of Lieut. Page of His Majesty's Corps of Engineers' (London, 1778).

Jefferys, Thomas, 'A Map of the most Inhabited part of New England' (London, 1774).

Marshall, Douglas W. and Howard H. Peckham, *Campaigns of the American Revolution An Atlas of Manuscript Maps* (Ann Arbor, 1976).

Nebenzahl, Kenneth and Don Higginbotham, *Atlas of the American Revolution* (Chicago, 1974).

Articles and Books

Anderson, Fred, *A People's Army Massachusetts Soldiers and Society in the Seven Years' War* (Chapel Hill, 1984).

Atwood, Rodney, *The Hessians Mercenaries from Hessen–Kassel in the American Revolution* (Cambridge, 1980).

Barck, Oscar Theodore, Jr., *New York City during the War for Independence with Special Reference to the Period of British Occupation* (New York, 1931).

Billias, George Athan, *George Washington's Opponents British Generals and Admirals in the American Revolution* (New York, 1969).

Black, Jeremy, *War for America: The Fight for Independence 1775–1783* (New York, 1991).

Blomfield, Reginald, *Sebastièn le Prestre de Vauban, 1633–1707* (New York, 1971).

Boatner, Mark M. III, *Encyclopedia of the American Revolution* (New York, 1958).

Bowler, R. Arthur, *Logistics and the Failure of the British Army in America 1775–1783* (Princeton, 1975).

Clinton, Sir Henry, *The American Rebellion Sir Henry Clinton's Narrative of His Campaigns, 1775–1782*, ed., William B. Willcox (New Haven, 1954).

Conway, Stephen, 'British Army Officers and the American War for Independence', *William and Mary Quarterly* (1984), pp. 265–76.

' "The Great Mischief Complain'd of": Reflections on the Misconduct of British Soldiers in the Revolutionary War', *William and Mary Quarterly* (1990), pp. 370–90.

'To Subdue America: British Army Officers and the Conduct of the Revolutionary War', *William and Mary Quarterly* (1986), pp. 381–407.

The War of American Independence (London, 1995).

Curtis, Edward E., *The Organization of the British Army in the American Revolution* (New York, 1969).

De Lancey, Oliver, *Orderly Book of the Three Battalions of Loyalists Commanded by Brigadier-General Oliver De Lancey 1776–1778* (New York, 1917).

Denton, Edgar III, ed., *Limits of Loyalty* (Waterloo, Ontario, 1980).

Duffy, Christopher, *The Fortress in the Age of Vauban and Frederick the Great, 1660–1789* (London, 1985).

Dull, Jonathan R., *A Diplomatic History of the American Revolution* (New Haven, 1985).

The French Navy and American Independence (Princeton, 1976).

Falconer, William, *An Universal Dictionary of the Marine* (London, 1789).

Fergusson, Bernard, *The Black Watch and the King's Enemies* (London, 1950).

Forbes, Archibald, *The Black Watch: The Record of an Historic Regiment* (London, 1910).

Ford, W. C., *British Officers Serving in the American Revolution* (Brooklyn, 1897).

Frey, Sylvia R., *The British Soldier in America: A Social History of Military Life in the Revolutionary Period* (Austin, 1981).

Great Britain, War Office, *A List of the General and Field-Officers, As they Rank in the Army; of the Officers in the Several Regiments of Horse, Dragoons, and Foot, on the British and Irish Establishments* (London, 1759–1783).

Greene, Jack P. and J. R. Pole, eds., *The Blackwell Encyclopedia of the American Revolution* (Cambridge [Massachusetts], 1991).

Gruber, Ira D., *The Howe Brothers and the American Revolution* (Chapel Hill, 1974).

'Britain's Southern Strategy' in W. Robert Higgins ed., *The Revoluitonary War in the South: Power, Conflict, and Leadership* (Durham, [N. Carolina], 1979).

'On the Road to Poonamalle: An Irish Officer's View of the War for American Independence', *The American Magazine* (1988), pp. 1–12.

Guy, Alan J., *Oeconomy and Discipline 1714–1763* (Manchester, 1985).

Hatch, Robert McConnell, *Thrust for Canada* (Boston, 1979).

Hayes, J., 'Scottish Officers in the British Army, 1714–1763', *Scottish Historical Review* (1956), pp. 23–33.

Higginbotham, Don, ed., *Reconsiderations on the Revolutionary War* (Westport, 1978).

Hoffman, Ronald and Peter J. Albert, eds., *Arms and Independence, The Military Character of the American Revolution* (Charlottesville, 1984).

Houlding, J. A., *Fit for Service: The Training of the British Army, 1715–1795* (Oxford, 1981).

Jackson, John W., *With the British Army in Philadelphia, 1777–1778* (San Rafael, 1979).

Jones, Thomas, *History of New York during the Revolutionary War*, ed., Edward Floyd De Lancey, 2 vols. (New York, 1879).

Klein, Milton M. and Ronald W. Howard, eds., *The Twilight of British Rule in Revolutionary America: The New York Letter Book of General James Robertson, 1780–1783* (Cooperstown, 1983).

Mackesy, Piers, *The War for America, 1775–1783* (Cambridge [Massachusetts], 1964).

Namier, Sir Lewis, and John Brooke, 'The House of Commons, 1754–1790' in Frank M. Stenton, ed., *The History of Parliament* (New York, 1964).

Palmer, Gregory, *Biographical Sketches of Loyalists of the American Revolution* (Westport [Connecticut], 1984).

Peckham, Howard H., *The Toll of Independence: Engagements & Battle Casualties of the American Revolution* (Chicago, 1974).

Riedesel, Frederika Charlotte Louise von, *Baroness von Riedesel and the American Revolution: Journal and Correspondence of a Tour of Duty 1776–1783*, trans. and ed. by Marvin L. Brown, Jr. with Marta Huth (Chapel Hill, 1965).

Scott, H. M., *British Foreign Policy in the Age of the American Revolution* (Oxford, 1990).

Simes, Thomas, *The Military Guide for Young Officers*, 2 vols. (Philadelphia, 1776). [The second volume of this work is *A New Military, Historical and Explanatory Dictionary*.]

Smith, Paul H., *Loyalists and Redcoats: A Study in British Revolutionary Policy* (Chapel Hill, 1964).

Smith, William, *Historical Memoirs of William Smith*, ed., William H. W. Sabine, 2 vols. (New York, 1956–1958).

Stewart, Charles H., *The Services of British Regiments in Canada and North America* (Ottawa, 1962).

Tiedemann, Joseph S., 'Patriots by Default: Queens County, New York, and the British Army, 1776–1783' *William and Mary Quarterly* (1986), pp. 35–63.

Ward, Christopher, *The War of the Revolution*, ed., John R. Alden, 2 vols. (New York, 1952).

Wickwire, Franklin and Mary, *Cornwallis: The American Adventure* (Boston, 1970).

Willcox, William B., *Portrait of a General: Sir Henry Clinton in the War of Independence* (New York, 1964).

Index

ARMY RECORDS SOCIETY
(FOUNDED 1984)

Members of the Society are entitled to purchase back
volumes at reduced prices.
Orders should be sent to the Hon. Treasurer, Army Records Society,
c/o National Army Museum,
Royal Hospital Road,
London SW3 4HT

The Society has already issued:

Vol. I:
The Military Correspondence of
Field Marshal Sir Henry Wilson 1918–1922
Edited by Dr Keith Jeffery

Vol. II.
The Army and the
Curragh Incident, 1914
Edited by Dr Ian F.W. Beckett

Vol. III
The Napoleonic War Journal of
Captain Thomas Henry Browne, 1807–1816
Edited by Roger Norman Buckley

Vol. IV:
An Eighteenth-Century Secretary at War
The Papers of William, Viscount Barrington
Edited by Dr Tony Hayter

Vol. V:
The Military Correspondence of
Field Marshal Sir William Robertson 1915–1918
Edited by David R. Woodward

Vol VI:
Colonel Samuel Bagshawe and the
Army of George II, 1731–1762
Edited by Dr Alan J. Guy

Vol. VII:
Montgomery and the Eighth Army
Edited by Stephen Brooks

Vol. VIII:
The British Army and Signals Intelligence
during the First World War
Edited by John Ferris

Vol. IX:
Roberts in India
The Military Papers of Field Marshal Lord Roberts
1876–1893
Edited by Brian Robson

Vol. X:
Lord Chelmsford's Zululand Campaign
1878–1879
Edited by John P. C. Laband

Vol. XI:
Letters of a Victorian Army Officer:
Edward Wellesley
1840–1854
Edited by Michael Carver

Vol. XII:
Military Miscellany I
Papers from the Seven Years War,
the Second Sikh War
and the First World War
Editors: Alan J. Guy, R. N. W. Thomas
and Gerard J. DeGroot

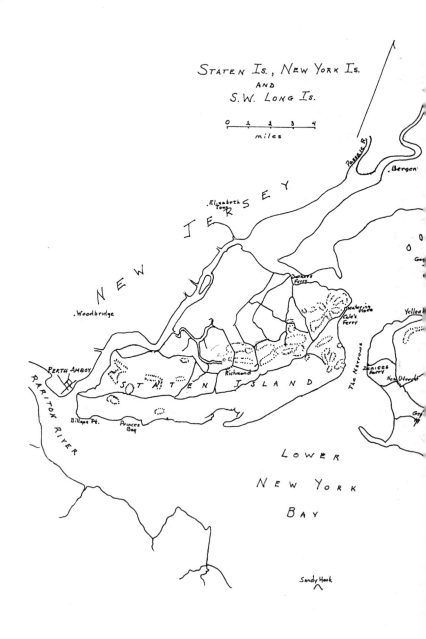

STATEN IS., NEW YORK IS.
AND
S.W. LONG IS.

0   1   2   3   4
miles

NEW JERSEY

Passaic R.

Bergen

Elizabeth Town

Woodbridge

Denkers Ferry

Cole's Ferry

Yellow

NEW JERSEY

PERTH AMBOY

RARITOK RIVER

STATEN ISLAND

Richmond

Billops Pt.

Princes Bay

The Narrows

Denices Ferry

New Utrecht

LOWER

NEW YORK

BAY

Sandy Hook